POWER

IN THE KREMLIN

POWER
IN THE KREMLIN

From Khrushchev to Kosygin

BY MICHEL TATU

Translated by Helen Katel

New York   The Viking Press

PUBLISHED IN 1969 BY THE VIKING PRESS, INC.
625 MADISON AVENUE, NEW YORK, N.Y. 10022

PUBLISHED IN CANADA BY
THE MACMILLAN COMPANY OF CANADA LIMITED

LIBRARY OF CONGRESS CATALOG CARD NUMBER: 67-10216

PRINTED IN U.S.A.

In a free society everything can be published –
and is forgotten because it is all seen at a glance.
Under absolutism everything is hidden, but may
be divined; that is what makes it interesting.

Marquis de Custine, 1839

Contents

FOREWORD   15

INTRODUCTION   19

PART ONE: THE U-2 AFFAIR AND ITS
          CONSEQUENCES

1 An Ill-fated Plane   41
  The Quarrel with China
  The Détente *at Stake*

2 A Month of Turmoil   53
  Moscow's Deliberate Silence
  Measured Indignation
  Embarrassment for Khrushchev
  Khrushchev under Attack at Home

3 Stir in the Top Leadership   69
  Demobilization, Purges and Control of the Armed
     Forces by the Party
  Malinovsky in the Forefront
  Mikoyan on the Decline
  The Changes
  The Newcomers: Kosygin, Podgorny, Polyansky

4 Aftermath of the Crisis   101
  A Private Talk in Pitsunda
  Prelude to Collective Leadership
  The Economy Seen from Backstage: Centralizers
     versus Regionalists

PART TWO: THE TWENTY-SECOND CONGRESS
1961–1962

1 The Pre-Congress Purge   127
The Larionov Case
The Man of the Hour: Gennady Voronov
No Special Favours for Anyone
Strange Coincidences

2 Destalinization   141
The Reasons
The Targets
Surprise Attack
Were Molotov, Malenkov, Kaganovich and
  Voroshilov Criminals or Not?
Operation Mausoleum
What Sanctions Should Be Inflicted on the 'Anti-
  Party Group'?
Another Stalinist Legacy: The 'Stronghold of
  Heavy Industry'
Berlin Crisis versus Agriculture

3 Power Problems   176
The New 'Cult'
The 'Three Terms' Rule
Collective Control
The Elections
The Co-optation Hurdle
The Young Men
Shelepin
An Ambitious Ideologist
The Balance Sheet

4 The Post-Congress Period – Wavering and   208
  See-sawing
Ilyichev on the Spot
What Was to Be Done with Molotov?
Switch in Agricultural Policy
The Military Assert Themselves
An Unexpected Comeback: Kirilenko

PART THREE: THE CUBAN FIASCO 1962–1963

1 The Gamble   230
   An Increase in Strength
   Moskalenko's Strange Fate
   The Hot Phase

2 Domestic Policy: Khrushchev on the Offensive   244
   New Destalinization Drive
   Help from Solzhenitsyn and Yevtushenko
   The Division of the Party
   A Decision Taken According to Rule
   Lenin to the Rescue (with Ampleyev's Help)

3 The Impact   261
   Tuesday October 23: A Wait-and-See Policy
   Friday October 26: The Start of the Bargaining
   Saturday October 27: The Switch
   Sunday October 28: Resistance at an End
   Khrushchev in Disgrace
   A Handy Target: Tumur-Ochir
   A Limited Objective
   Kosygin Defeated: The Shelving of Libermanism
   The November Plenum
   Losers and Winners

4 Restalinization Under Way   298
   From the Manège *Affair to Yermilov*
   Khrushchev in an Awkward Position
   The Ehrenburg Affair

5 February–March 1963: The Crisis   312
   Stalinists Triumphant
   An Easier Target: The Young Writers
   Appeasing China
   Trouble in the Police and Army: The Penkovsky Case
   The Supreme Sovnarkhoz
   Kozlov's Role
   Amendment of a Slogan

6 Kozlov's Illness: A Gain for Khrushchev   341
   Promoting Respect for Authority
   Two Would-be Successors Instead of One
   Plenary Session on Ideology
   Destalinization Again: Explanations by Khrushchev

PART FOUR: THE FALL 1964

1 The Premise: The Crumbling of Authority   364
  A Bad Moment for Suslov
  The 'Steel-Eaters' Again
  Shablon – *Pro and Con*
  An Alarm: The Orenburg Affair
  Lysenko on the Downgrade
  A Glorious Interlude – The Seventieth Birthday
  Brezhnev Becomes Heir Presumptive

2 The Last Straw   387
  The Rapprochement *with Bonn*
  Clash with the Planners
  The Real Danger Looms: The November Plenum

3 The Coup   399
  Suslov on the Warpath
  A Few Questions

PART FIVE: THE COLLECTIVE LEADERSHIP
          ON ITS OWN 1964–1966

1 The Lobbies   429
  The Apparatchiki
  The Managers
  The Party, Podmyena *and Producers' Initiative*
  The Future of the Sovnarkhozes
  Stepanov versus the 'Practical Men'
  The Confrontation of May 1965
  Disagreement between Suslov and Podgorny

2 From the September Plenary Session 1965 to   461
  the Twenty-third Congress March 1966
  An Enlightened Ideologist: Rumyantsev
  The Sinyavsky Case
  Destalinization Stopped

From Objectivity to Restalinization
The Spokesman of the Movement: Brezhnev
The Congress of Silences

3 The Power Structure   494
   Kosygin
   Podgorny
   Shelepin
   Is Suslov the Secretary in Charge of
       Organizational Problems?
   Brezhnev Consolidated
   The 'Secretary-General'
   'The Secretary Is Not a Chief'

EPILOGUE   525

POSTSCRIPT   532

MAIN EVENTS SINCE STALIN'S DEATH   543

BIOGRAPHIES   549

INDEX   559

*I would like to express my gratitude to Columbia University,
its Research Institute for Communist Affairs and its director
Professor Brzezinski, who gave me the opportunity to
devote over six months to this work. I am also grateful
for their sponsorship of the English-language edition of the book,
which could not have been written without their help.*

Foreword

People who, like myself, have been concerned with reporting the Soviet political scene for several years are bound to feel frustrated at some time or another. The régime offers a monolithic façade to its people and to the world. Everything seems serene, the Party declares itself to be united behind its leadership 'as never before'. And then, suddenly, the news breaks that a group of leaders have been in opposition for months or even years, or that the man believed to be a venerated leader has for a long time been execrated by those around him. Lesser revelations also seemingly come out of the blue, since all the discussions that precede them are held strictly in private.

There are two ways of reacting to these disconcerting zigzags. One is merely to record whatever happens and resign oneself to face an impenetrable façade once again until the next crisis; the other is to try to find out what lurks behind the blank walls. This is the purpose of this book, which attempts to reconstruct the main events on the Soviet political scene from 1960 to the present.

This survey is concerned only with the political scene. Economic, social, cultural and diplomatic problems have, of course, not been overlooked, but they are mentioned only in so far as they have a bearing on the political struggle at the top; in many cases this reduces them to a minor role. This will no doubt change, but as long as the power to make decisions remains concentrated in the hands of a few dozen persons in the Politburo, the Party Secretariat and the Government, and as long as their deliberations remain secret, Soviet political life will obey its own distinctive laws. This book, therefore, focuses on these few dozen people, the problems arising out of their mutual relationships and those of the institutions which they head. Experience has in fact shown that the importance of objective problems frequently depends on their relevance to power relationships. The ancient motive force of the thirst for power is something which Marxism overlooks.

This factor, then, will be kept in mind, as well as any other that may set off an internal crisis or determine its outcome. Sometimes this may be an event in the foreign field, such as the U-2 incident in 1960 or the 1962 Cuban blockade; these will be given the attention they deserve.

A few words of explanation about the techniques which I have used. In some cases, this book has drawn upon reports that circulated unofficially in Moscow or elsewhere as events unfolded. Such information has rarely been used, however, and only when the sources were judged to be thoroughly reliable. The Soviet press is the main source of the great bulk of the material used in this study. Here we are on more solid ground, provided we submit to the intellectual discipline which the interpretation of that press requires. It must be realized that, in a system where monolithism is the supreme principle, any dissent can be expressed only in an extremely oblique way. Any changes in the balance of power at the top must be the result of delicate manoeuvres and tacit alliances that can become visible only by equally subtle signs. At the same time, these signs cannot fail to become apparent in some way. The press does not merely relay directives, but also serves as the only peephole offering a glimpse into the closed world of power. Nuances of emphasis and silence itself are also signs for students of the press.

In short, one must sort out the items in order to identify and interpret the unusual – an exercise usually called Kremlinology. Assuming the term means 'science of the Kremlin', it is an unconscious tribute to the method I have described. At present there is in fact no other way of understanding what is going on in the centres of Soviet power. Are palaeontologists frowned upon for trying to reconstitute a skeleton from one vertebra? We shall be more cautious than they, but our curiosity is, at least, equally justified.

Once again, this reconstruction is only tentative. Some day, we may hope, archives will be opened – those of the Politburo and the Central Committee. The classic methods of historiography can then be applied and the present author for one will be delighted. But, in the meantime, scholars should not be deterred from using the fragmentary data at their disposal. In any case, the reader is free to evaluate for himself the hypotheses offered: for, at the risk of making too long a book, all the evidence for each assertion has been given.

This account starts in 1960, the year when Khrushchev's power began to decline. A better date, but unfortunately too remote, would have been the June 1957 crisis, when Khrushchev secured personal power and as a result aroused disagreements which will be discussed frequently in this study. The main facts of this crisis were: on July 4 1957 *Pravda* published a decision taken six days earlier by the Central Committee regarding the 'anti-party group of Malenkov, Kaganovich and Molotov' which was accused of having opposed a series of decisions during the previous 'three or four years'. All three men had long served in the Politburo under Stalin and at least one of them, Malenkov, had been Khrushchev's direct rival for top leadership. They were immediately stripped of all their functions. Only one other figure,

Shepilov, was charged with having 'joined the group'. Two other Presidium members, Saburov and Pervukhin, were removed without any explanation. Additional facts were divulged later: Khrushchev had been confronted not only by three main opponents plus another two men, but also by the head of the Government, Bulganin, and the chief of state, Voroshilov. That is to say, no fewer than seven out of eleven Presidium members had sought to expel him from his post as Party leader. Khrushchev, finding himself in a minority within the Presidium, managed to regain the upper hand only by taking the debate to a plenary session of the Central Committee called post-haste by his friends – in particular Zhukov, the Minister of Defence. After a week of discussion, the Central Committee reversed the Presidium's decision and vindicated Khrushchev as against his foes.

The case caused a great stir, partly because for the first time the Central Committee appeared to have acted as a Party parliament, which is its legal role. This should not be taken at face value, however, for it was later learned that, in the Central Committee debates, the opposition did not have its say on the essential point ('Not one speaker sided with the group', as Khrushchev noted at the Twenty-second Congress). It is clear, therefore, that the cards had been stacked, most probably through pressure by the military and by intensive lobbying. The Central Committee's prerogatives will presumably increase in the future. The process seems to have started owing to a return to collective leadership, but this scarcely existed in 1957 or even, as will be shown, in 1964.

Other events predating this survey, such as the campaigns to cultivate virgin lands and liquidate the machine tractor stations, will be mentioned in passing. The reader will find a brief outline of these developments in the appendix, which provides a summary of the main events in the Soviet Union after Stalin's death.

The term 'Politburo' has been used for the period following its official reinstatement in April 1966. For preceding years, we have used the term 'Presidium of the Central Committee of the Communist Party of the Soviet Union', or Party Presidium, or simply Presidium; this should be distinguished from the Presidium of the Supreme Soviet, a far less important body which is called here by its full name. The appendix also provides brief biographies of the chief members of the main administrative institutions for the period under survey.

A last word regarding the functioning of those institutions: everything would be infinitely simpler (and there would be no Kremlinology) if the lower administrative organs chose the members of the upper echelons by open selection. The practice of so-called 'democratic centralism' has, in practice, turned elections into appointments, since the members of each organ are elected on the basis of 'recommendations' from above which are accepted in the overwhelming majority of cases. It should also be noted that all appointments of any significance take place on the basis of the so-called 'nomenklatura', a system of rosters of officials of a given rank, which are drawn up and scrutinized by the immediate higher authority under the overall supervision of the Secretariat. This is a very effective means of controlling the careers of local officials and hence what takes place at their assemblies, including the Party congresses.

The author hopes that this account will help the reader to understand Soviet political life and its subtleties. Until facts come to prove or disprove its assertions, this study will, it is hoped, above all serve to illuminate from within some of the important events in Soviet history during the past few years.

Michel Tatu

Introduction

On the surface Soviet political life had never been as stable as at the beginning of 1960. The economic situation was satisfactory, and although the 1959 harvest had been markedly smaller than the previous one, the difference was not sufficient to shake the optimism of Khrushchev, who had taken full charge of agriculture. In foreign policy the picture was more complex but largely satisfactory. The prestige of Soviet Russia in the eyes of the world had reached its peak thanks to the launching of the first Sputnik in October 1957, which brought into prominence what the Americans still call the missile gap. Never had a head of the Soviet Government travelled abroad as widely as Nikita Khrushchev in 1959. In the second half of that year alone, the master of the Kremlin had been a guest of 'fraternal' Albania, Poland, Rumania, China and Hungary. Finally, to crown a whole year's labours, the United States of America, the fortress of capitalism, bestowed a lavish welcome on the visitor, confirming his image as a Head of Government of world stature.

It is true that despite Soviet demands, some of them quite peremptory, from the autumn of 1958 onwards, nothing had been achieved on Berlin; but the big four summit conference that Khrushchev had sought for over two years was about to open and President Eisenhower, with whom the Soviet leader maintained cordial relations, had acknowledged that the situation in the former German capital was 'abnormal'. It is true also that the policy of the Chinese leaders had of late become a cause for concern, but this, fortunately for Khrushchev, was not known to the public.

Khrushchev's victories were even more striking for the prestige and authority they brought him. No leader since Stalin had received as many tributes, awards and honours as the First Secretary of the Party and Head of the Government had in the course of a few months, particularly since his return from the United States in September 1959. All the cinemas in the country showed a long documentary of the tour in which America served as a mere background for the visitor's continuous triumph. A team of twelve prominent writers, including his son-in-law Adzhubey, the chief of 'agit-prop', Leonid Ilyichev, the chief editor of *Pravda*, Satyukov, and the official poet, Gribachev, put out a book of nearly seven hundred pages, the famous *Face to Face with America*, whose adulatory style is still unequalled. The latter-day 'personality cult' received a new impetus at the beginning of 1960, when the decision announced on January 30 to demobilize 1,200,000 men from the services was being discussed. *Pravda* featured 'letters from Soviet citizens' whose only object was to glorify Khrushchev, the 'maker of peace'. 'My sisters and I', said one of them on December 22 1959, 'have heard many people say that since Lenin we have never had in the Government a man so loved and respected by the people and so reassuring for the future.' A very unusual occurrence was the publication by *Pravda* in January 1960 of a cartoon showing Khrushchev himself attacking the snowman of the Cold War with an ice-pick.

On occasions the manifestations of the cult took on a more serious turn, verging on sacrilege or illegality. For instance, the trip to the United States dealt a blow to one of the régime's immutable traditions whereby the family of a Soviet leader keeps out of the limelight and certainly plays no political role. It is true that the name of Nina Petrovna Khrushchev disappeared from the press after mid-October 1959, but not so the name of Khrushchev's son-in-law Adzhubey, who was receiving ever greater publicity.

On September 11 1957 a ukase of the Presidium of the USSR Supreme Soviet had prohibited giving the name of any living statesman to any 'regions, cities, districts and other communities, to any enterprises, railway stations, kolkhozes, administrations and teaching establishments'. Such a rule was only prudent two months after the liquidation of the last leaders of the opposition. But it was being permanently violated in at least one spot, a small town in the Poltava area of the Ukraine which still bore Khrushchev's name. At the end of 1959 the decree was even more flagrantly infringed when the famous kolkhoz at Kalinovka, Khrushchev's birthplace, adopted the name *Khrushchev's Home* in a ceremony loudly publicized by *Pravda* on December 19 1959.

Then, also in 1959, a new phrase began to appear here and there amid the chorus of praise. To the uninitiated it may have seemed of no consequence, but to those involved it was of major importance. The phrase was: 'the Presidium of the Central Committee, having at its head [or sometimes even 'led by'] comrade Khrushchev'. Its novelty consisted in the quasi-official violation of the Party statutes whereby a collective deliberative and decision-making body such as the Presidium has no 'head'. The functions of the First Secretary might empower him to be 'at the head' of the Secretariat, or perhaps, to stretch a point, at the head of the Central Committee that endowed him with his powers. Within the Presidium, however, full equality is mandatory and, naturally enough, most of its members took care to avoid using the new formula. Nevertheless, it continued to turn up.

This first symptom of discord warrants a closer look at the other weak points in Khrushchev's position which analysis shows to have appeared at that time. Khrushchev had indeed won a brilliant victory in June 1957 over a coalition of his main political adversaries, but the abscess was very slow in draining. It took the whole of 1958 to eliminate Bulganin, who lost the chairmanship of the Council of Ministers in March, his membership of the Party Presidium in September, and was officially implicated in the 'anti-party group' only in November. Two other members of the 'group', Pervukhin and Saburov, were implicated only at the Twenty-first Congress in January 1959, and even then, as in June 1957, Pervukhin kept his seat as alternate member of the Presidium and Saburov his Central Committee membership. The last of the seven 'anti-party' men, Marshal Voroshilov, was still chief of state and member of the Presidium. Not until the Twenty-second Congress in October 1961 was he accused and forced to confess.

The thesis that Khrushchev felt strong enough to display indulgence was fairly prevalent among experts at the time, but does not stand up to investigation. It does not account for the periodic fresh outbursts of invective against a group that supposedly had been 'swept out of the way for good'. After the first wave in summer 1957 there was another in December 1958 and again in January and February 1959 during the Twenty-first Congress. The violence of the tone did not abate from one campaign to the next, but, strangely enough, the gravity of the charges lessened. Immediately after the 1957 victory a series of speeches, in particular by Khrushchev, Shvernik and Kozlov, had denounced 'crimes' committed by Malenkov, Kaganovich and their associates during Stalin's purges, in a way which suggested that very serious sanctions were in the offing. The subsequent denunciation, however, spoke only of political offences. As late as December 1958 Khrushchev had by implication demanded the men's expulsion from the Party, but at the Twenty-first Congress this sanction was hardly mentioned.

The issue of the 'anti-party group' provoked a serious political struggle behind the scenes, which erupted anew in 1961 during and after the Twenty-second Congress. Actually, it had less to do with the fate of the accused themselves than with the power structure as viewed on the one hand by Khrushchev and on the other by the rest of the top political leaders. For instance, did the First Secretary have to wield such a degree of personal power that any concerted opposition to him must entail extreme sanctions? Was it necessary to revert to the method used by Stalin – known as 'amalgamation' – when he indiscriminately labelled all his enemies Trotskyists, and was Khrushchev now going to apply the 'anti-party' stigma to anyone who had at any time hesitated to endorse any of his moves? Above all, did everybody's Stalinist past have to be scrutinized in order to settle not only political scores but criminal ones as well? Quite understandably, many of the senior leaders joined in answering 'no' to all these questions.

Another abnormal element in political life at the beginning of 1960 was that the membership of the Central Committee had not changed in the four years which had elapsed since the Twentieth Congress and no longer reflected the current balance of power. True, Khrushchev's supporters had been in the majority when the Central Committee was formed, but since his main opponents still sat in the Presidium at the time, the make-up of the Committee was inevitably the product of a compromise. It is known from an indication in *Partiynaya Zhizn* of July 1957 that, out of 309 participants in the June plenary session that ousted the 'anti-party group', 60 actually took the floor while 155 others handed in the texts of their proposed statements. Even assuming that all these speeches unreservedly and without any nuances supported Khrushchev's policy and style, it still meant that 94 persons had not seen fit to make their views known.

In any case, dismissals were fairly numerous. By January 1 1960, out of the 122 voting members of the Central Committee, 22 could be regarded as out of favour or at least demoted to functions incompatible with a seat on the Committee.[1] Most of them, seventeen in all, were purged after the June 1957 crisis, which fact sheds serious doubts on their loyalty towards Khrushchev. Nevertheless, they had retained their prerogatives as Central Committee members and, to judge from the verbatim records of the plenary sessions, exercised them to the fullest extent.

The Twenty-first Congress (January–February 1959) had provided an opportunity for changes. Although this was an 'extraordinary' congress, nothing in the Party statutes prevented it from holding elections. Thus an article published just before the Congress in a Party monthly, *Problems of History of the CPSU* (January 1959), had described the situation and reaffirmed the right of any congress to take any decision it wished concerning the elected organs of the Party, including decisions affecting their composition. This was not done, however, and neither that assembly nor any other plenary session even used its rights

---

[1] The officials demoted by January 1 1960 to functions that did not entitle them to Central Committee membership were: N. E. Avkhimovich, P. N. Alferov, N. K. Baybakov, I. A. Benediktov, I. P. Boytsov, D. D. Brezhnev, N. A. Bulganin, B. L. Vannikov, B. G. Gafurov, B. I. Deriugin, A. N. Zademidko, I. G. Kabanov, B. N. Kobelev, M. D. Kovrigina, V. A. Moskvin, Z. I. Muratov, I. D. Mustafayev, M. G. Pervukhin, S. G. Ragimov, M. Z. Saburov, V. M. Suslov, P. F. Yudin.

under the statutes to fill vacancies resulting from deaths or expulsions by drawing upon alternates. It is interesting that the only speaker at the Twenty-first Congress who thought it necessary to justify this state of affairs was Mikhail Suslov, who did so indirectly by claiming that the 'extraordinary' nature of the Congress precluded a 'Central Committee progress report' and hence, it was implied, the holding of elections. Another speaker advanced a similar point of view by emphasizing that the Congress had 'only one question' to discuss, namely the 'control figures' of the seven-year plan: this was Mikoyan. Neither he nor Suslov specified whether they welcomed or deplored the fact; but both of them had in fact far more to gain than Khrushchev from maintaining the *status quo*.

The situation was hardly to the taste of the First Secretary in any case. The Central Committee still included some of his declared adversaries (for instance Bulganin, Pervukhin and Saburov) or undeclared ones such as Baybakov and Benediktov, and did not include his most loyal supporters and strong men of the hour, such as I. I. Kuzmin, the Gosplan President, or I. V. Spiridonov, the First Secretary of the Leningrad region.

This anomaly produced another which, for a few years, affected the operation of the Central Committee. Throughout 1958 Khrushchev had visibly been trying to consolidate his victory without interfering with the normal procedure for calling the Committee into session. He ran into difficulties, as shown by the length of time it took him to evict Bulganin and, generally speaking, by the inordinately frequent plenary sessions – five between February and November 1958, a pace unequalled since 1927. After December 1958, most probably because the 'normal' methods had failed, he changed his tactics. The plenary sessions thereafter were held in the presence of a large audience of lower officials and shock-workers from the kolkhozes. Often several thousand persons attended in this way who did not belong to the Central Committee (and in some cases not even to the Party). Publicity also came into play for the first time: the sessions were announced several weeks in advance and the press reprinted the debates (theoretically *in extenso*). Naturally, Khrushchev and his supporters depicted the new procedure as more 'democratic'. This is not quite untrue, in so far as it made political life a little less secret, but understandably enough, the members of the Central Committee who retained some independence disliked seeing the 'Party parliament' invaded by people who were not entitled to attend. The non-members tended inevitably to be followers rather than leaders and this limited the work to the discussion of purely technical problems (generally involving agriculture). More serious discussions could, of course, be conducted outside these forums and occasionally the Central Committee did sit in due form, as in May 1960 and April 1962. On the whole, however, the so-called 'enlarged' meetings lasted through the Khrushchev years, although the frequency of sessions again dropped to the prescribed rate of two a year. Naturally enough the foremost concern of those members of the 'apparatus' who gained the upper hand over Khrushchev in October 1964 was to revert to the traditional pre-1958 type of sessions, i.e. closed ones where in all likelihood conflicting opinions could be voiced.[1]

In any case, the situation within the Central Committee was of secondary importance as compared to developments at the top of the hierarchy. Who were the fourteen full members of the Presidium? They can be divided into three categories, according to the closeness of their ties with the First Secretary:

The most loyal, who may properly be labelled *clients*, owed their entire careers to Khrushchev and their behaviour leaves hardly any doubt as to their total devotion to him. They were A. I. Kirichenko, Ye. A. Furtseva and L. I. Brezhnev.

The largest group, that of the *allies* whose careers had been largely or completely independent of Khrushchev and who were now in high places because they had supported him at the most crucial stage of his rise to power. Naturally this included the men promoted in June 1957 who did not belong to the first group. They were N. G. Ignatov, N. I. Beliayev, A. B. Aristov, F. R. Kozlov, O. V. Kuusinen and N. M. Shvernik.

A small heterogeneous group of *independents*. It included K. E. Voroshilov – the last 'anti-party' man, then chief of state and still, but not for long, in the Presidium – A. I. Mikoyan and M. A. Suslov. One should add N. A. Mukhitdinov, a leader of lesser stature (in 1960 he was Secretary to the Central Committee with responsibility for the Moslem republics). He was outwardly a strong backer of Khrushchev but his promotion had nothing to do with the 1957 crisis. He had been elected an alternate member of the Presidium at the Twentieth Congress and become a full member only in December 1957.

This picture is, of course, too cut and dried and calls for additional comment on some of the men. Thus L. I. Brezhnev belongs to the group of clients, since his entire rise within the Party (from 1938 to 1950) was directly promoted by Khrushchev in the Ukraine. However, in the last

[1] The verbatim records of the 'enlarged' Central Committee sessions reveal a curious detail. Until November 1962 Khrushchev went through the motions of obtaining the formal assent of the Committee members to the intrusion of outsiders by inquiring whether there were any 'objections'. After that date and at all ensuing sessions he no longer put the question but merely announced that 'the invited comrades are all present'.

years of the Stalin era, he had become a fully fledged leader in his own right. He had been First Secretary of the Moldavian Republic since 1950, and had entered the enlarged Presidium in October 1952 as an alternate. That was the Presidium that Stalin then counted on, in combination with the purge following the doctors' plot, to get rid of the old guard. (In this respect Brezhnev's case is akin to those of N. G. Ignatov and A. B. Aristov, also promoted in 1952. All three were demoted after Stalin's death. Brezhnev became deputy head of the Armed Forces Political Administration, Aristov the Chairman of the Executive Committee of the Khabarovsk Soviet, and Ignatov Second Secretary in Leningrad.) Like them, Brezhnev again began to rise in 1954 at the same time as Khrushchev himself, who at that time drew many of his recruits from this 'neo-Stalinist' reserve. It is not unreasonable, therefore, to place Brezhnev in an intermediate position between clients and allies, all the more so since he was far more restrained than Kirichenko and Furtseva in condemning the 'anti-party group' in the post-1957 period.

The group of 'allies' was even more disparate. Kuusinen and Shvernik were old-time Party members whose prestige must have been quite useful to Khrushchev in June 1957, but their age prevented them from playing a very active role (they were respectively seventy and seventy-two). Shvernik went on firmly supporting Khrushchev after 1957 by denouncing the criminal offences of the 'anti-party group'. The fact that he was Chairman of the Party Control Committee is significant here. Kuusinen, however, only spoke of their 'dogmatic errors'. A. B. Aristov, who was very discreet about the group at the Twenty-first Congress, took a markedly different line from N. G. Ignatov and N. I. Beliayev, who were far more violent. The spectacular manner in which all three entered the Presidium in June 1957, skipping the stage of alternate membership, leaves no doubt as to their role during the crisis, however, and it shows that the situation had changed a great deal in two and a half years. There was no longer any question of deciding whether to back the claims to power of Molotov, Malenkov and their associates, but rather to drag them before the courts and involve in their condemnation all who at one time or another had opposed the First Secretary. This in turn was tantamount to supporting his own claim to absolute power.

F. R. Kozlov's position is especially interesting, both owing to his past and to the importance of the role he was called upon to play throughout the ensuing years. Although still too young in the hierarchy to have sat in the enlarged Presidium of 1952, he may be regarded as a member of the neo-Stalinist reserve that was being built up during Stalin's last days. In January 1953 he published in *Kommunist*

(No 1 1953) a passionate call for vigilance, thus revealing himself the probable beneficiary of the purges destined to follow the doctors' plot. In consequence he was slightly downgraded at Stalin's death, relinquishing his post as Second Secretary of the Leningrad Oblast Committee to N. G. Ignatov, an outsider. Neither was this a promotion for Ignatov himself who, up to then, had been Central Committee Secretary. When in November 1953 the problem arose of replacing the head of the Oblast Committee, V. M. Andrianov, a client of Malenkov and too obvious a beneficiary of the Leningrad affair,[1] both the Second Secretary, Ignatov, and the Third Secretary, Kozlov, appeared likely candidates. Robert Conquest, in his excellent historical survey of the period,[2] expressed the opinion that Ignatov was the best possible candidate in Khrushchev's eyes and that Kozlov's appointment was the outcome of a compromise among the members of the then collective leadership. In fact, Ignatov's support of Khrushchev's policy never faltered throughout the years, which is more than can be said of his Leningrad rival. It should also be noted that Kozlov had entered the Presidium as an alternate as early as February 1957, that is to say with the assent of a majority that was far from favouring Khrushchev. It is also clear that he firmly picked the right side during the June 1957 crisis and was even among those who that summer suggested criminal proceedings against the 'anti-party group'. Later on, for instance at the Twenty-first Congress, he appeared far more moderate on the issue.

At all events, at the beginning of 1960 Kozlov was far from being the most important figure and held no position in the Party apparatus. He had been the First Deputy Chairman of the Council of Ministers since March 1958 and his speciality was industry, particularly metallurgy, in which he was well versed since he had worked for several years in the Izhevsk industrial combine and at the Kirov factory in Leningrad.

The other First Deputy Chairman of the Council, Anastas Mikoyan,

---

[1] The Leningrad affair was the last major purge of the Stalinist era. It started in February 1949 with the replacement of P. S. Popkov, the First Secretary of the Leningrad Urban Committee, by V. M. Andrianov. In the course of 1949 it led to the disappearance from the central bureaucracy of almost all the leading figures of the region and a number of officials who had originated or formerly worked in Leningrad. The most prominent were N. A. Voznesensky, President of the Gosplan and member of the Politburo, purged in 1949 and executed on September 30 1950; M. I. Rodionov, Chairman of the Council of Ministers of the RSFSR; A. A. Kuznetsov, Secretary of the Central Committee and member of the Orgburo; and I. V. Shikin, chief of the Main Political Administration of the Armed Forces (the only one who did not lose his life). Many of the victims were accused of Titoist sympathies, but many more, and in particular Voznesensky until 1952, were not charged with anything. The true motive seems to have been Malenkov's desire to rid the organization of followers of his rival A. A. Zhdanov, who had died in 1948, allegedly of natural causes.

[2] Robert Conquest, *Power and Policy in the USSR*, Macmillan, London, 1961.

was of a different stature altogether. To be sure, he was Khrushchev's ally if not his privileged confidant, especially on foreign policy where he himself played the role of roving ambassador. However, he enjoyed unquestioned independence owing both to his status as oldest Presidium member after Voroshilov and to his consummate mastery of the art of alliances and political manoeuvring. The best example was his attitude on the 'anti-party' issue. He firmly sided with the Khrushchev camp in the crucial days of June 1957 and probably even far earlier. At the Twentieth Congress he was the first to attack Stalin, preparing the way for the 'Secret Report' about to be delivered by the First Secretary. A year and a half later, he was delegated by the 'healthy segment' of the Presidium to hold a meeting, jointly with Bulganin, with the members of the Central Committee who were demanding explanations. Again it was he, together with Kirichenko, who put pressure on the wavering members of the 'anti-party group', such as Saburov, to come back into line, as Saburov testified at the Twenty-first Congress. Once the victory had been won, however, the subtle Armenian soon grasped the dangers of pushing it too far. Not only did his position as a member of the collective leadership induce him, like many others, to resist Khrushchev's yearning for personal power, but he also had his private reasons for trying to prevent matters from getting out of hand.

Having been a member of the Presidium since 1935, Mikoyan had participated in the succession of power struggles which followed Stalin's death. It is difficult to imagine that he did not at any time side with at least some of the 'anti-party group' and did not oppose Khrushchev on some point. Khrushchev incidentally disclosed later that Mikoyan was not particularly enthusiastic about the virgin lands programme. It is understandable that, under the circumstances, Mikoyan frowned upon the attempts by Spiridonov and other neo-Khrushchevian lower officials to implicate new 'accomplices' of the disgraced men. Indeed, after Bulganin, Saburov, Pervukhin and then Voroshilov, who were first supposed not to be involved but subsequently found themselves dragged in the mud, who could tell where the process would stop?

This is why, at the Twenty-first Congress, Mikoyan was particularly outspoken on the subject. He explained that during his recent trip to the United States the bourgeois journalists had insinuated in his presence that the new attacks against the group must reflect a strengthening of the opposition. Using this as an added argument for closing the issue, he declared: 'I answered them: no, absolutely not. Complete unity prevails within the Party and no struggle is going on. The group has not grown by one single member during this period'. As if to reinforce his statement, Mikoyan discussed the whole case without once naming the members of the 'group'. This enabled him to avoid implicating Bulganin, Pervukhin and Saburov, which indicates that the new policy of 'amalgamation' was not to his liking.

It follows that Mikoyan viewed attempts to fix criminal responsibility for the bloody purges of the past with even greater distaste. Not that he himself had been especially guilty in this respect. Unlike Kaganovich, Malenkov or Voroshilov, he does not seem to have personally taken a hand in the repression in general or in any specific 'case'. Nevertheless, he had entered the Party Presidium (then called the Politburo) in 1935, at a time when Stalin still made a point of associating the organ with his major decisions. It is known, for instance, that a vote was taken in the Politburo in 1937 on the punishment of the military leaders accused of treason – Tukhachevsky, Yakir, Uborevich and others – and Mikoyan, who was a member, must have taken part in this sinister procedure. Nor could he remain completely indifferent to the mention of Ordzhonikidze's suicide in 1937 (this case was brought up with odd insistence throughout the destalinization campaigns), especially since Khrushchev ascribed the action of Stalin's faithful lieutenant to the fact that he 'could no longer work normally with Stalin' and did not want to 'share the responsibility for Stalin's abuse of power' (Khrushchev's speech at the Twenty-second Congress, October 27 1961). Revelations of this kind tended to discredit all members of the then Politburo, and Voroshilov and Mikoyan were its sole survivors. Various attempts were in fact made later to justify the behaviour of some individuals during the purges. It was 'disclosed', for instance, that Khrushchev had been struggling against the 'personality cult' as early as 1935, that such-and-such a soldier had saved a colleague who had been unfairly accused, and so on. Nothing of the kind was ever said by way of exculpating Mikoyan.

It should be noted at once that Khrushchev was more at ease on this treacherous ground because he had become a full member of the Politburo only in 1939 (he gained a seat in January 1938, but without voting rights) when the great purges were over. The post-war purges (in particular the Leningrad affair) were decided outside the Politburo, and Khrushchev is free to say – as he does at every opportunity – that he did not know the truth. The only repression he can be charged with is that of 1938 in the Ukraine, although apparently all he did then was to replace the victims with his own people. In any case, Khrushchev, as the chief executive both in the Party and in the state, was freer than his colleagues in the collective leadership to present destalinization in the light that he chose and to engineer any trials that might be called for. [See footnote [1] opposite.]

At all events, as early as 1957 Mikoyan endeavoured to stop all investigation into criminal responsibilities and to protect the 'anti-party group' from legal proceedings. Neither then nor later did he speak of their 'crimes'. At the Twenty-first Congress in January 1959 he said plainly: 'We deemed it necessary, and still do today, to speak of the "anti-party group" at this Congress with one single aim – that of demonstrating once again, on the basis of facts, the incorrect and harmful nature of their political position.' Having said this much, he was more discreet than anyone else even as regards these political errors, and refrained from any insulting epithet, even that of 'factionaries' which most Presidium members used in their speeches.

In short, Mikoyan may be regarded as Khrushchev's ally on a large number of political issues and as his diplomatic supporter and adviser. For instance, his speech at the Twentieth Congress (1956) was an advance exposé of the entire peaceful coexistence programme that Khrushchev followed from 1957 to 1960. At the same time he opposed Khrushchev's concept of internal power structure. He simultaneously advocated freedom of opposition and opposed measures of destalin-ization that would implicate the Party's Stalinist cadres.

Another independent, M. A. Suslov, was and remained a subject of controversy among Kremlinologists until the events of October 1964, which at last convinced the sceptics that there could be no smoke without fire. Unfortunately in these matters one must be content for ever with the smoke because the fire is hidden. Even discounting the periodic rumours according to which Suslov's role was to make sure that Khrushchev was observing the Party traditions, many signs testified to his very special position. There were his many Stalinist backers; his probable role as organiser of the purges in Rostov and Stavropol from 1937 to 1939 and in Lithuania from 1944 to 1946; his part, although a minor one, in Zhdanov's drives against the writers and artists after the war and in the attack on Tito in 1948. But more importantly, because this has greater bearing on the analysis of his cur-

---

[1] The fact that Khrushchev had been less involved in the Stalinist purges did not prevent his opponents on the destalinization issue from mounting discreet counter-attacks on occasion. Thus on May 18 1962 *Izvestia* commemorated Yenukidze's birthday by writing: 'In 1937 Yenukidze was calumniated, arrested and condemned.' On the following day, May 19 1962, *Pravda* pointed out that Yenukidze had been 'one of the first victims of the personality cult', and added: 'As early as the beginning of 1935, Yenukidze was calumniated, stripped of his functions and later arrested and condemned.' Why the rectification as to the date? It so happens that Khrushchev was one of the first to attack Yenukidze in a speech made to Party activists in Moscow in June 1935. It may be, therefore, that *Izvestia*, which was much closer to Khrushchev at the time, was trying to gloss over the events of 1935. *Pravda*, on the other hand, was controlled by the Party Secretariat including people like Suslov and Kozlov, who could have set matters straight when performing their normal task of clearing the copy for the following day's issue.

rent position, he was a Central Committee Secretary since 1947 without interruption (consequently senior to Khrushchev, who only joined the Committee in 1949) and in this capacity launched the first attack (in *Pravda* of December 24 1952) against Voznesensky, the main victim of the Leningrad affair. In this respect, then, Suslov was particularly vulnerable.

We may assume that Suslov's supposed connections with Khrushchev in the early stages of his career are non-existent, except for one rather amusing exception. As a Professor at the Industrial Academy in 1930, Suslov may have had Khrushchev as a student! An odd twist.

As for his role in the years after Stalin's death, it is certainly ambiguous. He was elected a member of the Presidium in July 1955, when Khrushchev's opponents, even if not joined in a coalition, were nevertheless in the majority. And several indications suggest that Suslov was himself the candidate of the opposite camp:

1 He was promoted at the same time as Kirichenko and everything indicates that Kirichenko, whose case will be examined further, was then and always a loyal client of the First Secretary. As things stood in the Presidium, it is logical to assume that the majority must have favoured Suslov's promotion in order to preserve the existing balance of power. Suslov must have been chosen to offset three personalities far closer to Khrushchev who entered the Secretariat at the same time: A. B. Aristov, N. I. Beliayev and D. T. Shepilov. This certainly made it advisable to enhance the status of the only independent left in the Secretariat.

2 This deduction is confirmed by the declarations of Suslov himself about the 'anti-party group' after 1957. Assuming he joined the Presidium with the backing of at least a segment of the group in 1955, he could have been expected to depict his protectors as innocent of any serious fault at the time of his promotion, and as having engaged in factionalism only later. This, indeed, is what he said. As soon as he, too, was forced to give details about the group's activities (and that was not till 1961) he tried to show that it had all started only in 1956. His words were:

'In the first years after the Twentieth Congress (i.e. after 1956) the Party ran into stubborn resistance from the "anti-party group" of Molotov, Kaganovich, Malenkov, Voroshilov, Bulganin and others' (speech at the Twenty-second Congress, October 21 1961). A few months later, in a report delivered to professors of social science on January 30 1962, he further clarified his thought: 'The Party started to restore Leninist standards in social life immediately after Stalin's death. It revived the principles of collective leadership, increased the creative activity of the Party organizations and took decisive steps to restore socialist legality.' There followed a parenthesis on the Beryia case after which Suslov listed in idyllic terms all the achievements of the years 1953–1956. Again, it was only after speaking of the Twentieth Congress that he mentioned the opposition of those who then became 'anti-party' elements.[1]

Factually speaking, Suslov was, of course, right to assert that the 'Leninist standards in the life of the Party', and in particular the collective character of the leadership, were re-established as soon as the dictator died. If ever democracy did prevail at the top, it certainly was during that period when all opinions clashed, and vigorously so, within the Presidium, rather than after 1957 when Khrushchev had driven out his chief opponents. But Khrushchev and his supporters could not be expected to view the situation in the same light. They tended, understandably enough, to believe that things were in order only after their own power was secure, and hence they did not over-stress the slogan of collective leadership. For example, at the Twentieth Congress in February 1956, Kirichenko, the loyal Khrushchev supporter, only alluded briefly to the principle of collective leadership, whereas Kaganovich, Voroshilov and Malenkov laid special stress on it. There again Suslov sided with them and stood out as the staunchest advocate of collective leadership. It is true that, unlike Malenkov and Voroshilov for instance, in whose eyes this principle must 'continue to be applied and strengthened', Suslov, closer to Mikoyan in this respect, affirmed that it was already 'fully re-established'. Suslov gave the impression at the time of a man who was quite satisfied with the existence of an opposition and was keeping the score of the game.

In any case, the kind of absolution that Suslov was at pains to confer upon Molotov, Malenkov and their associates in respect of the period before the Twentieth Congress places him in opposition to the overwhelming majority of the group's critics. He particularly opposed Kirichenko, in whose opinion 'the members of the "anti-party group", *from the very day after Stalin's death*, attacked almost at each meeting of the Presidium everything that was new and progressive' (speech at the Twenty-first Congress, January 31 1959) and also Mikoyan who, speaking just before Suslov, denounced the group's conservative opposition *'during the two years preceding the Twentieth Congress'* (speech at the Twenty-second Congress, October 20 1961). Since these two men were the only other survivors of the pre-1957 Presidium, it is highly doubtful that Suslov was an old Khrushchev supporter.

3 Even if the Twentieth Congress and the year 1956 are taken as the

[1] *XXII syezd i zadachi kafedr obshchevstvennykh nauk, Moscow, 1962* ('The Twenty-second Congress and the Tasks of Professors of Social Sciences').

starting point, it is still difficult to agree unreservedly with the thesis that Suslov maintained no ties with the anti-Khrushchev members of the Presidium after that date. The trips by Suslov and Mikoyan to Budapest at the height of the Hungarian uprising at the end of October 1956 deserve special attention. The divisions within the Presidium had become so acute at the time that a delegation not representing both main tendencies at the top could not conceivably have been sent on an important mission abroad. This had been quite obvious a few days earlier, when Khrushchev was accompanied by Molotov and Kaganovich on his trip to Warsaw for his famous meeting with Gomulka. Everything points to the fact that, in the negotiations with Imre Nagy's Hungary, Mikoyan was Khrushchev's most faithful spokesman. It is most likely, therefore, that Suslov represented the opposite faction.

Another, still later episode casts some doubts on Suslov's loyalty to Khrushchev. This was the liquidation in March 1958 of the machine tractor stations (MTS). This involved selling agricultural machinery to kolkhozes and hence caused some dismay among ideologists. It was soon made known, however, that the measure had been contemplated as early as 1957, before the June crisis, and that the systematic opposition of the 'anti-party' elements had caused its postponement. It was then noticed that, alone among the Presidium members, Suslov failed to mention the measure in his election campaign speech of March 1958, at a time when the discussion organized by Khrushchev on the topic was at its height throughout the country. He did seem to approve it later, though half-heartedly, in his Twenty-first Congress speech, but his sincerity remains debatable.

In view of all this it would, of course, be very interesting to find out how Suslov behaved during the 1957 crisis. Alas, his personal attitude at that particular moment is the least known. However, there is no reason to doubt that he was on the right side. The mere fact that he retained all his functions after the historic purge while even such mild opponents as Pervukhin and Saburov were demoted is the best evidence. Apart from this, the only specific indication is provided by the *History of the CPSU* (1959 edition), where Suslov is numbered with those members of the Presidium, Secretariat and Central Committee who 'decisively intervened against the "anti-party group" and forcefully countered its desperate attacks against the Party's Leninist line'. (The same book omitted Voroshilov from the list, although he had not yet been officially 'unmasked' at the time.) But exactly when and how did Suslov make his stand? In the absence of further details, the following two incidental indications may be useful:

According to the Soviet press, Suslov was on a tour of the provinces at the time when the Presidium session that indicted Khrushchev opened on June 18 1957. Therefore he may not have attended the beginning of the proceedings.

According to the list in the *History of the CPSU*, what was later called the 'healthy segment' of the Presidium then comprised four persons out of eleven: Khrushchev, Kirichenko, Mikoyan and Suslov. The additional details that became known later about Mikoyan's and Kirichenko's activities against the group have already been noted (the former was the liaison man with the pro-Khrushchev members of the Central Committee and both tried to influence Saburov). Suslov has never been mentioned as having played a comparable role.[1]

The conclusion to be drawn from all this is that Suslov's part in saving Khrushchev cannot have been a major one. In any case, he has not since then been among the people who have tried to stir up fresh excitement over the case. His speech at the Twenty-first Congress, which could not have been terser on the issue, unquestionably places him among the advocates of the *status quo*.

Our analysis of the composition of the Presidium at the beginning of 1960 thus leads to the following conclusions – paradoxical ones considering that Khrushchev was then to all appearances at the pinnacle of his power:

1 The Presidium included only a tiny minority of his clients.

2 The majority consisted of 'allies' drawn from the 1957 anti-Molotov coalition who disagreed among themselves about the fate their opponents deserved and hence on the scope of the power that the First Secretary was entitled to arrogate to himself.

3 An old opponent of his, Voroshilov, was still a Presidium member.

4 Lastly, among the independents, one at least – Suslov – symbolized the continuity of the collective leadership both before and after the crisis, and therefore might become a pole of attraction for possible malcontents.

Not a very satisfactory situation for the First Secretary: moreover, it was going to become even less so with the downfall of A. I. Kiri-

---

[1] The count of 7 to 4 in the June 1957 session of the Presidium has been consistently given by Soviet sources since 1961, including Khrushchev himself in his talk with Guy Mollet in October 1963. It should be noted, however, that at the crucial session at least one of the seven, namely M. Z. Saburov, apparently did not vote with the group to depose Khrushchev from the headship of the Party. According to his own confession at the Twenty-first Congress, he declared on the contrary that 'the line of the Presidium is correct, collective leadership is a reality within the Presidium; but the policy of revenge should be forsaken and the case closed by noting and dispelling the minor shortcomings noted'. In other words, Saburov advocated no more than a kind of gentle warning to the First Secretary. Therefore it is rather arbitrary to include him among those who voted Khrushchev down in the Presidium and thus to speak of a majority of 7 to 4 – unless of course the seventh was someone else altogether.

chenko, who was not only one of his most faithful clients, but also a vital factor in his control over the Party apparatus. On January 13 1960, *Pravda* announced in a few lines that Kirichenko had on the previous day been appointed First Secretary of the Oblast Committee of Rostov-on-Don, replacing N. V. Kiselev who had 'been called upon to fulfil other functions'. This was Kirichenko the Presidium member, Central Committee Secretary in charge of cadres, Second Secretary and (since 1958) heir presumptive to Khrushchev as head of the Party. In May 1960 he was expelled from all the central administrative organs and a month later further demoted, as he lost even his Rostov post.

More than seven years later the entire episode is still highly mysterious. One version that circulated fairly widely in Moscow at the time ascribed the demotion to his defective 'style of work' with cadres. Kirichenko was rumoured to have clashed with influential Presidium members (Mikoyan's name was mentioned) who had chided him for his curt manner. It was also hinted that Kirichenko had opposed, at least on certain details, various decisions taken at the time regarding the armed forces and police (he was in charge of them as well), namely the demobilization of 1,200,000 men and the liquidation of the Ministry of the Interior (MVD) on the federal level.[1]

In his previously mentioned book, Robert Conquest suggests that differences on the nationalities policy had some bearing on the case. For example, the struggle against local nationalism was at a peak when Kirichenko was expelled, as shown by a Central Committee decree on propaganda published by *Pravda* on January 10 1960. Kirichenko had always been identified with a relatively liberal policy in this area and had risen to be head of the Party in the Ukraine in June 1953 as an opponent of the policy of all-out Russification favoured by his predecessor, L. G. Melnikov. In his speech at the Twenty-first Congress in February 1959, he also advocated self-government for each republic. If this hypothesis is valid, Kirichenko presumably fell from favour several months earlier, since it was in September 1959 that the campaign against nationalism took on new vigour in most republics, from the Baltic to Kazakhstan.[2]

[1] It is also quite possible that Khrushchev and Kirichenko disagreed as regards the right way to solve the Chinese problem. In September 1963 the Tirana daily *Zeri i Popullit* deplored the fact that no one had ever asked Khrushchev 'why Aleksey Kirichenko had been stripped of his functions and why Frol Kozlov was no longer heard about' (*New York Times*, September 10 1963). The Albanians must have had their reasons for mentioning Kirichenko and not others purged in the same circumstances, N. I. Beliayev for instance.

[2] The main episode in the drive against nationalism towards the end of 1959 took place in Latvia and involved the replacement of the First Secretary of the Republic, Ya. N. Kalnberzin, by his former deputy Arvid Pelshe. While Kalnberzin's disgrace was relatively mild (he was appointed head of state in Latvia and kept his seat as

Analysis of the unexpected return to favour of some individuals during 1959 brings us back to the same dates, and association with Kirichenko immediately springs to mind. For instance, on March 2 1959, I. V. Kapitonov and N. F. Ignatov were stripped of their respective functions as First Secretary of the Oblast Committee and Chairman of the Oblast Executive Committee of Moscow in the presence of Kirichenko and Aristov. By September 1959 Kapitonov reappeared as First Secretary of the Ivanovo Oblast Committee, and by January 1960 Ignatov occupied the corresponding post at Orel, although the criticism levelled at them in March 1959 had seemed to portend definitive disgrace.[1] Similarly, on April 16 1959, the Central Committee Secretary, N. G. Ignatov, was appointed Chairman of the Presidium of the RSFSR Supreme Soviet, a post which, for a man of his stature, definitely meant removal from real responsibility. Seven months later, he was relieved of his honorary functions to enable him 'to concentrate upon his essential work within the Secretariat of the Central Committee of the CPSU' (*Pravda*, November 27 1959).

In both cases the extremes of this swing of the pendulum correspond on the one hand to the period of Kirichenko's greatest strength just after the Twenty-first Congress and on the other hand to his deepening disgrace that autumn.

Whether all the explanations offered above are founded or not, they are not mutually exclusive. It is likely, on the contrary, that the fall of the 'number two man' was due to a combination of errors that aroused a heterogeneous coalition against him. It is not impossible, indeed, that Kirichenko clashed with Khrushchev himself, since the position

---

alternate in the Presidium and the CPSU Central Committee until 1961), this was not true of other local leaders who at this time were expressly charged with nationalist activities. The man who was later represented (in *Sovietskaya Latvia*, November 18 1961) as the chief of a 'nationalist group' was Edward Berclav, the deputy prime minister, who was stripped of his functions in the middle of July 1959. In September 1959 Pelshe launched a violent attack against Berclav's attempts to 'organize the development of the Republic in a spirit of narrowness and national autarky' (*Kommunist Sovietskoy Latvii*, No 9 1959). In November, in addition to Kalnberzin, the head of the government, Latsis, the trade-union chairman, and a number of other leaders lost their posts. Berclav was virtually exiled from Latvia by being appointed chief of the regional film rentals bureau at Vladimir in Central Russia (*Parliamentary Yearbook*, December 1959).

[1] Kapitonov and Ignatov were the targets of the following strange accusation in the bi-monthly *Partiynaya Zhizn*, No 8 April 1959: 'I. V. Kapitonov and N. F. Ignatov, the chairman of the Oblast Executive Committee, maintained incorrect relations outside the Party, which took up a great deal of their time and interfered with their work. . . . As a result the kolkhoz production reserves were insufficiently used' (sic). Ignatov was out of favour for a longer spell than Kapitonov. At the end of 1959, the *Parliamentary Yearbook* listed him as discharging the minor functions of assistant chief manager of the Moscow region sovnarkhoz.

of heir presumptive is apt to turn the most reliable of protégés into a pretender. On balance, however, it seems more likely that Khrushchev condoned the demotion rather than provoked it, and, moreover, that he lost a great deal in the process. Several signs reinforce this conclusion. 1 The only criticism of Kirichenko or explanation about him ever expressed was the following: in January 1961 Khrushchev disclosed to the plenary session of the Central Committee that Kirichenko and N. T. Kalchenko had 'lost their heads' during the summer of 1956 and requested permission immediately to harvest the crop that was 'scorching in the fields'.[1] But this was a very old business and too harmless to account for Kirichenko's abrupt demotion in 1960. Moreover, there were many reasons to believe that Khrushchev's chief target at that time was Kalchenko, the head of the Ukrainian Government and an old adversary of his. In February 1961, shortly after this new attack, Kalchenko relinquished his post. Kirichenko, after this, was mentioned only in favourable terms for his role during the war (for instance by General P. L. Batov in *Novoye Vremia* on February 1 1963).

Khrushchev was far more ruthless with the men he had made up his mind to sacrifice, even if they were his staunch allies (e.g. with N. I. Beliayev, a member of the Presidium and First Secretary of the Party in Kazakhstan, who was purged at the same time as Kirichenko).[2] Even if Khrushchev was not the instigator of Beliayev's demotion he had clearly decided to make him the scapegoat for the poor 1959 harvest in the virgin lands. In December 1959, at the plenary session of the Central Committee, he sharply criticized him for shortcomings in agriculture and, for good measure, even blamed D. A. Kunayev, who succeeded Beliayev as head of the Party in Kazakhstan.

2 If Kirichenko had been a personal victim of Khrushchev rather than of the Presidium as a whole, his fortunes could have been expected to improve after the First Secretary's downfall. As it turned out, he was not heard of after October 1964, and, moreover, some personnel changes suggest that Khrushchev's fall was used as an opportunity to eliminate the last traces of his influence. I. V. Kapitonov, whose ill fortune in 1959 has been noted, acceded to the important post of head of the Department for Party Organs of the Central Committee for the RSFSR (*Pravda*, January 26 1965) while another old adversary, L. G. Melnikov, whom Kirichenko had supplanted in the Ukraine in 1933, again rose

[1] This episode shows incidentally how flimsy was the independence of farming managers in general and the heads of Union Republics in particular. Even the First Secretary of the Party in the Ukraine could not order the harvesting without referring to Moscow for permission.

[2] N. I. Beliayev was appointed First Secretary of the Stavropol Regional Committee at the end of January 1960, was dismissed on June 25 1960 and disappeared without trace.

to the surface and obtained a government post in Moscow (Chairman of the State Committee on Work Safety for the RSFSR: *Pravda*, December 20 1964). As for the protégés of the former Secretary in charge of cadres, one at least has been identified. He was L. I. Naidek, appointed Second Party Secretary in the Ukraine in December 1957, when Kirichenko was promoted to Moscow, then demoted to the post of First Secretary of the Cherkassy Oblast Committee in February 1960, when Kirichenko fell from favour. Naidek lost even this minor post during the reorganization of oblast committees that followed Khrushchev's fall in the autumn of 1964.

3 It is enough to study Kirichenko's declarations, for instance at the Twenty-first Congress of January 1959, to note that he was at the time the most zealous supporter of Khrushchev in the entire Presidium. When the Khrushchev cult was only just getting under way, his praise for the 'outstanding activity, the Leninist firmness, the spirit of initiative and the immense organizational work' of the First Secretary was unequalled by any other Congress speaker. The insults he showered upon the 'anti-party group' – 'abject factionaries, political intriguers, contemptible dogmatists', etc. – matched the fervour of his tribute to the victor. Better yet, Kirichenko was the only speaker at the Twenty-first Congress who extolled the merits of Khrushchev's new technique of 'enlarged plenary sessions', extremely unpopular with the *apparatchiki* (members of the Party apparatus). Kirichenko described it as a 'convincing proof of the strengthening of the bonds between the Party and the masses'. All the others were silent on the subject.

In short, it is not likely that Khrushchev would have lightly resolved to part with such a wholehearted supporter. The cost of his removal, on the other hand, is obvious: Khrushchev lost not only a precious voice in the Presidium debates (with Beliayev's departure the group of protégés and close allies was whittled down to a narrow majority facing the 'independents') but, more important, a lieutenant who hitherto had been his right-hand man in maintaining control over the Party apparatus. Experience soon proved that Khrushchev would never again find another equally reliable helper. It is no over-statement that Kirichenko's fall in January 1960 opened a new phase in Khrushchev's reign.

Part One
THE U-2 AFFAIR AND
ITS CONSEQUENCES

1 An Ill-fated Plane

As everyone will recall, a serious international crisis was precipitated
in May 1960 when an American U-2 plane brought down over
Sverdlovsk by a Soviet rocket wrecked the Paris summit conference
even before it had begun. Outside Russia this looked like one of those
rare instances during Khrushchev's rule when Soviet policy changed
abruptly in the course of a few days. The main events of the crisis, as
reported at the time by the world press, were as follows:

May 1 1960: At 5.36 am (Moscow time) a Pakistan-based U-2 plane
piloted by Francis Gary Powers and flying at over 65,000 feet crossed
the Soviet border. Interrogation of the pilot and examination of the
plane's débris subsequently disclosed that his mission had been to fly
over Soviet territory along a route from Sverdlovsk to Murmansk
and to land at the Budö airfield in Norway. At 8.55 am the plane was
shot down over the Sverdlovsk area, in the Urals, by a ground-to-air
Soviet rocket. (Although a number of analysts have questioned some of
the details of the incident as reported by the Russians, there is no
serious evidence to contradict the Soviet version.) Powers, who managed
to parachute out of the plane, was almost immediately arrested. He
promptly made a full confession, including the fact that he was working
for the Central Intelligence Agency.

May 4: A plenary session of the Central Committee of the Communist
Party of the Soviet Union ratified several changes in the Soviet Govern-
ment and Party: F. R. Kozlov relinquished his post as First Deputy
Chairman of the Council of Ministers and became Secretary of the
Party; L. I. Brezhnev replaced Marshal K. E. Voroshilov as the Chief
of State; A. N. Kosygin was promoted to the post of First Deputy
Chairman of the Council of Ministers and became a full member of
the Party Presidium, together with D. S. Polyansky and N. V. Podgorny.

May 5: Khrushchev reported the U-2 incident in a speech to the Supreme Soviet, deliberately leaving out some details. He did not mention
where the plane had been brought down or the fact that the pilot had
been captured alive. On the same day, but after Khrushchev had made
his speech, the American Government released its own version of the
incident, later to be dubbed the 'cover version'. This was that the sole
mission of the U-2 had been to make high altitude tests for the National
Aeronautics and Space Administration. Powers had probably blacked

out from lack of oxygen and crossed the Soviet border accidentally. On May 6, in line with that statement, the State Department addressed a note to the Soviet Government requesting information about the incident and about what had happened to Powers.

May 7: In a second speech to the Supreme Soviet, Khrushchev disclosed the full details of the incident, derided Washington's 'meteorological' version and violently denounced American espionage activities. He added, however: 'I am quite willing to assume that the President [of the USA] did not know that a plane had been sent over Soviet territory and had not returned.'

That evening, the State Department released a statement disavowing the first 'cover version' and admitting that a 'flight over Soviet territory was probably undertaken by an unarmed civilian U-2 plane'. The statement claimed that 'the necessity for such activities is enhanced by the excessive secrecy practised by the Soviet Union in contrast to the free world', and added: 'As a result of the inquiry ordered by the President, it has been established that, in so far as the authorities are concerned, there was no authorization for any such flights as described by Mr. Khrushchev.'

May 9: Speaking in Moscow, Khrushchev called the American statement 'alarming', 'confused' and involving a 'highly dangerous explanation'. Referring to his statement of May 7, he added: 'I am not certain, but I do not exclude the possibility that the United States Government was aware of this flight.' He declared that the Soviet armed forces would strike at the bases used for take-off in territories adjoining the USSR if further incidents occurred.

That day, before Khrushchev's statement was made known in Washington, the United States Secretary of State, Mr. Herter, enlarged upon the May 7 statement by declaring: 'In accordance with the National Security Act of 1947, the President has put into effect since the beginning of his administration directives to gather by every possible means the information required to protect the US and the free world against surprise attack and to enable effective preparations to be made for their defence.

'Under these directives, programmes have been developed and put into operation which have included extensive aerial surveillance by unarmed civilian aircraft, normally of a peripheral character but on occasion by penetration. Specific missions of these unarmed civilian aircraft have not been subject to Presidential authorization.'

May 10: In reply to the statement of May 7 by the State Department, the Soviet Government addressed a forceful note of protest to the United States Embassy in Moscow, emphasizing that 'the State

Department's explanation that the flight had taken place without the knowledge and authorization of the United States Government does not correspond to the facts'.

May 11: Speaking to foreign journalists about the U-2 affair, Khrushchev said: 'Mr. Herter's declaration has raised doubts here concerning the accuracy of our earlier opinion that the President did not know about these flights.'

On the same day and virtually at the same time, Eisenhower held a press conference in which he fully confirmed Herter's revelations of May 9 about the American espionage programme, which in his opinion was 'distasteful' but a 'vital necessity'.

May 12: In reply to the Soviet note of May 10, which charged the United States with a 'calculated policy' of gathering information about the USSR, Washington confirmed in a note that: 'The United States Government does not deny that it has pursued such a policy for purely defensive purposes.'

May 14: Khrushchev, accompanied by Marshal Malinovsky, the Defence Minister, arrived in Paris for the summit conference.

May 16: Khrushchev, who was the first speaker at the meeting of the four heads of Government, demanded that Eisenhower publicly censure the flights over Soviet territory, officially repudiate such actions and such a policy aimed at the USSR and punish those guilty, failing which the Soviet Government would not take part in the summit conference. He suggested in the same statement that the conference be postponed for six or eight months, i.e. until after the American elections. Eisenhower announced that 'these flights were suspended after the recent incident and are not to be resumed', but he went no further.

May 19: Khrushchev was not pacified by Eisenhower's statement. and all efforts at mediation by de Gaulle and Macmillan were fruitless. Khrushchev left Paris after giving a stormy press conference and the summit conference never took place.

May 20: On his way back to the Soviet Union, Khrushchev stopped in Berlin. In Ulbricht's presence he announced that he would not sign the separate peace treaty between the USSR, East Germany and her other allies, which had been meant to terminate the occupation status of West Berlin, for another six to eight months – the period which he had suggested should elapse before a summit conference. 'We are realists,' he said, 'and shall never pursue a reckless policy.'

This statement eased the acute crisis that had shaken the world in the first two weeks of May. Unlike the Cuban crisis, this one brought no serious risk of military confrontation. Nevertheless, the fact that the summit conference had not taken place meant the abandonment of a policy to which Khrushchev had adhered resolutely for over two years – the policy of personal contacts and co-operation with the West which had culminated in the Camp David meeting in September 1959. Here, in May 1960, he had wrecked the very summit conference for which he had been clamouring since 1957. (True, he had once before, in 1958, turned down an opportunity for such a conference, probably under Chinese pressure.) There were to be no more opportunities during the rest of his reign except for the Vienna meeting with President Kennedy in 1961, which was held in very different circumstances.

Whatever the deeper reasons for the U-2 affair may have been, it played a decisive role in the reversal of Soviet policy. The succession of events, as reported above, illustrates a gradual stiffening of position. A major aspect was the significance attached by Moscow and Washington respectively to President Eisenhower's and his Administration's admission of espionage. It is quite clear that the decision taken in Washington on May 7 to avow and justify officially a policy of espionage against the USSR was the main factor in exacerbating the dispute. There were unfortunate coincidences as well: for example, the major declarations on the crisis, those of May 9 and May 11, were made simultaneously in Washington and Moscow, with each side unaware that the other was trying to outbid it at that very moment. In all likelihood, these factors were the direct cause of Khrushchev's behaviour on May 16, that is to say his decision to break off negotiations in such a dramatic fashion.

It does not follow, however, that if nothing had happened in Moscow and there had been no U-2, Khrushchev would have participated in the conference, pursued his Camp David policy and sought an agreement with the West. There had been several signs of a hardening of Soviet foreign policy well before Powers invaded Soviet air space on May 1. It became clear before many days had elapsed that the overflights had been only one element in the Soviet decision to delay negotiations with the West. Khrushchev proved this when, on May 16, he suggested deferring the conference for six or eight months, even before he knew how Eisenhower was going to react to his ultimatum. The Western press began to talk of disagreements within the Soviet leadership and with the military in particular. Curiously enough, Khrushchev decided to mention these rumours himself, something that he never did again in such detail. On May 28 1960, addressing a congress of communist workers' brigades, he said: 'American propaganda is circulating the silliest inventions about the situation in the Soviet Union. It is said, for instance, that instability is rife within the Party and the Government and that this has made difficulties for Khrushchev; that officers and generals who lost their jobs owing to a cut-back in the armed forces are opposed to him. The imperialists are also spreading

libellous tales according to which other socialist countries are demanding that the Soviet Union should abandon its policy of détente, and
so on. . . . Some bourgeois journalists even claim that there is a new
victim of dissension within the Soviet Government – that Mikoyan, the
veteran member of the Politburo, has been expelled from the Central
Committee, no longer attends receptions, was absent from a certain
dinner. . . .'[1]

After declaring that Mikoyan, far from being disgraced, was resting
at Pitsunda on the Black Sea, Khrushchev concluded: 'No, gentlemen,
let me answer you that you are blinded by class hatred and are indulging in wishful thinking. Mr. Allen Dulles's intelligence services must
be worthless if you have to base your policy on such crude and ridicu-
lous inventions.'

This is an excellent example of the difficulties which beset Kremlinology. In Moscow and elsewhere this statement made a great impression
on a number of well-intentioned people, who made haste to close the
discussion by saying: 'You see, Khrushchev himself has denied it. . . .'
This, however, was clearly wide of the mark. Without knowing the
views of Allen Dulles or belonging to the CIA, it was sufficient to read
Pravda and other Soviet publications to perceive serious indications of
disagreement. At the very least, Khrushchev's sharp denial should be
interpreted as a domestic policy manoeuvre to gloss over a period of
difficulty and bolster up his shaky authority. At most, it can be read
as an avowal of all the difficulties then confronting the leadership:
unrest within the Party and the Government, opposition from the
military, pressure from other socialist countries, Mikoyan's fall from
favour. These were in fact the problems that had arisen. Each of them
will now be discussed.

THE QUARREL WITH CHINA

The recent history of Soviet relations with China has demonstrated
better than anything else what Khrushchev's denial was worth. The
USSR and China had been at odds for several years and the background
of the problem will not be analysed here. At the end of 1959 and the
beginning of 1960 the matter came to a head. When the dispute was
made public in 1963 Soviet officials mentioned 1960 as the year in
which the conflict began. If this is true, Moscow certainly deserves a

[1] Collection of Khrushchev's speeches on foreign policy during 1960, published at
Moscow in 1961 under the title: *The Foreign Policy of the Soviet Union, 1960*, vol 1
p 622.

share of the blame. For example, the 1957 atomic co-operation agreement was broken off by the Soviets and Peking was so informed on
June 20 1959; the famous Tass statement on the border conflict between
China and India was released on September 9 1959 despite the opposition of the Chinese Government; at the Camp David meeting the
USSR, to say the least, did not seriously consider China's interests.
The talks between Khrushchev and Mao Tse-tung in early October 1959
were very cool, and from then on the situation as viewed from Moscow
was highly precarious.

However, until June 1960 when the Russians launched their veiled
attack on 'modern dogmatism', there were no outward signs of disagreement and the Soviet press was full of friendliness towards Peking.
'Chinese reactions' to events in the Soviet Union and the world were
always given prominence. On the anniversary of the friendship treaty in
February 1960 enthusiastic articles were published, including one in
Pravda of February 14 by a prominent Chinese personality, Mrs. Sun
Sin-lin (true, her analysis of the international situation was more or less
in keeping with the Soviet line). *Pravda* of April 27 1960 published an
article by the Albanian leader Enver Hoxha, although the crisis with
Tirana was already fairly serious. It transpired much later, from the
Chinese statement of February 27 1964, that Mikoyan had made a
secret trip to Albania in January 1960 'in order to engage in activities
hostile to the Chinese Communist Party'. Khrushchev himself made
some concessions to the Chinese by hinting during his trip to Indonesia
at the end of February that future summit conferences (not that of May
1960, whose list of participants was already closed) should include the
major Asian countries and in particular the People's Republic of China.

Some years later, it became known that negotiations behind the
scenes were far less friendly. On February 6, in a note to Peking, the
Soviet Communist Party denounced the attitude of the Chinese in the
conflict with India as 'narrowly nationalistic' (*Peking Review*, November
8 1963). This followed a series of protests (six between December 10
1959 and January 30 1960) by the Chinese Government to Chervonenko,
the Soviet Ambassador in Peking, against the neutralist attitude of the
Russians in this matter. Obviously, Moscow rejected the Chinese
complaints.

Khrushchev seems to have been jittery at the beginning of February
1960. On February 4, addressing the delegations of fraternal parties
at the closing banquet of a Warsaw Pact conference, he depicted Mao
Tse-tung as 'an elderly, crotchety person, rather like an old shoe, which
is just good enough to put in a corner to be admired'. Such, at any rate,
were his words as reported by the pro-Chinese minority of the Communist Party of Ceylon in a statement that the Chinese promptly

published (*Peking Review*, November 29 1962). The Chinese *People's Daily*, even better informed than the Cingalese dissidents, said that in the same speech Khrushchev had rudely criticized China's insistence on placing the USSR 'at the head of the socialist camp' (*Peking Review*, February 10 1964).[1] Whether Khrushchev actually spoke as reported or not, he does seem at that period to have been very off-hand, not only with the Chinese but with the other fraternal parties. In a speech on agricultural problems, on February 3, to the leaders of the European parties, he brusquely told his allies not to rely too much on Russian wheat and to seek other markets for their wine and vegetables.[2]

It is clear that the Chinese took advantage of the discontent among the allies caused by such statements, as well as the fears of being left in the lurch which the prospect of the summit conference had provoked in many quarters. In the second half of April, on the occasion of the ninetieth anniversary of Lenin's birth, a series of articles appeared in the major publications of the Chinese Communist Party, under the title 'Long Live Leninism'. For over three years these articles served as the platform of revolutionary communism in revolt against Moscow. Their interpretation in the West varied widely. Since they ended with enthusiastic declarations of Soviet–Chinese friendship, many analysts concluded that they did not prove anything. Soviet commentators were closer to the truth when – three years later – they described the articles as the beginning of the 'public quarrel'. Actually, it was only semi-public, since the only persons named by the Chinese were 'Tito and his clique'. But under each heading – the nature of imperialism, the struggle for peace, transition to socialism and the inevitability of wars – the Chinese made a sweeping critique of Khrushchev's foreign policy. Current events were not mentioned (there was not a word about the summit conference scheduled for the following month), but this omission was rectified by an editorial in the *People's Daily* of April 22 1960.

[1] Oddly enough, all through this stage of the dispute, the Chinese claimed that the USSR must remain 'at the head of the socialist camp', while pleading at the same time for the end of Soviet world hegemony. The most likely explanation of this is one which involves a Machiavellian attitude on the part of the Chinese, based on the principle that where there is a head there must also be a body. The Chinese, in fact, at this time wanted the communist movement to have a highly organized structure with permanent assemblies and secretariats in which China would naturally occupy second place after the Soviet Union. This would make it easier for Peking to influence Moscow's policy, and as soon as circumstances permitted China would move up to first place. Later, when the conflict sharpened, the Chinese gave up this demand, preferring to attack Moscow 'from the outside'.

[2] *Agricultural Speeches* vol 4 p 106. The eight-volume collection published between 1962 and 1964 under the title: N. S. Khrushchev: *The Building of Communism in the USSR and the Development of Agriculture*, comprises Khrushchev's speeches and notes on agricultural problems from September 1953 to March 1964. It will be referred to as *Agricultural Speeches*.

It listed thirty-seven 'aggressive acts or statements' by the United States Government between October 1959 and that date, and concluded that 'even after the Camp David talks and on the eve of the summit conference, we see no substantive change in the imperialists' war policy, the policy of the United States Government and of Eisenhower himself'. A report delivered by Lu Ting-yi on April 22 1960 added further thrusts aimed transparently at Khrushchev: 'Not only has our Party's general line of advance towards socialism been attacked by the imperialists and neo-revisionists, but it has also been reviled by some philistines who label it "petit-bourgeois fanaticism".'

Thus, just before the summit conference, Peking was putting strong pressure on Khrushchev to adopt a tougher line, by reminding him in every possible way that American imperialism was as aggressive as ever and had in no way been appeased by Khrushchev's smiles at Camp David.

Under these circumstances, the U-2 incident and particularly Washington's reaction could not have pleased Mao more or Khrushchev less. Mao summed up Chinese feelings to a group of Afro-Asian visitors on May 14 in a statement reported by the New China agency as follows: 'After saying that certain persons described Eisenhower as a lover of peace, comrade Mao Tse-tung expressed the hope that these facts [the U-2 affair] might awaken those people.'

As for the Soviet reaction to this Chinese offensive, the data available suggest that it was quite mild at the time (April and May 1960); indeed extraordinarily so if compared to Khrushchev's denunciation of the Chinese in February 1960 and the violence of his counter-offensive in June and July. A single timid rejoinder was contained in the report delivered by O. V. Kuusinen on April 22, when he took 'Western [sic] publicists' to task for recalling that Lenin 'had been opposed to peaceful coexistence'. 'To remain true to Marxism–Leninism today,' Kuusinen added, 'we must do more than merely repeat the old truth that imperialism is aggressive.' But the spate of Chinese proclamations at the end of April which, for the first time, publicly raised doubts about the very basis of Soviet policy, only provoked in the Soviet press new and fervent declarations of friendship for the great 'ally' in the East. Moreover, the Soviet leadership picked that moment to make a major conciliatory effort: on May 11, when, as we shall see, Moscow disarray was at its height, Mao was officially invited to the USSR. This invitation, which was declined, was disclosed by the Soviets three years later. It could, of course, be interpreted as a demand that Mao should give an account of himself rather than as a friendly gesture. It does indicate, however, a concern for diplomatic niceties that was certainly lacking in February, when Khrushchev insulted the Chinese head of state in front of delegates of the fraternal parties, and again in Bucharest in June.

It appears, then, that at the time of the U-2 incident, Moscow was in a weak position *vis-à-vis* the Chinese and that Mao certainly played a major role in wrecking the Paris conference, although the actual decision to break off the talks was undoubtedly taken in Moscow. The important fact is that, at the time, the Chinese point of view had its influence on Soviet political life.

THE *DÉTENTE* AT STAKE

Even before the May 1 incident, it had become obvious that Soviet foreign policy had stiffened. The guardians of communist orthodoxy had swung into action immediately after Khrushchev's return from Camp David. G. A. Zhukov, in charge of cultural relations with the West, had warned that these relations must not become a 'Trojan horse' of bourgeois ideology within Soviet society. Leonid F. Brezhnev had propounded an original view according to which the 'ideological struggle sharpens in proportion to the achievements of socialism'. Khrushchev himself, constantly caught between the desire for 'personal contacts' with the capitalist world and the preservation of his system, had drawn a sharp distinction in principle between 'peaceful coexistence between states', which he favoured, and 'coexistence of ideologies', which he rejected. But this distinction began to appear tenuous when Khrushchev advocated inter-state 'co-operation' instead of mere coexistence. Pushed to its logical conclusion, the appeal for 'co-operation' bordered on heresy which could not fail to arouse the vigilance of doctrinaire communists. One of them, P. M. N. Fedoseyev, writing in *Pravda*, rebuked *Literaturnaya Gazeta* (the writers' organ, which was relatively liberal at the time) for having treated over-leniently an article by the American Norman Cousins which painted an idyllic picture of a world without armies.

This was only an advance skirmish for, as the summit conference drew near, attitudes on the problems immediately at issue continued to harden. One of the first signs of this was a lengthy commentary by 'Observer' in *Pravda* of April 14 1960, which sharply criticized American views as outlined by Secretary of State Herter in a speech of April 4. Then, on April 25, Khrushchev himself made a long speech in Baku which was regarded by all the chancelleries as the toughest for several months. After expressing his 'alarm' at certain 'negative aspects' of Western policy during the past few weeks, Khrushchev rejected *in toto* the disarmament plan which the West had proposed to the Committee of Ten at Geneva. He also reaffirmed the most intransigent Soviet position on Berlin. Should negotiations fail, a peace treaty would be signed unilaterally with East Germany which, he said, would result in 'the loss of the right of access to West Berlin by land, water or air'. On April 27, the day after the publication of the speech, *Pravda*'s 'Observer' launched another major attack on various American declarations.

Clearly, this change of front was not solely the result of Soviet domestic developments. The fact is that the Western attitude had also stiffened, in particular over the Berlin problem. Herter's speeches already mentioned and those of the Under-Secretary of State, Dillon, had called for a firm attitude. Moreover, it was natural that the Head of the Soviet Government for his part should present his opening position in the summit negotiations in its hardest form. Khrushchev certainly did not then desire events to take the shape they eventually did. All the signs are that he was approaching the negotiations, if not in the hope of reaching important agreements, at least with the intention of taking further steps towards 'co-operative coexistence' with the West. It is quite possible that he would have been particularly exacting on the Berlin issue. His rash undertaking, in the autumn of 1958, to force the West to change the occupation status of Berlin made it imperative for him to achieve some success on this point. At the same time, he seems to have been eager to achieve some progress on disarmament. Pressed by the need to boost the Soviet economy and win the race for better living standards, he had used the *détente* created by his visit to the United States to persuade the military to accept a cut-back of one-third in the Soviet armed forces in January 1960. He undoubtedly wished to go even further, as indicated by his plan announced at the same time for the reorganization of the army on a basis of 'territorial militias'.[1] It is not to be excluded, either, that he contemplated concessions to the West on disarmament control – the traditional hurdle to international agreements and the point on which the Russians had always been adamant.

All in all, Khrushchev needed a success, if only to justify his insistence in demanding the conference and his notions about getting along with the West in political matters. At worst, even in the most probable event of the talks dissolving into pleasant generalities on coexistence,

---

[1] In the early months of 1960 there was a rumour in Germany that Moscow was about to curtail sharply its military forces stationed in East Germany. Apparently there was also a question of liquidating the Warsaw Pact organization. The rumours were never officially confirmed, but they seem plausible in the light of Khrushchev's statements of that time. He had more faith than ever in the supreme power of nuclear rockets.

Khrushchev's propaganda machine would, we may be sure, have presented them as a brilliant success for the policy of *détente*, and a major contribution to the victory of the 'realistic' forces in the West (represented especially by Eisenhower) over the 'warmongers'.

It may be wondered, therefore, whether the Baku speech itself, with its pessimistic undertone and its admission that the 'aggressive forces' in the West were 'still strong', did not go beyond the requirements of normal diplomatic outbidding before the approaching summit. Possibly some pressure was already being put on the First Secretary. The speech came after a prolonged period of political inactivity for Khrushchev, who was on holiday at Gagra on the Black Sea. But his whereabouts were announced only on April 20 after twelve days (an abnormal time lag for that period) during which no news about him was released. It was also noted that he had not returned to Moscow for the ninetieth anniversary of Lenin's birth on April 22, although this was celebrated as a major event in all the communist capitals. Furthermore, the scant attention given to Mikoyan (whose position will be discussed more fully later) also suggested that Khrushchev and his allies were losing some of their power. It may not have been sheer coincidence that Khrushchev's chief enemy, Molotov himself, chose that moment to attempt a political comeback. This came to light in November 1961 when Leonid Ilyichev made the following disclosure in a speech before the Twenty-second Congress: 'On April 18 1960 Molotov sent the editors of the journal *Kommunist* an article devoted to the anniversary of Lenin's birth. Its title was "About Vladimir Ilyich Lenin". Note that the article was written after the ideological, political and organizational defeat of the factionary anti-party group. The editors did not publish it.' Ilyichev went on to give several reasons for the refusal, which he regarded as 'correct'. They were that Molotov in his article had not said one word against the actions of the 'anti-party group' of 1957, 'as if it had never existed'. Molotov's thesis was that every country on the way to socialism had to deal with difficulties similar to those which Russia had experienced in the 'twenties, namely civil war and foreign intervention. This matched the Chinese views of the impossibility of a peaceful transition. As to foreign policy, Ilyichev commented: 'The article revised the principles of the Twentieth Congress on questions of international relations. It underestimated the new balance of power which had arisen after the Second World War, the growing power of the states of the socialist camp and primarily of the Soviet Union, as well as the increased political activity of the popular masses in the capitalist countries. Thus it ignored the real possibility of averting world war in our time.'

The striking fact, even more than the content of Molotov's article, was that a man of his experience had thought it possible to address it to the editors of *Kommunist* while he was in disgrace, and without a vestige of the traditional self-criticism. Did he really expect it to be published? It should be noted that on April 18 the issue of the magazine devoted to Lenin's birthday had already come out (it had been cleared on the 14th). It also contained an article by another Party member of long standing who in the past had been fairly closely associated with Molotov: namely A. A. Andreyev, who pleaded for a 'vigilant' foreign policy. It is possible that this precedent had encouraged Molotov to take such a daring step. It cannot be excluded, however, that he had received encouragement from other sources.

Such were the premonitory signs of a shift in foreign policy on the eve of the U-2 incident. Needless to say, the aerial intrusion of May 1 served to pour oil on the fires which were already smouldering. Two clearly distinct periods followed. They were:

1 The period of *decisions*, occupying roughly the first half of May, during which some wavering was perceived.

2 The period of *settling of accounts* in the second half of May, when Khrushchev was the target of some almost overt criticism.

2 A Month of Turmoil

MOSCOW'S DELIBERATE SILENCE

The embarrassment of the Soviet leaders on May 1 can be fully understood only if the U-2 incident is viewed in context. Powers's irruption into Soviet air space was not an isolated case but part of a plan pursued consistently since the U-2s had become operational in 1956. There is good reason to believe that the Soviets had been able to keep a close watch by radar on earlier flights over their territory, although their pursuit planes and anti-aircraft artillery were powerless to retaliate at high altitude. Khrushchev's misfortune was that the Americans did not bother to deny any of this after the scandal broke. Herter turned the knife in the wound when, on May 9, he declared that the American surveillance programme was no secret to the Soviet leaders.[1]

This was undoubtedly true, and apparently the attitude to be adopted towards United States incursions had already been discussed in Moscow: notably on April 9 1960, the date of the last previous intrusion 'from around Afghanistan'. Addressing the Supreme Soviet on May 5 1960, Khrushchev said:

'When these violations occurred, some of our comrades wondered whether a warning should not be issued to the United States . . . . There was an exchange of views within the Government and we decided then not to take any steps, not to send any note or memorandum because we knew from experience that they had no practical effect . . . . We warned our military that they should act resolutely and not let our air space be violated with impunity by foreign planes' (*Pravda*, May 6 1960).

In fact, the instructions given to the military must have been less categorical since, according to the same speech, Powers's U-2 was brought down only upon a specific order from the Soviet Government after Malinovsky in person had reported that a non-identified aircraft

[1] Khrushchev tried to deny this when addressing journalists on May 11: 'I did not know that such an intelligence-gathering programme had been worked out by the United States, and particularly a programme of reconnaissance flights over Soviet territory' (*Pravda*, May 13 1960). Nevertheless, in almost all his speeches during that period, he had to acknowledge that flights had been taking place for several years and that he had known about them.

was advancing across Soviet territory. According to a statement by Marshal Grechko, the order was issued 'by Khrushchev personally' (*Pravda*, May 7 1960).

The reasons why Moscow chose to keep silent about the incident of April 9 and a number of earlier aerial intrusions were later mentioned repeatedly by Khrushchev. It seems that, on at least one occasion, the decision not to broach the matter with the Americans was his own. In 1956, immediately after an official visit to Moscow by General Twining, the chief of the United States Air Force, an American plane was clandestinely sent to the USSR and penetrated as far as Kiev. Khrushchev referred to it in a speech at the Czechoslovak Embassy on May 9 1960:

'The question arose: should we protest or not? I suggested not sending any protest . . . . We learnt our lesson from the fact and stepped up our production of rockets and fighter planes.'

The reason adduced was always the same: namely, that a diplomatic protest would only 'gratify the adversary'. This is scarcely convincing, for Soviet diplomacy is not notably averse to making gratuitous protests. It is more likely that Khrushchev, in opposition to some of his colleagues in the leadership, intended to pursue his efforts towards a *rapprochement* with the United States despite the aerial intrusions. None of the earlier protests mentioned at the time of the U-2 incident were of more recent date than 1958. A more significant fact is that Khrushchev did not breathe a word about the overflights to Eisenhower at the Camp David talks. He was to be pointedly questioned on this subject when matters were aired in public.

Powers's interception on the morning of May 1 created an entirely novel situation since, for the first time, not only had a plane been brought down but full evidence of the misdeed was to hand. A large part of the aircraft was unharmed, the pilot was alive and co-operative to boot. Publicity appeared not only necessary but inevitable, although this point too seems to have been debated. One decision was taken officially during a Central Committee plenary session on May 4, which was probably preceded by an enlarged Presidium meeting. As early as May 3 most of the provincial alternate Presidium members – Andrei P. Kirilenko, First Secretary of the Sverdlovsk Oblast Committee, Demian S. Korochenko, head of the Ukrainian state, and V. P. Mzavanadze, First Secretary for Georgia, appeared in Moscow at a luncheon for Antonin Novotný, the leader of the Czechoslovak Communist Party. According to a reliable diplomatic source which claimed to have been given the information by Khrushchev himself, the U-2 affair occupied the Central Committee for the entire morning of May 4. This informant states that three speakers, one of them a Presidium member (unfortunately his name is not specified), were against bringing the case before the Supreme Soviet which was scheduled to meet on the following day. This is not many, but more than enough to indicate wavering in Government circles.

Another more concrete sign of indecision had appeared even before the Central Committee meeting. On April 28, a few days before the U-2 incident, Air Marshal K. A. Vershinin, the commander of the Soviet air force, had officially accepted an invitation from his American counterpart, General White, to visit the United States, in return for the visit to the USSR in 1956 of General Twining, General White's predecessor. The planning of the visit, however, had coincided with a clandestine overflight and this had particularly offended the Soviet officials (on May 9 Khrushchev compared General Twining to 'an animal prepared to shit on the very spot where he eats'). Hence it was to be expected that Marshal Vershinin would promptly cancel his acceptance after Powers's capture. As a matter of fact, on May 2 the Pentagon was requested to delay its official announcement of Vershinin's visit. Apparently the Soviets had not yet decided whether to cancel the visit (as the *New York Times* suggested on May 8) but wanted time to think the matter over. Cancellation indeed seemed the most likely prospect, but the reverse happened: on May 4 a communiqué in *Pravda* and the other chief Moscow papers announced that Vershinin had accepted General White's invitation and would be arriving in Washington on May 14 with six generals and three staff officers. On the same day a cable was received by the Pentagon authorizing the United States to make the same announcement.[1] The visit, of course, never took place. On May 12, at the height of the crisis, Vershinin informed his American counterpart that 'in the circumstances' he was reversing his decision (*Pravda*, May 14 1960). It is interesting to note, nevertheless, that three days after the May 1 incident, when the Soviet authorities must have been fully aware of the significance of their catch, they chose, albeit with some hesitation, to continue friendly contacts with the Pentagon 'warmongers'. Even the plenary session of the Central Committee does not seem to have altered this situation.[2]

[1] The details were published by the *New York Times* on May 14 1960 on the basis of information supplied by the Pentagon.
[2] This may be inferred from the fact that the *Pravda Ukrainy*, which was not published on May 4, reported Vershinin's acceptance on May 5, i.e. on the day after the Central Committee meeting.

MEASURED INDIGNATION

The Committee's failure to cancel the visit was probably no more than
an oversight, since decisions on a number of other problems, all pointing to a stiffening of attitudes, were ratified at that session. The so-
called 'organizational' questions, i.e. changes in the leadership decided
on that day, will be dealt with separately. They were the only decisions
announced, but it is not hard to divine the others from various signs,
including the report delivered by Khrushchev next day to the Supreme
Soviet.

In the first place, the Committee decided to give the U-2 incident the
widest publicity although, as already mentioned, some of the leaders
were not too eager for this. A ruse was even devised whose propaganda
success exceeded all expectations but whose later consequences were
fateful. This was Khrushchev's disclosure of only part of the truth in
his speech of May 5, and in particular his silence as to where the plane
had fallen, the pilot's capture and the existence of tangible evidence.
This made the Americans believe they could get away with an innocuous
'meteorological' explanation. Khrushchev's action may have been
suggested to him by a communiqué from the National Aeronautics
and Space Administration of May 3 stating that one of their research
planes had disappeared. In any event, the United States Government
fell into the trap by making its lengthy 'cover declaration' of May 5,
thus enabling Khrushchev to confound it two days later. In turn,
Khrushchev's triumph played a major role in Washington's decision
– a most embarrassing one for Khrushchev – energetically to defend
American espionage policy. The impulsive First Secretary had doubtless
not reckoned with this, and his eagerness for a big propaganda success
had overshadowed other considerations. If the ruse was not his own
idea, whoever suggested it to him may well have had ulterior motives.

In the second place, it was probably decided at the Central Committee meeting to wreck the summit conference. The proposals Khrushchev had intended to submit to the conference are not known. As
noted, he would probably have been tough on the Berlin issue but might
have been amenable to concessions on disarmament. His speech of
May 5 not only precluded any further shift in the Soviet position but
indicated for the first time, far more explicitly than in the Baku speech,
that the summit conference would achieve nothing. He said:

> 'I have been authorized by the Soviet Government to declare that
> the other side's latest moves, their speeches and some of their
> actions . . . unfortunately leave only scant hope that these Govern-
> ments . . . are seeking concrete solutions. . . . There are signs that

these [Paris] negotiations may not fulfil the hopes of the peoples of the world. . . . It would be a mistake to let oneself be lulled to rest by delusions. . . . If the talks bring no results, the nations will know who is to blame' (*Pravda*, May 6 1960).

A third sign, reported somewhat later by the Western monitoring stations, confirmed the stiffening of the Soviet line: on May 5 the jamming of 'Voice of America' broadcasts resumed, after a pause which had started in the autumn of 1959 and had lasted throughout the period of Soviet–United States *rapprochement*.

All this happened just after the Central Committee session of May 4, when no one in Moscow could yet suspect that Washington would react so uncompromisingly to the capture of the U-2. It is therefore clear that the incident in itself was only the last touch that enabled the advocates of a hard foreign policy to achieve what they had been seeking for several months.

Khrushchev's reference to 'delusions' already indicated a defensive attitude on his part. If anyone had entertained any 'delusions' about American imperialism, surely it had been he, both during and after his visit to the United States, with his lavish praise for the 'realistic' Administration officials and particularly Eisenhower, whom he portrayed as a 'sincere lover of peace', and 'courageous' to boot. During the entire crisis this friendly attitude towards Eisenhower was to be a serious source of weakness for Khrushchev and a trump card for his adversaries.[1]

This became obvious at the outset when the Tass agency, followed by all the Soviet newspapers, made a curious addition to its account of Khrushchev's report to the Supreme Soviet of May 5. At a point in the story regarded as particularly 'revolting', when Khrushchev mentioned that the national markings of the U-2 had been camouflaged, the following words depicted the 'reactions' of the audience: 'Cries of

---

[1] In the report on his journey delivered after returning to Moscow on September 28 1959, Khrushchev described Eisenhower as 'a man who enjoys the absolute confidence of his people'. He added: 'I had the impression that he sincerely wished to liquidate the cold war, create normal relations between our two countries and contribute to the improvement of relations among all countries of the world. . . . I do not doubt the President's desire to apply his will and his efforts . . . towards creating friendly relations between our peoples' (*Foreign Policy Speeches 1959* vol 2 pp 290–306).

He repeated the same tribute in Peking, in the presence of Mao Tse-tung himself, on September 30 1959: 'I had the impression that the President of the United States– supported by a considerable number of people – understood the need for lessening international tension' (*ibid.*, p 319).

And again in Vladivostok on October 6: 'I must say I liked talking with him [Eisenhower], an intelligent man who understands the seriousness of the international situation' (*ibid.*, p 328).

indignation. A voice: "How does this fit in with Eisenhower's unctuous speeches? This is sheer banditry!" ' (*Pravda*, May 6 1960). The present writer was at the meeting of the Supreme Soviet just described and has no recollection of any such 'exclamation' on the part of any deputy. *Pravda*, which is never at a loss to record any 'reactions' it wishes, as shown by its tailoring the volume of applause to fit the demands of protocol rather than facts, might quite as easily have 'reported' a different slogan. In this instance its choice was somewhat surprising, since Eisenhower himself was not yet implicated: on the contrary, Khrushchev had reaffirmed in the same speech: 'I do not doubt President Eisenhower's sincere desire for peace.'

The differences of opinion on this point were noticeable during the debate which the Supreme Soviet devoted to the issue on May 5 and 6. Khrushchev's supporters, for their part, refrained from mentioning Eisenhower's role (Ivan Spiridonov slipped into his speech a few barbs aimed at the Chinese and other detractors of 'peaceful coexistence') or even spoke of him in favourable terms: for example A. I. Struyev, an old Ukrainian Party member, recalled that the President of the USA was going to be the guest of the USSR in June, where he would receive 'genuine hospitality'. Others, however, boldly put their finger on the wound. Thus T. Ya. Kiselev, head of the Byelorussian Government, declared:

> 'The Soviet people are particularly revolted by this aggressive act of the American military clique after the people of the United States so warmly welcomed the chief of the Soviet state, and President Eisenhower proclaimed his love for peace. . . . This proves once again that it is indispensable to maintain strong vigilance against intrigues by the enemies of peace' (*Sovietskaya Byelorussia*, May 7 1960).

Others, without going so far as to mention Eisenhower and Camp David, achieved the same results by castigating those who 'speak of God and conscience, freedom and humanity, their sincerity and desire for peace, while indulging in vile and criminal acts against the Soviet people' (V. I. Dovgopol, First Secretary of the Urban Committee of Nizhni-Tazhil, Sverdlovsk region; *Pravda*, May 7 1960). V. I. Ustinov, who at the time was First Secretary of the Moscow Urban Committee, spoke even more plainly during a visit to Berlin: 'One cannot deceive the peoples of the world by empty talk about peaceful intentions. As the Russian proverb says: Do not look at what the mouth says, but at actions' (*Pravda*, May 8 1960).

So far, these were only generalities. It is worth noting, however, that the Chinese at that time were speaking in a similar vein. The picture became clearer a few days later, but Khrushchev was already trying to tone down the chauvinism of the hard-line officials. His closing speech to the Supreme Soviet session on May 7, while gloating over the Americans having been caught red-handed, is full of qualifying remarks; for instance: 'Even today I believe that the persons I met in the United States want peace and friendly relations with the USSR. . . . I am quite willing to believe that the President did not know that a plane had been sent to the Soviet Union and had failed to return. . . . For the present at all events, this is not a signal for war. . . . I would stress that this is not an appeal to stir up feeling in our country, but to observe calm, vigilance and reason' (*Pravda*, May 8 1960).

Had it not been for the American reaction which followed, Khrushchev might have succeeded in keeping things under control. The summit conference was doomed to fail, but it would have been possible to cloak the absence of practical agreements under a few reassuring generalities. The principle of personal contacts with the American leaders was not condemned outright and could have been revived after a reasonable interval.

EMBARRASSMENT FOR KHRUSHCHEV

The fragile compromise was at once upset by Washington's decision to accept full responsibility for the flight. As we have seen, the decision was announced in two stages: in fairly moderate terms in the State Department's declaration of May 7, and with more brutal frankness by the Secretary of State on May 9. Khrushchev apparently did his best not to take the first declaration at its face value. In an improvised speech at the Czechoslovak Embassy on May 9 – a rather confused one, obviously made in the glow of his propaganda success – Khrushchev began by suggesting that the blame lay entirely with the American military. He immediately added 'in confidence' and 'without being certain' that he 'did not exclude that the United States Government had known about the flight'. This was a negation of the version he tried to put across later, namely that he had constantly tried to leave the President 'a way out'. At the same time, but without undue severity, he criticized the State Department's declaration, calling it 'a highly dangerous statement. Dangerous because, instead of condemning such a flight, it justifies it and declares in advance, so to speak, that such over-flights are possible. . . . This, I repeat, is highly dangerous, besides being improper in principle and contrary to the spirit of peaceful international relations.'

Khrushchev thus described American policy as 'dangerous' rather than heinous. Marshal Malinovsky, speaking the same day at a victory commemoration rally, used an entirely different tone. He branded the American declaration as 'an even viler crime' of American imperialism, an 'insolent' gesture and evidence that the 'dark forces of the Pentagon have definitely lost their sanity' (*Krasnaya Zvezda*, May 10 1960).

In the upshot, the only decision announced that day was to warn the United States that the bases used for the take-off of reconnaissance planes would be attacked in the event of another similar incident. It took Herter's speech of May 9 to evoke the definitive Soviet response, which took the form of a spate of decisions in various fields.

The Party Presidium seems to have held a long meeting on May 10 and perhaps also on May 11. Apart from Podgorny, who made an official trip to Prague from May 6 to May 14, D. S. Polyansky, who was reported to be in Petrozavodsk on May 11, and Mikoyan, on holiday in Pitsunda (this point will be discussed later), all the members of the Presidium were in Moscow on those two days. In addition, on the evening of May 11, a Tass communiqué announced that a meeting of a Central Committee plenary session was being called for July 13 in order to hear a series of reports on industrial and technological problems. According to the traditions of the Khrushchevian era, such a call always seems to have been decided upon, or at least ratified, at a session of the Presidium. This body at the same time would usually approve the main outline of the theses to be submitted to the Central Committee, and would ratify a number of other measures on various issues. This duly happened between May 10 and 12. The decisions to invite Mao Tse-tung to Moscow (letter of May 11) and to cancel Vershinin's visit to the United States (letter of May 12) have already been mentioned. In addition, it is likely that another major decision was ratified on the same day by a hard-line majority of the Presidium; namely to wreck the summit conference.

It was not long before Khrushchev made it clear that things had gone one step further. On May 11, in a desultory conversation with journalists, he blurted out: 'And if the conference is not held, so what? We've lived many years as we are, we can do without one for another hundred years!' Khrushchev hastily added that, of course, he did want the conference and would even go to Paris two days before its scheduled opening, on May 14. But the hint, the only one dropped until May 16, suggests that something more had been decided: not, perhaps, to create the rumpus which actually took place, but at least to prevent the conference being held. Of course, the Soviet leaders did not yet know that Eisenhower would elect to back up his Secretary of State all along the line.

This view is confirmed by the extraordinary campaign launched by the Soviet press on the evening of May 13 against 'American aggression', etc. From then on everything indicated that the atmosphere would be utterly inauspicious not only for fruitful negotiations, but for any meeting at all. Conceivably Khrushchev, aware that the conference plan was moving towards failure in any case, accepted this course of action with good grace. But he may have had his reservations, and the whole matter is far from clear. Two points at this stage are noteworthy.

On the one hand, Khrushchev had hinted that the conference might not take place, yet here he was, going to Paris at the head of a large delegation. It would have been more logical to announce from Moscow, immediately after Herter's statement or at least after Eisenhower's on May 11, that the United States' position precluded any dialogue, instead of waiting till May 16. As it was, Khrushchev allowed doubts about his intentions to persist for five days. Eisenhower's declaration was not commented on during that time, which all suggested to public opinion that things were simmering down. The shock was all the more drastic when the conference opened, and the effect on Western opinion was disastrous.

Secondly, Khrushchev cast doubt upon the summit conference but not on another aspect of his foreign policy, although this was highly controversial – namely Eisenhower's proposed visit to the USSR from June 10 to 19 1960 (decided upon in January). Khrushchev did hint in his press conference of May 11 that 'unpleasant questions' would be asked the guest during the trip and that he 'would not like to be in his place', but he announced at the same time that there would be 'no excesses' and 'no insult by deeds' would be tolerated. In other words, the visit still appeared to him a reality. It was only on May 16, at the first summit meeting, that Khrushchev withdrew his invitation.

These contradictions may have been due simply to the confusion in Soviet policy during the period. It is also conceivable, however, that the solution arrived at in the discussions of May 10 and 11 was a compromise between Khrushchev and the hard-line members of the Presidium. The decision might have been taken to wreck the summit conference in deference to Chinese opposition, using the U-2 incident as a pretext, but not to call off Khrushchev's visit to Paris. What then was the purpose of his going? To meet Eisenhower and review the situation with him, particularly ways of maintaining personal contact. In the meantime, Khrushchev apparently persuaded his colleagues of the collective leadership to allow the President's visit to Moscow to remain on the agenda, just in case. This would explain, for one thing, why Khrushchev went to Paris to meet Eisenhower two days before the summit conference was to open. A study of Khrushchev's declarations of

May 11 shows that he expected and hoped for such a meeting. In answer to a question about Eisenhower's planned visit to the USSR, he declared: 'I shall discuss this with the President when I meet him in Paris.' This was confirmed by Malinovsky in a speech of May 30 1960, which is interesting since the Defence Minister was just then very critical of Khrushchev. The Marshal described Khrushchev's attitude in Paris, and even the fact that he went there at all, as evidence of his conciliatory attitude. 'The Soviet Government,' he said, 'would have been fully justified in not attending the Paris conference. Nevertheless, faithful to its peace-loving policy, the Government did decide to go to Paris and N. S. Khrushchev, the Head of the Government went there in the hope that the Government of the United States, *at a personal meeting between the Heads of Government* [Author's italics], would, with the courage and tact befitting gentlemen, openly condemn this aggressive act' (*Pravda*, May 31 1960).

The personal meeting never took place, except when the heads of the four powers were together at the Elysée on May 16. Probably this is where Khrushchev suffered his ultimate disappointment in his former Camp David friend. He may well have gone to what his Kremlin critics regarded as excessive lengths to arrange the meeting. At all events, within less than ten days, between May 28 and June 5, he deemed it necessary to justify himself three times on this score, first in a speech, then in the form of two interviews given on June 2 to *Izvestia* and on June 5 to *Pravda*. These statements were apparently addressed to Western opinion and meant to show that, contrary to the American claim, Khrushchev had not closed the door to bilateral talks. Possibly, too, they were designed to demonstrate that he had taken a firmer line than certain circles alleged. An interesting fact was connected with the third statement (*Pravda* of June 5 1960) in which he went as far as to quote excerpts from the verbatim record of the May 16 conference. *Izvestia*, whose chief editor at the time was Khrushchev's leading supporter, A. I. Adzhubey, published a summarized version which, as if by chance, stressed the toughest passages. On the other hand *Krasnaya Zvezda*, the army organ, was the only one of the Moscow and chief provincial newspapers which completely ignored Khrushchev's explanations.

To come back to the events of mid-May, it is clear that, whatever he may have achieved, Khrushchev's position was not strengthened. At the Presidium meetings of May 10 and 11 there must have been a barrage of criticism against his past diplomacy, since Herter had given unhoped-for ammunition to Khrushchev's adversaries. When Khrushchev met journalists on May 11, he had to make the following unprecedented confession:

'By sending a plane on an espionage mission, the American militarists have placed me, the man responsible for arranging the visit of the United States President to the USSR, in a very difficult position.' He was also compelled to admit that Herter's declarations had made him 'change his mind concerning the non-participation of the United States President in the affair' and also that his hopes had been 'to some extent unjustified'.

The present writer, who attended the press conference at which Khrushchev, who was unaccompanied by any other Soviet leader, spoke for over an hour standing on a chair surrounded by the débris of the U-2, recalls having experienced a peculiar feeling. For the first time, the ebullient Party chief gave an impression of genuine embarrassment. True it was far from evident that this was due to any political opposition. Since Khrushchev had a monopoly of making speeches on all issues, his utterances reflected the contradictions and fluctuations of Soviet policy, and it was possible to suppose that nobody was helping him to 'change his mind'. Actually, some suspicion arose on that very day when it was noticed that, for a good many hours, stories on the subject by all the 'bourgeois' (i.e. non-communist) correspondents were held up by the censorship. *Pravda* itself only reported his words, unaltered, on May 13, a delay of over twenty-four hours. Obviously they had been the subject of discussion in high places.

In the coming weeks Khrushchev's critics were to show less restraint.

KHRUSHCHEV UNDER ATTACK AT HOME

On May 18 1960 *Pravda* made a move whose significance eluded most of the foreign observers – including this writer – but must have caused a flurry among those people of the Party machine who were better versed in etiquette. On that date the Party newspaper published on page 1 the translation of a column by Walter Lippmann which had appeared in the *New York Herald Tribune* on May 17. In it, Lippmann criticized the American attitude in the crisis and noted that Khrushchev had endeavoured all along to leave the door open for Eisenhower. Although Khrushchev was certainly aware that the President had approved the general plan of the flights, Lippmann explained in substance, he had preferred to let the President say what was in fact a very sorry kind of truth, namely that he had not authorized this particular flight.

Noting that Eisenhower's attitude made it impossible for Khrushchev to by-pass the affair, Lippmann added: 'Had he done that, he would have been in the position of acknowledging to the world, to the Soviet people, *to his critics within the Soviet Union* [Author's italics], and to his communist allies, that he had surrendered to the United States the right to violate Soviet territory.'

There was no precedent for the mention by the Party newspaper, even under the signature of a foreign commentator, of the existence of Soviet criticism aimed at the Head of the Government. At least, *Pravda* ought to have preceded it by an editorial note, a fairly usual press practice at that time, stating that 'the content could not be fully endorsed' but that the article was 'interesting to Soviet readers'. Or better, it could have deleted the embarrassing sentence altogether. This is what a few provincial papers evidently more sympathetic to Khrushchev did, notably *Pravda Ukrainy* whose nominal head was then N. V. Podgorny, First Secretary of the Republic.[1] This was a typical Kremlinological oddity of which we shall meet more: using a perfectly harmless device that seemingly would not implicate anyone in the USSR (for how could anybody be made responsible for Walter Lippmann's views?), one or more of Khrushchev's foes were insidiously signalling to any Party people who cared to listen. Who those foes might be will be examined later. For the time being, let it merely be noted that they must have been in the Presidium or the Secretariat of the Party, the institution that has the last word as far as *Pravda's* make-up is concerned. (This was made easier by the fact that just then Khrushchev was in Paris with P. A. Satyukov and Adzhubey, the chief editors who ran the two large Moscow dailies for him.) As to the signal itself, it was meant to be taken literally, to show that Khrushchev was being criticized in the Soviet Union, and most probably at top level.

Naturally, the criticism could appear publicly only in this veiled form. Things being what they are in the Soviet Union, it is out of the question to make a frontal attack. Instead, the technique is to allude to some side aspect which, by reason of its historical implications, is particularly delicate. Several such insinuations were coupled with warm praise for Khrushchev. There is nothing astonishing about this, for at certain periods, personal tribute to him was as mandatory as under Stalin. Even then, however, it was one thing to praise the First Secretary's 'peace missions' in Camp David or elsewhere, and another to congratulate him on the 'firm attitude' he adopted on May 16.

As noted previously, at the session of the Supreme Soviet, the barbs began to be felt whenever Camp David and Eisenhower's personal role were mentioned, for this implicitly brought to mind the praise

---

[1] In addition to *Pravda*, the papers that published the full text were: *Izvestia* and *Sovietskaya Byelorussia* (then edited by K. T. Mazurov), and *Zaria Vostoka*, the main Georgian daily (First Secretary, V. P. Mzhavanadaze). Only the *Pravda Ukrainy* published it without the controversial sentence.

that Khrushchev had showered upon him at the time. Roughly speaking, the most embarrassing issues were these: if the flights had started so much earlier, why did Khrushchev not raise the matter with Eisenhower during the Camp David talks? Why had he depicted the President of the United States as a 'sincere lover of peace' and even a 'courageous' one, whereas at best he was no more than a pawn of the 'Pentagon military clique' and at worst – the most logical assessment on the part of the real doctrinaires – the conscious leader of 'monopolistic aggressive imperialism'? How did Khrushchev explain such a difference between the Camp David Eisenhower and the Eisenhower of May 1960 who was defending a policy of espionage against the USSR?[1] Behind these questions there loomed another, far more serious one: why, when all was said and done, did Khrushchev lend himself to this game of friendship with Eisenhower, why did he pay such a high price for a *rapprochement* with the biggest capitalist power in the world? All those who had looked askance at the dangerous fraternization of 1959 could now speak out.

The most notable of these was Vsevolod Kochetov, the acknowledged head of the conservative school in literature, who played an important political role at this time and throughout the Khrushchev era. In the spring of 1959 he had had to resign from the editorship of *Literaturnaya Gazeta*, officially for 'health reasons'. This had not prevented him from assuming a similar post in the journal *Oktyabr* at the beginning of 1961, which he kept for several years. In his article in *Pravda* of May 23 1960 he went as far as he possibly could, and in so doing provided a good example of the wiles used by oppositionists. He went straight to the point on the Camp David issue: 'It is, to say the least, hard to believe that a representative of the capitalist system is capable of seeing completely eye to eye with a representative of the socialist system on the basic questions of life on this earth. However people may seek to disguise the fact, capitalism . . . has, for a long time, meant nothing but reaction, it is morally a dead system. . . . We have known all this full well, ever since our school days. . . . Nevertheless, when Nikita Sergeyevich Khrushchev met Eisenhower and talked with him in Camp David, we should have liked to believe that the President of imperialist America was, if only to some extent, open, sincere and honourable.' The U-2 affair, however, had given the lie to this for, despite his smile

---

[1] Curiously enough, the most insidious – and at the same time the most orthodox – formulation of this question came from the correspondent of the East German *Neues Deutschland* at Khrushchev's press conference of May 18 1960: 'What in your opinion are the causes of Eisenhower's change of position since your Camp David talks? Can you explain the causes of the difference in the position of the President of the United States between Camp David and Paris?' (*Pravda*, May 19 1960).

and handshaking, Eisenhower 'could not betray the laws of his class, the imperialist community, which was capable of every infamy. . . . It is entirely possible that at the very time when the President of the United States was lavishing hypocritical politenesses upon N. S. Khrushchev, he was endorsing by a stroke of the presidential pen the day-to-day programme of high-altitude espionage flights over our territory.'

Kochetov hurriedly specifies that he for one was not deluded. 'Yes, we wanted to believe Eisenhower, we wanted to believe him for the sake of peace on earth. . . . We very much wanted to believe. But *unlike certain simple-minded persons [prostaki] we were not exactly moved to enthusiasm by the President's foggy, evasive statements.'* [Author's italics.]

In order to appreciate the outrageousness of such statements, it should be noted that the Chinese themselves went no further in their criticism of Khrushchev at this time, and occasionally used the same words. Kochetov's phrasing was strikingly reminiscent of Mao Tsetung's on May 14 quoted earlier. Probably because Kochetov's last quoted sentence represented the limit he had set himself, the article ended with warm praise for Khrushchev – naturally, for his attitude on May 16, when 'he accepted no concession or compromise when the honour of our homeland was at stake'. A belated tribute to a belated performance.

Kochetov had gone further than anybody else in the Soviet Union, and in all likelihood had done so with the agreement of prominent Soviet personalities. A few other commentators touched upon the thorny question of Eisenhower's role. It has already been shown that the most indulgent attitude towards Khrushchev was adopted by those who ignored the subject whenever it was discussed; the writers' analyses contradicted Khrushchev's explanations or, at best, preceded them. Khrushchev, who was aware of the implications for the evaluation of his past policy, had at first declared that Eisenhower had not known about the espionage programme and the schedule of U-2 flights. After the President of the United States himself affirmed the contrary, Khrushchev wavered, finally to grasp at the explanation conveniently offered by Walter Lippmann, namely that Khrushchev had denied Eisenhower's knowledge of the matter in order to leave the President an honourable 'way out'. This could be ascribed to diplomatic skill instead of complacent naïveté. Nevertheless, for the doctrinaire leaders, such an attitude meant ignoring the facts, whether the motive was guile or wishful thinking. An article by Professor Isakov in *Izvestia* of May 22 tried to resolve the ambiguities by ascribing in advance to Khrushchev the thesis of the 'diplomatic way out' (Khrushchev himself adopted it only in his speech of May 28). Isakov wrote: 'N.S. Khrushchev did everything he could to save the President's face, and he succeeded better than all Eisenhower's American supporters put together.' Thereupon the professor concluded that Eisenhower himself had 'swept away the last possible illusions as to his personal role'. He declared, just as Kochetov had done, that nothing else could have been expected from a man who was the mouthpiece of the monopolies and the American military caste.

Even Khrushchev's explanations in his speech of May 28 were not enough to clear matters up. While Khrushchev on that day again asserted that 'the President did not know about these overflights', a certain A. Nosenko wrote in the *Pravda Ukrainy* of May 31 that 'everything, absolutely everything was known to the President, the ultimate boss of the super-spy Allen Dulles'.

The accounts given by Khrushchev to a somewhat critical audience after his return from Paris were in any case belated. Khrushchev had returned on May 21 and was supposed to make his traditional report on the 25th, as the journalists were led to expect on the 24th. Instead, he did not speak till the 28th, to a conference of communist workers' brigades. On all points, his explanations seemed weak and defensive in tone. For example, he thought fit to add the following remark about his speech of October 1959 in which he had given an over-enthusiastic report on his mission to the United States:

'At the meeting held after my return to Moscow from the United States I again declared that there were forces there which sought to go on waging the cold war and the armaments race, and that it was not possible to tell for sure who would win, those forces or the ones seeking a *détente*' (*Pravda*, May 29 1960). As to his silence on the U-2 flights when he was at Camp David, Khrushchev repeated in substance the explanation given at his Paris press conference, which is worth quoting:

'While I was having a talk with President Eisenhower in Camp David I thought to myself: "I'll tell him." I was about to open my mouth to mention it. We were having a good talk and the President turned to me and said: "Call me my friend and I'll call you *moy drug* in Russian, just like a brother." That's when I felt like telling my friend: "It's not nice to fly over one's friends' territory without permission." Then I thought better of it and decided, no, it's no use talking about it. There's something in this friend that doesn't encourage absolute sincerity. So I decided not to bring it up.'

Obviously it is very difficult to take this explanation seriously, but Khrushchev had no other to offer. Neither had Gromyko, who, when the United States delegate at the Security Council, Mr. Henry Cabot Lodge, asked him the same question, said that Khrushchev had kept silent 'because he knew well the thoughts and habits of those he was negotiating with'.

Khrushchev elaborated upon the same argument on May 28, but added: 'I gritted my teeth at Camp David and did not bring up the matter of how inadmissible the flights were, because I knew with whom I was dealing, and not because I attached to them any less importance than I do now.' Thus, implicitly, he was invoking the argument provided by his adversaries – which was probably the only and true reason.

3 Stir in the Top Leadership

The ups and downs of the crisis have been reviewed. They show that Khrushchev had to veer, then reverse his foreign policy on several major issues. The criticisms listed here have shown on what issues clashes had occurred, or behind what formulae they were concealed. It remains to be seen who the protagonists in the debate were, apart from Khrushchev and the Chinese. The Chinese position has already been outlined, and in any event Peking only exerted an additional pressure, as did the various minor figures whose interventions have been mentioned in the preceding pages. Obviously, Kochetov, Kiselev, Ustinov and men of their calibre were the spokesmen of more important figures who alone took part in the decision-making. The role of the military chiefs will be reviewed before considering that of the political personalities.

DEMOBILIZATION, PURGES AND CONTROL OF THE ARMED FORCES BY THE PARTY

The demobilization measures announced by Khrushchev at the beginning of January 1960 undoubtedly caused serious discontent in the armed forces. Within two years, 1960 and 1961, 1,200,000 men, including 250,000 officers, generals and admirals, were to be discharged. Considering the past and present privileged position of the military cadres in the USSR, the sacrifice exacted from them was a major one.

One had only to read the newspapers to learn that complaints had poured into the central Government agencies and that the re-employment of the men concerned entailed many complications. Malinovsky himself had to remind the cadres of their sense of duty. 'One cannot approve,' he said in a speech, 'those demobilized officers who make unrealistic demands upon local authorities and seek highly paid top positions. . . . It must be explained to them that leading posts in the economy and the administration generally are occupied by deserving Soviet citizens who cannot be dismissed to make room for officers.' However, the Defence Minister invited the military cadres 'not to lose heart', even if they were discharged without pension (*Krasnaya Zvezda*, January 20 1960).

Another feature of this period is that the high military chiefs were probably divided as to the advisability of demobilization and the procedures used. Two army representatives expressed views on January 13 and 14 1960 at the session of the Supreme Soviet that ratified the decision. They were Malinovsky himself and Marshal M. V. Zakharov, who was later appointed chief of the General Staff but at this time was only the commander of the Soviet troops in Germany. True, they both approved of Khrushchev's initiative, but neither of Malinovsky's senior aides, Marshals V. D. Sokolovsky (chief of the General Staff) and I. S. Konev (commander of the Warsaw Pact forces), supported the demobilization at that session or later. They both lost their posts a few weeks later, which strongly suggests that they were at odds with Khrushchev and Malinovsky on this point.

As to Malinovsky, while 'whole-heartedly' approving the demobilization, as he said in his speech to the Supreme Soviet, he did not echo all Khrushchev's proposals, in particular his suggestion, 'for the future', of recruitment on a territorial basis which would avoid removing the military from civilian production. On the contrary, tempering Khrushchev's over-optimistic views on the invincibility of rockets and nuclear weapons, the Defence Minister stressed the thesis which the military were to uphold during the following years: 'We consider that one type of weapon cannot solve all the problems of war. The success of military operations, even in modern warfare, is possible only through the combined use of all military means and all weapons. . . . This is why we maintain all the branches of our armed services at a given strength, reasonably balanced and matching our needs' (*Pravda*, January 14 1960).

Malinovsky's rallying to the 'territorial system' proposed by Khrushchev occurred much later, in an article in *Pravda* of February 23 1960 on the occasion of the Armed Forces Day. It should be added that that was the last time the subject was mentioned. Neither Khrushchev nor anyone else later touched upon the idea, which seemed to evaporate together with the optimism that had produced it. The law on the cutback in the armed forces was suspended in the summer of 1961 (at the time of renewed Soviet pressure on Berlin) and was never re-enforced.

Nevertheless, the upheavals provoked by the law, probably coupled with disagreements on foreign policy, resulted in a reshuffle in the high military command in April 1960. The following posts were affected:

	Former holder	*New holder*
First Deputy Minister for Defence commanding the Warsaw Pact forces	I. S. Konev	A. A. Grechko
First Deputy Minister for Defence, Chief of General Staff	V. D. Sokolovsky	M. V. Zakharov
Commander of land forces	A. A. Grechko	V. I. Chuikov
Commander of Soviet troops in Germany	M. V. Zakharov	I. I. Yakubovsky
Commander of the Kiev military region	V. I. Chuikov	P. K. Koshevoy
Commander of the Byelorussian military region	S. K. Timoshenko	V. N. Komarov

As regards I. S. Konev there was some confusion in the date: it was only on July 25 1960 that *Pravda* officially announced his resignation 'on his own request, for health reasons' (although these did not prevent him from assuming command of the Soviet troops in Germany in August 1961). Actually it is clear that the change occurred in April, as it did with Sokolovsky and Timoshenko. The foreign military attachés in Moscow were informed of it on May 1 1960, and it was confirmed on May 9 when the report on the victory commemoration rally listed Grechko and Zakharov immediately after Malinovsky, in keeping with their new positions as 'First Deputy Ministers' for Defence – the former Ministers, Konev and Sokolovsky, being relegated to their alphabetical place in the list of marshals. The same procedure was used in following weeks (for example in *Krasnaya Zvezda* of May 28 1960 for the obituary of I. V. Markov). It is not clear why official confirmation for Konev was delayed. There might have been last-minute objections calling for a change, but this cannot be substantiated.

In any event, for the three main figures who gave up their positions without being appointed to higher ones, the demotion definitely appeared as a semi-disgrace. S. K. Timoshenko and V. D. Sokolovsky were named 'Inspectors-General for the Group of Defence Ministry Inspectors-General'.[1] In spite of the impressive titles, these were posts traditionally allotted to unassigned Soviet marshals. I. S. Konev obtained even less, being assigned no duties whatever from 1960 to the summer of 1961, when he received a new promotion. According to official information given to the military attachés in May 1960, he was simply retired, in the same way as Sokolovsky.

[1] This appointment was announced only two years later in the *Encyclopedia Yearbook* for 1962.

The reasons for the disgrace were probably different for each man. The case of Timoshenko, Stalin's former military deputy and Commissar for Defence in 1940 and 1941 (until the demands of war called for more capable leadership), paralleled the discreet removal at the same moment from the post of head of state of K. E. Voroshilov, one of Stalin's closest comrades in arms. Timoshenko was criticized in 1961 for his part in the defeats of the first war years, just as Voroshilov was for his 'anti-party' activities. As to Konev and Sokolovsky, their silence on the demobilization issue in January 1960 was a sufficient token of their attitude and probably the main reason for their disgrace.

The name of the new Chief of the General Staff, General Zakharov, calls for comment: he kept his post until March 1963, when he was suddenly appointed head of a military academy. The fact that he emerged from the shadow and resumed his functions as the head of the General Staff one month after Khrushchev's downfall, in November 1964, indicates that he was at odds with the latter. But nothing suggests that he already opposed him in 1960 or that his promotion had to be forced on Khrushchev. As mentioned earlier, Malinovsky and Zakharov were the only men to back the demobilization measures in January, and Zakharov's speech at the Supreme Soviet was one of the most flattering to Khrushchev personally. Zakharov had wished him 'many years of life, inexhaustible strength and robust health for the good of the Soviet people and the workers of the entire world'. (Even if a tribute to Khrushchev was almost mandatory, Zakharov was not obliged to be quite so enthusiastic.) It should also be noted that the man he was replacing at the head of the General Staff was less close to Khrushchev than he. Sokolovsky, who had held the post without interruption since 1952, owed far more to Stalin and even more to Marshal Zhukov, the former Defence Minister, who was removed in 1957 and whose Chief of General Staff he had been in Berlin during the war.

Unlike I. S. Konev, whose ties with Khrushchev were rather tenuous, A. A. Grechko, the new commander of the Warsaw Pact forces, was a Ukrainian and former comrade-in-arms of Khrushchev: they had taken part in the liberation of Kiev in 1943, Grechko as the deputy commander of the First Ukrainian Front; and Khrushchev as its political commissar. Grechko had commanded the Kiev military region throughout the post-war years, again under Khrushchev's auspices, and was very close to the First Secretary. In due course he became one of the most fervent devotees of the cult of Khrushchev's personality, and was one of the few people who called him 'Supreme Commander in Chief of the Armed Forces'.[1] On the other hand, like Zakharov, Grechko seems

[1] For instance, Grechko wrote in *Izvestia* of April 17 1964 on the occasion of Khru-

to have favoured a firm foreign policy and to have sided with the opponents of any agreement for a *détente* that might have come out of the Paris summit conference. He was the only military man who spoke at the session of the Supreme Soviet of May 5 and 7, and this is what he said on the issue:

'We are convinced that at the conference N. S. Khrushchev will know how to defend with honour the cause of peace, and how *to unmask and undermine the designs of aggressive circles*. We wish Nikita Sergeyevich success in the *difficult* Paris talks.' (Author's italics. *Pravda*, May 7 1960.)

This interpretation of the summit meeting as designed merely to 'unmask the designs of aggressive circles' indicates clearly enough that the speaker neither expected nor desired any serious result; it is very similar to the Chinese position. An editorial in *Jenmin Jih Pao* of May 16 also expressed the hope that the summit meeting would be 'a useful contribution to the denunciation of the American war policy and the cause of the strengthening of peace in the entire world'.

This was of course after the U-2 incident, at a moment when, as shown previously, the decision to wreck the summit meeting had, in all probability, already been ratified by the majority. It is quite likely that the military, Grechko included, belonged to that majority, for they were the first to rejoice at the decision. Konev's and Sokolovsky's

---

shchev's seventieth birthday: 'Credit for elaborating the present military doctrine of our state belongs to the Leninist Central Committee and N. S. Khrushchev personally. . . . N. S. Khrushchev knows the armed forces well: from the first days of the war, in his capacity as a member of the Military Soviets on various fronts, he endured all the hardships of war together with the troops and made an enormous personal contribution to victory over Nazism. As our Supreme Commander he often visits the troops and the fleets, is fully acquainted with their problems and the needs and aspirations of the soldiers. Soviet military men are full of affection and deep gratitude towards N. S. Khrushchev for having reinstated the Leninist principles in the life of our country, for boldly bearing the Leninist standard, for waging the ideological struggle against all renegades from Leninism.'

It is easy, but always entertaining, to observe the transition from one cult to another. For instance, this is what Grechko had said at the Seventeenth Congress of the Ukrainian Communist Party in September 1952:

'All the victories of the Soviet army are indissolubly linked with the name of our great leader and master, the greatest genius among the war leaders, comrade Stalin. Thanks to the Stalinist wisdom and insight, thanks to the Stalinist policy of industrialization of the country and collectivization of agriculture, our country was ready for active defence at the beginning of the Great Patriotic War. . . . Long live our leader and master, the genius of war, the great Stalin!' (Verbatim records of the Seventeenth Congress of the Ukrainian Communist Party, Kiev, 1953, pp 99–101.)

In the article of April 17 1964, quoted above, Grechko indicated that Stalin had taken up an 'erroneous position' on a number of questions relating to military organization, and that his 'cult' had impeded the development of military theory.

opinions are not known, but the April reshuffle in the high command shows that:

1 The two main figures who were demoted, Konev and Sokolovsky, had overtly opposed the demobilization measures.

2 Their successors, Grechko and Zakharov, seemed definitely closer to Khrushchev.

3 At the same time Grechko and Zakharov were the advocates of a rigid foreign policy and notoriously distrustful of any summit compromise.

Hence it is legitimate to suppose that the decisions taken during that period were the result of a compromise. Khrushchev obtained the removal of two 'undisciplined' military chiefs, re-established his authority over the armed forces and put through the military cutback programme. In return he agreed to go no further, not to conclude any 'dangerous compromise' with the West, in particular on the issue of supervised international disarmament, and to postpone his territorial militia plan. These concessions were probably all the easier for him to make in that the balance of power within the Party Presidium rendered them anyway inevitable.

All this is only a supposition as tenuous as the hypothetical compromise itself. The confusion in the top leadership that followed the U-2 incident swiftly spread to military circles. However, the existence of such a compromise would account for the seemingly contradictory changes that occurred during the month of May:

1 The attempt to take the army 'in hand' and to reaffirm the primacy of the political authorities over the military command.

2 Pressure by the military, and precisely those who supported the first move, for a stiffening of foreign policy. Their pressure verged on criticism of Khrushchev himself, as will be shown.

The attempts to regain control over the army took shape in April 1960, just at the time of the above-mentioned reshuffle. The prime mover was unquestionably Malinovsky, who in an article published in *Krasnaya Zvezda*, made a strong plea for total obedience by the military to the Party and its chiefs. Malinovsky began by declaring that the Party, its leaders, i.e. 'the Central Committee of the Party, its Presidium, the members of the Central Committee, the members of the Presidium and the First Secretary of the Central Committee, N. S. Khrushchev', co-operate closely with 'the military leaders' in all decisions affecting the army. He continued: 'We stress this fact in order that our military cadres may once again be imbued with the conviction that the leadership of the Party over the army and the navy is something without which we cannot live or work. . . . Leadership by the Party is the fundamental, unshakeable Leninist principle of the structure of the Soviet Army and Navy.'

In the same article Malinovsky also recalled an event which the military press was to emphasize for several weeks, namely the plenary session of October 1957. This served as a reminder of the demotion of Marshal G. K. Zhukov, Malinovsky's predecessor as Minister of Defence, whose main error had been to 'withdraw the army from Party control'.

These allusions do not appear to have been aimed at Zhukov personally, or to indicate any connection between him and the April reshuffle. Of the two principal personalities demoted, Sokolovsky could certainly be regarded as loyal to Zhukov, but Konev had been his main rival ever since the war years (they had competed for the capture of Berlin) and was Zhukov's chief accuser in October 1957. In other words, the mention of the 'October plenary session' was a reminder of penalties for lack of discipline, of which both Konev and Sokolovsky were to be found guilty much later. Their example, as well as that of Zhukov, was to serve as a warning to any would-be 'Bonapartists'. On April 15 an editorial in *Krasnaya Zvezda*, enlarging upon Malinovsky's article, warned any officers 'who do not want to accept criticism' against the machinations of 'demagogues' and against those who still displayed 'remnants of individualism'.

In April 1960 it was also decided to convene a large conference of the secretaries of Party cells within the armed services, in order to conduct a general review of political work among the military (Malinovsky had announced this in his article of April 14). The conference was held from May 11 to May 14 1960 in the Kremlin in the presence of three members of the Party Presidium, Leonid I. Brezhnev (the only one who took the floor), Nikolai G. Ignatov and Mikhail A. Suslov. Brezhnev's speech was not published, and *Krasnaya Zvezda* in its issue of May 15 1960 ran only a very vague summary of the two main reports, delivered by Malinovsky and F. I. Golikov, the Head of the Main Political Administration of the Army. It was also learned that the conference had 'unanimously supported the proposals submitted by the Main Political Administration of the Army for the solution of certain problems of organization'. From the statements and comments published on that occasion, it appears that the suggestions dealt with the structure of Party organization at the battalion, regiment and division levels and, more generally, with the perennial problem of the division of power between military chiefs and political commissars. The problem of reconciling the principle of 'unity of command', i.e. the right for a military chief to be obeyed unconditionally by his men, communists included, with the need for the Party to control the entire life of the country, military life included, has always been akin to the squaring of the circle. It appears that the conference cell secretaries merely confirmed the ambiguous directive which, according to the *Krasnaya Zvezda* of May 5, was issued just after Zhukov's demotion: the Party cells have the 'statutory right' to summon any member of the Party and criticize his conduct, but this right does not apply to the orders and instructions of the sole command, which 'may not be criticized'.

No further details are available, but the military press devoted its full attention to technical aspects of the Party–army relationship – 'Party work', 'political education', 'mass agitation' – and in *Krasnaya Zvezda* these even overshadowed the campaign of protest against the U-2. There is no doubt that the Party's programme to regain the upper hand over the armed forces was being carried out. The only new factor was that this no longer automatically enhanced Khrushchev's authority.

MALINOVSKY IN THE FOREFRONT

As we have seen, Grechko set the tone at the session of the Supreme Soviet just after the U-2 incident by wishing Khrushchev successes which were not exactly those that peace-loving public opinion expected from the Paris conference. This position seems to have been adopted by the Presidium, and ratified by the Central Committee on May 4. In addition the military apparently tried to exploit the incident to their own advantage, or so we may infer from the numerous speeches by Khrushchev in the first days of May in which he replied to arguments that must have been advanced by the military and their political allies. On May 7, in his second speech to the Supreme Soviet, Khrushchev insisted that:

> 'This [U-2] affair should not induce us to revise our plans so as to increase our appropriations for armaments and the armed forces, or to stop the cutback in military strength.'

On May 9 he enlarged upon this idea: 'When we have brought our armed forces down to 2,400,000 men [the figure specified in the law of January 1960] some time will elapse, after which, in all likelihood, we shall go on reducing their number.' Then, in a typical volte-face, Khrushchev said to the first general he spotted, A. S. Zhadov – who responded, as Khrushchev added, by 'scratching his head' – 'No, comrade general, it won't be straight away, but later. . . . Of course we won't reduce our armed forces to a point where it would endanger national security.'

The tone of the speech of May 9 was deliberately unfriendly to the military, whom Khrushchev was trying to reduce to the level of mere executives carrying out his orders. Hinting that Powers's flight was due to an ill-timed initiative by the Pentagon, he declared that, if a Soviet military man had been guilty of such a breach of discipline, he would have 'thrown him out on his ear'. Immediately afterwards he turned to the generals and said: 'On April 9, too, the spy plane should have been shot down, but our military missed the boat, to put it politely, and we gave them hell for it.'

All this indicates that the military were alarmed by the U-2 affair and a number of them took advantage of it to try to reverse the harsh treatment inflicted upon them since the beginning of 1960. Without going quite as far, their chief, Malinovsky, chose that moment to embark on a series of speeches intended to help him make a political comeback.

The differences between Khrushchev and Malinovsky on the interpretation of the State Department's declaration of May 7 and as regards the prospect of a meeting between Khrushchev and Eisenhower in Paris on the occasion of the summit conference have already been noted.[1] It is certainly no accident that Malinovsky was scheduled to go to Paris, officially as third member of the delegation ranking after Khrushchev and Gromyko, but actually as the main associate of the Head of Government. The significance of his going lends itself to endless debate. Optimists regarded it as a sign of unity between the Party and the military, while pessimists viewed Malinovsky as the man chosen by the hard-line group in the Presidium and among the marshals to watch over Khrushchev's every move. The truth is probably less simple than either view. While Khrushchev took advantage of Malinovsky's presence (whether he had wanted it or not) to make a noisy display of friendship towards him,[2] the latter's attendance was not quite according to the rules. In the six years of Khrushchev's power, the only other case of the kind occurred when the Head of the Government visited Albania in May 1959.

Finally, when Khrushchev's policy was criticized in the second half of May, Malinovsky was one of those who attacked his past policy. At the end of May, at the conference of communist brigades, he made one of the sharpest comments on the Camp David line:

'History teaches us that *one should not trust the words of the imperialists, sweet as they may be. The latest lesson of Camp David is too clear to allow us to forget history.* [Author's italics.] No, we do not

---

[1] See p. 60.
[2] In his press conference in Paris on May 18 Khrushchev introduced Malinovsky to the journalists as his 'friend', an 'outstanding soldier, a loyal son of the Communist Party and of his mother country', etc.

believe the imperialists. We are convinced that they are only waiting for a favourable opportunity to attack the Soviet Union and the other socialist countries, and the only thing that stops them is the risk of the total destruction of imperialism' (*Pravda*, May 31 1960).

Malinovsky, like Kochetov, immediately softened the blow by paying high tribute to Khrushchev: but it was to the tough Khrushchev of May 16, the man who had 'publicly, courageously, with energy and conviction defended the honour of our great mother country'. This type of compliment was mandatory, but apart from the particularly aggressive reference to Camp David, the implied criticism of Khrushchev was very much in line with the Chinese position. Such an intransigent attitude towards imperialism excluded any East–West *détente* such as Khrushchev had sought and was still seeking.

Malinovsky's attitude calls for a number of comments: he was also of Ukrainian background, had been fairly closely associated with Khrushchev during the war on the various Ukrainian fronts and, in October 1957, had been appointed Defence Minister with Khrushchev's backing and over Zhukov's head. According to rumour, he was even related to Khrushchev. He had in the past repeatedly proved his loyalty to Khrushchev and was to do so again in the future. In 1960 alone, as pointed out, he had not only ratified the demobilization measures but also the territorial militia plan initiated by the Head of Government, had sacrificed Konev and Sokolovsky and had led the movement to strengthen the Party's control over the armed forces. Yet that same man, at the end of May, was openly siding with Khrushchev's critics.

The contradiction is apparently due to two facts. First, all Soviet military men, even if Party members and even Khrushchev supporters, are primarily professionals. Their military and caste interests come before anything else. In this case, the summit prospects, and in particular supervised disarmament, could not possibly have been to their liking.

Secondly, it seems clear that, in the Presidium, Khrushchev was in trouble on at least two occasions after the U-2 incident owing to his past policy of *rapprochement* with the United States. This was on May 3 and 4 and then on May 10 and 11. His policy was largely reversed, which was a clear public indication of the attitude of the Presidium majority. On the other hand, submitting to the political power meant in essence supporting the majority view. This made it far easier for the military to adhere to the new line, since it was much closer to their own views than Khrushchev's. In the final analysis it might even be said that the attacks on the First Secretary did not conflict with the principle of loyalty to the Party since, at any rate in May 1960, Khrushchev no longer represented 'the Party line'.

In any event, this period was notable for something that was to prove of importance later, namely that when the First Secretary was in serious trouble, Malinovsky, Grechko and other marshals who were strong Khrushchev supporters, far from hastening to help their protector, kept their distance or even uttered criticism. This attitude was to be theirs also in the crisis of October 1964.

MIKOYAN ON THE DECLINE

It is unfortunately impossible to review the position of each Presidium member during this entire period. Not only did the façade of unanimity have to remain free of any too obvious cracks, but one of the characteristics of Khrushchev's reign was the enforced silence of almost all of the members of the team. Only the following scanty indications concerning some of them could be detected.

Two of the leaders seem to have pressed, well before the U-2 incident, for the stiffening in foreign policy that occurred in May: namely Mikhail A. Suslov and Frol R. Kozlov. Admittedly this deduction rests in part on the many rumours that circulated in Moscow throughout those years. Several of them emanated from reputedly trustworthy Soviet sources. Thus Suslov, who took the floor at the Supreme Soviet session of January 1960 as chairman of the foreign affairs committee of one of the houses, approved the demobilization law but stressed more emphatically than other speakers the fact that the Soviet peace policy must not be unilateral: 'We are by no means in favour of unilateral action' (*Pravda*, January 16 1960).

In a speech a few days later before the Italian Communist Party congress, he expressed reservations about the *détente*. Noting that the 'Western champions of the cold war . . . have not laid down their weapons', he added: 'It would be dangerous to give in to complacency and over-confidence on this issue' (*Pravda*, February 2 1960). Furthermore, the speech does not contain the reference, customary in all major Soviet texts of the period, to Khrushchev's 'historic visit' to the United States. The same omission is noticeable in two speeches by Kozlov, the only ones known to this writer to have been published between February and May. The first was made at a reception at the Chinese Embassy on February 12 commemorating the anniversary of the Sino-Soviet treaty. It is all the more remarkable since even Liu Sao, the Chinese Ambassador, had not refrained from praising Khrushchev's 'fruitful visit' to the United States (*Pravda*, February 13 1960). Kozlov's second speech, on April 13, a welcome to the chief of the Mongolian state visiting Moscow, also omitted any reference to

Khrushchev's visit to the USA. He struck a note of solidarity with China, coupled with a warning to the 'war-mongers' who 'will be broken, *in the West as well as in the East*, by the indestructible unity and cohesion of the socialist countries' (*Pravda*, April 14 1960). Finally, while Kozlov praised N. S. Khrushchev as 'the tireless fighter for peace', one cannot help noticing that at this time Leonid I. Brezhnev was far more emphatic on the subject. This is what he said during a visit to Helsinki:

> 'By his daring tireless fight for peace, *détente* and friendship among all peoples, comrade Khrushchev has earned the love and respect of all men of good will. He is rightly called the great fighter for peace all over the world' (*Pravda*, April 16 1960).

These nuances assumed deeper meaning when Kozlov turned out to be the main beneficiary of the May reshuffle and Brezhnev one of the losers. But the first, albeit hidden, victim of the crisis should be mentioned before the changes are reviewed.

Khrushchev's sharp denial, in his speech of May 28 1960, that there were grounds for 'speculation' about the 'very senior member of the Politburo, Anastas Mikoyan', had the desired effect. The issue seemed to be laid to rest. True, some analysts wondered why the Head of Government had deemed it necessary to make such an unprecedented remark. The fact was that a series of converging signs, even though they were of a typical Kremlinological subtlety, pointed to Mikoyan's fall from favour. Let us glance at the scheming that was going on backstage.

On March 17 1960 *Pravda* ran on page 1 the account of an interview given the day before by Mikoyan to Pappas, the Greek Ambassador, who was about to leave the country. The communiqué began as follows: 'The Deputy Chairman of the Council of Ministers of the USSR, A. I. Mikoyan, yesterday received . . .' Obviously, something was wrong: Soviet Government protocol always makes a distinction between the 'Deputy Chairmen of the Council' (who were D. F. Ustinov, A. N. Kosygin and A. F. Zasyadko) and the '*First* Deputy Chairmen of the Council', far more important figures whose authority extended to many fields, and who at the time were A. I. Mikoyan and F. R. Kozlov.

Could this have been a mere misprint? It is well known that the Party daily, scrutinized for hours by the Secretariat, proof-read several times over, is one of the most carefully produced newspapers in the world.

Furthermore, the same 'misprint' had been made by all the other papers, such as *Izvestia* of March 17 and *Krasnaya Zvezda* of the same date. The only papers that were not guilty of the error were those that did not report the interview at all, such as the provincial dailies. In any event, no one had dared to amend the Tass communiqué where the alleged misprint had originated.

Was the mistake of the official news agency an accident? The question is legitimate, for Mikoyan was soon referred to again by his proper title of 'First Deputy Chairman of the Council' (for instance by *Pravda* and the other newspapers of April 2 on the occasion of his departure for Baghdad. Still, the mistake of March 17 recurred on four subsequent occasions: in *Pravda* of May 7 1960 and May 8 (in the very midst of the U-2 crisis), and on June 15 and July 14. Once again all the other papers followed suit, and on the same dates referred to Mikoyan simply as 'Deputy Chairman of the Council.'

A confusing factor is that the situation returned to normal in the interval between these episodes, sometimes on the very same day. Thus, the mistake in *Pravda* of May 7 would appear side by side with another communiqué where Mikoyan was again referred to as 'First Deputy Chairman of the Council'. Therefore everything contributed to give the impression of a mere accident. In that case, however, it should also have happened to the other officials with the same rank as Mikoyan, whereas in this entire period the only one affected was Mikoyan: never F. R. Kozlov, who was also First Deputy Chairman of the Council until May 4 1960, and never Kosygin after that date, although their activities were at least as well covered by the press. This intent to harm seems sufficiently well established, although the meaning and limits of these subtle manoeuvres remain to be seen. Certainly it would be a gross exaggeration to say that Mikoyan had been relieved of his functions as First Deputy Chairman of the Council – a decision that would have required official notice, and was furthermore negated by his extremely varied activities. On the other hand, it cannot be regarded as mere pettiness on the part of an isolated individual. Unfortunately, the source of these variations of protocol, which must have required a number of accomplices in the Tass agency, is impossible to determine. They probably originated with the Party Secretariat, the ultimate controller of the press. But, as in the above-mentioned case where an article by Walter Lippmann was used to disclose indirectly the existence of an opposition to Khrushchev, these anomalies involving Mikoyan must have had a definite meaning for Party members and functionaries, viz. to indicate that Mikoyan's position was not quite as secure as in the past, and specifically that his peers in the Government (mainly Kozlov but also Kosygin) were to be regarded as outweighing him.

The same method, as we shall see, was used against other figures at other times. As far as Mikoyan was concerned, there were additional signs.

At the end of April 1960 the fortieth anniversary of the establishment of Soviet power in Azerbaijan was celebrated with great pomp. Normally, Mikoyan, the sole survivor among the twenty-six Baku commissars and a major figure in the events of 1920 in Azerbaijan, should have been in the limelight during the ceremonies. All his official biographies and particularly the most recent, which appeared in June 1959 in the *Concise Soviet Encyclopedia*, presented him as 'one of the leaders in organizing the Party in Baku, together with Kirov and Ordzhonikidze'. But as it turned out, not only was Mikoyan absent from Baku for the anniversary celebrations, but even his name was barely mentioned in the tributes. In his speech of April 25 in Baku, Khrushchev mentioned him only once, at the end of a long list of figures who 'had played a role at various times' during the revolution in Azerbaijan (Stalin headed the list). The same thing happened in the report of the First Secretary of the Republic, Akhundov, who had divided the personalities to be named into two categories, one consisting of VIPs and the other of lesser figures. Mikoyan's was the last name on the second list, after a series of forgotten people.

His eclipse was intensified in the last days of April and the first days of May, as is seen by comparing two articles about those celebrations written a fortnight apart. The first appeared in the journal *Kommunist* (No 6 of 1960, cleared for publication on April 14), signed by the same Akhundov, First Secretary of the Azerbaijan Communist Party; the second was in a periodical of the Central Committee, *Partiynaya Zhizn* (No 9 of 1960, cleared for publication on May 3), signed by T. Allkhverdyev, Secretary of the Baku Urban Committee. The first article listed some fifteen personalities who had helped the Party to victory in Azerbaijan (with Stalin still heading the list). Mikoyan was listed in eighth place, a relatively honourable one. The second article had the same men in the same order with one major difference: Mikoyan's name was not there.

The pitfalls of historical writing in the USSR are sufficiently well known, so that there is no need to go into the substance of the matter. The only fact to be retained from this episode is that, in April 1960, Mikoyan was on the way to becoming an 'unperson', one who has been deleted from history. Fortunately for him, he managed to extricate himself from his predicament.

During Khrushchev's reign it had become the fashion for observers of the Soviet scene to belittle the importance of physical precedence among leaders on Red Square and similar places on official occasions. The fetishism of hierarchy and protocol, it used to be said, was a feature typical of Stalinist times which had no place in destalinized Russia. This was a serious mistake, for the technique of observing who was present or absent on major occasions continued to yield excellent results, provided it was used with caution. Only the most important personalities were worth taking into account, and only conspicuous changes among them. Thus, by comparing the order of precedence of the eight main leaders on Red Square on May 1 1959 – Voroshilov, Khrushchev, Mikoyan, Suslov, Kirichenko, Kozlov, Furtseva, Shvernik – with the picture on November 7 1959 – Voroshilov, Khrushchev, Mikoyan, Suslov, Kozlov, Furtseva, Kirichenko, Shvernik – it became obvious that in six months only one man, Kirichenko, had been affected and, sure enough, he was purged in January 1960. Several other signs point to the fact that his decline had probably begun in the autumn of 1959.

To come back to Mikoyan, in 1959 he was consistently in third place, directly after Khrushchev. It would have been surprising, in view of the preceding remarks, if he had maintained his prominence in 1960. Actually, the order of precedence on the podium on May 1 1960 was as follows: Voroshilov, Khrushchev, Suslov, Kozlov, Furtseva, Mikoyan, Shvernik (*Pravda*, May 2 1960).

By descending from third to seventh place, Mikoyan was demoted even more than Kirichenko had been in 1959, and he occupied a place unprecedented for him.[1]

A partial return to normality occurred on May 5 1960, when Mikoyan appeared at the session of the Supreme Soviet in third position, after Khrushchev and Voroshilov but before Suslov and Brezhnev. It is true that this was a state ceremony and his Government functions entitled him to a higher rank for the occasion. Nevertheless, the old Bolshevik from Armenia was then at the lowest ebb of his career, and indeed he picked that moment, as if by chance, to leave the scene. On May 7, during his last public appearance (with a Mexican delegation) he had declared that he intended to go on holiday around the 9th. Whether this was voluntary or not, the result was a total blackout concerning him throughout the important period of the gathering U-2 crisis and the wrecking of the summit meeting. He reappeared in Moscow only on June 11, after an absence of over a month, and a fortnight after Khrushchev had disclosed his presence on the shores of the Black Sea in the denial quoted earlier.

Nothing was said about the reason for his ill-fortune since, according to Khrushchev, nothing was wrong in the first place. The only possible

[1] The manner in which the order of precedence is determined and carried out is a mystery. Under Stalin, the dictator alone probably decided how to place his comrades in arms. Under Khrushchev this seems to have been only partly true. Apparently a kind of consensus determined the decision, according to the momentary balance of power within the leadership.

hypothesis, and the most likely, is that Mikoyan was the victim of the change in Soviet foreign policy in the spring of 1960. It is well known that he advocated moderation. His predilection for trade, his negotiating talents, and especially the role he had played as Khrushchev's associate in the preceding few years, all contributed to this. He had paved the way for the Camp David talks by his visit to the United States in January 1959 and was regarded as Khrushchev's most trusted diplomatic adviser. It was logical therefore that he should have been the main target of the attack against 'compromise with imperialism', since he was the man most committed to that policy, together with Khrushchev but more vulnerable than he. The fact that the first 'misprint' involving him dated back to March 17 confirms that the reconsideration of the policy had started well before the U-2 incident, and it is reasonable to wonder whether Khrushchev himself was not already encountering some difficulties at that time.[1]

It is also significant that Mikoyan's ill-fortune was at its worst after the May 1 incident. Probably Khrushchev, in order to retain his authority, then sided at least partly with the majority by showing his readiness to sacrifice his second in command. When things simmered down somewhat at the end of the month, Khrushchev tried to restore the *status quo ante* and take Mikoyan under his wing again. This is, in all likelihood, the reason for the famous denial of May 28. In fact, it was not enough, since two of the newspaper 'errors' occurred afterwards, on June 15 and July 14 1960. In addition, it seems to have taken Mikoyan some time to regain the privileged position he had occupied in 1959. During the remainder of 1960 and even in 1961, he was usually listed after Suslov, and before him again only in the last years of Khrushchev's reign.

Mikoyan's case is interesting in that, more than any other, it seems to be linked with foreign policy issues, the main ones under debate at the time. In the end, he was not seriously affected, since he kept his post, but the same changes produced many other real losers.

THE CHANGES

The following changes were announced in *Pravda* of May 5 1960 after the Central Committee plenary meeting of the 4th:

---

[1] It may be no accident that the anomaly concerning Mikoyan coincided with the attack of 'influenza' which delayed Khrushchev's departure for France by one week (*Pravda*, March 14 1960). It should also be noted that the name of the distinguished invalid ceased to be mentioned in editorials and various articles in the Party daily between March 19 and 22, even on topics like maize crops (*Pravda*, March 22 1960) in which reference to him would have been natural.

	Demoted Members	New Members
Presidium of the Central Committee	N. I. Beliayev	A. I. Kosygin
	A. I. Kirichenko	D. S. Polyansky
		N. V. Podgorny
Secretariat of the Central Committee	A. B. Aristov	
	Ye. A. Furtseva	
	N. G. Ignatov	F. R. Kozlov
	A. I. Kirichenko	
	P. N. Pospelov	

So much for the Party. In the state apparatus, the following changes took place:

	Former Holder	New Holder
President of the Presidium of the Supreme Soviet (Head of State)	K. E. Voroshilov	L. I. Brezhnev
First Deputy Chairman of the Council of Ministers of the USSR	F. R. Kozlov	A. N. Kosygin
Deputy Chairman of the Council of Ministers, Chairman of Gosplan	A. N. Kosygin	V. N. Novikov
Deputy Chairman of the Council of Ministers of the RSFSR, Chairman of the RSFSR Gosplan	V. N. Novikov	K. M. Gerasimov
Deputy Chairman of the Council of Ministers, USSR		N. G. Ignatov
Minister of Culture of the USSR	N. A. Mikhailov	Ye. A. Furtseva

The main change within the Party was the entrance of Frol R. Kozlov into a Secretariat that had lost five, i.e. one half of its members. True, it was not stated at the time that Kozlov had become 'Second Secretary' (such a post does not exist officially) in Kirichenko's place. This was announced only in 1961 when, in the list of the Secretariat members chosen at the Twenty-second Congress, Kozlov was in second place after Khrushchev, instead of in alphabetical order. As soon as he was promoted in May 1960, it was clear that the new member was to be the strong man in the Secretariat. Among all the other members, only Khrushchev, Suslov and Brezhnev had a political stature matching their functions (one may discount Otto V. Kuusinen, who was too old to play any responsible role, and Nuriddin A. Mukhitdinov, whose only task apparently was to represent the Central Asian minorities in the principal organs). Suslov's role had always been mainly confined to ideological problems and relations with the foreign parties, and it is a safe bet that Khrushchev meant to keep him there, while Brezhnev had now been appointed head of state. The following plenary session of the Central Committee, in July 1960, threw light on the matter by deciding to 'free' Brezhnev from his work in the Secretariat 'owing to his new tasks'.

This two-stage removal and several other signs indicate that Brezhnev was Kozlov's chief rival at the time. The membership of the Secretariat just after Kirichenko's fall in January 1960 shows that only three candidates could possibly inherit the latter's functions. They were A. B. Aristov, L. I. Brezhnev and N. G. Ignatov. All three, as a matter of fact, seem to have been the victims of the May reshuffle, although not to the same degree.

A. B. Aristov left the Secretariat but retained the functions he had held for several years in the Bureau of the Central Committee for the affairs of the Russian Republic (RSFSR). In 1957 he had been appointed Deputy Chairman of the Bureau, its actual chairman next to Khrushchev. After the plenary session of May 4 1960 which removed him from the Secretariat, allegedly so that he might 'concentrate his attention on the Bureau of the Central Committee for the RSFSR', he actually continued to run the affairs of the largest republic in the country, for one thing by presiding over the replacement of the First Secretaries in the major regions. It was only in the beginning of 1961 that he suffered a much more serious blow, when he had to give his place to G. I. Voronov and was named Ambassador to Warsaw. Thus, the change of May 1960 was certainly no promotion but only the maintenance of the important if limited functions he was discharging.

N. G. Ignatov, as mentioned earlier, had competed with Kozlov as early as 1953 for the leadership of the Party organization in Leningrad, and might have been his rival again in 1960. However, his authority seems to have been confined to agriculture from 1957 to 1960, which did not make him the ideal candidate to succeed Kirichenko. Moreover, he did not seem to have a good foothold in the Party, as shown by the many reverses he suffered well before Stalin's death.[1]

---

[1] Ignatov had been elected alternate member of the Party's Central Committee by the Eighteenth Congress in 1939, and demoted in February 1941 for 'lack of ability' (no additional information was ever given about this). In 1952 the Nineteenth Party Congress made him an alternate member of the Presidium and a Party secretary. Six months later he lost these functions upon Stalin's death because, so it was stated, of 'his appointment to a responsible position in the Council of Ministers'. Actually

The last blow suffered by Ignatov came in April 1959 when he was elected to the honorary post of Chief of State of the RSFSR, which seemed to preclude any real responsibility. The assignment was to be cancelled in November 1959, probably because it was related to Kirichenko's rise and then his decline. In any case, all this pointed to animosity against Ignatov in various quarters. He was finally appointed Deputy Chairman of the Council of Ministers in charge of agriculture, which theoretically was his speciality.

For Brezhnev, on the other hand, being transferred to the post of Head of State, with all its apparent prestige, barely concealed a serious political defeat. Until 1959 his responsibilities in the Secretariat seem to have been mainly related to the problems of heavy industry, as indicated by his speech to the Twenty-first Congress in January 1959. It was soon noticed that Kirichenko's downfall had helped him, first by conferring upon him a large part, if not the bulk, of the prerogatives of the former Second Secretary. Thus, in January 1960 it was Brezhnev who went to Alma-Ata to supervise the purging of Beliayev from the leadership of the Kazakhstan Party – a major undertaking, since the victim was a member of the Presidium of the Party and the Republic is one of the most important in the country (*Pravda*, January 21 1960). Considering that changes of this kind had been carried out earlier by Kirichenko and later by Kozlov, it becomes clear that Brezhnev was acting as the official successor of Kirichenko as Party Secretary in charge of cadres. This new stature was emphasized during the session of the Supreme Soviet of January 13 1960, when, for the first time, Brezhnev made his appearance in the row of the 'big five', alongside Khrushchev, Voroshilov, Mikoyan and Suslov. Kozlov, although he was a member of the Government and the meeting was a state occasion, sat in the back row with the members of the junior leadership – in fact, just behind Brezhnev (*Pravda*, January 14 1960). The detail is noteworthy, for seven weeks later the situation was exactly reversed. On the occasion of a Women's Day rally on March 8 1960, held in the same place, the fifth man in the front row was Kozlov, while this time Brezhnev was behind him with the other junior members (*Pravda*, March 9 1960).

Between the two events, the situation had obviously changed in favour of Kozlov, who was still only First Deputy Chairman in the Government but already seemed to have a more promising future ahead. It would be tedious to list other examples of this kind. Suffice

---

he seems never to have taken up his 'appointment' and reappeared a few weeks later as Second Secretary of the Leningrad Oblast Committee. A steadfast ally of Khrushchev in the struggle against the 'anti-party group', he resumed his post as Central Committee Secretary after the June 1957 crisis.

it to note that, during March and April 1960, Kozlov's activities expanded to the point where he eclipsed Mikoyan – his peer though also his senior in the Government – and even infringed somewhat the formal principles of collective leadership. Thus, on April 15 *Pravda* 'overlooked' the alphabetical order and listed Kozlov ahead of N. G. Ignatov, another Presidium member, in reporting a ceremony, although nothing in the context required this.

No one could guess, of course, that Kozlov was going to leave the state apparatus to resume an even more promising career in the Party, but his rise was quite obvious.

Had Khrushchev prompted the choice? Considering what is known of the careers of the respective candidates and the conditions under which the reshuffle took place, it may be ventured that the candidate with the best chances of being picked by Khrushchev to succeed Kirichenko was Brezhnev. His Ukrainian background made him the man closest to Khrushchev. His statements showed infinitely greater loyalty to Khrushchev and to his policy than Kozlov's. On the other hand, the stiffening of foreign policy of April and May 1960, just after the U-2 affair, was clearly aimed mainly at Khrushchev and entailed strong criticism of his past policy. From the speeches made during that period it appears that Kozlov sided with the advocates of a tougher line. He was promoted just then, while Brezhnev on the contrary had been at the height of his influence in January 1960, when Khrushchev too had been in a strong position.

To sum up, at best Kozlov was a compromise candidate between the very pro-Khrushchev Brezhnev and a possible hard-line outsider favoured by the opposition (e.g. Suslov). Khrushchev accepted the decision, just as he had in 1953 for the leadership of the Party in Leningrad when it went against his protégé N. G. Ignatov. As things stood in 1960, he was probably not enthusiastic about it. The events of 1963 soon showed that relations with Kozlov were important, but none of this could have been foreseen in 1960.

The proof that Kozlov's appointment and Brezhnev's demotion had been considered was the lame decision of May 4 to appoint Brezhnev Head of State while maintaining him in the position of Party Secretary (a combination of functions which was not in the traditions of the régime). It does seem that Brezhnev tried very hard to keep the latter post. His speech to the conference of the army cell secretaries and his role in it between May 11 and 14 1960 (along with Suslov and Ignatov) were more relevant to his functions in the Secretariat of the Party.[1] It is

---

[1] The same holds true for Ignatov, who seemed propelled by the momentum of his position as former Secretary of the Party.

significant that when his departure from that post became official in July 1960 he was not replaced. Kozlov then became the only one in charge.

Although Brezhnev had been frustrated in his hopes of becoming the heir presumptive for the post of head of the Party, he was nevertheless achieving a sufficiently prominent position to retain a place in the group of senior members of the Presidium. As Head of State he had no serious responsibilities, but his vast experience as an *apparatchik*, Khrushchev's protection and also his relative youth (he was 54 in 1960) left him free to assume new tasks as opportunity arose, which turned out to be fairly soon.

Other lower-ranking members suffered worse blows.

Ye. A. Furtseva, the only woman among the leaders and a faithful follower of Khrushchev,[1] apparently underwent the same type of so-called transfer as Ignatov, i.e. she was called on to assume within the Government the tasks she had formerly performed at the Party Secretariat – those pertaining to cultural life, a field in which the Party unquestionably overrides any minister. Furtseva was to find this out very shortly, especially since the constant interference of the Central Committee's Agitation and Propaganda Department run by the dynamic Leonid F. Ilyichev was to reduce ever further the authority of her ministry in the years to come. However, even within the Secretariat her political stature was apparently never very large, and a few weeks before the May reshuffle some animosity towards her was detectable. Thus, at the end of March, Furtseva made an official trip to Byelorussia, spoke before the local Party cadres on propaganda questions and received the traditional official welcome from Mazurov and the other leaders of the Republic. The accounts appeared in *Sovietskaya Byelorussia* of April 1 1960, but contrary to a very widely observed tradition as regards travels by members of the Presidium, there was not one word about it in *Pravda*.

This gradual loss of favour was confirmed eighteen months later when, like Aristov and Ignatov, Furtseva lost her seat at the Party Presidium as a result of the Twenty-second Congress.

P. N. Pospelov was also ousted from the Secretariat, in the same way as A. B. Aristov, to enable him 'to concentrate his attention on the

---

[1] According to some experts, Furtseva's relations with the future Party chief dated back to the thirties, when she was an active young Komsomol member. She was first assigned to Kursk, Khrushchev's home, but Khrushchev was by then already a Party official in Moscow. In any event, Furtseva made her career under Khrushchev's auspices after 1950, when she was appointed Second Secretary of the Moscow Urban Committee while Khrushchev was the First Secretary. According to many sources, Furtseva played an important role in the June 1957 crisis, notably by rallying Khrushchev's advocates in the Central Committee. She was admitted to the Party Presidium as a full member after the crisis.

Bureau of the Central Committee for the RSFSR'. It is interesting to note that both men had entered the Bureau together in March 1956 in odd circumstances – a fortnight after the original membership had been decided by the Congress – and they left at about the same time, at the beginning of 1961. Pospelov, in May 1960, was entering the Bureau for the second time (he had left it at an undetermined date after 1956).[1] An old specialist in ideological matters, he had entered the Secretariat just after Stalin's death, at a time when promotion could only be the result of a compromise between rival factions. Later, however, he had evidently supported Khrushchev in his struggle for power, as shown by his promotion to alternate membership of the Presidium after the victory over the 'anti-party' elements in June 1957. His new functions in the Bureau for the Russian Republic were not made clear. In all likelihood he was to deal with ideological matters, but possibly also with questions of organization, for he supervised the replacement of the First Regional Secretary in October 1960 (*Sovietskaya Rossiya*, October 29 1960). For him, too, the reshuffle of May 1960 was the start of the decline. In February or March 1961 he was appointed Director of the Marxism–Leninism Institute (an honorary post that did not entail any political power) and he lost his seat as alternate member of the Presidium in October 1961, at the Twenty-second Congress.[2]

K. E. Voroshilov was another loser, but of a different kind. 'Upon his own request' and 'because of his unsatisfactory state of health', he abandoned to Brezhnev the post of President of the Presidium of the Supreme Soviet. The handing over of power was managed with the utmost delicacy and Voroshilov was immediately appointed member of the Presidium of the Supreme Soviet and awarded another medal as 'Hero of the Soviet Union'. Khrushchev in person spoke in praise of his past merits, carefully avoiding the slightest hint of what was to be disclosed publicly eighteen months later at the Twenty-second Congress: namely, not only that the old marshal had been one of the four 'founding'

[1] At any rate, this is what appears from the biographical yearbook of deputies to the Supreme Soviet of the USSR, issued in November 1962. The entry for Pospelov reads: 'Member of the Bureau of the Central Committee for the RSFSR since 1960.'
[2] As early as 1949 Pospelov had been appointed Director of the Marx–Engels–Lenin–Stalin Institute, and been replaced by Mikhail A. Suslov as Director of *Pravda*, a post he had occupied since 1940. That period seemed to have already witnessed a decline in Pospelov's influence. In 1952 he returned to *Pravda*, but only as Associate Chief Editor. His promotion to the post of Secretary of the Central Committee after Stalin's death was all the more spectacular. In this respect, his case is the opposite of Aristov's, Kozlov's and Brezhnev's and those of other neo-Stalinists, who were promoted in the wake of that purge and demoted when Stalin died. It was among them that Khrushchev recruited most of his allies.

members of the 'anti-party group' of 1957 but also that he bore 'personal responsibility for many mass repressions of the period of the personality cult'. In his speech, Khrushchev praised Voroshilov just as much as he did Brezhnev.[1] Considering subsequent events and Voroshilov's well-known conceit, it is most probable that he did not relinquish the highest state post of his own free will. Even if he was still among the First Secretary's opponents, it is legitimate to assume that his departure was the price exacted by Khrushchev in exchange for the other transfers. But the truth is probably more complex, for since his 'error' of 1957, Voroshilov had repeatedly given evidence of his submissiveness to the victor. Clearly at seventy-nine he was too old to be anyone's rival. It is possible, however, that he sided with Khrushchev's conservative opponents during the close vote at the Party Presidium, particularly on issues of foreign policy.

The logical result of the change came about only at the following plenary session in July 1960, when Voroshilov was 'freed' from his seat in the Party Presidium 'at his own request' and Brezhnev was removed from the Secretariat because of his new functions as Chief of State. These two-stage demotions seem to indicate that the decisions were difficult ones to reach.

THE NEWCOMERS: KOSYGIN, PODGORNY, POLYANSKY

The main losers in the reshuffle have been listed.[2] Among those who gained were, first, the three alternate members of the Presidium who were promoted to full membership: Aleksey N. Kosygin, Nikolai V. Podgorny and Dmitri S. Polyansky.

---

[1] The way in which Khrushchev presented Brezhnev's candidature is interesting too: 'Comrade Brezhnev', he said, 'is known by all as an experienced statesman. For the past three legislative sessions he has been a deputy to the Supreme Soviet of the USSR. He is also an experienced Party personality, for he was elected to the Presidium of the Central Committee as early as the Nineteenth Congress' (*Pravda*, May 8 1960). In other words, Khrushchev let it be clearly known that Brezhnev had been a member of the last Stalinist Presidium in 1952 and a deputy since 1950. Brezhnev's biography published in *Pravda* of the same day also stressed his seniority and did not say one word about the eclipse of 1953, after the dictator's death.

It is difficult to see any reason for Khrushchev to stress his protégé's good standing under Stalin, except for those resulting from the circumstances of the moment: as noted, Stalin was listed at the head of the heroes of the revolution in Azerbaijan and, since the winter of 1959, the press had practically stopped criticizing him. It was already a well-established rule that Stalin was extolled when things were not going well for Khrushchev.

[2] We do not take into account Nikolay A. Mikhailov, who was replaced by Ye. A.

In May 1960 Kosygin took a decisive step on his way to the highest Government post which he was to attain four and a half years later. Out of the three men promoted, he was the only one who advanced simultaneously in both hierarchies. At the same time as he rose to full membership of the Party Presidium, he became First Deputy Chairman of the Council of Ministers, the only other such post beside Mikoyan's. At the time, relatively little attention was paid to the promotion of this cold 'technocrat', for it was rightly thought that Party matters counted for more. However, his appearance in a major role was not negligible in the political balance of power.

He was, at least, an additional recruit to the group of independents in the Presidium. He did not owe anything to Khrushchev: under Stalin his position had been definitely more prominent than during the early years of Khrushchev's reign, since from 1948 to 1952 he had been a full member of the Party Politburo and, in the Government, a Deputy Chairman of the Council of Ministers. He had been demoted in October 1952: although the Nineteenth Congress had enlarged the membership of the Politburo to twenty-five, it had down-graded him to the status of an alternate. In the first post-Stalin Government, he was not reappointed Deputy Chairman of the Council of Ministers, but again achieved that post in December 1953. He was to keep it almost without interruption (except for a period in 1956–1957), serving with equal loyalty under Malenkov, Bulganin and Khrushchev.

His relations with Khrushchev during the 1957 crisis are somewhat obscure. On the one hand he benefited from the June decisions, when he once more became Deputy Chairman of the Council of Ministers, a post he had lost in December 1956, and was also made an alternate member of the Party Presidium.[1] There is no doubt that in the plenary session he sided against the 'anti-party group', as indicated by an article he published on the very first day of the affair in *Pravda* (July 4 1957). Nevertheless, although there were not a large number of technocrats hostile to Malenkov, Pervukhin and Saburov in the high circles of the state administration, Khrushchev did not call upon Kosygin at the

Furtseva as Minister of Culture, and on June 27 1960 was appointed Ambassador to Indonesia. Although the man had an interesting past (First Secretary of the Komsomol Central Committee from 1938 to 1952, Secretary of the Party Central Committee and head of Agitprop just before Stalin's death, First Secretary of the Moscow Oblast Committee until 1954) the change was not a serious blow to him, since for several years he had been playing only a very minor role. In 1954 his Party career had ended and he had become Ambassador to Poland.

[1] Even in this group of minor personalities, Kosygin was not particularly prominent. He was listed alphabetically, whereas three other alternates were named at the head of the list: N. A. Mukhitdinov, P. N. Pospelov and D. S. Korochenko (*Pravda*, July 4 1957).

time to run the economy, although he was manifestly the most qualified. In May 1957, before launching his major economic reform (elimination of a series of ministries and establishment of the sovnarkhozes or National Economic Councils), Khrushchev entrusted the chairmanship of Gosplan to an obscure official, I. I. Kuzmin, who was not a member of any leading organ of the Party and whose last known post was that of member of the Central Committee in charge of mechanical engineering. A month later, after the crisis that seems to have been precipitated by the reform, Kosygin was promoted, but Kuzmin even more so, since he retained the chairmanship of Gosplan and became First Deputy Chairman of the Council of Ministers. It was clear that Khrushchev wanted Kuzmin rather than Kosygin to take charge of the economy. It is also probable that Kuzmin seemed more trustworthy politically. At the Twenty-first Congress in 1959 he was more violent in berating Saburov and Pervukhin, whereas Kosygin only very briefly mentioned the 'anti-party group' and, when he listed its members, left out both these men.

Kosygin finally took Kuzmin's place at the head of Gosplan in March 1959, but the rivalry between them was settled for good only in the spring of 1960, when Kosygin won a complete victory and Kuzmin was definitely defeated. On April 22 1960, a few days before Kosygin's promotion, Kuzmin was replaced by A. F. Zasyadko as the head of the Scientific and Economic Council of State of the USSR, one of the short-lived agencies designed to 'co-ordinate' the economy. On May 21 he was appointed Ambassador to Switzerland (the decree appeared only in Pravda of June 9, which indicates some difficulty in reaching a decision). Kuzmin was recalled from Berne in February 1963 and was not heard of again.

The economic measures and the promotions of other planning experts decided upon at that time – all of them indicating that Khrushchev's traditional economic policy was also undergoing a major revision – will be analysed later in the present survey. Let it be noted first that politically:

Kosygin did not owe anything to Khrushchev.

Furthermore while he had supported Khrushchev against the 'anti-party group' in 1957, he was among those who wished to put a stop to the measures against Molotov, Malenkov and the others. As early as 1959, Kosygin had openly opposed extending the accusations to Saburov and Pervukhin.

Khrushchev was somewhat reluctant to let Kosygin assume the management of Gosplan and then of the entire economy, and obviously preferred Kuzmin to him.

In addition, of all the Presidium members, Kosygin was visibly the east willing to praise the First Secretary. Of all his statements during the last five years of the reign, the most laudatory seems to date back to July 15 1960, shortly after his promotion. Kosygin then paid tribute to Khrushchev's 'eminent merits' and described him as a 'tireless fighter for the cause of the working class, the cause of communism, a tireless fighter for peace' (*Pravda*, July 16 1960). This is tepid praise compared to what all the other members of the collective leadership without exception, even including Suslov, said at some time during this long period. It will be shown that, at the Twenty-second Congress, Kosygin was the man who most clearly expressed his reservations about the 'new cult'.

N. V. Podgorny, the First Secretary of the Ukrainian Communist Party, a Ukrainian himself, was bound to be a loyal Khrushchev supporter and remained so to the last. He especially had to appear as such when he entered the Presidium. His promotion was a two-stage affair: he was made an alternate member in June 1958 and a full member in May 1960. Everybody could not be promoted at once after the victory over the 'anti-party group' in June 1957 and, anyway, Podgorny was not senior enough in the hierarchy (he was then Second Secretary of the Ukrainian Communist Party after Kirichenko) to lay claim to a seat at the top. There is no doubt, though, that he actively backed Khrushchev during the crisis. When the attacks against Malenkov, Molotov and the others were renewed in December 1958, Podgorny took up an extreme position, denouncing the 'miserable attempts' of those 'factionaries'. He was even more outspoken at the Twenty-first Congress and was one of the very few leaders who used the expression 'Presidium of the Central Committee led by the First Secretary, N. S. Khrushchev', thereby supporting Khrushchev's claim to rise above the Presidium itself. Podgorny had also formally endorsed the First Secretary's questionable practice of stifling any serious debate in the Central Committee by bringing in hundreds of non-members. Addressing the Central Committee of the Ukrainian Communist Party in January 1960, Podgorny described this practice as an 'even clearer demonstration of the indestructible ties between the Party and the people, which are growing stronger day by day' (*Pravda Ukrainy*, January 20 1960). In short, Podgorny was one of the most zealous devotees of the new cult: at the December 1959 plenary session, for instance, he had recalled Khrushchev's visit to the United States in the following terms:

'Comrade Khrushchev's tireless activity, attachment to principles and ardent struggle for peace and the victory of communism have lent wings to millions of people in all corners of the globe. . . .

The Soviet people and the whole of progressive mankind warmly support and acclaim Nikita Sergeyevich Khrushchev's noble activity from the bottom of their hearts.'

All this places Podgorny in the group of Khrushchev's wholehearted allies. He even seems to have sided with him during the difficult period in May 1960, to judge from the restrained tone adopted by the Ukrainian press on foreign policy questions after the U-2 incident.[1] For several reasons, however, one should not consider Podgorny, like Brezhnev, Kirichenko or Furtseva, as a mere client of the First Secretary.

Although a product of the Ukrainian Party machine, Podgorny did not owe his promotion within the apparatus to Khrushchev's patronage. When Khrushchev was the First Secretary of the Republic, from 1938 to 1949, Podgorny's functions were decidedly humble. In 1939 he was a Deputy Chairman for the Ukrainian food industry, and after the war 'Permanent Representative of the Ukrainian Council of Ministers attached to the Government of the USSR' in Moscow. (There is no reason to think that such 'diplomats' play any significant role.) It was

[1] This conclusion emerges clearly if, for that period, one compares the *Pravda Ukrainy* and *Sovietskaya Byelorussia*, the official organ of the Byelorussian Republic, whose First Secretary at the time was K. T. Mazurov. Certain facts have already been mentioned. For instance, the speech made by T. Ya. Kisselev, the head of the Byelorussian Government, at the Supreme Soviet in the beginning of May was particularly critical of Khrushchev in connection with Eisenhower, whereas the Ukrainian speaker at the same session, I. S. Senin, carefully avoided this topic. Walter Lippmann's article mentioning 'critics of Khrushchev in the Soviet Union' was published in full in *Sovietskaya Byelorussia* of May 19 1960, whereas *Pravda Ukrainy* (May 18) deleted the controversial sentence. On May 5 the Ukrainian paper published the announcement of Vershinin's forthcoming visit to the United States when it was already in doubt. *Sovietskaya Byelorussia*, on the other hand, which had never mentioned the visit before, only announced on May 14 that it had been cancelled.

During this whole period *Sovietskaya Byelorussia* published a series of editorials on foreign policy, each more violently critical of American policy than the last, as well as accounts of protest meetings, in several of which Mazurov himself took part. It reproduced several articles from the Moscow *Pravda*, including a harsh editorial of June 19 1960 and an announcement on May 26 that a collection of documents on the U-2 case had just been published. The *Pravda Ukrainy* did not carry the latter two items and mentioned far fewer protest meetings, in none of which had Podgorny participated. He returned from a trip to Czechoslovakia on May 14 and no activity on his part was reported until the beginning of June. The few comments in the Ukrainian paper on the international crisis were moderate in tone. Thus, an article just before the abortive summit meeting, in the *Pravda Ukrainy* of May 15 1960, only mentioned the U-2 affair as a 'regrettable act' and a 'bad preparation for the important conference that is about to start'. The least one can say is that, at the time when that article appeared, the moderate tone was definitely outdated.

The only exception to this attitude was the article already mentioned, written by A. Nosenko in *Pravda Ukrainy* of May 31 1960 and referring somewhat unkindly to Camp David. Nevertheless, it seems clear that the Byelorussian leaders had none of the qualms experienced by the Ukrainian leaders in making the most of the U-2 affair, whatever the effect on Khrushchev. This may not be unrelated to K. T. Mazurov's attitude and his promotion in March 1965, after Khrushchev's downfall.

only in 1950, when Khrushchev was transferred to Moscow, that Podgorny entered the Ukrainian Party apparatus and rose rapidly: from 1950 to 1953 he was the First Secretary of the Kharkov Oblast Committee under Leonid G. Melnikov (an enemy of Khrushchev's, who had probably been appointed thanks to Malenkov, then the Party chief in the Ukraine); he then became Second Secretary of the Ukrainian Communist Party from 1953 to 1957 under A. I. Kirichenko and subsequently replaced the latter as First Secretary of the Republic in December 1957.

At times Khrushchev spoke very critically of Podgorny, which he never did *vis-à-vis* his real clients. This occurred in particular in January 1961, when it even seemed conceivable that Podgorny might be removed. The official reason then given was the poor harvest in the Ukraine in 1960.[1] The situation in this respect improved in 1961, and in the autumn of that year Khrushchev made a point of congratulating Podgorny. Political reasons may have been at the root of the attacks. We may observe that Khrushchev never reproached Kirichenko with agricultural failures, at least so long as he needed him politically.

These facts point to the conclusion that the relations between Khrushchev and Podgorny were those of allies rather than of patron and protégé. Political divergences may have existed between them: this is borne out by personal changes in the Ukraine carried out on several occasions, obviously against Khrushchev's own leanings.[2]

---

[1] The attacks reached their peak at the plenary session of the Central Committee of January 1961. When Podgorny started to report on the agricultural situation in his republic, Khrushchev curtly interrupted him by saying that half of the 1960 standing corn crop in the Ukraine had been stolen. Accusing Podgorny of having omitted that fact and many others from his report, Khrushchev added: 'Don't fool yourself or mislead the kolkhoz members and sovkhoz workers, because you'll pay the penalty for mismanagement sooner or later. Just bear that in mind.' Podgorny meekly replied: 'Nikita Sergeyevich, you are absolutely right' (*Pravda*, January 12 1961). A few days later Khrushchev went to Kiev to preside over a session of the Central Committee of the Ukrainian Communist Party and was somewhat gentler: 'We support the leaders of the Republic. But it must be stated that some comrades, while they worked honestly, did not fulfil our expectations. Our Party criticizes without pity. But the criticism will be useful if the leaders draw the right lessons from it. If they don't, so much the worse for them' (*Pravda*, February 1 1961).

[2] The clearest case is that of N. T. Kalchenko, appointed Head of the Ukrainian Government in 1954. Very soon Khrushchev became consistently hostile to him. He attacked him in a speech as early as February 1955. In January 1961 Kalchenko, even more than Podgorny, was the main target of Khrushchev's attacks. Khrushchev saw fit to express surprise that Kalchenko was still a member of the Central Committee and the USSR Supreme Soviet and a leader of the Republic. Kalchenko was finally demoted at the beginning of March 1961; however, he was immediately appointed First Deputy Chairman of the Ukrainian Government, kept his seat in the Presidium of the Ukrainian Party and remained in charge of the department of agriculture, a field in which Khrushchev judged him least qualified. Such treatment can be accounted for only by protection from on high, including that of Podgorny.

Nevertheless, proofs of Podgorny's loyalty on most major issues are far more numerous. Of all the new recruits to the Presidium in May 1960, Podgorny was undoubtedly the best as far as Khrushchev was concerned.

D. S. Polyansky, aged forty-three, in 1960 became the youngest man in the Presidium. (He was born on November 7 1917 new style, i.e. on the very day of the Bolshevik revolution.) His case is similar to Podgorny's inasmuch as they both became alternate members of the Presidium in June 1958.[1] It is known that, like Podgorny, Polyansky played an active role during the 1957 crisis in opposing Khrushchev's enemies, particularly Molotov, Kaganovich and Voroshilov. At the Twenty-second Congress of October 1961, Polyansky reported as follows on this episode:

'When, during the Central Committee plenary session (in June 1957), Kaganovich was charged with having ordered and personally carried out mass repressions in the Kuban, Voroshilov came to his defence. He sprang from his seat and shaking his fists shouted "You people are still young, we'll straighten you out yet!"' (verbatim record of the Twenty-second Congress, Moscow, 1962, vol 2 p 43).

The reverse happened to N. D. Bubnovsky. In a speech at Voronezh on March 31 1955, Khrushchev disclosed that he had been on the best of terms with this official for years, dating back to the days when he himself had been First Secretary of the Ukrainian Communist Party and Bubnovsky Secretary of a District Committee in the Republic (see collection of Khrushchev's *Agricultural Speeches*, vol 2 pp 67 and 93). After being promoted to the post of Secretary of the Ukrainian Central Committee in 1954, Bubnovsky was complimented by Khrushchev on several occasions. At the plenary session of January 1961 Khrushchev singled him out for praise among all the Ukrainian leaders, particularly for having protested in a note to the Ukrainian Central Committee against the agricultural practices that the Committee was trying to impose. In other words, Bubnovsky had criticised Podgorny's agricultural policy and Khrushchev congratulated him for it (*Pravda*, January 21 1961).

It would have been natural for Bubnovsky to receive an important promotion after this. Actually, just the reverse happened: in January 1963 he was appointed First Secretary of the Agricultural Oblast Committee of Khmelnitsky in the Ukraine, and two months later stripped of his functions in the Presidium and the Secretariat of the Ukrainian Central Committee of the Communist Party. In this case, Khrushchev's patronage had not outweighed Podgorny's hostility. This is an interesting illustration of the limits of Khrushchev's authority and prestige.

[1] The 1962 yearbook of the *Soviet Encyclopedia* wrongly indicated that Poliansky had served as an alternate member of the Central Committee Presidium from 1956 to 1960. Actually, at the time of the Twentieth Congress, he was the First Secretary of the Chkalov (Orenburg) Oblast Committee and had no reason to serve in the Party's supreme organ. It was only in April 1958 that he was promoted to an important post in Moscow, where he succeeded Kozlov at the head of the RSFSR Government. He still held this position in May 1960, when he was promoted to full membership of the Presidium. So far as can be seen, the mistake in the 1962 encyclopedia yearbook had no political significance.

The mention of youth, together with the fact that events in the Kuban were involved, suggests that the accusation against Kaganovich was put forward by Polyansky, who was at the time First Secretary of the Krasnodar (Kuban) Territorial Committee, and hence best qualified to raise the question. In his speech, Polyansky had reproached Voroshilov with having 'refused to meet the members of the Central Committee who demanded the convening of a plenary session'. It is very likely that Polyansky was himself among those Central Committee members.

Another confirmation of his role in this connection came shortly afterwards from the Albanian communist leader Enver Hoxha in a speech in Tirana on November 7 1961:

> 'In his speech against the "anti-party group" and against comrade Voroshilov in particular, Dmitri Polyansky did not, of course, reveal the details of his and his friends' backstage activities during the plenary session of the CPSU Central Committee in summer 1957. Polyansky kept this dark from the Congress, but he told their "friend" Lira Belishova[1] who told our Party about it' (*Zeri i Popullit*, November 8 1961).

Despite all this, the ties between Khrushchev and Polyansky, even more than those between Khrushchev and Podgorny, cannot be regarded as unconditional. Until Polyansky became Head of the Government of the RSFSR in 1958 he owed almost nothing in his career to Khrushchev, and despite his youth he had done brilliantly. A Ukrainian and an active member of the Komsomol in Kharkov before the war, he had left the region as early as 1940 to attend the higher party school in Moscow in order to become an *apparatchik*.[2] His biographies indicate that, from 1945 to 1949, he was an 'organizer responsible for the direction of cadres under the CPSU Central Committee, then a Central Committee Instructor' – in fact, one of the cogs at the very centre of the Stalinist organization. (It may be that he was then close to Kozlov, who was in charge of organizational work in the Central Committee, probably in the Cadres Directorate.) His rise was a normal one at the head of various Oblast Committees (Crimea, then Orenburg and finally Krasnodar) throughout the latter part of Stalin's reign and the beginning of destalinization.

We shall see later that a certain chronic weakness in his career entailed various reverses during the last years of Khrushchev's rule,

---

[1] Until 1960 Lira Belishova was one of the leaders of the Albanian Labour (i.e. Communist) Party. She was purged for pro-Soviet tendencies after the breach between Albania and the USSR.
[2] Polyansky's Ukrainian nationality is mentioned by the *Deputies' Yearbooks* of 1962 and 1959.

particularly in 1962 and 1964. Khrushchev, however, was milder in his criticism of Polyansky than he was towards Podgorny, although still fairly outspoken. In January 1961, for instance, the First Secretary curtly interrupted Polyansky several times when he was giving his report to the plenary meeting.

As to Polyansky's contribution to the 'cult' of Khrushchev, it was definitely in a lower key than Podgorny's, particularly in the latter years. The most Polyansky ever said on the subject was in January 1961, at a time when he himself was in difficulty:

> 'Thanks to his profound knowledge of life, his daring and clear-cut statement of problems, his gift for finding his way quickly and correctly in complicated situations, his wisdom and coolheadedness, he [Khrushchev] has earned the respect and love of the workers of the entire world.'[1]

There is nothing more complex than these 'organizational questions', i.e. those concerning personalities, and any conclusions call for great caution. By and large, the changes in the Presidium did not seem too unfavourable to Khrushchev. The entrance of an independent of some stature, Kosygin, was accompanied by the departure of another independent, Voroshilov, and the addition of two junior allies, Podgorny and Polyansky, from whom greater compliance could be expected. However, the reshuffle seemed to be the result of a compromise and a sign that Khrushchev did not have, or no longer had, the power to

---

[1] It should be added that, on one point at least, Polyansky openly opposed Khrushchev. In a note to the Party Presidium dated October 29 1960, Khrushchev had suggested that kolkhozes which were running at a deficit should be turned into state farms or sovkhozes, thus in effect having their debts absorbed by the state (*Agricultural Speeches*, vol 4 p 171). His suggestion applied in the first instance to the virgin lands, but he extended it to other regions in a remark made at the plenary session of January 1961. Polyansky, for his part, expressed hostility to the idea at the same plenary session, and declared: 'Anyone who tries to transform the lagging kolkhozes into sovkhozes is trying to evade the responsibility of strengthening the kolkhozes and is looking for an easier life for himself. . . . This is an absolutely incorrect position' (Verbatim record, pp 32–33).

A few months later the quarrel was resolved – in Polyansky's favour. In a speech made in Tashkent on November 16 1961, Khrushchev rejected his own earlier suggestion as 'being contrary to the policy of our Party' (*Agricultural Speeches*, vol 6 pp 87–88). It is not certain, though, that he did not go on encouraging the idea behind the scenes. In a note to the Presidium of July 31 1963 Khrushchev disclosed that during 'the past seven or eight years almost 19,000 kolkhozes . . . have been transformed into 3,131 new sovkhozes'. Once again he reprehended the practice while admitting that he had previously backed it. He justified himself by asserting that the calculations on the basis of which 'the Central Committee' (actually he alone) had reached the decision were 'more or less correct' and there were 'indeed possibilities of setting up sound farms in place of the inefficient kolkhozes', but that the local managers 'had forgotten their obligations' (*Agricultural Speeches*, vol 8 pp 66–67).

impose his own men at will. There were also weaknesses elsewhere:
1 The Secretariat was drastically reduced in numbers[1] and was, in effect, placed under the control of Kozlov, a man whom Khrushchev had good reason to regard as less reliable than his predecessor Kirichenko or his rival Brezhnev.

2 Besides Brezhnev, two other figures very close to Khrushchev had been removed from the Party apparatus, namely Furtseva and Ignatov. Furthermore, none of the newcomers, even Podgorny, was as loyal to the person and policy of the First Secretary as the men who had been dismissed.

3 Lastly and above all, this was paralleled by a serious setback for Khrushchev's policy. Not only had Khrushchev been forced to give up an international conference for which he had been clamouring for three years, but direct criticism had been levelled at him for his past activity (Camp David and other adventures). Moscow's Chinese ally had taken advantage of this to arraign him openly. At home his best ally on foreign policy issues, Mikoyan, had been defeated. Quite probably this was the first time since the 1957 victory that things had come to such a pass. That victory itself appeared less striking than had been supposed at first. It was no longer unthinkable that an opposition might rally behind men such as Suslov, Kozlov and Kosygin. There was no question of overthrowing Khrushchev – no one seems to have entertained such a plan at the time – but it had been proved that not only could Khrushchev be prevented from 'going too far', but that on occasion he could be forced to take a step backward. The lesson was worth pondering, particularly for his allies. Until then they had been unconditional ones, but now they saw another pole of attraction.

---

[1] A side-effect of the reshuffle was the return to a better ratio between Party representatives and Government in the new Presidium. Of the fourteen full members, seven were from the Party apparatus (Aristov, Kozlov, Kuusinen, Mukhitdinov, Podgorny, Suslov, Shvernik), and six from the state apparatus (Brezhnev, Ignatov, Kosygin, Mikoyan, Polyansky, Furtseva), while only Khrushchev belonged to both hierarchies. This reversed a trend that had reached its height in December 1957, when, out of the fifteen full Presidium members, ten were Party secretaries and only four represented the governmental machine (Bulganin, Voroshilov, Kozlov and Mikoyan). At that time, Khrushchev probably meant to affirm the crushing superiority of the Party over the Government, the head of which at that time was his unremitting adversary Bulganin. After he had ousted Bulganin and taken his place in March 1958 such a demonstration was less needed. Nevertheless, the upgrading of the governmental element in 1960 had the effect of giving even more power to Kosygin.

4 Aftermath of the Crisis

In his explanatory speech of May 28 Khrushchev was obviously trying to bury the U-2 affair. As far as he was concerned, the incident had blown over in the manner he had hoped for when the crisis was at its height, and he seldom mentioned it afterwards. On the contrary, he hastened to demonstrate by means of a fresh initiative that his policy of active coexistence had in no way been abandoned. On June 2 1960 he presented a disarmament plan to the Western powers which, he explained, had been drafted for the summit meeting. Its main new element was acceptance of the French proposal to liquidate the carriers of atomic weapons, namely the rockets and bombers, before disposing of the nuclear arsenal itself. The move was made in a spectacular manner, including a press conference on June 3, but remained a dead letter, firstly because the French Government showed no enthusiasm (the Soviet plan called for the liquidation of foreign bases at the outset) and secondly because the crucial problem of control remained unsolved. In any case, Khrushchev himself was shortly to backtrack: in less than a month, on June 27, he announced his Government's withdrawal from the Committee of Ten which was discussing disarmament problems at Geneva. This, it was noted, happened on the very day that he returned from Bucharest, where a communist summit had taken place which was almost as disastrous as the Paris one. It was clear that the attitude of Russia's 'allies' continued to weigh on Soviet policy.

As became known later, it was at the beginning of June 1960 that the CPSU, probably shaken by the rejection of its invitation of May 11 to Mao Tse-tung, suggested a meeting at Bucharest of the Party chiefs of the twelve socialist countries[1] on the occasion of the congress of the Rumanian Communist Party scheduled to open on June 20. The Chinese accepted but specified that this could only be a 'preparatory and preliminary' meeting which must in no way prejudice the decisions of the world forum of the parties that they wished to be convened. It is hard to tell whether, at the time they issued the invitation, the Soviet

[1] Namely the USSR, China, Poland, East Germany, Czechoslovakia, Hungary, Rumania, Bulgaria, Albania, Mongolia, North Korea and North Vietnam. Yugoslavia, which was still outside the movement because of her refusal to endorse the declaration of the last conference, in 1957, had not been invited, and neither had Cuba, whose régime was not yet Marxist–Leninist.

leaders had already decided upon the militant line which Khrushchev displayed in Bucharest. It is clear in any event that a stiffening on both sides occurred in the first days of June. In Peking a session, which had been postponed, of the General Council of the World Federation of Trade Unions opened on June 5 in an atmosphere of acute crisis between Soviet and Chinese delegates. The clashes at that session very soon began to reverberate in the 'bourgeois' press. On June 12 the Soviets replied to the semi-overt polemic on which the Chinese had embarked in April 1960 with their series of articles, 'Long Live Leninism!' N. V. Matkovsky, Deputy Director of the Institute of Marxism-Leninism, used the pretext of the fortieth anniversary of Lenin's book *Left-Wing Communism: An Infantile Disorder* in order to attack in *Pravda* the 'sectarianism' and 'dogmatism' that may 'represent a great danger at certain stages of the development of one Party or another'. Following this major lead, more or less veiled attacks on 'modern dogmatists' were to multiply in the Soviet press, until the preliminary meeting between the Soviet and Chinese delegations preceding the council of all the Parties led to a truce in September 1960.

Khrushchev arrived in Bucharest on June 18 together with Podgorny, Pospelov, Ponomarev, Andropov, Ilyichev (the last three being the heads of the Central Committee departments in charge of relations with the other parties and of ideology), Satyukov, the chief editor of *Pravda*, and Yepishev, the Ambassador to Rumania. The conference opened officially only on the 24th, but it was clear at the outset that Khrushchev had come not to surrender but to counter-attack. As early as June 21 he had circulated a 'CPSU Newsletter' sharply attacking Peking and, on the same day, he castigated those who 'parroted mechanically', 'like children', Lenin's principles on imperialism (*Pravda*, June 22 1960). It was also learned through the Chinese that the Albanian delegate Kapo had arraigned Khrushchev as a 'double-crosser'. On June 26 the Chinese delegation, in reply to the 'Newsletter', circulated a vehement statement against Soviet policy in general and Khrushchev's behaviour in particular (see *Peking Information* of May 8 1964 and other Chinese texts circulated after 1963).

The communiqué issued after the conference, which was terse and carefully worded, succeeded in masking the scope of the disagreement though not its existence. Not for several weeks did it become clear that Khrushchev had burnt his boats in that month of July 1960, being impelled to do so by the behaviour of the Chinese in Bucharest, and probably also by reports which his Albanian friend Lira Belishova sent to Moscow in early July[1] after a long stay in China. Moreover, the confer-

[1] Lira Belishova accompanied Hadji Lehi, the chief of the Albanian state, on an

ence was followed successively by the liquidation of the Chinese magazine *Druzhba* (friendship) printed in the USSR, which had begun to disseminate the more militant Peking statements among the Soviet public; the stopping of the delivery of other Chinese political publications, including the official illustrated magazine *Kitay* (China); the expulsion from Moscow of a non-identified Chinese diplomat (disclosed by Peking only in September 1963); and, most important of all, the recall from China of the Russian technical specialists and a series of economic reprisals listed as follows by the *People's Daily* in Peking in an editorial of December 4 1963:

'In July 1960 the Soviet authorities suddenly decided unilaterally to withdraw to the last man the 1,390 experts who were in China to help us with our work. They tore up 343 contracts concerning those experts as well as the annexes to the contracts, and they abolished 257 items under the head of scientific and technical cooperation. Since then they have substantially reduced the supply of complex and other key types of equipment of various kinds.'

According to the *People's Daily* of July 19 1963, the exact date on which all these decisions were made known to the Chinese Government was July 17 – i.e. directly after a plenary session of the Soviet Central Committee which had met from July 13 to 16 and had heard a report by Kozlov on the Bucharest conference. Hence there is almost no doubt that the Central Committee itself endorsed this momentous decision.[1] Besides, Party workers were shortly informed of the work

---

official visit to several Asian countries, including China. The Albanian delegation stopped over in Moscow twice, on June 1 and July 1. On July 1 they were luncheon guests of Brezhnev and Kozlov at the Kremlin (Khrushchev was then in Austria). *Pravda* at the time carried news of both Moscow visits, but the content of the actual talks was revealed only in 1964, when, in an official letter of February 22, the CPSU accused Liu Shao-tsi of having made outrageous statements about the Soviet Union to the delegation. 'Members of the delegation', the letter added, 'were indignant and informed the CPSU.' In its reply of February 27 1964, the Chinese Communist Party disclosed that among 'these members' was 'Belishova in particular, whom . . . you used as a tool to organize subversion against the leadership of a fraternal party. . . . The Albanian comrades treated the Belishova case as it deserved' (*Peking Information*, May 8 1964).

[1] In none of their later explanations did the Soviets ever deny that they were fully responsible for the technicians' recall. At most they sought to justify themselves by stating that the Chinese had made the experts' lives miserable, created a climate of suspicion and anti-Soviet propaganda around them, etc. As to the Chinese leaders, they declared that they had responded to the Soviet move by 'solemnly affirming their wish to have the experts continue their work in China and expressing the hope that the Soviet leaders would reconsider and revoke their decision' (letter of the Chinese Communist Party to the CPSU of February 29 1964, published in *Peking Information*, May 8 1964).

of the plenary session in dramatic terms. Suslov, the appointed rapporteur on the subject, addressed Party members on July 26 in Moscow and on July 27 in Leningrad. A few days later, this writer received echoes of the Moscow meeting from unofficial sources, which painted a startling picture.[1] According to these sources, Suslov had accused China of a bellicose policy and announced that henceforth relations with Peking would be restricted to government channels, while relations between the parties would cease. Consequently the Soviet technicians had been recalled and economic aid suspended. Suslov had added that a world conference of the parties at the highest level was planned 'for mid-September' and, should it fail, it was likely that the breach would be announced publicly. (There seems, indeed, every reason to think that a public breach was considered from this time on. The clumsy patch-up job achieved by the conference of the eighty-one parties in November 1960 merely delayed the public avowal by about three years.) Furthermore, according to the same source, the Presidium members 'unanimously' backed Khrushchev on this issue. The opponents, if there were any, were lower in the hierarchy and in any case they held their peace.

This particular statement may have reflected wishful thinking rather than an attempt to deceive. It should certainly not be taken on trust, but it does come fairly close to the conclusions arrived at by political analysis. It is tempting, naturally, to present these developments as a sign that Khrushchev, having surmounted the hurdles of the month of May, had again thrown his full weight behind his anti-Chinese policy and against his 'dogmatist' adversaries at the plenary session. But this would be an over-simplification.

As shown previously, the Chinese arguments seem to have met with some favourable response among the Soviet leaders in the first stage of the crisis, until about May 1960. There is no other explanation for the simultaneous warnings from Peking against the East–West détente and the stiffening of Soviet foreign policy throughout the spring of 1960.

The wreck of the summit meeting had been achieved by a hard-line majority in the Presidium whose unofficial spokesmen, i.e. Kochetov, the marshals and others, used arguments very similar and at times even identical to the Chinese. The pressure did not subside, as shown by the Soviet withdrawal from the Committee of Ten on Disarmament, directly

[1] Soviet censorship, then still in force for despatches by foreign 'bourgeois' correspondents, prevented the most sensational decisions announced by Suslov – e.g. the technicians' recall – from being reported, but permitted the growing Soviet–Chinese tension to be clearly hinted at. It seems therefore that the Soviet leaders, or some of them at least, wished the West to hear about the quarrel at that time.

after the Bucharest gathering. But it was one thing to sympathize with some Chinese theses on the impossibility of 'co-operating with imperialism' and the need to adhere to a rigid ideological line, and quite another to submit to the challenge now openly made by Peking against Soviet supremacy, or to accept the drastic sacrifices demanded by Mao Tse-tung in all fields (in particular the military and economic) for the sake of world revolution. After June 1960, and particularly after the conference of the World Federation of Trade Unions in Peking, it must have been clear to everyone in Moscow that China could no longer be appeased by minor concessions, and was demanding at least an equal voice with the USSR in Party policy. It is also a safe assumption that no one in the Kremlin was prepared to grant this, and Khrushchev's conservative foes least of all, since for them chauvinism and toughness were the major virtues. If, as it seems, the invitation to Mao Tse-tung of May 11 was an attempt at a compromise forced on Khrushchev by these hard-line elements, its unfavourable reception was likely to harden their attitude still further.

The problem was to recur at various periods of Khrushchev's reign, and analysis of the circumstances generally leads to the same conclusion. There is no doubt that differences arose as to the proper tactics, and it is likely that Khrushchev was among the most anti-Chinese of the Soviet leaders. There was an indication of this, for instance, in October 1960 – according to the Chinese themselves – when the First Secretary upon his return from New York raised once again the question of a draft statement which the committee of twenty-six parties had prepared for the November conference. Khrushchev apparently wanted the text amended in a 'revisionist' sense (*Peking Review*, No 37 September 1963). In his absence, Kozlov and Suslov had headed the Soviet delegation on the committee and it may be inferred that they had been more conciliatory towards the Peking viewpoint. There was similar wavering in 1963 and February 1964. The impression given each time, however, was that the main difference among the Soviet leaders lay elsewhere and that the squabble with the Chinese was at most merely one aspect of global policy among others, on some of which Khrushchev had had to make far more serious concessions. For instance, while the First Secretary met with effective resistance on destalinization, economic problems, etc., he seems to have been allowed, by and large, to have his way on the Chinese issue. It would seem therefore that on this point he met with only slight opposition.

In any case, on the major decisions of July 1960, there seems to have been broad agreement within the collective leadership.

It has already been noted in passing that men like Kozlov and Suslov played an important role in these decisions, as rapporteurs who presented the case to Party members. It is conceivable, of course, that Khrushchev was strong enough to compel both of them to defend a policy that they had not approved, but this is most unlikely, since it occurred just after his serious defeat in May, to which Suslov and Kozlov had strongly contributed. Furthermore, contrary to Khrushchev's pretence, the crisis was far from over. He was still forced to negotiate in order to govern. More than ever since the start of his reign, the period of June–July 1960 witnessed the triumph of collective leadership, with Suslov and Kozlov as the strong men. This is the conclusion to be drawn from certain anomalies in the political life of that period.

A PRIVATE TALK IN PITSUNDA

On June 2 1960, directly after Kosygin's return from a long journey to Argentina and Italy, the Party Presidium met in Moscow – or so we may assume, since three Presidium members from the provinces were known to be in the capital on that day. They were Podgorny, a full member, and two alternates, Korochenko and Kirilenko (the latter was in his Sverdlovsk stronghold only the day before). Evidently the meeting ratified the decisions announced a few days later – the resumption of disarmament negotiations under the new French-inspired plan, and the suggestion of a conference of the twelve party heads of the socialist camp in Bucharest.

No prominent personalities were reported to be elsewhere than in Moscow on June 2, but there is reason to believe that the following three members were not at the Presidium meeting: Mikoyan, who after the blow mentioned earlier had left Moscow around May 8 or 9 and returned only on June 11; Voroshilov, who was still a member of the Presidium but had also decided to take a long 'holiday' – his last appearance had been on May 14 and he was seen in Moscow again only on July 8; and finally Suslov, who had left more recently but also for a long time: on May 28 he had attended the opening of the conference of Communist brigades at the Kremlin and heard Khrushchev's speech. But he had not attended the final meeting of this conference on the 30th or been seen on any subsequent occasion, such as the art exhibition visited on June 1 by Khrushchev and all the Presidium members then in Moscow. Suslov returned to the capital only on July 9, at or about the same time as Voroshilov.

No doubt Suslov, like Mikoyan and Voroshilov, may have been consulted previously on the decisions about to be taken – a procedure frequently resorted to. Still, it is odd that he should have been away for so long when crucial decisions were being debated on issues of major concern to him, for instance relations with China. Did he have a voice in them?

The answer was forthcoming: on June 13 a front-page communiqué in *Pravda* announced that Khrushchev, who happened to be spending a short holiday on the shores of the Black Sea, had on the 11th visited a group of Soviet tourists at the Pitsunda holiday camp. 'At the same time as N. S. Khrushchev, the tourists were visited by M. A. Suslov and K. E. Voroshilov', the article went on. The three men, listed throughout in that order (the reverse of the alphabetical order in Russian), had been present at a ceremony for the bestowal of decorations, followed by a gay and lively theatrical performance where their appearance was greeted with 'loud applause'.

The first thing in the communiqué that caught the attention was that, while Khrushchev had in the past shared his holiday home with various Presidium members, most often Mikoyan, he had never been host to Suslov. This appearance of the chief ideologist by his side in such relaxed circumstances was the first of its kind and was to remain the only one. Furthermore, the twenty-four-hour delay with which the news was reported was not quite normal. The plot thickened when it was discovered that all the other papers in the country had ignored the event completely. Contrary to the time-honoured tradition whereby any news concerning the Head of Government was reported by all the newspapers, this item appeared only in *Pravda*. It was also noted that the communiqué did not come as usual from the Tass agency (the day before, on June 10, when Khrushchev had received Venizelos, the Greek political leader, at the same place, the news in *Pravda* of June 11 was attributed to Tass) but was presented as a kind of anonymous scoop by the Party daily.

There were two possible explanations. As June 13 was a Monday and *Pravda* was the only Soviet daily to appear on that day, the publication of the item in the other papers might have been scheduled for the following day and then cancelled. Or else the communiqué had been deliberately sent only to *Pravda* through other than the routine channels. In either case, the belated announcement and the unusual circumstances suggested that the move had been a unilateral one and had come under criticism.

While its source is hard to identify, its political purpose is easier to detect, as is the motive for the enjoyable meeting with the Pitsunda tourists. For any *apparatchik* who had for some time heard rumours of difficulties between Khrushchev and Suslov – and considering the previously mentioned events, it is quite likely that there were such – the point of the innocent communiqué was to show that the two men were disporting themselves together in the Black Sea, and that the rumours were therefore groundless. It would seem that, of the two, Khrushchev was the more interested in establishing this point after the blow to his prestige in May. At all events, when Suslov returned from his holiday in the following month, he did just the reverse to Khrushchev, as will be seen later.

Whatever the reason, staying together in Pitsunda must have given Suslov and Khrushchev an opportunity for important political talks. Khrushchev's intention seems to have been to deal separately with each of the factions in the Presidium as they had crystallized during the May crisis, and to gain control of that body as a whole after he had restored its unity. It is noteworthy that Mikoyan, whose views were probably quite different from Suslov's on a number of current problems, had already left Pitsunda when the latter arrived there.

It appears from Khrushchev's speech of May 28 that Mikoyan spent his 'exile' from Moscow at Pitsunda, where Khrushchev joined him immediately after his press conference of June 3.[1] But on June 11, when Suslov visited the tourists in the company of Khrushchev and Voroshilov, Mikoyan reappeared in Moscow and attended the funeral of Lavochkin, an aircraft constructor, together with other members of the Presidium (*Pravda*, June 12 1960).

Mikoyan was still under a cloud, as was shown a few days later by another *Pravda* 'misprint' concerning him – the fourth in three months: on June 15 he was listed as 'Prime Minister'. The fact that Khrushchev did not appear with him in public at any time during the holiday indicated that his company was still compromising. Evidently, being seen with Suslov and Voroshilov was far more profitable to Khrushchev, hence the touristic-political outing and the surrounding publicity. Above all, it was with Suslov that Khrushchev's relations needed patching up.

With what result? It was probably at Pitsunda that it was decided to retort to the Chinese arguments (Matkovsky's article in *Pravda* of June 12) and launch a strong counter-attack at the Bucharest conference. All signs indicate that Suslov had a part in these decisions.[2] If he was against them, his opposition was ineffectual, since Soviet policy continued to stiffen. Suslov's personal part in the public airing of the prob-

---

[1] One of the members of Khrushchev's personal bureau, V. S. Lebedev, was reported as 'absent from Moscow' on June 7 and was therefore unable to receive the Lenin prize awarded on that day to the co-authors of *Face to Face with America* (*Pravda*, June 8 1960). Probably his master needed him for important work at Pitsunda.

[2] V. V. Grishin, the President of Soviet Trade Unions and a USSR delegate to the conference of the World Federation of Trade Unions in Peking, had come back to Moscow on June 10. It is reasonable to assume that Khrushchev wanted to hear his report on the stormy session. If so, Suslov was in Pitsunda just in time to take part in the de-briefing.

lems in July suggests that he approved them. In any event, his later attitude was certainly not that of a man in a minority position like Mikoyan, but on the contrary, that of the strong man. As for the patching
up, it turned out to be less than profitable for Khrushchev. On June 16
Pravda announced, without further explanation or promises of other
assignments, that Kirichenko had on the previous day been demoted
from the post at Rostov to which he had been appointed five months
earlier. Ten days later N. I. Beliayev was removed from the Stavropol
Territorial Committee (*Kraykom*) (*Pravda*, June 26 1960). The final
disgrace of two men who had already been demoted at the same time,
in January 1960, could not be regarded as accidental. The reasons are
not clear, and it can only be assumed that current difficulties caused
their new punishment. Possibly they had tried to manoeuvre to be
reinstated, or perhaps they had talked too much and criticized the May
decisions. At any rate, these two close allies of Khrushchev were removed from the scene for good.[1]

PRELUDE TO COLLECTIVE LEADERSHIP

Another result of the changes was a marked downgrading of Khrushchev on the political scene. From June 14 to 16 a large conference of
agricultural experts met in the Kremlin in the presence of almost all the
Party leaders and, for the first time for years, the First Secretary was
not there to give his valued advice on this favourite topic. What made
his absence even more striking was the fact that V. V. Matskevich, the
Minister of Agriculture, who led the discussion, took some liberties with
the official viewpoint. He questioned the reasons for the enlargement of
farming enterprises, a policy initiated by Khrushchev several years
earlier, and stressed the importance of the *raykom* (district committee)
in the administrative hierarchy and agricultural inspection tours by
raykom officials – a system to which Khrushchev was to put a stop two
years later. In addition, Matskevich expressed scepticism about Ameri-

[1] The First Secretary's former allies were being removed, but his former foes also
were disposed of during the same period. The former Head of Government, Bulganin, who had been appointed chairman of the Stavropol sovnarkhoz in 1958, left
the region in the summer of 1960 and was retired – although he was allowed to settle
in Moscow (where Kaganovich also was living), whereas Malenkov was permitted
to do this only towards the end of Khrushchev's reign. Another coincidence was that
in the summer of 1960 it was decided to strip Molotov of his functions as Ambassador
to Mongolia. After unsuccessful attempts to secure the agreement of the respective
governments to his appointment to The Hague or Athens, he was finally sent to
Vienna as the USSR representative on the International Atomic Energy Agency.
The appointment was confirmed at the end of September.

can agricultural methods in general and those of Mr. Garst, a farmer and great friend of Khrushchev's, in particular. Finally, he had as little good to say of maize cultivation as of Khrushchev's achievements in general, to which he paid no tribute whatsoever (*Pravda*, June 15 1960).[1]

This was only a beginning of trouble for Khrushchev. After an inevitable spell of flattery during his visits to Bucharest and Austria (June 18 to July 8), there was a remarkable boosting of the principle of collective leadership. Most probably a new source of embarrassment was the RB-47 affair, an incident on July 1 in which an American reconnaissance plane was brought down by a Russian fighter in the Arkhangelsk area. Although much less serious than the U-2 incident, it placed the Soviet Government in an awkward position in view of their rash threat to bomb the take-off bases if a repetition occurred. Khrushchev extricated himself by stating in his protest note of July 11: 'Since the violation of Soviet air space was stopped in its initial stage, the Soviet Government deemed it sufficient to destroy the aircraft'.[2] The dilemma in question may account for the delay of eleven days in the Soviet reaction. There were other grounds for confusion too: according to the note from the Department of State of July 13, Soviet planes had been sent to take part in a search for the lost aircraft side by side with United States planes. It is hard to tell whether this was a machiavellian plot or a lack of co-ordination.

In any event, Khrushchev, who seems to have retained a monopoly of foreign policy decisions, referred to the subject in a press conference on July 12, but this was one of his few public speeches: on all other topics, Kozlov, Kosygin and Suslov had now taken over. The most surprising occurrence was on July 16, when the Central Committee heard a report on the conference of the twelve parties in Bucharest, delivered not by Khrushchev, the head of the Soviet delegation to the conference, nor by Podgorny, who had accompanied him, but by Kozlov, who had not been there. This may, of course, have been Khrushchev's way of showing the unity of the Soviet leadership in the face of the Chinese challenge – a demonstration to Peking that Kozlov approved of Khrushchev's

---

[1] This show of independence was to prove costly to the Minister of Agriculture. A few months later, in a note to the Party Presidium dated October 29 1960, Khrushchev criticized him for his attitude at the conference, attacking his 'incomprehensible' position and 'incorrect' plans for the organization of sovkhozes (see volume 4 of Khrushchev's *Agricultural Speeches*, p 175). In December 1960 Matskevich lost his post and was transferred to the virgin lands. It should be noted, however, that while opposing various agricultural schemes of Khrushchev's he was fairly close to him on many political issues, particularly that of the 'anti-party group'.
[2] Once again the pilots were captured alive, but these two men were far more discreet than Powers about their activities. They were not brought to trial and were returned to the United States a few months later, when President Kennedy took office.

attitude and had endorsed economic reprisals (these, as mentioned earlier, were made known to the Chinese Government on July 17). Still, a silent role of this sort was out of character for the First Secretary. Moreover, it extended to other matters: Khrushchev did not take the floor on economic problems, the main topic on the session's agenda, and left it to Kosygin to sum up the debate.[1]

Suslov, unlike Mikoyan, had come back from holiday on July 9 stronger than ever and eager to show it. It is doubtful whether this timing was accidental. Khrushchev, who returned from Austria the day before, had been greeted at the Vnukovo airport by most of the members of the Presidium. On the afternoon of July 9, he made a long report on his journey in the presence of the entire leadership. But Suslov appeared only a few hours later, at a reception given for the Indonesian Prime Minister Djuanda (he even startled foreign diplomats by sporting a Ukrainian peasant shirt without a tie). A very slight change in his schedule would have enabled him to hear the historic report of the tireless fighter for peace whom he had not seen since their Pitsunda meeting a month earlier. Another participant in the jollifications there had made the effort: after a two-month absence, Voroshilov made his first appearance in Moscow on July 8, just in time for Khrushchev's home-coming.

Suslov did not take the floor at the plenary session, but made his presence felt in other ways. On July 15 he spoke at a reception for delegates of the International Journalists' Union, welcoming the guests 'in the name of the Presidium of the Central Committee of the CPSU and of Nikita Sergeyevich Khrushchev'.[2] This formula was the only noteworthy feature of the speech, which was probably designed only to advertise the speaker's presence. (It was published by *Pravda* and *Krasnaya Zvezda*, the army organ, but not *Izvestia*.) Suslov further asserted himself, as already noted, by delivering his dramatic reports on relations with the Chinese to Communist Party members in Moscow and Leningrad. He also spoke on two earlier occasions, in Vilnius (Vilna) for the twentieth anniversary of the annexation of Lithuania and a few days before that at a large country excursion for writers, artists and scientists.

[1] Khrushchev apparently tried, as was his wont, to interfere in the discussion by hectoring the speakers from his seat. Kunayev mentioned in his speech to the plenary session a remark that Khrushchev had made in this way on the previous day concerning industrial development in Kazakhstan (verbatim record, Moscow 1960, p. 156). The new fact is that these interjections were not published. At the next plenary session, in January 1961, Khrushchev, who was obviously once again in a stronger position, resorted to the same practice on a much larger scale.
[2] The wording is not unimportant: a 'Khrushchev man' would have said 'In the name of the Presidium headed by Khrushchev', or simply 'in the name of Nikita Sergeyevich'. Suslov's intention was to show that the Presidium was still there and was not 'headed' by anybody.

This entertainment, held on the day after the Central Committee plenary session of July 17, reflected the triumph of collective leadership. The six senior members of the Presidium spoke in turn, each on a particular sector of the 'cultural front'. Suslov made the general report, thus discharging for the last time the functions of 'literary and artistic director' later assigned to Ilyichev. Then Brezhnev rose to salute 'science and the scientists'; Kozlov toasted the writers, Mikoyan the painters. Furtseva, the Minister of Culture, was allotted only the film writers, while Aristov cornered the musicians and Kosygin the playwrights. Khrushchev closed this odd symposium with a speech which *Pravda*, without publishing, described as 'powerful and lucid'. Several months later, in May 1961, a text appeared which was presented as an 'abridgment' (*Kommunist*, No 7 1961). Since it included extracts from other speeches he had made later at receptions for writers and composers, this text cannot be relied on as an account of what he had actually said in July 1960. Apart from routine appeals for *partiynost* (party loyalty) on the part of the writers, one feature is noteworthy, namely the veiled attack on 'certain dogmatists and lovers of theoretical disputes'; also the general emphasis on the minor nature of doctrinal problems as compared to the 'building of communism'. The hint was aimed at the Chinese, but perhaps at some people nearer home as well. As for Suslov's speech, published on the following day, it was a rather confused hotchpotch of old formulae.[1]

The other speeches were not particularly striking either. The dominant theme was unity and the need to rally around the chief in facing the outside world. Suslov, for example, extolled 'the unparalleled unity of Soviet society' and warmly praised the First Secretary, but only for his foreign policy.[2] Two days earlier, in the Central Committee, Kosygin also had found it necessary to praise Khrushchev in warmer terms than he ever had before, and to stress the theme of unity. 'Our Party', he said, 'is monolithic, united, more closely knit than it ever was around its

---

[1] The subtle Yermilov, a literary critic renowned for opportunism in a country where this is no rarity, used a devious method to 'reconcile' the two major speeches by Suslov and Khrushchev made at that meeting. After praising both in the *Literaturnaya Gazeta* of July 23 1960, he went on: 'The content of M. A. Suslov's speech must be considered in the context of the thoughts expressed in Comrade Khrushchev's speech, and, in particular, the principle that socialism is now proving its historic superiority over capitalism no longer only in theory, as was the case before socialism became the powerful reality it is today. . . .' The meaning of this delphic language seems to be: Suslov is a theoretician who is somewhat entangled in his own formulae. Better read Khrushchev to get a complete idea of what it's all about.

[2] 'An example of such firmness, consistency and energy in the struggle for peace is given us, comrades, by Nikita Khrushchev's tireless activity. It is with affection and respect, sincere gratitude and admiration that the common people in all countries speak of this noble activity of our Nikita Sergeyevich' (*Pravda*, July 18 1960).

Central Committee' (*Pravda*, July 16 1960). Such insistence is not accidental: not only did it reflect the need for cohesion *vis-à-vis* the Chinese, but also the clarification of the various groups' positions which had taken place during the previous weeks. Evidently the talks at Pitsunda or elsewhere among the main leaders had succeeded in shelving the May crisis if not in liquidating it. The effect had been to upgrade the role of the Presidium to a marked extent and correspondingly to downgrade Khrushchev. Only in this sense was it possible to speak of regained unity.

Within the Presidium itself there had been a reshuffle in the hierarchy, but evidently this was not accepted by all its members. The report on the meeting with the writers, as published in *Pravda* on July 18, was revealing in this respect. The speeches – their order, the space and category of applause meted out to each of them – were as follows:

Suslov:	5 columns	loud, prolonged applause
Brezhnev:	54 lines	tumultuous applause
Kozlov:	45 lines	friendly applause
Mikoyan:	5 lines	no applause mentioned
Furtseva:	10 lines	,, ,,
Aristov:	5 lines	,, ,,
Kosygin:	10 lines	,, ,,

The interesting thing is the preferential treatment given to Brezhnev and Kozlov, who were ranked immediately after Suslov and well above all the other Presidium members. Brezhnev had just lost his place in the Party Secretariat, but thanks to his new appointment as Head of State he retained his prestige as a senior member.

Mikoyan was dealt a severe blow, especially considering his past position. Typically, there was another 'error' concerning him in *Pravda* of July 14, which suggested that he was the object of a struggle. On the other hand, the photographs and captions published that day by most of the Moscow papers (*Pravda*, *Izvestia* and *Krasnaya Zvezda* for instance) showed 'Comrades Khrushchev and Mikoyan conversing with the writers'. This was odd since, according to the articles reporting the excursion, Mikoyan was in the modest position already mentioned, and the man who should have appeared in the photographs was Suslov, the principal rapporteur. Until then the press, or at any rate the Party daily, systematically presented Khrushchev with Kozlov on his right and Suslov on his left. This was done in particular by *Pravda* on July 14 and 15 during the Central Committee plenary session.[1]

[1] It is very difficult to explain these contradictions and their mechanism in each instance. To begin with, they may vary with circumstances. For example, at the meeting with the writers, Khrushchev may have made a point of having Mikoyan by his side most of the time rather than anybody else. They also depend on the level

Another sign that a struggle was going on was that the alternate members of the Presidium began just then to be listed in alphabetical order instead of in the preferential order as previously (*Pravda*, July 19 1960). Those who suffered by the change were the former Party Secretary, P. N. Pospelov, and a very old associate of Khrushchev in the Ukraine, D. S. Korochenko.

In short, the compromise reached by the protagonists of the May crisis created a situation entirely different to that of 1957–1959. Krushchev kept his post and most probably his privileged though not absolute voice in foreign policy. The praise of his activity by men like Suslov and Kosygin was intended to convince foreign opinion of this, but did not extend to any other field. Khrushchev, on the other hand, had had to give his fellow-members a larger share in all other public activities, ranging from agriculture to ideology. It was, of course, a precarious compromise, which Khrushchev soon tried to erode in every way he could. His great difficulty was that, after the May 4 reshuffle, his power no longer matched his ambitions.

The economic apparatus, in particular, was already slipping away from him.

THE ECONOMY SEEN FROM BACKSTAGE: CENTRALIZERS VERSUS REGIONALISTS

Everything in Soviet policy is linked together. It would be surprising indeed if the economic organs had not felt the after-effects of the upheaval in the top leadership in spring 1960. Objective factors contributed to this as well. No general survey of the economic situation is called for here; in any case, it was only in the last years of the reign that the year 1960 stood out as a turning point in that field. Suffice

---

at which decisions are made. An order from Khrushchev superseded anyone else's but Khrushchev might have found it embarrassing to give the entire press, through Tass or Agitprop channels, instructions concerning the cult of his own personality or the treatment of this or that member of the Presidium. For this reason he seems to have preferred to deal directly with his trusted men at the head of *Pravda*, *Izvestia* or the radio (significantly, these three officials – P. S. Satyukov, A. I. Adzhubey and M. A. Kharlamov – were demoted just after Khrushchev himself, whereas D. P. Goryunov, the director of Tass, was not affected). In the absence of an official order from Khrushchev, the Party Secretariat, i.e. Kozlov and Suslov, had the last word. They could give positive orders about the presentation of a given event, or else censor the material. If they abstained from doing so, the chief editor resumed his normal role. This subordination to various levels of the hierarchy explains how the same paper could from one day to the next, or even within a single issue, give conflicting indications concerning conflicts at top level.

it to say that, despite the delirious optimism which they professed at the time, the Soviet leaders must have been aware of impending trouble. On the one hand, spectacular measures such as the elimination of income tax and the institution of a six or seven hour working day were announced (May 1960), while on the other hand austerity measures were being taken discreetly to boost the revenue. Thus, on December 26 1959, the Presidium of the Supreme Soviet passed a decree whose details are unknown to us but which, according to the journal *Socialist Legality* for March 1960, aimed at 'suppressing certain excesses in the granting of pensions to some categories of pensioners'. A few days earlier, on December 10 1959, another decree 'severely limited' the accumulation of jobs (and hence of salaries) by one individual. This measure, affecting a large number of people, probably provoked a strong reaction, for on June 9 1960 another decree markedly restricted its effects.[1] Lastly, the transition to a six and seven hour working day was accompanied by a 'salary readjustment' which, despite official denials, meant substantial reductions in the pay of engineers and administrative employees, i.e. the 'middle classes'. The resulting discontent was clear to observers at the time.[2]

The acute budget difficulties were obviously part-cause of the decision to disband one-third of the armed forces. As already mentioned, the military tried to exploit the crisis of May 1960 in order to get the measure revoked or at least to resume the battle for military appropriations. As on several other occasions, they probably found allies among

---

[1] See the texts of the decrees of 1959 and 1960 in *Spravochnik Partiynovo Rabotnika* (The Party Workers' Handbook), 3rd edition, Moscow, 1961, pp 232 and 299.

[2] Popular discontent due to the pay cuts decreed in the autumn of 1959 clearly took on violent forms in several places. The Temir-Tau riots in Kazakhstan seem well documented by eye-witness reports. According to rumours in Moscow, similar demonstrations occurred in Kemerovo, the centre of the Siberian industrial basin of the Kuzbas, in early January 1960. At all events, on February 12 1960, A. B. Aristov conducted a major purge of the local leaders and removed in particular the First Secretary of the Kemerovo Oblast Committee, S. M. Pilipets, the Second Secretary, E. Z. Razumov, and the chairman of the local sovnarkhoz, A. N. Zademidko. In April 1960 the Bureau of the Central Committee for the RSFSR and the Council of Ministers of the Republic passed a special decree which was not published, with the object of 'developing industry and building and improving cultural and communal amenities for urban workers in the Kuzbas' (speech by L. E. Grafov to the plenary session of the Central Committee in July 1960, verbatim record, p 82).

The Temir-Tau riots brought even more brutal sanctions against local officials. The First Secretary of the Karaganda region, P. N. Isayev, was not only relieved of his post but probably expelled from the Party. The *Deputies' Yearbook* published in December 1959 does not mention his seniority in the Party and ignores his earlier work in the field of management. Isayev was appointed foreman in a metal factory in Sverdlovsk, which means that he was transferred from the region and demoted to worker's status, an extremely rare punishment in Khrushchev's Russia. The Chairman of the Karaganda sovnarkhoz, D. G. Onika, was also removed, but soon after became director of an institute in Moscow.

those whom Khrushchev once dubbed the 'metal-eaters' – the traditional economists who held to the hallowed rule of priority for heavy
industry. But Khrushchev was not as fully committed to a revision of
the principle as he became a few months later, and apparently this was
not at the time one of his major points of contention with the economic
managers.

Disagreements on management methods, however, were more serious.
In May 1957 Khrushchev had taken a crucial step towards decentralization by liquidating over twenty technical ministries and setting up
throughout the country about one hundred National Economic Councils
(sovnarkhozes) whose task was to run industry on a regional basis.
The decision had been taken, as was learned subsequently, over the
stubborn opposition of most of Khrushchev's foes in the Presidium –
notably Molotov, Shepilov and Pervukhin – and had played a large
part in arousing the 'anti-party' coalition of June 1957. In short,
Khrushchev's prestige was at stake on this issue as much as on the
virgin lands programme and other grand designs of his reign. And
the time had now come to reappraise all these questions.

In all fairness, the reform had yielded good results during its first
two years. The sovnarkhozes had made for better co-ordination of
economic activities within each region and had helped to rationalize
transportation problems. The new managers of enterprises were less
erratic than the former ministries because, as Khrushchev's propaganda
claimed, they really were 'closer to production'. Criticism was justified,
nevertheless, on the following important counts:

1 The reform had not come to grips with the basic problem that was
to grow more pressing during the ensuing years – that of the freedom
of the enterprises to manage their own production. They were smothered
under all kinds of controls, inspections and directives. It was a meagre
consolation for their directors to receive orders from regional bureaucrats instead of national ones. Moreover, it would be truer to say that
they were now harassed by both. The problem, however, was no more
capable of solution in 1960 than in 1962, when it began to be discussed
in earnest, or even in 1964. The opposition encountered by Khrushchev
and his reform lay elsewhere.

2 This opposition arose chiefly from the administrative departments
of the central planning agencies, who were more inclined towards
'centralist' conservatism than 'democratic' flexibility. Although the
sovnarkhozes were closely controlled by the republican and central
governments, they did arouse a certain amount of community spirit
among local cadres. Discipline was less automatic than in the past.
The need to cope with this danger, together with pressure from centralist-
minded economists, had already led to some undermining of the 1957

reform. First the departments of Gosplan supervising various branches of industry had been upgraded so as to become in effect surrogates for the disbanded ministries. Khrushchev's first cabinet of March 1958 had given ministerial rank to seven Gosplan members (in addition to that body's chairman, Kuzmin), three of whom were no more than department heads. Secondly, 'State committees of the USSR Council of Ministers' had soon afterwards been set up for various branches of industry. In principle, they had no direct managing power and their sole function was to lay down the technical policy of the industries in question. Nevertheless, the committees were strongly tempted to take matters directly in hand just as the former ministries had done. In any case they multiplied in numbers during the ensuing years.

The criticism aimed at Khrushchev on other issues in the spring of 1960 provided the centralizers with a favourable terrain for their new offensive. They won a point on April 7, when the Central Committee and the Council of Ministers passed a decree on 'the further improvement of planning and management of the economy'.[1] On the ground that the problem was to 'combine as far as possible centralized state management with the development of initiative by local bodies', the decree divided the powers of the two large central planning agencies that had been competing until then. Gosplan, then headed by Kosygin, was to be in charge of so-called current planning, i.e. outlining and supervising the execution of annual plans. The Gosekonomsoviet, or scientific–economic Council of State, headed by I. I. Kuzmin, was to be in charge of long-range planning, i.e. drawing up the five and seven-year plans then under consideration. In addition, it was to submit to the Government a twenty-year plan – no doubt the one made public in 1961 at the Twenty-second Party Congress.

Overlapping of management and planning was one of the perennial flaws of the planning system set up by Stalin. The latest attempt at a division of powers was not the first or the last. In this instance, however, one of the immediate effects was to relieve Gosplan of part of its traditional functions, thus enabling it to intervene more actively in the work of the sovnarkhozes. This, indeed, was just what the decree aimed at, since it was explained that 'the growing and deepening ties among economic regions make it necessary to strengthen current planning . . . in particular to harmonize the development plans of different economic regions among themselves'. Another result was to strengthen the Gosekonomsoviet and hence the 'centre' in relation to the periphery. (The first Gosekonomsoviet chairman, A. A. Goreglyad, was promoted

---

[1] For the decreee of April 7 1960 on economic planning, see *Spravochnik Partiynovo Rabotnika* (The Party Workers' Handbook), 3rd edition, 1961, p 262. The Moscow newspapers did not mention the subject at the time.

'Minister of the USSR' on June 11 1960. Another Minister, E. S. Novosyolov, was transferred from Gosplan to Gosekonomsoviet, thus enhancing the latter's status. Two other prominent officials, N. A. Tikhonov and S. M. Tikhomirov, also joined Gosekonomsoviet during the year.) It is interesting that the personalities singled out to head the agency during the reshuffle were not drawn from among Khrushchev's close supporters. Kosygin's promotion on May 4 to the top of the state economic machine (supervising both his former Gosplan domain and the Gosekonomsoviet) has already been mentioned. The others promoted were:

1 A. F. Zasyadko, a man with a chequered career who had suffered a serious blow in March 1955 just after the downfall of Malenkov, with whom he seems to have been associated. Demoted then from USSR Minister for the coal industry to the same position in the Ukraine, he had returned to the centre in May 1957, when the industrial reform that he had strongly advocated came into favour. But his ties with Khrushchev were looser than his Ukrainian background would have suggested. In November 1962 he opposed the First Secretary's reforms and again fell from favour as a result. From 1960 onwards, in fact, he was a much less ardent supporter of Khrushchev than I. I. Kuzmin, whom he replaced at the head of Gosekonomsoviet. The change was most probably decided at the same time as the reorganization of the planning bodies, and was announced on April 22.

2 V. N. Novikov, promoted Chairman of the USSR Gosplan instead of Kosygin. He had enjoyed the cloudless career typical of the senior managers of the most sacred branch of Soviet industry, that of armaments. His entire career since 1928 had been in that area. He was Deputy Minister for Armaments from 1941 to 1948 and again in 1954 and 1955. His immediate superior during all those years, D. F. Ustinov, will be mentioned again more than once. Both attended the military mechanical engineering institute in Leningrad and graduated in 1934. Novikov may also have had ties with F. R. Kozlov, for in 1957 he had taken over the management of the Leningrad sovnarkhoz when Kozlov was in charge of the Party organization in that region. He owed nothing whatever to Khrushchev except that, in May 1958, he had been chosen over his old adversary N. K. Baybakov to take charge of the RSFSR Gosplan. Like Zasyadko, Novikov clashed with the First Secretary in 1962 and fell from favour. Zasyadko died not long afterwards, but Novikov resumed his brilliant career after the palace revolution of October 1964.

3 K. M. Gerasimov, who succeeded Novikov as head of the RSFSR Gosplan, belonged to the same group. He had also worked in the defence industry since before the war, and under D. F. Ustinov's pro-

tection had been Deputy Minister of Armaments almost uninterruptedly from 1941 to 1957. He too had been sent to the provinces
after the 1957 reform and had since 1958 been in charge of the Gorky
sovnarkhoz. It was a sign of the times that those men were the first
to return to Moscow.

Although the promotion of the veterans of the war industry was
compensated by the leading role given to Kosygin – who for a long time
had favoured light industry and consumer goods – it could not be
regarded as accidental at a time when leading circles were in the grip
of a violent chauvinistic and conservative reaction. These were the type
of men who, with many others, had prevented Khrushchev not only
from cutting the military appropriations as much as he would have
liked, but also from abandoning the principle of priority for heavy
industry – a problem which bedevilled him till his last day in power.

It is also likely that the newly promoted men backed the centralizing
tendencies which were manifested in the debate on management. Far
from abating after the decree of April 9 1960, this debate grew in inten-
sity in the ensuing weeks.

In addition to the provisions on the jurisdiction of Gosplan, that
decree introduced a completely new element. Article 4 stated that, in
order to ensure 'the strengthening of economic ties among sovnarkhozes', it was necessary to 'set up, in the country's major economic
regions, Economic Councils to co-ordinate and plan the work of the
sovnarkhozes'. Thus the latter bodies were to be regrouped within larger
economic regions and a new administrative echelon – the 'co-ordinating
council' – was to be added to the already lengthy chain of command.

It would be interesting to know how this provision came to be
adopted, since not only was it never applied, but it was not even mentioned again for a year. The 'co-ordinating councils' were set up only
on April 26 1961, under a decree of the Central Committee and the
Government that was not even published at the time.[1] Khrushchev
mentioned them fleetingly in his progress report to the Twenty-second
Congress in October 1961, when he spoke of the 'recently created' enlarged economic regions that are called upon to play 'a major role in
modernizing the economy' (Verbatim record of the Twenty-second
Congress, vol 1 p 64). Here again the declaration was premature, for it
was only in February 1962, i.e. almost two years after the supposedly
'firm' decision of April 1960, that a map of the regions was published
and the composition of their 'co-ordinating councils' made known

---

[1] The economic 'co-ordinating councils' are mentioned only in another decree of
February 15 1963 ordering their liquidation and disclosing the date of the decree
under which they were set up (*Spravochnik Partiynovo Rabotnika*, 5th edition,
Moscow, 1964, p 95).

(*Pravda*, February 23 1962, and *Sovietskaya Rossiya*, February 28 1962). The councils proved to be short-lived, and a few weeks later they ceased to be mentioned. The question of larger economic regions was in fact settled only at the end of 1962 and in an entirely different way: far from 'co-ordinating the work' of the sovnarkhozes, many of them were simply liquidated.

All this pointed to a major struggle. The opposition of sovnarkhoz officials was probably compounded by that of Khrushchev, who did not care to see his grand design of 1957 being gradually eroded. After a long controversy there was clearly a marked change in orientation leading to a shaky compromise which itself was soon questioned.

The decision of April 9 had entrusted the USSR Gosplan, in cooperation with the governments of the republics, with working out a draft text on the enlarged regions, to be submitted to the Council of Ministers within one month. Actually it took two months instead of one, and produced a different project: on June 18 1960 a decree announced the creation of a sovnarkhoz of the RSFSR whose task was to 'co-ordinate the work of the sovnarkhozes' within that republic and to watch over the 'observance of state discipline in the fulfilment of supply plans'. The chairman of the new body was V. M. Ryabikov, himself a former leader in the war industry, the First Deputy Minister for Armaments from 1940 to 1951, and a close associate of D. F. Ustinov who, like him, had been trained in Leningrad.

It is not clear whether the creation of a 'super-sovnarkhoz' at the head of the largest republic in the country – a pattern that was followed by the Ukraine and Kazakhstan – was a step towards greater concentration as compared to the enlarged economic regions contemplated earlier, or a step away from it. In any case, it was a further infringement of the prerogatives of the original sovnarkhozes and a step backward from the 1957 reform. There are many signs that the new measure was not accepted and carried out without recriminations, even at top level.

At the July 1960 plenary session only four speakers mentioned the RSFSR sovnarkhoz. They were K. M. Gerasimov, I. S. Senin, G. I. Gaile and P. F. Lomako. These were the first four rapporteurs of the first day. All other speakers ignored the question, even Kosygin in his closing speech. Neither was it mentioned in the resolution adopted at the end of the session. As to Ryabikov, not only did he not take the floor at the session, but he was not even a member of the seventy-member drafting committee elected on July 15 to prepare the resolution. It seems likely therefore that a change of mind at the very outset of the session had made the matter taboo. Moreover, the corresponding sovnarkhozes for the other republics were set up only after some delay.

N. A. Sobol, the chairman of the Ukraine sovnarkhoz, was appointed only on July 30.

While the measure of June 18 was thus contested, the 1957 reform did not fare better. An analysis of the debates at the plenary session shows a visible wavering on the issue. Of the twenty-five political and economic leaders who took the floor, only eleven supported it. All the others refrained from broaching the subject and even in some cases from uttering the word sovnarkhoz. This applies to A. P. Kirilenko, First Secretary of the Sverdlovsk Oblast Committee, who managed to speak for half an hour about industrial activity in his important region without once mentioning the existence of the Sverdlovsk sovnarkhoz. Here again, the speakers who were silent on the subject were definitely more numerous at the end of the session than at the beginning, and they included almost all those who spoke on the last day, including Kosygin.[1] It thus seems that the backstage discussions resulted in making the leaders more cautious as regards not only the RSFSR sovnarkhoz but also on the subject of sovnarkhozes in general. As to the final resolution, it did pay the customary tribute to the 1957 reorganization – 'a truly revolutionary measure . . . that accelerated the development of productive forces', but it no longer praised the reform for having 'swept away administrative barriers', as had been claimed for instance after a similar plenary session in June 1959. The resolution was also more incisive than the earlier one in calling on the plenary session to put a stop to the harmful tendencies of certain leaders towards economic autarky.

Clearly none of these questions had been settled. The struggle between centralizers and regionalists was to go on behind the scenes for years to come, leading to compromise agreements that only worsened matters. Rather than touch the sovnarkhozes, it was decided to multiply administrative hierarchies, thus increasing still further the gross unwieldiness of the bureaucratic machine. The most glaring effects of this policy, however, did not make themselves felt till 1963.

---

[1] The attitude of K. M. Gerasimov is interesting. He was the first and main rapporteur at the session, and not only did he not pay tribute, even rhetorically, to Khrushchev's 1957 reorganization, but he voiced certain veiled criticisms of it. For instance, he deplored the fact that the sovnarkhozes insisted on having industrial 'branch managements', something that had been regarded as legal from 1957 onwards. He also noted that the problem of relations between the various economic regions was 'far from solved'. Since Gerasimov had been one of the few people who welcomed the creation of the RSFSR sovnarkhoz, he can probably be counted as one of the staunchest opponents of decentralization. It should be noted also that he pleaded for 'further rapid development of the steel industry' (he had earlier deplored the 'metal shortage' from which the country was suffering and stressed the 'all-important' problems of mechanical engineering as opposed to those of the chemical industry, whose champion Khrushchev had become at the time).

Considerable attention has been devoted to the events of the first half of 1960 because they appear to set a precedent for some other crises that Khrushchev was to face before his final defeat. An embarrassing political reverse (the U-2 incident) served as a catalyst for the latent opposition. Grievances long suffered in silence came tumbling forth, both from the military, who had been by-passed in appropriations, and from the top planners yearning for greater centralization. All their demands, which constituted the background of the struggle for power, found political expression in the Party Presidium where the balance of profits and losses was swiftly drawn. Thus 1960 witnessed a serious blow to Khrushchev's ambitions and forced him to accept some sharing of power. His decline seems definitely to date from this period.

Whether all this would have happened if the U-2 had not overflown Soviet territory a fortnight before the summit meeting and if President Eisenhower had not accepted responsibility for it is a moot point. It is likely that the detractors of Khrushchev's policy, ranging from the Chinese to the Soviet marshals and including the conservatives within the state and party apparatus, would eventually have found an opportunity for action. But the best chance was given them by a foreign country. Instances when decisions in the West have had such clear-cut repercussions on the situation in the Kremlin are sufficiently rare for this one to be given all the emphasis it deserves.

No opinion will be expressed here as to whether this event was salutary from the Western point of view. United States policy was in any case influenced by domestic motives, particularly the fact pointed out by Allen Dulles,[1] that secrecy could not have been maintained for long under American conditions. But such motives should not have been the only ones. No policy of relations with Moscow can be planned intelligently without regard to the capital question of how it affects the struggle for influence at top level in the Soviet Union. For this purpose, the symptoms of that struggle which are visible to the outside world must be taken seriously however slight they may seem. Even before May 1 1960, these signs showed clearly enough that Khrushchev, despite his self-assurance and the cult that surrounded him, was far from being the absolute master he had been taken for. This fact seems to have been generally underestimated. Before considering whether or not it was in the Western interest to help him consolidate his power, it would have been useful to have been aware of its limitations.

[1] Allen Dulles, *The Craft of Intelligence*, Harper & Row, New York, pp 197–198.

Part Two
THE TWENTY-SECOND CONGRESS 1961–1962

Nothing particularly striking occurred in the second half of 1960 or the early months of 1961. Some events, such as the council of the eighty-one communist parties or Khrushchev's visit to the United Nations in the autumn, are connected with the story already told and are only its logical outcome. However important their repercussions abroad may have been, they were less significant domestically. They only showed that Khrushchev was going about his normal business in his usual manner. Other happenings in this period, however, point forward to the next major stage of his reign, namely the Twenty-second Congress. This will accordingly be the starting-point of our analysis.

A Party congress is not necessarily a salient event. In Stalin's time, when he had the whole apparatus under his thumb, the congress, like the Supreme Soviet, existed to do his bidding. They merely provided the dictator with a convenient platform to proclaim his major decisions while the so-called 'elections' with which they concluded helped to record the favours and demotions meted out between sessions. That was the pattern for about twenty years, from the Seventeenth Congress in 1934 to the Nineteenth in 1952. But when the leader's authority is insecure, congresses are a different matter; and this was the case at the famous Twentieth Congress of 1956, when a fierce clash occurred behind the scenes between Khrushchev and his adversaries. The cause was Khrushchev's intention, which met with strong opposition, to bring criticism to bear on Stalin's record. However, after Khrushchev's victory over Molotov and his allies in 1957 it should have been possible to revert to the formula of rubber-stamp congresses – the demonstration of monolithic unity around the man at the top.

This did happen, outwardly at least. The Twenty-first Congress in the spring of 1959 was a quiet one. It was convened to display concerted support for the launching of the seven-year plan rather than because of internal political strife. Khrushchev did try to consolidate his earlier gains by resuming his 'anti-party' campaign, but since the congress decided – against Khrushchev's wishes in all likelihood – that the membership of the Central Committee would not change, there was not much he could do. The Congress only showed to close observers that the problem of the 'anti-party group' was not quite settled and that powerful forces were against exploiting it for political purposes. This had a strong bearing on Khrushchev's position, as the Twenty-second Congress confirmed beyond all expectations.

The Congress was prepared well ahead of time. The opening date – October 17 1961 – was announced in January of that year. The main documents to be discussed – the Party programme and statutes – were published at the end of July and commented on in the press for two and a half months. They will be discussed later, but another less publicized aspect of the preparation for the Congress deserves analysis first. This is the extensive reshuffle at various levels of the Party apparatus that started at the end of 1960 and continued throughout 1961.

1 The Pre-Congress Purge

One difference between the Twenty-second Congress and those of the Stalinist type should be mentioned at the outset. The defunct dictator purged anybody whenever the fancy took him, with or without a congress, while in this instance it was the forthcoming elections to the Central Committee that provided the occasion for the purge. This was indeed a long-awaited opportunity to settle certain accounts. It was also imperative for the leaders if they did not want to wait four more years, i.e. until the next congress, before getting rid of interference. The plural 'leaders' is used deliberately, since Khrushchev was not the only one eager for a purge. And the best way of getting rid of people was to strip them, before the congress, of the functions that entitled them to membership of the principal Party organs. This was done on a large scale. Between 1956 and 1960, for instance, the composition of cadres had remained relatively stable, whereas the changes in the eighteen months preceding the Twenty-second Congress affected hundreds of officials and involved the demotion of at least twenty full members of the Central Committee. G. I. Voronov indicated the scope of the purge at the Twenty-second Congress when, reporting for the RSFSR, he said: 'Over one-third of the Territorial Committee and Oblast Committee Secretaries have been replaced during this year.'

All purges have their own laws: they need a propitious climate, a slogan and the existence of heretics – who are not necessarily those denounced publicly. Under Stalin, for instance, there were the purges of political opponents, saboteurs and 'pro-Japanese Trotskyist spies'. Under Khrushchev, fortunately, both the slogans and the methods were milder. In this case agriculture provided the setting, while incompetence and bureaucratism were the targets.

The issue was far from being a mere pretence. Not only was Khrushchev's passion for agriculture well known, but he was then entering his period of organizing frenzy that was later dubbed *prozhektorstvo* or project-mongering, the mania for incessant drives, reforms and changes in the administrative set-up. Since the results of his agricultural policy of the preceding two years had been disappointing (the 1959 and 1960 crops had been mediocre and stockbreeding was on the decline) Khrushchev had concluded – in good faith it seems, if somewhat naïvely – that the whole trouble was due to the bad execution of a good policy.

'The cadres decide everything' became the motto. Let a good organizer, a Party man preferably, take a lagging kolkhoz in hand, and miracles could be expected. Starting at the end of January 1961 a new system was devised for the harvesting of agricultural products and a group of inspectors 'responsible to the Party' was appointed. Khrushchev wanted many of them to be placed on the roster of the federal Central Committee, which meant that their recruitment would be subject to decision by Moscow. In fact, this was the start of the trend towards authoritarianism that prevailed almost continuously until 1964. Peremptory and detailed directives were drafted at top level on all the technical aspects of cultivation and agricultural production. Party officials at all levels were to supervise the daily execution of the work and answer personally for its results. Obviously, this provided a powerful means of pressure upon reluctant officials.

THE LARIONOV CASE

At the same time another 'front' had been opened which proved even deadlier for the cadres. This was the drive against swindling, falsification of agricultural statistics and other machinations whose scope had previously been underestimated, although the evil itself was ever-present.

The sad demise of Alexis Larionov was the starting point of the campaign. Larionov was a very old *apparatchik*, the First Secretary of the Riazan Oblast Committee since 1948. He had been acclaimed as a hero at the December 1959 plenary session, when Khrushchev had praised him to the skies in all his speeches and proclaimed him a Hero of Socialist Labour for having made and fulfilled the commitment to triple in one year the supplies of meat for his region. Following his example the promise of 'three plans a year' became a quasi-official slogan and several regions adopted it for 1960. Suddenly, on September 22 1960, Larionov died. The papers carried suitable obituaries, but a few weeks later a rumour started in Moscow that he had shot himself in the head to avoid an impending scandal. It turned out that the high production he had been praised for resulted from wholesale cattle slaughter not only around Riazan but in other regions as well. In other words, he had simply been buying up his neighbours' cattle. A great deal of the meat had been bought at high prices in state stores by the kolkhozes and entered in the books twice over. In many other instances, the entries were altogether fictitious and had been arranged by bribing accommodating bookkeepers. It took over two years for all these facts to be confirmed (see the journal *Problems of History of the CPSU*, No 3 1963, and *Kommunist*, No 13 September 1963). At the time the matter was only hinted at, but some of Khrushchev's speeches published later indicate that behind the scenes it caused violent dissension.

The subject was indeed embarrassing for the First Secretary. Although it did not take an agricultural expert to grasp that a region's meat production could not be tripled in one year without jeopardizing the livestock or resorting to shady devices, the man who had most enthusiastically backed Larionov was none other than Khrushchev himself. In January 1959 he had been asked whether he thought it advisable to publicize Larionov's extravagant commitments, and he had personally given the green light. Disclosing this in December 1959 (before the scandal broke), Khrushchev boasted of having overridden the advice of some 'sceptics' who were completely discredited. He had rashly added: 'I know comrade Larionov to be serious and reliable. He is not the man ever to make an unrealistic commitment, to shine today only to come to grief tomorrow. He just isn't that kind of man.'[1]

In the event, Khrushchev had to fight a rearguard battle in several stages. In a note dated October 29 1960 to the Party Presidium, a month after Larionov's suicide, he had to admit that complaints about the man's obnoxious behaviour had been made as early as 1959 and that an investigation was called for. But he hinted at the same time that the charges must be libellous and that Larionov's promise to triple the deliveries had been realistic. Two months later, in his 'theses' (still confidential) distributed to the participants of the January 1961 plenary session, Khrushchev had to admit the bitter truth which the investigation had evidently disclosed, that the 'three plans' commitment had been imposed from above without any discussion with the region's kolkhozes and sovkhozes, which had no means of fulfilling them. He also had to acknowledge that the figures had been falsified. The culprits, he declared without any further details, had received the punishment they deserved. All this came to light only in 1963 (in the collection of agricultural speeches), possibly because the matter was no longer topical,

---

[1] Speech by Khrushchev at the Central Committee plenary session of December 1959: see *Pravda*, December 29 1959 and Verbatim Record of that plenary session, p 381. It is interesting that subsequent versions of the speech after the 1960 fiasco were substantially altered. The compliments paid to Larionov and particularly those quoted here were not included in the collection of Khrushchev's agricultural speeches (vol 4 p 61), published in January 1963. The famous promises of the Riazan region were not reprinted there and it was only stated that the kolkhozes and sovkhozes of the region had made 'extensive commitments'. The reports about performance were also changed: the 'three plans a year' were changed to two. Clearly, Larionov did not hold the monopoly for tampering with records.

or else because the First Secretary was then in a particularly weak position.[1]

In general, Khrushchev was not one to be embarrassed by such discrepancies, and in 1961 he was strong enough to use the campaign against the falsifiers to his own advantage. He depicted the Riazan events as one link in a chain affecting a number of regions, involving very many officials and not restricted to agriculture. His attitude at the plenary session of January 1961 was that of an irate teacher, bluntly admonishing the regional leaders and repeatedly hectoring the speakers from his seat, without even sparing the Party Presidium members Podgorny and Polyansky. Needless to say, he was even less civil with the Oblast Committee Secretaries, the main target of his attacks at that stage of the battle. He told one of them, G. I. Vorobyev, First Secretary of the Krasnodar Territorial Committee, that the woman kolkhoz shock worker Dolinyuk would make a better regional secretary than he. In his 'theses' he had made a strong plea for the purging of officials who had failed to make the grade, refusing 'to break out of the vicious circle of their own ideas'. Of course, these appeals were coupled with a plea for the promotion of younger people. 'I don't remember a single case', he lamented, 'of a Territorial Committee Secretary being promoted to First Secretary of an Oblast Committee.' By these words Khrushchev was trying to forestall a procedure often used in the past, namely transferring people instead of dismissing them. The idea of bringing in recruits from the districts appealed to him because they were likely to be more malleable. For the Oblast Committee Secretaries of the old Stalinist apparatus who were still in the majority, the drive betokened final disgrace.[2]

---

[1] On March 17 1963 Khrushchev again brought up the Larionov case in a note to the Presidium, this time in a tone verging on self-criticism. He wrote: 'The Oblast leaders (of Riazan) slyly misled the Central Committee. That was an oversight (*niedosmotr*) by the Central Committee of the CPSU, the Central Committee Bureau for the Russian Federation, and the Council of Ministers of the RSFSR' (*Agricultural Speeches* vol 7 p. 482).

[2] The atmosphere of the pre-congress purge rapidly involved the population as well. It was in the spring and summer of 1961 that the now famed ukases were promulgated which revived the death penalty for serious economic crimes such as counterfeiting and traffic in foreign currency, and that the so-called 'comradely tribunals' were set up with power summarily to remove undesirables from the cities. A penalty of five years' deportation to 'specially assigned places of residence' was instituted for all idlers (*tuneyadtsy*), i.e. persons whose activities were outside the official channels. In the ensuing months wide publicity was given to the sentences passed on a number of people guilty of illegal traffic. As an example, the law on currency dealings was applied retroactively to the Muscovite Ian Rokotov, who was removed from the jail where he was serving his sentence, retried, sentenced to death and executed on express orders from above. Over 100 death sentences for economic crimes were officially announced during the following two years. As to the number of

A purge needs not only the proper climate but also the means to carry it out. Before reviewing the results of this one, let us consider the changes that preceded it within the top leadership, or rather in the central apparatus in charge of personnel. There were no major demotions, except in a single case, but rather a series of discreet, albeit complex transfers, a fact which increased the number of beneficiaries.

The first item was Kozlov's confirmation in his position as Second Party Secretary through his appointment as rapporteur to the forthcoming congress on the subject of the reform of statutes. He was assigned this task in effect at the plenary session of January 1961, although the post has no legal basis and is only a long-standing tradition (Khrushchev had assumed the same role at the Nineteenth Congress in 1952, and by so doing became the third man in the Party after Stalin and Malenkov). This meant not only that if Khrushchev disappeared Kozlov would succeed him at the head of the Party, but also that, for the present, Kozlov would be the general supervisor of cadres. This, as we have seen, was nothing new after May 1960, but the consolidation of his position gave him a major role in the pre-congress purge.

Another feature of the purge was the elimination of A. B. Aristov, who, while remaining a member of the Presidium, was appointed Ambassador to Warsaw just after the January 1961 plenary session. The reasons for his concealed demotion are completely obscure to this day.

It is unlikely that Khrushchev was its instigator, since, as mentioned earlier, Aristov's entire career after Stalin's death showed his close ties with the First Secretary; nor did Khrushchev's fall in 1964 lead to any upturn in his fortune. On the other hand, Kozlov might have had something to gain from Aristov's removal. Aristov's position as Vice-President of the Central Committee Bureau for the Russian Federation – i.e. its *de facto* president, second only to Khrushchev – had given him control for several years over the assignment of personnel within the republic and had enabled him to carry out many purges in the provinces, particularly in 1959 and 1960. In all likelihood, he had had arguments on this problem with Kozlov who, from May 1960, was in charge of the same department for the entire Soviet Union. Kozlov must have had some difficulty in imposing his authority on a man of equal political stature who, moreover, was senior to him in the Party apparatus. (Aristov was a First Regional Secretary in 1944, when Kozlov was only starting in the Stalinist central apparatus.) A sign that the conflict

---

people sentenced to deportation for 'idleness', it was of course never made public. In his report to a conference on ideological matters held on December 25 1961, L. F. Ilyichev mentioned 'several thousand' for the 'last few months'.

had centred on personnel issues was the fact that Aristov's removal was shortly followed by that of M. T. Yefremov, who had been his right hand in personnel affairs as head of the 'Party organs' department for the RSFSR since 1959. It is also characteristic that Aristov's successor, G. I. Voronov, continued to persecute Yefremov for months after the latter was banished to Cheliabinsk as First Secretary.[1] He was obviously trying to have him eliminated for good, but did not succeed.

THE MAN OF THE HOUR: GENNADY VORONOV

Voronov, the only new man admitted to the Presidium in 1961, was distinguished as a fanatical 'purger', and in this respect his promotion came at the right time. Unlike his predecessor, Voronov could boast of some background in agriculture (although in view of his later career, his real competence is debatable), and this had brought him to Khrushchev's attention even in 1954, when he was First Secretary in Chita in the Far East. Voronov owed to Khrushchev his first promotion, an extremely modest one it is true, to Director of Egg Farming in the USSR Ministry of Agriculture in 1955. Afterwards, when he took charge of the Party in Orenburg in 1957, Voronov became known for his authoritarian methods in agriculture. He did all he could to impose the so-called Orenburg system of soil management. Discussing it at the December 1958 plenary session, Voronov had declared: 'We insist upon the acceptance of all these measures by the kolkhozes and sovkhozes. Those who violate the prescribed agricultural techniques make themselves liable to stern administrative action. We demand the unconditional execution of a whole system of agricultural techniques.' In short, he adopted an attitude which, a few years later, was reprehended under the name of *shablon*, i.e. the use of authoritarian methods to enforce hidebound directives. This will be discussed in more detail later, in connection with certain signs in 1964 of Khrushchev's impending downfall. In any event, when Voronov was promoted in 1961 his

---

[1] Throughout the second half of 1961 and all of 1962 the region of Cheliabinsk, and M. T. Yefremov personally, were criticized repeatedly by the press and particularly by *Sovietskaya Rossiya*, the organ of the RSFSR that Voronov had taken over. The Central Committee Bureau for the RSFSR attacked Yefremov personally in July 1962 for industrial shortcomings (*Pravda*, July 17 1962), and two months later again for agricultural delays (*Sovietskaya Rossiya*, September 23 1962). Lastly Voronov himself attacked him in *Pravda* (November 4 1962) for having mismanaged the harvest. However, D. S. Polyansky, writing the same day on the same topic in *Izvestia*, was more indulgent. He did not name Yefremov and ascribed the poor harvest in Cheliabinsk to 'an unprecedented drought'.

characteristics were such as to please Khrushchev, especially as the newly fledged agricultural expert (his training had been in industrial engineering) was pliant enough to indulge all the First Secretary's agricultural fads. For example, he was zealous in castigating the advocates of letting land lie fallow or growing grass, which he had himself propounded for years.[1] He also declared himself to be an admirer of Lysenko, the biological pundit and Khrushchev's protégé.[2] For all these reasons, and mainly because agriculture was very much in the news, Voronov was likely to strike Khrushchev as a more than adequate replacement for Aristov at the head of the Bureau for the RSFSR.

However, the affinity between Khrushchev and Voronov stopped there. Politically Voronov was in no way a client of the First Secretary's, to whom he owed nothing in his career in the Stalinist era. He had not helped Khrushchev against his foes and kept almost complete silence, in 1957 and later, on the 'anti-party' issue. Furthermore, even though Voronov supported Khrushchev on the technical aspects of his agricultural policy, he differed from him on broader political issues. This 'agricultural expert' became one of the few outspoken advocates of priority for heavy industry and one of the staunchest opponents of the necessary appropriations for agriculture. Finally, there is no doubt that, while admitting only to the modest ambitions of a technologist, he sought to use the agricultural purges to his own advantage. His strong appeals for the 'promotion of young people' were not merely an echo of Khrushchev's pleas, nor did the two men always back the same people. Thus two officials promoted in 1962 with Voronov's help to supervise the collection of agricultural products in the Russian Federation, N. I. Smirnov and V. P. Mylarshchikov, had shortly before come

[1] At the plenary session of December 1958, Voronov had strongly advocated that more land be allowed to lie fallow and had even asked for sanctions against those who dared to cultivate fallow land. In 1961, after Khrushchev had launched a long-postponed drive against the practice, which he regarded as insufficiently productive, Voronov hastily changed his tune. In December 1961 he cited the Cheliabinsk region (his personal adversary M. T. Yefremov was in charge there) in order to censure the practice of leaving land fallow as 'land-robbery, squandering of public property' (*Sovietskaya Rossiya*, December 22 1961). He suggested 'replacing those who do not want to understand this principle and resist it, by people capable of successfully fulfilling the Party's demands' (*Sovietskaya Rossiya*, December 2 1961). He was probably asked questions concerning his own change of heart, for in March 1962 he explained at Orenburg that 'it used once to be thought that in the dry regions of Orenburg the land must be left fallow before the autumn work. I also believed this until recently' (*Pravda*, March 13 1962).

[2] At the Twenty-second Congress, Voronov described Lysenko as the most prominent of the 'eminent scientists who have substantially helped the sovkhozes and the kolkhozes'. At that time many prominent figures had already stopped praising Lysenko because his views were so controversial.

under violent personal attack by Khrushchev, who had managed to have them removed from their former post.[1]

NO SPECIAL FAVOURS FOR ANYONE

All in all, Khrushchev did not fully trust Voronov, nor did he want anyone to monopolize the benefits of the purge. Consequently, early in 1961, he made other changes within the Central Committee Bureau for the RSFSR. Alongside Voronov a second Deputy Chairman, V. M. Churayev, was appointed, no doubt at the direct instigation of the First Secretary. Churayev, an old member of Khrushchev's apparatus in the Ukraine, First Secretary of the Kharkov Oblast Committee from 1944 to 1950, was in 1956 one of the first recruits to Khrushchev's stronghold, the newly founded Bureau of the Central Committee for the RSFSR. From the start, he had dealt with cadre appointments. He now regained a major role in management of personnel and, although on a lower level than Voronov, was well placed to carry out Khrushchev's orders. Another somewhat unexpected promotion to the Bureau for the RSFSR was that of M. D. Yakovlev (the former Ambassador to the Congo, expelled by Mobutu a few months earlier), who took charge of the ideological sector. Although his past and his loyalties were less clear-cut, he also had a post-1938, hence pro-Khrushchev, Ukrainian background. However, the difficulties made for Voronov in the beginning were short-lived. When the latter officially became First Deputy

---

[1] N. I. Smirnov, who for four years had been Chairman of the Executive Committee of the Leningrad Soviet, had in October 1961 been appointed Vice-President of the USSR Gosplan in charge of agriculture. The appointment obviously displeased Khrushchev, who bluntly told Smirnov in a speech in Moscow on December 14 1961: 'You don't understand basic agricultural questions'. In March 1962, shortly after this admonition, Smirnov was relieved of his functions, only to reappear a few days later as Minister of Agricultural Production and Transportation of Agricultural Products in the RSFSR. In this capacity he was Deputy Chairman of the Committee for Agriculture of the republic, a newly created body of which Voronov was chairman. This did not deter Khrushchev from continuing to harass Smirnov until he was finally removed for good at the beginning of 1964. The decisive factor in Smirnov's retention of his post may have been that, besides Voronov, Kozlov, his former chief in Leningrad, was also protecting him. As for V. P. Mylarshchikov, he ran the Agricultural Department of the Central Committee for the RSFSR until the summer of 1959, when he was replaced, apparently because he had clashed with Khrushchev on plans to 'force' the agricultural targets of the seven-year plan. In December of that year he made an appearance in the minor post of Director of the Trust for Vegetable Production Sovkhozes of the Moscow region. Then he was no longer mentioned until May 1962, when he was promoted to First Deputy to Smirnov at the Ministry for Transportation of Agricultural Products of the RSFSR. Again, Voronov was behind this unexpected promotion.

Chairman of the Bureau after the Twenty-second Congress, Churayev was demoted to ordinary member and Yakovlev resumed his diplomatic career as Ambassador to Iraq. It was only in April 1962, with the surprise promotion of Kirilenko, that Voronov was faced with a serious rival for the leadership of the Bureau.

Again it was at the same time – February and March 1961 – that another Ukrainian, V. N. Titov, took over the key post of supervisor of Party organs in the Federal Republics. This made him the 'technical' organizer of purges under the 'political' supervision of Kozlov and Khrushchev. Titov, an old member of the Party apparatus in Kharkov, a former associate of Churayev whom he succeeded, was fully qualified to continue Khrushchev's policy in this sensitive area. His ill-fortune a few months after Khrushchev's downfall, in March 1965, is an even clearer reflection of his ties with the ex-First Secretary. It is almost certain that his relations with Kozlov mirrored those of Churayev with Voronov: that is to say, he watched closely if discreetly the behaviour of his immediate superior on behalf of the supreme chief. The Soviet system provides many examples of this technique, and it is only natural that under Khrushchev the old Ukrainian hands were found best suited for the task.

The cadre system after the early 1961 reshuffle was thus many-faceted. At the top, Khrushchev, Kozlov and Voronov, all senior members or on the way to becoming so, had strong motives for using the purge for their own ends. A little lower were men such as V. N. Titov and Churayev, who enjoyed Khrushchev's confidence but were restricted to executive tasks. It should be added, however, that even men at this level were not entirely independent in their decisions. As stressed in the preface to this work, everything suggests that all important appointments, and in particular the filling of posts that entitle the beneficiary to a seat in the Central Committee, are ratified by the Party Presidium. This does not diminish the role of the specialized apparatus and of the department heads who prepare each applicant's file, or of the Party Secretaries who propose candidates. But the positive role of some of the men in charge is counterbalanced by the negative role of other leaders in the Presidium, who cannot be prevented from objecting to this or that applicant. Under the conditions prevailing after the 1960 crisis, it is likely that this privilege was not overlooked and that the men who objected to Khrushchev's personal power were careful to restrict the promotion of his creatures.

Thus it would be a gross over-statement to regard the pre-congress purges and promotions as the work of Khrushchev alone. Any scrutiny of the hundreds of changes made during that period shows that the picture was extremely complex and the result of conflicting influences.

While it would be highly risky to draw cut-and-dried conclusions from it, the following aspects may be noted:

1 It is obvious that Khrushchev could engineer the removal of an official on the regional level when he used all his authority. The clearest case is that of the First Secretary of the Tula Oblast Committee, O. A. Chukanov, who was purged in mid-July 1961, just after Khrushchev's trip to that region. The two men had had a talk that Khrushchev described as 'difficult' because, as he put it, Chukanov 'knows very little about agriculture'. It is interesting that the conversation was reported to the Presidium in a note of July 20 1961, i.e. after and not before Chukanov's demotion had been carried out in Voronov's presence on the 17th.[1] The personality of his successor, I. Kh. Yunak, is also interesting – a Ukrainian who was rocketed direct from Dniepropetrovsk to Tula. When Khrushchev took a hand in such matters it was not hard to detect his preferences.

Again, the seemingly definitive fall from favour of L. G. Melnikov was apparently due to Khrushchev's personal intervention. Melnikov was a former head of the Ukrainian Party and is believed to have had close ties with Malenkov. In July 1961 he was removed from the post of Chairman of the Kazakhstan Gosplan, a modest one which he had occupied since 1957 and which might have saved him from losing his seat as an alternate on the Central Committee. Only after Khrushchev's downfall did Melnikov reappear in Moscow at the head of a technological ministry.

A few other instances can be quoted of long-standing grudges thus settled by the First Secretary: I. P. Ganenko in Astrakhan, P. F. Cheplakov in Sakhalin and N. T. Kalchenko in the Ukraine, all of whom he had attacked personally during the preceding years. However, there are not many cases of this kind. Furthermore, while Khrushchev's dislike of a particular official might be decisive, he apparently had more trouble at this time in securing favourable treatment in matters of recruitment. Hence the promotion of Ukrainians, which played such a major role in Khrushchev's rise between 1953 and 1957, was apparently negligible in this pre-congress reshuffle. Apart from Yunak, mentioned above, there was Zarobian, a former associate of Khrushchev's in the Ukraine, who became First Secretary of the Armenian Communist Party in December 1960. There was also the even more striking example of Z. T. Serdyuk. This man had become a leader in the Ukraine at Khrushchev's side in 1938 and was then appointed First Party Secretary in Moldavia. In May 1961 he was promoted to the post of

---

[1] See Khrushchev's *Agricultural Speeches* vol 5 p 418. Chukanov reappeared in January 1963 as First Secretary of the 'industrial' Oblast Committee of Tula.

First Deputy Chairman of the Party Control Committee, a particularly important body because it was in charge of all expulsions from the Party. At the Twenty-second Congress, Serdyuk played a major role in the offensive against Molotov and the other enemies of the First Secretary.

2 Most of the other men promoted during this period had less obvious connections, or none at all, with the First Secretary. On the other hand, the backing of some of the newcomers by other strong men of the moment is clearly discernible. First there was Kozlov's influence: at least three of his former associates – N. G. Korytkov, N. S. Konovalov and A. S. Drygin became heads of Party Regional Committees, in Kalinin, Kaliningrad and Vologda respectively.

In addition the influence of the Party's Second Secretary seemed particularly strong in high economic circles, partly owing to the links he reputedly enjoyed with the leading figure of the armament industry, D. F. Ustinov.[1] Two of Kozlov's former deputies in Leningrad – I. A. Grishmanov and S. A. Afanasyev – rose within the central administration, one of them to the summit of the building industry (Gosstroy) and the other to the head of the RSFSR sovnarkhoz. The second had also been an executive in the armament industry, two other representatives of which rose to prominence in 1961. They were V. M. Ryabikov, already promoted in 1960 and now appointed First Vice-President of Gosplan, and K. N. Rudnev, who became head of the scientific research co-ordinating committee with the title of Deputy Chairman of the Council. In this way, Khrushchev met with increasing difficulties from so-called 'steel-eaters' throughout the ensuing years. Moreover, in some instances these promotions resulted in the dismissal of Khrushchev appointees. Thus V. A. Kucherenko, a personal friend of the First Secretary and the head of the building industry for almost six years, was relegated to an honorary post early in 1961, while K. D. Petukhov, a former factory director in the Ukraine under Khrushchev and a member of the Central Committee, lost his post at the head of the Moscow sovnarkhoz on the eve of the congress.

STRANGE COINCIDENCES

The above-mentioned changes call for one more remark. Surprisingly enough, from May 1960 onwards a series of high Party officials, most of them members of the Central Committee since 1952 or earlier, were

[1] Kozlov's ties with the economic leadership seem to be suggested by the fact that Ustinov was consistently elected deputy to the Supreme Soviet for Izhevsk in the Udmurt Autonomous Republic, a city where Kozlov had served from 1936 to 1944 and had been active in organizing war industry.

discreetly removed from posts of real responsibility although not the slightest mistake was ascribed to them. They were G. A. Denisov, former First Secretary of the Saratov Oblast Committee and later head of the Agricultural Department of the Central Committee, who became Ambassador to Bulgaria in May 1960; S. D. Ignatiev, First Secretary of the Tatar Oblast Committee, relieved of his duties 'for health reasons' in October; and S. Tovmasian, First Secretary of the Armenian Communist Party, relieved of his functions 'in connection with another assignment' in December 1960 and appointed Ambassador to North Vietnam a few months later.[1] They were a mixed group and may have incurred disfavour for any number of reasons. Closer scrutiny, however, revealed a somewhat unexpected link among them: each one had stood out by the violence of his attacks against the 1957 'anti-party group' on the two main occasions when the issue was debated, namely at the plenary session of December 1958 and the Twenty-first Congress in 1959. At the Congress in particular all four had strongly attacked the two figures newly associated with the group, Pervukhin and Saburov, whereas most speakers had repeated the standard phrases about 'dogmatists' without implicating additional men. Could this be sheer coincidence?

Who were the other salient attackers of the 'anti-party group' on these two occasions, and what fate befell them? There was, to begin with, I. V. Spiridonov, First Secretary in Leningrad, the first speaker to attack Pervukhin and Saburov; then T. Uldzhabayev, who demanded the expulsion of both from the Central Committee; E. P. Kolushchin- sky, a member of the 1956 Central Committee, who went still further and was the first to suggest that the whole group be expelled from the Party; and lastly I. I. Kuzmin and V. V. Matskevich, who gave addi- tional details on the 'shameful' doings of Molotov and his allies. Study of the position of all these people just after the pre-congress purges reveals further coincidences. As mentioned earlier, Kuzmin was removed in April 1960 and Matskevich in December. In April 1961 Uldzhabayev was abruptly stripped of his functions of Party chief in Tajikistan and expelled from the Party, an extremely rare occur- rence. Finally, in the summer, Kolushchinsky was relieved of his functions in Omsk for having, among other things, 'violated the principles of collective leadership'. Thus, as the Twenty-second Congress

---

[1] The title of ambassador, even to a 'friendly' country, should not give rise to any illusions. In the Soviet system after Stalin it was the traditional way of gently remov- ing undesirables. Molotov and Aristov are the best examples. Many Stalinist digni- taries were swept aside in the same way after the dictator's death. They included P. K. Ponomarenko, I. A. Benediktov, I. K. Zamchevsky and N. S. Patolichev, who were all relegated to the diplomatic corps between 1953 and 1956.

was about to open, the only one among the earlier attackers of the 'anti-party group' who was not in trouble was Spiridonov, whose turn was to come in 1962.[1]

This cannot be pure chance. Of course, there may have been other contributing factors. For instance, Kuzmin was a long-time rival of Kosygin for leadership of the economy, and Matskevich disagreed with Khrushchev's agricultural policy. On the other hand, even admitting that Uldzhabayev was a swindler as *Pravda* stated, or that Kolushchinsky's behaviour violated 'Leninist standards', it would be naïve to think that these factors alone accounted for their demotion. In the Soviet system there is nothing easier than to discover all kinds of 'objective' mistakes in a man's behaviour once it has been decided to get rid of him. There is ample evidence that this follows rather than precedes the decision. Another interesting factor in this instance was that, of all the officials listed above whose removal had been accompanied by public criticism, only Matskevich, the Minister of Agriculture, had been attacked by Khrushchev personally. The others had been censured by other members of the Presidium or anonymously in *Pravda*. Obviously the instigator of their removal was not Khrushchev.

It would be an exaggeration to conclude that the friends of Molotov, Malenkov, Kaganovich and others were powerful enough to come to their aid, for instance by reopening the decision of June 1957. It is quite likely, on the contrary, that the same purge affected a sizable number of former associates of the 'anti-party group' and people whose behaviour during the 1957 crisis had seemed suspicious to Khrushchev. This appears to be the case with several old *apparatchiki* eliminated in 1960–1961, whose political position had started declining as Khrushchev became stronger. There was, for example, I. D. Yakovlev, the former First Secretary in Kazakhstan, who was transferred to Ulianovsk in 1958 and eliminated for good in August 1961; P. F. Cheplakov, who in 1938 was one of the deputies of Bagirov, one of 'Beriya's henchmen' in Azerbaijan, and many others. In short, Khrushchev was not so weak that he could not purge his notorious opponents from the local Party apparatus; but on the other hand, he could not save his most outspoken allies from suffering the same fate.

The conclusion is subtler but not ambiguous. The principle of the settlement of the 1957 crisis was not questioned. It was recognized by

---

[1] The turn of events after Khrushchev's downfall confirms the hypothesis put forward here. Except for Matskevich, who recovered his post of Minister of Agriculture, and Spiridonov, whose position remained unchanged, none of the men listed above re-emerged from obscurity after October 1964. Two of them, in fact, fell lower still. G. A. Denisov and I. K. Zhegalin were relieved of their ambassadorial functions a few weeks before the Twenty-third Congress, which then deprived them of membership of the Central Committee, which they had held uninterruptedly since 1952.

almost everybody that Molotov, Kaganovich and Malenkov, aided by Shepilov, had formed an 'anti-party group' of dogmatist and conservative tendency whose elimination had been justified. But unanimity was confined to this specific point. Attempts by Khrushchev and his friends to revive this formula, to broaden it for their own purpose and, in particular, to implicate others by association or to extend the accusations in certain dangerous directions met with powerful resistance then and later. The effects of this resistance during the 1960 and 1961 purges clearly show that it came from Khrushchev's immediate associates: the Presidium and the Secretariat of the Party. This is what gives meaning and interest to the struggle which started at the Twenty-second Congress, and which centred on whether the terms of the 1957 settlement should be revised. The background of the struggle was destalinization, the main theme of all Soviet political life since 1953.

2 Destalinization

If Khrushchev were to be remembered in history for one single reason, the word 'destalinization' would suffice. Although never officially so labelled in the USSR, Khrushchev's policy, from the delivery of his famous 'secret report' to the Twentieth Congress in 1956 until his public report of October 27 1961 and afterwards, was rightly called destalinization in the West.

THE REASONS

The first problem is to discover why Khrushchev embarked on this course, why for years he worked so stubbornly at destroying the 'cult' of his predecessor. Why, in particular after the first destalinization drive of 1956 proved so dangerous to the cause of communist unity in the world, in the Soviet bloc and in the USSR itself, did he noisily revive the campaign five years later, when the Chinese (to mention no others) had clearly shown that they regarded this as a provocation? Granted that Stalin's methods and 'excesses' had to be abandoned – which few disputed – could it not have been done quietly, discreetly and by degrees? After all, Pope John XXIII had modernized the Church without the slightest hint of criticism for his predecessor. Why, in a country of such orthodox believers as the Soviet Union, where continuity is the rule and words often weigh more heavily than deeds, deliberately offend the faithful by the sacrilegious profanation of the former idol?

Clearly some explanation is called for as to the motives of the destalinizers and above all their leader, Khrushchev. To begin with, idealism should not be discarded outright; for Khrushchev often showed his honest desire to rank as a humane leader, bringing his people peace with foreign countries, an abundance of material goods and security from the arbitrary methods of a police state. It is conceivable, although very unlikely, that he sincerely thought he had to proclaim Stalin's crimes 'in order to guarantee that such methods were abandoned for ever'. But this clearly was not the only reason.

Even the desire to be recognized as the man favouring domestic

relaxation was not free from demagogic overtones. To listen to Khrushchev one would have thought that, but for him, Russia would have
remained in the dark era of arbitrary repressive rule and that his advent
had been a gift of Providence. People tended to forget that Malenkov,
too, had been in favour of a loosening of control, that destalinization
had in fact begun as soon as the dictator had died, with the restoration
of collective leadership, the end of mass arrests, the freeing of those
inculpated in the 'doctors' plot' and the ban on police methods as a
solution for political conflicts among the great man's successors. It soon
became clear that Khrushchev sought to exploit these developments
for the sake of his own popularity.

Closer scrutiny showed that destalinization, originally aimed at promoting a sense of security among cadres, was having the opposite
effect. It was, in fact, a singularly dangerous weapon in the hands of the
First Secretary, who was using it to purge his would-be rivals and consolidate his own power. Any newly established leader is obliged to
renovate the political machine and promote young men who are more
docile because more dependent upon him, rather than to rely on the
old cadres whose prestige and authority might sap his own. But to
eliminate the latter he needs the right arena and has to create, more or
less openly, an atmosphere of witch-hunting to make them feel vulnerable. For Stalin in the 'twenties and 'thirties the arena was the class
struggle and the watchword was the unmasking of spies and saboteurs.
A quarter of a century later, in a Russia wounded to the core by these
excesses, could there be a better motive force than the weight of dammed-
up resentment against those responsible for the earlier purges?

How is it then, it might be objected, that in the destalinization drive
as it had developed so far, only the victims of the crimes had been
mentioned and not the culprits? But this was not quite so, and we know
today that the culprits had been kept constantly in view behind the
scenes if not in public. This was so in the Beriya case and also in the
crisis of June 1957, when Molotov, Malenkov and Kaganovich were
arraigned for their past misdeeds. True, the resolution denouncing their
'errors' did not mention this aspect any more than the terser one a year
later announcing Bulganin's downfall. But even in his case it was learned
subsequently that many charges had been brought which dated back
to the Stalinist era. The new element in the Twenty-second Congress
was that for the first time a set of people were being accused publicly,
and they also happened to be Khrushchev's political foes.

This shows more clearly the close link in Khrushchev's mind between
destalinization and his fight with his personal opponents among the
post-Stalin collective leadership. He had associated the two causes long
before, no doubt as soon as he realized how he could turn to his own

use the bitterness of the victims of forced labour camps and the population's yearning for justice, felt as strongly by the new generation as by what remained of the Old Bolshevik cadres purged by Stalin. When did he decide to become the mouthpiece of their aspirations? Not as early as he claims. Until 1955 at least, Khrushchev gave the impression of being a relatively orthodox Stalinist in opposition to Malenkov's attempts to push the production of consumer goods. This brought him support from Molotov and Kaganovich in ousting Malenkov, then his most formidable enemy. It is not even quite certain that Khrushchev was actually the initiator of the famous 'secret report' on Stalin's crimes at the Twentieth Congress, although he delivered it himself.

Khrushchev had been very vague on the subject in all his earlier speeches and it is not impossible that he was urged on by a group of extremists outside the Presidium. However this may be, from the Twentieth Congress onwards Khrushchev resolutely took the lead of the anti-Stalinist movement and used it to blackmail his political foes. On October 27 1961 he spoke as follows of 'the manner in which the "anti-party group" reacted to the suggestion of raising at the Twentieth Congress the question of abuses of power during the period of the cult of personality':

> 'Molotov, Kaganovich, Malenkov, Voroshilov and others categorically opposed that suggestion. In reply we told them: "If you object to the question being raised, we shall ask the delegates at the Congress for their opinion". We did not doubt that the Congress would favour discussing the question. It is only then that these persons agreed, and a report was duly made to the Twentieth Congress on the question of the personality cult.' (*Twenty-second Congress* vol 2 p 583).[1]

Thus at this time Khrushchev already threatened to outflank the opposition of his fellow-members of the Presidium by appealing over their heads to the rank-and-file delegates. By thus violating the unwritten rules of collective leadership, he showed his hostile intentions. These appeared even more clearly in the discussions that followed, even when outwardly they were concerned only with rehabilitating the memory of a dead person. Thus Furtseva gave the following account of an enlarged session of the Party Presidium held 'shortly before the plenary session of June 1957' whose purpose was to decide upon the rehabilitation of the military chiefs executed in 1937: Tukhachevsky, Yakir, Uborevich, etc.

[1] In the present volume the reference *Twenty-second Congress* denotes the three volumes of the *Twenty-second Congress of the Communist Party of the Soviet Union*, verbatim records, published in Moscow in 1962.

'Their innocence was so evident that even Molotov, Malenkov, Kaganovich and the others favoured their rehabilitation, although at the time they had had a hand in their tragic demise. And then, during the discussion, Nikita Sergeyevich asked them very quietly but directly: "When were you right, then? At the time when you voted on their fate with such a tragic result, or today when you claim to rehabilitate them? Answer me, on which occasion were you right?" This plain, straightforward question infuriated and embarrassed them' (*Twenty-second Congress* vol 1 p 396).

The episode is highly interesting in that it shows not only how Khrushchev sought to precipitate the crisis in 1957 (the 'anti-party' plot was not a unilateral affair) but also for what highly personal ends he was using the struggle 'for the liquidation of the consequences of the personality cult'.[1] As already noted, he may have felt more at ease than his adversaries on the subject of criminal responsibilities because officially he had not taken part in any decisions until he joined the Politburo as a voting member in 1939. The mechanism of this gradual behind-the-scenes escalation becomes easier to understand. Reference to the 'cult' meant raising the issue of repressions and camps; naming the victims of past injustice meant pointing at culprits who were still alive. The hunt for the guilty was a pretext for the settling of political scores.

This also explains why destalinization had to be conducted in public, noisily, even stormily. The emotion stirred up by the 'tears of the victims' and the indignation of the masses were meant to create the climate, to provide the leverage for the purge about to be conducted. It was not going to be easy for the First Secretary to get rid of his Stalinist foes, especially those in high positions, but the more Stalin's crimes were talked about, the closer he would be to his goal. In comparison, the salvage of Tukhachevsky's honour was a minor objective indeed.

Even so, any rash value judgment would be out of place. Though Khrushchev may have had ulterior motives, objectively his action did rid the political system of a number of Stalinists, from Molotov, Kaganovich and Voroshilov downwards, who undoubtedly would have done the country greater harm than Khrushchev. If the latter had been left to his own devices, if the promises of the Twenty-second Congress had

---

[1] Other examples of Khrushchev's use of destalinization could be cited. According to a statement at the Twenty-second Congress by N. A. Mukhitdinov, the former dictator of Azerbaijan, Bagirov had 'enjoyed the protection of Malenkov, Kaganovich and Molotov'. Now, the trial and execution of Bagirov occurred in April 1956. Even admitting that Mukhitdinov exaggerated the extent of the 'protection', this fact confirms that the trial was aimed at Khrushchev's adversaries.

not been buried or if his reign had lasted a few years longer, the movement would have led to more spectacular purges and to a far larger turnover in political personnel. Power would have grown even more personal and collective leadership would have been forgotten. But, paradoxically, the régime would probably have been less conservative than it is now. In its broad outlines, destalinization, even though monopolized for the benefit of one man, undoubtedly echoed the country's deep yearnings. The camp gates in all likelihood would have been thrown open with or without Khrushchev's action; but the search for the men responsible, the punishment of the culprits remains an abscess that will have to be lanced some day. A modest step was taken in that direction by the First Secretary, and though his action was limited both by circumstances and by his own motives, it did conform to the 'movement of history'.

THE TARGETS

Such was the background. But why were Khrushchev and his friends so eager at the opening of the Twenty-second Congress on October 17 1961 to return to the charge over destalinization and launch a major attack on foes who allegedly had been 'rejected with contempt by the entire Party' over four years earlier? We may safely discard the official explanations casually given to the Congress, according to which these were matters pertaining to the Central Committee's activities for the period under review, or that the Party ought to be 'fully informed' about them, or that it was important to demonstrate the 'monolithic unity of the Party around its Leninist Central Committee'. The Party only knew what the leaders saw fit to tell it, and if mention of the issue demonstrated anything at all, it was precisely the absence of unity in the top leadership. The two genuine reasons were more specific.

The first was that the 'anti-party group', despite their disgrace, were showing signs of activity. The most 'incorrigible', as several speakers put it, was Molotov. In 1957 he had been the only participant in the plenary session who abstained on the resolution condemning him. Subsequently he had admitted to his Party cell (at the Soviet Embassy in Ulan Bator) that the resolution was justified. This apparently was a 'hypocritical' confession, for two days later, in a conversation with a member of a Soviet delegation, he expressed doubts about the advisability of liquidating the Machine Tractor Stations. This was in February 1958, at the moment when a plenary session of the Central Committee had approved the decision. (Speech by N. G. Ignatov at the

Twenty-second Congress vol 2 p 107.) As already mentioned, in April 1960 Molotov submitted to the editors of *Kommunist* an 'erroneous' article on the occasion of Lenin's birthday. And now, in October 1961, on the eve of the Congress, the former Chairman of the Council of People's Commissars was falling back into evil ways: in a letter addressed to the Central Committee he criticized the Party programme as 'anti-revolutionary, pacifist and revisionist'. In other words, he was extremely close to the Chinese theses. If he criticized Stalin at all, it was only for his thesis on the victory of communism in one country, which Molotov deemed impossible. But the programme in his opinion contained the same mistake, because it 'did not link the building of communism in the USSR with the prospects for the revolutionary struggle of the working class in the capitalist countries and for socialist revolution on the international scale'. Moreover, Molotov was playing the role of the child in 'The Emperor's New Clothes' by remarking that 'Lenin nowhere said anything about peaceful coexistence among states with different social régimes'. For the same reasons he rejected Khrushchev's thesis that socialism would be victorious all over the world 'through force of example' (speeches of P. A. Satyukov and P. N. Pospelov at the Twenty-second Congress vol 2 pp 355 and 460).[1]

All these details throw interesting light not only on Molotov's sympathies for the Chinese but also on the tactics of his official critics, who made no bones about linking the 'anti-party group' with foreign heretics. O. V. Kuusinen was the most outspoken on this point, declaring that Molotov, through the 'writings he had been concocting lately [more than one evidently], was trying to fish in troubled waters . . . if not here at home, then in some foreign waters'. He also declared that the 'sectarian platform' so created was to serve for 'future anti-party speculations', thus hinting that Molotov entertained hopes of a political comeback (*Twenty-second Congress* vol 2 p 390).

As for the other members of the group, fewer specific details were mentioned. According to Mikoyan, they had sent letters of self-criticism to the Party leadership 'a year or eighteen months' after the crisis of June 1957, i.e. in the second half of 1958, and no evidence was adduced of any subversive activity on their part. It seems, however, that their meekness had its limits. According to information from a reliable source, one of Khrushchev's objectives was to call to the Twenty-second Congress Molotov, Malenkov, Kaganovich and Bulganin so that they might confess their past errors *urbi et orbi* and proclaim the

---

[1] According to information obtained at the time, Molotov's letter to the Central Committee meeting of October 1961 was distributed to all the delegates as a 'congress document'.

'Leninist' wisdom of the then leadership. Definite pressure had allegedly been put on them for this purpose, without success, in the summer
of 1961. Their silence, together with Molotov's contumacy, is sufficient
to explain why Khrushchev and his friends showed renewed hostility
towards them.

However, this cannot be the only reason. Despite Molotov's letters,
his 'Chinese' sympathies and Kuusinen's foreboding tone, one cannot
seriously entertain the thought that the four leaders purged in 1957
could by themselves have threatened the Party leadership. This cannot
have been the only reason why the issue overshadowed the entire
Congress proceedings. On the foreign policy issue, Khrushchev had
already decided to attack the Chinese more violently by coming to grips
with the Albanians. Criticism of Molotov's pro-Chinese theses added
practically nothing new. Domestically, the danger was even less evident:
in the Soviet political system as it has existed up to now, there is no
possible return to favour for a major political figure, and under Khrushchev's domination this was even truer. On the other hand, as mentioned
previously and as the Congress confirmed, despite all divergences
within the collective leadership as to the degree of punishment called
for, nobody thought of reconsidering the June 1957 decision to strip
the men of all leading functions. (This decision was maintained even
after Khrushchev's downfall, despite a few measures of indulgence.)
In other words, in October 1961, neither Molotov nor any of the chief
members of the group was anything more than a political corpse. Why
then this flood of insults that overshadowed the main agenda, surprised
foreign public opinion and in the end laid bare serious differences for
the whole world to see?

The answer lies in the same principle of escalation which we saw at
work over destalinization. When Khrushchev was attacking Stalin in
1956, he was really aiming at Molotov, Kaganovich and his other
adversaries in the Presidium. Similarly his 1961 attacks against these
men, now defeated, were really aimed at other opponents, still in the
saddle, whom he was trying to eliminate. The accusation, true or
false, of complicity for a longer or shorter time with the men who fell
from power in 1957 was the most convenient way of getting rid of his
present opponents. And who were they? To begin with, probably
Suslov, whose ambiguous behaviour in the period before 1957 has
been noted and who seemed a likely candidate for 'guilt by association'.
But even men like Mikoyan and Kosygin might eventually feel threatened, especially since the concomitant anti-Stalinist drive was directed
against the whole of the 'old guard' of which they were the most
prominent representatives. In any case, these were the men who were
about to oppose the First Secretary's policy most firmly.

One more reason made it advisable to unleash the offensive at the Party Congress. A plenary session of high-ranking *apparatchiki* is not especially tractable, whereas the Congress provided Khrushchev with a unique opportunity to impose decisions which he knew to be unpopular with his colleagues, by appealing over their heads to the lower echelons of the Party. He had used the same method at the Twentieth Congress in 1956 so as to force his Presidium opponents to ratify his 'secret report'. This type of blackmail was in theory highly democratic, since the Presidium has no legal standing *vis-à-vis* the Congress, which is the supreme decision-making body. But in practice, who in the audience would have dared object to a proposal put forward by Khrushchev himself in the presence of all the 'fraternal Party' delegations from the bloc and even foreign journalists? In the long run, the device was not only demagogic but dangerous, since others might be tempted to use it to their own advantage. But Khrushchev could not refrain from trying it again since it had worked so well at the Twentieth Congress.

SURPRISE ATTACK

There was no advance indication that destalinization, the question of 'violation of legality' and the 'anti-party' affair were going to occupy the centre of the stage at the Twenty-second Congress. All through the summer of 1961 only the 'grandiose programme of the building of communism' was publicized, with hardly any mention of the 'cult of personality' and none whatsoever of Stalin. Khrushchev himself, when he spoke at Erevan and Tbilisi in May 1961, extolled the former dictator, as in the past, as the first of the 'eminent revolutionary figures' who had worked to establish bolshevik power in those regions. Only on the eve of the Congress did a few observers notice the portent that Soviet television showed Chukray's film *Clear Skies*, the most anti-Stalinist work of the preceding months. It was little enough to go by in forecasting developments in the large hall of the brand-new palace erected in the Kremlin enclosure for the purpose of this and future congresses. The assembly consisted of 4,393 delegates 'with a deliberative voice', i.e. the right to vote, and 405 delegates 'with an advisory voice', about a thousand distinguished guests and the representatives of eighty-three 'Marxist–Leninist' or friendly parties from outside the Soviet Union.

The offensive developed slowly. Khrushchev's two marathon reports delivered during the first two days did contain a few new references to Stalinism and the 'anti-party group', but there was still no sign that the issue was going to overshadow everything else. The new references were:

As regards Stalin: a justification of the condemnation of the 'cult of personality' at the Twentieth Congress, and the quotation of the passage in Lenin's testament dated 1922 in which the founder of the Soviet state suggested replacing Stalin as the Party's Secretary-General because he was 'too rude'. But the report contained this reservation – soon to be discarded – 'Of course J. V. Stalin deserved well of the Party and the communist movement, and we give him his due for this'.

As regards the 'anti-party group': for the first time Voroshilov was openly implicated (until then he had only been under suspicion). Furthermore, a new accusation was added to the official indictment (factionalism, attempt to deviate from the 'Leninist course' etc.). This new charge, which had not been put forward since the speeches during the 1957 crisis, was that Molotov, Kaganovich, Malenkov and Voroshilov bore 'personal responsibility for many large-scale repressions against the Party cadres, the Soviets, the economy, the army and the Komsomol, and other similar events during the era of the personality cult'.

Finally, the attack against the Albanian leaders was closely linked with the struggle against Stalinism by being delivered under the same heading as the above two points and in similar wording: attachment to the 'methods of the personality cult', repressions, opposition to the line of the Twentieth Congress, etc.

Nevertheless, apart from the Albanian issue whose international implications were of such significance, nothing had been said which in any way exceeded what might have been expected of a progress report on the part of the country's leadership for the preceding five years. The space devoted to the subject in the first day's report was modest, while the second day's report, dealing with the Party programme, did not mention it at all. The first speakers – A. F. Gorkin, rapporteur for the Party's Auditing Committee, and P. N. Demichev, First Secretary of the Moscow Urban Committee, barely mentioned the 'personality cult' or ignored it altogether and censured the 'group' in routine phrases, far milder than Khrushchev's the day before.

The man who opened the full-scale attack was Podgorny. His task, and that of the others who spearheaded the prosecution, was to repeat Khrushchev's accusation on the responsibility of the group's chief members for the repressions, and to back it up with specific examples. As a Ukrainian and loyal follower of Khrushchev, Podgorny naturally passed over the 1937 and 1938 repressions in the Ukraine and concentrated on 1947 instead. Kaganovich had then been for a few months First Secretary in that republic, and according to Podgorny had behaved as a 'sadist' and a 'degenerate'. Podgorny's main demand was for Kaganovich's expulsion from the Party, and this introduced what turned into the main issue at stake.

The next speaker was I. V. Spiridonov, who in 1959 had taken the lead in implicating Pervukhin and Saburov and who consistently behaved as an out-and-out anti-Stalinist. He focused his attack on Malenkov, branding him as responsible for the repressions linked with the 'Leningrad affair' in 1949, but did not demand his expulsion from the Party. This was done by the following speaker, K. T. Mazurov, First Secretary for Byelorussia.

These three speakers had set the tone, but it was several days before the criminal charges overshadowed everything else. Furtseva, Polyansky and Ignatov devoted most of their speeches to the issue. But it was left for Ignatov, who took the floor on the sixth day of the Congress, to make the crucial demand on behalf of Khrushchev and his followers, namely the simultaneous expulsion of the three 'anti-party' leaders, Molotov, Kaganovich and Malenkov. Then the tone grew even more strident as N. M. Shvernik, A. N. Shelepin and Z. T. Serdyuk filled their speeches with 'revelations' concerning the Stalinist repression and the sinister role of the three accused. Other speakers, such as Ilyichev and Satyukov, also concentrated on that subject and drew up a formal indictment against the group's latest political crimes. Towards the end of the Congress, demands for their expulsion multiplied to a point when they became almost routine. As will be shown, however, this at no time represented the views of the majority.

The peak was reached on October 27, the ninth day of the Congress, when Voroshilov made an abject speech of self-criticism. When Khrushchev took the floor to close the debate he hardly mentioned the Party programme or the rest of the official agenda, but instead delivered what was really the public version of his 'secret report' to the Twentieth Congress. He gave a dramatic account of the highly suspect assassination of Kirov, Ordzhonikidze's suicide and Tukhachevsky's execution – all Stalin's worst misdeeds, or at any rate those most resented by Khrushchev. Among the most spectacular conclusions of his speech were a proposal to erect a monument in Moscow 'to the memory of the comrades who fell victims to arbitrary power', and also an emotional promise for which, short-lived as it was, he does deserve credit. This is what he said:

'Comrades! Our duty is to investigate carefully such abuses of power in all their aspects. Time passes, and we shall die since all of us are mortal, but as long as we have strength to work we must clear up many things and tell the truth to the Party and people. Our duty is to do our utmost to establish the truth here and now, for the longer it is since these events, the harder it will be to reconstruct them as they really were. Of course, as the saying goes, you cannot bring dead men to life again. But this whole story must be recorded with full candour in the history of the Party. This must be done, so that such things shall never happen again in the future.' (*Twenty-second Congress* vol 2 p 584).

Another crucial point was reached on October 30, two days before the end of the Congress, when the decision was taken to remove Stalin's body from the Mausoleum in Red Square, where it had lain since 1953, and to bury the bloodthirsty dictator 'in another place'. This was a highly symbolic decision that deeply stirred the entire population. It was also practically the only decision of the Congress that was carried out, because no time was lost in doing so. As for all the other promises to the victims (the monument was never built and nothing more is known to this day about Kirov's murder or the mechanism of Stalin's purges) and, above all, the punishment of the guilty, the inescapable conclusion is that the destalinization offensive of October 1961 was a fiasco. The reason is, of course, that it was impossible to speak of the victims without speaking of the guilty. And even when the threat was aimed at 'political corpses' like Molotov, Malenkov or Kaganovich, it touched so many vested interests that it could never be carried out and resistance was all too obvious. However, although the debate was conducted in the usual roundabout way – an elaborate construction of nuances, omissions and shifts in emphasis – it was one of the most overt and interesting conflicts among Soviet leaders that has taken place in the past few years. Two issues were at stake here, which should have been linked together but were not. One was the criminal responsibility of the former Stalinist leaders, and the other the punishments to be meted out.

WERE MOLOTOV, MALENKOV, KAGANOVICH AND VOROSHILOV CRIMINALS OR NOT?

Khrushchev's first report and his statement that these four men bore 'personal responsibility for many mass repressions . . . during the era of the cult of personalty' afford a touchstone of the attitudes of other speakers. Which of them endorsed his remarks and thus answered the above question in the affirmative?

1 Among voting members of the Presidium (the names of those who ceased to belong to the Presidium after the Congress are in italics; we

shall deal later with G. I. Voronov, the only speaker promoted to voting membership): N. V. Podgorny, *Ye. A. Furtseva*, M. A. Suslov, D. S. Polyansky, *N. G. Ignatov*, *N. A. Mukhitdinov*, N. M. Shvernik, F. R. Kozlov and of course Khrushchev.

Other major speakers were: I. V. Spiridonov, K. T. Mazurov, L. N. Yefremov, Ya. N. Zarobian, M. A. Sholokhov, A. P. Kirilenko, P. A. Satyukov, A. N. Shelepin, B. P. Beshchev, A. V. Georgiev, N. N. Rodionov, A. T. Serdyuk and F. S. Goriachev.

Some differences existed among the above. Shvernik, one of the most vehement denouncers of the group, did not accuse Voroshilov of criminal acts. Neither did Kozlov or Mazurov, the latter simply forgetting to mention this new victim – who, by the end of the Congress, had in fact practically been cleared of criminal responsibility. As for Suslov, he laid the blame for repressions on 'many personalities in the anti-party group' without naming any of them. His position is suspect, for, of all the officials listed above, he was the only one to slip in those few words without adding any details (his attack on the 'anti-party group' was singularly brief).[1] What he did say may have simply reflected 'disciplined' obedience to the Presidium majority, since it was included also in the collectively approved report.

2 A second group of speakers may be classed as 'ambiguous'. These men, without endorsing the key sentence of Khrushchev's report, mentioned the 'crimes' of the 'anti-party group' without going into details. The word 'crimes' is itself ambiguous, since the inflation characteristic of Soviet parlance easily turns into crime (*prestuplenie*) what may be no more than a mistake or a marginal deviation from the Leninist line. In this instance, the uncertainty was increased by the fact that these speakers, like Suslov, refrained from giving any details of their own. The fleeting mention of unspecified 'crimes' showed that they had no wish to take an active part in the campaign and preferred a middle-of-the-road position. Brezhnev, then Head of State, also belongs in this category. He depicted Molotov and the others as 'bent under the weight of the past and the mistakes and crimes committed on that basis'. He was followed, with very slight variations, by V. V. Grishin, R. Ya. Malinovsky (who spoke of the repressions and even torture inflicted on the military chiefs, but without accusing anyone by name, and not even mentioning Voroshilov, who must have felt implicated);

---

[1] It is also interesting that, referring to the 'anti-party group' at the Twenty-second Congress, Suslov listed only 'Molotov, Kaganovich, Malenkov, Voroshilov, Bulganin and others', omitting Shepilov and especially Pervukhin and Saburov, two men who had also been members of the Presidium until 1957. He had done the same at the Twenty-first Congress and in all his other speeches. This systematic omission may have been due to the fact that Pervukhin's and Saburov's reactions to Khrushchev's moves were scarcely cooler than his own.

and also P. N. Pospelov ('criminal actions during the period of the cult of personality'), N. G. Yegorychev, I. I. Bodyul, A. M. Shkolnikov and others who merely referred to previous speeches. This applies to B. N. Ponomarev, while G. G. Abramov spoke of 'direct crimes', as if to show that 'crimes' was a relative term.

3 A third group consisted of those who refused to speak of responsibility for the repressions or even of 'crimes' in general, thus showing that they answered 'no' to the vital change. These were among the voting members of the Presidium: A. I. Mikoyan, A. N. Kosygin and O. V. Kuusinen; and, among other speakers: P. M. Demichev,[1] A. F. Gorkin, D. A. Kunayev, Sh. Rashidov, V. P. Mzhavanadze, G. I. Voronov, V. N. Titov, L. F. Ilyichev, V. S. Tolstikov etc.

Out of a total of 77 political leaders heard by the Congress (taking into account only the most prominent figures), 44, i.e. a majority, belong to the third category, as compared to 23 who answered *yes* and 10 whose position was ambiguous.

There were differences within the 'no' camp also. They ranged from those who dared not say a single word about the 'anti-party group' (I. G. Kebin, First Party Secretary in Estonia) to those, like L. F. Ilyichev and O. V. Kuusinen, who devoted most of their speeches to it and even called for sanctions against its members. Again, Mikoyan was more eloquent and tougher than Suslov, for instance regarding the political errors of Molotov and his allies. Unlike Suslov, who had criticized the group essentially for its opposition to certain Party decisions, Mikoyan specified that the disagreements 'had not concerned specific organizational or political questions but . . . the definition of the entire Party policy and its general line in the new stage of historical development'. On this point he actually went further than Khrushchev himself by being the first to declare that Molotov's confession to his Party cell was sheer hypocrisy and that the former Head of Government 'remained true to this day to his conservative and dogmatic views'.

It was the speakers in the last category, whose leader was unquestionably Mikoyan, who meant to confine matters to a political 'trial' and not instigate one on criminal responsibility for the Stalinist era. Mikoyan, of course, did not support the 'methods' of the past any more than anyone else, but he realized that Khrushchev and his staunch supporters would endeavour to turn this hunt for the guilty into an instrument of new purges or even 'repressions'.

---

[1] It was in his first and main Congress speech that Demichev opposed the fixing of criminal responsibility for the repressions. Speaking a second time on October 30 to approve the transfer of Stalin's body from the Mausoleum, he specifically implicated Stalin and Malenkov in the 'Leningrad affair'.

'The struggle against the dogmatic conservative group', Mikoyan complacently declared, 'has been waged by democratic methods within the Party, without any state repression'. By this he sought to intimate that the same methods should be maintained in the future, and that the idea of criminal prosecution, which the furious attacks of Spiridonov, Shelepin and the rest seemed bound to lead to, should be rejected. His denunciation of the Albanian leaders was also typical: he reproached them mainly with threatening to shoot 'all those who, on any issue, do not agree with the leadership' and with the expulsion of many old Party members. Kosygin took a similar stand.

Mikoyan clearly felt in an awkward position as an old associate of Stalin, probably only slightly less involved in the repressions than Molotov, Kaganovich or Voroshilov. As noted previously, he was bound to feel implicated by references to the cases of Yakir and Tukhachevsky, whose fate had been settled in the Politburo, or that of Ordzhonikidze who, as Khrushchev pointed out, had committed suicide 'in order not to share the responsibility for Stalin's abuses of power'. This is why Mikoyan was intent on restricting the charges to the group's 'conservative dogmatism' and also why he differed from Khrushchev himself as regards the causes of the group's opposition. Khrushchev ascribed it to their 'personal responsibility for the repressions', in other words their fear of being 'unmasked' by destalinization, while Mikoyan's position was markedly different. According to him, the resistance of the 'dogmatic conservative group' was due 'first and foremost, to their organic attachment to the cult of personality . . . their lack of understanding of the fact that the country is entering a new stage of its development, the period of the building of communism over a wide front, and that the world socialist system is becoming the dominant factor in the evolution of mankind' (*Twenty-second Congress* vol 1 p 447).

Directly afterwards Kosygin took a similar line, his boldest statement being that the members of the group had been 'contaminated' by the 'cult of personality'. All these psychological analyses were of course far milder than Khrushchev's report, or even than the avowals of Voroshilov, himself one of the accused. In his confession of October 27, Voroshilov had said: 'I entirely agree with the great work performed by the Party for the restoration of Leninist standards in Party life and the disavowal of the violation of revolutionary legality during the period of the personality cult, and I deeply regret that I too made mistakes under those circumstances'. The word 'mistakes' instead of 'crimes' and the phrases 'I too' and 'under those circumstances', were of course meaningful, especially since Voroshilov did not elaborate upon the identity of the other culprits. The old Marshal nevertheless did admit, in part at least, something which a large section of the Presidium (Mikoyan, Kosygin and Kuusinen as well as Shvernik, Kozlov and possibly Suslov) had refused to charge him with.[1]

This insistence on referring to 'dogmatic errors' when far more was at stake could not go unnoticed. Obviously, Khrushchev's warmest supporters found it distasteful that what they persisted in calling a plot, namely the activities of Molotov and his associates and their scheming in 1957, should be treated in such euphemistic terms. One of them, N. N. Rodionov, Second Party Secretary in Kazakhstan and former aide of Spiridonov in Leningrad, openly expressed his disagreement: 'The participants in the "anti-party group" are termed dogmatists. So they are. But what they tried to do in June 1957 was more than mere dogmatism: it was banditry and criminal practice, which calls for the full rigour of the law[2] (*Twenty-second Congress* vol 3 p 130).

In short, even apart from the problem of sanctions, a major struggle was going on behind the scenes as regards the definition of the crime. Its details are not known, but the result is clear, not only from the events of the following months and years but from the resolution voted by the Congress itself on the evening of October 31. This contradicted Khrushchev on two key points:

1 As regards Stalin, the strongest words used were 'abuse of power', 'mistakes', 'distortions' and 'methods alien to the spirit of Leninism'. There was no question of 'repression' or even of the fact that people had lost their lives (the monument to the victims was, of course, not mentioned). Moreover, the resolution stated: 'The Party told the people

[1] On the other hand, what Voroshilov did strongly deny was his very participation in the 1957 'anti-party group'. He only admitted that 'at the beginning of the struggle against that group, he had supported certain mistaken harmful acts by some of its members . . . .' Then he added: 'But I had no inkling of its factional activities until, as a result of the examination of the behaviour of the group's members at the June Plenary session, their true face was revealed and they themselves confessed. . . . After that I immediately declared that I had known nothing, had never been part of any group and at no time had any dealing or contacts with people of that kind.' The statement shows well enough how Voroshilov changed his tune, but it is also a study in ambiguity. It is clear that the opprobrious phrase 'anti-party group' which emerged after the defeat of Molotov and his allies was simply the victor's terminology. Until then the so-called 'group' was nothing else than the majority of the Presidium.
[2] Rodionov also regarded Molotov, Kaganovich and Malenkov as 'adventurers whose hands are red with the blood of the best sons of the people'. But, as mentioned, sanctions have an odd way of backfiring, and as had happened before to zealots of his kind, Rodionov was soon punished for his temerity. In December 1962 he was relieved of his functions in Kazakhstan 'in connection with another assignment'. Apparently he reappeared some time later as Deputy Chairman of the Leningrad sovnarkhoz, his former stronghold. He was, however, the only man in that category to make a brilliant come-back after Khrushchev's downfall. In October 1965 he became First Secretary of the Cheliabinsk Oblast Committee. This exception is probably due to the settling of the Kozlov–Brezhnev rivalry for leadership of the Party in Kazakhstan, as will be shown in Part Five (p 515n).

the full truth about the abuses of power during the period of the cult of personality'. Khrushchev, on the other hand, in his speech of October 27 quoted above, had said that many matters remained to be elucidated (the Kirov affair to start with) and that it was the Party's duty to go on doing so 'as long as we live'. The resolution, by contrast, signified 'This is enough'.[1]

2 As regards the 'anti-party group', the resolution stated that Molotov and his allies were 'renegades' and 'intriguers', but there was no mention of their 'crimes' and the key sentence of Khrushchev's original report, on their responsibility for the repressions, was missing. This too was a long step backward.

What was the reason for Khrushchev's defeat? As we have shown, the 'no' camp constituted a majority of speakers at the Congress, but this alone does not fully account for it. The resolution was ostensibly drafted by an *ad hoc* committee of ninety-one members, but was certainly approved first by the Party Presidium, all of whose members sat on that committee. On the other hand, the Presidium had previously ratified Khrushchev's progress report and his dramatic speech of October 27 on the crimes perpetrated by Stalin and the 'anti-party' elements. In his speech Khrushchev had even specified the nature of those crimes, and we shall see later that he was probably telling the truth. What then could have caused the switch?

The explanation may be that a few Presidium members changed their minds, but more probably that the composition of the Presidium itself had changed between October 27 and the last days of the Congress. This change had singularly strengthened the 'no' camp (on the criminal responsibility of Molotov and his friends) as against Khrushchev and those who had answered 'yes' to the key question. As indicated above, out of the 14 members of the former Presidium, 9 had approved the thesis of the guilt of at least the three chief accused (Khrushchev, Furtseva, Ignatov, Kozlov, Mukhitdinov, Polyansky, Podgorny, Suslov and Shvernik); 3 had answered 'no' (Mikoyan, Kosygin and Kuusinen), and one was ambiguous (Brezhnev). Information is lacking about A. B. Aristov, the Ambassador in Warsaw since January 1961 and the only Presidium member on leave of absence, who did not take the floor at the Congress. But even assuming that he would not have backed Khrushchev on this point, and even if Suslov is not counted (as he

---

[1] The statement in the Twenty-second Congress resolution that the 'full' truth had been told about the era of the cult of the personality was such a blatant exaggeration that it was slightly qualified later. The second edition of the *History of the CPSU*, published in October 1962, contains the following statement about the Twenty-second Congress: 'The Congress told the Party and the people the truth about Stalin's abuses of power. . . .'

probably should not be) in the 'yes' camp, this still meant a majority of 8 to 6 who, on the eve of the Congress, favoured mentioning the group's responsibility for the Stalinist crimes.

Nevertheless, on October 31, the day when the resolution was submitted and ratified, Furtseva, Ignatov, Mukhitdinov and Aristov had already been eliminated, while an eloquent opponent of prosecution, G. I. Voronov (who in his speech had merely slipped in a conventional phrase about 'renegades to Marxism–Leninism, revisionists and dogmatists', without even specifying whether he meant the Albanians, the Yugoslavs or Molotov) had joined the Presidium. This created the following new balance of power:

For recognition of guilt: Khrushchev, Kozlov, Polyansky, Podgorny, Shvernik, Suslov (?).

Against it: Mikoyan, Kosygin, Kuusinen, Voronov and probably Brezhnev.

Thus, in the new Presidium, Khrushchev could count on a majority of six to five which, however, would turn into a minority if Suslov sided with the 'noes' – assuming he had left their ranks in the first place. It is clear that Suslov and Brezhnev, who had been the most reluctant to commit themselves one way or the other, must have played the role of arbitrators. Another who may have withdrawn his support was Polyansky. In his speech, he had implicated Voroshilov (quite strongly) and Kaganovich, without mentioning the others. Kozlov had also been tough (according to him, the three chief accused 'had had a hand in the extermination of many innocent people'), but a sound sense of political opportunism and of feeling amongst the lower levels of the Party apparatus may have helped them change their minds.

In any case, the conclusion was clear: the drive for destalinization and the unmasking of the culprits had never been easy and, with the new leadership which emerged from the Twenty-second Congress, it was becoming even more difficult, if not impossible. A striking result, considering the emphasis with which the Stalinist crimes had been denounced.

OPERATION MAUSOLEUM

The resolution whereby the Congress decided on the morning of October 30 to remove Stalin's remains from the place of popular veneration calls for further remark. (He was buried finally alongside other dignitaries of the régime, in an honourable site in the Kremlin cemetery.) A persistent rumour circulated in Moscow that the decision had been taken over the heads of the Presidium members by means of a 'surplus vote' by the full Congress.

There is reason to believe this, not only because approval would have been difficult to secure from the Presidium as it has just been described. The actual procedure was as follows. The proposal was introduced by I. V. Spiridonov, the traditional anti-Stalinist champion, who was at pains to represent it as a petition from the rank and file. It had, in fact, been rumoured the day before that such a proposal had been made at factory meetings, but it is not clear whether this took place to order and, if so, whose. Spiridonov also disclosed that the Leningrad workers had made the same request in 1956 just after the Twentieth Congress.

Spiridonov was seconded by Demichev in the name of the Moscow Urban Committee and by Dzhavakhishvili, the head of the Georgian Government. This was a prudent arrangement in view of the riots with which the dictator's homeland had reacted to the first destalinization drive in 1956. Dzhavakhishvili was the most cautious of all the speakers and ascribed the crimes of the past to 'anti-party elements and other adventurers' rather than to Stalin himself, whose name passed his lips only once. A former inmate of a prison, D. A. Lazurkina, next took up the tale, followed by Podgorny. The only other leader who gave his opinion was Khrushchev himself, who shouted 'Quite right!' from his seat when Lazurkina declared that Stalin's body ought to be moved.[1] The plan was adopted by a show of hands and carried out the same night. It is true that everyone voted for it, including the members of the Presidium; but, in a public meeting there was hardly any alternative, short of violating a tradition of several decades' standing. Secondly, the wording of the decision did not tally with the rest of the Congress's work. This particular decision mentioned 'mass repressions against honest Soviet citizens', which were directly ascribed to Stalin, whereas, as noted above, the strongest expression used in the final Congress resolution was the much vaguer wording 'abuse of power'.[2]

---

[1] Lazurkina created a stir by declaring that she used to consult Lenin every day, and her ultimate argument was: 'Yesterday I consulted Ilyich as if he were alive in front of me, and he told me "It is unpleasant for me to lie next to Stalin, who brought so much misfortune to the Party" ' (*Twenty-second Congress* vol 3 p121).

[2] The wording of the Congress resolution is important. 'Mass repressions', affecting 'honest Soviet citizens' indiscriminately, reflected the plain truth, namely that the régime of terror had been one affecting the entire population. The term 'abuse of power', on the other hand, was closer to the version that tended to present the Stalinist repressions as relatively isolated phenomena striking mainly at Party dignitaries. This version had prevailed after 1956, with the result that the destalinization and rehabilitation measures were presented as affecting leading figures in the Party and state. Not until Solzhenitsyn published his *Day in the Life of Ivan Denisovich* was it acknowledged in Soviet literature that the régime of the labour camps had been a

All this bears out the hypothesis that Khrushchev in this instance used the method he had found so successful in 1956. Or, at least, it may be assumed that, as at the Twentieth Congress, he blackmailed opponents in the Presidium by threatening to 'lay the question before the Congress', thus obtaining their unwilling consent. It is even conceivable that he did not 'consult' the Presidium at all.[1]

WHAT SANCTIONS SHOULD BE INFLICTED ON THE 'ANTI-PARTY GROUP'?

Paradoxically, this question has to be considered separately from the previous one, although logically any proof of criminal responsibility should have resulted automatically in prosecution and trial. Evidently Khrushchev and his chief followers tried to obtain this.[2] Had they had their way, in the ensuing months there would have been a 'Molotov (or Malenkov or Kaganovich) trial', just as the Bagirov trial followed the Twentieth Congress. But, as we have seen, the mere mention of those men's guilt met with strong resistance from various quarters. Under the circumstances, Khrushchev could hardly count on obtaining from the Congress more than the first step towards a future prosecution, namely the expulsion of the culprits from the Party.

Appearances notwithstanding, this kind of sanction is far from being purely symbolic. Even apart from the underlying threat of prosecution, this was the ultimate political and moral disgrace for these Party dignitaries of ancient standing. Traditionally, expulsion of one of the old leaders from the Party has always been a delicate matter in communist circles. It took Stalin several years to have his foes expelled during

---

mass phenomenon and that its victims had been ordinary Soviet people, whether Party members or not. At the Congress itself, almost everything said about the victims referred to the Party 'comrades'. It was for them specifically that the famous monument was to have been erected.
[1] The decision to move Stalin's body was accompanied by all the ritual consequences. Stalin's posthumous disgrace meant that cities, villages, kolkhozes and enterprises of the Soviet Union were forbidden to bear his name. The change began at once. Stalingrad with all its prestige became Volgograd, Stalino became Donetsk and Stalinsk, Novokuznetsk. But the process was slower than might have been expected, and months or even years later announcements were still being made that kolkhozes and villages were discarding Stalin's name.
[2] A clear indication of attempts by Khrushchev and his followers to obtain a trial was given when *Pravda* reported on a speech made by Gomulka to a plenary meeting of the Polish Communist Party in November 1961. He declared that Molotov and the rest of the 'anti-party group' would not be brought to trial. Although *Pravda* of November 25 1961 reported the speech in detail, this sentence was deleted.

the 'legal' stage of his rise to supreme power. In the case of Molotov and his allies, the possibility of expulsion had been mentioned during the crisis of June 1957, then by Khrushchev himself in December 1958 and finally in 1959 at the Twenty-first Congress. All these efforts had been in vain, most probably because they raised a number of major questions. Did Molotov's opposition to Khrushchev's policy, already punished in 1957 by his elimination from leadership, justify this extreme sanction? Would it not set a precedent for punishing any and every objection to the acts of the First Secretary? True enough, Molotov was being 'stubborn', as shown by the 'erroneous' writings he was sending to the Central Committee. But was he not entitled to express his personal opinion? Why not a milder punishment, 'censure' for instance? Lastly, even his responsibility for the repressions, as it had been outlined, was perhaps not as conclusive as it seemed. At worst, even if Molotov had participated in sinister doings at the time of the 'cult', he had not been the only one, and it behoved the Party as a whole to take responsibility for them. Expulsion on that score might set a damaging precedent.

This accounts for the wealth of contradiction on the issue. It was paradoxical enough to hear Shvernik describe Malenkov, Kaganovich and Molotov as being stained with the blood of innocent people and then tamely conclude: 'They cannot remain in the ranks of our Party'. It was paradoxical too that some of the main accusers, such as Furtseva, said nothing whatsoever about sanctions, whereas Kuusinen, who had refrained from mentioning Molotov's criminal responsibility, nevertheless called for his expulsion from the Party as a 'political speculator'. Finally it is possible that some officials were prevented from fully expressing their opinion on this point by outside factors, e.g. the attitude of other members of their delegations. This seems to have been true of Spiridonov (Leningrad) and Podgorny (Ukraine).[1] In any case, the picture in regard to sanctions was markedly different from that regarding criminal responsibility. This is how the delegates stood on the issue of expulsion from the Party:

1 The following expressly called for it:

In the Presidium: N. V. Podgorny (for Kaganovich only); O. V. Kuusinen (for Molotov only); N. G. Ignatov (for Molotov, Kagano-

---

[1] There were striking differences between the speeches of Spiridonov and Podgorny and those of the Second Secretaries for their respective regions, V. S. Tolstikov and I. P. Kazanets. While the former were violent in their attacks against the group, the latter were soft-spoken, mentioning the matter in routine terms without mentioning crimes or listing names. This would account for the fact that Spiridonov, despite his violent language, did not demand any sanction against the group and Podgorny even tempered his position between the beginning and the end of the Congress. After having first called for Kaganovich's expulsion from the Party, in his last speech on October 30 he merely advocated 'severe punishment'.

vich and Malenkov); N. M. Shvernik (for Molotov, Kaganovich and Malenkov); and of course Khrushchev.

Other important speakers: A. P. Kirilenko, B. N. Ponomarev, G. G. Abramov, I. I. Bodyul, N. G. Yegorychev, Z. T. Serdyuk, N. N. Rodionov, P. N. Pospelov, M. T. Yefremov and F. I. Golikov also called for the expulsion of these three leaders of the 'group'. So did P. A. Satyukov, who added for good measure Shepilov, his former chief at *Pravda.* Another three speakers, K. T. Mazurov, L. N. Yefremov and Ya. N. Zarobian, asked only for Malenkov's expulsion. Altogether, out of the seventy-seven political speakers at the Congress, thirty-three favoured expulsion.

2 The following refrained from mentioning punishment directly or indirectly:

In the Presidium: A. I. Mikoyan, A. N. Kosygin, M. A. Suslov, Ye. A. Furtseva, N. A. Mukhitdinov.

Other speakers: C. I. Voronov, R. Ya. Malinovsky, V. V. Grishin, I. V. Spiridonov, V. P. Mzhavanadze, Sh. Rashidov, V. N. Titov, V. S. Tolstikov, D. A. Kunayev, etc.: altogether thirty-two speakers.

3 Finally, a third group, which also must be classed as 'ambiguous', consisted of speakers who mentioned 'sanctions' or even 'punishment', rather than 'responsibilities', but did not further clarify their thought. This was a middle-of-the-road stand, since 'Party sanctions' could well mean something different from expulsion. The newly adopted statutes, like the old ones, provided for a graduated scale ranging from 'warning' (*postanovka na vid*) to 'censure', then 'severe censure', then 'censure with notation on the Party card' (also the case with 'severe censure'), and finally expulsion, the 'supreme punishment measure'. It is true that some also spoke of 'responsibility toward the people', which, construed literally, could mean a trial. But again, the first measure in that direction would be expulsion from the Party. It does not seem that these speakers intended to use the expression in a legal sense: more likely they were striving to create confusion as to what they wanted. These officials were:

In the Presidium: L. I. Brezhnev (the 'anti-party group' should 'assume responsibility before the Party and people for their errors and crimes'); F. R. Kozlov ('grave responsibility to the Party and people'); D. S. Polyansky (must 'take full responsibility for their anti-party actions').

Among other speakers: A. N. Shelepin, who spoke of 'severest responsibilities', and L. F. Ilyichev, who further enlarged upon this delicate subject. The Party, he explained, had shown great 'magnanimity' towards Molotov and his associates by 'keeping them in its ranks' and 'giving them work' although they had 'not been worthy of it'. Self-criticism on their part was imperative but had not been forthcoming. Failing this, 'whoever persists in his mistakes must take responsibility before the Party and people'.

Comparing the three groups, we reach the interesting conclusion that neither in the pre-Congress Presidium nor in that elected on October 31 was there a majority favouring the expulsion of Molotov and his associates from the Party. Even if Kuusinen and Podgorny are counted as advocates of expulsion, which they demanded for one only of the accused, and even if Aristov is counted in that group (he did not speak at the Congress and considering his earlier position it is doubtful if he belongs here), on the eve of the Congress the group consisted of not more than 6 out of 14 Presidium members. In the new Presidium their number had dropped to 3 (Kuusinen, Shvernik and Khrushchev) out of 11, since at that point Podgorny wanted only 'severe punishment'. This is a paradoxical conclusion, considering that in the first Presidium the members in favour of declaring the 'anti-party group' guilty of repression were in the majority. What emerges clearly is the wavering and deep division of the collective leadership on this issue. Although the partisans of expulsion were in the minority, those who wanted no sanction whatsoever were a minority also: 5 out of 14 in the first Presidium, 4 out of 11 (Mikoyan, Kosygin, Suslov and Voronov) in the second. The only possible consensus was for unspecified sanctions, and this on the assumption that the three men whose positions were ambiguous (Brezhnev, Kozlov and Polyansky) sided with the first group. In short, a majority, if a narrow one, favoured some kind of action, but did not quite know what.

This is why the question of expulsion from the Party was not raised in the progress report, whereas that of responsibility for the repressions was. Since Khrushchev could not make the demand for expulsion appear as the position of the top leadership, he by-passed the difficulty by letting his most loyal lieutenants, Podgorny, Spiridonov, Ignatov and others, raise it in their own name. In a sense, this was one issue on which each man was free to vote as he saw fit. The requests for expulsion were presented by individual speakers – fairly numerous, but nevertheless a minority. Moreover, they were fewer in the top leadership than in the lower hierarchy, probably because the former could better foresee the dangers of the procedure and the political implications for themselves.

Khrushchev very probably tried to foil them through a surprise vote as he had on the mausoleum issue. As on that occasion, all the delegates would probably have raised their hands eagerly if someone had come to the rostrum to propose a resolution for expulsion. Nothing in the statutes would have prevented such a fresh demonstration of grass-roots democracy. This possibility was indeed mentioned: the writer Mikhail

Sholokhov, who at the time did not hide his 'personal friendship' or even his 'manly love' for 'dear Nikita Sergeyevich', concluded his particularly virulent attack on the 'anti-party group' with the words: 'Aren't we being too tolerant towards those who have on their conscience thousands of loyal sons of our mother-country and Party who perished, thousands of their kin sacrificed? *The Congress is the supreme organ of the Party; let it proclaim its stern but just verdict on the factionalists'* [Author's italics] (*Twenty-second Congress* vol 2 p 164).

Sholokhov was supported by P. N. Pospelov, whose conclusion, although vaguer, followed the same line: 'Molotov, Malenkov and Kaganovich must not remain members of our great Party. There is no doubt that the Twenty-second Congress will unanimously approve the proposal of a number of delegates for the expulsion of those schismatics and factionalists' (*Twenty-second Congress* vol 2 p 464).

Things were obviously moving towards a show-of-hands decision; the lower echelons of the Party being once again manipulated by long-distance command in order to circumvent the large majority in the Presidium. In the meantime, however, another proposal was made by none other than A. N. Shelepin, the head of the KGB, the man who had most dramatically inveighed against the bloody crimes of the 'anti-party group', but who was already displaying his high skill in manoeuvre. His concluding words were:

'The time has come for the Party Control Committee attached to the Central Committee of the CPSU to consider the question of making the members of the anti-party group bear the most severe responsibilities.'[1]

The Party Control Committee (KPK) was an organ appointed by the Central Committee to watch over the discipline of Party members, determine necessary sanctions and consider appeals against sentences of expulsion pronounced by regional committees. It was presided over by Shvernik (who on the eve of the Congress had been assigned a deputy, Z. T. Serdyuk, a loyal client of Khrushchev). As far as Khrushchev was concerned, the Committee was in good hands for the purpose of ousting his foes; but it was clear also that the Party Presidium had an even stronger grip on the Committee. On a matter of such importance it would have its say, and probably the final one. Furthermore, recourse to the KPK meant playing for time. As a stop-gap measure, this would

---

[1] We apologize to the reader for this over-literal translation from the Russian, which political analysis demands. The word 'responsibility' (*otvetstvennost*) used by almost all the 'ambiguous' speakers of course carries the idea of sanction, but does not go as far as 'punishment' (*nakazanie*), demanded for instance by Podgorny. The effect of Shelepin's speech was to urge that Molotov and his associates should be called to account, while not specifying the degree or even the nature of the sanction advocated.

prevent a surprise vote by the Congress and would instead steer the matter into a maze of bureaucratic procedure.

Although not stated in so many words, that was the decision taken. It satisfied everybody – not only the 'ambiguous' Presidium members or the opponents of any sanction at all, who under the circumstances could hope for nothing better, but quite probably even most of the few advocates of expulsion, starting with Shvernik, the Chairman of the Control Committee. It satisfied everybody, that is, except Khrushchev himself, who was virtually robbed of his main weapon. He was far more isolated on the issue of sanctions than he had been on destalini-zation as a whole, and he could not or dared not try the 'mausoleum' technique again. The question of expulsion was not mentioned in his speech of October 27,[1] nor in the final resolution nor any other Congress decision. A few weeks later, when this writer had the opportunity of asking Khrushchev point-blank whether Molotov was still a member of the Party, he answered with some irritation: 'Why don't you ask Shvernik? He's taking care of it.' Shvernik, of course, was not available for questioning, but it soon became obvious that he was not doing very much. Meanwhile, the quarrel was shortly to erupt with added violence, as will be shown later.

ANOTHER STALINIST LEGACY:
THE 'STRONGHOLD OF HEAVY INDUSTRY'

Although of capital importance, the two problems just discussed were not the only controversial ones at the Congress. Many things were said and many problems touched on in the flood of speeches, documents and resolutions that occupied the public, or rather the experts who had the time to scrutinize them, during that fortnight. Spectacular topics which drew particular attention in foreign countries were not always the ones which caused the greatest turmoil within the leadership. For instance, notwithstanding Enver Hoxha's statements,[2] there is no trace

---

[1] This speech, however, did not indicate that the *status quo* would be maintained. By asking for indulgence for Voroshilov and suggesting that his case be dealt with 'differently from those of the other active members of the anti-party group', Khrushchev hinted that something would be done about the latter. It has been shown that a consensus to this effect existed in the Presidium, and it was natural that this collectively approved speech should reflect it.

[2] In his speech in Tirana on November 7 1961 Enver Hoxha, the leader of the Al-banian Communist Party, observed with satisfaction that, according to his reckon-ing, only fourteen Soviet speakers had criticized Albania. The figure was correct, but Hoxha refrained from mentioning that those fourteen reflected the overwhelming majority of the Party Presidium and in particular all its senior members including

of serious disagreement having arisen on the Albanian question.

A few speakers made some reservations about nationalities policy, an issue on which the Party programme followed a strongly 'integrationist' line, not to say one of intensive russification (the dissemination of the Russian language in the various ethnic republics was specifically encouraged, as well as a 'continuing exchange of cadres', the creation of inter-republic economic organizations and lastly the 'rapprochement and fusion of national cultures'). Not only were a few non-Russian republican leaders singularly discreet on that part of the programme (for instance I. G. Kebin from Estonia, V. Yu. Akhundov from Azerbaijan and D. A. Kunayev from Kazakhstan), but pleas for caution on this issue were made by two members of the Presidium, Mikoyan and Mukhitdinov, each of whom in his own way warned against administrative 'prodding' (podtalkivanie): the latter recalled that Lenin himself had opposed compulsory dissemination of the Russian language.

It was officially acknowledged that friction existed on another issue: that of 'the State of the whole people' and 'the Party of the whole people', the new slogans which the official ideological line had substituted for 'dictatorship of the proletariat' and 'the Party of the working class'. Needless to say, the new terminology had no effect whatsoever on the actual state and party structure. Obviously, the changes in wording were prompted by the needs of foreign propaganda rather than by actual developments at home.[1] Nevertheless, the ideologists brought up on the old formula were obviously restive, and Khrushchev had to reply in his report to 'certain comrades' who wanted to maintain the dictatorship of the proletariat 'until the complete victory of communism' and buttressed their arguments with 'arbitrarily culled quotations from Marx, Engels and Lenin'.[2] Most probably this was why

---

Suslov, Kosygin, Mikoyan and Kozlov. (The latter in particular, in his direct answer to Chou En-lai, used the latter's own formula to assert that public criticism of the Albanians was 'the only correct, serious Marxist–Leninist way of approaching the question'.) The only leaders who had not spoken on the subject were Podgorny, Shvernik, Aristov (who did not take the floor) and the future member of the Presidium, Voronov. Later they too, with the noteworthy exception of Shvernik, publicly criticized not only Albania but the Chinese as well.

[1] O. V. Kuusinen indicated clearly that the new ideological slogans were dictated by foreign propaganda needs when he said complacently: 'The State of the whole people puts an end to the speculations [of Western social-democrats] on the maintenance of the dictatorship of the proletariat until the victory of communism'. In other words, the formula put an end to the embarrassing fact that the Soviet régime officially acknowledged itself to be a dictatorship.

[2] 'Certain [other] comrades' asked for the liquidation of the 'kolkhoz market' (a semi-free market for agricultural produce which plays an essential part in supplying Soviet cities) or even the elimination of all trading and of the 'money–goods relationship' in favour of a barter system. All these utopian 'demands' were strongly remini-

some noted speakers were tepid in their defence of the new line: Brezhnev, for instance, who, as Head of State, should have been particularly interested in 'the State of the whole people', hardly mentioned it and let Mikoyan and Kuusinen expatiate on the subject. On the other hand, the chief ideologist, Suslov, wholeheartedly backed the new formula, although cautiously pointing out that it meant neither 'liberalism' nor 'anarchy', which indeed was quite plain.

However, these controversies, if such they were, were of minor importance. The nationalities question was of no immediate concern. It had been included in the same form in the programme published in the preceding summer, and the prospective 'fusion of nationalities' naturally belonged to the very distant future. The 'State of the whole people' likewise called for no immediate decisions, to say the least. The problem of economic priorities, on the other hand, was far more serious. It was hampering government activity almost at every turn, and was bound to continue doing so. It is easier to understand this feature of the situation in October 1961 if a closer look is taken at a somewhat earlier period.

In the autumn of 1960 Khrushchev began a serious assault on one of the most sacred tenets of the Soviet system as Stalin had shaped it, namely the dogma of priority for heavy industry. The division of industrial production into 'group A' (capital goods) and 'group B' (consumer goods), the unwritten law conferring priority on the former, the pre-eminence of steel and coal and the hectic industrialization of the first five-year plans, the cult of patriotism and the armed forces, the sacredness of the war industry – all these were axioms for a whole generation of political leaders, ideologists, planning experts and economists. It was going to be very difficult, if not impossible, to change course.

Khrushchev did not in fact mean at this time to question industrialization or the priority of defence needs as he understood them. But the mission he had assigned himself, of reforming the country's agriculture and then catching up with the living standard of the United States, could not be achieved without diverting huge funds towards the consumption sector, mainly agriculture and light industry.

Somewhat naïvely, Khrushchev had thought at first that he could avoid this. Quite apart from his clash with Malenkov in 1955, when

---

scent of the 'theoretical controversies' that Stalin enjoyed arbitrating, and they showed that nostalgia for the dictator was still strong in the middle ranks of the Party apparatus (far more than at the top, at least on that point). The theses were rejected, of course, by Khrushchev who reminded 'those comrades' that they were trying to run too fast.

the latter questioned the dogma of priority for heavy industry, Khrushchev still believed early in 1960 that he could increase agricultural production by so-called 'voluntary' methods. Explaining to his friends of the socialist camp on February 3 1960 that he had raised the agricultural targets of the seven-year plan despite the objections of his 'agricultural apparatus', he asserted that those new targets could be attained 'by raising even higher the enthusiasm of the masses for work, by further developing socialist emulation'.[1] It was an attractive notion, since it did not cost anything, and the First Secretary often toyed with it subsequently. The stagnation of agricultural production reflected by the 1960 harvest did induce him, however, to consider sterner measures. In a note to the Party Presidium dated October 29 he announced that radical steps would have to be taken and added: 'Clearly, the estimated allocations will not be sufficient. Therefore some thought should be given to the problem of increasing appropriations to agriculture out of the accumulations available to our economy owing to the over-fulfilment of plans' (*Agricultural Speeches* vol 4 p 162).

He then produced the following plan: Soviet industry, and heavy industry in particular, fairly regularly over-fulfilled the provisions of the 1959 seven-year plan, and Khrushchev estimated the value of this excess production at about 90 billion roubles from 1959 to 1965. This sizeable revenue should, he believed, be used to develop agriculture and light industry. In other words, henceforth industry was to finance agricultural development instead of the reverse as formerly. Later Khrushchev went even further, asking that heavy industry production be held down to the plan targets while those of agriculture and light industry should be substantially raised. This was a major infringement of the 'law' on priorities.

Orthodox believers certainly did more than frown upon this. On December 31 1960 the press censored part of the First Secretary's New Year toast in which he had made flippant remarks about heavy industry. A few days earlier, on December 26, the planners were 'instructed by the Party and the Government' to review the figures of the seven-year plan as Khrushchev had requested. But the instructions were curiously non-committal: the excess revenue, it was stated, would be channelled 'towards the development of *industry and agriculture* in order to satisfy the growing demand of the population' (*Party Workers'*

[1] Khrushchev's *Agricultural Speeches* vol 4 p 109. Among the 'agricultural organs' whose estimates he had rejected, Khrushchev mentioned the agricultural departments of the Central Committee for the Federated Republics, including the RSFSR. This probably accounts for the fall from favour at the end of 1959 of the head of one of those departments, P. E. Doroshenko. Generally speaking, departments changed heads, on the average, every eight months between 1959 and 1962.

Handbook, 1961, p 325). Meanwhile, Khrushchev was overtly coming to grips with the 'steel-eaters'. On January 17 1961 he declared to the Central Committee that it would be 'very satisfactory', meaning 'quite enough', if, in 1965, 86 to 91 million tons of steel were produced, as estimated. He deplored the fact that an 'appetite has developed in some of our comrades for giving more metal to the country', adding pictures- quely: 'One should not be like a fish that can see only on one side'. The new slogan accordingly was: 'agriculture must keep in step with industry'.[1]

On the whole, the Central Committee plenary session held in January 1961 satisfied him on that score. The resolution voted at the end of the session proclaimed: 'The building of communism . . . today calls for a different and swifter rate of development of agriculture. . . . The plenary session believes that today our country is able to increase ap- propriations well beyond the estimates of the seven-year plan for the development of agriculture and for the industry that services agricul- ture. . . .' The resolution repeated almost word for word Khrushchev's declaration of January 17, which was to be the leitmotiv of the new policy. Its gist was that the days were past when belts had to be tightened and all efforts bent on the creation of heavy industry. 'Today', Khrush- chev declared, 'our country has such a powerful industry, such a power- ful defence force that it can, without jeopardizing the development of industry and the strengthening of its defence, devote more funds to the development of agriculture and increase the production of consumer goods'.[2] To put it more plainly, the plenary session was taking a first set of measures to help the kolkhozes. This included lower prices for spare parts and petrol, tax cuts and an extension in the time-limit for the repayment of certain loans. The total value of this assistance was roughly 860 million roubles, a modest sum. Khrushchev announced optimistically a few days later at Rostov that far more important Gosplan projects were afoot for the production of tractors and agri- cultural machines. The Government and the Party, he added, will do 'everything possible to solve the problem'.

These hopes were doomed to bitter disappointment, and the manner in which they were buried shows the necessity of pessimism in all that has to do with Soviet agriculture.

Firstly, the higher levels of the economic apparatus almost openly opposed the measures. We have no accurate data on the revised esti- mates based on the instructions given to Gosplan on December 26 1960 to review the figures of the seven-year plan. They were scheduled

[1] Plenary session of the Central Committee, January 1961, Verbatim records p 528.
[2] *Ibid.*, pp 527 and 615.

to be ready by April 15 1961 and, as shown, Khrushchev was still optimistic about them at the beginning of February. Two months later, in a note of March 13 1961 to the Party Presidium, he did not conceal his bitterness. He said:

'Leading officials, including some in Gosplan, have not properly studied the actual situation with a view to meeting the needs of the kolkhozes and sovkhozes for machines. *They have erroneously concluded that the equipment now used in agriculture is fully adequate*' [Author's italics] (*Agricultural Speeches* vol 5 p 319).

Thus in 1961 Gosplan (its chairman being V. N. Novikov, formerly in charge of war industry) dared to interpret the agricultural situation in a manner radically different from Khrushchev's and to maintain that the kolkhozes did not need anything. Needless to say, the First Secretary strongly contested this assertion. During his tour of the provinces, Khrushchev wrote, he had been asked for financial help 'in all regions without exception'. And he asked again that the Central Committee and the Government should take a special decision on the increased production of agricultural machines. There is no trace of such a decision in any of the official texts for the ensuing months. And, even if such a directive had been issued, the chances are that it would have remained a dead letter. The combination of red tape, the planners' more or less overt hostility and the dogma of priority for heavy industry was more than enough to make officials 'lose sight of' the instructions by means of which Khrushchev was trying cautiously to reverse the trend. Whenever funds were unexpectedly needed in a sector of industry, whenever the State had to meet an unforeseen expense, the required funds were always quietly but firmly abstracted from the poor relations of the Soviet economy, agriculture and the industrial 'group B'. In this way, the appropriations for agriculture were unobtrusively cut several times during 1959 and 1960. Khrushchev disclosed this in his note of October 29 1960, specifying that 'the future investments earmarked for irrigation and the supply of agricultural machinery under the seven-year plan were eventually cut by over 13 milliard roubles' (*Agricultural Speeches* vol 4 p 181). Another result was that the appropriations per acre to sovkhozes (state farms) were lower in 1959 than in 1956.

All this was being done underhandedly, 'by nibbling' as Khrushchev put it later, and it did not stop even after he launched his campaign for aid to agriculture. When, early in 1961, the First Secretary of the Kemerovo region, L. I. Lubennikov, looked at the plan handed to him for the current year, he suddenly discovered that he was to receive only 580 tractors as against 1,284 for the preceding year, and 400 harvester-threshers instead of 820. Revealing this fact to the plenary session of January 1961, Lubennikov begged the 'comrades in the Presidium of the Central Committee' to reconsider the decision. The modest measures decided upon at that plenary session apparently met a similar fate. At the Twenty-second Congress, nine months later, K. T. Mazurov said: 'The January plenary session recognized the need for much higher investments in agriculture out of the accumulations resulting from over-fulfilment of certain branches of heavy industry. This decision of the plenary session should be carried out with greater speed' (*Twenty-second Congress* vol 1 p 301).

Another example illustrates the ill-will of the administrative agencies: on February 23 1961, upon a suggestion by D. S. Polyansky, it was decided to allow the farms to be connected to the state electric network. According to A. M. Shkolnikov, First Secretary of the Stalingrad Oblast Committee, nothing had been done to implement this by the opening of the Twenty-second Congress. Shkolnikov laid the responsi-bility on 'the Gosplan apparatus' and specifically on its then chief, V. N. Novikov. In all fairness it should be stated that Novikov had been encouraged in his policy by the best possible authority, namely Khrushchev himself.

BERLIN CRISIS VERSUS AGRICULTURE

From the summer of 1961 onwards – specifically since his Vienna meeting with President Kennedy in early June – Khrushchev had launched one of the strongest campaigns of intimidation of the Cold War, based on the Berlin issue. He announced that he was going to sign a peace treaty 'before the end of the year', with the Western powers and West Germany if they were willing, or else with East Germany alone. In either case the treaty would terminate the occupation status of West Berlin: all communications with the former capital would have to be renegotiated with the German Democratic Republic, and any attempt to ignore the treaty would be met by force. Throughout August 1961 Khrushchev poured forth some of the most chauvinistic speeches any Soviet leader had ever made, openly mentioning the possibility of a third world war and brandishing his rockets with unprecedented fierceness. The acutest stages of the crisis were the building of the Berlin wall on August 13 and, at the end of that month, the unilateral resump-tion of nuclear testing by the USSR. Khrushchev topped it all off during the Congress with the blast of the super-bomb of over 60 megatons, the most powerful ever tested.

We need not pursue the diplomatic intricacies of the crisis, which subsided in the same way as it had broken out, i.e. when its instigator so willed. The West stood firm, and Khrushchev, who had said privately during the summer that he knew how to 'cool off metal after tempering it', announced at the opening of the Twenty-second Congress on October 17 that the date of December 31 1961 for his peace treaty 'was not so important as all that'. Actually the issue was left dormant for several months under the guise of negotiations and Khrushchev reverted to it only in the following year, in a fresh approach which will be reviewed later. What concerns us here is the effect of the crisis on the Soviet economy. Khrushchev soon had to accept that he could not pursue two goals at once.

It is hard to tell whether it was the Berlin crisis that brought about an increase in military expenditure, as the official version has it, or conversely whether the need of the military to strengthen the armed forces prompted the crisis. In other words, was the crisis the pretext or the cause of the armed forces' good fortune? It may be noted that the marshals had been advocating for a long time the resumption of nuclear testing which was suspended in 1958. As early as June 21 1961, more than two months before the resumption and less than three weeks after the Vienna meeting, Khrushchev announced: 'Several devices have been perfected in the Soviet Union and require testing'. He warned that if the United States resumed testing the USSR would follow suit 'immediately', and he would not have been displeased, to say the least, if the occasion had thus been provided. Apart from this, Khrushchev had the most to gain from a success in his personal area, namely foreign policy, and deliberately took the initiative in bringing about a crisis. While he may not have been the instigator of all the military measures taken at the same time, he did have to pay the bill for his foreign policy. At the beginning of July the suspension of the 1960 demobilization measures was announced at the same time as an increase of 3,114 million roubles in the defence budget.

In keeping with established tradition, no information was given about what other categories of the budget would be used to finance this. In all likelihood, however, agriculture and light industry were sacrificed once again. This did not solve anything, for the leaders of heavy industry did not feel sufficiently compensated for the new efforts they were being asked to make. The Magnitogorsk combine, for instance, one of the largest metallurgical enterprises in the country, was instructed in 1961 to increase its output of steel by 16 per cent, of rolled steel by 18 per cent and of metal pipes by 32 per cent, although it was not allocated one extra kopek to expand its plants. The result was described in the following terms by M. T. Yefremov, First Secretary of the region, at the Twenty-second Congress: 'The metal workers started using the existing equipment at a forced pace, sometimes violating plant regulations. . . . This led to the premature wearing out of equipment and also some accidents' (*Twenty-second Congress* vol 2 p505).

In short, this crisis of the summer of 1961 showed the Soviet leaders more clearly than ever what acute problems the distribution of capital among the various sectors of their economy could create. This helped to dispose them to seek cheaper means of changing the strategic balance of power in their favour. The idea of installing nuclear rockets in Cuba was very probably one of the consequences.

Three reasons – namely, the declared hostility of the 'steel-eaters', their clandestine nibbling at appropriations and, lastly, Khrushchev's own diplomatic ambitions – explain why the diehard exponents of priority for heavy industry defended themselves so successfully. As we have seen, the most formal decisions and instructions were carried out perfunctorily or not at all. Nevertheless, the battle in terms of formulae went on. The documents of the Twenty-second Congress teem with ambiguous sentences, veiled disagreements and laboured compromises.

A marked success over heavy industry was the draft Party programme published in the summer. This highly authoritative text, the expression of the 'general line' for the coming twenty years, contained no explicit affirmation of the 'law' of priority for heavy industry. This priority, however, was presented as 'the basis of the country's technological progress and economic power', and the programme stressed the need 'to continue tirelessly to promote its growth'. The development of the metallurgical and fuel industries, 'the foundation of modern industry', was 'to remain as previously one of the foremost economic tasks'. It was added that the mission of heavy industry was 'to satisfy the needs of the country's defence and the development of the branches of the economy producing consumer goods'. In other words the priority of heavy industry was not reaffirmed, although nothing was said to deny it either.

In his report on the programme on October 18 1961 Khrushchev went further by introducing two new points not included in the programme. 'Over the next twenty years,' he announced, 'we are considering bringing closer together the respective rates of development of the means of production and of the means of consumption.' (It is true that he immediately added: 'Heavy industry has always played the leading role in increasing production and will continue to do so.') He was, however, opening a breach in the predominance of heavy industry by making for the first time a distinction between two sections of the famous 'group A': that which supplied machinery to the means-of-production industry, and that which supplied it to the consumer industry. As between, for example, producers of rolling mills and those of looms, he intended to give a marked advantage to the latter: the rate of increase from 1961 to 1980 was to be 8 per cent and 13 per cent respectively. Although these details were not part of the Party programme, since they were included in a collectively approved report it was likely that a consensus on that point existed in the top leadership. At least as far as long-term planning was concerned, Khrushchev had managed to have some of his designs prevail.

In the short run, however, a complete deadlock had occurred and the First Secretary had had to back down on certain points. In January 1961, as already indicated, he asked that the figure for steel production set for the seven-year plan be kept at 86 to 91 million tons. This took some doing, for the 'steel-eaters' wanted 100 ('We held them back', Khrushchev declared). He also asked on the same day that 'the revenues accumulated as a result of the over-fulfilment of industrial production plans be channelled towards agriculture, light industry and the food industry'. He even repeated the sentence in his progress report of October 17, but added the word 'mainly' after 'channelled', meaning that some of the revenues would go elsewhere. The resolution adopted at the end of the Congress embodied this passage without any change but maintained neutrality on the priorities issue. It called for 'continuing to develop heavy industry at an accelerated pace . . .' and at the same time for 'the stepping-up, in all its aspects (*vsemernoye*), of the production of consumer goods'. In fact it did not promise one extra kopek for agriculture. Khrushchev confirmed this when, speaking a few days later to the agricultural workers of Uzbekistan, he as it were, turned his pockets inside out to show they were empty. 'I have brought with me only good wishes', he told them, and tried to cheer them up by assuring them that 'the human brain is worth more than money' (November 16 1961: *Agricultural Speeches* vol 6 p 88).

The refusal to take sides seems to have reflected the views of a large sector of the Party Presidium, and particularly its senior members. Kozlov, Brezhnev and Suslov did not mention the matter in their Congress speeches. Mikoyan merely asked for 'some redistribution of manpower' in favour of the consumer sector, but refrained from discussing the broader problem of investment priorities. Kosygin touched upon the substance of the matter but with singular caution. According to him the problem was to provide for the 'faster [*operezhayushchy*, literally 'out-distancing'] growth of the main branches of heavy industry' and also for the 'accelerated development of light industry and the food industry'. The 'advantages of the socialist system' enabled 'large funds to be channelled towards the accumulation fund', while 'the consumption fund is also being increased'. In other words, both could be done at the same time and there was no need for a choice. On the other hand, Kosygin noted that consumption investment since 1960 had been 'very much higher than estimated in the seven-year plan'. This could be regarded as an answer to the rank-and-file demand for consumer goods and also contradicted Khrushchev's lament that appropriations for agriculture had been cut instead of raised since 1959. Coming after Kosygin, Polyansky was even more specific: by his reckoning, investment in agriculture 'had been tripled' in the last few years. (All this, be it noted in passing, raises many questions as to the reliability of statistics.) Polyansky also insisted that the agricultural failures resulted mainly from personnel weaknesses, which obviously placed him among the advocates of the *status quo* in appropriations.

Several of these officials changed position later, and what they said at the Twenty-second Congress should not be regarded as their last word on the subject. On the other hand, a difference was perceptible between those who, then and later, systematically advocated greater sacrifices for the sake of agriculture, and those who sided with the 'steel-eaters'.

The main member of the first group was Podgorny, who from January 1961 onwards had been keener to help agriculture than Khrushchev himself and had stood up to the First Secretary on that point.[1] At the Twenty-second Congress he went further than all the others, questioned the Gosplan estimates and asked for greater effort. This is what he said:

'We understand that it is not easy to satisfy growing needs all at once. It does seem, however, that in keeping with the prospects for the development of agricultural production, Gosplan should . . . once again carefully assess the possibility during the coming years of stepping up the production of tractors, automobiles, machines and . . . fertilizers . . . for the needs of agriculture, and should submit proposals on this point to the Central Committee and the Council of Ministers' (*Twenty-second Congress* vol 1 pp 276–277).

Podgorny's appeal was supported by a sizeable number of representatives of the regions and republics, among them K. T. Mazurov,

---

[1] A particularly sharp clash occurred when, in his report to the plenary session of January 1961, Podgorny requested more tractors for agriculture in the Ukraine. Khrushchev interrupted him with the helpful suggestion that he solve the problem by increasing the speed of the tractors he had. Podgorny retorted: 'I said in my speech that we are working on speeding them up. But we must be given what we ask for.'

'In that case', Khrushchev countered, 'say "given" in a louder voice.'

'Nikita Sergeyevich, I think that when I mentioned in my speech the shortage of machines I only confirmed what you said about the abnormal situation that has arisen in the production of a number of agricultural machines. The problem is to increase the production of material in short supply.'

'You see, comrades, how he is making me side with him!'

(Plenary session of January 1961, verbatim records p. 63.)

First Secretary for Byelorussia, and a few specialists including M. A. Olshansky, the Minister of Agriculture, who had succeeded V. V. Matskevich in December 1960 and who stressed, not unreasonably, that the campaign against fallow lands and grass-growing made it 'extremely necessary' to increase the production of mineral fertilizers. But those were isolated appeals. Where fertilizers in particular were concerned, it took some time for Khrushchev to decide, or be able, to adopt radical methods. For, meanwhile, the heavy industry lobby was not idle. While the VIPs were silent, the lower echelons were all the more vocal. The spokesmen of the group were not those who might have been expected. Strangely enough, the head of Gosplan, V. N. Novikov, did not appear at the Congress. V. E. Dymshits, one of his closest aides and future successor, spoke on behalf of the planners but did not make any clear-cut statement. On the other hand, N. G. Ignatov, although in charge of agriculture as Deputy Prime Minister and a faithful ally of Khrushchev on all other issues, was the first to rejoice that the Party had 'as in past years, firmly maintained priority for the development of heavy industry'. After him L. F. Ilyichev, the Agitprop leader, was the only one to reproach Malenkov with an all but forgotten sin, that of having in 1954 made the 'anti-Leninist assertion that priority for the development of heavy industry was not mandatory'. On that point both went beyond the Party programme which, as noted, no longer explicitly stated the 'Leninist' view. Other speakers implicitly backed them, some by deploring the 'shortage of metal' afflicting the economy (G. I. Voronov), others by asking for larger appropriations for heavy industry (M. T. Yefremov), etc.

Thus, despite the fervour of advocates on both sides, the question remained deadlocked at the Congress. The practical result was that agriculture received nothing more. Judging from the position taken up by men as close to Khrushchev at the time as Ignatov and Ilyichev, the First Secretary was not then deeply committed on the issue. Compared to his stand at the end of 1960 and the beginning of 1961, however, it is clear that he had retreated to some extent. The fortress of heavy industry stood firm, and, although Khrushchev seemed to accept this, it could not be forgotten that it was he who had dealt it the first blow a year earlier. This signified that the economy was another of the areas in which Khrushchev could not do everything he wanted.

3 Power Problems

Khrushchev had been checked on three major issues. Destalinization had been stopped at the end of the Congress, the campaign to expel Molotov and his associates from the Party had failed and the problem of agricultural investments had remained deadlocked. These were serious defeats and in turn raised a broader question: to what extent was the First Secretary the actual master? How did his colleagues in the Presidium assess his authority? How much were they willing to contribute to his cult? How did Khrushchev himself view these problems?

In such highly delicate questions no spectacular revelations could be expected from the Congress. There were nuances and variations in emphasis which will be reviewed presently, but these should not mask the main fact, namely, that for the period under survey no one was thinking of replacing Khrushchev as First Secretary. Although in principle the Congress was supposed to have ended his term of office, neither he nor anyone else had the slightest doubt, before or during the proceedings, that he would be triumphantly 're-elected'. Whether everybody was satisfied or whether would-be successors' personal ambitions were beginning to show themselves is another matter. These questions could not be asked in so many words, even behind the scenes. Meanwhile, Brezhnev, Kozlov, Suslov and Kosygin reconciled themselves to seeing Khrushchev entrenched 'at the head of the Central Committee' (the formula officially used throughout the Congress). If they acknowledged the existence of any problem, it was not whether there should be a leader but what were their relations with him.

This should be kept in mind when considering the cult of the leader. In a system as authoritarian as the Soviet, the fact that the authority of a man 'at the head of the Party' is accepted inevitably entails glorifying him. The 'monolithic' principle, the immutable image of the Party 'closely knit around its Leninist leadership', makes it mandatory to extol the wisdom of its decisions and therefore that of the chief. The picture could be different only if the chief expressly forbade any tribute to himself or if, instead of one leader, there were several men jealously watching over one another (as after the triumph of the collective principle in October 1964).

Neither of these situations existed in 1961, and it would not be fair to blame Khrushchev for having failed to ban the cult of his own personality. In the USSR as elsewhere, personal prestige helps to consolidate one's authority, and the First Secretary needed it even more than Stalin if he was to make his views prevail over a reluctant Presidium. Actually, he was more than tolerant towards the cult. Starting in 1959 he awarded himself the laurels of 'peace-maker' and, when his popularity sank markedly after the 1960 crisis, he took energetic steps to revive it during the preparations for the Congress. The plenary session of January 1961 devoted to agriculture, followed by interminable tours all over the country,[1] helped him propagate the image of the leader 'close to the people' – which was at least partly true – and versed in every subject, which was less so. Gagarin's space flight in April was heavily exploited, and Khrushchev even arranged to have the Order of Lenin awarded to himself on July 17 (it is true that Brezhnev and Kozlov received it at the same time).[2] The Berlin crisis and the anniversary of the German attack of 1941 gave him an opportunity to sport a general's uniform and display his solicitude for the men in the armed forces. At Stalingrad in September he made a point of embracing Marshals Yeremenko and Chuikov, the two heroes of the historic battle, and reminding the public about his own part in it as a political commissar.

There were other signs of the cult: during the summer a long film documentary was shown entitled *Our Nikita Sergeyevich*, depicting his life 'in the service of the people' with special stress on his popularity abroad. It was learned also that the most famous kolkhoz in Uzbekistan, whose chairman was the threefold 'hero of labour' Tursunkulov, had been named after Khrushchev (curiously enough the kolkhoz 'Khrushchev's Home' had again become the Kalinovka Kolkhoz at an undetermined date, probably in 1960). Lastly, an unusual biography appeared in the summer of 1961 under the discreet title *The Story of an Honorary Miner*. It was a fictionalized biography of Khrushchev during his youth in the Donbas and contained a wealth of illustrations and hitherto unpublished photographs, in particular portraits of the

---

[1] The following is a list (probably incomplete) of Khrushchev's travels in 1961. January to March: Kiev, Rostov, Tbilisi, Voronezh, Sverdlovsk, Kurgan, Novosibirsk, Akmolinsk, Alma-Ata, Sochi. May: Erevan and Tbilisi, Batum, Rostov. June: Leningrad, Alma-Ata, Sochi, August: Kharkov, Stalingrad, Yalta. Then there was his visit to Czechoslovakia and Vienna at the beginning of June. No sooner did the Congress end than he resumed his 'agricultural' tours, this time in Central Asia and Siberia.

[2] Here, for instance, is what appeared in *Pravda* of August 26 1961 under the signature of Vladimir Orlov: 'N. S. Khrushchev directs the broad trends of technological progress of the country, the working out of the basic directives and overall plans for the development of space science and techniques. . . . He visits all the plants and sectors of the giant space sites and knows all their leaders by sight and name. In periods of difficulty he takes part in the discussion of the most important experiments.' Gagarin himself made similar statements.

hero starting at the age of eighteen, and one taken in 1925 showing him and Stalin with a group of Party functionaries. The book was officially alleged to have been prompted by local initiative. It had been published at Stalino, the capital of the Donbas, in connection with a decision of the miners' union, taken on April 5 1960, to name Khrushchev an 'honorary miner'. Despite its modest number of copies (50,000) it was put on sale in Moscow, but as far as is known to this writer the central press was silent on the subject. This was in fact Khrushchev's only official biography and, needless to say, could not have been published 'without his knowledge'. The discreet manner in which it was brought out indicates that the cult was running into difficulties.

THE NEW 'CULT'

The huge amount of praise heaped on Khrushchev at the Congress should be considered against this background. It was practically mandatory in the case of a recognized chief, and his exalted role in the proceedings contributed to the same effect. Khrushchev delivered the two marathon opening reports and held the floor for two consecutive days.[1] Enthusiasm for the reports necessarily extended to the person who had delivered them. Besides, the offensive against the Albanians and their Chinese ally required an even more signal demonstration of 'monolithic cohesion' around the man singled out for their attacks. In short, everybody paid tribute to him, although there were various ways of doing so.

It is worth quoting the personal tributes bestowed by various leaders at the Twenty-second Congress. Tedious as they may appear, the situation cannot be correctly assessed without taking into account the sheer volume of praise. This was the picture:

Brezhnev: 'An eminent personality of the State and the Party. . . . His inexhaustible energy, his revolutionary fervour, inspires us all to carry on the struggle. What distinguishes comrade Khrushchev is his faith in the people and in the strength of our Party, his unshakeable firmness in carrying out the Party line, his intolerance towards the enemies of communism, his daring and decisiveness. These qualities above

[1] Long afterwards, it was learned that Khrushchev's oratorical monopoly at the Twenty-second Congress had struck some of the foreign delegates adversely. Thus Georges Marchais declared in November 1964 to the Central Committee of the French Communist Party: 'On several occasions our Politburo had been worried about this [Khrushchev's role]. For instance, we could not understand why comrade Khrushchev had delivered both reports to the Twenty-second Congress himself and why he took the floor on every question' (*L'Humanité*, November 9 1964).

all characterize comrade Khrushchev as a faithful Leninist, developing consistently and creatively the great lessons of Marxism–Leninism. . . . He displays endless activity . . . tirelessly upholds the cause of peace and of freedom for all nations. . . . For all of us the daily activity of Nikita Sergeyevich Khrushchev is a magnificent example of tact and sympathy . . . towards the suggestions from the workers. . . . We all know how he can explain to the people in a clear and intelligible way the most complex questions, how he maintains close ties with the people, drawing from this pure clear source his inspiration and folk wisdom; we all know his enormous talent as an organizer. These qualities have rightly earned Nikita Sergeyevich the love and profound respect of our Party and of the whole Soviet people.'

Kozlov: 'True Leninist, eminent political personality and theoretician of Marxism–Leninism.'

Kosygin: 'True Leninist.'

Mikoyan: 'It is impossible not to appreciate what efforts the Head of the Soviet Government, comrade Khrushchev, has exerted in the cause of peace. . . .'

Podgorny: 'Eminent statesman and Party personality . . . Comrade Khrushchev's whole activity, his ebullient energy, his truly revolutionary Leninist attitude towards the solution of complex theoretical and practical problems, his indissoluble ties with the people, his humanity and simplicity, his capacity to learn continuously from the masses and to teach them, are an uplifting example for the whole Party and for each and every communist.'

Polyansky: 'The successes of our country in the last few years . . . are indissolubly linked with the name of N. S. Khrushchev, a faithful Leninist, an eminent political personality of our time. A man of great soul and inexhaustible energy who knows life well and draws fresh strength from contact with the people, Nikita Sergeyevich has earned the deep respect and great love of the broad masses.'

Suslov: 'An eminent Leninist and great personality of our Party.'

Voronov: 'A remarkable example . . . of creative approach· to the solution of the most complex questions . . . is given to us all . . . by the Central Committee and N. S. Khrushchev personally.'

Kuusinen: 'The new programme had to be worked out under the guidance of a Marxist–Leninist who knew how to combine theoretical audacity and insight . . . who was distinguished by fidelity to principles, who did not for one second lose sight of the final goal of historical evolution and at the same time would never cut himself off from the grass roots; who knew the lives of the workers as well as his own, who believed in the people and reflected their cares and hopes. Considering all this, one sees clearly how important it is that the drawing up of the new programme was directed personally by a Leninist such as comrade Khrushchev.'

Shvernik: 'Nikita Sergeyevich has shown great wisdom in the solution of the most important questions in domestic and international life, he has acted as a fearless champion of our Party's correct Leninist policy. . . . There is today no corner of the globe where comrade Khrushchev is not known as a great fighter for peace and friendship among all nations.'

Furtseva: 'Our dear Nikita Sergeyevich . . . a faithful Leninist, a tireless and selfless fighter for the Party.'

Ignatov: 'He . . . studies with indefatigable energy the achievements and experience of the foremost workers . . . selects bit by bit everything that is valuable and carries on a great, passionate campaign for whatever is progressive. . . . He has personal ties with thousands of people, knows their thoughts, encourages them with advice when needed, teaches them to improve production indices. . . . He has revealed to the country the Herculean strength to be drawn from maize, and has aroused love for its cultivation.'

Mukhitdinov: 'Continuer of Lenin's work.'

Shelepin: 'He played an eminent role in the unmasking and defeat of the factionalists [Molotov and others]. Comrade Khrushchev performed that task masterfully, in a Leninist manner. In complex circumstances Nikita Sergeyevich displayed personal courage and intellectual firmness, showing himself to be a faithful, intrepid Leninist for whom there are no other interests than those of the people, of Leninist unity and the cohesion of our great Party.'

Mazurov: 'Inflexible Leninist . . . who personally displayed great initiative, firm will, audacity and courage in the working out and execution of the decisions of the Twentieth Congress.'

There would be no point in undertaking a detailed exegesis of these phrases, although praise for a specific action or a single aspect of Khrushchev's political role does not have the same value as indiscriminate praise for all the hero's personal virtues. However, the gamut of praise we have quoted roughly corresponds to the reactions we have already described in regard to two major issues, viz. the criminal responsibility of the 'anti-party group' for the Stalinist repressions and the question of their eviction from the Party. Essentially those speakers who had been discreet on those two issues were also discreet in their cult of the First Secretary, and this tends to confirm that siding with him on the points in question entailed allegiance to his person and complicity in his ambitions. The only exception was Brezhnev, whose equivocal position on the 'anti-party group' has been noted but who, on the other hand, was conspicuous by his truly dithyrambic praise of Khrushchev.

It is not clear whether the one was intended to make up for the other, but it should not be forgotten that, earlier in his career, Brezhnev had been a client of the First Secretary, and that he still owed him a great deal at the time of the Congress.

In any case, the reserved attitude of four of the most prominent members of the Presidium was striking. They were Kozlov, Kosygin, Mikoyan and Suslov. Of the four, Kosygin was unquestionably the most discreet, and this, as noted, was a characteristic attitude on his part. Typically, he was also the most outspoken in warning against the new cult, which he did in the following words:

'The lessons of history must never be forgotten. We must and will do everything we can so that in future there shall be no place in our Party or in our society for the cult of personality, so that it shall be destroyed root and branch. . . . There must be no place for the cult of personality in the building of communism' (*Twenty-second Congress* vol 1 p 577).

True, everyone else was also criticizing the cult of personality, but Kosygin was more pessimistic than most. According to him the cult still had 'roots' and 'branches' and something needed to be done about 'the future'. And what is more, it should be remembered that Kosygin had not spoken of the repressions or the abuse of power and had not even recalled Stalin by name. Therefore, coming from him, the expression 'cult of personality' was meant in a direct and literal sense, namely the cult of any personality. If the cult was still a threat, what 'personality' could be in question?

Evidently Kosygin disliked this adulation of the First Secretary by one Congress speaker after another. He was certainly not alone in this: towards the end of the Congress there was a sterner reaction against the new cult, clearly emanating from the collective leadership and not from its beneficiary. Before analysing this, we must consider another feature closely affecting the prerogatives of power and its holder: namely certain new provisions of the Party statutes.

THE 'THREE TERMS' RULE

The Party statutes, another basic text submitted to the Congress together with the programme (this time with Kozlov instead of Khrushchev as the rapporteur), had given rise to an anomaly that summer. A plenary meeting of the Central Committee on June 19 1961 had 'unanimously' approved the draft programme but had ratified the new statutes only 'in principle' (*v osnovnom*). Probably because this was not full approval, their publication was postponed. The plenary session decided to publish both texts on July 31, that is, six weeks later.

The contested points cannot be identified, since the version released on the specific date is the only one known to us and was not amended subsequently. Evidently, if any corrections were made, it was during those six weeks. There is good reason to believe nevertheless that the discussions centred on fairly radical provisions that distinguished these statutes from the previous ones. First, a fixed proportion of all the leading Party organs, from the Central Committee Presidium down to the cell committees, was to be replaced at each election. The proportions were: one-quarter for the Presidium and the Central Committee, one-third for the same bodies at the republic and regional levels, and one-half at the lowest level. Secondly, the principle was established that, in the ordinary way, no one could be elected more than a certain number of times to membership in the principal organs of the Party. The number was: three times for Presidium members, three times at the regional level and twice for a cell Secretary. Two exceptions were allowed, however:

1 The 'three terms rule' did not apply to the Party Central Committee, whose members could be elected an indefinite number of times. Consequently, one could be a Party Secretary for an unlimited time, since these rules applied only to the deliberative bodies (Presidium or bureaux) and not to the secretariats (except at the cell level).[1]

2 In the paragraph dealing with the Presidium the statutes added: 'Some Party personalities may, by virtue of their recognized authority and their outstanding political, organizational or other qualities, be elected to the leading organs for a longer period.' This required a three-quarters majority.

It is hard to tell who profited most by the new rules. In theory they markedly restricted Khrushchev's power, or at least its duration. If the three-terms rule was given its broadest interpretation, the two personalities who should have been swept aside in 1961 were Khrushchev and Mikoyan, who had entered the Presidium after the 1939 Congress and been kept on by the 1952 and 1956 Congresses. But both of them, especially Khrushchev, obviously felt covered by the exception granted to 'recognized authorities'. The First Secretary might regard the rule of replacement of one-fourth as a convenient means of purging the central and regional apparatus of people who were in his way and

---

[1] Traditionally all the Secretaries at the regional level and below are at the same time members of the deliberative body (bureau). This does not apply to the upper hierarchy, but the exception could only benefit the junior Secretaries who were not members of the Presidium after the 1961 Congress, for instance Shelepin, Demichev, Ilyichev, etc.

appointing in their place the compliant elements he held in reserve, under guise of promoting the young. He made this clear in his report on the programme on October 18 1961. Commenting on the new statutes he declared:

'An order has to be established whereby comrades elected to the leading posts should not bar the way to new recruits but should clear the path for others. . . . Some cells die, others are born. . . . It is no secret that there are comrades among us who in their time were duly appreciated and elected to leading posts and who have now been holding them for decades. Over the years some of them have lost the ability to run things in a creative manner, have lost the sense of what is new, and they have become a brake. It would be a mistake to leave these men in their posts merely because they were elected long ago. Must we confine ourselves to the circle of persons elected long ago to the leading organs? That is not our custom' (*Twenty-second Congress* vol 1 p 252).

This call for a purge was nothing new coming from Khrushchev, and it showed that he viewed the new statutes favourably provided they received this interpretation. But interestingly enough, this was not how they were understood by the collective authors of the Congress documents. According to the Party programme the rules on replacement and on the three terms aimed at '*excluding the possibility of an excessive concentration of power* in the hands of some Party officials [*rabotniki*] and at preventing these people from *eluding collective control*' [Author's italics] (*Twenty-second Congress* vol 3 p 332).

Legally these rules did not make much sense, for it is not clear how any of them could, for instance, prevent a person elected to the top leadership of the Party for twelve years (the space of time covering three congresses) from concentrating vast powers in his hands. Their political motivation was much more understandable. If anyone should have felt aimed at by the reference to an 'excessive concentration of power' it was certainly Khrushchev, who, in addition to being First Secretary of the Party, had 'concentrated' in his hands the leadership of the government apparatus by becoming Chairman of the Council of Ministers in 1958, was also Chairman of the Central Committee Bureau for the RSFSR and, generally speaking, was deliberately taking over leadership in all areas. The allusion was pointed enough in all conscience: was it conceivable that anyone would have dared to make it in Stalin's day? Its authors in fact chose not to expose themselves by laying too much stress on it. The only speaker who mentioned this 'concentration of powers' was Kozlov, who quoted the above passage in his report on the statutes. Khrushchev recalled it once, in his speech of

October 27, but in a different vein. According to him, concentration of power was inevitable and the only remedy was watchfulness to prevent the leader from abusing such power. 'Naturally, for many reasons, great power concentrates itself in the hands of a man who occupies a leading post. . . . The leader . . . must not abuse that power.' No one else, not even Kosygin, again raised this highly sensitive question.

COLLECTIVE CONTROL

The reference to 'collective control' was equally significant. The wording admitted of two interpretations: control of the elected leader by the body of his electors, or else control of the elected leader by his colleagues. In standard Soviet terminology, and particularly in matters involving the rank and file, the difference between the two interpretations is generally blurred. Where the top leadership is concerned, however, the distinction is of the utmost importance. What 'collective' body was to control Khrushchev? The Central Committee that had elected him, or the Presidium elected at the same time as he?

There is no doubt whatever that Khrushchev was a systematic advocate of the first interpretation only. Not that he ever explicitly and officially denied the second one, which would have been an overt provocation to his peers – something he could not afford, at all events in public. But he so often and so insistently expounded the thesis of the responsibility of the leader towards his electors that this cannot fail to be regarded as designed to exclude the other thesis. He, the First Secretary of the Central Committee, had been elected by the Central Committee, hence he was responsible to it. Only the Central Committee was entitled to settle all questions of power. All power must derive from the rank and file. These in substance were the themes that he developed throughout his rule in a series of public speeches and before many of his foreign visitors – in particular the French socialist leader, Guy Mollet, in a very frank private talk in October 1963. In theory these were lofty ideas and the First Secretary's claim to be a good democrat should not be rejected out of hand. Actually, the Soviet system being what it is and the Central Committee being restricted by long tradition to the role of a rubber stamp, Khrushchev felt infinitely freer in dealing with it than with the Presidium. This theory of plebiscitary democracy suited him all the better in that the electors were people loyal to him or supposed to be, and in any case far more tractable than his peers in the Presidium. What could have been simpler than to have his quarrels with his equals resolved in his favour by a well-orchestrated plenary session, or better still one swollen by hundreds of enthusiastic kolkhoz members? The thesis of 'power deriving from the rank and file' was less innocent than it might have seemed; clearly it was aimed against the Presidium and had no other purpose.

This interpretation of Khrushchev's motives is strengthened by the example he always quoted of the 1957 crisis, when he was kept in power by the Central Committee overriding the majority of Presidium members who had joined forces against him. He was fond of recalling the incident, and on one such occasion at the Twenty-second Congress he expressed his faith in control 'by the rank and file'. As Ignatov, his faithful ally, described from the rostrum the machinations of Molotov and his associates to prevent the First Secretary from receiving his Central Committee friends in the initial stage of the crisis, Khrushchev cut in to explain:

'They wanted to deprive me of the possibility of meeting the members of the Central Committee and appointed Voroshilov to discharge the task. I answered: It's the plenary session that elected me First Secretary and nobody can deprive me of the right to meet with members of the Central Committee of the Communist Party. I was elected by the plenary session of the Central Committee and that body must make the decision. Things will stand as the plenary session decides' (*Twenty-second Congress* vol 2 p 106).

All this concerned the past, but nothing prevented Khrushchev from saying the same thing to his current Presidium if the latter were to oppose his moves. It is likely that he did so more than once. The First Secretary's most fervent backers also made derogatory remarks against the Presidium, the 'so-called arithmetical majority' (N. G. Ignatov) or the 'certain arithmetical majority' (P. A. Satyukov) which in 1957 had emerged within the Presidium against Khrushchev. These phrases showed disrespect both for the plain facts of arithmetic and for the right of the collective leadership to vote on any issue that concerned it. Mikoyan, who had himself been in the minority at that time, merely noted objectively that the members of the 'anti-party group had reckoned up the votes they could muster against the Party leadership within the Presidium of the Central Committee'. He did not go out of his way to call an actual majority 'so-called' or to deny the formal correctness of the treatment meted out to the 'anti-party group'.

More audacious still were the remarks by certain other followers of the First Secretary about the 'Presidium of the Central Committee headed by comrade Khrushchev'. The illegality of this phrase has already been pointed out. It was used by very few speakers at the Congress, but one of them was L. F. Ilyichev, one of the men Khrushchev was holding in reserve to counter Suslov and probably supplant him in a future Presidium.

All this, coupled with the spreading of the new 'cult', must have prompted some stocktaking within the collective leadership. There were no public statements pro or con and no senior member of the Presidium said anything to support Khrushchev's thesis of democracy based on the rank and file.[1] A reaction probably set in behind the scenes for, at the end of the Congress, an attempt was made to get matters into focus. This was done by Khrushchev in the concluding speech of the first part of the debates, delivered on October 27. This was a fierce denunciation of Stalin's crimes and those of the 'anti-party group' and it reflected, as Khrushchev pointed out, the views of the collective leadership. As we have seen, the Presidium as it was then constituted did support the denunciation of those crimes. The speech also represented the majority opinion on other issues; indeed, some of the things Khrushchev said that day very probably did not represent his own views.

First he protested, or pretended to protest, against the cult of his own personality. After observing that it had been the object of 'special emphasis' and that his role had been played up in speeches at the Congress 'and also often in our press', he added: 'I understand the kindly sentiments that inspire those comrades. Permit me neverthe-less to emphasize that everything said regarding me should be addressed to the Central Committee of our Leninist Party and to its Presidium.' Such modesty was belated: at no time during the Congress or at any other period of the cult had Khrushchev made any move to curb his zealous admirers. Perhaps in this instance it was an affectation meant to improve his image still further, but he used an argument that went to the heart of the matter: the cult, he said, had the effect of 'alienating

---

[1] In practice the tendency to resort to plebiscites was countered, but at another level of the hierarchy. For instance, a proposal was made during the discussion of the statutes whereby the Party committee secretaries at various levels of the hierarchy would have been elected directly by the Party plenary assembly for the region in question instead of by the committee itself. If this had been applied to the supreme organs for instance, Khrushchev and the other Party secretaries would have been elected by the entire congress of 4,000 delegates instead of the 175 members of the Central Committee as hitherto. But the proposal was not likely to please anyone, even Khrushchev, because its effects were dangerous. The Congress votes by secret ballot while the Party committees, including the Central Committee, vote by show of hands. The suggested procedure would, to say the least, have introduced an element of uncertainty into the proceedings. The counter-argument used by Kozlov is interesting. 'This would mean,' he said, 'that the Secretaries would be endowed with higher powers than the other members of the Bureau or the Committee. Such a proposal contradicts the principle of collective leadership and there are no grounds for accepting it.' (*Twenty-second Congress* vol 3 p 30.)

one personality from the leading collective . . . of isolating it from the leading group of comrades' (*Twenty-second Congress* vol 2 p 592).

In other words, Khrushchev had to admit that the new cult offended the Party Presidium. If the confession was spontaneous it indeed showed remarkable deference to his fellow members for the first and only time.

On the question of 'collective control' he was much more specific. Discussing the issue in far greater detail than in his earlier report, he first repeated his favourite interpretation: any authority, 'even the most august', should never 'cease to reckon with the opinion of those who elected it'. He then, surprisingly, added the second interpretation. The leader 'needs a collective'; if he overlooks this truth, he runs the risk of 'no longer listening to the voice of the other comrades elected, like him, to leadership and he may take it into his head to crush them. Our great master Lenin decisively opposed this. . . .' (*Twenty-second Congress* vol 2 p 593).

There is, of course, no way of proving that Khrushchev was forced to include these words in his speech, but, until disproved, we shall take this as a hypothesis. Everything he had said previously, and at the Congress itself in commenting on Ignatov's speech, showed his determination to recognize solely the authority of his electors of the Central Committee and not that of his peers. All the attacks against the manoeuvres of Molotov and his associates during the 1957 crisis followed the same line. As for his protests about the 'cult', they were platonic and short-lived. In the following days of the congress other speakers, for instance P. A. Leonov, First Secretary in Sakhalin, heaped ecstatic praise upon Khrushchev, who made no attempt to stop them. Obviously he had been compelled to 'elucidate matters' or, let us say more politely, it had been 'suggested' to him. He had complied but did not feel obliged to go any further. He did nothing to check the eulogists whose 'kindly sentiments' he had expressly acknowledged.

The other representatives of the 'leading group' could hardly press the offensive on that point. Nobody could yet think seriously of attacking the First Secretary directly; and it would have been tantamount to an attack to ask openly and insistently about something that had never been actually settled by the power centres of the communist apparatus – namely, where does collective leadership stop and the authority of a single leader begin? This was another aspect of the same problem and everybody acknowledged that it would have to be solved; but the best they could do for the present was to watch the leader and resist some of his specific moves. This they did with respect to the destalinization measures, the witch-hunt against the 'anti-party group', and economic matters. But when it came to the basic problem – namely, the division of power between Khrushchev and the 'collective' leadership – it was to continue festering beneath the surface for three years longer.

THE ELECTIONS

Electing the Party's ruling bodies, the Central Committee and Auditing Committee, is one of the prerogatives of the Congress, the 'supreme authority' in all matters. The statutes require a secret ballot and there is no evidence that this has ever been contravened, even under Stalin. But no one acquainted with Soviet political life will imagine that this in itself could give rise to any surprises. The average delegate, like any local dignitary 'elected' by the rank and file, is in reality a Party member 'recommended' by his superiors, that is to say co-opted. He is chosen in the first place for his utter docility, as a good communist, towards the current leadership. He is made a delegate to the Party Congress so that he may display his loyalty to the leaders, not oppose them. This may change some day, but that is how it was in 1961 and is even now. Furthermore, it is not the delegate's business to select the leader. He is 'free' only to place in the ballot box a list of 100 to 200 names carefully prepared beforehand and 'recommended' by the Party leadership. This is the list of the future voting members of the Central Committee, listed in alphabetical order in token of equality. It is they, meeting in closed session and voting by show of hands, who in due course elect the members of the Presidium, the Secretaries and the First Secretary.

Thus the procedure of the secret ballot is irrelevant to any power struggle within the leadership, the only type of contest that is conceivable under the present rules. If, for instance, a delegate to the 1961 Congress had favoured a 'Suslov group' or a 'Kozlov group', his vote would still have been exactly the same as that of a Khrushchev supporter, since the names of his favourites would also have been on the list. He could, it is true, have crossed out Khrushchev's name, and it is possible that a handful of people did so. This, however, would have meant going against the wishes of Suslov and Kozlov themselves, since they too had ratified the list. In any case, the average delegate to the Twenty-second Congress was definitely no anarchist in the making.

Everything in fact went according to plan, since P. N. Demichev, the chairman of the Accounts Committee who gave the result of the vote on the morning of October 31, announced that 'all the comrades registered on the lists of candidates for the secret ballot had been elected to the central organs of the Party'.[1] The new Central Committee comprised 175 full members and 155 alternates, and the Auditing Committee 65 members. All the members of the outgoing Presidium were full members of the Central Committee – which incidentally left open the question which members of the supreme body would be affected by the rule of replacement of one-fourth. The membership of the Central Committee, too, had been substantially enlarged as compared to 1956. It consisted of an additional 42 voting members and 33 alternates.

It would be both unnecessary and hazardous to attempt a political analysis of its make-up. It is true, of course, that while the preceding Central Committee had saved Khrushchev in 1957, this new one was to oust him three years later. But it would be misguided to attempt to discover in its composition reasons for its changed attitude. As we have noted and shall see again, in 1964 as in 1957, the Central Committee only ratified – unanimously or virtually so – the decision proposed to it. When the Committee was elected, nobody was thinking of getting rid of Khrushchev; its composition was negotiated at length during the summer by the members of the collective leadership, and reflected the balance of power as it then was at the top. It also had to mirror the state of the central and regional hierarchy as it had evolved since the Twentieth Congress. The changes were in fact more far-reaching than after the previous elections of 1956, but this meant simply that the purges, in particular those of 1960 and 1961, had been more numerous and thorough than those carried out between 1952 (the Nineteenth Congress) and 1956, and also that the interval which had elapsed since the last elections was almost twice as long. Consequently there were no major surprises in October 1961 : all those eliminated from the principal bodies had been stripped months or years earlier of the functions that would have entitled them to a seat.

It would, in fact, be risky to assert that the new Central Committee was either more or less pro-Khrushchev than the 1956 one. True, the new one was formed at a time when Khrushchev was far stronger, when many of his personal enemies were quitting the scene, including Bulganin, Pervukhin, Saburov and Voroshilov, as well as the group of old regional committee secretaries whom he had recently stripped of their functions. On the other hand, a few Stalinist dignitaries known

---

[1] This Committee, which is separate from the Credentials Committee that checks the delegate's accreditations, also helps to prevent possible surprises. It is the only organ of the Congress whose composition, except for the name of Demichev, its Chairman, was not disclosed. Furthermore, judging from the Congress verbatim records, Demichev did not announce the number of votes received by each person elected, but only listed their names.

to be at odds with the First Secretary were confirmed in their seats despite a marked downgrading of their functions: for instance, I. A. Benediktov, former Minister of Agriculture, currently Ambassador to India, and N. M. Pegov and N. A. Mikhailov, both Party Secretaries under Stalin, who were now relegated to ambassadorial posts in Iran and Indonesia. In addition, several officials closely associated with Khrushchev were eliminated for good, for example, A. I. Kirichenko, N. I. Beliayev, and also General I. A. Serov, the former head of the secret police.

The existence or absence of a Ukrainian background is not a reliable criterion either. However, it is interesting to note that, out of the 175 full members of the Central Committee, about 36 were old Ukrainian hands or people who had worked in that republic while Khrushchev was First Secretary there (1938 to 1950), as against only 20 in 1956. But this must be qualified: the increase comprised chiefly men of the present-day Ukraine, that is those who, although they had probably been connected with Khrushchev in the past, had risen in the hierarchy after his departure and constituted the élite of the republic by 1961. This group, who might be called the 'Podgorny Ukrainians', increased strikingly from 8 to 20. It should be noted, however, that all the republics had more representatives since the Central Committee membership itself had been increased. At the same time, the more interesting category of old Ukrainian hands who had been promoted to responsible posts in Moscow or elsewhere under Khrushchev's auspices rose only from four to five, so that his latest accession of strength did not suffice to balance the departures.[1] Moreover, some of these 'Moscow Ukrain-

---

[1] This group of 'Moscow Ukrainians' was not, in fact, very large. Apart from Brezhnev and, to stretch a point, Polyansky, the following could be placed in that category in October 1961: A. A. Grechko, Marshal of the Soviet Union, Commander of the Warsaw Pact; A. F. Zasiadko, Deputy Chairman of the Council of Ministers (his relationship with Khrushchev had had its ups and downs and around 1955 he apparently was associated with Malenkov); Z. T. Serdyuk, recently appointed First Deputy Chairman of the Party Control Committee; V. N. Titov, head of the 'Party Organs' department of the Central Committee for the Federated Republics; V. M. Churayev, member of the Central Committee Bureau for the RSFSR, apparently in charge of personnel; G. V. Yeniutin, Chairman of the State Control Committee; R. A. Rukenko, Prosecutor-General; V. A. Kucherenko, President of the Academy of Architecture. In addition, there were the holders of certain important peripheral posts: S. V. Chervonenko, Ambassador to Peking; A. M. Rumyantsev, an ideologist who spent the longest stretch of his career in Kharkov and was currently Chief Editor of the international journal *Problems of Peace and Socialism*; A. P. Kirilenko, First Secretary of the Sverdlovsk Oblast Committee; I. Kh. Yunak, First Secretary of the Tula Oblast Committee; A. V. Kovalenko, First Secretary of the Belgorod Oblast Committee; and also V. P. Mzhavanadze and Ya. M. Zarobian, Party chiefs respectively in Georgia and Armenia, who, while remaining nationals of their republics, had also served in Khrushchev's Ukraine.

All these men were elected to full membership of the Central Committee in 1961,

ians', including Brezhnev and Polyansky, were beginning to stand on their own feet. When all is said and done, no Presidium contained as many Ukrainians as the one that evicted Khrushchev in October 1964.

A few statistical data are of interest as illustrating certain constant features of Soviet political life.

Out of the 175 voting members of the Central Committee 88, that is, exactly half, were Party *apparatchiki* – whether federal secretaries like Khrushchev or Kozlov, or local secretaries, Party press officials and other 'ideologists'. Another 56, that is, one-third, were dignitaries in the state apparatus – ministers, ambassadors or planning experts; 14 were military men, all marshals and generals. The remainder – scientists, writers, factory managers – were no more than a handful. If one adds to the above figures those for the alternate members of the Central Committee and the Auditing Commission (395 persons in all), one reaches a similar conclusion: all these bodies comprised the political élite of Soviet society, and primarily those who bore the title of Secretary.

Classification by seniority also leads to interesting conclusions. Listing the members of the 1961 'élite' according to whether they figured in the principal bodies as constituted at previous Congresses (1956, 1952 and 1939), one obtains the following result: (see table on page 192).

The turnover was thus particularly high: out of approximately 400 members of this élite, close to 60 per cent were joining its ranks for the first time. The proportion is, however, less marked in the uppermost ranks of the hierarchy: out of the voting members of the Central Committee, the newcomers remained in a minority. Their 66 colleagues of 1956 vintage represented half those elected at the previous congress

---

but many of them had been members since 1956 or even 1952. Moreover, a few of them had been downgraded in recent months, for instance V. A. Kucherenko and V. M. Churayev. Lastly, as noted in Zasyadko's case, they did not by any means always act as loyal clients of Khrushchev. This also applies to A. M. Rumyantsev, whose rise in the central apparatus dates back to 1952 and who, after the First Secretary's downfall, again stepped into a more important post. The picture therefore was varied.

Two promotions due to Khrushchev's direct personal patronage were those of his son-in-law, A. I. Adzhubey, Chief Editor of *Izvestia*, who was elected full member of the Central Committee and thus became the youngest member of that body (he joined the Party only in 1954); and G. T. Shuysky, who apparently was the director of Khrushchev's executive office throughout his reign. Shuysky had been an editor of the journal of the Ukrainian Komsomol, had gone into the First Secretary's service in that republic in 1941 and followed him to Moscow in 1950. Under the title of 'official in charge of the Central Committee apparatus', he was in 1961 elected member of the Party Auditing Commission. This was not much, considering that Stalin had had his private secretary, Poskrebyshev, appointed full member of the Central Committee. Needless to say, Shuysky completely dropped from sight at the same time as his master, in October 1964.

	1961	1956			1952			1939			Completely New
		C.C.	Alt.	Audit.	C.C.	Alt.	Audit.	C.C.	Alt.	Audit.	
Members of C.C. ..	175	66	27	5	40	19	4	9	4	1	74
Altern. C.C. ..	155	3	31	7	1	14	4	3	1	—	113
Auditing Comm.	65	—	1	19	1	1	5	—	1	1	45
Total ..	395	69	59	31	42	34	13	12	6	2	
			159			89			20		232

(133). Of these 66, no fewer than 40 dated from 1952, thus constituting the hard core that had been running the country all along regardless of the ups and downs of destalinization.[1]

Furthermore, almost all the top Party leaders belonged to that core. Out of the eleven Presidium members elected by the 1961 Congress all but one, D. S. Polyansky, had been in high positions in 1952, when most of them were already voting members of the Central Committee (only Podgorny was then in the Auditing Committee). Many dated from before the war: Khrushchev, Shvernik, Mikoyan and Kosygin were members of the 1939 Central Committee, while Suslov was a member of the Auditing Commission elected that year. This should not cause undue surprise: careers are slow in the Party, and after the purges of the thirties it took about twenty years' service in the 'apparatus' before a man had any chance of rising to the top.

This continuity in the supreme leadership accounts for certain important features. Apart even from Khrushchev himself, whose motives we have examined, the task of destalinization was clearly not in the best possible hands. The 'hard core' could be counted on to obstruct it, not only because some of its members were implicated in the 'excesses' of the defunct dictator, but because any break with the past was likely to jeopardize the continuance of their careers. The principle of co-optation that governs recruitment to any high office was naturally the trump card. Used to its fullest extent it can operate in a highly restrictive manner, to prevent the entry of new recruits and enable the leaders to sit tight. This is what happened when the new Presidium was formed at the Twenty-second Congress.

[1] It should be stated at the outset that the Twenty-third Congress as well hardly touched this 'hard core'. Its membership had dwindled to 37 as some of the original members had died in the meantime, and it lost 4 more of its members at the April 1966 elections (Khrushchev, N. A. Mukhitdinov, G. A. Denisov and I. K. Zhegalin), but 3 veterans of 1952 made their comeback at the same time. They were Voroshilov, N. K. Baybakov and M. V. Zimianin. Therefore, 36 of the fully fledged members of the 1966 Central Committee were at the same post in 1952.

THE CO-OPTATION HURDLE

There must have been interesting discussions when the Presidium members came to decide who should be sacrificed under the new rule of replacement of one-fourth of their membership. Since there were fourteen of them, four had to leave. In fact, most of the victims had been branded some time earlier and the new rule may have been devised on their account in the first place. As noted previously, A. B. Aristov, N. G. Ignatov and Ye. A. Furtseva had been stripped of their posts in the Secretariat in May 1960 and demoted to new ones that no longer entitled them to a seat in the Presidium. Only Ignatov, who was a Deputy Prime Minister responsible for agriculture, still qualified as a member (Polyansky was later in a similar situation for years).

The removal of N. A. Mukhitdinov, on the other hand, was unexpected. He lost both his seat in the Presidium and his rank of Party Secretary – two posts he had occupied since 1957 – and, despite his membership in the Central Committee, found himself relegated to the humble functions of Vice-President of Soviet co-operatives. The sudden demotion suggests punishment for some mistake, but there are no indications of its nature. The only clue may be afforded by the lukewarm tone of his Congress speech on the 'rapprochement among nationalities', a subject which, apparently, was his speciality in the Secretariat. According to people who knew him, he was in fact an unassuming figure who had always played a lowly role in the leadership; besides, his Uzbek nationality foreshadowed no great future. His and Furtseva's departure meant nevertheless that the Presidium was losing two of its younger members. The only man who entered the inner circle was of greater stature. He was G. I. Voronov (an alternate since January 1961), who could boast as much seniority as Kozlov and Podgorny and, like everybody else concerned, had served in the Central Committee since 1952. The 'replacement', incidentally, had the effect of raising the average age of the Presidium membership from 59 to 60.

A few minor changes occurred among the Presidium alternates: in addition to P. N. Pospelov and Ya. N. Kalnberzin, who had previously been demoted, two Ukrainians were removed. They were D. S. Korochenko, the head of the Ukrainian state and a former close associate of Khrushchev's (he was, however, elderly), and A. P. Kirilenko, the First Secretary of the Sverdlovsk Oblast Committee, who was also very close to Khrushchev. Kirilenko, as we shall see, made a striking comeback six months later. M. G. Pervukhin of the former 'anti-party group' was also ousted, almost four years after his 'crime', which did not prevent him from remaining Ambassador to East

Germany. As against these five departures, only two men were promoted to alternate membership of the Presidium: Rashidov, the head of the Party in Uzbekistan, and V. V. Shcherbitsky, the Chairman of the Ukrainian Government.

It could scarcely be claimed truthfully that one-fourth of the Presidium had changed as the new statutes required. Four voting members had left, but they had not been replaced and the Presidium had merely been reduced from fourteen to ten members. The hard core remained solidly entrenched, all the senior members in particular. The principle of co-optation had shown its restrictive effects and reaffirmed the continuity of the leadership. However, it is harder still to suppose that the proceedings were to Khrushchev's liking, for the following reasons.

1 The four departures were certainly not those he most wished for. Furtseva was not only a client who owed her career to him, but a devoted follower and a reliable voter on all controversial issues in the Presidium. Ignatov, as we saw, had also been a loyal ally before and after 1957, and his speech at the Twenty-second Congress itself – except for the reference to heavy industry – had been just what the First Secretary wished to hear. Indications regarding Aristov and Mukhitdinov are less clear, although the former's loyalty had been amply demonstrated at least until 1959, and the latter's minor role also bespoke compliance. Why had they been removed instead of Suslov, Kosygin or Mikoyan, for instance, who, as we know, disagreed with the First Secretary on various occasions?

2 Even supposing that Khrushchev resigned himself to the departure of these four, and that Voronov, despite his neutrality on Stalinism, found favour in the First Secretary's eyes for other reasons, it must have been painful for him to receive so little satisfaction. For almost a year, Khrushchev had been calling repeatedly for a purge and for the infusion of young blood. He had succeeded in bringing about a wide reshuffle in the regional hierarchy, in introducing a few reliable Ukrainians (V. N. Titov, Z. T. Serdyuk) into the Central Committee apparatus, in replacing half of the membership of the Central Committee, and, as will be shown presently, even in reforming the Secretariat. But he was helpless when it came to the Presidium, the summit of the hierarchy, and source of all decisions. While everything was in a flux around these eleven men, or rather the six or seven who held the keys to power, including that of Khrushchev himself, they remained in their posts more firmly than ever. Was it for this – for the entry of a single man, Voronov – that the Party chief had gone to all that trouble? Clearly not. Before him, Stalin had demonstrated that problems arise first at the top and that that is where the first blow must be aimed: the rank and file can come later. Khrushchev, lacking his predecessor's police

apparatus, had inverted the order, but when he struck at the lower echelons he had the top in mind. Since he could not summarily evict his adversaries from the supreme body, he tried at least to double its membership by bringing in his own men, of whom there was no shortage. But even there he ran into the hurdle of co-optation.

All through the ensuing years he laboured to remedy the situation by eliminating his adversaries or bringing in new blood, or both. To the very end of his reign the results were negligible. During the five years of his decline, from 1960 to 1964, the Presidium remained by far the stablest of all Soviet political institutions. And it was precisely because it was stable that Khrushchev's power dwindled.

THE YOUNG MEN

The marked changes in the Party Secretariat as compared to the Presidium should be viewed against the background of this impasse. Evidently in the Secretariat Khrushchev had a freer hand, probably because he was the *First* Secretary, hence the nominal chief of the institution, whereas the Presidium, despite what Ilyichev and a few others might say, had no head. It is hard to tell how the co-optation rules affected Khrushchev's prerogatives in regard to the Secretariat. Probably the candidates, like those for any other major post, were discussed by the Presidium, but the First Secretary's voice was dominant if not decisive. As a result Khrushchev was able to do for the Secretariat what he would clearly have liked to do in the Presidium. Nobody, it is true, was dismissed except Mukhitdinov, and all the old members, Suslov, Kozlov and Kuusinen, were untouchable because of their membership of the Presidium. But five new Secretaries were brought in, five 'young' ones not merely in age but chiefly in the sense that mattered to Khrushchev, that is, new to the top hierarchy and hence more malleable. All of them but one – B. N. Ponomarev, who apparently had ties with Suslov – were at the time close to the First Secretary, and some of them were also ready to help him in his struggle against the rest of the Presidium. Another interesting fact is that all except Shelepin became Secretaries without relinquishing the posts they already held in the Party apparatus – such as heads of departments in the Central Committee or Secretariat or Urban Committees in Moscow and Leningrad. It looked as if the status of each of these officials was being enhanced *vis-à-vis* the other Secretaries who had hitherto supervised their work. Although these new men did not sit in the Party Presidium they appeared, within the Secretariat at any rate, as the equals of Kozlov, Suslov and the others.

This must certainly have given the latter food for thought about the future.

The five 'young men' were I. V. Spiridonov, P. N. Demichev, A. N. Shelepin, L. F. Ilyichev and B. N. Ponomarev. The case of Spiridonov does not call for close analysis, since his stay in a higher post was short-lived and his violent anti-Stalinist position has already been noted (in particular his leading role in the matter of the Red Square mausoleum, his accusations against Malenkov and, back in 1959, his attempt to implicate Saburov and Pervukhin with the 'anti-party group'). He was so consistently outspoken on those issues that at times he appeared keener on destalinization than Khrushchev himself and may even have disagreed with the First Secretary about it. His responsibilities in Leningrad also suggest association with Kozlov, whose deputy he had been for many years before succeeding him. Kozlov, too, after the 1957 crisis, was one of the fiercest accusers of the 'anti-party group' (Kozlov was still very firm on this issue at the Twenty-second Congress, but Spiridonov went much further). In any event, at the time under discussion Spiridonov apparently was ready to do Khrushchev's bidding even when this involved a threat to the members of the collective leadership. His removal in April 1962 can probably be traced to this excess of zeal. The sad fate of previous anti-Stalinists speaks for itself.

The other new Secretaries fared better. P. N. Demichev, like many others, managed to change ground in time to reap the benefits of Khrushchev's downfall in 1964 – even though in 1961 he was the typical protégé whose entire career had unfolded under the auspices if not the direct patronage of the First Secretary. It is true that Demichev had only started out in 1950 and had no Ukrainian background. He was only 32 when he entered the 'apparatus' in that year (the Moscow Oblast Committee, of which Khrushchev had just become the head). He was later reported to be 'in the apparatus of the Central Committee' at an unspecified date between 1950 and 1956; everything suggests that the transfer occurred after Stalin's death, just when Khrushchev was 'concentrating' upon his tasks of Central Committee Secretary. Demichev received another interesting assignment in 1958 and became the executive aide (*upravlyayushchy dyelami*) of the Council of Ministers of the USSR when Khrushchev became Prime Minister. The exact nature of this job is not known (it is probably administrative rather than political) but clearly the post is always occupied by a man trusted by the Head of Government. The first thing Kosygin did when he took Khrushchev's place in October 1964 was to replace the then executive aide, G. S. Stepanov, by M. S. Smirtiukov.

Demichev, in March 1959, had been promoted from this post to head of the Moscow Oblast Committee, replacing I. V. Kapitonov, whom Kirichenko had just dismissed. This was a signal promotion for a man of 40 who was not even a member of the Central Committee. In all likelihood Kirichenko helped in this, and probably Khrushchev did so as well. Demichev's transfer from the Moscow Oblast Committee to the Urban Committee in 1960 was of no personal significance for him, since the Urban Committee itself had just been upgraded over the Oblast Committee. He was serving on the Urban Committee when he was appointed Secretary. As in Spiridonov's case, this was a return to an intermittent Stalinist tradition whereby the Party chiefs for the two largest cities in the country were entitled automatically to a seat in the Secretariat. Demichev's rise stopped there, but he retained the seat.

One more remark: at the Twenty-second Congress, as already noted, the large-scale attack against Stalinism, the 'anti-party group' and its crimes was not launched by Demichev, the first speaker, but by Podgorny, Mazurov and Spiridonov. This indicates that Demichev had become slightly cooler towards his patron and protector. At any rate, he had not been chosen for, nor had he sought, the role of reconnaissance man for the First Secretary's personal battles. After events took the turn that has been described, he duly spoke for a second time at the end of the Congress to approve Stalin's eviction from the Mausoleum; he also recalled in stern words the repressions and crimes of the past, implicated Stalin and Malenkov in the Leningrad affair, and called for the expulsion of the three leaders of the 'anti-party group'.

SHELEPIN

A. N. Shelepin and Demichev were the same age, 43 in 1961, but similarities stopped there. Demichev's career was indeed of recent vintage, but Shelepin, despite his youth, had been in the Stalinist apparatus for a long time, almost as long as Kozlov and other much older men. During the war, for instance, when Demichev was in the services like everyone else, Shelepin was too valuable to be sent to the front. (Even in the Finnish war he was already serving as a political commissar.) In the komsomol apparatus in Moscow he did so well that within a few months he was promoted to instructor, then department head, then secretary and finally in 1943 Secretary of the Komsomol Central Committee, after which he became Second Secretary. He held the latter post for almost ten years under N. A. Mikhailov, the First Secretary, whom he succeeded in 1952. Thus, in the last year of Stalin's reign, Shelepin was already a major figure in the régime, responsible for the whole youth movement, certainly a more important post than heading a provincial Oblast Committee, and in that capacity he was already a full Central Committee member.

Under the circumstances his successive promotions under Khrushchev suggest an alliance carefully cultivated by him rather than a relation of patronage. This does not detract from their importance, for Shelepin, by some miraculous gift, seemed to attract assignments to key posts. In 1958 he left the komsomol to become head of the Central Committee department dealing with Party organs. A few months later he took over the direction of the secret police or KGB, then vacant owing to General I. A. Serov's removal. He remained in this post for three years, during which he apparently managed to allay the fears of the Party leaders over possible encroachment on their jurisdiction by the police. Assuredly it was the kind of post that enabled a man to play his own game to some extent, and there were repercussions of this in the diplomatic sphere.[1] These, however, were less numerous than under his predecessor, and during his tenure the slogan 'the police under Party control' was a reality. In 1961 Shelepin managed to please not only Khrushchev but everybody else as well. His promotion to the Secretariat was even more spectacular than for the others since, as mentioned, he was the only official for whom a new post was created.[2]

A question arises as to his role at the Twenty-second Congress: of all the speakers, except perhaps Shvernik and Khrushchev himself, Shelepin was the most scathing accuser, the author of the most dramatic disclosures about the crimes of Stalin and the 'anti-party group', each of whom in turn he arraigned for bloody misdeeds (including Voroshilov, whom even Shvernik had spared). The tone may be judged from his conclusion: 'How can these people sleep in peace? They must be haunted by nightmares, they must hear the sobs and curses of the mothers, wives and children of innocent comrades done to death.' (*Twenty-second Congress* vol 2 p 405). We have already noticed that misfortune generally befell the authors of reminiscences such as these: for anybody but the Presidium untouchables, it was risky to take that line or to be too ruthless with the 'anti-party group'. Why then did

[1] Shelepin's hand can be detected particularly in the Russell A. Langelle affair which broke out in the autumn of 1959 in the very midst of the Camp David euphoria, with the arrest and expulsion of an American Embassy employee in Moscow. The calls for vigilance then sounded in the press were so out of keeping with the diplomatic atmosphere of the moment that the timing cannot be regarded as accidental.
[2] Shelepin's jurisdiction within the Secretariat seems to have been extensive: after being replaced at the head of the KGB at the end of the Congress, and until he was appointed to head the Party–State Control Committee a year later, he was dealing with transportation, justice, para-military problems (which suggests that he was still supervising the 'administrative organs', that is, the police) and commerce as well, while also receiving some foreign communist delegations and heading a party delegation to Hungary.

Shelepin later escape Spiridonov's fate? Why instead was he promoted just after Khrushchev fell, overcoming the co-optation difficulties? Why, above all, did such a skilled politician assume such a daring stance in 1961?

The 1964 promotion is, of course, a special matter to be discussed later, but some remarks may be made on the other points. First, it cannot be excluded that Shelepin, as chief of the KGB, was ordered by Khrushchev to produce at the Congress a few of his files on Molotov and his associates. This was in line with his job, just as it was for Shvernik or Serdyuk, who were also in charge of personal matters involving the 'comrades'. Secondly if, as is likely, Shelepin did this of his own free will, this was not necessarily a bad political calculation at the time. In the Presidium as it existed before the Congress and during the first stage of the debates, the majority did favour public denunciation of the Stalinist crimes. Shelepin, though well informed, might not have known that the new Presidium would be much more cautious on the issue (it took over only on the last day of the Congress and, while some expulsions had been decided long before, other changes were probably the outcome of last-minute decisions). Thirdly, the dramatic tone of his speech did not exclude certain nuances. As already mentioned, he was vague on the expulsion issue and only spoke of 'gravest responsibilities'. He was the only speaker who made a suggestion that satisfied everybody and was adopted in the end, namely, to refer the problem of 'sanctions' to Shvernik's Control Committee. Moreover, at no time did he implicate Pervukhin and Saburov (any more than he had at the 1959 Twenty-first Congress). Apparently he did not endorse the 'guilt by association' policy, and on this point he was close to Suslov. Finally, he deemed it useful to warn his comrades against the anti-Soviet agitation that the destalinization drive was arousing in the Western press, thus enabling the latter to 'distract world public opinion from what is important, decisive and fundamental in the work of our Congress – the grandiose programme of our Party'. This was an odd warning, coming precisely from the man who had spoken of practically nothing but crimes, blood and tears. But it was calculated to reassure those who wished to revert as soon as possible to the safe points of the official agenda – the programme and the statutes.

Thus Shelepin had already taken some steps to appease the adversaries of Khrushchev's line that he was upholding so strongly. Needless to say, when the wind shifted, he was wise enough to trim his sails. No doubt it was difficult for him to erase the memory of his speech, but he never mentioned the issue again.

Anyway, neither that speech nor his earlier ones can be taken as a key to his deepest convictions, since judicious opportunism is of course the indispensable requisite for a successful political career. In this respect his career is a model one, and Shelepin's promotion in 1961 rightly caught the attention of Western opinion. He held better cards than any of the other 'young men' who reached the top. In spite of his age he had Party seniority and was part of the Stalinist 'hard core': he was among the forty Central Committee members of 1956 who were still seated in 1961, and was thus a reassuring figure for the advocates of 'continuity in leadership'. He had wasted no time in provincial posts and was in constant touch with the men in the central leadership and the nerve centres of power. As the head of the komsomol he was a former associate and leader of most people who then or later occupied key posts in the régime. He had already drawn freely upon this reserve of support.[1] The Party organs, the police and the 'Party–state Control Committee', of which he became the head in 1962, were important and at the same time relatively secure sectors. A man in a post of that kind could watch and intervene in other parts of the apparatus without being blamed, as were so many regional heads, for economic or other failures. As the chief of the Committee, Shelepin for many years was the one man in the country besides Khrushchev who had a foothold both in the Party and the state apparatus, and his transfer to the KGB helped him to make useful contacts with the military. For all these reasons, Shelepin was very well placed in the struggle for power, barring mishaps and reserves which, as will be shown, are always possible.

AN AMBITIOUS IDEOLOGIST

L. F. Ilyichev was also a promising candidate eager to better his chances, but if Khrushchev were ousted he was almost sure to suffer. Unlike Shelepin, who was supporting the First Secretary while also reinsuring with the collective leadership as much as he could, Ilyichev backed Khrushchev *against* the collective leadership and particularly against Suslov. He also tried to force his way into the Presidium too soon. This was tackling too formidable an adversary.

[1] The following are examples of interesting connections with Shelepin: V. E. Semichastny, komsomol Secretary from 1950 to 1958, who in 1958 succeeded Shelepin at the head of that organization and in 1961 did so as head of the KGB. V. S. Tikunov, an official of the komsomol central apparatus during the war, then a deputy of Shelepin at the head of the KGB from 1959 to 1961, and finally Minister of the Interior for the RSFSR; A. N. Aksionov, komsomol Secretary until 1959, then appointed Minister of the Interior in Byelorussia; V. I. Zaluzhny, deputy of Shelepin at the head of the komsomol until 1958, and also after 1962 at the head of the Control Committee.

Ilyichev's case is a classic example of an alliance made with ulterior motives: in the beginning he did not appear as an eager Khrushchev supporter but rather as a former Stalinist paying for past mistakes. For years he had been Chief Editor of *Pravda* and *Izvestia* and assistant head of Agitprop (in 1948–1949), and after Stalin's death he was given the politically minor post of head of the press department of the Foreign Ministry. He was kept there for five years, which enabled him to show his zeal in supporting Khrushchev during the latter's trips abroad. Even when he was put in charge of Agitprop in May 1958, his stature grew only as a reflection of Khrushchev's personal power. Khrushchev kept Ilyichev at his side as a member of his 'press group' during all the well publicized trips of 1959, ranging from Camp David to Djakarta and from Paris to Bucharest. It was in that capacity that, along with the rest of the 'court' – Adzhubey, Satyukov, Zhukov, Troyanovsky and others – Ilyichev did his share to enrich Russian culture by using the tours as material for, *inter alia*, *Face to Face with America*, awarded the Lenin Prize for literature in 1960.

It was only in 1961 that Ilyichev's standing improved in the political apparatus – in the Central Committee – and that he emerged as a leader of special weight in ideological affairs. His promotion to Party Secretary at the Twenty-second Congress was decisive in this respect. Since the Twentieth Congress he had held only a minor post in the Party Auditing Commission, whereas in 1961 he rose to the very top of the Party executive. He took advantage of this to expand the activities of his department (which a year later assumed the better sounding title of 'Ideological Service'), and finally won a quasi-monopoly in that area. One of the victims of this encroachment was Suslov, who in the former Secretariat was evidently in charge of these matters. There is no doubt that Ilyichev fully intended to squeeze in next to Suslov, short of dislodging him from the Central Committee and the Presidium. Khrushchev, too, probably used Ilyichev to this end, at least from 1961 onwards.

Ilyichev's rivalry with Suslov seems well established, judging from his reference to the Voznesensky case at the Twenty-second Congress, already mentioned in passing. The brilliant economist Voznesensky was the main victim of the so-called Leningrad affair. He had been a member of the Politburo and Deputy Chairman of the Council of Ministers, but was stripped of all his functions in 1949 and arrested. All his works were withdrawn from circulation, in particular his book, *The USSR War Economy during the Great Patriotic War*, which had received a Stalin Prize in 1948. Oddly enough, neither the book nor the author was criticized publicly for over two years. The first official who embarked on the task, as far as this writer is aware, was Suslov. In an article signed by him in *Pravda* of December 24 1952 the book was dubbed 'anti-Marxist' and all those who, following the general line, had four years earlier given it enthusiastic reviews were sternly reprimanded.[1] In 1961 the article was less than ten years old and must have been fresh in many memories. And Ilyichev commented upon the matter at length. He did not mention Suslov, to be sure, and pretended to ascribe the responsibility to Stalin alone. But as he deplored the withdrawal from circulation of Voznesensky's book because it was supposed to be 'anti-Marxist and anti-scientific', he used the very words Suslov had uttered in 1952. Since there had been no other attacks, the implication was clear. There were, however, no other references to this highly delicate question either during the Congress or later, except for an indirect allusion by P. A. Satyukov.[2] It was broached again only in December 1963, when the fiftieth anniversary of Voznesensky's birth was commemorated posthumously.

---

[1] In his article on the Voznesensky affair, Suslov was particularly sharp with P. N. Fedoseyev, who had been director of the Party's theoretical journal *Bolshevik* (now called *Kommunist*) and was relieved of his post in 1949 for having praised Voznesensky's book to the skies. At the same period the chief of the Agitprop service of the Central Committee, who was none other than D. T. Shepilov, was reproached for 'not having been up to his task as regards control of the journal *Bolshevik*' and having promoted the dissemination of Voznesensky's book. In making these disclosures, Suslov also attacked two renowned economists, L. M. Gatovsky and G. M. Sorokin. Finally, he saw fit to name the members of the editorial board of *Bolshevik* after its 1949 reorganization, although there had been other changes since. Fedoseyev had been replaced by S. M. Abalin and five other members of the board had been replaced; however, a few of the earlier ones had remained, including L. F. Ilyichev and P. N. Pospelov.

Thus the affair had implicated or at least affected most of the nation's ideologists and Suslov's article seemed to foreshadow a sterner purge among them. Several analysts have established, correctly it would seem, a connection between this belated attack and the dictator's plot which was also held in reserve and broke out a few days later. Stalin's death put an end to both, but the implications of the reopening of the case in 1961 were only the greater. After suffering disgrace in varying degrees, all those concerned were still alive and holding respectable posts. Fedoseyev was the director of the Institute of Philosophy of the Academy of Sciences and was elected full member of the Central Committee by the Congress; Gatovsky was Chief Editor of the journal *Problems of Economics*; Sorokin was his associate and it was he who, in *Pravda* of December 1 1963, commemorated Voznesensky's anniversary. Only Shepilov was in a difficult position for having joined the 'anti-party group' in 1957.

[2] Speaking about the Voznesensky case Satyukov said: 'The stand taken by eminent personalities of our Party on various problems of the building of the economy has been discussed here and you know what repressive measures were taken against them by Stalin.' (Twenty-second Congress vol 2 p 350). Altogether, the speech of *Pravda's* Chief Editor seems very close to Ilyichev's. They were the only two people who openly accused Stalin of dictatorship in theoretical and ideological matters. Satyukov attacked Molotov for the same reasons and almost in the same words as Ilyichev and even quoted Ilyichev to document his criticism of Shepilov.

The Suslov–Ilyichev rivalry, which erupted again just after the Congress, ended only in 1964, when Suslov won. For the time being it is enough to note that Ilyichev had chosen the dangerous path of opposing one of the most powerful members of the collective leadership. Since he naturally needed the backing of the supreme chief if he was to gain the upper hand, he did not hesitate to support Khrushchev's efforts to rise above his colleagues. As noted previously, Ilyichev was one of the handful of speakers at the Congress who described the First Secretary as being 'at the head of the Presidium'. Coming from such a skilled politician the phrasing was certainly no accident. Moreover, he used it again several times, even as late as in June 1964, a few months before Khrushchev's head rolled (see *Kommunist* No 11 1964). His repeated appeals for the safeguard of the 'leader's authority' should be interpreted in the same way. He said, for instance: 'It would be incorrect and harmful to confuse the authority of our leaders with the cult of personality.' This meant that praise and whatever else enhanced Khrushchev's prestige and authority was not a bad thing in itself.

This, again, was a tactful alliance dictated by self-interest and had its limits (as noted, Ilyichev was silent on the 'crimes' issue; paradoxically, he was tougher as regards sanctions for the 'anti-party group' and even mentioned the possibility of expulsion). As his stature grew, so did his pretensions. His mistake, apparently, was over-estimating Khrushchev's strength *vis-à-vis* the rest of the Presidium. He probably assumed that the First Secretary could always carry off an operation of the 1957 type and correct an unfavourable situation at the top by appealing to the Central Committee or other forces. Had this been the case, Ilyichev would without fail have entered the Presidium at the expense of an 'anti-party' Suslov. In all fairness, Ilyichev was not the only one who thus miscalculated.

The role of B. N. Ponomarev, another ideologist, was less important. The International Department of the Central Committee which he had headed since 1955, and which dealt with the problems of relations with fraternal parties in countries where they were not in power, could not compare with the mighty organizations run by the other functionaries promoted at this time. It is true that Ponomarev was also the official historian and chief editor of a new Party history. But for years before and after 1961 his task was to be a self-effacing witness at countless meetings with foreign delegations at which the main speaker was generally Suslov. Ponomarev's promotion to Secretary, unlike Ilyichev's, was never accompanied by the slightest sign that he might possibly eclipse his patron and protector. The fact that he probably did enjoy Suslov's protection is attested by an interesting 'Letter from Moscow', whose other details stand up under scrutiny, published in a Russian émigré newspaper in Paris in December 1964.[1] There is also other evidence. Ponomarev was not a Khrushchev man by career or outlook, and it will be shown later that his historical work was not always calculated to suit the First Secretary's policy. At the Twenty-second Congress, his speech was singularly close to Suslov's, not only because they covered roughly the same ground. True, he went further than Suslov by calling for the expulsion of the 'anti-party group' after referring, without details, to 'the shameful and illegal acts . . . that comrade Shvernik spoke of' (the tone of the debate had risen after Shvernik's indictment and the demands for expulsion were more frequent). Ponomarev justified his appeal in the following curious terms: 'The members of the anti-party group must answer . . . for their anti-party actions committed in the period of the cult of personality as well as after the Twentieth Congress.' As is known, the period of the 'cult of personality' had ended in 1953 and the Twentieth Congress had been held in 1956. Thus he seemed to imply that between those years the slate was clean. Suslov, as noted, was systematically expounding this thesis and he probably had good reasons for it. Ponomarev was the only one who backed him on this point.

Suslov's victory in 1964 did not bring Ponomarev any of the inconveniences suffered by Ilyichev. He could have done better for himself, of course, but the diplomatic sector of the Central Committee is evidently a poor starting point for climbing to the summit. What he lacked mainly was stature and ambition.

Ponomarev's promotion showed that Suslov was still strong. But the promotions of Demichev, Shelepin. Spiridonov and Ilyichev more than compensated for Ponomarev's. Evidently these were the men that Khrushchev would have liked to push into the Presidium, then or later, and they were good recruits. Short of reconstructing the deliberative body as he wanted to, he had an executive body, the Secretariat, whose composition was more to his taste and where those likely to hamper him were now in a minority. This was about the only success of which he could boast.

---

[1] See *Russkaya Mysl* (Russian Thought) of December 3 1964. The details given in the (naturally unsigned) article indicate that it could have been written only by a person within the Central Committee machine. The author states that it is thanks to Suslov's patronage that Ponomarev joined the Central Committee in 1948, after having conducted a wide purge within the Sovinformburo over which he had been presiding since 1946. It also contains many revelations about the role of Suslov, who is depicted as the man chiefly responsible for Khrushchev's downfall. The document is vulgar in style, but the dates and other verifiable details tally with existing information.

THE BALANCE SHEET

It may seem paradoxical to have stressed the internal struggle for power in describing a Congress which the entire world communist press and a sizable sector of the free press reported as a striking display of unity, a triumph for Khrushchev and so forth. But the fanfare accompanying conclaves of this kind tends to divert attention from actual controversies. In all fairness too, many things were far from being as clear at the time as they are now. In order to grasp the real problems one must strip the most eloquent proclamations of their ritual phrasing, discount the conventional professions of solidarity and unity, and concentrate on the details and nuances that betray the true conflict. The optimism and enthusiasm, even when sincere, should be disregarded because they are secondary.

For example, there has been and still is talk about the Party programme and future communist society. But it is evident that for Khrushchev and those around him it was infinitely more important to settle the problems of the day than to worry about what was going to happen twenty years hence. This is not to say that the struggle for power was the only problem, but it certainly was the main issue of the Congress. Nothing else of any significance was in fact touched on apart from the Albanian and Chinese problem, which was only a form of the struggle for power projected on to the international scene, and the problem of economic priorities, which was deadlocked and not openly debated.

There were real internal problems, of course, and destalinization brought fresh ones, but this was not the first time that the Soviet leaders set them aside to settle their own scores first.

Things were not the same now as in 1960, when differences had last been aired in public. In that case an external incident, the U-2, had precipitated a crisis instigated not by Khrushchev but by his opponents, who had widened the debate, imposed decisions in various areas and reshuffled the top leadership according to their own wishes. This is normal behaviour on the part of an opposition whose means of direct action are limited and which therefore prefers to wait for the leader to suffer a reverse before itself taking the offensive. Khrushchev, on the other hand, was freer in 1961 to pick the time and place for the confrontation. Like a Western Prime Minister who can time elections to suit his own party, he was better placed than anyone else to use the régime's official ceremonies for his own purposes. The Party Congress, with its opportunities for directly influencing the rank and file and for encouraging the worship of his person, provided the ideal setting. Above all, if the *status quo* at the top no longer satisfied him, that, if ever, was the occasion to modify it to his taste thanks to the election of the principal Party organs.

The 'aggressor' in this instance was therefore Khrushchev. The ground he chose – destalinization – was the same as in 1956. Officially, his adversaries were again the same, but his real attack was on the men close at hand who were hemming him in. We know the outcome: destalinization got off to a fairly good start, and after two weeks of congress debates the climate was favourable enough for a decision as dramatic as the transfer of the late dictator's remains from the Mausoleum. But this set off a reaction whose meaning was: 'Enough!' If Khrushchev had counted on producing an atmosphere in which the leadership could be reshuffled without further ado, he had miscalculated. It was probably not in spite of his offensive but because of it that the instinct of self-preservation operated. In the result, the new Presidium turned out to be less eager for destalinization than the previous one. Incidentally, it was new only in the sense that its most turbulent members had left it. All the old-timers were solidly entrenched and only a few younger men, the 'junior' Secretaries, were drawing purposefully close to them. The attempt at purges implied by the demands for the expulsion of the 'anti-party group' from the Party had not yielded the expected results. For various reasons, the large majority of the leaders opposed extreme sanctions against Molotov, Malenkov and Kaganovich.

This meant two things for the future:

1 The problems had not been settled as Khrushchev desired, but on the other hand the decisions had been carried by a narrow margin. On the issues of destalinization and the public denunciation of the crimes of Molotov and his associates, a shift of a vote or two could tilt the scale either way. Moreover, the man in charge was an 'activist' who was bound to try again at the next opportunity. This explains the to-ing and fro-ing on this issue until the end of Khrushchev's reign, and explains why the struggle came to an end when he fell. It will resume only when another leader wants and is able to make a bid for supreme power and uses the slogan of destalinization as a means.

2 At the same time, this premeditated attack on the *status quo* must have shown the collective leadership, or at least its many members who intended to preserve the full prerogatives of the Presidium, which way the wind was blowing. It was clear to them that Khrushchev would no longer be content with the victory, a slim one at that, which he had won in 1957, and that he meant to expand his personal power at their expense. In order to do this he had not even hesitated to question some dogmas which were essential to the continuity of the Stalinist leadership and its hard core. There is little doubt that the Twenty-second Congress

markedly contributed to the stiffening of what was probably not yet an overt opposition but already a powerful resistance conscious of its strength. The offensive of the First Secretary and his henchmen had indeed swollen the ranks of this resistance. Mikoyan himself, hitherto the privileged confidant, had on this occasion, perhaps for the first time, found himself in serious disagreement with Khrushchev. As to the others, Suslov and Kosygin, the experience was most likely to heighten their vigilance. The two rivals for the succession, Brezhnev and Kozlov, would also have to reckon with this. Brezhnev, then in a position of inferiority, believed he had to kowtow to the chief, but Kozlov, now entrenched at the head of the Party as heir presumptive, was growing aware of the scope of the resistance to Khrushchev and learning how best to use it. He and many others grew increasingly cool towards the leader.

4 The Post-Congress Period: Wavering and See-sawing

The Twenty-second Congress had shaken the country's political life so severely that the vibrations did not die away immediately. The following months, until about the spring of 1962, were a troubled period. As was to be expected, the contradictions appeared mainly in the areas in which controversy had erupted at the Congress itself.

The conflicts arose first among the ideologists, whose task it was to disseminate the Party's directives throughout the country and to explain to the masses what had happened at the Congress as regards destalinization. They also had to repress any thoughts of independence that the shock might have awakened in the intelligentsia. The effects among the writers showed only later, but as early as November a well-known economist, Leon Leontyev, dared to write a resounding article in which he questioned 'the fundamental economic laws' formulated by Stalin and sought to rehabilitate some theories which had been in force before 1930 (*Ekonomicheskaya Gazeta*, November 20 1961). He had to be cautioned, which was done without delay, for then as now all the ideologists agreed that it was dangerous to let the debate spread to circles outside the Party. 'We must decisively oppose', said a *Pravda* editorial on December 24, 'the slightest attempts aimed, under guise of eliminating the consequences of the cult of personality, at distorting the essence of the Party's decisions and policy.' For the same reason a drive was launched, to all appearances unanimously, against those who, ignoring the Congress, still insisted on giving Stalin more than his due. For instance, two history professors at the Moscow University, P. B. Zhibarev and M. D. Stuchebnikova, had concocted, early in 1961 it is true, a 'review of the sources of the history of the CPSU' in a tone over-flattering to the former dictator. According to Suslov, the assessment of some of his acts was 'even more laudatory than at the height of the personality cult'. They were criticized for it by everybody including Suslov, Ilyichev, Ponomarev and all the major Party journals.

ILYICHEV ON THE SPOT

One point not settled at the Congress, however, was how to evaluate the activities of the ideologists under Stalin. It had not been decided whether the work done by them was valid and whether theoretical work had progressed at all under the dictator. L. F. Ilyichev, the most daring of the speakers on this point, answered both questions in the negative. Speaking of the period of the cult he had declared:

'A situation was created where *a single man in the Party was entitled to have the last word* on all theoretical questions. . . . It is no accident that *for decades no work of any significance* has been achieved in our country in political economy or history. . . . It is only after the consequences of the cult of personality were overcome that it became possible to do Marxist–Leninist work in the main branches of theory and history.'[1] [Author's italics.]

This drew a scathing reprimand upon Ilyichev. On December 20 and 21 1961 *Pravda* published an immense editorial in two instalments, the second dealing specifically with the activities of ideologists during the 'cult'. After stating that the Party could not have withstood the hardships of the building of socialism and war if it had not 'continuously developed and enriched the theory', it concluded:

'This is why *assertions that during the* period of the cult of personality *the Party achieved nothing* in the field of theory and did not advance theory *are untenable*. Anyone who takes up such a position supports, whether he means to or not, *the pernicious view that one man could,* during that period, *settle all questions pertaining to practice and theory*. This is a gross distortion of reality, a deviation from the Marxist–Leninist theory of the role of the Party and of the people as the decisive force in the building of socialism. To adopt such a point of view is to drift rapidly towards idealist positions' [Author's italics] (*Pravda*, December 21 1961).

The text was not signed, that would have been too much to ask, but pending any information to the contrary it is difficult to attribute it to anyone but Suslov. To start with, it was a way of paying Ilyichev back for his perfidious allusion to the Voznesensky affair. In addition, Suslov was the only man wielding enough authority on the subject to contradict someone who was now a Party Secretary. Moreover, his speech at the Congress, unlike those of Ilyichev and his associate Satyukov, was striking in that it did not contain one word about Stalin's errors on theoretical problems during the period of the 'cult'.

[1] Text of Ilyichev's speech published by *Pravda* on October 26 1961, two days after he delivered it. The verbatim records of the Congress published three months later give a slightly watered-down version. Instead of 'decades' the text reads 'many years', and at the end 'Marxist–Leninist writings' was altered to 'good, useful writings' (*Twenty-second Congress* vol 2 p 182).

It is true that much later, in a report delivered on January 30 1962, Suslov did broach the question in a way that verged on heresy in view of *Pravda's* condemnation. He said:

'Stalin's pretension to exercise a *kind of monopoly* in the development of revolutionary theory, *the right to the last word* which he arrogated to himself in theoretical matters and his tendency to settle theoretical questions by administrative methods seriously *impeded* and *hampered* the development of social sciences. . . .' [Author's italics] (*Pravda*, February 4 1962).

Thus Suslov appeared fairly close to Ilyichev in the first part of his analysis, by admitting that Stalin had enjoyed 'the last word' – obviously a difficult thing to deny. But he departed from Ilyichev's conclusion inasmuch as he declared that this monopoly had only 'hampered' theoretical thought instead of making it completely sterile. This may have reflected a compromise accepted by both sides since, shortly after the *Pravda* attack, Ilyichev had modified his own position. In his report to an ideological conference held on December 25 1961, that is, four days after the *Pravda* editorial, he no longer asserted that the Party had done 'no work'. His strongest wording was: 'Under circumstances where a single man legislated on literally all theoretical and ideological questions . . . creative thought was naturally exposed to great difficulties.'[1]

At all events, the confusion and rivalry among the ideologists were emphasized by their considerable and increasingly similar activities, and also by some new anomalies. The December conference at which Ilyichev played the leading role, and which opened in the presence of Khrushchev and 2,700 officials dealing with ideological matters, ended in a strange manner. An unidentified chairman brought the conference to a close on December 28, although only two speakers had registered for that morning and not one resolution had been adopted. Had Suslov anything to do with this? It was noticed that one of the last major speakers, Satyukov, had attacked a resolution of 1948 condemning the opera *Bogdan Khmelnitsky* and several Soviet musicians, a resolution in which Suslov seems to have been involved at the time as head of Agitprop. For whatever reason, Suslov disappeared from circulation on that day.[2] His absence from the New Year festivities was explained to diplomatic circles as caused by a 'serious illness'. He reappeared on

---

[1] *XXII Syezd KPSS i voprosy ideologicheskoy raboty* (The Twenty-second Congress and Problems of Ideological Work), Moscow 1962, p 14.

[2] Suslov's activity dwindled markedly after the Congress. From December onwards Kuusinen received all foreign communist delegations instead of Suslov, whose speciality this had been.

January 6, when he received a Polish delegation, but this was reported in the press only on the 9th. After that he vanished again until January 30, the opening date of 'his' ideological conference attended by Kozlov and 2,600 professors of social sciences and other theoreticians. His report was published – in part – five days later in *Pravda*, and it took eleven months for a fairly complete text to appear in *XXII syezd KPSS i zadachi kafedr obshchestvennikh nauk*, December 1962 (*The Twenty-second Congress of the CPSU and the tasks of professors of social sciences*).

A week before that conference, yet another ideological conference had met, this time under P. N. Pospelov's chairmanship with V. I. Snastin as rapporteur. The press had reported its opening on January 23 but nothing further was heard of it. Obviously things were not at their best among the ideologists.[1]

WHAT WAS TO BE DONE WITH MOLOTOV?

The ideologists were not the only ones in trouble. At about the same time another matter caused an even greater stir. Once again, it concerned the 'anti-party group'. As noted, there was no majority in the Presidium for their expulsion, although a consensus favoured some unspecified sanction, and this apparently was implemented. According to information gathered by the Yugoslavs at the time, the question was settled in the Presidium in December. There had been no majority for expulsion, let alone for a trial, but, according to the same sources, agreement was reached 'unanimously' to inflict a 'Party reprimand' (*partiyny vygovor*)

---

[1] An even more obscure quarrel broke out among the ideologists. In an anonymous editorial in *Pravda* of November 21 1961 the following sentence appeared, obviously added without regard to the context: 'Those who today are uttering banalities by proclaiming that we must start enriching theory, and who do not notice how fast the evolution of theory is already developing in the Soviet Union in close conjunction with the practice of the building of communism, are laughable and pitiable.' A check reveals that at least four speakers at the Twenty-second Congress had stressed (with varying degrees of insistence) the need for the enrichment of theory: viz., Suslov, Ilyichev, Ponomarev and lastly Khrushchev himself in his report. This is probably why *Kommunist* shortly thereafter (No 18, December 1961) countered in an editorial by quoting the First Secretary: 'We would be betraying the spirit of our doctrine . . . if we did not enrich it with new principles and theoretical deductions.' Nevertheless, the same attack against the 'enrichers' appeared in a reply to the economist Leontyev, already mentioned above, in the journal *Problems of Economics* (No 1 1962). The reply was signed by five economists, but since they carried little political weight their names are not indicative. In any event, they merely repeated the sentence in *Pravda* quoted above. Even today it is impossible to know or even to guess who could have been the hidden instigator of this odd attack.

upon the three leaders of the 'group'. This was not confirmed, but is very likely considering the mood at the Congress. In any case, two facts seem certain:

1 There were no expulsions from the Party. In the autumn of 1962 it was rumoured again that proceedings to that effect had started, but apparently nothing came of it. Only from Suslov's report in February 1964 was it learned incidentally that Molotov and his allies had been 'thrown out of the Party ranks'. It is highly probable that the fact would have been known earlier if the expulsion had occurred in 1961 or 1962.

2 Some of those in authority believed the matter to have been settled for good by this decision of December, and since, after all, a reprimand is not a death sentence, promptly sent the 'anti-party' people back to their former posts. One of them, Molotov, still held the official function of Soviet representative at the International Atomic Energy Commission in Vienna. He had been recalled (unofficially) just after the Twenty-second Congress, obviously pending a decision on his fate. A remarkable succession of moves occurred in this connection.

On the afternoon of Monday, January 8 1962, the Soviet Press Department, which is normally impervious to any requests for information, spontaneously told the assembled Western newspapermen that Molotov was about to resume his duties in Vienna 'and is already there'. The news was spectacular considering all that had been said at the Congress about the man's 'crimes', and it created a sensation abroad. Actually, Molotov was still in Moscow, but on the 9th the same officials announced that he would leave the following Saturday. On the 10th it was announced that no further information was available. Molotov never did leave for Vienna, and it was probably at that moment that he went into peaceful retirement in his apartment in Granovsky Pereulok street near the Kremlin.

In any case, the incident showed the ambiguity of the sanction decided upon in December. To the advocates of clemency, the 'reprimand' was evidently a victory which they intended to consolidate by demonstrating publicly that Molotov had remained at his dignified post in Vienna and that his crimes had been forgiven. To the others, and in particular to Khrushchev, who probably engineered the cancellation of Molotov's departure, a reprimand was better than nothing and was at least ignominious for its victim. Probably to destroy the psychological effect of the 'false news', a decree was passed on January 15 rescinding all decisions under which the names of Molotov, Voroshilov, Kaganovich and Malenkov had earlier been bestowed on Soviet towns, villages and enterprises. (Decree published in *Gazette of the Supreme Soviet of the USSR*, No 3 of January 19 1962.) This decision was purely academic, since all these places, even those named after Voroshilov, had been changing their names as far back as 1957. But even though the issue was no longer of practical importance, the authors of the decree persisted in hammering it home.

Khrushchev also seemed to be having his troubles during that difficult start of the new year. At the New Year's Day reception his behaviour surprised the diplomats. After letting Brezhnev propose the first toast, he read casually a trite text prepared in advance and made none of his usual improvisations and jokes. Finally, he left the gathering as soon as he could, without speaking to a single foreigner. Shortly afterwards he was rumoured to be 'ill', which delayed a long-planned trip to Byelorussia. He left only on the evening of the 9th (the day on which Molotov's departure for Vienna was countermanded). Khrushchev's first speech of the year, delivered on January 12 in Minsk, sounded for the first time a note heard later during his spells of gloom: 'I am myself at the retirement age, and it is highly disagreeable when one finds oneself without an occupation, when one can no longer feel as useful to society as previously. This is the state of mind that is most painful to a man' (*Pravda*, January 13 1962).

Prophetic words to be sure, but which for a man of his temperament probably indicated no more than discouragement. Be that as it may, shortly after this speech, Khrushchev disappeared from the scene for a fortnight, which had not happened for a very long time. The press reported him to be in Kiev on January 28, then in Sochi on February 7. But, even after these brief appearances, a rumour went on circulating in Moscow that an attempt on his life had occurred in Byelorussia.[1] There were two versions, one of them dramatic (a police officer had shot him when Khrushchev reprimanded him for failing to keep order during one of his appearances), the other more moderate (a madman had shouted something at him during a theatre performance in Minsk). While neither can be verified, a very well informed foreign communist made this comment when repeating the second version: 'Some highly-placed people have their reasons for spreading the rumour of an attempt on his life.'

Altogether, things were not going well for Khrushchev. It clearly appeared during that month of January 1962 that the Twenty-second Congress had raised far more problems than those, if any, which it had solved. Destalinization had caused ripples abroad, the attack on the Albanians had backfired instead of bringing either them or the Chinese to heel, while the abandonment of the prospect of a German peace treaty distressed even Ulbricht (this point will be discussed later). The stiffen-

---

[1] The Italian communist daily *L'Unità* reported the rumour of an attempt on Khrushchev's life on February 6 1962.

ing of the domestic opposition, a normal consequence of Khrushchev's offensive at the Twenty-second Congress, had apparently made itself felt before the end of 1961 as regards the issues of Stalinism and the 'anti-party group'. All these signs indicate that the possibility of a violent clash having taken place at this time should not be ruled out.

SWITCH IN AGRICULTURAL POLICY

For a while, apparently, the leadership managed to smother those problems, but another controversy arose immediately. This was on the problem of economic priorities, and it created fresh turmoil. The question had come up a year before, but despite Khrushchev's efforts the *status quo* had endured throughout 1961. This time something really had to be done. Immediately after the Congress Khrushchev threw himself wholeheartedly into a violent drive against grass-growing and fallow-lands which, he said, caused Soviet agriculture to waste millions of hectares of fertile land. The 'inter-tilling' (*propashnaya sistema*) that he advocated or rather demanded in its place was one of intensive cultivation. It was risky, however, to embark upon such a venture without supplying the mineral fertilizers, weed-killers and machines that the farmers badly needed. Khrushchev himself had admitted this in the past and, although more intensive cultivation was an old idea of his, he had acknowledged in a speech on July 11 1954 that it was impossible to think about it as things stood. 'If we insisted on a higher grain yield in the regions already under cultivation', he said, 'by intensifying agriculture and improving management, we would need at least ten years and huge funds for the building of chemical plants to produce the mineral fertilizers. . . . We would need a lot of money and a lot of time.' (*Agricultural Speeches* Vol 1 p 344.) This, however, is just what he did in 1961: for nearly six months after the Twenty-second Congress he went around demanding in and out of season that all agricultural workers should give up the system of fallow-lands and grass-growing, although he did not promise them the slightest help in exchange. He even insulted scientists and agronomists who objected to his schemes.

The strong resistance put up by the agricultural workers had some effect, however. In March 1962 Khrushchev condescended to look into the matter seriously. His report to a special new 'agricultural plenary session' even conveyed the impression that the Presidium had agreed to large investments in agriculture. This is what he said:

'If we merely appeal to people to grow corn and sugar beet or to introduce mechanical milking, but do not organize the production of machines to harvest corn and beetroot, milking machines and other equipment, we shall simply remain babblers. One cannot call for high productivity and cut maize with hatchets' (Plenary session, March 1962, verbatim records, p 83).

Then the First Secretary elaborated upon the disclosures he had made in the autumn of 1960. The supply of equipment to agriculture had fallen instead of rising in the preceding few years. Between 1957 – when, he said, far greater attention had been given to mechanization problems – and 1960, the supply of machines for maize harvesting had fallen from 55,000 to 13,000 and that of motorized cultivators from 208,000 to 79,000. Agricultural machine factories had been reconverted to other types of production; the output of fertilizers had increased only by 2.9 million tons in the preceding three years, whereas the plan provided for an increase of 23 million tons for the current seven-year plan. The fault lay, Khrushchev said, with the 'leading officials of Gosplan and other economic management organs, who regard all the problems of mechanization of agriculture as solved and even think that something may be withdrawn from the agricultural machine industry to be given to other branches of the economy'. For good measure, he blamed the 'Central Committee departments that do not provide effective Party control over the execution of measures decided by the Party . . .'.

This was his conclusion, and not just his personal one:

'The Presidium of the Central Committee considers it urgent to work out a concrete programme for increasing the supply of equipment to agriculture.' Still in the name of the Presidium, he outlined the 'broad features' of the programme, including the building of 'at least three powerful new factories for agricultural machinery'. This, of course, would take time, but must be started 'immediately'.

Such were his words on March 5 1962, at the opening of the plenary session. Exactly four days later at the close of the debate, an unprecedented switch occurred. Taking the floor for the second time, Khrushchev declared:

'The officials in charge of agriculture, and primarily those at the head of Republics and regions, must understand that the measures envisaged for strengthening agriculture do not mean that we shall immediately divert funds away from industry and the reinforcement of the country's defence' (Plenary session of March 1962, verbatim records, p 426).

The remainder of the speech, the tone of which was completely different from the previous one, urged workers in agriculture to be content with what they had:

'The most urgent objective today is to obtain maximum use from the material and equipment. . . . Otherwise one might lull oneself with the hope of receiving extra help, new material. . . . Can we, by relying on the material and the degree of mechanization already reached in the kolkhozes and sovkhozes, raise agricultural production at once and to an important extent? Yes, comrades, it can be done. . . . Let us agree, then, to talk less about the shortage of machines, and to make better and fuller use of the material in the kolkhozes and sovkhozes. As the saying goes, it takes no great brains to shout: Give, give, give!' (Plenary session of March 1962, verbatim records, pp 427–428.)

The switch was so marked that Khrushchev was constrained to explain: 'This does not mean that I am going back in any way on the report. . . . No, the question of increasing aid to agriculture must and will be solved.' But he made only two concessions on that score: he promised an increase in the supplies of tractors and truck trailers, and mentioned the possibility of calling a new plenary session to discuss the chemical industry and fertilizer production. On the second point the promise was for a very distant future. Only towards the end of 1963 was the fertilizer question considered.

The question then was firmly shelved and the plenary session resolution merely requested without further details 'that new investments for agriculture be sought'. They were found a little later in the consumers' pockets. But before this problem is reviewed, the cause of the shift deserves consideration.

Khrushchev had announced in his report of March 5 that the Presidium had agreed to increase appropriations to agriculture. Actually the statement made at about that time by the various members of the leadership in their electoral speeches (part of the Supreme Soviet was then being replaced) were notable for their lack of unanimity. Among advocates of help to agriculture at the plenary session were Podgorny ('The new tasks imperatively demand rapid mechanization of agriculture and extensive financial and technical aid to kolkhozes and sovkhozes'), and Kozlov ('Urban industry can and must considerably increase its aid to agriculture'). In the opposite camp were again Voronov ('industry is the essential base of our economy', coupled with utter silence about agricultural investments); apparently Suslov (who stressed all that had been done for agriculture in the preceding five years and thereby contradicted Khrushchev, according to whom help to agriculture had been cut); and Brezhnev, who was completely silent on the subject. Kosygin maintained his neutrality, pretending to believe it possible to reinforce defence, industry and agriculture all at once. Kuusinen, Mikoyan and Polyansky were vague on the question. It was not till April that the Presidium officially confirmed the old line of priority for heavy industry in the collectively approved report for the commemoration of Lenin's birthday. Significantly, the report was delivered (on April 22) by L. F. Ilyichev, an overt advocate of priority for heavy industry.

'Our Party,' he said '. . . consistently pursues the policy of developing heavy industry as the essential base of the material and technological foundation of communism, of the country's defence and the progressive increase of the people's welfare. Only doctrinaire and revisionist bunglers can oppose heavy industry to the production of consumer goods, or industry to agriculture. The theory of broadened socialist production demands the harmonious and well-proportioned development of all branches of the economy, the leading role being given to heavy industry' (*Pravda*, April 23 1962).

That was the thesis that the Presidium had adopted. It is not very likely, though, that the switch was decided within the Presidium itself within four days, during the March plenary session, since its members had had ample time to discuss and approve the First Secretary's original report. Exceptions do occur, and it seems that in this instance outside forces intervened. Khrushchev himself had named the 'leading officials of Gosplan' (still under V. N. Novikov at the time). His repeated references to the needs of defence in his speech of March 9 were not accidental. The military had obviously made themselves heard, and some agitation on their part was in fact noticeable in the ensuing weeks.

THE MILITARY ASSERT THEMSELVES

Marshal Malinovsky, the Defence Minister, published no less than three major articles during the month of May 1962 (in *Kommunist* No 5, *Pravda* of May 9 and *Krasnaya Zvezda* of May 24). Also on the 24th a book on military strategy came out, edited by Marshal Sokolovsky, former chief of the General Staff, and written by several specialists. The book, like the Minister's articles, stressed one theme: that rockets and atomic armament are only part of a country's defence equipment and that all the other sectors must be strengthened as well. Malinovsky had already said this at the Twenty-second Congress, but the wavering of the political leadership prompted him to make it quite plain in the following words: 'Our military doctrine', he wrote in *Kommunist*, 'is that, however important the role of nuclear armaments and rockets may be, it does not in the least follow that there is no longer any need for other means of armed combat involving mass forces. Victory cannot be secured in modern war without the combined efforts of all types of armed forces, which must therefore be developed as required.'

Malinovsky thereby contradicted the Head of Government, or at least the position Khrushchev had held in 1960 with his favouring of push-button warfare and the territorial militias, which Malinovsky had also approved at the time. The military went even further, and painted the international picture in the blackest colours in order to gain their ends. For instance, President Kennedy had unfortunately declared in an interview given to the American columnist Stewart Alsop that under certain conditions the United States might take the initiative in a nuclear conflict with the Soviet Union. Khrushchev, who was then in Bulgaria, did his best to tone down the repercussions. Quoting a clarification from the White House, he asserted on May 19 that 'the President subsequently tempered his declaration to some extent'. But that was not the view of Malinovsky, who wrote in *Kommunist:* 'Subsequently the President confirmed this statement and stressed that it represented the traditional position of the United States.'

Needless to say, the Marshal used this episode to request 'an even greater reinforcement' of Soviet military potential and to express his opinion in the most bellicose terms. One who suspects that the adversary is entertaining thoughts of aggression naturally advocates preventive warfare. Accordingly, the military press featured Malinovsky's ominous declaration at the Twenty-second Congress: 'We must study all means of foiling the enemy's aggressive designs by dealing him a timely and devastating blow.'[1] It may also be wondered whether V. A. Zorin's sharp rejection at the Geneva disarmament conference on May 29 1962 of a draft agreement to ban 'war propaganda', which he had previously accepted,[2] was not also due to military intervention.

We do not know whether the military obtained all they wanted,[3]

---

[1] *Twenty-second Congress* vol 2 p 118. This formulation of military doctrine was never repeated by Khrushchev or any civilian. It was reiterated by Malinovsky in the beginning of 1964, but by then, to the 'devastating blow', the qualification 'retaliatory' (*otvyetny*) was added, which changed its meaning radically (see *Krasnaya Zvezda* of January 9 1964 and *Pravda* of February 23 1964).

[2] The text of the Geneva draft agreement banning war propaganda had been published in full by the Tass Agency and reprinted by a few provincial papers, in particular the *Pravda Ukrainy* of May 27 1962, which announced that 'at last an initial concrete result has been reached'. The counter-order had probably been received by the Moscow papers earlier, so that they ignored the agreement altogether.

[3] The gradual downgrading of Khrushchev in the eyes of the military in 1962 is documented by the *History of the Great Patriotic War (1941–1945)*, whose five volumes came out between 1960 and 1963. Volume III, which appeared in 1961, mentioned Khrushchev's role in World War II no less than 41 times as against 28 times for

but the result of their action, coupled with that of the 'steel-eaters', was to protect their sector from any sacrifices that the agricultural programme might have entailed for them in March. Since the industrial programme had to be financed in some way and since, in spite of Kosygin's optimistic statements to the contrary, the shortage of funds had never been so formidable, cuts had to be made right and left, mostly in the categories of consumer goods and prestige expenditure. Between March and May 1962 it was decided to suspend the law voted in May 1960 for the elimination of income tax, to cancel plans for holding a world fair in Moscow in 1967, and not to take part in the New York fair. Although it was not announced officially, there was much talk of curtailing appropriations for housing,[1] culture and education. Lastly, on June 1, 1962, a rise was announced of 20 to 30 per cent in the price of meat and butter. Thus, the people themselves were to pay for the increase, judged necessary by the authorities, in the price paid by the state to the producers of meat and dairy products.

It was certainly without enthusiasm that the Soviet leaders took this step, especially considering the loss of prestige that it entailed for Khrushchev's agricultural policy in the eyes of world opinion. Moreover, it also caused a stir at home and, specifically, a serious riot in Novocherkassk in the Rostov region.[2]

Stalin. Volume IV, which came out in 1962, had only 15 references to Khrushchev and 16 to Stalin. Volume V, which appeared in 1963, further accentuated the difference, Khrushchev receiving 16 references to Stalin's 21.

[1] There was another anomaly with respect to building: on December 23 1961 *Pravda* had announced the calling of a large 'builders' conference for the entire Soviet Union', to take place in Moscow in February. The conference was never held, although no official explanation was given. The reason must have been the general review of financial problems undertaken at the beginning of 1962. A drive against the dispersion of building sites and the 'scattering of capital' was launched at that time and must have slowed down investment in that branch of industry. Therefore it was not a good moment to convene building specialists in a solemn congress.

[2] The wealth of evidence leaves no doubt as to the riot in Novocherkassk following the rise in food prices, although the number of casualties cannot be estimated. In this case too, a careful analysis of the official indications is quite conclusive in itself. On June 2 1962, i.e. the day after the riots, Khrushchev denounced in a speech 'the anti-social elements who impede our forward movement, the grabbers [*rvachi*], the idlers and criminals'. 'We must slap down [*odyorgivat*] those who do not or will not understand,' he concluded, thereby showing that the first reaction was to stamp out the movement (*Pravda*, June 3 1962). After this, K. R. Kozlov was dispatched to the area. An Oblast Committee plenary session was held in his presence and *Pravda's* account of it on June 9 was fairly clear despite the official euphemisms. 'Certain Party organizations', it was reported, 'have weakened their ties with the masses and fallen down on their ideological and didactic tasks'. Denouncing a 'contemptuous attitude towards workers' needs and requests', the Party organ called for 'decisively improving the work of commercial enterprises and those concerned with collective feeding and public services', while 'reinforcing the struggle . . . against manifestations of bourgeois ideology, idleness, cupidity, drunkenness and hooliganism'.

AN UNEXPECTED COMEBACK: KIRILENKO

The moment has now come to go back a little and take a closer look at personality problems arising from the Congress. As early as February, surprisingly enough, Voroshilov was entered on the list of candidates for the new Supreme Soviet, although the old 'anti-party' Marshal had been attacked at the Congress. On the other hand a member of the government, the Minister of Culture, Furtseva, was not on the list. After attracting attention by her zealous support of Khrushchev and her attacks on the 'group', she had lost her seat in the Party Presidium and by November had almost vanished from the scene for good.[1] Her expulsion from the Supreme Soviet, which traditionally includes every minister, was a sure sign of her impending departure from the Government. Ignatov's position also seemed in jeopardy. He had been expelled from the Party Presidium and, although elected deputy, seemed about to lose the chairmanship of the State Committee for Agricultural Stocks, a body whose elimination Khrushchev had in effect suggested in his report of March 5. Anyway, Ignatov did not participate in any of the countless agricultural conferences that the First Secretary and his lieutenants were organizing throughout the country, although he was in charge of agriculture in the government hierarchy.

Both Furtseva and Ignatov, however, were still in their posts in the new Government formed at the end of April 1962 after the elections.

The Novocherkassk local paper, *Znamya Kommuny*, managed to continue publication as if nothing had happened but, starting in mid-June, it contained the same appeals for the control of 'hooliganism', particularly among the 16,000 young people in the city living in municipal dormitories, among whom 'instances of disorder were noted'. Finally on July 27 the newspaper published a decree of the local Soviet dated July 12 1962 'on the maintenance of public order in the city of Novocherkassk'. One article of the decree 'forbids children and adolescents under 16 years of age to go about in the streets after 9 p.m. in summer and 8 p.m. in winter unless accompanied by their parents'. The decree was to remain in force for *two years*.

Furthermore, starting on June 1, foreigners were refused permission to visit Rostov and the surrounding area. The official reason was an epidemic – which did not prevent athletic teams from Rostov coming to Moscow to take part in a competition.

[1] At the start of the Congress, Furtseva's fortunes already appeared shaky. The foreign journalists allowed to attend the proceedings were requested to wait for the publication in *Pravda* of the speech of the Minister of Culture before reporting on its content. It was rumoured that she did not attend the Central Committee meeting that elected the Presidium at the end of October. After this she disappeared for over six weeks. There was talk of a serious clash between her and her deputy ministers (particularly A. N. Kuznetsov, the First Deputy), of serious illness and even of attempted suicide. The fact is that when she came back in mid-December she looked physically shaken.

The new cabinet was indeed remarkable for its stability. Except for one minor change, everybody was in the same place.[1] In this instance, too, it was hardly likely that the *status quo* suited Khrushchev. After all, he had attacked often and at length the top Gosplan officials, as well as the leaders of the State Committee for Chemistry whom he had charged on March 5 with 'sheer irresponsibility'.

It may reasonably be assumed that 'consultation' regarding the new cabinet caused the unexpected postponement of the Supreme Soviet session. It had been scheduled to open just after the elections, on April 10 1962, but a brief communiqué on the evening of April 5 announced its postponement till the 23rd. Apparently the Party Presidium had been meeting since the beginning of the week (Podgorny, then First Secretary of the Ukrainian Communist Party, was reported in Moscow on Monday the 2nd) to plan the proceedings of the Supreme Soviet meeting and the composition of the Government, but had failed to reach any agreement. The delay did not solve anything, as was shown by the fact that things were again left as before. What Khrushchev thought of this may be judged from his statement a few days later against the 'bureaucrats' and especially – a newer feature – their protectors:

'In any opinion, those who pose as defenders of parochialism and of the honour of the uniform are doing anti-communist work. They are siding with the bureaucrats and covering up the activities of those who impede the building of communism. *Those people won't stay in the saddle anyway: sooner or later the horse will throw them off. . . .'* [Author's italics] (*Pravda*, May 11 1962).

Paradoxically, at the same time a reshuffle of some consequence had occurred in the top Party leadership. While the March plenary session had left things unchanged, when the Supreme Soviet met on April 23 it became evident that two changes had been made. Spiridonov was elected President of the Union Soviet, which was a barely polite way of

---

[1] The only cabinet change in April 1962 involved G. A. Zhukov, who was replaced by S. K. Romanovsky as Chairman of the Committee for cultural relations with foreign countries. Subsequently, it was put about that this was to enable him 'to resume his activities as a journalist'. It may be noted that he had been better off a few years earlier as an acknowledged member of Khrushchev's entourage during the First Secretary's trips abroad, when he was occasionally even entrusted with confidential missions – for instance in the United States at the end of 1958. This downgrading in 1962 contrasted with the brilliant rise at the same moment of a man who had been roughly in the same position at the start, namely L. F. Ilyichev. A few days after leaving the Government, Zhukov received the order of Lenin in honour of the fiftieth anniversary of *Pravda* – but, strangely enough, the Party daily forgot to mention his name among 76 recipients of the award, the list of whom was published on the following day, May 5 1962.

announcing his removal from responsible office in Leningrad and in the Central Committee Secretariat. At the same time, a new name, A. P. Kirilenko, figured in the Party Presidium. *Pravda* confirmed this three days later and indicated his new functions: First Deputy Chairman of the Central Committee Bureau for the RSFSR, a new post alongside and at the same level as G. I. Voronov's.

Both these changes upset the order established by the Twenty-second Congress. Spiridonov had been promoted in October 1961 to the post of Party Secretary from which he was now removed, and it was at that same time that Kirilenko had been demoted. The Congress had deprived Kirilenko of the seat of alternate member he had been holding in the Party Presidium since June 1957, and at one point it was not even certain that he had kept his functions of First Secretary in Sverdlovsk.[1] This made his promotion now even more spectacular.

It also meant a gain for Khrushchev, since Kirilenko was a 'client' *par excellence*, having made his entire career in the Ukraine under Khrushchev's auspices. He owed Khrushchev his first promotion to Oblast Committee Secretary in 1939 and to First Secretary in 1947 (incidentally, for two years he had also been Brezhnev's associate as Second Secretary of the Zaporozhie Oblast Committee when the latter was First Secretary there, in 1946 and 1947). Kirilenko's breakthrough from the confines of the Ukraine to head the large industrial region of Sverdlovsk had occurred in 1955, most probably under Khrushchev's patronage. Kirilenko had thus been one of the first Ukrainians to move into a key post at the centre. In this way he had entered the Bureau of the Central Committee for the RSFSR as soon as it was formed, in 1956, when it was a notorious Khrushchev stronghold. A year later, after the 'anti-party' crisis, his loyalty to the First Secretary earned him an alternate seat in the Party Presidium – a handsome promotion for the head of a regional organization. His eulogy of the First Secretary had always been immoderate:[2] like the most faithful clients,

---

[1] Like most of the officials demoted after the Twenty-second Congress, Kirilenko was not heard of again for the rest of the year. In December 1961, for instance, he failed to take part in an agricultural conference for the Urals, attended by Voronov. The rapporteur for the region was the Chairman of the Oblast Executive Committee, K. K. Nikolayev, who was not very flattering in his account of 'certain work' in agriculture performed by the regional Party organization. Kirilenko reappeared only at election time, in March 1962.

[2] Here are excerpts from some of Kirilenko's speeches indicating his attitude towards Khrushchev personally:

At the plenary session of December 1959: 'Comrade Khrushchev . . . who has gone through a rich school of life, embodies the great wisdom of ordinary people. Each day of his activity affords an outstanding example of the manner in which we should work in order to improve the life of the Soviet people. Nikita Sergeyevich has earned the deepest respect and love of our people and Party through his firm execution of

he had spoken (at the 1959 Congress) of the 'Presidium of the Central Committee led by comrade Khrushchev'. It is barely necessary to add that he backed the Party chief in his 'personal' campaigns. His speech at the Twenty-second Congress was a model in that respect: he strongly attacked, and supplied details about, the criminal activities of the 'anti-party group' (all without exception, apparently) and explicitly demanded the expulsion from the Party of Molotov, Malenkov and Kaganovich. There was only one shadow in the picture: in latter years Kirilenko seemed somewhat cool about the 1957 industrial reform and the sovnarkhoz system. All his speeches on industrial questions – his main subject – were distinguished by silence on that point.

In spite of this shadow, it is difficult to understand how Khrushchev succeeded in introducing such a reliable recruit into the Presidium despite the co-optation hurdle. The other Ukrainians, Brezhnev, Podgorny and probably Polyansky, had good reasons for backing Kirilenko's candidacy, but that was not enough. Evidently a package deal was made since, at the same time, a particularly vociferous ally of Khrushchev on the destalinization issue, I. V. Spiridonov, was evicted from the Party apparatus and replaced in Leningrad by the more moderate V. S. Tolstikov.[1] Also at that time, Voroshilov was maintained in his functions at the Supreme Soviet Presidium, which helped further to heal the blows he had suffered from the Congress.[2]

In addition there was probably a fairly widespread reaction against the main victim of the reshuffle, G. I. Voronov. As the sole First Deputy Chairman of the Bureau for the RSFSR (its actual head immediately after Khrushchev) Voronov had given free rein to his authoritarian

---

the Leninist policy for peace and his selfless struggle for the strengthening of peace throughout the world.'

At the plenary session of July 1960: 'The ebullient activity of Nikita Khrushchev, his speeches on the Soviet Union's foreign policy, the creative development he imparts to Lenin's ideas . . . arouse the pride and admiration of all Soviet citizens and the whole of progressive mankind.'

At the Twenty-second Congress: 'Our dear N. S. Khrushchev . . . who carries on Lenin's work with such talent, the eminent theoretician and practititioner of the building of communism . . . the tireless fighter for peace and for the triumph of the Leninist principles of peaceful coexistence . . .'

[1] Tolstikov came from Leningrad and was a relative newcomer to the Party apparatus (until 1960 he was only Deputy Chairman of the Executive Committee of the city's soviet). His promotion to Second Secretary of the Oblast Committee in 1960 might have been due to Kozlov, who had just gained the upper hand in the Secretariat. Unlike Spiridonov, Tolstikov was very discreet on destalinization and the 'anti-party group' throughout Khrushchev's reign.

[2] Contrary to what took place on November 7 1961, Voroshilov was admitted to the saluting base at the Mausoleum for the 1962 May Day parade, and of his own volition he stationed himself on Khrushchev's right. His appearance was ignored by television, but on the following day he was in *Pravda*'s photographs.

tendencies and used Khrushchev's agricultural campaigns for an energetic purge of the regional apparatus. At the March 1962 plenary session he had let it be understood that the setting up of 'territorial agricultural boards' – a new system devised by Khrushchev to solve the agricultural problem – would enable him to extend his bureau's authority down to the rank and file personnel. This in turn would lead to further concentration of power in his hands. Since Voronov dealt with practically nothing besides agriculture, industry was neglected. P. F. Lomako, an economic expert, had in theory taken charge of industry within the Bureau after the Twenty-second Congress, but he bore only the title of plain Deputy Chairman, and was not a member of the Presidium, hence did not carry sufficient political weight.

All these factors must have led to a consensus for a better division of powers. Thus the creation of a second post of First Deputy Chairman given to a member of the Party Presidium was a means of re-establishing the balance and promoting 'healthy' competition. Voronov, it seems, was not particularly happy about it (he was reported to be on holiday during the negotiations in April) and devoted the ensuing months to securing his position. The result was not conclusive, for in November 1962 he lost the leadership of the Bureau in exchange for another post, a responsible if slightly lower one, of head of the RSFSR Government which downgraded him to simple membership of the Bureau. This did not make him lose his seat in the Party Presidium, but it became clear at that point that not all its members were his friends.

In any event, it was from the end of April 1962 that the Party Presidium assumed the complexion which remained unchanged until Khrushchev's downfall two and a half years later, except for two important changes brought on by fate itself: namely Kozlov's heart attack in April 1963 and Kuusinen's death a year later.

To judge from the order of precedence at the saluting base on May Day 1962 and the volume of 'nominations' by the 'masses' to various posts during the Supreme Soviet elections that year, two well defined groups seem to have emerged within the Presidium:
1 The senior group headed by Khrushchev, then Brezhnev and Kozlov almost on a par, and, a little further down, Mikoyan, Suslov and Kosygin.
2 The juniors, among whom precedence was variable and of no great importance: Voronov, Polyansky, Kuusinen, Kirilenko, Podgorny and Shvernik.

The composition of these groups did not change much, except in the summer of 1963 when Podgorny rose from the second to the first. The grouping was not quite in keeping with functions: for example, Kuusinen held exactly the same titles as Suslov in the Presidium and the

Secretariat. It was a fact nevertheless: a 'senior' was never on the same level as a 'junior' at official gatherings, which shows that prerogatives often derive from subtler forms of political influence rather than official functions alone.

The grouping also had a political meaning, for while the Presidium included many friends of Khrushchev, its three most independent members, those who showed most reserve as regards some of Khrushchev's actions and who obviously did not hesitate to let him know their views on occasion – namely Kosygin, Suslov and Mikoyan – were all in the senior group.

Part Three
THE CUBAN FIASCO
1962–1963

The Cuban crisis of October 1962 was not only a crucial moment in world history but also a turning point for the Soviet régime, both in its dealings with the West and with respect to its inner functioning. Even though the decision secretly to send strategic missiles armed with nuclear warheads to an island off the American continent may be regarded as reckless, it was a truly dynamic move – the last, hitherto, that Stalin's successors have undertaken in order to alter the world balance of power in their favour. The hasty withdrawal of the weapons under American pressure during the last week in October may have been a prudent act or a shameful capitulation, but it was assuredly a set-back – a spectacular and bitter one – for Soviet diplomacy. For several years afterwards, Soviet diplomacy entered a stage of self-containment. The demands on Berlin were shelved and, in general, the *status quo* provided the basis for an unwritten pact of peaceful coexistence with the United States; some previously proclaimed principles were even infringed in the process. The Moscow treaty on the suspension of nuclear tests and the 'hot line' were among the results. This meant a complete change from cold war psychology. At the same time, the Cuban crisis was the starting point for another cold war in the East, as the quarrel with China now came into the open, while some of the ties among communist parties loosened and Moscow's prestige declined.

The Cuban crisis also marked a turning point in Soviet internal policy. This aspect of the problem, which has not been explored thoroughly, will be dealt with at greater length in the present survey. The dynamic stage which lasted until the autumn of 1962 was accompanied by impetuous moves by the First Secretary – his last: a spectacular revival of destalinization and an open attack on the Party apparatus, culminating in the sacrilegious dividing of the Party into two separate branches and the subordination of the economic planners. Then the retreat from Cuba gradually but ineluctably led to an ebbing of the tide. As a direct if distant outcome of the Cuba fiasco, in February–March 1963 Khrushchev had to face his most serious crisis since 1957. This is why the internal as well as the external aspects of events must be analysed at each stage of this turbulent period.

1 The Gamble

As far as the world knew, the Cuban crisis started in the evening of October 22 1962 when President Kennedy announced that a 'quarantine', a blockade in fact, was being set up around Cuba, where Soviet intermediate and medium-range ballistic missiles (IRBMs and MRBMs) had been detected. Clearly, the story began earlier: for the Americans on October 14, when a U-2 took the first convincing photograph over San Cristóbal, and for the Soviets, naturally, well before that date. Therefore, the first question is, when and how Moscow decided to place these forty missiles in Cuba.

It is safe to ignore the reason consistently adduced by Khrushchev, namely that he wished to defend Castro and him alone. In his major speech to the Supreme Soviet on December 12 1962, Khrushchev even asserted that it was the Cubans and not the Russians who had taken the initiative. The Cubans, he said, 'had asked the Soviet Government for extra help'. This was denied by Castro in the interview he gave a little later to Claude Julien, the correspondent of *Le Monde*,[1] and even more explicitly after Khrushchev's downfall, in a speech on March 13 1965. In the second speech, which *Pravda* reprinted, the Cuban leader indicated clearly that the rockets had been offered to him, that accepting them had meant a 'risk', but that he had not hesitated to do so 'for the sake of strengthening the socialist camp'.

It is possible, of course, that Khrushchev believed the rockets would help the defence of Cuba as a deterrent. If the United States Government detected them and resigned itself to their presence, any thought of aggression would have had to reckon with the threat of thermonuclear retaliation. But this was a minor consideration: had Cuba's defence been the main object, it would have been far simpler to extend the Warsaw Pact guarantees to cover the island, or else for the USSR to

[1] Castro gave the following explanation to Claude Julien as to why he accepted the Soviet missiles: 'We had discussed among ourselves the possibility of asking the USSR to provide us with rockets. But we had not reached any decision when Moscow offered them to us. It was explained that by accepting them we would strengthen the socialist camp on the world scale. And since we were already receiving a large amount of help from the socialist camp, we decided that we could not refuse. That is why we accepted them. It was not in order to ensure our own defence, but primarily to strengthen socialism on the international scale. That is the truth, even if different explanations are given elsewhere' (*Le Monde*, March 22 1963).

commit itself to declare war in case of aggression against its ally. Khrushchev, however, had consistently avoided any outright commitment. In September 1960, when a journalist in New York had asked him point-blank: 'Is it true that you stated that in case of a United States intervention against Cuba, the USSR would strike at the United States?' he had evasively replied: 'More or less true . . . ' then added: 'You need not worry. . . . Since America is not going to attack Cuba, there can be no danger' (Khrushchev's *Foreign Policy Speeches* 1960 vol 2 p 382). Later, the mention of retaliation was termed a 'symbolic' one. In short, the Soviet remained non-committal, even after the Bay of Pigs fiasco in April 1961 had shown a similar half-hearted attitude on the part of the United States. Even at the height of the crisis, during the summer and autumn of 1962, the Warsaw Pact guarantee was not extended to Cuba, nor was any official military alliance concluded with that country. Evidently Cuba was only part of a bigger game.

As Castro had said, the rockets were intended to 'strengthen the socialist camp' as a whole – in other words, to provide the USSR with an inexpensive means of altering the strategic balance of power in its favour. If, as the Americans claimed, the Russians then had only a very small number of intercontinental ballistic missiles, the placing of the forty smaller devices in Cuba turned them into intercontinental missiles trained on the United States. More importantly, they escaped the United States early warning system, thus upsetting all retaliation plans. Such a strategic advantage, achieved with a relatively small expenditure, represented a leap forward in the armaments race. This was a great boon for the Soviet economy, overburdened as it was by the quickening pace of arms production set by Kennedy.

There is no doubt that the move was a gamble, but it was not necessarily bellicose. At that stage of the balance of terror, Khrushchev had no new motives for wanting actually to use the weapons. The missiles, like the rest of his arsenal, were meant to intimidate, not to be fired. They were to serve as a formidable instrument of pressure on the United States in future negotiations and it is conceivable that Khrushchev himself meant to withdraw them some day – in exchange for substantial concessions, of course. Therefore the secrecy surrounding the operation was not meant to last. Although rockets were not mentioned, Soviet declarations did not conceal the stepping-up of military assistance to Cuba during the summer and autumn of 1962. According to President Kennedy's adviser, Theodore Sorensen,[1] Mikoyan later assured the President that Moscow had meant to inform Washington of the missiles'

---

[1] Theodore C. Sorensen, *Kennedy*; Harper and Row, New York, 1965. See also *Look* magazine of September 7 and 21 1965.

presence, but 'not till after the American elections, to prevent it from becoming a campaign issue'. Apart from the excuse of the elections, Mikoyan was probably telling the truth: the secret was not supposed to, and could not in fact, last longer than the time needed to confront the U.S. with a *fait accompli*, after which the card would be disclosed. Khrushchev had in fact casually announced his intention of visiting the United States in November, probably with the intention of springing the surprise himself.

The objective of the manoeuvre was clearly Berlin. Ever since Khrushchev had raised the issue in 1958, the Russians had tried all possible tactics: first pressure (the six-month ultimatum), then smiles (at Camp David), then pressure again and even the fist-banging session (during Khrushchev's summer offensive of 1961). Everything had been in vain. In the spring of 1962 an entirely fresh approach was needed. Khrushchev's prestige was largely at stake and his adversaries in the communist camp were using the issue as a weapon against him. It was learned later that during a Warsaw Pact meeting in Moscow in the summer of 1961 the Albanians had demanded that the USSR sign the German peace treaty. Ulbricht, who was most directly concerned, was also showing signs of impatience.

At the end of 1961 and the beginning of 1962 Moscow's relations with East Germany were deteriorating, especially since Khrushchev had tried the new device of an overture to Bonn. On December 27 he addressed a somewhat unusual memorandum to the West German Ambassador in which he warned the German Federal Republic against its allies and expressed hope for better political relations. Strangely enough, while the text was reprinted in full by the East Berlin *Neues Deutschland* and in Bonn, it was completely ignored in Moscow. On January 17 a spokesman on East German television acknowledged for the first time that differences existed with the USSR, by saying in effect that the Soviet Union was trying to preserve peace on the international level, whereas the German Democratic Republic also had national problems to settle.

Another oddity was that on January 26 1962 *Izvestia* published an article on the German problem by the commentator Polianov, specifying that it reflected only 'the author's personal point of view'. The article contained nothing that had not been written a hundred times, in particular on the impossibility of constantly postponing the signing of the peace treaty. Did this mean that the problem was being reviewed? In any case, Ulbricht came to Moscow at the end of February and was probably promised that 'something would be done'. Some new way of forcing a success had to be found, and Cuba provided it.

It might be objected to this theory that, if Berlin was the real goal, and if the entire plan rested on the assumed absence of any American reaction, Khrushchev could have simply helped himself to Berlin by signing his separate peace treaty, thereby ending the occupation status of the former capital. If he was so bold in the Caribbean, why was he so cautious on Berlin? The answer is that the respective risks were of a different nature. Although he denied this, Khrushchev was quite aware that unilateral action on his part in Berlin would be illegal. And above all, the lengthy negotiations conducted with the West for years had convinced him that the Atlantic camp would regard any violation of freedom of access to West Berlin as a *casus belli*. By placing his rockets in Cuba, on the other hand, Khrushchev was doing nothing illegal and was on the contrary forcing his opponent to act illegally if he wished to react at all. Khrushchev may have genuinely believed on the strength of the preceding months' experience that Kennedy would not take such a step. In 1961 Kennedy had in fact appeared much firmer on Berlin – where he held out against the very violent pressure of that summer by taking military measures, and so forth – than on Cuba, where he had not dared push his Bay of Pigs operation to its logical conclusion. As seen by the resolute gambler in Moscow, Cuba was the weak spot.

This background will help to establish the date when the decision was probably taken. According to Khrushchev (speech of December 12 1962), it was in August 1962 that the Russians and Cubans agreed, through the mediation of Che Guevara during his visit to Moscow, on the installation of thermonuclear rockets in Cuba. It is quite possible that the formal agreements were concluded on that date, but the real decision, with everything it entailed in the way of preparations and plans, had certainly been taken earlier by Moscow – probably in April 1962, to judge from the diplomatic situation and certain changes in the Soviet General Staff.

AN INCREASE IN STRENGTH

On the diplomatic front, and assuming that the operation was indeed aimed at Berlin, the logical result should have been a stiffening of the Soviet attitude and a harsher tone in dealings with the West from the time at which the decision was taken. This in fact occurred from the end of April till the end of May. Here are a few examples.

During the first three months of 1962 talks took place in Moscow about Berlin between Gromyko and the American Ambassador, Llewellyn Thompson, supplemented by contacts in Washington. The result from the Soviet angle was meagre. On March 16, in a speech to his constituents, Khrushchev referred to the Berlin talks in an extremely sceptical vein, implying that nothing would come of them. On April 12 he wrote in a message to the British Prime Minister, Macmillan: 'I no longer trust in the wisdom of those quarters which today determine the policy of the Western powers.' In the meantime, the Berlin problem was relegated to the background, which signified a *détente*. On April 24 Gromyko made a very moderate speech to the Supreme Soviet, pleaded for continuation of the talks and even acknowledged the few positive results achieved. Just before this, the Soviets stopped their harassment in the Berlin air corridor, while Marshal Konev, who had been placed in command of the Soviet forces in Germany at the height of the tension during the previous summer, was recalled to Moscow 'in order to resume his functions at the Ministry of Defence' (*Pravda*, April 20 1962).

However, the tone again changed within a week. On May 3 *Pravda* carried a very tough three-column article by 'Observer' dealing exclusively with the Berlin problem, which said *inter alia:* 'The Soviet Union may not confine itself to meeting the test of force if it comes. Let the West be warned that whoever sows the wind will reap the whirlwind.' On May 19 the Party organ reverted to the subject in the same tone. On the 21st Khrushchev signed a Soviet–Bulgarian communiqué in Sofia that was particularly aggressive on the Berlin issue, advising the West to forsake any illusions, and again flaunting the threat of a separate peace treaty. In June the tone grew even more strident: while the communiqué of the Warsaw Pact leaders assembled in Moscow contained the same threat, the *Pravda* 'Observer' promised 'a bitter awakening' to the Western politicians who 'believe that might is right' (June 10 1962).

Meanwhile, some interesting facts involving Cuba were emerging. On April 28, during the week in which Moscow changed course, Khrushchev received the Cuban Minister for Public Works, Cienfuegos. A week later, on May 5, he saw the Cuban Ambassador in Moscow – for a preliminary sounding, perhaps. A few weeks later, he publicly stated for the first time that arms were being supplied to Cuba. (Not that they had not been sent before this, but the Soviet press had never acknowledged supplying anything but tractors and other civilian equipment.) Speaking to a group of young Cubans on June 2 Khrushchev remarked: 'Besides, we are helping Cuba with weapons and other things. . . . If a socialist state enjoys a strong economy as well as good-quality armaments, this has an even better effect on the minds of those who are thinking of starting a new war.' The Havana newspaper *Noticias de Hoy* responded with a grateful editorial on June 8 (reprinted by *Pravda* on the 11th), which stated with reference to the weapons: 'We know

that this aid is invaluable. But we also know, and Khrushchev emphasized it very aptly, that this aid cannot in itself solve all the problems,
and can help only when it falls into the people's firm hands.' Possibly
it would be going too far to regard this as foreshadowing the disagreements with Castro that broke out, after the crisis, as to the ownership of
the equipment and in particular of the IL-28 bombers. All this must be
recorded, nevertheless, together with the trip to Cuba at the end of
May by Rashikov, a Presidium alternate who headed a delegation 'to
study irrigation problems'. Upon his return, Rashikov spent an unusually long time in Moscow instead of returning to his Uzbekistan
domain (his presence was noticed in the capital on June 11, 15 and 16).

To sum up, preliminary analysis yields the following results:
1 a definite stiffening in tone on the Berlin issue between April 24 and
May 3;
2 a first hint about the shipping of arms to Cuba at the beginning of
June.

Another curious detail: at the end of June and the beginning of July
the Chinese Ambassador to Moscow, Liu-Siao, indicated on several
occasions to ambassadors from neutral countries that the Chinese were
glad that the Soviets had at last found the right way to solve the Berlin
crisis. He did not explain further, but looking back, it is not impossible
that the 'new way' consisted of turning Cuba into a strategic base in
order to put pressure on the United States. No other known event of the
period could have justified such optimism on the ambassador's part.
This would mean that the Soviet Union had informed the Chinese of its
decision, which is quite possible, considering the more relaxed atmosphere that prevailed between the two countries from the spring of
1962.[1]

---

[1] There had been no Sino-Soviet reconciliation or even any genuine *détente* in the
spring of 1962, but rather a quiet spell after the tumult caused by the Twenty-second
Congress and the Albanian affair. A few signs were visible, specifically the publication in *Pravda* of April 3 of the full text of an editorial in the Peking's *People's Daily*
on the Urumtsi river development (its general tenor was that progress had to be
achieved step by step rather than by leaps – which was clearly acceptable to Moscow).
Moreover, a dialogue was maintained between the two capitals: on April 7 the Chinese
Communist Party backed the suggestion of various Eastern bloc countries for a new
conference of the Communist Parties, to which it is known that Moscow responded
favourably in principle, in a letter of May 31. We also know that Moscow kept
Peking informed about some of its diplomatic moves and American proposals. For
instance, on August 25 the Soviets advised the Chinese of the American offer to
conclude an agreement on the partial suspension of nuclear tests, and of their intended
refusal. (At the same time, it is true, the Soviets were declaring themselves ready to
accept another American proposal aimed at stopping the proliferation of nuclear
weapons, to which the Chinese strongly reacted in their reply of September 3 1962.)
Similarly, starting that spring, the Russian press began to give more coverage to
news from Peking.

MOSKALENKO'S STRANGE FATE

The analysis of certain changes in the military high command supports the above hypothesis as to the date of the crucial decision. Although the ground here is less certain, it is worth examining.

During the spring of 1962 three marshals lost some of their functions and influence. They were I. S. Konev, who, as mentioned, was recalled from commanding the Soviet forces in East Germany; K. S. Moskalenko, who was succeeded by S. S. Biryuzov in charge of strategic rockets; and F. I. Golikov, who was replaced by A. A. Yepishev, one of Khrushchev's Ukrainian clients, at the Main Political Administration of the Armed Forces. Pending further information, it is reasonable to ascribe the first change to the ending of the Berlin crisis (Konev's American counterpart, General Clay, was recalled at the same time); in any case, Konev had fallen from favour as early as 1960. On the other hand, it is not at all unreasonable to link Moskalenko's case with the Cuban affair. The decision affected him directly as commander in chief of strategic rockets. It is a safe bet that a man anxious to preserve his equipment intact could not have been happy at the prospect of having his most secret weapons shipped with their nuclear warheads to a highly exposed site such as Cuba. Later events were to show that the Americans had been within a hair's breadth of capturing the devices, and Moskalenko must have worried about this more than anyone else. Moreover, these rockets had to be withdrawn from current supplies, or, if they were only on order, diverted from their original destination. Moskalenko assuredly had definite ideas on the subject, which did not necessarily coincide with those of the politicians. Golikov's role in the matter is less certain; but his task would have been to explain to the officers and men involved the reasons for this 'agonizing reappraisal' of traditional Soviet policy with respect to foreign bases. In any event, like Moskalenko, he suffered spectacular ups and downs in the course of 1962, and these corresponded with the development of the Cuban crisis.

Moskalenko was relieved of his command in April 1962, but this was learned only in July. Until then, the news was withheld, as was the mention of his successor, Biryuzov. The disgrace apparently was gradual, judging from a few anomalies in the press. For instance, on May 18,

---

It is true that at the same time Moscow was denouncing Chinese support to Albania (in particular in a letter of February 22) and that, apparently for the first time, border incidents took place. In April and May 1962 'tens of thousands' of Kazakhs from Sinkiang sought refuge in the USSR and were not sent back despite Peking's requests. All these details were disclosed a year later, generally by Chinese sources (see the *People's Daily* of August 15 and September 6 1963).

when *Pravda* published an obituary of Admiral Golovko, Moskalenko was one of the signatories – far below Malinovsky and the Deputy Ministers of Defence to be sure, but in an honourable place none the less, and before the other marshals such as Rokosovsky, Konev and Sokolovsky. But at the end of June, when the death of General Antonov called for another obituary, Moskalenko was last on the list of the seven marshals who signed, coming even after the 'anti-party' Voroshilov (*Krasnaya Zvezda*, June 22 1962). Things looked worst in July when the *Encyclopedic Yearbook* for 1962 (dated July 12) described him as 'From 1960 to 1962, commander in chief of the rocket troops, Deputy Minister of Defence of the USSR; since April 1962, chief inspector of the USSR Defence Ministry.' In July, then, Moskalenko had lost not only the rockets command but his title of Deputy Minister of Defence as well. A change for the better came a few months later. The Supreme Soviet *Deputies' Yearbook*, published at the end of November 1962, contained the following entry: . . . after 1960, commander in chief of rocket troops, Deputy Minister for Defence; at present, Deputy Minister of Defence of the USSR, Chief Inspector.' Thus Moskalenko's rating had gone up since July and he had regained his post of deputy minister.

Golikov's fortunes were similar. His fall from favour was not officially disclosed until May but had occurred in April, roughly after Gromyko's trip to Yugoslavia in the second half of that month. That was when Golikov's successor Yepishev, hitherto Ambassador to Belgrade, returned to Moscow with Gromyko and revisited Belgrade only to pay his farewell calls. On April 25 the Supreme Soviet elected Yepishev to the committee on the drafting of a new constitution (the only ambassador to serve in that capacity). Golikov was not a member of the committee, and Yepishev must have already replaced him at the head of the Armed Forces Political Administration. On May Day, Golikov did not attend the rally in Red Square and the foreign diplomats were told that his absence was due to illness. The decree on his transfer, dated May 11, was published only on May 21 (*Pravda*, May 22).

Golikov's fall from favour was apparently even more drastic than Moskalenko's, since nothing was heard of him throughout the summer of 1962. The 1962 *Encyclopedic Yearbook* published in July reported no activity at all on his part after his departure from the Armed Forces Political Administration. But here again, at the end of November, the picture changed. The *Deputies' Yearbook* declared that he 'at present discharges functions of responsibility in the Defence Ministry', which shows that the 'health reasons' mentioned earlier were of short duration. His name reappeared among signatories of obituaries in December 1962, and this continued at fairly regular intervals thereafter.

To sum up, both men's careers for the year 1962 present two interesting characteristics:

1 A fall from favour in April, the official repercussions of which were clearest in the second half of May;

2 A return to influence in November, i.e. after the Cuban débacle.

What makes the coincidence so striking is that the analysis of Soviet diplomatic activities indicates that these were stepped up at the very moment when the two men fell from favour. It is tempting to reconstruct events as follows: in April 1962, contemplating the futility of all previous efforts to obtain a settlement on Berlin, Khrushchev devised a new means of pressure on the United States – the shipment of nuclear missiles to Cuba. The matter may have been discussed at the formal Party Presidium meeting held on the occasion of the Supreme Soviet session between April 22 and 25, and this may have heightened the difficulties of that agitated period. It is safe to assume that Moskalenko opposed the plan, and Golikov probably did too, hence their resignation (either at their own request or imposed from above). Assuming also that the diplomatic stiffening was connected with the Cuban affair, this means that a decision in principle had been taken at that stage, since the first sign came on May 3. It was probably during the month of May, before or after Khrushchev's trip to Bulgaria from the 14th to the 20th, that the necessary preparations were begun.[1] These must also have had an effect on the efforts of Malinovsky and other military leaders (mentioned in the preceding section of this book) to obtain larger military appropriations, in particular for the development of conventional armaments. It is reasonable to assume that the heavy cost of the Cuban operation had to be met, at least in part, by cutting the so-called 'conventional items' in the defence budget.

No information is available on the discussions among the Soviet leaders, but one may safely make the following comments.

Khrushchev was undoubtedly the instigator. It was a gambler's move, and Khrushchev's attitude on Berlin and other issues had clearly shown him to be a gambler by temperament. The move was also consistent with what the Chinese later called 'an excessive reliance on atomic weapons'. Moreover, everything points to the fact that he

---

[1] American accounts provide no accurate data on the exact timing of the decision to ship missiles to Cuba, but Sorensen estimates that it was taken in the spring. In his book *Kennedy* he writes: 'Judging from the rapidity with which they [the missiles] had been assembled, the planning and preparations for this move had been under way within the Soviet Union since spring and within Cuba all summer. The sites had been selected and surveyed, the protective anti-aircraft missiles moved in, the roads improved and the local inhabitants evicted' (p. 668).

The author also discloses that over one hundred communist bloc and bloc-chartered vessels had unloaded equipment in Cuban ports during July and August.

had the last word in the formulation of foreign policy – until the fiasco, that is. A decision of such magnitude could not have been taken against his will or even without his support. It will be shown subsequently that he and he alone was damaged by the failure in October, when Kennedy proclaimed the blockade. Khrushchev was reproached for having overreached himself as an adventurer on the 22nd, rather than for backing down on the 28th. Altogether, Khrushchev's entire attitude that summer showed that he was conducting the operation and meant to reap the full benefit himself.

At the same time, the Presidium could not conceivably have been left out of the decision. The collective leadership discussed many lesser matters. However, there is no sign of any opposition to Khrushchev's move, nor are any of the leaders known to have been overridden in a discussion, as Mikoyan had been in 1960. In fact, Mikoyan himself was not much in evidence before the crisis. He had gone on a long holiday on 21 August and returned only after the Americans reacted over Cuba. (He was back in Moscow on October 23.) He had suffered no ill effects from the decision in April; on the other hand, in May, Kosygin was upgraded and became the number two man in the Government, definitely overshadowing Mikoyan, the other First Deputy Chairman of the Council of Ministers. Since the situation was reversed around the end of the year and since Kosygin was the only member of the collective leadership besides Khrushchev who played host to Che Guevara in August, one is tempted to ascribe a special role to Kosygin in the Cuban venture. But as his fall from favour came long after the crisis, it is much more likely to have been due to the industrial reorganization that will be discussed later.

No special signs can be detected during this period with regard to other top officials. Kozlov was out of view for nearly two months in June and July, after leaving the Rostov area. Suslov took his holiday in August and September, at about the same time as Khrushchev. It may be noted that when Raul Castro, the Cuban Defence Minister, was in Moscow at the beginning of July, Khrushchev was his host at a luncheon on the 8th, also attended by Kirilenko, Mikoyan and Suslov. To sum up, the activities of that summer of 1962 do not prove that full agreement prevailed about the move that was under way, but, equally, there is no firm evidence to the contrary.

THE HOT PHASE

The hot phase of the operation started in September, when the missiles had to be shipped to their faraway exposed sites. Khrushchev's diplomacy fitted the situation and showed what his intentions were in case of success. They were twofold:

1 Khrushchev wished to discourage the United States from attempting any intervention in Cuba. Since the Soviet preparations could hardly go unnoticed, he disclosed just enough to give the Americans pause but not enough to provoke a crisis. For instance, no communiqué was issued after Raul Castro's visit early in July, while the visits of Guevara and Aragonez were followed on September 3 by the announcement of a stepping-up of arms deliveries. A Tass statement of September 11 denied any shipment of missiles but was more emphatic than any previous communiqué about Khrushchev's promises to Cuba in case of aggression.[1] Simultaneously, efforts were made to dissuade the United States from taking too close a look at Cuba. A strong anti U-2 drive was launched, for this purpose. An incident over the Kurile islands was the subject of a protest on September 4 which the press exploited for several days, even after an apology by the United States. *Pravda* had not even waited for this incident to denounce the overflights in a tone reminiscent of 1960.

Khrushchev took advantage of the usual summer influx of foreign visitors to define his position. On September 17 in a talk with Pitterman, the Austrian Vice-Chancellor, he emphasized the firmness of Soviet commitments to Cuba and 'disclosed' that the USSR would fight any blockade of the island. He proclaimed to all and sundry that the Americans had lost their fighting spirit. For instance, he spoke disparagingly about the weakness of the Western democracies to the poet Robert Frost, who was a guest at the Kremlin on September 7. They were 'too liberal to fight', Khrushchev explained. In short, he seemed confident at the time that all he had to do was raise his voice a little. Khrushchev's heightened self-assurance of those days was that of the gambler who has made his move.

---

[1] The big lie about Soviet missiles shipped to Cuba was worded as follows (*Pravda*, September 12 1962): 'The Soviet Government has authorized Tass to declare that the Soviet Union does not need to ship to any country, to Cuba for instance, any actual equipment in order to repel aggression and deal a retaliatory blow. The explosive force of our nuclear capabilities is so powerful and the Soviet Union has such a large number of powerful rockets for the delivery of these atomic warheads that there is no need to seek any site for their installation outside the borders of the Soviet Union.'

The same declaration affirmed that any attack against Cuba 'will start war' (the absence of articles in Russian makes it impossible to tell whether this meant *a* war or *the* war).

The declaration is remarkable in many other respects – its jumbled contents (it mentions the Russian Civil War and foreign intervention, the Soviet cosmonauts, Hitler, Mussolini and the Suez affair) and its vulgar style ('don't poke your nose where it doesn't belong'). Many experts believe it was written by Khrushchev himself.

2 On Berlin, his tactics were subtler. Officially the problem of a German settlement was set aside, although his intentions were made quite clear. On September 6, A. F. Dobrynin, the Soviet Ambassador in Washington, invited Theodore Sorensen to the Embassy and dictated to him the following message from Khrushchev to President Kennedy: 'Nothing will be undertaken before the American Congressional elections that could complicate the international situation or aggravate tension between our two countries . . . provided there are no actions by the other side which would alter the situation. This applies also to a German peace settlement and West Berlin' (Sorensen, p 677). The message also mentioned Khrushchev's plan, apparently made during the summer, to visit the United States and address the United Nations General Assembly. It said: 'Such a trip, if it proves necessary, would take place only in the second half of November. The Chairman does not wish to become involved in your internal political affairs'[1] (*ibid.*, p 667).

Khrushchev confirmed both these points to his many September visitors (Pitterman; the West German Ambassador, Kroll; the Belgian statesman Raymond Scheyven and others). He declared that he would be patient about Berlin till November but that, if the West then persisted in its negative attitude, the situation would grow serious. He also hinted that the United Nations trip might (as could have been guessed) provide the opportunity for a summit meeting and fruitful agreements.

Under the circumstances, it is fairly easy to picture what would have happened if the Cuban coup had succeeded. At the beginning of November most of the missiles shipped to Cuba would presumably have become operational. With this formidable weapon levelled at the heart of America and with the added prestige that accrues to the bolder player, Khrushchev could have faced Kennedy with something approaching triumph. If the Americans had not by then detected anything in Cuba, the chances are that Khrushchev, instead of Kennedy, would have brought the matter up and displayed the photographs. He would then have tried to bargain, primarily on Berlin and perhaps also on the American bases system as a whole, not only in Turkey. Even if he had not obtained anything by this means, he would at least have retained the strategic benefit of his advanced base and the prestige of the man

---

[1] The only surprising thing in the message from Khrushchev to Kennedy on September 6 was the timing of the planned visit to the United States in the 'second half' of November. In September the date of the Central Committee plenary session had already been set for November 19, and Khrushchev himself announced it on September 29 in a speech delivered in Central Asia and published later (*Agricultural Speeches* vol. 7 p. 189). The plenary met on schedule and sat until the 23rd, so that the second half of November was a busy period. A better time to visit the United States would have been immediately after the November 7 celebrations or else after the plenary session, at the end of the month.

who has scored a crucial point. It is certain therefore that, while the last week in October was a hot one, without it there would have been an even longer and hotter winter.

Did Khrushchev have last-minute doubts? It is possible, since he had no lack of warnings toward the end. As early as September 4, Kennedy, while denying the information put about by the Republicans on the presence of offensive weapons in Cuba, had declared: 'Were it to be otherwise, the gravest issues would arise.' Replying on September 13 to the Tass declaration of the 11th, President Kennedy had added: 'If at any time the Communist build-up in Cuba were to endanger or interfere with our security in any way ... or if Cuba should ever ... become an offensive military base of significant capacity for the Soviet Union, then this country will do whatever must be done to protect its own security and that of its allies.'

Even more significantly, Kennedy re-read this warning to Gromyko during a conversation with him in Washington on October 18. (Kennedy was by then aware of the presence of the rockets but, since the American reaction had not yet been decided upon, gave no inkling of this to Gromyko.) Furthermore, the Soviets must have been warned by the repeated overflights (up to six or seven a day) over their Cuban bases.

Possibly this was why Khrushchev never publicly announced his intention of going to New York in November. Besides, the date of the plenary session of the Central Committee, although decided on in September, was confirmed much later than usual – on November 9, only ten days before the opening. Khrushchev was probably waiting to see how his plans would unfold in Cuba before making definite arrangements. At the risk of further angering Kennedy, he chose to lie. At the interview of October 18 Gromyko read a declaration giving assurances that the USSR was working solely for Cuba's defence (while affirming that Moscow would sign a separate peace treaty with Germany if no settlement on Berlin were in sight after the American elections). A few days earlier, Khrushchev had instructed one of his unofficial emissaries, G. N. Bolshakov, to hand to the Americans a message stating in so many words: 'No missile capable of reaching the United States will be placed in Cuba.'[1] When Khrushchev received the American Ambassador, Foy Kohler, in the Kremlin on October 16 he was equally reassuring but, in preparation for the impending events, took care to mention the American bases in Turkey and Italy. Possibly Washington's concern forced Khrushchev to speed up work on the Cuban bases in the fairly reasonable hope that the American reaction

[1] The information that no device threatening the United States existed in Cuba, as well as that on the Kennedy–Gromyko talks and the other details of American moves, is to be found in Sorensen's book.

would be deterred by operational missiles. From the middle of October the Americans noticed that the missiles were mushrooming on Cuban soil, even before any adequate anti-aircraft defence had been set up. If this feverish activity was not a sign of war (and Kennedy was entitled to wonder about this) it already showed an undercurrent of panic.

2 Domestic Policy: Khrushchev on the Offensive

A great many events of the spring and summer of 1962 on the domestic scene must be viewed in the light of the Cuban gamble. If everything had gone according to plan as regards Cuba and the United States, Khrushchev could have expected a badly-needed diplomatic victory in the coming autumn. To all those who reproached him with having acted too boisterously over the years, jeopardizing the nation's prestige to no purpose, he could at last have shown results. The occasion would have been favourable for a consolidation of his position and he could have settled old scores with some people who were in his way, or at least extricated himself from the impasse into which he had been plunging ever deeper since 1960. In 1962 – for the last time – he made more moves than at any time since 1957. Some of them, such as dividing the Party, succeeded despite the crisis. Others, such as the resumption of destalinization and the drive against the economic planners, came to a halt after a short while. But for the Cuban fiasco at the end of October, it is quite possible that the plenary session of November 1962 would have been even more impressive and there would have been more changes in the top leadership.

The fact is that 1962 was a bad year for many *apparatchiks*. Khrushchev and his allies devised a number of schemes to whittle down their prerogatives.

NEW DESTALINIZATION DRIVE

First, destalinization was revived. If there was still any need to prove that the First Secretary's aim in this was his yearning for personal power rather than his humanitarian ideals, 1962 provided the evidence. In the course of that year, Khrushchev's 'liberalism' on the home front matched his recklessness in foreign policy: that is to say, his liberalism was as aggressive towards his domestic adversaries as the Cuban operation was towards the West.

Destalinization had barely progressed since the Twenty-second Congress. It may even be said to have regressed, since the attack against the 'anti-party group' had ceased. A new approach was needed. First, the offensive against Stalin himself was resumed. From the spring of 1962, even the phrase in Khrushchev's report to the Twenty-second Congress in which he paid lip-service to Stalin, saying that the dictator 'naturally did a great deal for the Party and the communist movement and we give him his due', fell into disuse. All references to the former idol had to be disparaging. Khrushchev took pains to show this at every opportunity in his speeches, particularly during his visits to Bulgaria in May and Central Asia in September. At a conference of ideologists under Ilyichev's chairmanship in the middle of October, just before the Cuban crisis, the 'struggle against remnants of the cult of personality' in every field was given a prominent place in all speeches. The general impression was that anything – from errors in doctrine to economic and military mistakes – could be used as a stick to beat the former ruler. Stalin's police excesses were not overlooked either, as was shown by the flood of obituaries of his victims in the newspapers.

A few measures of wider scope were taken quietly. On April 4 a decree promulgated without any fanfare cancelled awards, dating back to March 1944, to 700 NKVD officers for the 'exemplary execution of government missions'. The men's specific merits were not spelled out, but it is likely that they related to mass deportations from the territories recovered from the Germans at the end of the war. Among those affected were General Serov, former KGB chief and a close associate of Khrushchev's in the Ukraine, and also Beriya, Abakumov, Kruglev and evidently some former police officers who were still living. Thus, for the first time, a semi-public sanction was taken against those guilty of repressions.

As to rehabilitations, a major step was taken in the autumn of 1962. According to many unimpeachable sources, about September Khrushchev received Bukharin's widow to inform her that her illustrious husband had been cleared of the crimes for which he was executed in 1938. Financial compensation was promised to the family. True, the gesture did not mean that his political 'errors' were expunged, but, the system being what it is, any indulgence towards a former adversary is bound to have serious psychological repercussions. Significantly, no similar measures were reported about Trotsky, Kamenev or Zinoviev: their deviations were leftist ones, whereas Bukharin's was rightist, that is, closer to the line that Khrushchev was now trying to promote. It should be noted that Bukharin's name was uttered only once at the Twenty-second Congress, namely by Suslov, in a disparaging manner (verbatim records, vol 1 p 518).

In short, revisionism was in the air, and it is no accident that during the same period another move was made: the attempt at reconciliation with Tito, which achieved lasting success. In May, Khrushchev had taken the opportunity of his visit to Bulgaria to advocate better relations, affirming that Yugoslavia was 'building socialism'. The *rapprochement* was consolidated by a visit by Brezhnev to Belgrade at the end of September, which Tito returned in December. This was one of the few aspects of 'pre-Cuban' policy which endured almost unchanged in the months and years to come.

HELP FROM SOLZHENITSYN AND YEVTUSHENKO

Literature was also widely used to promote destalinization. This calls for comment on the relationship between it and politics. As we have emphasized, Khrushchev's motives in conducting his destalinization drive had little to do with ideals of liberty. But liberal Soviet writers saw things in their own way and, very rightly, took advantage of the situation. For them the attack on Stalin was, and would henceforth be, an opportunity to shake off controls and to write with true realism rather than in the vein of forced optimism labelled 'socialist realism'. In fact, they saw a chance of paying old scores. All the liberals to be found in Russia justly regarded destalinization as an attack upon dogmatism, administrative control and lies, in short any interference with independent thought. On both sides of the argument, Stalin himself was merely a symbol to serve wider purposes.

The urge for freedom on the part of Soviet intellectuals was, of course, too strong to be confined within any boundaries acceptable to Party leaders. Whatever had happened over Cuba, Khrushchev would have been forced to prevent the writers blowing off steam, as he had in 1957 and again in March 1963. But this time more was at stake and the reaction spread beyond literature. This was because Khrushchev had made the writers, or some of them at least, part of his political game.

In point of fact, he had only climbed on the bandwagon. As soon as the Twenty-second Congress was over, liberal Soviet artists and writers had naturally burst forth, taking advantage of the new climate to put stronger pressure on the Stalinist conservatives who ruled the roost in intellectual life. The culmination came early in April 1962, when the elections to the steering committee of the Moscow section of the Writers' Union yielded spectacular results: eight out of seventy-six candidates were defeated, including L. S. Sobolev, the head of the writers' organization of the Russian Republic, and N. A. Abalkin, *Pravda's* literary columnist. The climate was so unhealthy for the conformists that three of their leaders – V. A. Kochetov, N. M. Gribachov and A. V. Sofronov – had preferred not to stand in the first place. On the other hand, the two most articulate spokesmen of the new generation, the poets Yevtushenko and Voznesensky, had been elected. Shortly thereafter, Yevtushenko and another outspoken writer, Aksyonov, were admitted to the editorial board of the literary journal *Yunost*.

The summer and most of the autumn of 1962 were a golden inter-lude for *avant-garde* youth. There were mass poetry readings, laudatory articles on the young writers and endless discussions on the 'fathers and children' theme in Soviet literature. Even the black sheep of im-pressionism and abstract art, the arch-heretics of the Soviet art scene, began timidly to raise their heads.[1]

For a long time the Party leadership appeared neutral, letting the 'children' express themselves while it also allowed the 'fathers' to have their say. However, considering the success of the children in the free discussion with the fathers, the Party's neutrality amounted to compli-city. At the gathering of Moscow writers already mentioned, P. N. Demichev, the Urban Committee First Secretary, had even departed from neutrality so far as to declare that a very conservative article pub-lished a little earlier by *Kommunist* did not represent the official point of view. It must have represented at least the views of V. P. Stepanov, an ideologist who had just taken over as editor of the journal, for throughout the summer it was followed up by articles in the same vein. Only in September did Khrushchev enter the controversy by making two very far-reaching moves.

The first was the decision to force the publication of Aleksandr Solzhenitsyn's tale, *A Day in the Life of Ivan Denisovich*. This moving account of life in the Stalinist camps is known well enough the world over not to require further comment. Suffice it to recall that its powerful style and psychological insight made it the most crushing account yet published of the concentration camp régime. Politically it set the Stalinist 'phenomenon' in proper perspective as a mass phenomenon and not merely a matter of individual 'excesses'. Moreover, it belied the fiction propounded later, according to which faith in the Party had remained strong despite the barbed wire. The characters depicted by Solzhenitsyn yearned for justice pure and simple – not the brand dis-pensed by the Party. For all these reasons, the book was not entirely

---

[1] As early as February 14 1962, *Izvestia* published an article by the critic Alpatov who cautiously but firmly defended modern art. Later the critic Turbin published a book (later roundly criticized) entitled *Comrade Time and Comrade Art*. It contained such remarks as: 'The twentieth century is witnessing the triumph of abstraction.' After this, private exhibitions of abstract art started emerging from the shadows. It was one of them that provoked the fracas on December 1 1962.

to Khrushchev's liking. The shock it caused, however, was just what he needed to recreate the anti-Stalinist climate – something he had been working towards for the past few months.

Solzenitsyn's story was published in Number 11 of *Novy Mir*, which came out in the second half of November, that is, after the Cuban crisis; but the decision to publish it must be dated at the end of September, for the material had gone to the printer on September 21. Rumours of a forthcoming sensation were already going about Moscow. According to reliable information, two men were instrumental in getting the story published. They were Tvardovsky, the director of *Novy Mir*, who had the manuscript and eagerly fought for its publication, and Khrushchev's personal lieutenant, V. S. Lebedev, who read the main passages to the First Secretary. Khrushchev was won over and allegedly had twenty copies of the text distributed to the Presidium members and alternates. The Presidium probably met towards the end of September to discuss the matter, and some dissent was almost certainly voiced. One widespread version was that Kozlov and Suslov had objected. It also seems that Khrushchev himself reported these objections in his speech of November 23 to the plenary session of the Central Committee. It allegedly took two Presidium meetings for a unanimous decision to be reached, and probably strong pressure by Khrushchev on the reluctant officials. According to one source, the First Secretary pointed his finger at Kozlov and Suslov, declaring: 'How can we fight against remnants of the cult of personality if Stalinists of this type are still in our midst?'

This, if true, seems to show that Khrushchev was bellicose towards his adversaries, just as in 1957 the posthumous rehabilitation of Tukhachevsky had served him as a pretext to join issue with his opponents in the presence of their colleagues. Was he again trying to use Stalin as a weapon against enemies close at hand? His next move suggested this even more clearly.

Yevtushenko's poem *Stalin's Heirs* appeared in the literary section of *Pravda* on October 21, on the eve of the Cuban blockade. Although of much less literary value than Solzhenitsyn's work, it was of great political import, since the young poet was the first to go to the core of the destalinization issue. Instead of the dictator's ghost, his 'errors' or his crimes, he spoke of the heirs, who were Stalinists alive and biding their time. He wrote:

> *Some of his heirs are in retirement pruning their rosebushes,*
> *and secretly thinking that their time will come again.*
> *Others even attack Stalin from the rostrum but*
> *   at home, at night-time, think back to bygone days . . .*

No wonder they suffer heart attacks.
For these former champions of his, the times are not right.

To a number of people, these verses suggested that the pensioned-off 'heir' pruning his rosebushes was Bulganin and the heart attack victim Kozlov, who was in fact so stricken in 1961. However this may be, Yevtushenko's poem, much more than Solzhenitsyn's book, was what Khrushchev wanted to hear and to make public. The circumstances of its publication are not known, but it took place when Yevtushenko had been in Cuba for many weeks as a *Pravda* correspondent. The poem, which he had read in public more than once that summer, seems to have been written immediately after the Twenty-second Congress and the transfer of Stalin's body which provided its theme. Printing was delayed because a top-level decision was necessary. All information points to the fact that it came from Khrushchev,[1] and apparently this time the Presidium had no part in it.

The offensive against Stalin and his heirs went on under its own momentum even after the Cuban fiasco. Then, during the winter, it collapsed before the upsurge of conservatism it had helped to provoke. If destalinization had lasted a few months longer instead of being cut short by the Cuban crisis, it would have borne results. The November plenary session might have turned out differently and prominent 'heirs' of Stalin might have been overthrown.

THE DIVISION OF THE PARTY

The dividing of the Party was the first of the 'hasty, unplanned and unjustified organizational moves' about which so much was heard after the palace revolution of October 1964. The reorganizing mania typical of Khrushchev's 'subjective' style was given free play. This last major drive of his coincided with the Cuban adventure and the revival of anti-Stalinism. Khrushchev was attacking on all fronts at once.

His object was to change the traditional methods of the Party apparatus rather than the apparatus itself. The major reform in this 1962 series, namely, the division of the Party into industrial and agricultural branches, did not mean a streamlining of the machine but, on the contrary, an extreme bureaucratic hypertrophy. Khrushchev's purpose was not to curtail the Party's prerogatives, but to reinforce them by endowing it with quasi-total control over the economy. The

---

[1] Yevtushenko writes in his autobiography: 'I sent the poem [*Stalin's Heirs*] to Khrushchev and *Pravda* published it.'

main features are well known: each Party Oblast Committee, or regional hierarchy, was split into two such Committees covering respectively agriculture and industry. The same procedure was carried out at the level of regional soviets and their executive committees. At a lower level, the basic administrative unit, the *rayon*, was replaced by territorial agricultural units and 'zones of industrial production'. On a higher level again, the Republic Central Committees set up two bureaux in charge respectively of industry and agriculture. The same applied to the RSFSR and to the Central Committee apparatus for the USSR.

Many of the scheme's consequences were easy to foresee, but some of those responsible may have realized them only after some time. It meant the arbitrary carving up of a modern society into separate watertight segments. In actual fact, outside agriculture and industry, there is a whole range of intermediate activities and some of a higher order, such as education, science, justice and commerce, and it was impossible to determine under which of the two sections they should come. The system of administrative barriers (*vedomstvennost*), which was already found irksome as between regions, was now to be implanted in the very core of the former administrative units and further breed bureaucratic red tape. These were practical difficulties that undoubtedly contributed to the rapid elimination of the system after its initiator fell, and they may have aroused objections when it was first introduced. But they were probably not the sole factor determining the respective attitudes adopted when the plan was discussed at top level.

Politically, the effects of the plan were different for different people. Those most severely hit were the Oblast Committee Secretaries. Instead of managing a whole region, as formerly, they were henceforth entitled only to half an Oblast Committee (less than half in fact, since their traditional functions of political, ideological and police control – whether or not the reformers had intended this – were downgraded merely by being divided). For the overwhelming majority of the political Oblast officials, the loss was compounded by an additional factor: almost all the Oblast Committee First Secretaries had been recruited during the previous years on the basis of their competence in agriculture, to satisfy Khrushchev's quasi-exclusive interest in that sector. In many cases these officials found themselves after the reform at the head of the agricultural unit, which was the one most reduced in size, while an outsider took over the more important Oblast Committee for industry. Had a Party congress been held between 1962 and 1964, these functionaries of long standing would have run a serious risk of losing their seats in the Central Committee, or at any rate of finding themselves swamped by the mass of newcomers.

The other victims were the Rayon Committee Secretaries and their aides – an army of several tens of thousands – whose posts had simply been eliminated. Those who could not be employed in the new Oblast Committees could hope for nothing better than technical work entailing even less political influence than formerly. The picture was hardly any rosier for the high economic officials. A plant manager, for his part, might view with equanimity this new extension of the bureaucratic maze; and the prospect of an Oblast Committee tailored to the needs of industry might well seem attractive to him as providing stronger backing for his requests to the state bureaucracy. But for the top officials of Gosplan and other central administrative agencies, the scheme meant a further loss of autonomy to the specialized Party bureaux and departments.

At the very top, the effect was not too drastic. The top men in the state apparatus were of course affected by the Party's encroachment on economic management; but the heads of the Party machine within the Presidium – Kozlov, Suslov and others – suffered no diminution of influence. True, the upholders of orthodox theory tended to regard the reform as an infringement of the fundamental principle of 'the alliance of workers and peasants'. But in so far as they had feared – and this was always their foremost concern – that the economic managers would escape Party control, they received ample assurances. More than ever, the Secretariat was to function as the General Staff of the country in all sectors. The top officials in charge of ideology, of 'Party organs' and of 'control' (this last was set up a little later) were to have their own chain of command within the Party industrial and agricultural machines, and even the state machine as far as 'control' was concerned. Some high officials might have been sensitive to the grievances of their clientele amongst the Oblast and Rayon Committee officials, but the major reshuffle that was under way enabled them to replace this following by another.

All this should be taken into account in analysing the background of the decision and the opposition which it encountered. When, in November, 1964, an outcry was raised about the dividing of the Party in 1962, the impression given was that it had been pushed through hastily and arbitrarily by a 'subjectivist' Khrushchev over the opposition of a 'scientifically' minded collective leadership. Actually, the truth seems to be that, while Khrushchev was the originator of the reform, he secured wide agreement to it within the Presidium, and the decision was taken with due regard to the democratic standards, such as they were, then prevailing in Moscow. The texts of his many speeches about the reform and in particular his 'notes to the Presidium' were released only afterwards, in the spring of 1963, in volume 7 of *Agricultural Speeches*. They provide a fairly detailed account of the procedure followed in the months before the decision was officially announced in November 1962.

A DECISION TAKEN ACCORDING TO RULE

Khrushchev first outlined his plan on September 10 1962 in a note (*zapiska*) of some fifteen pages addressed to the Presidium (*Agricultural Speeches* vol 7 p 163). He was in Gagra on the Black Sea at the time and claimed that, during his holiday, he had 'given a great deal of thought to improving the structure of the Party and Soviet apparatus'. The starting point had been a Presidium meeting in August at which he had 'suggested ways of improving the work of industry'. He said no more of this, but other facts give some idea of what happened at this initial discussion. The meeting took place about August 20, just after the reception in Moscow for the cosmonauts Nikolayev and Popovich (apart from this, Khrushchev spent August in the Crimea). Not long before, from July 27 to 30, a conference of 'officials of local RSFSR Party organizations' had met under Kozlov's and Kirilenko's sponsorship. The main topic of discussion was the 'strengthening of Party control over industry and building, including the widening of the role and responsibility of the Oblast and Urban Committees' (*Pravda*, July 31 1962). The conference had deplored the 'superficial and hidebound' attitude of local Party organs in dealing with industrial matters – a hint as to the crux of the problem. In the preceding few years, under pressure from Khrushchev, agriculture had become the dominant, not to say exclusive concern of local cadres. Regional Secretaries were kept in a permanent state of battle-readiness by the First Secretary's incessant agricultural drives. If it was not maize growing, it was 'square-cluster sowing', intertilling (*propashnaya systema*) or a combination of all of them. Officials simply had no time left for industrial problems. To top it all, at the March 1962 plenary session Khrushchev insisted on placing the First Secretaries of Oblast Committees in charge of 'committees for agriculture' to be set up in each republic and region[1] in order

---

[1] In his report of March 5 1962 about the 'committees for agriculture' which were about to be set up, Khrushchev stated: 'During the preliminary discussion of this matter, some comrades advocated that the chairman of the committee for agriculture in each republic should be the Central Committee Secretary in charge of agriculture. This suggestion seems to me difficult to accept. . . . The Secretary (in charge of agriculture) would be powerless if he were alone. The entire Party organization must concern itself with agriculture.'

Khrushchev won, but the committees for agriculture, at least at the regions and republics level, were apparently short-lived.

to impress upon them that they were personally responsible for agricultural production.

Complaints were undoubtedly heard during the Presidium meeting of August 20 and Khrushchev apparently upheld them, since in his note of September 10 he used this as the main argument in support of his plan. This was both radical and seemingly equitable: if each Oblast Committee were split in two, neither industry nor agriculture could be slighted. An additional motive was not mentioned: in all likelihood, the officials who sincerely wanted to rationalize industrial management, especially Kosygin who, two years later, advocated some economic liberalization, used the August discussion to bring up the real problems. Their foremost concern was not the 'reinforcement of the Party's role in running the economy' but rather the actual management of the economy, coupled perhaps with stronger Party controls. This meant giving some substance to the concepts of price, profit-earning capacity and profit, as well as granting plant managers sufficient autonomy to enable them to cope with bureaucratic red tape.

Khrushchev's 'note' on the dividing of the Party appeared the day after *Pravda* published the now famous article by the hitherto unknown Kharkov economist, Professor Liberman (September 9). With *Pravda*'s backing, Liberman called for a broad debate on the role of profit-earning capacity (*rentabelnost*) and profits in the Soviet economy. His suggestions will not be discussed in detail here, especially as they were not followed up at the time. They did not, as often supposed in the West, constitute a grandiose plan, but rather a fresh approach, an effort to lighten the controls and interference of bureaucratic planning bodies by means of a rational manipulation of the laws of supply and demand. What we are concerned with here is the political impact of Liberman's ideas, in particular on the always delicate problem of Party–state relationships. Any increased autonomy for local managers worries the central planning officials, who are used to the traditional chain of command: it is also bound to worry Party officials, who live in fear of a managerial class emerging and escaping their ideological and political grip. If nevertheless, pressed by circumstances and the need for efficiency, the Party leaders agree to the relaxation of state control, it must be on condition that the Party's control over these sectors is strengthened. Khrushchev's plan of 1962 for dividing the Party was clearly intended to fulfil this condition.

This, of course, was not the only reason the plan was adopted; in any case, Liberman's suggestions were eventually shelved while the price paid for them remained. But this was certainly not foreseen during the August discussion. It is more likely that the pressure Kosygin exerted in favour of management reform found enough supporters

in the Presidium on its own merits. In 1962 the bureaucratic strangle-
hold over the economy was indeed just as bad as in 1964 and 1965.
Although no basic remedy was decided upon, it was agreed to encourage an open debate among experts, which began with the publication of Liberman's theses on September 9 and lasted until November.
At the August 20 meeting of the Presidium, some members must have
expressed their personal concern about the effect on the Party's role.
Khrushchev certainly understood this kind of thinking much better
than Liberman's theses. Characteristically, all his correspondence and
all the speeches of that period contain not a word on the professor's
ideas or the press debate. From the conference held by Kozlov and
Kirilenko in July, it is clear that he was not alone in feeling apprehen-
sive. The threat represented by Liberman's theses enhanced the attraction of Khrushchev's proposal to divide the Party so as to strengthen
its hold over economic cadres.

Actually his plan was somewhat more moderate than that finally
adopted in November. It grudgingly hinted at 'some co-ordinating
agency' to be maintained in each region as a link between the two Oblast Committees (*Agricultural Speeches* vol 7 p 173). We do not know
whether this proviso was suggested to Khrushchev by others, but in
any case it was later eliminated, which would not have happened if the
original plan had aroused strong indignation among the top leaders.
The procedure recommended for carrying out the plan was fully
'democratic'. Khrushchev modestly concluded his note of September 10
as follows:

> 'If the suggestions outlined in the present note are acceptable, if
> the members of the Presidium agree that they will create new condi-
> tions for improving the country's management . . . then it would
> be possible to deliver a report on that subject to the Central Com-
> mittee at its plenary session. But it would be advisable beforehand
> to request the Oblast and Territorial Committees and the Party
> Central Committees of the Republics to give some thought to work-
> ing out the requisite plans. . . . The scheme should then be discussed
> by the Presidium and these important questions brought to the
> attention of the Central Committee' (*Agricultural Speeches* vol 7
> p 177).

While the plenary session was again to operate as a mere rubber-
stamp, the Presidium's rights remained intact. Khrushchev came back
from holiday about the middle of September and an enlarged Presidium
meeting was held in Moscow between the 17th and the 22nd. (Three
of the provincial alternates – K. T. Mazurov, V. P. Mzhavanadze and
V. V. Shcherbitsky – appeared in Moscow on the 20th, at the same time

as the full member, N. V. Podgorny, fresh from Kiev.) The substance of the debates is not known, but a few days later, on October 1, Khrushchev said in a speech at Ashkhabad: 'The Presidium of the Central Committee discussed this suggestion (the dividing of the Party) and approved it. It has been decided to convene a Central Committee plenary session' (*Agricultural Speeches* vol 7 p 220).

After the Presidium meeting, and not before, Khrushchev started circulating the text of his note to the Presidium among the regional cadres. He first mentioned it only on September 28, to members of Turkmenia sovkhozes (*Agricultural Speeches* vol 7 p 190).

It might be objected that Khrushchev may have been lying when he declared that the Presidium had approved the plan, just as he lied to President Kennedy about the presence of rockets in Cuba. However, he was probably speaking the truth, and not only because it was harder to dissemble on such a topic. For, in these same speeches in Central Asia (published only six months later, which made it easier for him to be candid), Khrushchev had no qualms about ignoring the Presidium's stand on other issues and about saying so. The most clear-cut example of this occurred in connection with a scheme he devised a little later for setting up a Central Committee Bureau for Central Asia (*Sredazbyuro*) to oversee the Party machines of the Republics in question. His first reference to it dates back to the same October 1 speech before a gathering of Turkmen 'activists': 'I have had an idea, and when I am back in Moscow I shall take it up with the members of the Presidium. Perhaps it would be desirable to set up a Central Asia Bureau of the Central Committee of the CPSU' (*Agricultural Speeches* vol 7 p 215).

He duly outlined the plan in another note to the Presidium on October 5 (*Agricultural Speeches* vol 7 p 249), but before this, during his tour, he tried to secure public support for the project in cheerful disregard of the collective leadership. The most striking instance was his statement on October 3 in Tashkent to a group of cotton experts – not even a Party audience:

'I have not yet submitted the idea to the members of the Presidium of the Central Committee. This is why I am consulting you. I want to know your opinion. And when I am back in Moscow I shall report to the Presidium. If you agree, I would like to draft a note to the Central Committee on the basis of your views. What do you think, would this be useful or not?' Voices: 'Useful!' (*Agricultural Speeches* vol 7 p 232).

The Central Committee for Central Asia was in fact set up after the plenary session, together with several other bodies designed to increase the economic centralization of this area. In his report to the plenary session on November 19, Khrushchev depicted his proposal as a reflection of 'the Presidium's opinion' (*Agricultural Speeches* vol 7 p 332). It is possible that the collective leadership did agree to it in the end, but its assent had been extorted by means of the summary plebiscites Khrushchev had carried out at local meetings under the guise of practising direct democracy.[1] Nothing of the sort occurred with his plan for dividing the Party. In the latter case, the rank and file were most probably 'consulted' in a similar way, but only after the Presidium had studied and approved the plan.

It is interesting to compare the ways in which the two plans were amended. The plan for dividing the Party became more drastic in November, whereas the one for setting up the Central Asia Bureau was weakened as regards the power of its chief. In his note of October 5 regarding the Bureau, Khrushchev had stated that it was to be headed by an 'authoritative official (*avtoritetny deyatel*) of our Party' (*Agricultural Speeches* vol 7 p 259). Obviously it did not occur to him then that in December an obscure Rayon Committee First Secretary from Moscow, V. G. Lomonosov, who was not a member of the Central Committee or of any superior organ of the Party, would be picked to head the new organization. This shows that, especially after Cuba, the scope of the First Secretary's moves was reduced to some degree. If this did not happen with the dividing of the Party, it was because wide agreement on the subject prevailed within the Presidium.[2]

[1] A glaring example of Khrushchev's high-handed behaviour towards the collective leadership and the methods he used to force his views upon others was provided on October 5 in Tashkent at a conference of Central Asian cadres. Mentioning (for the first time in public) his plan for setting up a single 'cotton production administration' in the three large cotton-producing republics of Central Asia, he added: 'It is possible that the Kazakhstan cotton-producing regions should also come under this administration. What is your opinion, comrade Kunayev?' (Kunayev was then First Party Secretary for the Kazakhstan Republic.) 'Quite right!' Kunayev replied, whereupon Khrushchev declared: 'You see, *the Kazakhs agree*.' (*Agricultural Speeches* vol 7 p 245.) [Author's italics.]

[2] The scant explanations supplied after the event indirectly corroborate the thesis that the First Secretary's moves were to some extent restricted. For instance, V. P. Mzhavanadze declared at the March 1965 plenary session, after having remarked that the 1962 reforms ran counter to Party statutes:

'It is known that *many members* of the Central Committee brought this up when the Oblast Committees and Oblast Executive Committees were divided. The *members of the Central Committee* of the Party with whom I spoke expressed their indignation. They told Khrushchev that this would make work more complicated, that it should not be done, but he refused to listen.

'The *members of the Central Committee* of the Party had put up with everything, but they did not tolerate interference with the Party, they refused to accept it and they acted in a perfectly correct manner' (Plenary session of March 1965, verbatim record, p 89). [Author's italics.]

The fact that Mzhavanadze laid stress on the 'members of the Central Committee'

LENIN TO THE RESCUE (WITH AMPLEYEV'S HELP)

The lower hierarchy, for its part, was far from pleased with the reforms. Advocates of the Rayons emerged in March 1962 when it became clear that Khrushchev and his allies were set against them. Men like G. I. Voronov or P. E. Shelest (then First Secretary of the Kiev Oblast Committee) came out, some of them more firmly than others, for the maintenance of the Rayons, their Party committees and prerogatives.[1] Khrushchev had opposed them verbally from June onwards ('It must be stated frankly: the Rayons as they exist at present are a passing phenomenon,' he said on June 27 1962 in Moscow), and in November he proceeded to act.

The division of the Party probably came as an even greater shock to the old-timers in the regional apparatus. This is shown not by any direct statements – true to tradition, the 'debates' at the November plenary session reflected a gratifying unanimity – but by the intensive propaganda carried on immediately after the session against invisible opponents. For instance, the ideologists were mobilized to explain that the 'alliance between the workers and the peasants' was, of course, not being weakened by the reform but 'reinforced'.[2] At the same time it had

---

is of course not accidental. It is likely that he would have included the Presidium in this belated praise, had its members deserved it.

It should also be noted that the same Mzhavanadze had declared in November 1962: 'We share and fully support the proposals of N. S. Khrushchev on the new structure of Party organs' (Plenary session of November 1962, verbatim record, p 218).

[1] Voronov and Shelest, who advocated keeping the Rayons in existence, had none the less disagreed on a minor point – that of whether or not the Rayon Committees should be entitled to publish their own newspapers. Voronov, while advocating the maintenance of the Rayon Committees 'which were, are, and will be the agents of political leadership in every aspect of economic and cultural life of the Rayons', had asked for the elimination of these newspapers and their replacement with newspapers serving several Rayons. Shelest, on the other hand, had not been awed by Voronov's status as a Presidium member and had frankly opposed him on that point. Taking the floor at the March plenary session, he had declared: 'It is difficult to agree with the proposal of comrade Voronov and comrade Nuriev (First Secretary in Bashkiria) on the liquidation of Rayon newspapers. It seems to me that this way of posing the problem is premature. The Rayon Committee remains, as it was heretofore, an important element in our party's organic structure.' For the same reasons, Shelest had made reservations about the '*partorgs*' (Party organizers) whom Khrushchev had installed to control agriculture, thus further weakening the Rayon Committee's authority. This system, Shelest contended, 'should be studied further in all its details' (Plenary session of March 1962, verbatim records, p 314).

[2] P. N. Fedoseyev wrote in *Pravda* of December 9 1962 about the division of the Party: 'Of course dogmatists will be found to claim that the new system may lead to a slowdown in the *rapprochement* between industry and agriculture, between town and village. It can be authoritatively stated, however, that the reorganization will not only not slow this process down, but will strengthen it. . . .'

to be explained why the power of the local Party bosses had to be reduced to strictly economic problems.

Miraculously, the founder of the Soviet state himself came upon the scene to give a hand to his 'faithful disciples'. On September 28 1962 *Pravda* gave a full two pages to 'a new document by Lenin' called 'Current [*ocheredniye*] tasks of the Soviet state'. It was explained that this was the 'first version' of part of a text dictated by Lenin in March 1918 and newly discovered by specialists. A document bearing the same title had for a long time been part of the *Complete Works* of Lenin, but it so happened that the new version departed markedly from the original and bore a strong resemblance to Khrushchev's line. Its main point was that the Party had reached a stage where 'the emphasis must be laid on the economy rather than politics', that 'political tasks must be subordinated to economic ones' and that 'the problem of state management today consists primarily in solving purely economic problems'. A *Pravda* editorial stressed the importance of the discovery and wrote: 'The production principle has been placed in the forefront of the new system of agricultural management. The Party consistently applies and will continue to apply the Leninist directive giving priority to the economy over all other activities of the Soviet state.'

In his letter of September 10 Khrushchev had used this very same 'production principle' (*proizvodstvenny printsip*) as an argument for the division of the Party, whose new structure would contrast with the territorial principle hitherto applied. As mentioned, his plan was approved by the Presidium around September 20 and the publication of Lenin's text a week later was obviously aimed at winning the assent of diehards in the Party bureaucracy. Seldom had history so directly stepped in to serve the needs of day-to-day politics.

It is impossible to tell whether the document was in fact authentic. The account of the circumstances under which it was dictated and then forgotten, only to be found and deciphered forty years later by a young researcher at the Marxism–Leninism Institute, N. A. Ampleyev, is not very convincing.[1] Signs of unease about the matter were in fact notice-

---

The chief editor of *Kommunist*, V. P. Stepanov, wrote in *Izvestia* of February 8 1963: 'In letters to the editor it is sometimes asked: under these conditions what will become of the alliance between workers and peasants? Won't the Party leadership of the alliance be weakened? Such concern on the part of comrades is understandable, but it is unfounded and rests on a misunderstanding. . . . The constitution of two independent Party organizations in the regions and territories can in no way weaken the Party's leadership of the alliance between workers and peasants.'

[1] Two days after the publication of Ampleyev's document, *Izvestia* carried an account of the discovery. According to the Government daily, in order to 'save time', Lenin had dictated his text to five different stenographers, who took down different parts of each sentence: one would take the first part of a sentence, the second the middle and so on.

able. For instance, on October 10 Ampleyev was awarded a 'badge of honour' by the Presidium of the USSR Supreme Soviet for his 'success in preparatory research work towards the publication of an important historical document'; but the decree announcing the award was not published by the Moscow press, and appeared only in the 'Bulletin of the USSR Supreme Soviet' dated October 12 1962, and in those provincial newspapers that had published Lenin's document in September. This included the Ukraine, Uzbekistan and Georgia, but not Byelorussia or Kazakhstan, where both Lenin's newly discovered writing and Ampleyev's achievement were ignored. Apart from this, publicity about the find was limited in volume and fairly mixed in tone. After having published and commented on the text on September 28, *Pravda* said no more on the subject, nor did other papers. It was also strange that the ideologist Yu. P. Frantsev published a detailed commentary on 'Current Tasks of the Soviet State' in *Pravda* of November 29, with reference to the 1918 text and without a single allusion to Ampleyev's new version. E. I. Bugayev, the chief editor of *Partiynaya Zhizn*, also took up a strange attitude: although in *Pravda* of December 26 he enlarged upon the need to give the economy priority over politics, he ignored the Ampleyev version of Lenin's essay, although it provided excellent material in support of the thesis. On April 28 1963 *Pravda* commemorated the forty-fifth anniversary of the publication of 'Current Tasks' without one word about the new version, whereas *Izvestia*, *Sovietskaya Rossiya* and a few other provincial papers did mention it.

Before long, the hesitation died down. The new text was included in Lenin's *Complete Works* (volume 36) and, even after Khrushchev fell, the consensus seems to have been that it was indeed authentic.[1] If any differences remained, they probably concerned the significance of the text rather than its authorship (after all, the version published in the

---

The text had thus been cut into meaningless fragments. The whole thing had been forgotten and the five parts of the cryptogram (taken down in an obsolete form of shorthand) had remained a mystery. It was only in 1962, according to *Izvestia*, that Ampleyev had started working on the puzzle and had finally solved it.

[1] P. N. Pospelov and G. D. Obichkin, respectively Director and Deputy Director of the Institute of Marxism-Leninism, referred favourably in *Kommunist* (No 5 April 1965) to the newly published chapters of 'Current Tasks'. 'These chapters', they wrote, 'are particularly relevant to current problems because in them Lenin stresses the importance of solving economic problems, which are fundamental and crucial for the life of the Soviet state'. It is worth noting that these writers did not go quite so far as the text itself, which clearly advocated the *primacy* of economics over politics.

In April, P. Zeven referred in *Pravda* to the original version (April 16 1965) and added an even more cautious commentary: 'These chapters shed light on a series of problems in greater detail than the definitive version and make it possible to gain a deeper understanding of the substance of this inspired work of Lenin's.'

writer's lifetime was presumably the most authoritative) and, more important, the use to which Khrushchev meant to put it. As early as 1963, the theoretician G. E. Glezerman acknowledged in a somewhat apologetic article in *Kommunist* (No 7 1963) that Lenin was not above contradicting himself on occasion, and recalled that his other slogan: 'Politics cannot fail to dominate economics' was still valid. For all these reasons, the number of top Party leaders who agreed to endorse Ample-yev's discovery and uphold the primacy of economics remained small. In the Presidium, they were Khrushchev (in his report to the November plenary session), Kosygin (in his report on the anniversary of the revolution on November 6), Brezhnev (before the Congress of the Czechoslovak Communist Party on December 5 1962) and Podgorny (at the plenary session of the Ukrainian Central Committee on December 6).

Altogether, it had not taken a coup to bring about the division of the Party, as was suggested in 1964. In the summer of 1962 industrial managers and economists, encouraged by Kosygin, were pressing the top Party leaders to relax planning regulations. The leaders responded by trying to reinforce their control over industry, especially since agriculture had become the cadres' full-time occupation. Khrushchev's solution was a plan that drastically upset the habits of the regional apparatus without disturbing any vested interests of the top hierarchy. His approach was somewhat more aggressive than seeking mere relaxation of controls, since the primacy of economics in the Party's local activity was openly asserted, and this certainly caused his colleagues some concern. Destalinization, however, was still Khrushchev's main weapon against them, particularly in its new aspect involving Stalin's 'heirs'.

Such was the picture in October 1962, when Khrushchev's other aggressive move, the Cuban gamble, was coming to fruition. We now turn once again to foreign policy.

3 The Impact

President Kennedy's announcement of the blockade of Cuba on the evening of Monday October 22 (in the early morning of the 23rd, Moscow time) was the 'bitter awakening' for the Soviet leaders that, a few months earlier, *Pravda* had promised the West.

The vicissitudes of the crisis and its ending on October 28 with the withdrawal of the missiles from Cuba have been described and commented upon at length in all parts of the world. We shall, however, concentrate on the waverings and perhaps even conflicts that the crisis provoked in Moscow.

The broad change in Soviet policy in the face of the American challenge is not difficult to reconstruct. *Pravda's* headlines during the crucial week are a good starting point:

Wednesday 24: 'The unleashed American aggressors must be stopped!'
'Hands off Cuba!'

Thursday 25: 'The aggressive designs of United States imperialists must be foiled. Peace on earth must be defended and strengthened!'

Friday 26: 'Everything to prevent war.' Below, an editorial with the title: 'Reason must prevail.'

Saturday 27: No headline, but only the motto used on November 7: 'Peoples of all countries, be vigilant; unmask the imperialist warmongers! Struggle more actively for the preservation of a durable and indestructible peace!'

Sunday 28: 'We must defend and consolidate peace on earth.'

Monday 29: 'We must ensure the peace and security of all peoples.'

These indications make it possible to trace a 'belligerence curve' showing two main peaks – the higher on the 24th and a slightly lower one on Saturday the 27th. From these peaks there was a steep decline toward two decidedly pacific low points – the first on the 26th and the second on the 29th of October, just after the final retreat.[1] This indeed fits in with the course that events took.

---

[1] The dates given are those of the *Pravda* issues. The headlines therefore reflect official views in the late hours of the preceding evenings.

TUESDAY OCTOBER 23: A WAIT-AND-SEE POLICY

The (albeit decreasing) aggressiveness of the first three days corresponds to the period of waiting. The Kremlin must have taken some time to size up the situation, for the first official reaction to the announcement of the blockade did not come until 5 pm on Tuesday the 23rd, while the news had reached Moscow not later than 2 am. The reaction took the form of a government statement. It was firm in tone, a little too much so in the light of what was to follow, since it 'decisively' rejected American claims 'which naturally no State concerned with preserving its independence can accept'; it described the American move as 'a step towards the unleashing of a thermonuclear world war', and warned against its 'catastrophic consequences'. Apparently this was also Khrushchev's tone in the two letters he sent Kennedy on Tuesday afternoon and Wednesday evening. These were never published, but Sorensen reports that they showed Khrushchev 'to be manoeuvring, to be seeking a consensus among the top Kremlin rulers, uncertain whether to admit that missiles were there [in Cuba] or not'. 'We were wondering', Sorensen adds, 'whether their [the Soviets'] inconsistent positions reflected a possible internal struggle.'

Actually, it does not seem likely that any serious internal struggle occurred at that stage (except, naturally, for reproaches to Khrushchev for his reckless move). The Soviet rulers were certainly manoeuvring and hesitating, but circumstances themselves were the cause. At first, the blockade disguised as a 'quarantine' must have seemed to them a half-hearted and rather vague response. We know that Kennedy had deliberately chosen it owing to its flexibility, for it left him free to tighten the blockade gradually if need be. His first object was to play for time and discover whether his adversary was telling the truth.

If, as we believe, no Soviet leader then wanted a direct military confrontation with the United States, the line adopted by Khrushchev at that stage probably did not arouse any controversy. The only concession made was to avoid or at least postpone any resort to force by ordering sixteen of the eighteen freighters en route for Cuba not to sail farther. This apparently happened on Wednesday the 24th[1] and was

---

[1] Sorensen reported that sixteen freighters on their way to Cuba had been ordered to stop. Another collaborator of President Kennedy, Arthur M. Schlesinger Jr. (*A Thousand Days*, New York, 1965) states that the news about the Soviet freighters being re-routed only reached him on Thursday the 25th. The first version seems more likely, for Sorensen was constantly at the President's side during the crisis whereas Schlesinger had been assigned to assist Adlai Stevenson, the American Ambassador to the United Nations. Anyway, the order must have been given in Moscow several hours before the Americans could observe the actual results.

confirmed the following day by Khrushchev in a message to U Thant, the Secretary-General of the United Nations.

At the same time, however, Soviet diplomacy was fully deployed for the purpose of intimidating the United States. On Wednesday, Khrushchev replied to the British philosopher Bertrand Russell that it was out of the question to 'appease the bandit', which would only make him 'increasingly insolent'. When on the same day he was host to the American businessman William Knox, Khrushchev warned him that Soviet submarines would sink any vessel attempting to hamper traffic with Cuba. His simultaneous pleas for a summit conference were obviously a play for time, since what had been and still was the main purpose of the operation – namely, the installation of nuclear missiles in Cuba – was going on faster than ever. Sorensen describes the results of aerial reconnaissance flights over Cuba during those days as follows: 'Work was going ahead full speed. All the MRBM's would be operational by the end of the week, with the IRBM's ready about a month or so later.'

It is obvious that if this work could be completed under cover of diplomatic negotiations over broader issues, for example the general problem of foreign bases, Khrushchev would have won all he wanted: not only strategic reinforcement as a result of his newly built Cuban base, but also the diplomatic initiative resulting from his greater strength. At the same time, the Soviet leaders set to work to secure their rear, a sign that they were preparing for a confrontation. This was the meaning of *Pravda's* editorial of Thursday October 25, echoed by *Izvestia* that same evening, supporting the Chinese in their border conflict against the Indians. The Soviets judged it necessary to strengthen the 'cohesion of the socialist camp' on the eve of the tense diplomatic game that was about to start.[1] Later, having chosen the line of 'shameful compromise

---

[1] Actually, perhaps because Khrushchev had foreseen for some time the possibility of a diplomatic confrontation with the United States after his Cuban operation, he made a point of assuring the Chinese of his sympathy even before the opening of the hostilities with India (of which he had been given prior information). This at least was the version given by Peking in November 1963 (see, for instance, *Peking Review* of November 8 1963). The Chinese Government, according to Peking, had, as far back as October 8 1962, notified the Soviet Embassy that the Indians 'were preparing an attack on the border' near the Himalayas. Peking also informed Moscow that the presence of Soviet weapons in the hands of Indian soldiers made 'a bad impression' on the Chinese soldiers.

What Khrushchev replied about the arms is not known, but his attitude on the problem as a whole was quite clear. *Peking Review* wrote: 'On October 13 and 14 1962 [that is, before the Cuban blockade] Khrushchev made the following statement to the Chinese Ambassador: "Information received by the Soviet Union on India's military preparations is identical to that received by the Chinese. If the Soviets were in the place of the Chinese they would have made the same decisions. A neutral attitude is impossible in the Sino-Indian border conflict. If China were attacked and the Soviets declared themselves to be neutral, this would be an act of treason." '

with imperialism', Moscow no longer saw any need to play up to the Chinese and switched abruptly to the Indian side.

The Soviets started to back down during Thursday the 25th under the influence of three factors. First, they had had time to realize that Kennedy was not bluffing about the blockade. The only replies that Khrushchev had received to his secret letters of Tuesday and Wednesday, Sorensen reports, were 'firm restatements of our position'; the Americans' foremost demand, to 'withdraw the missiles', meant what it said, and this was confirmed through all possible diplomatic channels. At dawn on Thursday a Soviet tanker was allowed to continue towards its destination; but it had been hailed by an American Navy vessel and ordered to identify itself.

Secondly, an unprecedented military pressure was converging from all quarters on the Soviet Union. All the United States armies and fleets in the world were deliberately displaying their war preparations, while the Polaris missile submarines throughout the seven seas were exchanging with their bases uncoded messages about targeting. This could all have been bluff, of course, and there were no doubt people in the Kremlin who said as much. But to those who had to make the decisions and knew the quantitative superiority of the American strategic capabilities, it was no trifling matter.

Thirdly, a much more definite danger was looming: the Americans might strike at the Cuban bases, invade the island, take Castro prisoner and destroy his régime, and most probably all of these things at once. It will never be known whether this might actually have happened. Neither Kennedy nor anyone in his entourage ever knew for certain. Sorensen merely writes that 'the pressures for such a move (air strike or invasion) on the following Tuesday [October 30] were rapidly and irresistibly growing, strongly supported by a minority in our group [of Presidential advisers]'. In any event, Khrushchev contemplated the risk with the utmost seriousness, as he later confirmed himself.

The danger of invasion, incidentally, showed up the worst weakness of Khrushchev's gamble. For the socialist camp as a whole, the prestige of the USSR and the future of the communist movement, the destruc-

---

The *Pravda* editorial of October 25 (five days after the beginning of hostilities in the Himalayas) confirmed this stand in more moderate terms: it attacked sharply 'certain reactionary circles in India' and even 'certain progressive-minded personalities' who 'might be led . . . to take up chauvinistic positions'. China's suggestions for a settlement – published in full elsewhere in *Pravda* – were welcomed as 'constructive' and as constituting 'an acceptable basis for the opening of negotiations for a peaceful settlement'.

This line was in sharp contrast with that adopted during the first Sino-Indian conflict in the autumn of 1959. The reason obviously was that Khrushchev was then striving for a *rapprochement* with the Americans, while in 1962 he was defying them.

tion of Castro's régime would have been a world-shaking catastrophe. On the other hand any attempt to resist it by conventional means at such a distance from Soviet territory was bound to fail. The risk could be countered only by thermonuclear retaliation, which no Soviet leader wanted or could afford unless he was himself ready to die. This was enough to provoke bitter recriminations against the instigator of the operation. It may be, again, that some of the Kremlin rulers were less convinced than others of the Americans' determination and the risk of an invasion of Cuba. This view found expression in a tougher policy of stretching out the negotiations and extracting as many concessions as possible in exchange for the missiles' withdrawal. This and the more conciliatory line in fact prevailed in turn.

FRIDAY OCTOBER 26:
THE START OF THE BARGAINING

The message of October 25 to U Thant (released that evening) already implied retreat, since Khrushchev intimated that he would acquiesce in the blockade, while Kennedy had not departed from his position. This was confirmed by *Pravda's* pacifist headlines of the 26th, coupled with the strong appeal to 'reason'. All the developments of Friday the 26th more or less confirmed the predominance of a soft line at Moscow.

First, there was Khrushchev's letter delivered to the American Embassy that afternoon.[1] Its text was never released by either side and its substance remains a subject of controversy. Schlesinger, the most categorical among the American aides, affirms that it offered in unequivocal terms to withdraw the missiles in exchange for a mere pledge of non-invasion. Khrushchev, he writes, 'declared his profound longing for peace. "Let us", he said with visible emotion, "not permit this situation to get out of hand. If the United States would give the assurance that it would not invade Cuba and if it would recall its fleet from

---

[1] Witnesses declare that Khrushchev had his letter delivered to the American Embassy on Friday the 26th between 2 and 4 pm Moscow time. It then had to be translated, enciphered, sent to Washington and deciphered, so that by the time it reached President Kennedy's desk it was already past 9 pm Washington time, that is, more than twelve hours later. The American Embassy had no direct line to the United States and had to transmit its telegrams through Soviet channels. This situation prompted the Soviets to resort to a swifter procedure for their ensuing messages: viz. to have the text broadcast by Radio Moscow at the same time as the message reached the Embassy. The 'hot line' agreement signed a few months later remedied this shortcoming.

the quarantine, this would immediately change everything. Then the necessity for a Soviet presence in Cuba would disappear." '

The other witnesses are not so positive. Sorensen grants that the offer in Khrushchev's letter 'in essence appears to contain the germ of a reasonable settlement', but adds that it was a bit vague. 'It seemed to vary from one paragraph to the next and was accompanied by the usual threats and denunciations.' Other well-informed American observers have confirmed this impression. A book recently published in New York contains a long analysis of the note:[1] the author, who obviously draws on excellent sources, also finds it ambiguous. Khrushchev did indeed ask Kennedy to stop the blockade and promise not to invade Cuba, but did not specify what he would do in exchange. At one point he said that the situation in this event would be 'transformed from one day to the next', and in another that: 'in that case the need for the presence of our military experts in Cuba would disappear'. He did, to be sure, declare himself prepared to do something to ease the crisis, but seemed above all to be playing for time. Furthermore, nowhere was there any mention of international control.

In any case, Sorensen must be right when he states that, in their reply to the letter on the 27th, the Americans chose to interpret it as they saw fit. Apparently in order to read Khrushchev's note as an indication that he was prepared to withdraw his missiles against a pledge that there would be no invasion, the letter and even the spirit of the message had to be stretched.

Whether Khrushchev did have some such bargain in mind when drafting his message is a moot point, but on that very day what may have been a half-formed idea took concrete shape under strange circumstances. At 1.30 pm Washington time (9.30 pm in Moscow) A. S. Fomin, the counsellor of the Soviet Embassy, telephoned to a friend of his – John Scali, an American newspaperman – and asked to see him immediately. When they met, Fomin made a suggestion which is thus reported by Schlesinger[2]: 'What would you think of a proposal whereby we would promise to remove our missiles under United Nations inspection and Khrushchev would promise never to introduce such offensive weapons into Cuba again? Would the President of the United States be willing to promise publicly not to invade Cuba?' According to Schlesinger, Fomin asked for a quick reply, which was returned through Scali at 7.30 pm (3.30 am of the 27th in Moscow) upon instructions from Secretary of State Dean Rusk. The United States regarded the proposal as offering 'real possibilities' for negoti-

[1] Elie Abel, *The Missile Crisis*, J. B. Lippincott Company, Philadelphia and New York, 1966.
[2] *A Thousand Days*, p 726; also *Life*, November 12 1965.

ation, but 'they [the Soviets] must understand that time was short, not more than forty-eight hours'. Fomin went back to his office to transmit the information 'after a brief attempt to introduce the idea of United Nations inspection of Florida as well as Cuba'. It was to be learned a little later that V. A. Zorin had made a similar proposal to U Thant, also on Friday the 26th.

This episode leaves no doubt that the possibility of a retreat arose definitely on that day, being conveyed in vague terms in Khrushchev's message and transmitted to the Americans later that evening through unofficial channels. Possibly Khrushchev was pushed in that direction by fresh American pressure, specifically by a declaration made at 8 pm (Moscow time) by a State Department spokesman to the effect that 'further action will be justified' if the installation of missiles continued in Cuba. (The spokesman, according to Sorensen, had overstepped the President's instructions.) In any case, in view of Washington's favourable reception of Fomin's proposal, the crisis could have been settled on that basis on Saturday.

SATURDAY OCTOBER 27:
THE SWITCH

What actually happened was just the opposite. Moscow's attitude stiffened markedly on Saturday, and at the same time betrayed such confusion that serious clashes must be assumed to have occurred among the top leaders.

First, it is far from certain that Fomin's feeler was unanimously approved by the Kremlin. On Friday evening, while Khrushchev was awaiting the results of his overture to the United States (he had taken time off and gone to a Cuban concert with Brezhnev, Kozlov, Polyansky and Shvernik), the Moscow papers were preparing their Saturday issues. To keep in line with Khrushchev's message and Fomin's move they should have maintained the pacific tone of Friday morning, or at any rate emphasized Cuba's defence as Khrushchev had done in his message, rather than the issue of America's foreign bases. But that was not the case. *Pravda* came out on Saturday morning with a headline definitely tougher than that of the day before. The tone of *Krasnaya Zvezda*, the Army organ, was not conciliatory either. Its commentator, Leontyev, wrote: 'The United States is demanding the evacuation of Soviet mily tary equipment from Cuba. . . . But why then not evacuate militari-equipment and troops from the hundreds of bases that surround the Soviet Union?' Particular stress was laid on the presence of bases 'close to the Soviet borders'. It was not clear whether Leontyev had in mind Turkey alone or a broader exchange; but this is irrelevant. If the possibility of a deal limited to Cuba had been accepted by all the Soviet rulers, such a comment would have had no object.

Much clearer signs of stiffening reached the United States on that Saturday: in the morning, a U-2 was shot down over Cuba – the first incident of its kind since the crisis started. This could not be regarded as accidental, since two other American planes were subjected to anti-aircraft fire over Cuba at about the same time. In Washington, Zorin and Fomin started pressing for an inspection of American bases. Fomin had already mentioned it the day before, but only in passing. Naturally the emphasis on this issue cast the gravest doubts as to the prospects of a settlement that had seemed conceivable only the day before. Furthermore, early on Saturday afternoon, a protest demonstration took place in front of the American Embassy in Moscow, whereas such action had not been deemed expedient at the start of the crisis, despite the 'indignation' then prevailing.

Finally, at 5 pm Moscow time, the Kremlin proposed to evacuate the Cuban bases in exchange for America's liquidation of its bases in Turkey. That was the most important Soviet blunder during the entire crisis. It surprised the Americans because it bore no relation to the previous day's proposals. It surprised the public still more next day, when it was noticed that its authors had forgotten all about it.

The confusion reached its height late on Saturday afternoon, when *Izvestia* came out. On page one was Khrushchev's message proposing the Cuba–Turkey deal, and on page two the following comment by V. Matveyev: 'Measuring things by their own cynical bargaining standard, some persons in the United States are plotting schemes whereby, in exchange for the abandonment by Cuba of the means to counter an American aggression, some American base near Soviet territory might be abandoned. . . . Such "proposals", if they deserve the name, only reveal the impure conscience of their authors' (*Izvestia*, October 27 1962; October 28 in the foreign edition).

Apart from the fantastic contradiction that made Khrushchev himself a 'cynical bargainer', another point was worth noting. Matveyev concluded with a quotation from the Government's declaration of October 23, as a retort to the advocates of the bargain in question. It stated that if the United States wished to 'reinforce friendly relations with the Soviet Union' it should accept Moscow's proposals for the withdrawal of 'all foreign troops' to their own national territory, and should liquidate 'the military bases on foreign territory in various parts of the world'.

This position was as tough as could be, even more so than the one

Krasnaya Zvezda had taken up that morning. Not only did it rule out exchanging one base for another, but the crisis was to be used as the occasion for negotiations over the problem of American bases throughout the world. Far from relinquishing anything, the USSR was reviving – with better chances for success, apparently – one of its oldest demands. Almost one week after the beginning of the crisis, and after Khrushchev's unofficial overture of the previous day, this indeed reflected a radical stiffening.

Matveyev, of course, had not written an article of such importance on his own. His commentary must have been dictated by the Ministry of Foreign Affairs, or even higher quarters, on Saturday morning or in the early afternoon. Furthermore, it fitted in with the other signs of stiffening, the sudden interest in the inspection of American bases and the grave decision to shoot at American planes over Cuba. The contradiction between this commentary and the note on Turkey is due to the fact that the latter was handed to the newspaper at the last minute and the editors had no time, or forgot, to jettison their columnist's article.

The last piece of evidence concerning Saturday, far from clearing matters up, only adds to the confusion. It is Khrushchev's report to the Supreme Soviet, delivered on December 12 1962:

> '*On the morning of October 27* we received, from our Cuban comrades and from other sources, definite information that this attack [the invasion of Cuba] would take place within two or three days. The telegrams we received displayed *extreme alarm, which was well founded.* Immediate action was required to prevent an attack on Cuba and to preserve peace. A message was addressed to the President of the United States suggesting a decision that would naturally be acceptable. . . . We declared that if the United States pledged itself not to invade Cuba and also prevented an aggression against Cuba by its allies, the Soviet Union would be prepared to withdraw from Cuba the armaments that the United States regarded as offensive' (*Pravda*, December 13 1962) [Author's italics].

The confusion had reached its peak: Khruschchev claimed in this report to have been the initiator of the final settlement, but if he really did make the proposal just described (and this is not certain) he did so on the 26th, not on the 27th. The only message he sent to Kennedy on the 27th was about the bases in Turkey, and now he was not even mentioning them. In any case, why did he speak of 'the morning of the 27th' as the turning point on the way to conciliation when precisely at that moment the Soviet attitude was at its hardest?

The answer is not easy but can be tentatively suggested on the basis, first, of a fact, second, of a hypothesis.

The fact is that the Turkish diversion was not a sign, or the sign, of stiffening, as was believed for a while, but merely an intermediate stage between a much more extreme stiffening and complete retreat. The stiffening occurred in the morning of Saturday; all the signs listed, and in particular Matveyev's article, go to prove it. Its substance was that the withdrawal of Soviet missiles from Cuba could only take place as the outcome of broad negotiations – lengthy and difficult ones – on the problem of American bases the world over. In the afternoon, on the other hand, the Soviets declared their readiness to discuss the Turkish bases alone – a significant step backward.

The hypothesis is that Khrushchev, who favoured conciliation, was outvoted on Saturday, that he did not approve of anything that was done that day, not even the Turkish proposal, and chose subsequently to regard the events of the day as an interlude of no significance. His explanation of December 12 was both a defence plea and a belated recital of the facts – not as they actually were, but as they should have been if his advice had been heeded.

His hints, on Friday the 26th, of a possible retreat must have aroused some opposition, since the press did not follow suit. Khrushchev may even have acted without consulting his colleagues when he made his most specific offer to President Kennedy (through the Fomin–Scali channel). In any case, after being notified of Washington's favourable response during the night of Friday, he had tried to talk his colleagues into a settlement on that basis. Not only did he fail, but he probably ran into sharp resistance. The problem was not of course that any of the leaders were determined to lay down their lives for Cuba, but that disagreement arose between those who did not believe in an impending invasion of the island and those who did. Khrushchev, the principal pessimist, had to adduce the secret information received that morning and containing the signals of 'extreme alarm' he mentioned later. Evidently the majority still refused to share his misgivings, at least for a few hours, and succeeded in making a firm line prevail. There must have been sharp disagreement on that score. In the afternoon, a solution was apparently found in the form of the lame compromise over the Turkish bases. The notion might have been considered earlier, then discarded only to be brought out again.[1] The gesture was a concession on the part of the hard-liners, but was not satisfying to Khru-

[1] Both Sorensen and Schlesinger venture the opinion that the 'Turkish' message of 27 October had actually been drafted before Khrushchev's letter of the 26th. They point out that the style of the message of the 26th bore the mark of haste and of Khrushchev's personal impulsiveness, whereas that of the 27th obeyed the rules of protocol and traditional style and was no doubt drafted by the Ministry for Foreign Affairs. Anyway, the important point is the date when they were sent out – the only indication as to the timing of the decision.

shchev, since it disavowed his earlier position. All this may explain Khrushchev's burial of the 'Turkish' proposal, his mention of the detail regarding the bad news received 'on the morning of the 27th' and his insistence that 'the alarm was well-founded'. His aim was to record for history the thesis that he had unsuccessfully defended before his colleagues that day and to vindicate his own line, not theirs. He did not explain, naturally, why he had determined on this course on the 26th, that is the day before the intelligence about the 'extreme alarm' had been received. But at least he was bringing a semblance of consistency into a series of chaotic happenings.

SUNDAY OCTOBER 28: RESISTANCE AT AN END

Subsequent developments were far more logical. In the diplomatic sphere, the 'Turkish' solution – a compromise among the various tendencies in the Kremlin – was not worth much attention.

This attempt at bargaining bore the seeds of the crucial concession, namely the abandonment of the missiles in Cuba and hence of all the grandiose diplomatic prospects that had inspired the gamble.[1] Furthermore, since Khrushchev's present offer fell short of what he had imprudently hinted at the day before, Kennedy had sound reason to ignore it. No serious resistance could be contemplated for the sake of what had now become a mere symbol. Kennedy's crucial message on the evening of the 27th (which must have reached Moscow in the morning of Sunday the 28th) evidently struck the right note at the right time. Accompanied by a strongly-worded note from Robert Kennedy announcing massive reprisal action if the withdrawal of the missiles was not announced 'immediately', it forcibly outlined the minimum demand: withdrawal in exchange for a promise of non-invasion – and no more than that.

The exact moment when Khrushchev ordered work to be stopped on the Cuban bases is not known. He disclosed only that it was 'before' the order to remove the rockets and ship them home, which was announced in Moscow at 5 pm on Sunday the 28th. This shows that the resistance of some colleagues to his move lasted a few hours longer, owing perhaps to the fact that the United States had not retaliated for the attack on its planes the day before. Since one concession leads to another, Khrushchev had to give in afterwards on the IL-28 bombers that Kennedy had

[1] Another sign of Soviet disarray in the Cuban crisis was the note of the 27th containing the first official acknowledgment of the presence of missiles in Cuba. (Khrushchev had admitted it on Wednesday the 24th to the American businessman William Knox, but this was not public knowledge.) This admission, made under pressure after so many denials, greatly weakened the Soviet position.

added to the list of equipment to be evacuated. Khrushchev had to wait for more than three weeks for the lifting of the blockade (November 21) and agree to a symbolic but humiliating inspection of Soviet vessels on the high seas. In the meantime, Mikoyan had left for Cuba to try to patch things up with Fidel Castro.

Altogether, these events show that the turmoil in Moscow was at least as great as in President Kennedy's entourage. Probably even greater, since this time a threat hung over the Soviet leaders, the reverse of what had so often happened in the past. Moreover, Kennedy had the last word in any American decision, while Khrushchev did not: clearly the Presidium was not content to resign itself to a consultative role. The most crucial days in this respect were undoubtedly Saturday the 27th and probably the days just before the first concession (Friday the 26th). Incidentally, the only two days when no leader made any public appearance were Thursday and Saturday, except for Kosygin who received a visitor on Saturday.

The information so far available does not make it possible to ascertain which of the leaders assumed a given stance in the discussions. Khrushchev almost certainly adopted a soft line early in the game. He blundered by giving in too quickly, or at any rate by showing too soon that he was prepared to give in, and this may account for the switch to a harder line in the early hours of the following day. The instigators of the switch apparently included Kozlov, whose position just after the crisis appeared definitely more rigid than Khrushchev's.[1] He could not have been the only one, since the hard line prevailed for a few hours.[2]

---

[1] Kozlov's tough line over the Cuban crisis is shown by his speech to the Congress of the Italian Communist Party in December (*Pravda*, December 4 1962), which was particularly rigid on foreign policy. Also Kozlov remarked to a foreign ambassador at the November 7 1962 reception, after Khrushchev had made a conciliatory speech on the happy outcome of the crisis, that the situation was 'still very tense' and could bring the world once more to the brink of thermonuclear war.

[2] During the debate on the Cuban crisis some members of the Presidium were not present. G. I. Voronov and A. P. Kirilenko had both been on holiday since the end of September and returned to Moscow only for the November 7 celebration. They were not seen at any official gathering during the crucial week. Podgorny was not seen in public, either in Kiev or in Moscow. The alternate members, who have a consultative vote in all deliberations, did not come to Moscow during the debates. Mzhavanadze was reported in Tbilisi on 23, 24, 25, and 27 October, and Rashidov in Tashkent around the same time.

Only Mikoyan, as mentioned above, was recalled from a holiday that had started at the end of August. In general, the men who seem to have been most closely associated with the decisions of the crisis week were Khrushchev, Brezhnev, Kozlov, Kosygin, Mikoyan, Suslov and Polyansky. The first four apparently played the major role, as will be shown. It is not surprising that, in that tense period, there was no full Presidium meeting and a few senior members made all the decisions. For the same reasons, formal votes are unlikely to have been taken, since group pressure was sufficiently effective.

It need scarcely be recalled that the settlement was indeed a defeat for the Soviet Union and for Khrushchev. Some people – particularly in the United States – contended, and still do so, that it was the opposite. Such a position can stem only from an over-estimation of, if not an obsession with, the Castro movement. True, Khrushchev himself hastened to picture the settlement as a victory, by asserting that his main object, the survival of the socialist régime in Cuba, had been secured and had even been underwritten by the United States.

He had no other way out, of course, but the argument is not convincing. Even admitting for a moment that the defence of Cuba was his foremost objective, it was an odd way and certainly a costly one to reach it by hurriedly withdrawing a huge amount of equipment, when a formal treaty of alliance would have done just as well in the first place. Khrushchev's real motives, as confirmed by his behaviour through the preparatory stage of the operation, were far more ambitious. The liquidation of the venture brought back the *status quo ante* with a very slight gain for Khrushchev on Cuba, but an infinitely greater loss for him internationally. All he had obtained was the promise – not in a particularly solemn form – that Cuba would not be invaded, whereas Kennedy had gained immeasurably greater prestige, authority and power. Moreover, these were enhanced by the fact that Kennedy had not sought them. It became clear subsequently that the Cuban affair marked the end of the great Soviet design on Berlin, of the rocket-rattling that had served Khrushchev so well since his 1957 space achievements – in short, of a long period of Soviet initiatives. The Chinese, in fact, were quite right when they accused him of sinning first through 'adventurism' and later through 'capitulationism'.

KHRUSHCHEV IN DISGRACE

The differences about the way to solve the crisis blew over, but resentment within the collective leadership against the man who had caused such embarrassment was more lasting. The signs of Khrushchev's diminishing influence and prestige during and after the Cuban fiasco can naturally be detected only by the groping methods that Kremlinology entails. Nevertheless, they add up to one of the most impressive series in the whole reign. Moreover, they began to appear not after the capitulation of October 28, but on the very day that the United States blockade of Cuba opened the crisis, the 23rd. They lasted for about a month, which may be regarded as the period of the impact. Here, in chronological order, is what happened:

Starting on October 23, the wording of reports on Khrushchev's official activities changed. His talks with foreign statesmen or delegations, according to Soviet protocol, might be reported in one of two basic ways. In the first, the meeting was stated as having been held 'at the Central Committee of the CPSU', a banquet as having been given 'by the Presidium of the Central Committee' or by 'the Soviet Government', and so forth – the procedure adopted after the triumph of collective leadership in 1964. In the second form, the main figure was in the limelight and his entourage relegated to the background.

It hardly need be said that Khrushchev favoured the latter. For years the custom was to present him as the only authoritative personality with whom contacts on any subject were warranted. Without going very far back, on October 15 1962, one can find a report in *Pravda* headed: 'Luncheon given by N. S. Khrushchev' and going on to state that the First Secretary and his wife N. P. Khrushcheva had entertained the Chinese Ambassador Liu-Siao. All the members of the Presidium then in Moscow had also been present at the luncheon, but this fact was barely mentioned. Similarly, *Pravda* of October 18 1962 reported a 'luncheon given by N. S. Khrushchev for Urho K. Kekkonen', although Kozlov and Kosygin also attended. The term 'given by Khrushchev' should not be misunderstood: banquets were held in the Government reception rooms at the Kremlin.

On October 23, however, on the first day of the crisis, Gheorghiu-Dej, the head of the Rumanian Communist Party, stopped in Moscow on his way back from Asia. A luncheon was given for him – this time 'on behalf of the Central Committee of the CPSU, the Supreme Soviet of the USSR and the Council of Ministers'. Such was the formula used by *Pravda* on the 24th, under the equally impersonal headline: 'In honour of the Government delegation of the Rumanian People's Republic.' Khrushchev was mentioned, to be sure, but in his alphabetical order among the guests, well down the list. Incidentally, it appears on closer inspection that on the first day of the Cuban crisis, *Pravda* mentioned Khrushchev's name only once – in a dispatch from New York reporting a speech by V. A. Zorin. It was not in the editorial (about the crisis) or any other story by staff writers, which is quite unusual. Only on the 26th was Khrushchev named in the editorial and on the 28th in the staff writers' articles. (This does not refer to texts of official messages and telegrams, which are naturally reprinted with their signatures.)

Another example: on October 30 the head of the Czechoslovak Party, Novotný, had a meeting at the Kremlin with Khrushchev, Brezhnev, Kozlov and Kosygin (who were listed in that order), followed by a luncheon. *Pravda* of the 31st reported this under the heading:

'Talks at the Central Committee of the CPSU' and stated that the luncheon had been given 'by the Presidium of the Central Committee'. Here again Khrushchev is listed in his alphabetical place. In order better to understand the anomaly of the wording, suffice it to consult *Pravda* of February 2 1963, reporting the welcome given to Novotný, who was back in Moscow after a trip. The talks were now reported under the following title: 'Meeting of N. S. Khrushchev with Novotný', although Kosygin was also present. The luncheon this time was stated to have been given 'by N. S. Khrushchev' even though the entire Presidium attended it. In other words, the situation was back to normal.

It had become normal in fact by December 1962, on the occasion of Tito's arrival in Moscow.[1] But the emphasis on collective leadership introduced in the last week in October lasted throughout November, especially the first half of that month. The talks with Ulbricht, Gomulka and Kádár were reported by *Pravda* of November 3, 5 and 9 respectively, in the same manner as for Novotný on October 3. This unusual heading in *Pravda* on November 3 should also be noted: 'Meeting of comrades Khrushchev and Suslov with comrade Zhivkov'. Normally, Suslov would have received only an incidental mention, as Kosygin did in February 1963 on the occasion of the talks with Novotny, and Mikoyan on the occasion of Tito's visit.

In short, the mere opening of the Cuban crisis caused Khrushchev suddenly to lose ground within the collective leadership. Although the grave situation and the danger to the country might have been expected to enhance the chief's stature, the result was the exact opposite.

On October 25 1962 the town of Khrushchev in the Kirovgrad region changed its name, by decree of the Presidium of the Supreme Soviet of the Ukraine, to 'Kremges' (i.e. 'Kremenchug hydro-electric station'). The town was not an important one and had not distinguished itself in any way. It had been listed under the name 'Khrushchev' since 1958 in the directory of Soviet communes. It was at first in the category of 'urban boroughs', then became a 'town' on March 17 1961 after absorbing the nearby 'town' of Novogeorgievsk (see *Vedomosti Verkhovnovo Sovieta SSSR*, April 6 1961). In other words, it had risen to a higher status eighteen months before, during the preparations for the Twenty-second Congress. But, more important, it was the only town in the entire USSR to have borne the First Secretary's name. As previously mentioned, at an undetermined date – probably in 1960 – the

[1] See *Pravda* of December 7 1962 for the report of Tito's reception in Moscow, headlined: 'Talks of N. S. Khrushchev with Josip Broz Tito' – although Mikoyan also was present. As for the luncheon reported in the same issue of the paper, it was given 'by the Government of the USSR', although Khrushchev was listed first among those present.

Kalinovka kolkhoz also lost its name of 'Home of Khrushchev'. This apparently happened at the same time to a number of plants and institutions, although a new 'Khrushchev Kolkhoz' appeared in Uzbekistan in 1961. At all events, in 1962 no other place of any significance bore the First Secretary's name, and it may be no accident that this last toe-hold of the latter-day personality cult happened to be in the Ukraine. Its disappearance on October 25, two days after the American reaction to Cuba and in the climate just described, is presumably even less accidental.[1]

A HANDY TARGET: TUMUR-OCHIR

On November 1 1962 (two days after the retreat on Cuba) *Pravda* reprinted on page three the full text of an editorial published 'recently' by *Unen*, the daily newspaper of the Mongolian Party. The article spelt out the charges brought by Tsedenbal and his friends against Tumur-Ochir, a former member of the Politburo and Secretary of the Party, who had been stripped of all his functions on September 10, 1962. The domestic implications of this list of charges, such as the defendant's nationalistic leanings, his exaggerated admiration for Genghis Khan and so forth may be set aside. The other charges deserve closer attention:

> 'Comrade Tumur-Ochir tried to use the struggle against the remnants of the cult of personality for his own far-reaching purposes. His aim was to use the condemnation by the Party of certain serious mistakes committed by Choibalsan,[2] in particular in 1937–38, and to inflate this issue in a sensational way in order to drag Choibalsan's revolutionary work in the mud and thereby exclude from leadership the cadres of the older generation who had worked with Choibalsan.'

All this sounds very familiar, and it is tempting to substitute Stalin for Choibalsan and Khrushchev for Tumur-Ochir. The article goes on as follows:

> 'In order to achieve his perfidious objectives, comrade Tumur-Ochir asserted that the struggle against the cult of personality was not being pursued energetically enough. He wanted each meeting or conference, whether at the top or at the bottom of the hierarchy, to be devoted mainly to this issue. He made it the chief point on the

[1] The text of the decree renaming the town of Khrushchev appeared only three weeks later in the *Vedomosti* of the Supreme Soviet of the Ukraine, No 46, dated November 16 1962.
[2] Choibalsan, the 'Stalin of Mongolia', died in 1952.

agenda for the next Republican conference of officials in charge of ideology, which he hoped thereby to turn into a forum for his libellous attacks against the Central Committee and leadership of the Party.'

In the Soviet Union, too, a man was trying to push the 'cult' issue into the limelight, had used it in the past and was planning to continue using it as a weapon against his colleagues. Against a background of attacks against the Stalinist camp and the dictator's heirs, Khrushchev was preparing to turn the November plenary session into exactly the kind of gathering Tumur-Ochir was planning for his ideological conference. The following remark of Tsedenbal's also struck home:

'Demagogically picturing himself as the only fighter against the cult of personality, Tumur-Ochir was deliberately reviving the sorrows of the relatives and friends of the victims of past repressions. He was thereby trying to foster unhealthy tendencies in public opinion and to create an atmosphere of suspicion and distrust vis-à-vis the policy and leadership of the Party.'

This was just what had happened at the Twenty-second Congress and what Khrushchev had recently started doing again by lending his support to Solzhenitsyn. Such a list of charges could hardly fail to embarrass some people in Moscow, starting with Khrushchev and all those who, following his lead, had engaged in reopening old wounds.

True enough, the editorial had been written in Mongolia about a purely Mongolian quarrel. The loyal Party head in Ulan-Bator, Tsedenbal, was not likely to have wanted to make trouble for his chief patron in Moscow. But why had *Pravda*, which could easily have ignored the details of this minor matter in a faraway place, suddenly decided to write about it? Tumur-Ochir's removal had been announced in Moscow at the time (*Pravda*, September 12) and, strangely enough, the reasons given were entirely different. According to *Pravda* then, Tumur-Ochir was a man 'detached from life' who displayed a timid, hidebound attitude towards Marxist theory – the normal type of charge that Khrushchev himself would level at his adversaries. Furthermore, the *Unen* editorial about Tumur-Ochir was dated October 18. *Pravda* therefore had waited two weeks before mentioning it, and these two weeks had been important ones for Khrushchev.

Evidently this was another blow against Khrushchev and also a fresh illustration of the methods used. When a frontal attack is not possible, the only way to vent criticism is to publish, allegedly for information's sake, anything suitable for the purpose, regardless of the source and original object of the story. One example, as we have seen, was Walter

Lippmann's column in 1960. The report about Tsedenbal, while subtler, was undoubtedly a more stinging blow. Khrushchev himself, of course, had done no less when he had suddenly 'discovered' Yevtushenko's mediocre poem, *Stalin's Heirs*.

Pravda of November 3 had another surprise in store for its readers: a lengthy article by K. E. Voroshilov, the old marshal who, a year earlier, had been dubbed a member of the 'anti-party group'. It differed from the previous indications in that it was not directed against Khrushchev, who had in fact probably commissioned it. Ostensibly, Voroshilov was only commemorating the forty-fifth anniversary of the Revolution, but actually his article was an endorsement of Khrushchev's line in the Cuban crisis. Quoting the First Secretary several times, Voroshilov expressed his 'deep gratitude' to the man who had 'prevented a world catastrophe'. But to rely on praise from such compromised personalities was in itself a signal anomaly. Backing from outsiders, which it is quite normal to seek in the Western democratic system ('Even the opposition is supporting me'), is not the rule in the USSR. Under the Soviet régime, the only right which remains to a man who has 'sinned against the Party' is the right to applaud in silence. Voroshilov had not spoken out since his 'confession' of October 31 1961 and, despite his membership of the Presidium of the Supreme Soviet, the occasional honours bestowed upon him were due to his own insistence rather than to the benevolence of the powers that were. For instance, while on October 18 he had been permitted to join the other marshals at the ceremonies commemorating the battle of Borodino (*Pravda*, October 19 1962), at the rally in the Kremlin afterwards he had been relegated to the public section and wore civilian clothes. His 'mistakes' were still being cited in articles on historical problems (for instance in *Pravda* of June 24 1962).

Voroshilov's article did not contain a word about his past mistakes (under normal circumstances, at least that much would have been expected) or about the 'anti-party group'. None the less, his fortunes took a turn for the better: on November 1, the press had already published the letter of a Soviet Air Force veteran who expressed his high esteem for his 'dear respected K. E. Voroshilov', whom he had known 'for forty years'. On December 28 *Krasnaya Zvezda* published a photograph of him in marshal's uniform, the first since the Twenty-second Congress.

The last sign may be regarded as summing up the series. It expressed the views of the collective leadership more frankly, without underhand remarks. It consisted of an unsigned article in *Pravda* of November 15 1962 on the second edition of the *History of the Party* which had just come out. Nearly half of the fairly short article laid stress on the collective nature of the leadership. Furthermore, the accent was not on collective leadership at the rank and file level, as it had been in most earlier articles on the topic, but definitely concerned the top hierarchy. And it did not refer to the past, but to the present and the future. In the eyes of the anonymous authors, 'the principle of collective leadership for the solution of *all* political and practical problems confronting the Party and the state constitutes *the most important feature* of the Leninist approach'. This was linked with the problem of the cult of personality and its possible 'recurrences' (*retsidivy*), and it was asserted that the application of the principle of collective leadership 'helps to overcome successfully the baneful consequences of the cult of Stalin's personality'. In other words, the foremost duty of anyone who claimed to destalinize was to pay heed to the opinion of others; and it was for 'ceasing to heed the collective opinion of the Party and its Central Committee' that Stalin was being blamed, even more than for having killed innocent people in the repressions.

The article ended with this single but most eloquent quotation from the new history book: 'The criticism of the cult of personality made by the Party on the basis of Marxist–Leninist principles serves as a warning against the abuses of power and the use of power for personal ends. Much is given to the leaders, but much is expected from them in return. The decisions of the Twenty-second Congress teach Party and state officials to take full cognizance of their responsibility to the Party, the people and history, so that the power entrusted to them by the masses may be used only for the sake of their socialist motherland and the victory of communism. Any leader who forgets this strays from the principles of communism. The Party and people will always assess justly the historical role of any man who assumes political responsibility.'

These prophetic words assume their full meaning when read in the context of the Party's historical textbook,[1] where they form the conclusion to a long disquisition on the need to put a stop to the manifestations of the cult 'for all time' and to prevent 'any recurrence'; the main passage is a long quotation from Khrushchev in which, under the circumstances already described, he protested against the 'cult' of himself at the end of the Twenty-second Congress in October 1961.

There is another indication that this new edition of the Party history was hardly a pro-Khrushchev one. The slant given to relations between the Soviet Union and Yugoslavia was markedly at variance with that in favour at the time of the book's appearance (the text was cleared on October 23 1962, almost one month after Brezhnev's visit to Yugoslavia, when Tito's visit to Moscow was already being prepared). For

[1] *Istoriya KPSS*, Moscow, 1962.

instance, on page 630 it is stated that the 1948 Kominform resolution against Tito was 'correct in all its basic principles' and gave 'a Marxist–Leninist critique of the basic errors of the Yugoslav Communist Party leaders'. Stalin is accused of having committed a 'serious mistake' by completely breaking off government relations with Yugoslavia ('under Beriya's influence'), but this does not signify a political rehabilitation of the Yugoslav leaders. For instance, in a further reference to the attitude of the Yugoslav Party in 1957, it is stated that it 'placed itself in opposition to the international communist movement'. The book adds (in the present tense):

> 'This shows that the leaders of the Communist League of Yugoslavia have not renounced their anti-Leninist views, that they scorn the good will of the CPSU and the other Marxist parties. . . . Their renegade attitude towards Marxism–Leninism finds its fullest expression in the programme adopted in 1958 by the Seventh Congress of the Communist League of Yugoslavia. All communist and workers' parties in the world have labelled this programme a revisionist one. . . . But the leaders of the League have rejected the criticism and have engaged in new hostile acts against the CPSU and the other fraternal parties, thus finding themselves isolated in the ranks of the international communist movement.'

All the above passages already figured in the first edition of the textbook, which appeared in 1959 just after the Twenty-first Congress of the Soviet Communist Party, when attacks against Yugoslavia had been increasing. By leaving them unchanged in the 1962 edition, the authors of the textbook were deliberately ignoring all efforts at *rapprochement* made in the meantime.

The personalities of the authors (a 'collective' of historians headed by B. N. Ponomarev, the Central Committee Secretary, who was probably closer to Suslov than to Khrushchev) are not of major importance. Such so-called 'scholarly' projects undergo all kinds of checking, re-reading and correction by political bodies. In this case there must have been many consultations, since the material was sent to the printer on February 15 (which means that the bulk of the work was finished) but the actual order to print was given only on October 23 – the first day of the Cuban crisis. The actual date may be coincidence, but if, as appears, the manuscript was held up for approval at the top level, October 23 was the best possible day for overriding any resistance on Khrushchev's part.[1]

---

[1] The malaise aroused by this *History of the Party* was evinced in other ways as well; for instance, the very scant publicity surrounding its publication. *Pravda* published only an anonymous commentary on November 15, and other newspapers were even

A LIMITED OBJECTIVE

All these signs of disfavour, the dates of which are striking in themselves, show without any possible ambiguity that Khrushchev was being held responsible for the Cuban gamble and its failure. At the same time, the indirect reproaches – especially the Mongolian editorial and *Pravda's* article of November 15 – were far more serious than on any previous occasion of this sort, even in May 1960. They reflected the magnitude of the fiasco itself, as well as the gradual whittling down of the chief's authority and prestige since 1960.

Is it possible that Khrushchev's actual removal was contemplated after Cuba? While this cannot be entirely discounted, it is not very likely. The triumphant operation of October 1964 has created a somewhat distorted image of what the Soviet Union is really like. The Soviet régime has come to be viewed as a kind of Western system where the leader 'falls' on a given issue, just as a Prime Minister is overthrown by Parliament because of opposition to a bill. And since Khrushchev's downfall looked on the surface like a straightforward change of Government, it was tempting to suppose that it might have happened two years earlier as well – after a fiasco such as few democratic Governments, after all, could have survived.

But this would be a gross oversimplification. The palace revolution of October 1964 was not as simple as it looked. It succeeded because there was a plot, and a well-organized one, and Khrushchev was not on his guard. This combination of circumstances did not exist in 1962. It is quite possible that, at that moment, it occurred to Suslov or Kozlov, for instance, that it would be a good idea to get rid of Khrushchev. But they are not likely to have tried to put it into effect then and there. If the operation was to succeed – and the stakes were high enough to make success imperative – the advance preparations would have had to be carried out in secret. Khrushchev would have had to be prevented from using his position to pull any strings. In other words, this required action behind the scenes, as far as possible during a quiet period. To begin with, even veiled attacks could not be permitted lest they might put the victim on his guard. Therefore, the signs of late 1962 should be taken at their face value, viz. that Khrushchev was under strong but limited attack owing to his drive for personal power. They

more discreet. It was only in April 1963 that the journal *Problems of History of the CPSU* (No 4 1963) devoted an article to it, although the subject should have been one of major interest. Even this contained some criticism (of 'repetitions' and 'insufficiently precise formulation') that is not normally exercised upon books of such an official nature. The first edition, in 1959, had been greeted by far more numerous and wholly laudatory reviews.

represented a step forwards towards collective leadership in decision-making, and a further reaction against the 'excesses' of destalinization. It does not appear that his opponents could, or wanted to, do more at that stage.

Khrushchev, in fact, was on his guard and determined to yield as little as he could. The moment the crisis was settled, he tried to resume command of the situation, and he succeeded up to a point. First, he exploited to the full the role of peacemaker conferred on him by world opinion thanks to his gesture of October 28. (Naturally, he was less eager to dwell upon his less fortunate move of April.) A press campaign on the peace theme was launched with the help of Voroshilov among others. In addition, Khrushchev was extolled for his achievements in another realm. In the summer of 1962 the State publishing company had started bringing out all the speeches on agriculture he had made since 1953, and each volume was hailed with high praise (e.g. in *Pravda* of November 11 1962, No 16 of *Kommunist*, *Ekonomicheskaya Gazeta* of November 24 etc: many of the articles were reprinted by provincial papers). Oddly enough, the phrase 'the Presidium of the Central Committee headed by comrade Khrushchev' reappeared in these articles and some editorials. This was how the First Secretary and his friends chose to hint that collective leadership had its limits.

Khrushchev's most potent weapon of all – destalinization – was not yet laid aside. *Novy Mir's* issue No 11, with *A Day in the Life of Ivan Denisovich* by Solzhenitsyn, came out in mid-November. As if on cue, the entire press responded with wholehearted praise. This was not surprising, since it was well known that the story had been given the green light at the highest level on Khrushchev's insistence. Only one bastion of conservatism kept silent, Kochetov's magazine *Oktyabr*, which was awaiting better days to vent its ire.[1] Those who spoke at all gave new impetus to destalinization whether they meant to or not. As the young poets gave one public reading after another, the theme

[1] The critic Aleksandr Dymshits, until then deputy chief editor of *Oktyabr*, left the editorial board in December 1962. According to information from a reliable source, this was because he had wanted *Oktyabr* to publish a favourable review of *Ivan Denisovich*, which angered Kochetov. Dymshits did write a review some time later in the weekly *Literatura i Zhizn*. The playwright Sheynin might have left *Oktyabr* for the same reason at that very time. He had been the first deputy chief editor of *Oktyabr* before Kochetov took over the magazine in the beginning of 1961; he was subsequently demoted to the position of mere deputy chief editor (March 1961) and then to simple editor (July 1961).

Oktyabr commented upon Solzhenitsyn's story only after the 1963 'restalinization', and did so in a consistently critical vein. The silence it maintained in 1962 was manifestly out of tune with the conformism of the day. This can only be accounted for by encouragement in high places. In Moscow's literary circles, Kozlov was spoken of as Kochetov's protector.

of 'Stalin's heirs' again moved into the foreground. For instance, the following comment by *Pravda* of November 23 1962 showed which way the wind was blowing:

'Yes, Stalin's heirs are trying to hamper the Party and the people in their struggle and their task of enlightenment. . . . They are trying to fob us off with superficial tirades in place of the stubborn and effective struggle that must be waged against the remnants of the cult of Stalin's personality. They are trying to hide the truth about themselves by means of hollow, meaningless phraseology. By their very nature, people of that ilk remain faithful to the customs, ideas and methods of the cult of personality that have been condemned and unmasked. . . . They are ready to renounce the whole past and yet to preserve all of it. They have learned nothing and forgotten nothing.'[1]

These signs of a come-back on Khrushchev's part, which were at the time mingled with the effects of his discomfiture, indicate great confusion. The conclusion is that nothing had been decided yet, and that Khrushchev was trying to regain lost ground despite the criticism levelled at him. In order to do so, he was deliberately pursuing his destalinization drive. One thing probably helped him: the advocates of collective leadership were far from united. Other problems existed at the time, and this made for divergent interests and attitudes on the part of the chief personalities. Kosygin's short-lived mishap should be viewed against that background.

KOSYGIN DEFEATED:
THE SHELVING OF LIBERMANISM

On November 8 1962 Kosygin suffered a blow. Until that day, he had been in excellent standing. In September, owing to Mikoyan's lengthy holiday, he had attended all the Government functions as the number two man, and stood in for Khrushchev whenever necessary. Throughout the Cuban crisis he had been a member of the ruling quartet (Khrushchev, Brezhnev, Kozlov, Kosygin), particularly in all the negotiations with East European Party and government leaders: Novotný on

[1] Amusingly enough, the commentary in *Pravda* of November 23 1962 about 'Stalin's heirs' was signed by V. V. Yermilov, the same man who in January 1963 violently attacked Ehrenburg (see p. 301). On the surface, he was writting on the same topic or one closely related to it, but the change of target shows how much the line had shifted within a few weeks.

October 30, Ulbricht on November 2 and Gomulka on the 4th. On November 6, Kosygin delivered the official report at the meeting commemorating the anniversary of the Revolution, an honour traditionally reserved for personalities in high favour. On the 7th, at the saluting base on Red Square, he was in fourth position, after Khrushchev, Brezhnev and Kozlov.[1]

Then, on November 8, Kádár was invited to the Kremlin, and his hosts were – Khrushchev, Brezhnev and Kozlov. The quartet had turned into a trio: Kosygin attended only the banquet that followed the talks, together with the junior Presidium members. Neither was he seen on November 9 at the Militiamen's Day parade which the trio attended.

This in itself would not warrant any definite conclusions, although, as will be seen, November 8 was a significant date. But, a surer sign confirmed that something actually had happened. On December 2 Mikoyan returned to Moscow from his long and difficult mission in Cuba and the United States. The Tass agency and the radio, followed by *Pravda* and the other newspapers of December 3, published the following communiqué: 'On December 2 the *First Deputy Prime Minister of the USSR, A. I. Mikoyan,* returned to Moscow from a voyage to Cuba. A. I. Mikoyan was met at Vnukovo airport by the *Deputy Prime Ministers of the USSR,* A. N. Kosygin and M. A. Lesechko, by the Ministers of the USSR, A. A. Gromyko and S. V. Kurachev', etc. [Author's italics.]

The analysis of the Mikoyan case in 1960 has shown the meaning of such infringements of protocol, although this one did not last so long for Kosygin as for Mikoyan two years earlier. On December 7 *Pravda* again listed Kosygin with his correct title of 'First Deputy Prime Minister' and the matter ended there. But once is enough.[2] In this particular case, the 'oversight' of which Kosygin had been a victim, in contrast to the proper wording with reference to Mikoyan, simply meant that henceforth Mikoyan ranked above the other First Deputy

---

[1] This writer glimpsed the quartet in action at the November 7 reception at the Kremlin. Khrushchev stood to the fore, with Brezhnev, Kozlov and Kosygin directly behind him and in front of the remaining leaders. This position was maintained while Khrushchev made his speeches. Before each toast he actually consulted with the trio, which was certainly not his custom.

Although it might not have suited Mikoyan and Suslov, the composition of this super-Presidium was a logical one, since it included the chief of State and the second men of the Party and the Government. Evidently, as an outcome of the Cuban crisis, these three were being associated with all decisions more closely than in the past.

[2] On November 8 1962, when Kosygin's status was downgraded in press and radio communiqués, some Moscow and provincial papers published the communiqués and others abstained. But none of the former dared correct the 'mistake'.

Prime Minister. This was confirmed during the two Khrushchev–Tito conferences held on December 6 and 7: in the absence of Brezhnev and Kozlov (who were heading delegations abroad), the sole member of the leadership allowed to attend was Mikoyan, not Kosygin. At the end of October the picture had been exactly the opposite: for instance, the talks with Novotný were attended by Kosygin, and Mikoyan was left out although he was in Moscow at the time (*Pravda*, October 31).

The reasons for Kosygin's downgrading are not far to seek. On the evening of November 9, Tass announced the convening of a plenary session of the Central Committee for the 19th – a date already set in September, but hardly mentioned during the Cuban crisis. It is likely that after the November 7 celebrations, the time had come to resume preparations for the plenary session and take the final decisions on it.

What decisions could these be? The plan for the division of the Party had been approved several weeks earlier, and the practical details were already worked out in the republics and regions. As far as the top leadership was concerned, that matter had been settled. But one current problem remained: how to sum up the September debate on the Liberman theses. The discussion in the press and meetings of economists had ended only a few days before. Towards the end of October a consensus seemed to favour some degree of orthodox centralization (this was the indication gathered from a round-table discussion organized at the time by the weekly *Ekonomicheskaya Gazeta*). Nevertheless, a variety of suggestions had been made for a cutback in the number of 'indices' (*pokazateli*) used in the administrative aspect of planning, a change in the pricing system, resort to 'economic levers', and so forth. Until at least the first week in November, the press gave the impression that the major theses at the forthcoming plenary session were those of the economy and management methods, and not the bureaucratic reshuffle which, in the event, superseded any basic reforms.

It is quite likely that the decision to bury the suggestions of the Liberman school was taken by the Presidium on November 8 or 9, at the same time as the final decisions regarding the plenary session. Khrushchev announced it only in his report of the 19th (after paying lip-service to the 'valid suggestions' put forth during this 'serious discussion', whose analysis was postponed).[1] The decision itself would have been taken some ten days earlier, when the debates ended.

---

[1] Regarding the economic reforms, in his report of November 19 1962 Khrushchev instructed the 'planning agencies and the Economics Institute of the Academy of Sciences to study the proposals carefully' and, on the basis of their analysis, to 'draft recommendations of an economic nature aiming at improving planning and the scientific organization of labour'. It was learned at the beginning of 1963 that committees were at work on this task. Apparently no results were achieved as to

The actual size of the forces that advocated reform is not known. They were probably a fairly large minority, since the question again arose two years later with a roughly similar Presidium (minus Kuusinen and Kozlov). In any case, Kosygin was on the side of the minority, as shown by the attitude he adopted just after Khrushchev's downfall. This means that Kosygin was defeated on November 8, which is the most likely explanation of his downgrading. The opposite camp probably included Khrushchev – whose attitude throughout the preceding months had shown his scant interest in any real reform of the Soviet economic structure – but also Kozlov, Suslov, possibly Kirilenko and other members of the Party apparatus. As noted, their foremost and traditional concern was to reinforce the grip of the Party over the industrial managers. The forces represented by Liberman obviously would have led in the opposite direction. The plan to divide the regional apparatus may have originally been intended to outweigh any possible danger from that quarter; at any rate, it was quite sure to eliminate any such threat.

All the economists and planners found themselves in difficulties at that stage. On the evening of November 9 the resignation of A. F. Zasyadko, the President of Gosekonomsoviet (the State body in charge of long-range planning) was announced. The health reasons invoked cannot be completely discarded, since he died suddenly of a heart attack on September 5 1963. Nevertheless, the date of his resignation, on the very day when the final decisions for the plenary session were taken, can hardly be a coincidence. Besides, although Zasyadko was a Ukrainian, he seems to have been associated more closely with Malenkov than with Khrushchev. He had apparently come close to Kosygin in the past few years and had been promoted to his present post in April 1960, about the same time as Kosygin, and in preference to Kosygin's chief rival, I. I. Kuzmin. Zasyadko's successor, P. F. Lomako, had previously been Deputy Chairman of the Central Committee Bureau for the RSFSR and had no ties whatsoever with Kosygin.

The fate of another prominent planner, V. N. Novikov, was apparently settled at the same time. On July 17 1962 he had relinquished the presidency of Gosplan to V. E. Dymshits and became head of the Soviet delegation to Comecon, the Mutual Economic Assistance Council of the Eastern bloc. The post was just then upgraded by Khrushchev, who was advocating closer economic integration abroad as well as at

---

planning reform or placing of price schedules on a sounder basis (a precondition of any improvement of management). Not until the summer of 1964, when an article by Trapeznikov, a member of the Academy, was published (*Pravda*, August 17 1964), was what is called Libermanism considered again.

home;[1] in addition, Novikov remained Deputy Prime Minister. However, some signs already indicated that this was no promotion.[2] This was confirmed by the November plenary session, which demoted him to the rank of minister and appointed M. A. Lesechko to replace him as Soviet representative at Comecon (*Pravda*, November 25 1962 and *Izvestia*, December 15 1962). A few months later, it was learned that Novikov had inherited Lesechko's functions at the head of the 'Committee on Foreign Economic Problems of the Presidium of the Council of Ministers of the USSR' (*Pravda*, June 2 1963), an important body but less prominent than Comecon.[3] Novikov, like Zasyadko, had been promoted in 1960 together with Kosygin. Both men had since worked in close co-operation with him.

The disquiet among planners was easy enough to understand when a reform intended to bring them under even tighter Party control was afoot. Besides setting up specialized Oblast Committees, Khrushchev's plan provided for instituting bureaux to deal respectively with agriculture and industry, in all the republics and the central apparatus. In addition, the plenary session instituted a 'Central Committee Bureau for Chemical and Light Industries' under a Party Secretary, P. N. Demichev, and a mixed Control Committee combining the Party and the State apparatus, under Shelepin. The latter body had closer links with the Party than with the State, and enjoyed broad powers of intervention within the State hierarchy.

Khrushchev did not conceal in his statements that he, and probably other Party officials as well, regarded all these measures as a means of getting the economic machine well in hand. True, attacks on Gosplan are quite common in Soviet political life but, in the autumn of 1962, Khrushchev was more outspoken and specific than ever before

[1] A Comecon summit meeting had been held in Moscow in June and Khrushchev presented to it a far-reaching plan for economic co-ordination. But this did not satisfy him, for in a long article published by *Kommunist* in August (No 9 1962), he again advocated close integration under the guise of 'international socialist division of labour'. In his report to the November plenary session, he even suggested the revival of joint agencies for the exploitation of common resources (such bodies had existed under Stalin). He also advocated the setting up of a common planning agency for all Comecon countries, and finally another summit meeting of all its members. None of these plans was carried out. Their only result was a period of tension between the Soviet Union and Rumania.

[2] When Novikov was appointed to Comecon in November 1962, it was noted that the appointment of his successor at Gosplan, Dymshits, was announced before his own, and with greater fanfare. For more than three days there was no announcement about Novikov – something that does not happen when an official is on the up-grade.

[3] The connections of Lesechko, who from 1956 to 1957 was Minister of Systems Engineering and Automation, cannot be clearly established. He had, however, suffered a set-back in 1957 when he became Vice-President of the Ukrainian Gosplan. This was at the time of the industrial reform launched by Khrushchev, when Zasyadko, on the contrary, moved from Kiev to Moscow.

on such matters as the lack of discipline of the bureaucrats in the planning agency, the metal lobby, favouritism in recruitment and 'young university graduates who lay down the law'.[1] The link that, for the first time, was alleged to exist between Gosplan's lack of co-operation and remnants of the 'cult', as well as the new calls for purges, showed what Khrushchev was driving at. Novikov and Zasyadko bore the brunt of the blow, but inevitably Kosygin was implicated.

THE NOVEMBER PLENUM

The plenary session of November 1962 aptly illustrates a besetting weakness of Soviet political life. When confronted with a concrete problem – in this case the entanglement of the economic machine in bureaucratic red tape – the leadership takes one step towards a solution (the Liberman debate) but withdraws as soon as the complexity of the problem, and particularly its potential dangers, become evident. The inevitable panacea – strengthening of Party control over the sector involved – then comes into play. The moment this happens, the debate spreads to the Party bureaucracy and is fought out among its various branches. The outcome is a reshuffle favouring the top group of the moment, while the real problem is by-passed. Those who truly desire reform can only wait for better days.

[1] Khrushchev made the following attacks on Gosplan. In October 1962 he wrote in a note to the Presidium, after having explained that Gosplan's erroneous decisions must be rescinded: 'What is the cause of such miscalculations by our planning bodies? Obviously the trouble is due to hidebound thinking. Earlier, some young people joined the Gosplan. They did their work honestly, but gradually detached themselves from life, and for some of them the passing of time blunted the sense of what is new. For these people, work in Gosplan and Gosekonomsoviet has become a kind of juggling. Just as circus artists juggle with swords and knives, so these officials juggle with figures which they sometimes take out of thin air, without analysing them, without acquainting themselves with the actual case, without looking into the matter. . . . This is why it might be better to think about replacing these entrenched officials and hire new ones who, after graduating from the Institute, have actually worked in a factory or on a farm...' (*Agricultural Speeches* vol. 7 p 265.)

On November 19 1962 against the 'steel-eaters': 'Steel production is like a path already traced with a deep furrow: even a blind horse will not deviate from it, because the wheels would break. Similarly, some officials have put on steel blinkers. They see and act as they were taught to long ago. Let a new material appear that is better than steel and costs less, and they all start shouting: 'Steel! Steel! . . .' (*Agricultural Speeches* vol 7 p 362.) And in the same report: 'The problem of cadres recruited for our main planning agencies needs serious reviewing. Often, people are hired directly after graduating from the universities and institutes. . . . Those people have never heard the hum of a motor, and already they are uttering economic maxims and trying to plan production in a country as huge as the Soviet Union. Why is this? Obviously, in many cases, officials hire their friends and pals. As in the fable, someone is appointed thanks to Friend Fox who has slipped a word to Mother Lioness.'

Main Changes in the Party and Government in November–December 1962

Party Posts	Former Holder[1]	New Holder
Sec'y of CC, CPSU, Chairman of Central Committee Bureau, CPSU for Industry and Building	–	A. P. Rudakov
Sec'y of CC, CPSU, Chairman of Central Committee Bureau, CPSU for Agriculture	–	V. I. Polyakov
Sec'y of CC, CPSU, Chairman of Committee on Party Organization problems attached to CC, CPSU	–	V. N. Titov
Sec'y of CC, CPSU	–	Yu. V. Andropov
Chairman of CC Bureau, CPSU for Chemical and Light Industries	–	P. N. Demichev
Chairman of Ideological Committee attached to CC, CPSU	–	L. F. Ilyichev
Chairman of Party–State Control Committee of CC, CPSU and of the USSR Council of Ministers	–	A. N. Shelepin
First Deputy Chairman of the CC Bureau, CPSU for RSFSR, alternate member of the Presidium of the CC, CPSU	G. I. Voronov	L. N. Yefremov
First Secretary of the Moscow Urban Committee	P. N. Demichev	N. G. Yegorychev
Chairman of CC Bureau, CPSU for Central Asia	–	V. G. Lomonosov
Chairman of CC Bureau, CPSU for Transcaucasia	–	G. N. Bochkarev

In each federated republic there were set up a 'Central Committee Bureau for Industry and Building', a 'Central Committee Bureau for Agriculture' and a 'Party-State Control Committee of the Central Committee and of the Council of Ministers'.

In each region: liquidation of the Oblast Committees and Territorial Committees and setting up of an 'Oblast Committee (or Territorial Committee) for Industry' and of an 'Oblast Committee (or Territorial Committee) for Agriculture'.

[1] A dash in this column indicates a newly created post.

Main Changes in the Party and Government in November–December 1962

Government Posts	Former Holder	New Holder
Deputy Chairman of the Council of Ministers, USSR (in charge of agriculture)	N. G. Ignatov	D. S. Polyansky
Chairman of the Council of Ministers, RSFSR	D. S. Polyansky	G. I. Voronov
Deputy Chairman of the Council of Ministers, USSR, President of Gosplan	A. F. Zasyadko	P. F. Lomako
Deputy Chairman of the Council of Ministers, USSR, Chairman of State Council for Building (Gosstroy)	I. A. Grishmanov	I. L. Novikov
Deputy Chairman of the Council of Ministers, USSR	V. N. Novikov	M. A. Lesechko
Deputy Chairman of the Council of Ministers, USSR	–	A. N. Shelepin
Chairman of the Presidium of the Supreme Soviet of the RSFSR	N. N. Organov	N. G. Ignatov

The Gosekonomsoviet or Economic State Council (in charge of long-range planning) was changed into the USSR Gosplan (Chairman: P. F. Lomako).

The former Gosplan (in charge of short-range planning and of management) was changed into the National Economic Council or Sovnarkhoz of the USSR (Chairman: V. E. Dymshits).

In each region, the soviet executive committees (Oblast Executive Committees and Territorial Executive Committees) were liquidated; an 'Oblast (or Territorial) Executive Committee for Industry' and an 'Oblast (or Territorial) Executive Committee for Agriculture' were set up.

This does not mean, of course, that the apparatus and its chiefs had no trouble in settling their quarrels. In the huge upheaval caused by the November plenary session, many anomalies occurred, as shown by the table on p 289 and above. Khrushchev did not succeed in pushing through all the plans he had announced in his earlier speeches. Other, hitherto unmentioned, ideas were adopted. The setting up of inter-republic administrations, a plan that had been opposed in October, was postponed. At the end of December 1962 the Central Committee Bureau for Central Asia was instituted (the delay was probably caused by disagreements over its prospective head, V. G. Lomonosov); in February 1963 a similar bureau was set up for Transcaucasia and the Central Asia sovnarkhoz. In his November 19 report Khrushchev had suggested other Central Committee bureaux for each enlarged economic region (*Agricultural Speeches* vol 7 p 331) and this was not followed up. Neither was anything said about the Central Committee bureaux for RSFSR industry and RSFSR agriculture. These were mentioned by Khrushchev in his notes from September onwards, and possibly existed at some point, but the officials who headed them were never identified. On the other hand, no sign had heralded the creation of a 'Committee on Party Organization Problems' (whose chairman was V. N. Titov), of an 'Ideological Committee' (with L. F. Ilyichev as Chairman) and of a 'Central Committee Bureau for Chemical and Light Industries' (under P. N. Demichev), all of which resulted from the plenary session. These waverings may indicate not only resistance to some of Khrushchev's moves but also rivalry among different branches of the apparatus. The two main bodies likely to have competed were the Central Committee Secretariat and its Bureau for the RSFSR, although both were headed by Khrushchev himself.

The Bureau ranked lower than the Central Committee, but this had not stopped it from developing some independence. Kirichenko, the head of the cadres administration, when at the peak of power, had been strong enough to remove officials in the RSFSR as well as in the other Republics. But in the preceding two years his successor Kozlov had been able to touch only officials outside the RSFSR. In the meantime, new specialized services for the RSFSR had sprung up within the Central Committee, under the Bureau's control. In each instance, this had resulted in whittling down the traditional powers of the federal bureaucracies. After A. P. Kirilenko was promoted First Deputy Chairman of the Bureau in April 1962, the trend became more marked.[1] Another result of his promotion was to place the Bureau representatives on a par with Secretariat representatives within the Presidium itself. Facing the three Secretaries on the federal level – Kozlov, Suslov and Kuusinen – were now three representatives of the Bureau – Kirilenko, Voronov and Polyansky (not to mention Khrushchev, who belonged to both).

Although the November reshuffle did not eliminate all these rivalries, it somewhat enhanced the federal Secretariat. The setting up of the Committee on Party Organizational Problems and the Ideological

---

[1] During the summer of 1962, there appeared a 'Central Committee of the CPSU Building Service for the RSFSR' headed by A. V. Gladyrevsky, and a 'Central Committee of the CPSU Mechanical Engineering Service for the RSFSR' headed by I. I. Kozlov.

Committee, which were above the corresponding Central Committee departments, not only enhanced the stature of their heads, Titov and Ilyichev, but consolidated their authority over the corresponding Bureau services: for, while the chiefs of the Bureau services presumably became 'members' of the committees, Titov and Ilyichev were their chairmen. The fact is that, from then on, most of the services directly supervised by the Secretariat, and in any case those under Titov and Ilyichev, were no longer described as working merely 'for the Federated Republics' but as the 'Party Organs' or 'Ideological Department' of the Central Committee. Furthermore, the corresponding RSFSR services were divided into two sections, one for industry and the other for agriculture, which did not enhance their prestige. For instance, V. I. Stepakov, with his odd title of 'Chief of the Central Committee Ideological Department for RSFSR Agriculture', no longer represented a threat to Ilyichev.[1] The latter also extended his empire in other directions, and successively took over the departments of 'Science, Institutions of Higher Learning and Schools' and then the Cultural Department of the Central Committee. The chiefs of those departments, V. A. Kirillin and D. A. Polikarpov, were permitted to become his deputies.

At the top, the strengthening of the federal Secretariat *vis-à-vis* the

---

[1] The downgrading of the Central Committee Bureau for the RSFSR in November 1962 is confirmed by the analysis of precedences. Thus the obituary of the Second Secretary of the Communist Party of Georgia, D. P. Zemliansky, published in *Pravda* of September 24 1963, bore the signature of the following dignitaries listed as shown below (with their titles added by this writer):

L. I. Brezhnev (chief of State and Secretary of the Central Committee, CPSU):
V. P. Mzhavanadze (First Secretary of the Central Committee of the Georgia Communist Party);
V. N. Titov (Secretary of the Central Committee, CPSU);
L. F. Ilyichev (Secretary of the Central Committee, CPSU);
G. D. Dzhavakhishvili (Chief of the Georgia Government);
P. F. Pigalev (First Assistant Chief of Party Organs Department of the Central Committee, CPSU);
G. N. Bochkarev (Chairman of the Central Committee Bureau for Transcaucasia, CPSU);
M. A. Polekhin (Chief of the Central Committee Party Organs Department for RSFSR Agriculture);
V. I. Stepakov (Chief of the Central Committee Ideological Department for RSFSR Agriculture).

It will be seen that an *assistant chief* in the federal service, Pigalev, came before two departmental *chiefs* for the RSFSR, Polekhin and Stepakov, which confirms the subordinate position of the latter two men after the 1962 reform. Bochkarev's fairly low position is also worth noting. These inter-republic bureaux of the Central Committee had never achieved the high status that Khrushchev planned for them, nor did their chiefs.

This hierarchy has nothing to do with the rank of the same officials within the elected Party bodies. For example, Polekhin was an alternate member of the Party Central Committee, i.e. slightly higher than Pigalev, who was only a member of the Auditing Committee. Bochkarev did not belong to any Party hierarchy.

Bureau also brought about a few changes. The First Deputy Chairman of the Bureau, G. I. Voronov, whose downgrading in April 1962 has been noted, had to give up his key post in exchange for that of mere head of the RSFSR Government. True, the post was a prominent one, but it was not normal for an official of his rank to leave the Party apparatus just when the State apparatus was losing ground to the Party. Moreover, Voronov was henceforth only a 'member' of the Bureau for the RSFSR. His successor as First Deputy Chairman of the Bureau, L. N. Yefremov, was at the same time elected an alternate member of the Presidium – not a full member like Voronov. This meant that Kirilenko, who had received a spectacular promotion in April, was confirmed in a privileged position at the head of the Bureau. The Bureau itself, however, would now have only two representatives on the Presidium, facing the three federal Secretaries.

All these details may seem forbidding, but so was the situation itself. Seldom had a shake-up been so complex, seldom did there appear to be such overlapping of interests and functions. With a good deal of simplification, one might draw the following picture. On top of a fairly old rivalry between Voronov and Kirilenko for leadership of the Bureau for the RSFSR, a rivalry had arisen between Yefremov and Voronov, as well as new potential conflicts between Kirilenko and Yefremov. All three, however, had a common interest in maintaining some autonomy for the Bureau *vis-à-vis* the federal Secretariat, which was trying to whittle down the Bureau's powers. Then, within the Secretariat, there was jockeying between Suslov and Ilyichev for leadership of the ideological sector, together with competition for cadres leadership between Titov, who was less influential among the Secretaries but closer to Khrushchev, and Kozlov, who was in the reverse position. Nevertheless, the Secretaries as well as the members of the Bureau strove to preserve the Party's standing *vis-à-vis* Government officials, while the latter were certainly no less anxious to ward off encroachment by the Party.

Meanwhile, within the Government, a rivalry had just sprung up between Mikoyan and Kosygin. Brezhnev, to be sure, should have felt above such contingencies as Chief of State, but how could he forget that he would have become the second man in the Party had it not been for Kozlov? And we already know of the attempts of a large section of the collective leadership to exact its fair share of power from a nominal leader, Khrushchev, who was too eager for personal power. A difficult situation, which must be our excuse for depicting it at length. But these details may help to understand a little better how Khrushchev managed to survive the Cuban fiasco and his other difficulties.

LOSERS AND WINNERS

The period was one of confusion, but it is useful to keep the names of the chief losers and winners in mind. The losers belonged essentially to the State apparatus, as could have been expected. Kosygin ,Zasyadko, V. N. Novikov and Voronov, who was about to be relegated to the Government machine for a long time to come, have already been mentioned.

Polyansky should be added to the list. He was Voronov's predecessor at the head of the RSFSR Government and was appointed Deputy Chairman of the USSR Council of Ministers. For a member of the Party Presidium, the post was an unusually humble one. Until then, according to tradition, a seat in the highest Party hierarchy entitled the holder at least to the post of First Deputy Prime Minister, as with Kosygin and Mikoyan. Whenever things took a different turn (as for Malenkov, who had been simply Minister of Electric Power Stations from 1955 to 1957, and N. G. Ignatov and Furtseva, who after 1960 were respectively Deputy Prime Minister and Minister of Culture) ejection from the Presidium had always ensued. Within the Government, Polyansky was now on a par with seven other officials, none of whom was a full or alternate member of the Presidium. True, his functions were more important. For instance, it was noticed later that he had taken charge of agriculture, evidently as a successor to N. G. Ignatov, who once again was relegated to the honorary post of Chief of State (Chairman of the Presidium of the Supreme Soviet) of the RSFSR. In view of what is known about Polyansky's and Ignatov's views, Khrushchev probably did not favour the changes. In all likelihood, he intended eventually to eliminate Polyansky from the Presidium, as had been done with Ignatov, if for opposite reasons. It is also clear that Polyansky did not have unanimous backing within the collective leadership. The fact that it took him a year after Khrushchev's downfall (until September 1965) finally to be promoted to *First* Deputy Prime Minister is evidence enough. In addition, like Voronov, Polyansky had suffered an initial setback in April 1962. A regional Party official, G. I. Vorobyev, had been elected, instead of him, as Chairman of the Committee on the Drafting of Government Bills for the USSR Soviet.

On the winners' side, L. N. Yefremov had been promoted to the post of First Deputy Chairman of the Bureau for the RSFSR in charge of agriculture, with the rank of alternate member in the Party Presidium. He had belonged to the Party for a considerable time and was also a member of the 1952 Central Committee, but his connections are difficult to trace. In view of his past attitude as regards the 'anti-party group' and the warmth of his praise for Khrushchev, he may be listed among loyal Khrushchev supporters. However, during the U-2 crisis, he adopted a very militant attitude; moreover, his role in the Orenburg purge in April 1964 – unofficially directed against Voronov and ultimately against Khrushchev – is significant. After the First Secretary fell, Yefremov suffered a serious set-back, but later events showed that his fate was far from settled. In 1963 he had his ups and downs.[1] In short, he apparently owed his position to a compromise – an unsuccessful and contested one at that – having a few backers but also strong foes.

All the winners of this round belong to the Party Secretariat. The November reshuffle strengthened most of the new Secretaries elected at the Twenty-second Congress, whose careers have already been analysed (for instance L. F. Ilyichev with his Ideological Committee). Others were transferred to posts of equal or higher rank. Shelepin became the head of the new Party–State Control Committee, while Demichev was moved from his post of head of the Moscow Urban Committee to the Bureau for Chemical and Light Industries.

---

[1] Indications of the ups and downs in Yefremov's status starting in 1963 are as follows. At the Twenty-second Congress, he heatedly denounced the crimes of the 'anti-party' elements during the repressions, and attacked Malenkov particularly for the Leningrad affair. He called for Malenkov's expulsion from the Party, but his alone.

Khrushchev mentioned Yefremov several times in his speeches as a 'good comrade', particularly on June 30 1962 and at the December 1959 plenary session. However, the praise was coupled with minor criticism, and at the January 1961 plenary session he repeatedly interrupted Yefremov's speech with unfriendly remarks.

On foreign policy, Yefremov declared at the Supreme Soviet session held after the U-2 incident: 'It is not in order to make concessions to capitalism that we were born and are living. The Soviet Union will never accept the proposals of the West aimed at weakening our positions or those of any other country of the socialist camp' (*Pravda*, May 7 1960). At the plenary session of July 1960 Yefremov was practically the only one who mentioned the RB-47 incident – this 'new gross violation of Soviet airspace by an American military espionage aircraft'.

Throughout 1963 the problem of how to list L. N. Yefremov on the roster of Presidium alternates – in the alphabetical order or last as the most recent member – kept recurring. The *Agitator's Guide*, cleared for printing on March 11 1963, listed him last; the *CPSU Guide* (May 31 1963) in his alphabetical place; the *Encyclopedic Yearbook* (July 1963) likewise; but the *Party Activist's Notebook* (October 5 1963) had him in last place. The *Verbatim Record* of the June 1963 plenary session had it both ways: Yefremov figured at the end of the list at both meetings of June 20 and in his alphabetical place everywhere else.

In December 1964 Yefremov was sent to Stavropol as First Secretary of the Territorial Committee (*Sovietskaya Rossiya*, December 23 1964), which would normally indicate his forthcoming eviction from central posts in Moscow – the Bureau for the RSFSR as well as the Party Presidium. This did not occur, however. The *Encyclopedic Yearbook*, cleared for printing on June 3 1963, listed him as First Deputy Chairman of the Bureau for the RSFSR. Just a few days later, however, in *Izvestia* of June 15, he was still listed as First Secretary of the Stavropol Territorial Committee. Not only is this contrary to all traditions, but it is not quite clear how in practice Yefremov could have combined the two functions. The conflict was actually settled only in April 1966, when the Bureau for the RSFSR was liquidated.

Four other new Secretaries belong in this first group. They are V. N. Titov, in charge of 'Party Organs' since the beginning of 1961, who also became a Secretary and was awarded a committee; Yu. V. Andropov, who joined the Secretariat and retained leadership of the Central Committee Department 'for relations with the Communist and Workers' Parties of the socialist countries'[1] (his rise was a normal one after the promotion, a year earlier, of B. N. Ponomarev, who had been in charge of relations with the fraternal parties in non-socialist countries); and V. I. Polyakov and A. P. Rudakov became Chairmen respectively of the new Central Committee Bureaux for Agriculture and Industry, as well as Party Secretaries. For them, the promotion was even more spectacular, since up to then they had been only alternate members of the Central Committee. The plenary session co-opted them as full members – the only case of this kind during Khrushchev's stay in power.

Apart from Andropov, who owed nothing to Khrushchev and whose only protector was apparently O. V. Kuusinen,[2] all these men were very close to the First Secretary. Rudakov, like Titov, was an old Ukrainian hand. His many years of service in the Ukrainian Central Committee apparatus between 1938 and 1954 made him an early protégé of Khrushchev. V. I. Polyakov had not been in the Party so long but made up for it by his zeal. As head of the agricultural section of *Pravda*, he had come to Khrushchev's attention in December 1958 at the latest.[3] At the request of the First Secretary he was made editor of *Rural Life*, a paper newly created by the Central Committee. In March 1962 he also became chief of the Central Committee Agricultural Department for the Soviet Union. Khrushchev liked to choose his lieutenants among journalists, as he had with Adzhubey, Lebedev and Shuysky, to mention only a few. Like them, Polyakov was abruptly dismissed in November 1964 after the leader was overthrown.

[1] There was never any official announcement of Andropov's promotion as head of the department for relations with communist and workers' parties in the socialist countries. The name of the committee was indicated only once (in the *Party Worker's Handbook*, 1959 p 500). However, in view of his activities for many years, his promotion to the post may be taken for granted.
[2] Andropov had made his entire career in Karelia and Finland (in part as First Secretary of the Republic's Komsomol from 1940 to 1944, then in the Party apparatus until 1953) under the auspices of Kuusinen, who, during all those years, was the Republic's Chief of State. After having been assigned to diplomatic functions after Stalin's death (he was Ambassador to Hungary during the 1956 rising), Andropov took over the Central Committee service for relations with the Parties in the socialist countries in 1957 – at which time Kuusinen had again joined the Presidium and the Secretariat, also to deal with the problems of the international communist movement.
[3] It was at Khrushchev's personal request that Polyakov was included in the Committee for the drafting of the resolution of the plenary session of December 1958, when he was neither an alternate nor a full member of the Central Committee (verbatim record p 260).

All this confirms the conclusions formulated on the basis of the 1961 promotions. The Secretariat was becoming even larger (increasing from eight to twelve members); this was logical considering that the Party was encroaching upon the role of the state. Khrushchev, who was obviously freer to manipulate the Secretariat, was taking advantage of this to promote his own men, thereby whittling down the power of the old members such as Suslov or Kozlov. But no more than in 1961 was he able to alter the composition of the Presidium, even where junior members like Polyansky or Voronov were concerned. Once again, experience showed that whenever a man had been allowed into the inner sanctum, it was extremely difficult to get him out.

4 Restalinization Under Way

The November plenary session of 1962 marked the end of the troubled period that followed the Cuban crisis. Khrushchev had apparently weathered the worst of the storm, since no more personal attacks occurred such as were levelled at him directly after the blockade. However, his troubles were not over; in fact they were just starting and were at once subtler and deeper than before. His adversaries no longer aimed merely at paring down the chief's authority but at imposing a real shift in policy, especially in the area where his action was most threatening to those in high office, namely destalinization. At the end of November the current started moving in the opposite direction and, in March and April 1963, this produced a situation that bore all the markings of a leadership crisis. Even though some details have not been elucidated and all the experts do not agree in their conclusions, no one denies that these six months of the 1962–1963 winter were among the most troubled of the Khrushchev era. In the eyes of this observer, there is no doubt that, following the 1960 crisis, the counter-offensive at the Twenty-second Congress and its failure, a new stage began in the undermining of Khrushchev's power.

FROM THE *MANÈGE* AFFAIR TO YERMILOV

It is not in the least surprising that the reaction affected art and litera-ture. The effervescence among the intelligentsia after the new destalini-zation campaign in the autumn has been outlined. Even barring any political crisis, Khrushchev would have had to take some repressive steps. His mistake had been to believe that he could use the liberal intellectuals according to his whims and for his own political ends. He had not realized that his drive against Stalin and the 'heirs' would rapidly turn against the authority of the Party as a whole and hence against his own. His other mistake was to have overlooked (or to have been helpless against) the fact that, in order to regain his grip over the intellectuals, he would have to rely on those Stalinist forces which he was trying to subdue. A tyro in cultural matters, he was caught in this twofold contradiction, which must be remembered when one attempts to sort out what was deliberate from what was not in his statements of this period. Just as Khrushchev had viewed the liberal writers merely as a weapon in his campaign against Stalin and the 'heirs', his adversaries used the literary conflicts as a pretext in order to promote restalinization. This in turn was to help them maintain their own position and the policy they deemed best for the country. Khrushchev gradually became a helpless prisoner of these reactionary forces.

It is not within our scope to explore the details of these events from the literary and artistic standpoint.[1] The psychology of the quarrels, the acrimony with which grudges of long standing were vented through this channel (going back forty years where painting was concerned) warrant a special study. These pages will merely provide a broad outline of the main stages of the struggle, and particularly their political implications.

It all started, officially at any rate, when on December 1 1962 Khrushchev and a group of Presidium members went to a large painting exhibition in the *Manège* building (the former Tsarist riding-school) near the Kremlin. It had been organized by the Moscow section of the Artists' Union. Two thousand paintings were on view, and a small number were less representational than was customary under the rules of 'socialist realism'. They were by painters who had been censured in the 'thirties (Falk and Sterenberg) or by bold young men such as Nikonov, Andronov and Andrey Vasnetsov. In the course of his visit, and under the vigilant escort of V. A. Serov, the head of the Artists' Union and high priest of conformism, Khrushchev was led to an adjoining room where young abstractionists grouped around Professor Belyutin had been invited to exhibit. Khrushchev, who had already expressed strong criticism of the 'formalists' mentioned above, now exploded and hurled vulgar abuse at the 'culprits', ending with a 'declaration of war' on abstract art. The event was reported in a long communiqué (*Pravda*, December 2) and was the start of a violent campaign against the 'contortions' of modernism in painting and also music.

All the philistines of official painting inveighed whole-heartedly against the timid manifestations of anti-conformism, while liberal circles in turn voiced their anxiety. Khrushchev received many pleas on behalf of artistic 'pluralism' and warnings against the exploitation of the new witch-hunt by Stalinist elements.[2] To allay the storm, on

---

[1] There are many accounts of the artistic scene in the autumn and winter of 1962–1963. Special attention may be drawn to Priscilla Johnson's (*Khrushchev and the Arts, the Politics of Soviet Culture, 1962–1964* (Boston, Mass., M.I.T. Press, 1965).
[2] One of the letters received by Khrushchev in the first half of December 1962 after the *Manège* outburst, expressing fear that Stalinist elements would exploit the incident, was signed by seventeen personalities of arts and literature. It said in part:

December 17 Khrushchev assembled the four hundred most prominent representatives of the arts and letters in the presence of the entire Party leadership and allowed spokesmen of the various groups to have their say. The sharp controversy did not assuage passions and showed that the Party line had not been determined. The Party spokesman, L. F. Ilyichev, cited impassively the expressions of concern brought to his attention from the right as well as from the left. He was, to be sure, sterner towards the liberal protests, which he interpreted as advocating the 'coexistence of ideologies', in other words permissiveness toward 'bourgeois' ideals – something the Party could never countenance. But he concentrated on painting and music, ignoring literature except for an attack on the underground author Yesenin-Volpin. Since the discussion was far from conclusive, a new debate was scheduled for 'after the New Year'. One untoward incident occurred: G. I. Serebryakova, a concentration-camp victim, violently attacked the writer Ilya Ehrenburg, who appeared as champion of the liberal school. She accused him not only of having been 'Stalin's mouthpiece' but also of having caused the deaths in 1948–1952 of members of the Jewish Anti-Fascist Committee. As evidence, she brought up the testimony of A. N. Poskrebyshev, Stalin's former private secretary, who had fallen from favour since his master's death in 1953. But this outburst was naturally not published.

Within a week the drive was beginning to affect literature too. On December 24 and 26 Ilyichev assembled one hundred and forty young artists and writers under the auspices of his Ideological Committee. He attacked the singer-poet Bulat Okudzhava and the writer Yury Nagibin. A few days later Ehrenburg was again arraigned, this time by two notorious Stalinists – the painters Laktyonov (*Pravda*, January 4 1963) and Aleksandr Gerasimov (*Trud*, January 9). The latter, however, so overstated his case, embracing in his accusations even the weekly *Nedelya* edited by A. I. Adzhubey, that he had to make a self-criticism (in the magazine *Ogonyok*). In the case of both Nagibin and Ehrenburg, the attacks were directed at amateurs of formalist art, the protectors of the modernists in painting and sculpture, rather than at the writers. V. A. Kosolapov, the chief editor of *Literaturnaya Gazeta*, had to relinquish his post at the end of December for having been too soft in the war against abstract art, and was replaced by a far more conservative figure, A. B. Chakovsky.[1]

'We are witnesses of how artists belonging to the only tendency that prospered under Stalin, which refused to others the chance to work or even to live, are beginning to interpret the statements you made at the art exhibition. We firmly believe that you did not wish for this and that you are opposed to it' (quoted by L. F. Ilyichev on December 17: *Pravda*, December 22 1962).

[1] The pretext for Kosolapov's removal as chief editor of *Literaturnaya Gazeta* in

The writers were still faring well enough, particularly the young ones. Their poetry readings went on through January. On December 28 *Pravda* published a story by Yury Kazakov, whose writings had been shelved since 1957, and on January 3 it paid a glowing tribute to young literature under the signature of the highly respected Korney Chukovsky. Ilyichev himself had liberally praised the young luminaries Yevgeny Yevtushenko and Andrey Voznesensky. The first left in mid-January, as scheduled, for a protracted semi-official tour in West Germany and France.

The second stage of the movement of reaction, which ended by sweeping everything before it, started in the second half of January. The events in chronological order were as follows: an attack by *Izvestia* on January 20[1] against the novelist Nekrasov (charged with not having sufficiently slanted against the United States the account in *Novy Mir* of his trip there a few months earlier); the publication by *Pravda* on January 27 of a vicious pamphlet by the chauvinistic N. M. Gribachov, 'No, Young People!', clearly aimed at Yevtushenko and hinting that the fashionable young poets were ready actually to betray their country; a fresh attack by *Izvestia* on January 31 against the bulwarks of progressive art, the magazines *Novy Mir* and *Yunost*, and their editors, Tvardovsky and Boris Polevoy, for having published respectively a pessimistic story by Aleksandr Yashin on country life and 'mean, trivial verse' by Voznesensky. All the big names were gradually being dragged into the limelight.

At the same time, Ehrenburg got his share. On January 30 *Izvestia* – again – published a long article by the critic V. V. Yermilov (who had performed a few other questionable missions of the same kind before). This time he attacked Ehrenburg not only for his liking for formalistic art, but for his attitude toward the Stalinist purges, as he had described them in his memoirs (those passages had been published by *Novy Mir* in May 1962, so this was a delayed reaction to say the least). In substance, the charge was that Ehrenburg had sinned against 'ethics' by stating that he had known or at least guessed the arbitrary nature of the 1937 and 1938 arrests, but had merely 'gritted his teeth' in silence. Yermilov's thesis was an original and ingenious one: the

---

December 1962 was an article against abstract art which a particularly militant conservative, the sculptor E. V. Vuchetich, had sent to the magazine and which the magazine published on December 18 1962 – one day too late. The author had meanwhile taken advantage of the conference of the 17th to complain to Khrushchev that the editors of *Literaturnaya Gazeta* had refused to publish such newsworthy material. He succeeded in rousing the First Secretary against the magazine, and, a week later, Kosolapov was removed.

[1] The dates given in this section of the book all refer to the newspaper's Moscow edition.

Soviet people had been shocked in the 'thirties at learning that so many 'enemies of the people' had slipped into their midst, but they had not doubted that the arrests in general were justified. Whenever they had happened to believe in the innocence of an accused person, they had not hesitated to say so publicly. 'There were even', Yermilov added, 'a number of statements made at meetings and in the press . . . regarding what was in fact the very essence of the cult of Stalin.' If Ehrenburg had had doubts about the campaign, it was merely because he enjoyed 'a great advantage over the enormous majority of average Soviet people'.

Ehrenburg lost no time in retorting in a letter which *Izvestia* published on February 6. He was in a position to assert flatly something that Yermilov could not contradict: viz. 'I did not attend a single meeting where people came to the platform to protest against the arbitrary arrest of comrades they believed to be innocent. Nor did I read a single article of protest in a case involving one or more people on the subject of what Yermilov calls "the very essence of the cult of Stalin".' While fully maintaining all his previous statements, Ehrenburg accused Yermilov of 'seeking through insinuations to insult him as a man and as a Soviet citizen'.

The reply, published the same day by the same paper, was a new exercise in acrobatics by Yermilov. Ehrenburg, by his thesis on silent awareness in the face of arbitrary power, was 'insulting a whole generation of Soviet people in his attempt to give himself a clean bill of health'. *Izvestia*'s editors ran the two letters in the same issue with a short comment openly approving Yermilov and censuring Ehrenburg; the latter, however, was blamed only for his refusal to discuss his formalistic leanings and the problem of artistic creativity. 'Ehrenburg's letter', the paper declared, 'indicates that the author is more concerned with accusations he has invented himself than with the substance of these problems.'

The second 'encounter' between the Party leaders and the intellectuals on March 7 and 8 brought the crisis to a head. A few aspects of the intervening period should, however, first be reviewed. To begin with, the relatively slow course of events is noteworthy. The waverings of December ended in the first stalemate in January, followed by a resumption of the anti-liberal drive, again followed at the end of January by an unstable *status quo*. No striking fact occurred in February after the renewed attack on Ehrenburg on the 6th. The sequel to the debate of December 17, at first fixed for early January, was postponed several times. 'Circumstances prevented it', Ilyichev said later, 'and the interval lasted longer than expected.'[1] (*Pravda*, March 9 1963.) What could these circumstances have been?

[1] The time lag with which the major Party statements on art and literature in the

First, the time lag may have been due to external factors: Khrushchev spent most of January (from the 9th to the 28th) away from Moscow, travelling successively in Poland, East Berlin and the Ukraine. Relations with China, which had been exacerbated by the Cuban affair, must have worried him more than literary problems at this point. Nothing, however, prevented him from deciding upon a clearer line upon his return, which was in the first half of February (after the Ehrenburg affair).

Another external reason should not be overlooked: resistance from the people involved. The December discussions had shown how closely knit the liberal group was. It was obviously not going to be as easy to get it back into line as Khrushchev had imagined at the time of the *Manège* episode. The petition by the seventeen, which has been quoted in part, bore the signatures of some of the greatest names in the arts and literature: not only Ehrenburg and Paustovsky, but even personalities who apparently were less committed, such as the sculptors Konenkov and Favorsky, the writers Kaverin and Chukovsky, and probably Konstantin Simonov.

The second letter, advocating the 'peaceful coexistence' of the various tendencies, had been supported, for a while at least, by officials hitherto completely loyal to the Party, such as A. A. Surkov and N. S. Tikhonov. The most prominent living Soviet composer, Dmitri Shostakovich, had not only signed the first petition but had refused to disavow his *Thirteenth Symphony* inspired by some of Yevtushenko's poetry (in particular his poem *Babi Yar* against anti-semitism). It was performed for the first time, despite an official boycott, on December 18, the very day after the celebrated discussion.[1] Finally, while most of the artists criticized on December 1 had retreated into silence, the few who had agreed to come forward had been more than ambiguous in their self-

---

winter of 1962–1963 were released to the public is interesting. Ilyichev's report of December 17 was published – with large omissions – only on December 22 in *Pravda*. His second speech of December 26 at the Ideological Committee came out only on January 10 1963 and only in *Literaturnaya Gazeta*. Khrushchev's remarks at the first conference were never officially reported. True, they were hardly fit to print, particularly where they concerned anti-semitism.

It is noticeable that the press kept up with the statements much better after the line had been officially decided upon. Ilyichev's introductory speech of March 7 appeared in *Pravda* two days later, and Khrushchev's within the same interval.

[1] In an article published in the winter of 1962 and based on the above information (*Le Monde*, December 28 1962), this writer, owing to a slip made by his source, ascribed to Sholokhov a public gesture of sympathy for Ehrenburg after the latter was attacked by Serebryakova on December 17. In fact, the man who backed him was Shostakovich. Sholokhov, on the contrary, had joined the official chorus by declaring on March 7: 'For a long time now, I have been thinking what has just been said about Ehrenburg.' It is true that Sholokhov, the future Nobel Prize winner, played a very small part in the ensuing outcry against the liberals.

criticism. Ehrenburg's riposte to Yermilov's insinuations was also calculated to discourage any over-impetuous attacks.

KHRUSHCHEV IN AN AWKWARD POSITION

A harsh campaign was nevertheless launched, so that the above reasons
were not decisive. It is, indeed, hard to picture Khrushchev changing
his mind about a large-scale offensive once he had determined to carry
it out, especially in a sector which he obviously regarded as minor
compared to serious political issues. Moreover, despite all the steps
taken since 1953 toward a régime of enlightened dictatorship, such
moves are decided in high political quarters and not as the result of a
dialogue with the prospective opponents. Hence the cause of the protracted wavering must have lain in the Party Presidium itself, and
specifically in the reluctance of Khrushchev, who realized the dangers of
the counter-offensive to himself. The final decision, as we shall see,
coincided with other retreats or setbacks in his main policy. The
political implications of the literary episode should therefore be
examined at this point. Khrushchev had several reasons to be
embarrassed.
1 He had not been the instigator of the crackdown on the artists and
writers. The conservative camp had asked him to step in, in a tone
verging on recrimination. There is no doubt that Khrushchev's outburst against the abstract paintings at the *Manège* was spontaneous,
though the visit itself was not. It had been organized by Serov and a
few other veterans of official Stalinist art, and followed a petition by a
'large group of artists' addressed to the Presidium of the November
plenary session; that is, approved between November 19 and 23. Its
peremptory tone is significant:

> 'At the present time the formalists are questioning the value of
> realist art and are claiming that Lenin's precepts and the Party's
> decisions on the subject are obsolete. By their acts and declarations,
> the formalists are seeking to revive the trends condemned in the
> Party's decisions. *We request the Central Committee of the Party*
> to determine what in these decisions has become obsolete. If they
> are not obsolete, the declarations against these decisions made in
> the *press*, the *radio*, and *television* must be regarded as *revisionist*
> and as aiming to infiltrate an ideology alien to us.' (Quoted by
> Ilyichev on December 17, *Pravda*, December 22 1962.) [Author's
> italics.]

The 'request' was directed at the encouragement the formalists were receiving from most official propaganda media, even more than at their actual work. It is noteworthy that it was addressed to 'the Presidium of the plenary session' (according to Ilyichev) or to 'the Central Committee' (according to the text) – but at all events to the collective leadership. The petition of the seventeen, on the other hand, which warned against neo-Stalinist elements, was addressed to 'Dear Nikita Sergeyevich,' 'the person who had done most to extirpate Stalinist arbitrariness from the life of our country'. True, a member of the opposite camp, the arch-Stalinist Yevgeny Katsman,[1] also chose to address 'Comrade Khrushchev' personally, but his letter in *Pravda* of December 16 1962 was a barely disguised reprimand. Quoting Lenin, who had allegedly said about art, 'We must not just sit idle and let chaos develop', Katsman went on: 'V. I. Lenin *believed that art must be controlled, and he controlled it.*' The current situation was far darker, according to Katsman: 'The absence of control (*neupravliayemost*) in art has created a breach through which alien artistic notions are penetrating. The representatives of the bourgeois world are trying, by ideological means, to capture a segment of our youth.' He, too, accused radio and television[2] and concluded tartly: 'The Leninist standards of our social life are being brought back into the country at large. The question is: when will the Leninist precepts and principles be fully restored in our art? . . . It is high time to remember what Lenin said about art and to apply his principles.'

In short, Khrushchev, the 'faithful Leninist' and the 'continuer' of Lenin's work, was being reproached for having forgotten the lessons of his master. He could hardly have found such warnings pleasing or even normal.

2 Khrushchev's first reaction to these neo-Stalinist demands was apparently adverse. The first petition from the 'hard-liners' was submitted during the November plenary. At the end of the session, on the 23rd, Khrushchev made an important speech which, after many rumours to the contrary, was not published. Its text remains unknown, but it is known that it dealt at length with literature and painting. As stated

---

[1] Yevgeny Katsman, an old champion of socialist realism (he had attacked Mayakovsky on the subject in the 'twenties), had been privileged in the 'thirties to paint the official portraits of Stalin and the top men in his entourage. A colleague who went to see him in 1962 found a portrait of the late dictator on his desk. One of his obsessions was that the abstract painters were paid spies of foreign countries.

[2] Since February 1962 the Radio and Television Committee was run by M. A. Kharlamov, the former head of the press department at the Foreign Ministry. More important, he was a member of Khrushchev's retinue during all major trips abroad, and a co-author of the famous *Face to Face with America*, written just after Camp David (he had edited the book). His swift removal after the October 1964 coup leaves hardly any doubt as to the closeness of his ties with Khrushchev.

previously, other information corroborates that Khrushchev expressed admiration for Solzhenitsyn and approval of Yevtushenko's *Stalin's Heirs*. He also spoke of destalinization and his tone is easy to imagine, considering the excitement aroused by *Ivan Denisovich* and Khrushchev's ulterior motives in these matters.[1]

In any case, Khrushchev's speech was surely not of the kind that the militant conservatives had expected. Not that Khrushchev was a devotee of abstract art, of course; but it was the destalinization climate he was promoting that had stirred up the liberal elements, and it could only encourage them to push forward on all artistic fronts. At all events, the plenary was not followed by any order to stop the agitation of the abstractionists and formalists generally. It was on November 26, three days after Khrushchev's speech, that Belyutin organized his exhibition of abstract art for foreign journalists, and only on the 29th that an order was issued forbidding the same exhibition at the Yunost hotel. 3 Under the circumstances, Khrushchev's visit to the *Manège* appears rather as a reversal of policy, showing that the wind had shifted during the preceding week. Khrushchev's speech of November 23 must have aroused deep anxiety among the 'heirs', who already saw themselves under pressure in all areas of culture. Their agitation must have been used by some more highly placed 'heirs', who imposed the first major decision of the counter-movement – namely, not to let the speech be published. That week's debates must have been lively, so much so that Khrushchev could not refrain from letting a Western ambassador, whom he saw on November 28 1962, catch a glimpse of the picture. According to the diplomat's statement to this writer, Khrushchev said in substance: 'I favour greater freedom of expression, since the level we have achieved in the economy and technology demands this. But some of my colleagues in the Presidium think we must be cautious. Obviously, we shall have to wait a while before going ahead any further'. The First Secretary could not have admitted more candidly that he had suffered a blow. He probably did not yet realize that having been prevented from going forward, he would be forced to go back.[2]

---

[1] The *Unità* correspondent in Moscow, who at the end of March 1963 reported on the 'general debate' of the winter of 1962–1963, corroborated the fact that the November plenary had indeed been a turbulent one. Stating that the debate had started at the plenary, he wrote: 'The session was unruly, eager for change, anti-Stalinist' (*Le Monde*, April 3 1963).

[2] Khrushchev had used earthier language when he addressed a small gathering of writers in November 1962 (before the plenary session apparently) on the subject of destalinization. According to a reliable source, this is what he said on that occasion: 'Some people are waiting for me to croak (*zdokhnut*) in order to resuscitate Stalin and his methods. This is why, before I die, I want to destroy Stalin and destroy those people, so as to make it impossible to put the clock back.'

4 As soon as the first stage of the reaction in literature set in, it became obvious that restalinization was its accompaniment. On December 12, in his speech before the Supreme Soviet, Khrushchev spoke these revealing words: 'Our Party,' he said, 'subjected Stalin's errors and abuses to strong, energetic criticism, *although it does not deny his merits* vis-à-vis *the Communist Party and movement*' (*Pravda*, December 13 1962). Until 1960, and even as late as the end of 1961, such a statement would have been entirely normal. But after the destalinization drive of the summer and autumn of 1962, it was no longer so. For many months, not one good word had been uttered about Stalin, and his 'merits' were no longer mentioned, even in passing.

These words did not fall on deaf ears. B. N. Ponomarev declared to a conference of historians on December 18: 'We acknowledge, as N. S. Khrushchev did once again emphatically before the Supreme Soviet, Stalin's merits *vis-à-vis* the Communist Party and movement.' 5 The attacks on certain well-known protégés of Khrushchev's were so many indirect attacks against his own authority. Yevtushenko's *Stalin's Heirs* had been published by Khrushchev's order, as everybody now knew, and the young poet's position was thereby enhanced. In October and November, Yevtushenko was *Pravda's* special correspondent in Havana. The lively if courteous discussion he had had with Khrushchev on December 17 about art had apparently not altered this, since ten days later Ilyichev had complimented the poet. Gribachov's attack against Yevtushenko (still a veiled one) was bound to hit the man who had bestowed his favours upon him.

Solzhenitsyn's case is even more clear-cut: Khrushchev was strongly committed to this writer, having supported him against opposition within the Presidium and publicly boasted about doing so. On December 17 Khrushchev had made a point of personally introducing the author of *A Day in the Life of Ivan Denisovich*[1] to the four hundred assembled writers, while Ilyichev confirmed the blessing of the authorities.[2] But as early as January 11 1963 the same *Ivan Denisovich* was

---

[1] It was Tvardovsky who disclosed later that Khrushchev himself had introduced Solzhenitsyn to the gathering of writers. Tvardovsky did this in the interview he gave to Henry Shapiro, the UPI correspondent, which was reprinted in *Pravda* May 12 1963. Tvardovsky said: 'At the first meeting, Nikita Sergeyevich mentioned Solzhenitsyn in his speech and introduced him to all the participants at the Palace of Receptions on the Lenin Hills.'

[2] Ilyichev spoke as follows about Solzhenitsyn at the gathering of writers on December 17 1962: 'In the art of socialist realism, our Party supports the sound critical trends that affirm life. Artistically and politically powerful works, which boldly and truthfully expose the arbitrariness that prevailed in the period of the cult of personality, have recently been published with the approval of the Party's Central Committee. Suffice it to mention Solzhenitsyn's *A Day in the Life of Ivan Denisovich*' (*Pravda*, December 22 1962).

being criticized. Lydia Fomenko in *Literaturnaya Gazeta* brought up, timidly as yet, the argument that later became the key one used by the conservatives, namely that the book did not 'bring out the total dialectic of the period . . . did not achieve the level of generalization on which its conflicting phenomena could be reconciled'. In other words, Solzhenitsyn had 'forgotten' to say that the Party had advanced despite Stalin, that the period of the 'cult' had not been one of utter despair. This correctly reflected what the 'heirs' were thinking, but it was too early to say so. Lydia Fomenko was contradicted by V. V. Yermilov in his article of January 30 against Ehrenburg. On the other hand, it was easier to attack Solzhenitsyn for his other writings, for instance, *Matryona's House*, an impressive description of rural life published in January by *Novy Mir*. The first critical review appeared on March 2 1963 in *Literaturnaya Gazeta*, before the big storm. But this too was only the beginning.

6 Ehrenburg enjoyed a less obvious but nevertheless real protection. Not only had his memoirs been published in 1962 with some measure of assistance at the top, but Khrushchev had mentioned his encouragement of the book to the American poet Robert Frost on September 7 in the presence of A. A. Surkov, the leader of the Writers' Union. This official support was partly withdrawn in December because of Ehrenburg's too overt backing of the formalist painters. Ilyichev took a dig at him on December 17, though without naming him, when he denied that Lunacharsky and Lenin had had a liberal attitude in artistic matters. (Ehrenburg had argued this in his memoirs.) This was nothing, however, compared to what Serebriakova on that day and Yermilov later said about him. The episode deserves a closer look.

THE EHRENBURG AFFAIR

The attack on Ehrenburg diverted destalinization from the path that Khrushchev had planned. The 'heirs' devised a stroke of genius in order to deflect the dangerous campaign from themselves. Khrushchev was trying to smoke out the hardened Stalinists who were hampering 'the forward movement' by which he sought to bring about the 'restoration of Leninist standards' (in fact the consolidation of his own power). These people, according to the First Secretary, were the 'dogmatists' and the 'sectarians' (the critics of his policy). It now became apparent that destalinization could hit other targets as well, namely the destalinizers themselves.

Ehrenburg was ideally suited to demonstrate this fact, since he too had been a protégé of Stalin, had also contributed to the 'cult' and had since become a leader of the liberal wing. The occasion was especially fitting since his 'formalistic' misdeeds made him more vulnerable just after the *Manège* incident.

This explains the attack on Ehrenburg at the meeting of December 17. The conservative right wing had the good fortune to have a camp victim, Serebryakova, as an ally. Was her intervention spontaneous? No one in Moscow could think that an individual acting alone would take the responsibility of bringing criminal charges against a highly placed figure in the presence of Khrushchev and all the Party leaders.[1] The reference to the testimony of Poskrebyshev, the strong man of the Stalinist régime, the man who not only was best informed about the purges, but had sponsored the careers of many leaders and high officials who were still well entrenched, could not be free from ulterior motives either. Various observers believe that this was direct blackmail against Khrushchev himself. It is difficult to be sure, since a considerable number of others, whose particular views covered a wide range, might also have been aimed at. The fact to be kept in mind is that, for the first time, the sharpest edge of the destalinization weapon – the threat of criminal charges – was being aimed at a destalinizer.

In substance, Yermilov only repeated what Serebriakova had said, but with all the diplomatic nicety required in a written document. Yermilov's insinuations were clear: the 'great advantage' ascribed to Ehrenburg during the period of the 'cult' meant that he knew a great deal about arbitrariness, and hence was to some extent an accomplice. In his second letter, of February 6, Yermilov feigned to withdraw the charge by declaring that Ehrenburg had 'invented' it against himself. Actually, this was further blackmail: either Ehrenburg was to give up the liberal form of anti-Stalinism and rally to the thesis of the 'good Stalinists' who opposed 'unjust excesses', or else he would be placing himself in the posture of a defendant, in which case matters could go much further: for if he had indeed been an accomplice, the matter must be cleared up. In his first letter, Yermilov had opposed Ehrenburg's thesis according to which 'memories' should be allowed to 'melt away'. In support of this Yermilov, with supreme skill, had quoted Khrushchev's well-known promises to the Twenty-second Congress: 'Our duty is to unravel carefully every aspect of affairs of that kind connected with the abuse of power. Time will go by, we shall die since all of us

---

[1] It is not possible, nor is it within the scope of this book, to judge the substance of the charge brought against Ehrenburg by Serebryakova. It should be noted, however, that he had intended to devote a chapter of his memoirs to explaining in detail his attitude during the anti-semitic repressions of 1948–1952. That chapter was censored when the rest of the work was published in spring 1963.

are mortal, but as long as we work we can and must elucidate many things, tell the truth to the Party and to the people. . . .'

In other words, the movement had come full circle: these words uttered by Khrushchev eighteen months earlier against his 'anti-party' adversaries were now backfiring against his allies. It cannot be excluded that ultimately they might apply to Khrushchev himself, since, in this roundabout way, it was the first time that his adversaries came so close to challenging him with the question: 'And where were you at the time?'[1] This, of course, was only a remote possibility: an Ehrenburg trial appeared as unlikely as a Molotov trial had earlier. The present move was, none the less, the most reliable means of preventing either, and thereby any other settlements of scores that Khrushchev might have been planning.

Curiously enough it was *Izvestia*, under Khrushchev's son-in-law Adzhubey, the organ that should have been closest to Khrushchev in all respects, which printed the attacks. Generally speaking, this newspaper played the most 'reactionary' role in the intensified reaction at the end of January. For instance, it carried the attacks of the 20th against Nekrasov and of the 31st against Tvardovsky and Polevoy. It should be noted once again that the chief editor's role may be curtailed under certain circumstances, depending on the status of the official or institution that sends in the copy. Moreover, Adzhubey had accompanied his father-in-law on his visit to Poland and East Germany. If he was with him till the end of the journey, Adzhubey could have returned to Moscow only on January 28, that is, the day before Yermilov's first attack on Ehrenburg, after the new line had been adopted. The editorial note of February 6 brushed aside the 'ethical' aspect of the Ehrenburg case – allegedly fabricated by the writer himself – and reproached him solely for his association with the formalists. The impression created was that the earlier incident was to be regarded as closed; but the subtleties of Yermilov's reasoning must have been noted by some people.

At all events, when Khrushchev returned at the end of January, he found the situation much deteriorated. In his absence, the wave of Stalinization in cultural matters had gathered momentum. His personal prestige, despite the improvement after the Cuban crisis, was again

[1] The 1963 attack against Ehrenburg for his silence during the purges takes on a more concrete significance if one recalls a story about the Twentieth Congress which circulated fairly widely in Moscow after 1956. According to the story, Khrushchev was reading his famous Secret Report when the following anonymous note was handed to him: 'Why didn't the Politburo and you do anything to prevent these awful things?' Khrushchev allegedly broke off, read the note aloud, and then asked: 'Will the writer identify himself?' When no one in the audience stood up, Khrushchev went on: 'There, comrades, is the answer to the question.' In other words, he then espoused Ehrenburg's thesis.

showing signs of weakness. The many foreign journalists assembled in Stalingrad at the beginning of February for the twentieth anniversary of the great victory waited for him in vain, despite firm indications given them only the day before from official sources. Judging from the way in which Khrushchev had in the past used any tribute to himself in various articles commemorating the event,[1] it is more than doubtful that this sudden attack of modesty was voluntary. Another unexpected event: on February 2 Moscow broke off the nuclear-test-ban talks, although in December a solution had seemed very near (Khrushchev had accepted the principle of three inspections per year on Soviet territory to detect undergound explosions). More serious shifts were at hand.

---

[1] On January 27 1963 *Pravda* published a photograph showing Khrushchev at the command post of the Stalingrad front, leaning over a map with Marshal A. I. Yeremenko, the front commander. The same newspaper carried an article by Yeremenko about the battle, in which Khrushchev was mentioned more than any other personality. Another photograph of him at Stalingrad appeared in *Pravda* of January 30. On February 2 S. S. Biryuzov, then commander in chief of the strategic rockets force, published an article in *Komsomolskaya Pravda* in which he praised the 'iron logic and breadth of strategic views of N. S. Khrushchev', displayed 'in all their brilliance' at Stalingrad. According to another article by the same author published in *Politicheskoye Samoobrazovanie* (Political Self-Education), No 2, February 1963, Khrushchev had displayed 'immense energy and wisdom in the formulation and execution of plans for the defeat of the enemy'.

Malinovsky was more reserved in the article he published on February 2 in *Pravda*. He mentioned Khrushchev only for his role in 'political work'; as to the plans for the counter-offensive, they had never been 'the work of one individual'. The allusion was meant specifically for Zhukov, but could apply as well to any other would-be monopolizers of glory.

5 February–March 1963: The Crisis

On February 15 or 16 1963, or perhaps on both days, an 'enlarged' meeting of the Presidium was held in Moscow. The evidence for this is that two of the provincial members, Podgorny and Rashidov, were seen at a reception in Moscow on the 16th. Their colleagues K. T. Mazurov, V. P. Mzhavanadze and V. V. Shcherbitsky were not with them, but neither were they reported to be in their domains of Minsk, Tbilisi, and Kiev.[1] A few weeks later, amid speculation about the change of line on various issues, a rumour circulated that in the course of a Presidium meeting in February, Khrushchev had found himself in the minority and that his resignation had even been considered. It was reported at the same time that the attack had been led by Kozlov. No details about the course of events are available. As to the personalities involved, many indications do point to Kozlov. In any event, the matters debated at the session are no longer a mystery. They centred on the following problems.

STALINISTS TRIUMPHANT

The pro-Stalinist reaction, launched in a roundabout way via art and literature, triumphed in the celebrated second 'encounter' of March 7 and 8 between Party and intellectuals. The decisions in this field were almost certainly taken earlier, that is, at the mid-February Presidium session. Technical reasons, namely the elections to the soviets of the republics on March 3, which required campaigning by the officials in the second half of February, precluded any immediate gathering of judges,

---

[1] Rashidov, who may be presumed to have attended an enlarged Presidium meeting on February 15 and 16 1963, was still in Tashkent on February 14, and was back there on the 18th, according to his newspaper *Pravda Vostoka*. Obviously he went to Moscow for a specific purpose. In general, a study of the movements of the various officials shows that the 15th and 16th were the only days in February (except perhaps for the 6th and 7th) when they could all have congregated in Moscow. And the fact that the two officials from the provinces were seen in Moscow on the 16th supports the theory that the meeting was held in mid-February.

prosecutors, and victims. However, as early as February 28, Yevtushenko was instructed to cut short his visit to France.[1]

The major speech delivered by Khrushchev on March 8 (*Pravda*, March 10 1963) is already history. We need not comment on its references to literature or to such 'normal' features as his call for discipline and Party loyalty (*partiynost*), for the rejection of 'ideological co-existence', and for the concept of art as a tool of propaganda. He was also no doubt sincere in his liking for the marches composed by the Pokrass brothers and for Laktyonov's trite paintings.[2] Khrushchev was only expressing in slightly stronger terms something that all the Party leaders had always thought, namely, that literature was meant to serve the powers that be. The only difference was that the character of its mission now differed radically from the one Khrushchev had assigned to it in 1962.

Still, a political leader is a prisoner of his own statements – or at least those of recent months. Even if he tries to forget them, his audience is not fooled, and the speaker cannot ignore this fact. Khrushchev could not have indulged in such an outright recantation of his own words just because he had changed his mind, as some people contend; and even if he had so changed it, one would have to ask why. The essential point is that Khrushchev was reversing himself on his pet issue of anti-Stalinism, which he had made into the basis of his power.

Stalin, for whom he had not had one kind word in eighteen months (save for the phrase about his 'merits' in his speech of December 12 1962), was suddenly again discovered to have had great qualities indeed, and now Khrushchev was confessing that he had wept at his funeral. The man accused of having committed serious mistakes as early as 1912 was now receiving the stamp of approval for his contribution to the revolutionary struggle 'before and during the Revolution, and in the following years of the building of socialism'. The dictator was hailed not only for having ensured the opponents' political defeat but also for having 'led the struggle to rid the country of plotters and for having waged victorious war against the enemies of the people. In this he had been believed in and supported.' 'It could not have been otherwise', Khrushchev added, 'for in the past there had been more than one instance of deceit and betrayal. . . . The class enemies . . . had begun to use methods such as sabotage, subversion, assassination, acts of terror-

[1] Priscilla Johnson, *Khrushchev and the Arts, the Politics of Soviet Culture, 1962–4*. But Yevtushenko, although he was ordered to return at the end of February, left Paris only on March 4 1963.
[2] The Pokrass brothers had composed a melody, *Moscow on a May Morning*. Khrushchev had good grounds to declare himself moved by it, since he confessed that he had commissioned it. Laktyonov was an official painter of the 'photographist' school, which set store by meticulous accuracy of detail.

ism and revolt.' This was little short of a white washing of the purges. Khrushchev did not deny, however, that 'excesses' had been committed, but to do so he reverted to a formula practically abandoned since 1957, namely Stalin's illness 'in the last years of his life'. Apart from Yakir's case, the only instances of arbitrariness he mentioned were the Leningrad affair (1949) and the Doctors' Plot (1952–1953) – that is, the last ones. Even then he found excuses for them: 'Knowing Stalin's pathological distrust, the intelligence services of the imperialist countries were fabricating these cases by forging documents that seemed fully authentic.'

There were many other disavowals. The man who had promised the Twenty-second Congress to 'unravel many things as long as we live and work' now asserted that the Party had told 'the people *the whole truth* on the subject.' For the first time, then, he endorsed the wording of the Congress resolution which was so anomalous that, as noted previously, even in Ponomarev's *History of the Party* the word 'whole' had been deleted. The man who had approved and even insisted on the publication of *Ivan Denisovich* was now admitting that this kind of literature drew 'the fat bourgeois flies from abroad'. He did manage to pay passing tribute to Solzhenitsyn, but he was in effect crying 'Enough!' to all other writers who were eager to deal with this 'highly dangerous theme'. The man who, six months earlier, had tried to console Bukharin's widow and had repudiated his trial was now saying that the line advocated by the 'right wing' leader 'might have led to the restoration of capitalism in our country . . . disarmed us militarily in the face of hostile and aggressive capitalist encirclement'. This was tantamount to saying that 'objectively' Bukharin was a traitor. The man who for several years had never spoken of the Leningrad affair without mentioning Malenkov now no longer implicated anyone in it. Only Kaganovich was mentioned in connection with a purge, or rather the threat of a purge, in the Ukraine in 1947. Gone were the days of the 'anti-party group' and their 'personal responsibility for mass repressions'.[1] The man who had told Frost that he approved of Ehrenburg's memoirs all of a sudden was discovering that 'in reading them one cannot help noticing that he paints everything in gloomy colours'.

The Ehrenburg case was too important to be left at that. The writer was attacked at length by both Ilyichev and Khrushchev, although the approach was not the same. Ilyichev endorsed all Yermilov's charges and mentioned Yermilov in the process. For instance, he repeated and expanded Yermilov's insinuations about Ehrenburg's 'advantages' over

[1] Malenkov was censured once by Khrushchev in his speech of March 8 1963, but for a political sin: with Beriya, Malenkov had allegedly been tempted to sell out East Germany after Stalin's death.

most people during the Stalin era, and made it a point to quote several of Ehrenburg's tributes to Stalin in 1951.[1] In short, Ilyichev, who obviously had less to fear in raking up the past, had no qualms about calling things by their true names and turning the destalinization weapon against the destalinizers themselves. Khrushchev had good reason to be more cautious: he did not mention Yermilov or the 'theory of silence', and carefully refrained from condemning Ehrenburg's attitude towards Stalin. The furthest he went was to say dispassionately that 'comrade Ehrenburg was not persecuted or restricted during the period of the cult of personality', whereas a writer 'like, let us say, Galina Serebryakova' had suffered 'an entirely different fate' (this was significant considering the incident between the two writers in December). For the rest, his criticism of Ehrenburg was directed mainly against the liberal writer who had been content to observe the Revolution but had refused to take part in the struggle.

Khrushchev did uphold the defensive aspect of Yermilov's theory: 'The question arises whether the leading cadres of the Party knew, let us say, about the arrests carried out during that period. Yes, they did know about them. But did they know that absolutely innocent people were being arrested? No, they did not. They believed in Stalin and could not even imagine that repression might be exercised against honest people devoted to our cause' (*Pravda*, March 10 1963).

Later in his speech Khrushchev also upheld, though without especial emphasis, the view that some 'courageous communists' had not hesitated to report to Stalin the excesses known to them. In addition to Sholokhov, who had protested against the abuses of the 1933 collectivization, Khrushchev mentioned in passing two other instances. Stalin 'had not been supported' when he sought to fabricate a case against a 'counter-revolutionary centre' in Moscow, and this had saved the cadres concerned from a repetition of the Leningrad affair. In addition, the 'Ukraine bolsheviks' had stood up to Stalin, Beriya and Kaganovich when they had tried to engineer a 'Ukrainian nationalists' case which would have decimated the local intelligentsia. Khrushchev did not give any dates, but it was easy to verify that, each time, he was at the head of the administration involved. This was tantamount to a plea in his own defence.

We shall never know how acute were the quarrels roused by the

---

[1] Naturally, Ilyichev, who was no less vulnerable than Ehrenburg for his past attitude towards Stalin, hastened to add after repeating Yermilov's indictment: 'If I am quoting you [Ehrenburg], it is not in order to set you apart from others or to criticise what you said. We all spoke and wrote in that vein at the time, without hypocrisy. We wrote what we believed. But it appears that you did not believe, although you did write. This is an entirely different thing.' (*Pravda*, March 9 1963.)

'Ehrenburg affair', but the above details show by and large that its instigators achieved their object. After having used destalinization one-sidedly against his enemies for so many years, Khrushchev was practically rehabilitating almost the whole generation of 'leading cadres' and hoisting Stalin himself back on to his pedestal. He had threatened Molotov, Malenkov and other 'heirs' with criminal prosecution and now was in the position of humbly pleading his own cause. One of his favourite weapons, the search for responsibilities, had backfired.

There is hardly any doubt that this issue had caused a great deal of turmoil behind the scenes in the preceding months. For example, the correspondence of 1933 between Stalin and Sholokhov had, Khrushchev said, 'been found recently in the archives'. Now, no one, especially in the Kremlin, goes digging into archives without a specific purpose. Moreover, Stalin's archives could hardly be a quarry of exclusively pleasant memories for anyone. Poskrebyshev's odd appearance in the news a few weeks earlier was also significant. In short, a great deal of dirty linen was being washed, but by no means all of it was of Khrushchev's choosing.

AN EASIER TARGET: THE YOUNG WRITERS

This, apparently, is why it was suddenly decided to stop. The decision was probably taken by common consent: Khrushchev's adversaries had made their point, their object having been to stop Khrushchev's one-sided destalinization rather than to conduct counter-purges. Khrushchev and the destalinizers had even better reasons for stopping the drive. After the major speech of March 8 there was a complete *volte-face*: Ehrenburg and his 'theory of silence' were completely forgotten, as was the whole question of Stalinism and the purges.[1] Then, since an outlet had to be found for the persecuting zeal of the triumphant conservatives, a safe target was found in the young writers, whose success was arousing jealousy and who had to be brought to heel without delay. Henceforth the campaign could again concentrate on the more tractable themes of patriotism, Party discipline and heroic tradition – a flare-up in public temper, easier to control, in fact almost an everyday phenomenon in a conservative, chauvinistic society.

[1] After March 8 1963, Ehrenburg was mentioned sporadically and in passing, in a long list of blameworthy writers. (For instance, in *Komsomolskaya Pravda* of March 22 and in a speech by M. Sokolov to a plenary session of the Steering Committee of the Writers' Union (*Literaturnaya Gazeta*, April 2 1963). But no other charges were brought against him.

Khrushchev, who hardly differed in this respect from the other members of the top leadership, could have no major objection to this new form of the campaign. He must have preferred it by far to the previous phase of neo-Stalinism, although for reasons similar to those outlined in our account of that phase, it did not enhance his prestige.

In the first place he had to sacrifice at least Yevtushenko, one of the men he had publicly supported. Even on March 8 he was indulgent in his references to the young poet. He praised his anti-Stalinist work and acknowledged that (with some reserve concerning an interview given to *Lettres Françaises*) 'comrade Yevtushenko behaved in a dignified manner' during his visit to Paris. Yet at the time Khrushchev made his speech, half of Yevtushenko's *Precocious Autobiography* had been published in Paris by the weekly *L'Express*, and this somewhat flippant piece of writing was already known in all political circles. Obviously, Khrushchev had had no objection to it up to then. He probably had not foreseen that its mere publication abroad, unusual though the procedure was, could become a 'case', or else he would not have spoken so rashly. At the end of March, however, a week after *L'Express* published the last instalment, G. A. Zhukov's attack at the plenary session of the Steering Committee of the Writers' Union opened an unprecedented campaign against this 'act of treason' by Yevtushenko. There was even a request for his expulsion from the Union. In the meantime, Andrey Voznesensky, the only young writer whom Khrushchev had berated on March 7, was practically overlooked.

Solzhenitsyn, another protégé of Khrushchev's, was also under a cloud. *Ivan Denisovich* was still immune to attack for a while, but his other writings, and especially *Matryona's House*, were overtly criticized from then on. Sokolov, for instance, said that the 'writings' of Solzhenitsyn (he did not specify which) 'deserved no more than a shrug' (*Literaturnaya Gazeta*, April 2 1963).

Secondly, the conservatives had sound motives for persisting in and even emphasizing their fractious attitude of November and December 1962. In effect they were now saying to Khrushchev: 'It is your fault that we have had to intervene by main force to clear up the mess in cultural life. None of this would have happened but for your scandalously liberal attitude in 1962.' That was the accusation underlying the indignant recollections of the recent past, the praise for the 'timely' crackdown, the complaints about the 'strange' complacency of the press towards the tendencies now censured. All these points occurred repeatedly in the declarations made at the time by the militant conservatives.[1] The complaints voiced in those circles about over-frequent

---

[1] This is what the conservatives said about the Government's excessive leniency

trips abroad by young writers belong in the same category, for after all it was the Government that had given them their passports.

Naturally the movement could not be allowed to go too far in the opposite direction either. The quarrel had unleashed such passion that total victory by the 'right wing' might have resulted in violent reprisals that would have jeopardized domestic equilibrium. (After all, the 'left' represented practically everybody who was anybody in Soviet literature.) Moreover, it might have exposed the Party leadership to pressure by unruly extremists whose Stalinist feelings went beyond the desired level. They could not be permitted to gain control any more than the liberals before them. This does not mean that the extremists did not have their spokesmen in the Presidium – and if they did, Kozlov was probably one of them. But in the upshot a consensus emerged in favour of limiting the practical results of the conservatives' victory.

In addition to silencing the young poets for many months, the right wing gained V. A. Serov's appointment as head of the Academy of Fine Arts to replace B. V. Yohanson, regarded as too soft (this took place in December 1962); the removal of S. P. Shchipachov, who had supported the young authors, from the Moscow writers' organization and his replacement by G. M. Markov (March 1963); and the crackdown on films through the setting up of a special State Committee on March 23. (Actually this step was at least equally aimed at further whittling down the powers of Furtseva's Ministry of Culture – she was the main loser in the whole campaign – in favour of Ilyichev. This was shown by the fact that the new minister for film production, A. V. Romanov, remained assistant head of the Ideological Department. Lastly, a few precautionary measures were taken in the field of education.[1] But,

---

in cultural matters. E. Serebrovskaya: 'The meetings [between the Party leadership and the intelligentsia] were the long-awaited event that had been due for a long time and radically refreshed the ideological atmosphere' (*Literaturnaya Rossiya*, April 5 1963). A. B. Chakovsky: 'Generally speaking, when one reads certain things published a few months ago, one is bewildered as to how all this could have appeared in the columns of the press' (*Komsomolskaya Pravda*, March 29 1963). M. Sokolov: 'Obviously, everything is not quite right as regards Party leadership (*partiynoye rukovodstvo*) over magazines, newspapers, and our Writers' Union itself' (*Literaturnaya Gazeta*, April 2 1963). S. Baruzdin: 'The essential point is that this major discussion on literature came just at the right time. I would even add that it had to come just now and could on no account have been postponed. . . . Let us confess that this workshop [the literary sector] has been producing just about anything during the last two or three years' (*Literaturnaya Gazeta*, March 15 1963).

[1] Among the measures taken at the beginning of 1963 to restrict art education, which are less well known than those aimed at the artists themselves, were the reduction 'from 250 to 200' in the number of students in the higher schools of art; the transformation of the Gorki Institute for Literature into a correspondence school; the reconversion of most graphic arts schools into institutions for applied and industrial art; and the exclusive teaching of 'easel painting' at the Repin Institute in Leningrad and the Surikov Institute in Moscow (in December 1962 a new director, A. Laktyo

despite the threats from those who wanted 'acts instead of words' (V. A. Kochetov in *Literaturnaya Gazeta* of March 16), the campaign hardly went beyond words. Tvardovsky and Polevoy, the directors of *Novy Mir* and *Yunost*, were castigated several times at the end of March and may even have been close to dismissal; but they survived, although neither uttered a word of self-criticism. Even Yevtushenko, the principal scapegoat, kept his post in the Writers' Union as well as on the editorial board of *Yunost*, despite pressing pleas for his removal.[1]

Such was the picture at the beginning of April, after the severest visitation that Stalin's ghost had inflicted on the country since the Twentieth Congress. We must now look more closely at the other decisions of the important Presidium session of February 15, 1963.

APPEASING CHINA

As we saw in discussing the events of 1960, the Chinese ceased to have any partisans at Moscow within a short time of disclosing their ambition to supplant Soviet hegemony. This does not mean, however, that there was unanimity on tactics among the Soviet leaders or that Khrushchev was not prevented from reacting as strongly as he would have wished. February–March 1963 was one of the periods in which this happened. Exasperation against Peking was suddenly followed by a friendlier line, and this, in all probability, was forced on Khrushchev.

The Cuban fiasco had given the Chinese ample ground to revert to the aggressive attitude they had never really abandoned, despite occasional spells of appeasement in 1962. Their accusation of 'capitulationism' succeeding 'adventurism' was broadcast to the four corners of the earth for weeks on end, to Khrushchev's great embarrassment.

The Soviet leadership's initial reaction is not known, but it became clear later that the problem had been discussed at the plenary session of November 1962.[2] The result was a marked stiffening on the part of the

---

nov, was appointed to head the latter). All these measures are contained in a decree of the Central Committee and Government dated May 9 1963 but published a full year later (see *Spravochnik Partiynovo Rabotnika*, 1964, pp 240–248).

[1] Yevtushenko's expulsion from the Writers' Union was demanded by Vladimir Fedorov before the Steering Committee of the RSFSR Writers' Union (*Literaturnaya Rossiya*, April 12 1963) and four other speakers at the same meeting. His removal from *Yunost* was suggested in an editorial in the issue of that magazine for April 1963.

[2] The fact that the November 1962 plenary session was called upon to deal with the stiffening on the part of the Chinese is clear from the following remark made by M. T. Yefremov to the February 1964 plenary session (verbatim record, p 594): 'This is the fourth occasion on which the Central Committee during its plenary

Soviet Union and its allies. Novotny and Togliatti attacked the Chinese outright at the beginning of December at the Czechoslovak and Italian Party Congresses. On December 10 1962 *Pravda* reprinted the attacks, thereby breaking with the custom of not mentioning the Chinese by name. On December 12 Khrushchev went further than he ever had in the attack by insinuation, when he compared the Albanians to brats to whom 'somebody' had given three kopeks to shout rude words at their mother. He also suggested that the Chinese communists were even more 'capitulationist' than he, since they tolerated Hong Kong and Macao, 'foul-smelling enclaves' of colonialism, at their very doorstep.

The Chinese retorted by hinting that the unequal treaties of the past had also left traces of colonialism in the Soviet Far East, and the tone of the dispute rose even higher. On January 7, *Pravda* published a huge editorial (twelve columns) violently attacking the Albanians 'and those who support them'. The Chinese answered in the same tone in *Jenmin Jih Pao* (the *People's Daily*) (January 27) and, in Khrushchev's presence, through their delegate at the Congress of the East German Party. Khrushchev used the same forum to propose a truce. But did he really believe it was possible? This is doubtful, for on February 10 *Pravda* criticized the stand taken by the Peking press and said so outright. The unusual editorial was intransigent on the tactical issue and placed the entire burden of resuming contacts on the adversary. Where the Albanians were concerned, for example, it reaffirmed without any change the position adopted by Khrushchev at the Twenty-second Congress, namely that the Tirana officials must, if they wanted a *rapprochement*, 'renounce their mistaken views and return to the path of unity'. This can hardly be regarded as an 'open door' to reconciliation, as its authors would have it.

The exact timing of the shift was notable. The anniversary of the Soviet–Chinese friendship treaty on February 14 would have provided a most suitable opportunity for a gesture of *rapprochement* if it had been desired, but no such thing happened. The ritual article in *Pravda* mentioned in harsh tones the 'enormous aid' given by the USSR to the Chinese; none of the top leaders attended the traditional rally at 'Friendship House', leaving this duty to A. A. Andreyev, the aged chairman of the Soviet-Chinese Friendship Society. On the following day, February 15, however – when, according to our belief, the enlarged Presidium met in Moscow – a noticeable change occurred. At a recep-

sessions has considered the situation within the international communist movement.'
Unless there was a secret plenary session – a rather unlikely possibility – the Chinese problem must have been 'considered' at the plenary sessions of November 1962, June and December 1963, and February 1964. The fact had been made public only twice, in June 1963 and February 1964.

tion given for the King of Laos late in the afternoon, Khrushchev rushed towards the Chinese Ambassador, Pan Tsin-li, and in front of the assembled diplomats and journalists, gave him a spectacular embrace. His toast was devoted almost exclusively to the 'friendship and brotherhood' of the Soviet Union and China and the solidarity of both peoples in the face of the common enemy. 'When capitalism has been buried,' Khrushchev declared, 'the USSR and China will together cast the last shovelful of earth on to its coffin'. It was Gromyko, incidentally, who went to fetch the Chinese diplomat from his corner and pushed him into the arms of the First Secretary. The gesture was well planned and had the desired effect, for the entire foreign press wrote about it the next day. Why not have timed it twenty-four hours earlier, to mark the anniversary of the treaty? The only possible explanation is that the new attitude had been decided upon that very day.

The symbolic move would not have deserved such attention had it remained an isolated one. But subsequent developments followed the same line and went even further. On February 21 1963 a letter from the Soviets to the Chinese Communist Party announced what was described as 'a new step'. It was an invitation, an unconditional one this time, to reopen the dialogue through a bilateral meeting. In addition, Moscow accepted the principle of a world conference of the communist movement. Until then the Soviet leadership had politely dodged Peking's proposals for such a meeting.[1] Even on the substance of the disputed issues, the letter was infinitely more conciliatory than anything said before. It mentioned 'common views on all fundamental questions, and asked the Chinese 'not to overestimate' differences or 'lay undue stress' on whatever divided the two Parties. (The phrase used later was 'set aside' differences, which is not quite the same.) Hinting that the Soviets were prepared to strive for *rapprochement* even on thorny issues, the letter said: 'It would be advisable to agree on measures likely to contribute to a narrowing of differences'. Finally, listing the problems that would have to be the 'centre of attention' in a future world council of the Parties, the letter spoke of 'common tasks in the struggle against imperialism and its aggressive plans, for the development of the world socialist community and the strengthening of its influence throughout the world, and for the strengthening of unity within the communist movement' (*Pravda*, March 14 1963). The 'struggle for peace', and especially what had been the leitmotiv of all Soviet

---

[1] In a letter of April 7 1962 the Chinese had officially accepted the proposal for an international conference which had been addressed to them by the Parties of Vietnam, Indonesia, and others. In their reply to the proposal on May 31 1962 the Russians had accepted 'in principle' but had made many conditions, including a capitulation by the Albanians (this was revealed by Peking on March 9 and September 6 1963).

declarations since 1960 – the 'prevention of thermonuclear war' – were not even included.

This indeed was a new attitude, confirmed by similar invitations sent at the time by Moscow to all the Parties allied with the Chinese: on February 22 to the Japanese Communist Party, at the end of that month to the New Zealand Communist Party and also at 'the end of February' to the Albanians who, for a year and a half, had been ostracized. (The invitation to the Albanians was disclosed by *Pravda* on April 3 1963, the invitations to the Japanese and New Zealand Communist Party only in 1964. See *Partiynaya Zhizn*, August 17 1964.) Coming after the acid remarks about Tirana two weeks earlier, the gesture was particularly significant. This really was an overall attempt at reconciliation with the whole 'renegade' wing of the communist movement.

The Chinese were visibly taken aback by the move. At first they did not take it seriously, or, in any case, were reluctant to abandon the polemical course they were engaged in. Starting on February 27, *Jenmin Jih Pao* started publishing a series of venomous articles which had been announced earlier. Then the allies of the Chinese must have informed them that they had received similar proposals from the Soviets, and perhaps the Chinese began to realize that something had happened in Moscow.

In their reply of March 9 they 'welcomed' the Soviet proposal and noted with satisfaction that Moscow had agreed 'firmly' to the plan for the conference; they also accepted the offer of bilateral talks and made a further accommodating move. On February 23, Mao had indicated to the Soviet Ambassador, Chervonenko, that it was up to Khrushchev to make the journey and that he was welcome to stop in Peking 'on his way to Cambodia'. (In fact, Khrushchev had never contemplated going to Cambodia and the Chinese knew it.) But now the Chinese Communist Party agreed to send a delegation to Moscow. Even better, it agreed to suspend the polemic. True, it made clear that a real armistice would have to be negotiated later, but 'for the time being' it would not exercise its right of reply. The series of *Jenmin Jih Pao* editorials did suddenly stop at that moment. A similar change was noted in Albania. After first rejecting Moscow's letter, the Albanians changed their minds and a little later responded to the Soviet overture.[1]

[1] The letter from the CPSU to the Chinese Communist Party of March 30 1963, published by *Pravda* on April 3 1963, commented on the Albanian reaction to the Soviet invitation as follows: 'At the end of February of this year the Central Committee of the CPSU took a new initiative and addressed to the Central Committee of the Albanian Labour Party a proposal to hold a bilateral meeting between the representatives of our two Parties. However, this move, prompted by the spirit of friendship, did not meet with an appropriate response. The leaders of the Albanian

The Chinese reply was reprinted in full in *Pravda* on March 14 1963, at the same time as the Soviet message of February 21. Here again Moscow had done its best to show complaisance by breaking an old diplomatic tradition and letting the other side have the last word (of course, the Chinese reply was satisfactory enough to show that the initiative had paid off). Later, things deteriorated rapidly enough, when each Party enlarged upon its starting position. The Russians tried to keep the polemic in a low key in their long programme letter of March 30, handed to Mao on April 2 and published the following day by *Pravda*. That letter represented a partial return to the Khrushchev line, inasmuch as it reaffirmed at length the policy of peaceful co-existence, and contained the highly controversial statement that Yugoslavia was a 'socialist country'. This was the letter that the Chinese answered much later in their famous '25 points' during the great summer quarrel. However, their view of it was made clear on April 11 in a violent article in the Albanian *Zeri i Popullit*.

Nevertheless, the basic fact is that, from mid-February 1963 at least until mid-March, Moscow was exceptionally conciliatory towards Peking and its allies. The political circumstances of the time suggest that this new attitude was imposed upon Khrushchev. Although in theory the two areas are separate, this new line was, naturally enough, coupled with a stiffening in domestic policy The neo-Stalinists obviously hoped this would make a good impression on the 'ultras' of Peking.

At the same time, the diplomatic language used towards the West also hardened. On February 22 Malinovsky, the Defence Minister, thought fit to announce that 'an attack on Cuba will mean the start of World War III'. Khrushchev pretended to endorse this unprecedented declaration in his speech on February 27, but in fact he softened it in some measure. The rash promise was in fact out of step with reality, since on February 18, that is, shortly before Malinovsky spoke, Moscow had secretly informed Washington that 'several thousand troops' would be withdrawn from Cuba before March 15 (this was disclosed later by the United States). Apart from the suspension of talks on nuclear tests, which has already been mentioned, the only acts were of the kind that appear striking but cost little to carry out. For instance, the decision

---

Labour Party did not even deem it necessary to accept our letter. Later, having evidently thought it over, the Albanian leaders sent a letter in which, while making all kinds of reservations and setting conditions, they did refer to such a meeting. If they really desire it, we are prepared to held the meeting.'

The Japanese Communists also accepted the Soviet offer of a meeting in a letter of March 6 1963, but postponed the dialogue until the autumn, allegedly because of Japanese elections.

announced on March 13 to suspend coal deliveries to France as a sign of solidarity with the striking French miners – a notorious departure from the traditional principle of separation between Party and Government action – was meant to demonstrate the Soviet 'revolutionary' attitude as a rebuttal to Chinese accusations. In fact, the Chinese paid it no attention whatsoever. Neither did they have one word of approval or even of comment regarding the cultural restalinization. Those who had imagined that this campaign might disarm Chinese attacks were wasting their time, but they only discovered this later.

TROUBLE IN THE POLICE AND ARMY: THE PENKOVSKY CASE

This case was already a fairly old one, but the Party Presidium must have debated it at the same session on February 15 and 16. This can be inferred from the fact that certain concrete moves connected with it were made in the days that followed.

The main facts are well known: on October 22 1962 O. V. Penkovsky, officially an assistant head of department in the State Committee for Co-ordination of Scientific Research (KNIR), probably a member of Soviet military intelligence, and certainly an agent of the United States and British intelligence services since 1961, was arrested in Moscow after having been detected and followed for several months. The date – the eve of the American blockade of Cuba – does not seem directly significant, though it is conceivable that the imminent confrontation with the United States prompted the KGB to put a premature end to the cat-and-mouse game. On November 2 two of Penkovsky's foreign contacts were arrested. They were the British businessman Greville Wynne in Budapest and the American diplomat Richard Jacobs in Moscow (who was expelled from the USSR two days later). At that stage nobody apparently suspected any future political repercussions, since nothing happened to those who were later involved. For instance S. S. Varentsov, the senior marshal of the artillery, was honoured by having an article on the use of tactical rockets in *Izvestia* of December 1 1962; while General I. A. Serov made an official appearance a few days earlier when he greeted a North Korean military delegation in Moscow (*Pravda*, November 30).

A change was noted on December 11, when Tass announced Penkovsky's arrest. The communiqué was the signal for the first blast. *Pravda* ran a lengthy account of the conspiracy in two instalments, on December 15 and 16, with special emphasis on the role of American diplomats in Moscow. Neither Varentsov nor any other Soviet citizen besides Penkovsky was mentioned at that stage.

Even for propaganda purposes such publicity had its drawbacks. The image of 'monolithic' Soviet society was marred by the news that one of its privileged members, one of the few actually allowed to travel abroad regularly, had betrayed his country and gone undetected for almost two years. The admission meant a break with a rigorously respected tradition of many years' standing. Never since the Beriya affair and its consequences had there been any mention of a 'spy' who was not a foreigner and, as such, open to denunciation. Even though the charges against Wynne, the Englishman, required some explanation, nothing forced the Kremlin to lay such stress on his Soviet 'contacts'. The campaign must have had some other object besides the classic call for 'vigilance'.

Outwardly, there were no other developments in the Penkovsky case until his and Wynne's trial, announced on April 17 1963 and held in Moscow from May 7 to 11. Not until after the trial, through an article in *Izvestia* of May 29, were the names of some of those implicated announced officially. These were S. S. Varentsov, the former commander of tactical rockets, 'demoted in rank and functions' for having protected Penkovsky;[1] Major-General A. Pozovny, subjected to 'severe disciplinary measures' as a 'close acquaintance of Penkovsky,' and for having 'communicated to the spy information gathered in the course of his work in violation of existing regulations'; a Colonel V. Buzinov, and V. V. Petrochenko, a member of the Committee for Scientific Research, who were punished for the same reasons (only the latter appeared at the trial as a witness). One may safely add General I. A. Serov, although he was never officially implicated. According to all the information available at the time, the former KGB chief was removed in February or March 1963, in connection with the Penkovsky case, from the post of chief of Military Intelligence (GRU) that he had occupied since 1958. His removal was logical if, as we believe, Penkovsky had worked for those departments. On the other hand, there was

---

[1] The *Izvestia* article of May 29 1963, about the Penkovsky trial, was in fact an interview with Lieutenant-General A. G. Gorny, a military prosecutor at the trial. Gorny disclosed that Varentsov had met the future spy at the front during the war and had backed him in his appeal against removal from the Army cadres. 'Varentsov,' Gorny added, 'obtained a review of Penkovsky's unfavourable record and, in the last analysis, helped him to gain entry to the State Committee for the Co-ordination of Scientific Research'.

At the June 1963 plenary session, Varentsov was expelled from the Central Committee (he had been an alternate member since 1961) 'for having relaxed his political vigilance and committed unworthy acts' (*Pravda*, June 22 1963). On the same grounds, at the end of September, he lost his seat as Deputy to the Supreme Soviet (*Vedomosti Verkhovnovo Sovieta SSSR*, November 6 1963).

no corresponding purge in the Committee for Scientific Research (KNIR), where the political repercussions might have been considerable. Penkovsky's direct superior, the assistant head of KNIR's foreign branch, was D. M. Gvishiani, none other than Kosygin's son-in-law, while K. N. Rudnev was a Deputy Prime Minister.[1]

Varentsov's first unusual absence was noted on February 22, on the occasion of Army Day. This means that his fate, like Serov's, was sealed during the agitated period when all the other decisions were taken. It is not known whether others were in trouble because of him, or who they might have been. As to Serov, however, the political implications were very clear: he was the only police professional with whom Khrushchev had been allied constantly throughout his career, in the Ukraine as well as in Moscow.[2] One way and another, the Penkovsky case, revealing as it did a huge network of officials who, if they were not accomplices, had at least covered up for the culprits, was causing serious ripples in high political circles. Those who decided to give it such publicity were bound to have taken this into account from the outset. Suffice it to add that the affair coincided with the Stalinist reaction and further compounded the confusion.

Times of trouble always mean agitation within the police force. As if by accident, an old case was revived at the same time. On March 11 and 12 1963 *Izvestia* published a story in two instalments on the case of Russell Langelle, an American Embassy official who had been arrested and expelled in mid-October 1959. At first sight this had nothing to do with the Penkovsky case, which the author only touched on in a footnote. But some of the fresh details concerned a 'Colonel P.', recruited by Western intelligence as early as 1957. In other words, here was another instance of treason. And there was no explanation of why this old story, which had been so awkward for Khrushchev's policy at the time, had to be dug up just now.[3]

It is not clear whether the KGB went too far over Penkovsky, or whether, to keep it from being carried away by success, a decision was

[1] Some foreigners who are familiar with KNIR had the impression that Gvishiani had not engaged in any activities from November 1962 to May 1963. This cannot be confirmed, but later he was somewhat emphatically cleared of suspicion. On May 9 1963 he was reported by *Pravda* to have been present at an audience given to British businessmen by Khrushchev. On May 18 he wrote an article for *Izvestia*.

Rudnev, on the other hand, was carrying on his normal official activities throughout the 'difficult' period and, for example, had an article published in *Izvestia* on January 15.

[2] According to a UPI dispatch, Serov was expelled from the Party in the spring of 1965 for his excesses during and after Beriya's rule (*New York Times*, May 26 1965). This further punishment, coming after Khrushchev's downfall, would tend to confirm that the two men had been closely connected.

[3] It should be pointed out that the editor of *Izvestia*, Adzhubey, was not in Moscow

taken to strengthen discreetly its competitor, the 'Ministry for the Protection of Public Order', the former MVD. At all events, a decree of April 6 1963, aimed at 'broadening the democratic basis of penal procedure', authorized officials of the Ministry to conduct judicial investigations in the same way as the office of the public prosecutor and the State security agencies (KGB). 'Large-scale profiteering and plundering' were no longer to come within the exclusive jurisdiction of the KGB, as they had since 1961 (*Spravochnik Partiynovo Rabotnika*, 1964, p. 202). This provision was most probably at the root of the 'war between the police departments' of which there were evident signs in 1963.[1]

---

at the time of the publication of this story. He had left on February 14 for Rome where, after having been received in audience by Pope John XXIII, he had met the Italian President, Gronchi, on March 12. Only this last meeting was reported by the Soviet press (*Pravda*, March 14 1963).

[1] The most revealing episode in the rivalry between the two police services was the so-called 'Shakerman–Roifman' case of the summer of 1963. The two men, accused of having bribed unspecified officials, had been sentenced to short terms of imprisonment at the same time as a number of other swindlers, after a trial about which the newspaper *Sovietskaya Rossiya* carried a story by a militia officer, Zapylayev, on September 11 1963. The investigation which the MVD had conducted under its new powers had supposedly closed the case. But a month later, on October 20, a violent article in *Izvestia* changed the whole picture. Shakerman and Roifman, it appeared, were not confederates in a minor case but the chiefs of a powerful gang, the leaders of a network whose underhand dealings extended to fifty-two plants and kolkhozes in several areas of the country. The damage did not amount to a mere few thousand roubles, as established by the first trial, but to three million 'new' roubles, or over three million dollars. Curiously enough, the new investigation had been conducted by the 'glorious Chekists', that is, the KGB. The authors of the article did not explicitly blame the original investigators for their error, but they might just as well have done so. This is what they wrote: 'It is our glorious Chekists who uncovered the affair. Before it came within the purview of the KGB, the swindlers had been operating for a very long time. To our sorrow, they were unmasked only after the Chekists had taken the matter in hand.' *Izvestia* then explained that the Cheka, the predecessor of the KGB, had been created by Lenin in order to fight not only counter-revolutionaries and spies, but also 'profiteers, bandits and thieves of socialist property, i.e. all those who were trying to undermine the economy of our young Republic. And the Cheka did not regard this as a minor task.' This was a barely disguised protest against the decree of April 6.

The KGB, however, did not obtain all it wanted from the Shakerman–Roifman case. In the article of October 20, *Izvestia* had demanded 'an exemplary public trial, open to all and with wide publicity'. They also wanted the indictment to be read by the public prosecutor of the USSR in person. None of this was done. The swindlers were tried in February 1964 with a minimum of publicity, and *Izvestia* reported their death sentence in a few lines on February 28 1964. Simultaneously, the entire press was giving full coverage to an achievement of the MVD. This was the eventful capture of the bandit Oganessian, who had committed several murders in Moscow. The investigation had been conducted personally by V. S. Tikunov, the RSFSR Minister of the Interior.

THE SUPREME SOVNARKHOZ

The drive for a renewed concentration of the economy had followed a 'normal' course during the preceding months. At the plenary session of November 1962 Khrushchev had apparently accepted this and in his report had strongly urged that the number of State Committees be increased and their authority strengthened. He said:

'We must finish the work of setting up committees in all key sectors of the economy. . . . The Presidium of the Central Committee has discussed these matters several times and reached the unanimous conclusion that the management of scientific research organizations and study bureaux should be centralized within committees for the sector in question, i.e. that its structure should be a vertical one.'

Khrushchev had had more difficulty in justifying the formation of enlarged economic regions, which meant reducing the number of sovnarkhozes (National Economic Councils) to less than half. He alleged, however, that this had been considered when 'his' reform was put into effect in 1957, but 'it had been decided to reconsider the matter later, when sufficient experience had been acquired. We now have this experience' (*Pravda*, November 20 1962).

One thing that Khrushchev certainly had not considered in 1957 was the creation of the 'Supreme Sovnarkhoz' announced on March 13 1963. Or to be more accurate, he had forcibly opposed it, as he had the setting up of State Committees. He told the Supreme Soviet on May 8 1957:

'During the debate on these questions, some comrades proposed the establishment of a Supreme National Economic Council (sovnarkhoz) or else specialized economic institutions, such as committees attached to the USSR Council of Ministers with the duty of running the principal branches of heavy industry. These proposals met with valid objections. . . . A supreme sovnarkhoz with overriding powers of management would have resulted, like the federal ministries, in duplicating the activity of the sovnarkhozes and the corresponding industrial divisions of Gosplan. The management committees would be wasting their time and energy over current problems that can be successfully dealt with by the republics and the sovnarkhozes; this would also divert many officials from their proper tasks' (*Pravda*, May 9 1963).

It can, of course, be contended that Khrushchev may have changed his mind. True, but the change must have occurred in less than one week rather than over a six-year period. Everything points to the fact that the creation of this new super-administration was decided upon within the few days preceding its official announcement, after an enlarged meeting of the Presidium and of members of the Government held on March 13: the matter was probably not even considered at the preceding meeting on February 15. One of the effects of the change, for instance, was to withdraw a number of State Committees from Gosplan's authority and attach them directly to the Supreme Sovnarkhoz. As late as March 2, however, the President of Gosplan, P. F. Lomako, had commented in *Izvestia* on a decree of January 11 which extended his authority to these committees, without suspecting for a second, obviously, that part of his new power was going to be withdrawn. Again, on March 5 1963 a new decree provided for an exchange of staff among the Committee for Scientific Research (KNIR), Gosplan and the Sovnarkhoz (no mention of 'supreme') of the USSR, in order to ensure better liaison (*uvyazka*) among these agencies (*Spravochnik Partiynovo Rabotnika*, 1964, p 224). Clearly, there was no inkling that one week later all these people would be gathered within one single bureaucracy, so that 'liaison' would be far more drastically ensured. Why was the change of policy so sudden?

The answer lies in an important political by-product of the decision of March 13. This was a mass promotion of all the top officials in the defence industry, the heavy industry lobby and other 'steel-eaters' against whom Khrushchev had been fighting ever since 1960. The suddenness of the reorganization shows that they were determined not to waste a moment in taking advantage of Khrushchev's political weakness in March 1963 in order to gain a victory over him.

Let us look at the two aspects of the reorganization:

1 Administratively, the only effect of the decision of March 13 was to increase concentration a little further. The Supreme Sovnarkhoz, which topped the whole structure, was given jurisdiction over all the existing institutions. ('Within the limits of its competence, it issues directives and instructions that are binding on all State organs regardless of the authority to which they are normally subordinate', the constitutive decree stated.) Primarily, the Supreme Sovnarkhoz was supposed to eliminate the disputes and rivalries that had developed among Gosplan, the federal Sovnarkhoz, Gosstroy and KNIR, in short the profusion of central agencies that had blossomed as a result of the 1957 reform. At the same time, a number of State Committees were turned into 'production' committees: i.e. they acquired direct managerial powers, which further increased their resemblance to the former ministries. Since, on the other hand, obvious political considerations forbade the pure and simple cancellation of a reform in which Khrushchev's prestige was involved, the local sovnarkhozes, now 'enlarged', continued to display a semblance of activity. They were even to be further complicated by the setting up within most of them of a 'planning committee' of twenty to forty people and a 'council for the co-ordination of regional develop-

ment' in which Party officials were to be included (decree of May 30 1963, *Spravochnik Partiynovo Rabotnika*, 1964, p 109). The outcome was the most spectacular bureaucratic tangle in the history of the Soviet economy. The system of vertical and horizontal compartmentalization was infinitely more cumbersome than anything heard of in the past, even under Stalin. Never had there been such an inflated Government apparatus (nearly one hundred federal ministers), never had the drive to codify everything led to the creation of such a labyrinth.[1]

2 Politically, the March 13 reform resulted in a spectacular promotion of the war industry leaders. The most prominent of them, D. F. Ustinov, was entrusted with the management of the Supreme Sovnarkhoz. Since he was going to be in charge of five out of the eight Deputy Prime Ministers,[2] he was promoted to First Deputy Prime Minister, on an equal rank with Kosygin and Mikoyan, although this did not entitle him to a corresponding place in the Party hierarchy. (As we shall see, for a long time this point was under debate. Ustinov did not enter the Presidium, however, and remained a simple member of the Central Committee.) L. V. Smirnov, who had served under Ustinov as Chairman of the State Committee for Defence Technology, became Deputy Prime Minister, while his deputy, S. A. Zverev, took over Smirnov's post with the rank of Minister. This entailed more than a reshuffle of officials: Ustinov was attaching directly to his Supreme Sovnarkhoz the State Committees for defence technology, aeronautics, electronics, radio-electronics, naval construction, atomic energy and medium-scale mechanical engineering, to name only some of them. In other words, he retained direct control over all defence industries, so that the entire war industry was being promoted at the same time as its chiefs. The impression created was that, while the country floundered in political and economic confusion, men who knew what they wanted were taking over the command posts. They had broken out of the honourable confinement imposed on them by Khrushchev when he took over the

---

[1] An illustration of the new problems created by the reform of March 13 1963 is a decree of the USSR Council of Ministers of August 22 1963, aimed at 'settling' the problem of adjusting production to demand for consumer goods. The decree, published in *Spravochnik Partiynovo Rabotnika*, 1964, p 140, covers nine pages of close print which defy the wits of the ablest experts. It should be mentioned, however, that the text also aimed at establishing 'direct links' between suppliers and customers in light industry. To this effect, it referred to another decree of August 8 1960 and called for its 'strict application'. Obviously, the problem was not a new one.

[2] The five Deputy Prime Ministers placed under D. F. Ustinov's authority by the reform of March 13 1963 were: P. F. Lomako (Gosplan), V. E. Dymshits (Sovnarkhoz), I. T. Novikov (Gosstroy), K. N. Rudnev (KNIR) and L. V. Smirnov (Defence). Only D. S. Polyansky, A. N. Shelepin, and M. A. Lesechko remained outside his jurisdiction.

economy, and were capturing a large section of the latter without relinquishing their own specialized preserves.

It is not surprising that the other men promoted during this period were either the natural allies of the war industry, such as the 'steel-eaters', or personalities well known for their hostility to Khrushchev. On March 10 1963 N. K. Baybakov left the Krasnodar sovnarkhoz to take over a sector in which Khrushchev was particularly interested at the time – the State Committee on Chemistry. The return to Moscow of the man who had been the last President of Gosplan before the 1957 reform and had clearly opposed the latter was naturally not to the liking of the Head of the Government. When Khrushchev succeeded in asserting his 'chemical line' in December 1963, he again managed to remove Baybakov from top responsibility.[1] V. F. Zhigalin, a veteran in heavy mechanical engineering (the *narkomtyazhmakh* of the Stalin era), left the Moscow sovnarkhoz to become First Deputy Chairman of the USSR Sovnarkhoz (as assistant to Dymshits) and Minister of the USSR. His rivalry with the Ukrainian K. D. Petukhov in 1961 has already been noted. Zhigalin's promotion to full membership of the Central Committee just after Khrushchev's fall also shows the nature of his relations with the ex-First Secretary. As for A. M. Tarasov, who on March 13 was appointed deputy to Ustinov at the Supreme Sovnarkhoz – the only such deputy appointed at that time – he had made his career in Byelorussia since 1951 and owed nothing to Khrushchev.

In these circumstances, budgetary priorities were most likely to follow similar lines. In November 1962, the issue again seemed to have been sharply debated. In his speech to the plenary session, Dymshits had promised substantial increases in agricultural appropriations. This was mentioned by Tass, but on the following day (November 24) *Pravda* omitted it from its report of the meeting. Khrushchev had announced a 'recent decision' to increase the production of mineral fertilizers to 41 million tons in 1966 (as against 17 million in 1962), but the matter was not mentioned again for almost a year.[2] There were no new developments on this front during the crisis of February–March 1963, except for the fact that Khrushchev's chemical programme

[1] In January 1964 the Committee on Chemistry, which in the meantime had become the 'Committee for the Petroleum and Chemical Industry', was divided into three sections: (1) chemical industry; (2) refining and petrochemistry; (3) petroleum extraction. Baybakov was put in charge only of the latter and least important section, whereas management of the chemical industry went to an outsider, L. A. Kostandov, and petrochemistry to V. S. Fyodorov (*Pravda*, January 28 1964).

[2] In the same report in which he mentioned the planned increase in mineral fertilizers, Khrushchev stated that in future the 'Leninist line of priority for the development of means of production' would nevertheless be 'continued' (*Agricultural Speeches* vol 7 p 316).

was deadlocked and, as we shall see, he did not succeed in having a plenary session called to deal with the problem. His speech to his constituents on February 28 1963 shows how acrimonious the discussion had become. He said: 'This must be stated outright: when in the Government we examine the problems of distribution of appropriations . . . we are often confronted with agonizing problems.' The hardest task, he added, was to reconcile the needs of civilian and of defence industry 'so that there is no exaggeration on either side'. Clearly he was in no position at that time to start a war with the 'steel-eaters', but had to appease them: 'No sane person, I am sure, will reproach the Central Committee and the Soviet Government for following such a policy [reinforcement of military potential]. On the contrary, if defence were neglected for the sake of extraordinary achievements in the fulfilment of daily human needs, the electors . . . would be entitled to regard this as a crime' (*Pravda*, March 1 1963).

KOZLOV'S ROLE

Restalinization and the takeover of key economic posts by Khrushchev's adversaries were a sure indication of his sorry position. Khrushchev was at a low ebb indeed in February–March 1963. A feeling of helplessness about economic problems was obvious from his statements of February 28. In the same speech he referred to his age for the first time since the spring of 1962 (another difficult period): 'You know how old I am going to be soon' (69 on April 17). This was censored in *Pravda's* account but the conclusion was left in: 'Thank you for having gathered here to cheer me up, as it were'. Paradoxically, there were none of the indirect attacks on him such as had immediately followed the Cuban fiasco. But this was merely because there had instead been an overt attack: evidently the Presidium meeting of February 15 and 16 and subsequent ones had resulted in a formal indictment by the collective leadership of his policy and its results – destalinization, the break with China, the relaxation of 'vigilance' in security matters – and had forced him to change his line on the issues in dispute. Khrushchev's surrender was so manifest that there was no need for special signals to Party members. It was deemed sufficient to show that the most important decision – the neo-Stalinist campaign against the intellectuals – was truly the work of the collective leadership as a whole. This was done by *Pravda* of March 10 1963, which contained the full text of Khrushchev's celebrated speech of February 28, by including a photograph of the entire Presidium standing behind him, instead of showing the speaker alone, as was customary.

So much for *Pravda*. But the photographs in the other newspapers were equally noteworthy: four of them – *Sovietskaya Rossiya, Selskaya Zhizn, Moskovskaya Pravda* and *Komsomolskaya Pravda* – showed Khrushchev alone talking with one literary figure or another.[1] The more important papers presented a different picture, as these captions show:

Sovietskaya Kultura of March 9 1963: 'Comrades N. S. Khrushchev and F. R. Kozlov'; *Izvestia* of March 10: 'N. S. Khrushchev and F. R. Kozlov talking with writer S. V. Mikhalkov and scenario writers G. N. Chukhray and I. A. Pyriev' (compared with the *Sovietskaya Rossia* caption: 'N. S. Khrushchev conversing with writer S. Mikhalkov and scenario writers G. Chukhray and I. Pyriev' – in other words, the same scene minus one person); and *Krasnaya Zvezda* of March 10: 'Comrades N. S. Khrushchev and F. R. Kozlov at the conference'.

It was not very common for the collective leadership to be honoured in such a way and still more unusual for one of its members to be singled out and placed almost on a par with Khrushchev. Other signs confirm the trend: on the evening of March 3, five days before meeting the intellectuals, Khrushchev and Kozlov went together to the Bolshoy to a performance of *La Traviata*. This was not a première or an official occasion, and the reasons, circumstances and instigators of this singular appearance of the ruler with the heir presumptive are matters for speculation. *Pravda* carried the news (March 4 1963), followed by that evening's *Vechernyaya Moskva;* but *Izvestia* ignored it, as did all the other newspapers next day.

Kozlov spent the period from February 26 to March 1 'campaigning' in his former Leningrad stronghold. Each day *Leningradskaya Pravda* reported on his activities. It carried his photograph on the first page with the entire regional leadership around him, and altogether gave him the kind of coverage usually reserved for Khrushchev himself. Moreover, the occasion provided more than the beginnings of a new 'cult': V. S. Tolstikov, First Secretary of the Oblast Committee, introduced the candidate to his constituents on February 26 in the following terms: 'The breadth of view and the practical turn of mind that are the hallmark of the bolshevik, the art of bringing a creative spirit to the solution of any problem, the burning desire to devote all his strength and wisdom to the struggle for the happiness of mankind, for com-

[1] Among the newspapers concerned, one at least could be regarded as the Khrushchev organ *par excellence*. This was *Selskaya Zhizn* (Rural Life), which was run by V. I. Polyakov, a loyal client of the First Secretary. *Sovietskaya Rossiya*, the organ of the Central Committee Bureau for the RSFSR, was under the control of A. P. Kirilenko and G. I. Voronov. To put it mildly, these men had no reason to give Kozlov privileged treatment.

munism – this is what characterizes our candidate, Frol Romanovich Kozlov' (*Leningradskaya Pravda*, February 27 1963).

For a local campaign speech this might have been common form, but on the same day the Moscow *Pravda* echoed Kozlov's praises. In its report of the same meeting, it quoted another speaker as saying: 'F. R. Kozlov has gone a long way, from textile worker to major (*krupny*) leader in the State and Party. He possesses outstanding qualities: lofty ideas and principles, the gift of organization, practical sense, perseverance and firmness in the execution of Party and Government decisions' (*Pravda*, February 27 1963).

This was infinitely more than anything said in the same issue about the other main candidates who had addressed their constituents the day before, viz. Brezhnev, Kosygin, Mikoyan, Podgorny and Shvernik. Brezhnev, for instance, although mentioned first by virtue of his post of Chief of State, was only described as a 'worthy candidate'.

The large number of campaign meetings naturally prevented *Pravda* from reprinting the speeches in full. Kozlov's was briefly summarized, although it was mentioned that the candidate had concluded by paying tribute to 'the faithful Leninist, the tireless fighter for peace and communism, N. S. Khrushchev'. Curiously enough, the full text of the speech, which took up a whole page in *Leningradskaya Pravda*, did not contain that particular sentence. There were altogether five references to Khrushchev, but no praise whatsoever. The rest of the speech was of no great interest. It was noteworthy only by its assurance and rapturous optimism about the state of the country, which was in singular contrast to Khrushchev's dejected tone on February 28.

All this amply confirms the information spread about by the Moscow intellectuals that Kozlov, their number one enemy, was behind the February and March decisions, and in particular the neo-Stalinist campaign.[1] His privileged treatment by the press and his strange attitude towards Khrushchev suggest that he was not only the natural heir presumptive but also a rival for power. After having succeeded in inflicting a signal defeat on Khrushchev, was Kozlov trying to press his advantage and to evict the harassed leader either suddenly or gradually? Was there any idea, as some rumours had it, of stripping Khrushchev of one of his functions – leadership of the Party or of the Government? Khrushchev declared a little later that he could not 'for ever' fulfil his functions in both hierarchies. It must be assumed that if Kozlov had

[1] With regard to rumours that Kozlov had instigated the restalinization campaign: as early as December 3 1962, in a speech to the Congress of the Italian Communist Party, Kozlov accused the 'bourgeois press' of distorting the spirit of the Twenty-second Congress by laying the greatest stress on denunciation of the 'cult' and overlooking the grandiose programme of the Party (*Pravda*, December 4 1962).

not been stricken by illness, events would have taken a different turn in 1963. Khrushchev's reign would in all possibility have ended earlier, either in law or in fact.

What was the attitude of the other members of the collective leadership during the crisis? What is known of Suslov suggests that he supported Kozlov in his offensive, especially on restalinization and in the attempt at a *rapprochement* with Peking. At any rate, he seemed to grow in stature during that period. At official functions he regularly took precedence over Mikoyan, contrary to the earlier situation.[1] Mikoyan for his part again chose to withdraw. After visiting his Rostov constituents on February 26 he was not heard of again until April 2. (He was the only Presidium member, apart from the aged Kuusinen, who did not attend the celebrated meeting with the writers on March 7 and 8.) As for Brezhnev, he could not have been happy about the spectacular rise of the man who had been his successful rival in 1960 for the position of heir presumptive. Although Brezhnev's position as Head of State entitled him to first place at official functions, in matters of real importance he was treated in accordance with his true political weight. For instance, when he last went abroad, to the Congress of the Czechoslovak Communist Party in December 1962, not one member of the Presidium took the trouble to see him off at the airport or to meet him on his return (*Pravda*, December 2 and 13 1962). Kozlov, on the other hand, who went to Italy around that time, was seen off and met on return by Suslov (*Pravda*, December 1 and 13 1962).

Another victim may have been A. P. Kirilenko, also a 'Ukrainian' member of the Presidium, although the signs affecting him defy the sharpest Kremlinological insight. *Pravda* made a new type of 'misprint' concerning him on March 12 1963 by thus listing the members of the Presidium who attended an RSFSR agricultural conference: 'Brezhnev, Voronov, Kozlov, Kosygin, Kirilenko, Kuusinen, Polyansky, Suslov, Khrushchev . . .' This followed Russian alphabetical order throughout except for Kirilenko, who should have come between Voronov and Kozlov. No other newspaper followed *Pravda's* example, which did the same thing next day, on March 13. A month later the same anomaly

---

[1] Kozlov's precedence over Mikoyan was particularly noticeable in the first days of April 1963. While Khrushchev was 'resting' in Gagra, Kozlov was the strong man in Moscow. The listing: Brezhnev, Kozlov, Suslov, Mikoyan, was the only 'legal' one (see in particular *Pravda*, April 5 and 11). On April 22, after Kozlov's illness and Khrushchev's return to Moscow, Suslov was once more listed before Mikoyan, but on and after the 25th the order was reversed. On the tribune on May Day the order was the following: Khrushchev, Brezhnev, Mikoyan, Suslov, Kosygin. On February 22, after the major Presidium session, the listing had been the same except that Suslov preceded Mikoyan.

This confirms that Mikoyan was affected by blows aimed at Khrushchev. Normally he was in a better position when Khrushchev was present than when he was away.

occurred in *Izvestia*, on April 22 and again on the 23rd. This time the error was copied by other newspapers, but not *Sovietskaya Rossiya*, the daily controlled by Kirilenko. This was a remarkably original 'signal', but until further information is available it is safer merely to observe that it does not seem to indicate any rise in Kirilenko's stature. A more reliable 'signal' was that the 1963 *Spravochnik Partiynovo Rabotnika* (cleared for printing on March 30) faithfully reprinted the text of the decisions providing for the changes in the principal Party organs, adopted at the Twenty-second Congress and the plenary session of November 1962, but 'overlooked' those of April 1962 whereby Kirilenko was elected a member of the Presidium. This spectacular promotion has already been discussed earlier, as well as the role that Khrushchev obviously played in it. After the latter's defeat in the spring of 1963, some circles must have been at pains to serve notice on all his protégés that sudden demotions were no less possible than sudden promotions.

AMENDMENT OF A SLOGAN

All these developments made the first fortnight in March a highly agitated one. After so many difficult decisions and manoeuvres a pause must have been welcome. After the enlarged session of the Presidium and the Council of Ministers which ratified Ustinov's promotion on March 13, public life quietened for two weeks. Khrushchev left Moscow for the south, stopping in Tula, Kursk and in the Ukraine to visit chemical plants. From March 17 until the beginning of April he dropped out of sight. Kozlov made an appearance in Moscow around the 22nd and then left for Ashkhabad, where he dismissed various officials.[1] Kosygin, Brezhnev and Suslov each made one public appearance, and Mikoyan was still on 'holiday'.

The only notable events were the letter of the Central Committee of the CPSU to the Chinese on March 30, and the agreement (announced only in the West) on April 5 for a 'hot line' between the White House and the Kremlin. Thus the principle of a dialogue with the United States, strongly advocated by Khrushchev after Cuba, was maintained.

---

[1] Both before and after the November plenary session, Kozlov conducted purges only outside the RSFSR. He did a great deal of this throughout the period, removing D. A. Kunayev and other Kazakhstan leaders in December (*Pravda*, December 26 1962); the First Secretary of the virgin lands territory, T. I. Sokolov, in February (*Pravda*, February 22 1963); and lastly the head of the Turkmenian Government, the Head of State and the Second Secretary of that Republic in March (*Pravda*, March 26 1963).

After the dangers of the October confrontation, this technical improvement presumably met with no objection from the collective leadership.

From the beginning of April, that leadership was under the growing authority of Kozlov, while Khrushchev in his Gagra retreat appeared more and more in disgrace. He was visited by a delegation from Somalia on April 1, and by Vukmanovich-Tempo, the head of the Yugoslav trade unions, on the 3rd. But during the same period, more important figures – Waldeck-Rochet of the French Communist Party and Max Reimann, the leader of the West German Communist Party – had lengthy talks in Moscow, where no one apparently suggested their going to Gagra. One of the problems, and a difficult one, was how to explain to the 'allies' the reversal of the Soviet cultural line in March. Sure enough, this was handled by Kozlov, with the help of Suslov where the French were concerned. Kozlov even attended with Mikoyan two luncheons given for a Finnish Government delegation on April 5 and 6, which showed that his Party functions did not prevent him from taking part in State and diplomatic affairs. One might well ask where all this was leading.

Actually, the political career of the energetic heir presumptive was coming to an end. But before he left the stage two facts occurred that obviously were connected with his person.

First, on April 10 *Pravda* announced a Central Committee plenary session for May 28 to discuss 'current ideological tasks'. It was unusual for a decision of this kind to be taken in Khrushchev's absence, which had now lasted almost a month. Furthermore, the programme clashed with Khrushchev's plans, since for a long time he had wanted the next plenary session to be devoted to the growth of the chemical industry. He had said so publicly as early as March 1962 and again at the November plenary session (*Agricultural Speeches* vol 6 p 449, and vol 7 p 364). In February 1963 the question even seemed to have been settled, for at the beginning of that month a reliable Soviet source told a foreign diplomat in Moscow that the next plenary session would be held 'at the end of March' and would be devoted to chemistry. Two weeks later, however, the same source gave entirely different news: the session was to be held 'at the beginning of June' and would deal with ideology.

This suggests that the Presidium meeting of February 15–16 interfered with Khrushchev on this issue too and forced him to change his plans. Efforts were indeed made later to dissipate the malaise. Ilyichev in his report to the plenary session on June 18 1963 went as far as to say that the First Secretary had been its instigator: 'When the Presidium of the Central Committee discussed the matter of the next plenary session (i.e. probably in February), N. S. Khrushchev suggested that questions of the Party's ideological work be considered.' The journal *Kommunist* also declared at the same time: 'The plenary session was called on the proposal of Nikita Sergeyevich Khrushchev' (No 10, July 12 1963).

Such emphasis is suspect: Khrushchev had every reason to prefer a plenary session on the subject of chemistry, not only because he had publicly advocated it for a year, but also because an ideological debate in the Party 'parliament' meant breaking with all the traditions established during his reign. He had always preferred dealing with the 'practical tasks of building communism', and he had even better reasons in the spring of 1963 to avoid any contact with 'ideologists' after the bitter blow to his destalinization policy. Furthermore, Khrushchev never himself mentioned any plenary session on ideology, even in his March 8 speech to the intellectuals. He mentioned it for the first time on April 24 1963, that is after the plenum had been summoned. Even then his lack of enthusiasm was obvious. He first spoke of what interested him most – the plenary session on chemistry; then added: 'It is known that *the Presidium* of the Central Committee has decided to call a plenary session devoted to a discussion of the Party's ideological tasks for the end of May. . . . Since the plenary sessions of March and November [1962] have examined the basic problems of industry and agriculture, the discussion of ideological problems is *entirely legitimate*' (*Pravda*, April 26 1963. Author's italics). This was a tepid form of approval, and he could not, of course, avoid supporting a step that had already been announced officially. One cannot be certain, however, that the decision was openly taken against his wishes or without his knowledge. Probably it had been adopted in his presence in February but he had still hoped that it would be reconsidered. After all, the 'encounter' of March 7 and 8 with the writers might have passed as a plenary session of sorts, thus closing the matter. Anyway, there was still time to think things over until 'the beginning of June', if that date was indeed decided upon in February (a longish time ahead, whereas the plenary session on chemistry had been planned for the end of March). Thus it is conceivable that the calling of the plenary session, announced during his absence on April 10, was meant to put pressure on him. It is hard, in fact, to tell what part Khrushchev, now sitting in Gagra, had in the decision, but it is quite clear that Kozlov, who was taking charge of everything in Moscow, was its instigator.

The next day, April 11, *Pravda* had another, even greater surprise in store for its readers. At the very bottom of page one, under the modest heading 'Correction' (*utochnenie*), was the following note:

'The May Day slogan addressed to the workers of Yugoslavia should read as follows: "Fraternal greetings to the workers of the Socialist

Federal Republic of Yugoslavia who are building socialism! Long live the eternal and indestructible friendship and co-operation between the Soviet and Yugoslav peoples!" '

Experience of the Soviet press teaches that it is up to the reader to do the thinking. Looking up the text of the slogans as it appeared in *Pravda* three days earlier, on April 8, we find that the workers of Yugoslavia were greeted as follows: 'Fraternal greetings to the workers of the People's Federal Republic of Yugoslavia! May friendship and co-operation between the Soviet and Yugoslav peoples develop and strengthen in the interests of the struggle for peace and socialism!'

The changes were twofold and at first made for some confusion. It so happened that on April 7, the day before the slogans were published, Yugoslavia had adopted a new constitution whereby the 'People's Federal Republic' had been changed into 'Socialist Federal Republic'. This fact, officially communicated by the Yugoslav Embassy to the Soviet Ministry of Foreign Affairs on April 8, had been acknowledged immediately. On the evening of the same day, the wording of the slogan had been changed accordingly in *Izvestia* as well as in the English language bulletin of the *Novosti* press agency .

On the other hand, what the Yugoslavs had neither suggested nor foreseen was the rest, namely, the phrases 'who are building socialism', 'eternal and indestructible friendship', etc. And this was the main point, because the first version of the slogan followed the pattern of greetings to 'friendly' peoples who were not part of the 'family', such as the Indians and Indonesians. But the second version, which strictly adhered to the formula used for the Poles, Czechs, Hungarians, etc. – not to mention the Chinese and Albanians – made Yugoslavia a full member of the socialist camp. The point could not have been stated more clearly. Moreover, this had been done in such a way that the Kremlinologists and even more the host of experts who had always refused to believe in 'signs' really had something to ponder over.[1]

The affair is still obscure, even more so than appears at first sight. One should not, for instance, link the two stages of the episode – the initial publication of the slogan and its correction – in order to construe it as a mere exercise in civility. It is true that, after Tito's visit to the USSR, after the lengthy pleas in January and February in defence of Belgrade, after the letter of March 30 stating unequivocally that Yugoslavia was 'a socialist country', the original slogan was an anomaly. It is possible, however, that it did not imply a deliberate infringement

---

[1] On April 13 1963, *Pravda* spelt out the meaning of the correction in the May Day greetings to Yugoslavia by giving a full list of the fourteen 'socialist' countries, in which Yugoslavia was included.

of the official line. It was the text used in the lists of greetings published in 1962, on May Day as well as on November 7, and it is possible that it was reproduced in the same form through an oversight. The mistake, if any, was of omission rather than commission, and had been shared by the friends of the Yugoslavs, with Khrushchev in the lead; for otherwise they would have given the proper instructions in the first place, and, since they had the authority to make corrections, they would have been obeyed. The fact that three days elapsed before the correction indicates that they were not on their guard concerning this specific issue.

In the last analysis, once the 'harm' had been done, and the initial greetings published, it might have seemed hardly worth stirring matters up. After all, who took seriously those tedious lists of exclamation marks spread out twice yearly over a whole page of *Pravda*? If perchance a Kremlinologist in the West, in Belgrade or in Peking had raised an eyebrow, he would have consulted the previous lists and noted that there had been no deviation. The significant point was the change of April 11, not the routine of April 8. It is unlikely that anyone could have seriously regarded the earlier version as the sign of a rebellion against Khrushchev's policy. If there had been any doubts on this score, the text of the letter of March 30, published only five days earlier by the same *Pravda* and obviously approved by the collective leadership, was an infinitely more reliable indicator of the official line.

The correction of the slogan, on the other hand, had a perfectly clear meaning. It could have come only from Khrushchev, the most outspoken partisan of a *rapprochement* with Yugoslavia and the only person who could have given an order of such dramatic impact to the press.[1] Moreover, the correction dealt a sharp blow to the drafters of the slogans, whoever they may have been; and it was an overt slap in the face to Kozlov – the man who had assumed overall responsibility for Party affairs during the First Secretary's absence, and who therefore, deliberately or through oversight, had let the erroneous version slip in.

It has already been noted that Khrushchev, like everyone else, cared little for May Day slogans, before or after their publication. It was three days before he reacted, on April 10 – the very day on which *Pravda* announced the convening of the plenary session on ideology. If this news was vexatious to Khrushchev it called for revenge or a retort. The temptation was to look for some pretext or to inflate some past incident. This may have prompted the slogan episode. This, of course, is only a hypothesis.

---

[1] It is hard to conceive that a major correction such as in the May Day 1963 greeting to Yugoslavia, if it were given to the press by anyone but Khrushchev himself, could 'slip by' in *Pravda* without its director consulting him. The correction was announced by Tass on the evening of April 10 but appeared next day in *Pravda* only. Perhaps it was thought inadvisable to revive old wounds by running it in all the newspapers.

6 Kozlov's Illness:
A Gain for Khrushchev

According to rumour, Khrushchev and Kozlov had a violent clash over the telephone on the evening of April 10 about the Yugoslav slogan and other issues. It was further rumoured – no one knows for certain to this day – that Kozlov was so sharply upbraided that it was too much for his heart, so that his fateful illness was brought on by a political attack. The hypothesis is attractive, even plausible, but it cannot be verified.

What is certain, on the other hand, is that the departure of the heir presumptive from the scene coincided with the slogan incident. Kozlov's last public appearance was on Wednesday, April 10, in the daytime, at a congress of artists where he was accompanied by Brezhnev, Kirilenko, Mikoyan, Polyansky and Suslov (*Pravda*, April 11 1963). The next day, April 11, when the correction in *Pravda* appeared, was a blank day: not a single official appearance by Kozlov or any other member of the Presidium was reported (only Podgorny was seen in Kiev). The reason is not known, and possibly the unusual quiet was due precisely to Kozlov's sudden collapse. By Friday, April 12, there was no room for doubt: on 'Cosmonaut Day' (the anniversary of Gagarin's flight two years earlier) all the leaders present in Moscow solemnly gathered at the Kremlin, but Kozlov was not there. The same thing happened next day at a meeting to commemorate the poet Demyan Bedny (*Pravda*, April 13 and 14 1963). Kozlov was never seen in public again.

It is also clear that he was genuinely ill (of a stroke). Not only was this reported by all possible sources and then announced officially, but the victim died less than two years later, on January 30 1965. He had had several heart attacks before, in April 1961 in particular. The present one was far more serious, although for several months there was talk of possible recovery. Kozlov did seem better in July 1963; on the 11th, Kádár, the chief of the Hungarian Party, visited him in hospital and had 'a friendly chat' (*Pravda*, July 12)'. The *Encyclopedic Yearbook* (*Yezhegodnik*) for 1963, brought up to date at the beginning of July, restored him to his proper place in the Party Secretariat – second after Khrushchev – whereas an earlier listing, cleared for printing on May 31, had demoted him to his alphabetical place for the first time since the Twenty-second Congress (*Spravochnik KPSS*, or CPSU

Handbook, 1963). But this favourable situation did not last: by October, Kozlov was again listed as a Secretary on a par with the others (see *Zapisnaya Knizhka Partiynovo Rabotnika*, or *Party Worker's Notebook*, cleared for printing on October 5 1963, p 79), and on October 31 Khrushchev answered Guy Mollet's question about him with the words 'Oh, he's a very sick man!' He spoke 'with a broad smile', as the head of the French socialist party himself told this writer.

One point is not debatable: whatever its cause, the illness of the heir and would-be supplanter meant a substantial gain for Khrushchev. Kozlov, the spearhead of the opposition, the strong man of the February–March crisis, had been determined to press his advantage. Had he remained on the scene, he, rather than Brezhnev, would presumably have found himself heading the Party on the day the succession opened; and if he had not vanished when he did, it might have opened much earlier. His disappearance did not paralyse the opposition, but it did rob it of its impetus.

Discussing individuals is of course a 'subjective' approach; but who was facing Khrushchev now? Suslov had in all likelihood been Kozlov's ally throughout the crisis and was probably next in line as the spokesman of the *apparatchiki* and the upholder of orthodoxy. But his major quality was caution: his career and long coexistence with Khrushchev indicate that his main gift was devising alliances and manoeuvres, rather than launching frontal attacks or conceiving grand designs. Kosygin was not very different. He was a strong opponent of 'personal power', to be sure, and concerned with efficiency and stability. He was quite capable of backing various groups that opposed Khrushchev, but not of leading them. Moreover, he wielded no power over the Party. Mikoyan, who was neither ambitious, powerful nor 'orthodox', was capable, no doubt, of supporting some manoeuvre, but he was the least likely challenger. Beyond this circle were the still dependent clients and allies. Brezhnev was not likely to grieve over the departure of the man who, in 1960, had prevented him from becoming the heir apparent. Brezhnev rose later on, but for the present he needed help from Khrushchev in order to step into Kozlov's place. He still had time to think about his later plans. The very pro-Khrushchev Podgorny was still in Kiev. The other, 'junior' Presidium members had even less reason than the 'seniors' to push themselves forward.

To sum up, it was going to require exceptional circumstances, or rather some threat, to induce these men to take the offensive and pick a chief. For the time being, Khrushchev did not have too much to worry about. Provided he kept his energy, he would not only be able to hold on to power, but to recover lost ground. The opposition was still strong enough to hold him back, but not to enforce a major political shift as in February–March. It again went underground, so to speak, and started to manifest its existence by indirect Kremlinological 'signs'. For lack of anything better, it sought to invoke the 'ghost' of Kozlov. The events of the ensuing weeks define this new phase.

Starting in mid-April various indications showed that Khrushchev was working to enhance his image. The publication of volumes 6 and 7 of his *Agricultural Speeches* was hailed by a burst of laudatory articles in most newspapers. The first in the series appeared in *Pravda* of April 17 – the sixty-ninth birthday of its author, as it happened (not being a round figure, it was not celebrated officially). The speeches were now described more importantly as 'works' (*trudy*) which, it was learned, represented a 'major contribution' (*krupny vklad*) to Marxist–Leninist science'. V. I. Poliakov, Khrushchev's ghost-writer on agricultural subjects, wrote an even more complimentary article in *Kommunist* (No 6 1963) in which he spoke of the 'Presidium of the Central Committee headed by N. S. Khrushchev'. All this was widely reproduced in the provincial press.

The author of the 'works' reappeared in Moscow on April 20 after a six weeks' absence, just when a piece of good news, namely Castro's visit, was announced. This was most welcome, not only because it effaced the October fiasco and provided for a highly needed show of unity in the face of the Chinese, but also because signs of friendliness from the most celebrated contemporary revolutionist would enhance Khrushchev's authority at home. He almost completely monopolized the guest, allowing only Brezhnev – on the second day of the visit, May 4 – to attend the large *dacha* party that marked the start of the talks.[1]

Earlier, on April 24, Khrushchev had made his 'comeback' speech before a conference of RSFSR industrial cadres. This was a cautious start, but parts of the speech deserve attention.

He mentioned the Supreme Sovnarkhoz and D. F. Ustinov's promotion without any enthusiasm. Since he could not cancel the decision, he affirmed that it would 'make it possible to provide better management for State organizations'. He immediately pointed out that the 'Supreme Sovnarkhoz would operate under the direct supervision of the Party Central Committee and the Council of Ministers'. Then, using the 'bourgeois press' as a stalking-horse, he proceeded to upbraid the armament producers and Ustinov in particular. He explained that it

---

[1] Mikoyan was honoured with a private visit by Castro on May 2 owing to his long-standing friendship with the Cuban leader, and also because he had fallen ill. He disappeared until the middle of June and had to undergo surgery. The British opposition leader, Harold Wilson, confirmed this after he visited Mikoyan on June 13.

was out of the question for the Soviet economy to manufacture 'nothing but rockets'; the reform, on the contrary, would make possible closer control over the defence industry as a whole: 'Comrade Ustinov has been appointed Chairman of the Supreme Sovnarkhoz, and it is he who happened to be responsible for the defence industry. He knows the situation there, and we may hope that he will enforce even better order in that domain.'

After mentioning the existence of 'reserves' – that is to say, wastage – in that industry, Khrushchev went on: 'Comrade Smirnov has been appointed in Ustinov's place. He is younger than comrade Ustinov and we can prod him just as successfully as we have prodded comrade Ustinov, who used to be answerable for the defence industry.'

Khrushchev did not hesitate to 'prod' in the same manner the other traditional upholders of centralization, the chairmen of State Committees, and to chide them for their tendency to assume managing powers like those of the former ministries. 'This is an old disease and is caused by the fact that certain State Committees are headed by former ministers, good ministers no doubt – but even good ministers are not always free from mistakes. The heads of State Committees who not only want to be in charge of science and study bureaux, but also to manage enterprises, are actually pulling us backwards.' And he concluded: 'Committee chairmen, carry out the decisions of the Central Committee and of the Government! These decisions have defined the committees' tasks with precision and clarity' (*Pravda*, April 26 1963).

The result of the chiding was not long in coming. Ustinov, who since his appointment had always been listed in the press under his correct title of First Deputy Chairman of the Council (see *Pravda* of March 23 and 31), was next listed as a Deputy Chairman on a par with the others, in his alphabetical place after M. A. Lesechko and K. N. Rudnev (*Pravda*, April 30 1963). Subsequently, he experienced a series of ups and downs – periods of decline alternating with fitful promotions within the principal Party organs.[1] On the whole, until the end of Khrushchev's reign – and even for a few months thereafter – an intermediate position was maintained. Ustinov was a kind of 'first among

[1] Here is one sign of Ustinov's promotion within the Party: on May 11 1963 he attended a 'Party' luncheon given for the chief of the Uruguayan Communist Party, and was listed immediately after the Central Committee Secretaries (*Pravda*, May 12 1963). On the other hand, in July, for three consecutive days, he was downgraded without any explanation and was last on the list of 'Deputy Chairmen' of the Council of Ministers (*Pravda*, July 20, 21 and 23 1963).

Only in March 1965 was Ustinov promoted to alternate member of the Presidium. He then left the Government to become Party Secretary. His Supreme Sovnarkhoz was liquidated after the reform of September 1965, which was better designed to bring about the desired concentration.

the Deputy Chairmen' (or vice-presidents) in the Government (listed as Deputy Chairman but preceding the others of that rank), rather than a titular First Deputy Chairman like Mikoyan or Kosygin. His Supreme Sovnarkhoz was mentioned only sporadically, half a dozen times at the most in two years, and never as playing any outstanding role. Furthermore, on May 9 1963, a new 'first deputy' to Ustinov was appointed at the head of the Sovnarkhoz. This was S. M. Tikhomirov, a chemist. Khrushchev was probably trying to give a voice to the 'new technology'.

PROMOTING RESPECT FOR AUTHORITY

Khrushchev at this time made interesting, if cautious, allusions to the February–March crisis. He mentioned neither destalinization nor restalinization but evoked the problem of authority. He again summoned the writers and artists to obey (this may be called the most sincere and 'normal' part of his speech of March 8), and then went on to speak of 'leaders' generally. 'It is a poor leader indeed whose interpretation of the role of personality in society is restricted to his own interests, his position, his person. . . . There are still people among us who do not understand this *and lump everything together. In their opinion, if the Party takes a stand against the cult of personality, this means that one may also take a stand against the authorities. There is nothing Marxist, nothing Leninist, in this interpretation*' (*Pravda,* April 26 1963 [Author's italics]).

For additional clarity, one may refer to the statement in the *History of the Party* that *Pravda* so helpfully quoted on November 15 1962. The collective nature of leadership, it said, 'helps to overcome the nefarious consequences of the cult of personality'. This we interpreted as meaning that the main duty of anyone who claimed to destalinize was to co-operate with his peers in fulfilling leadership functions or, more simply, to take the views of others into consideration. This, evidently, was what Khrushchev had been reminded of in February and later; and this was also what he now called 'lumping everything together'. In reply to those who were telling him: 'As you are so eager to criticize Stalin, don't do as he did, but observe democratic methods', he was saying or at least thinking: 'I will destroy Stalin without your help and, if necessary, against your opposition; what is needed here is a chief, and I am he.'[1]

[1] Khrushchev let it be known in much clearer terms that he meant to remain the chief, during a meeting he had on April 20 1963 – the day of his political comeback –

Whom did he mean to warn? Who were the leaders who were so attached to their 'personal interest'? Kozlov no doubt, but who else? One detail is worth noting: on the day when Khrushchev delivered his speech, the members of the Presidium were seated together with him at the official table as usual, except for two of them who, as though by way of punishment, were relegated to the back with the alternates and the Secretaries. These were Polyansky and Suslov. For Polyansky, a 'junior' member, this happened once or twice later, but for someone in Suslov's position it was quite unheard of.[1]

In any case, the above analysis should be taken into account in considering the part of the speech that had the most pronounced repercussions abroad:

'I believe no one will suspect me of thinking, when I speak this way, of anyone's specific position in the Party, least of all my own. I am sixty-nine and I am entitled to say this. After all, everybody understands that I cannot for ever occupy the posts I hold at present in the Party and in the State. This is why, when I say these things, I am not thinking about myself but about our great Party, the Soviet people, the great cause of communism' (*Pravda*, April 26 1963).

He had said this on purpose. A few hours after the speech, before it had even appeared in print, the American and British Ambassadors, whom he received in audience, ventured to question him about the rumours circulating in the Western press. Khrushchev merely replied that his speech was indeed going to add to the rumours. The passage in question was in fact deliberately circulated abroad by Tass, whereas other remarks he had made were played down.[2]

It is conceivable that Khrushchev was forced by someone to make the statement – although it is hard to imagine by whom and how – but this is unlikely. Both its substance and its context served his immediate

---

with Italo Pietra, the director of the Italian paper *Giorno*. When Pietra congratulated him for having toppled Stalin off his pedestal, and added that 'the times of the Caesars had ended all over the world', Khrushchev replied: 'Yes, the times of the Caesars are past. Here we have a collective leadership. But there are times when the rule of one far-seeing man is better than that of several who cannot see.' This detail, which was not included in the official report of the meeting, was told to this writer by his colleague Raffaello Uboldi, who was present at the interview.

[1] A photograph in *Pravda*, April 25 1963, shows Polyansky and Suslov sitting at the back with the alternate members of the Presidium and the Secretaries, rather than at Khrushchev's table with the other full members of the Presidium.

[2] The English translation of Khrushchev's speech of April 24 1963, supplied by APN (Novosti Press Agency), did not include his remark that 'comrade Smirnov can be prodded as successfully as we have prodded comrade Ustinov'.

purposes to perfection. He was striving hard to climb back and re-affirm his badly shaken authority. He was reminding all those who had had wind of the crisis, and especially those who were eager to hold on to their gains of February–March, that he was still in charge. To justify himself he added: 'It is not for myself that I am working, but to make authority respected.' This show of altruism was in no way a sign that he was preparing to relinquish power, but only a means of disarming his adversaries.

Although Kozlov was gone, resistance had not stopped. It was merely being toned down. Instead of attacking overtly, as they had when the energetic would-be heir was on the scene, Khrushchev's opponents were reverting to hints and signs. At the end of April and the beginning of May, several of these appeared.

There is, for instance, the sudden publicity given to Ponomarev's *History of the CPSU*, which had been completely forgotten since its publication in November 1962. Commenting on the book in a lengthy article, *Kommunist* (No 7, cleared for printing on May 4 1963) congratulated the authors on having criticized Stalin's mistakes 'without any attempt at sensationalism'; it also laid great stress on the principle of collective leadership. An example of that principle given by G. I. Shitarev in the latest issue of *Partiynaya Zhizn* (No 8, cleared for printing on April 29) was too vivid not to catch the eye. Quoting the testimony of an old bolshevik, Shitarev observed: 'Vladimir Ilyich [Lenin] seldom spoke at discussions of the sovnarkom (Council of Ministers). Clearly he did not want to overshadow others with his authority, but waited for them to declare themselves. If no one took the floor, he would often ask: "What does comrade so-and-so say about this?" That is the Leninist approach to leadership . . . an approach that all Party leaders should follow and study.'

No one who knew about Khrushchev's habit since 1958 of interrupting speakers at Central Committee plenary meetings at every turn could miss the point. In any case, Khrushchev took a step down from his pedestal. On April 28 the Tass agency quoted Castro's toast 'to comrade Khrushchev, an eminent figure in the Communist Party and the Soviet Government'. In *Pravda* of the 29th this was rendered as: 'The eminent activities of Comrade Khrushchev, who leads the Leninist Central Committee of the Communist Party and the Soviet Government.' There was no longer any 'eminent figure', and the 'Leninist Central Committee' had been rescued from oblivion.[1] Another sign noticed at the time was that *Pravda* of May 3 published a telegram

[1] Only V. I. Polyakov's paper, *Selskaya Zhizn*, published the Tass version of Castro's toast to Khrushchev in April 1963.

signed by Khrushchev, 'Secretary of the Central Committee of the CPSU'. Here the interesting thing was that for the first time in many years the adjective 'First' had been left out. Then, on April 22 and 23, there were the curious signs already noted with respect to Kirilenko.[1] All this points to the fact that the situation was still confused.

All these issues must have been brought out into the open just after the May Day celebration, when two new things occurred:

On the evening of May 3, the following communiqué was sent to *Pravda:* 'In reply to queries received, the Central Committee of the CPSU advises that the Presidium member and Secretary of the Central Committee of the CPSU, comrade F. R. Kozlov, was not able to take part in the May Day celebrations because of illness' (*Pravda,* May 4 1963).

This could only have been a political gesture. It was not the first time or the last that health reasons had prevented a member of the Presidium from taking part in the major celebrations of the régime. For example, this had happened to Shvernik on November 7 1962, to Suslov on November 7 1963, and to Kozlov himself on May 1 1961 when he had had another stroke. Never had it been deemed necessary, however, to give the slightest explanation about them. The rule was probably being broken to reassure those who knew Kozlov was in bad shape, rather than to inform the public. Although the heir presumptive was seriously ill, he was still a member of the Presidium and Secretary of the Central Committee and was to be reckoned with. But if Khrushchev and his friends had hoped to close the unpleasant chapter so easily, they were soon undeceived.

In fact, Kozlov's ghost went on consistently haunting the top hierarchy. His picture remained in a good place in the official gallery; his signature still appeared on certain documents (for instance, the letter of congratulation to Khrushchev on his seventieth birthday on April 17 1964); and he was mentioned in all reference texts (with some fluctuations in rank as noted). This ended only in November 1964, two months before Kozlov's death and one month after Khrushchev's fall. It might almost seem as though Khrushchev was himself responsible

[1] Conceivably, another figure who might have played some part in April 1963 was N. M. Shvernik, the oldest Presidium member, about whom there had been nothing special to report until then. On April 28, at the ceremony organized for Castro in Red Square, Shvernik had occupied the abnormally high position of number three, coming before Suslov and Kosygin. His seventy-fifth birthday, on May 19, was apparently to be celebrated with some pomp: the illustrated magazine *Ogonyok* No 21, dated May 19 and cleared for printing on the 15th, had a large photograph of Shvernik on its fly-leaf. But the birthday came and went without any special ceremony or even an award. On May 23, at another rally for Castro, Shvernik was in last (eighth) place among the rulers, after Voronov and Polyansky, whom he usually preceded.

for Kozlov's mysterious continued presence, as if he had actually been protecting him in some way. Actually, the reverse was true: Kozlov was being mentioned only as a counterpoise – a symbolic one at least – to Khrushchev's power. Hence, after the latter was gone, the former was no longer needed. (It is probably not by accident that this happened just after Brezhnev – Kozlov's chief rival – had taken power.) Even so, the forms were respected, and the eviction was presented as 'sick leave' for the purpose of 'extended treatment' (*Pravda*, November 17 1964).

The second decision was the postponement of the 'plenary session on ideology' which, as noted, had been called at Kozlov's instance for May 28. Strangely enough, the decision was publicized only later. *Pravda* announced on May 14: 'On May 3 the Central Committee decided to postpone the meeting of the plenary session until June 18.' Why the delay, and why was it specified that the decision had been taken ten days earlier? The answer probably had to do with diplomatic problems, for in the meantime an agreement had been reached with Peking on the date for bilateral talks. On May 9 the Chinese had suggested June 15, and the Russians replied two days later that they would prefer to postpone the meeting till July 5. Peking accepted, and the final agreement, concluded on May 14, was announced by *Pravda* two days later. Possibly the Soviet rulers wished to intimate to the Chinese that the plenary session had not been timed with the express object of delaying the bilateral conference, since its date had been fixed earlier. Castro's visit, which lasted until the beginning of June, may have accounted for the fixing of both dates.

At the same time, the postponement of the plenary session coincided with the communiqué of Kozlov's illness. Obviously, on May 3 there had been a discussion not only about the laying of Kozlov's ghost, but also on the interim handling of his important functions until his possible recovery. Who was going to become the second man in the Party? The question was important enough to warrant an additional three weeks for thinking it over.

TWO WOULD-BE SUCCESSORS INSTEAD OF ONE

The June plenary session provided an ingenious solution to the problem (*Pravda*, June 22 1963): Kozlov's powers went to two people instead of one. They were Brezhnev and Podgorny, who, while remaining members of the Presidium, were appointed Secretaries. For Brezhnev, this was a re-entry into the Party's General Staff after a three-year eclipse: a normal gesture of 'reparation'. For Podgorny, who was leaving the

Ukraine after nearly six years as the head of that Republic, the advance to Moscow somewhat recalled Khrushchev's rise in the Stalin era.

Which of the two did Khrushchev favour? Both appeared infinitely closer to him than Kozlov, even if they were not to be considered still dependent on him. Possibly Podgorny had a slight edge, since on most controversial issues (for instance the 'anti-party' affair at the Twenty-second Congress), he seemed closer to Khrushchev. Moreover, as a newcomer to the central hierarchy, he was in a slightly more dependent position. Brezhnev, thanks to his past functions, had already been introduced, so to speak, into the high Party, State, and Army circles. In any event, caution forbade Khrushchev to allow anyone to hoist himself into the position of 'challenger' as Kozlov had done. His true interest was to maintain the equilibrium between the two men.

In fact, it was clear from the start that the former pretender's example would be very difficult to follow. Kozlov had purged the people around him as soon as he joined the Secretariat in 1960, and had thus turned it into a formidable stronghold within a very short time. Brezhnev and Podgorny, on the other hand, were only further inflating the large membership of fourteen persons (the previous record of eleven had been set in December 1957). Moreover, Brezhnev remained Chief of State. Despite the possible advantage in terms of protocol, this prevented him from being fully effective in his new functions.

During the first few months it was hard to tell whether Brezhnev or Podgorny was ranked higher in the Party hierarchy. Or more accurately, there were fluctuations that the press did its best to smooth over, as if the matter were to be left open as long as possible.

Just after the plenary session, Brezhnev seemed to be well ahead of Podgorny. At the welcoming rally for the cosmonauts, Tereshkova and Nikolayev, on Red Square on June 22, Podgorny was in sixth place – his usual one as a junior member – while Brezhnev was in second position, where he was photographed as part of the intimate group of the cosmonauts with Khrushchev. But this was not noticeable un-less one watched the television coverage or saw the photograph – in *Kazakhstanskaya Pravda* of all places (June 25). Contrary to tradition, the Moscow press had refrained from reproducing it or any close-ups of the platform. Several weeks later, when Brezhnev appeared in his new capacity conducting negotiations with foreign communist leaders, Podgorny was seen with him on a few occasions (on August 26 with Aydit, the head of the Indonesian Communist Party and on October 2 with Max Reimann, the head of the West German Communist Party). However, shortly afterwards, Podgorny grew in stature and was able to act on his own. He conducted the talks with the head of the Nor-wegian Communist Party, assisted by Kuusinen who, despite an identical title, was listed after him (*Pravda*, October 21 1963). At the time Podgorny appeared with increasing frequency as the third-ranking man at official functions. Moreover, when the Congress of Soviet Trade Unions opened in the presence of the leaders on October 28, Podgorny took a seat on Khrushchev's right, and Brezhnev on his left – a reversal of the order of June 22. This apparently was again over-doing things: for *Pravda*, followed by the other major newspapers, did not publish any close-ups of the platform so as to prevent the faces from being scrutinized. Only *Trud* and a few other minor papers reproduced this 'detail'.

In short, the Brezhnev–Podgorny rivalry remained unsettled for a long time. It is likely that it was only after July 1964, when Brezhnev was divested of his functions as Head of State, that he became a 'pretender'; until then the picture remained very confused, as regards the division of labour for instance. In an interview given in Paris to Bernard Féron (*Le Monde*, March 7 1964), Podgorny explained that his work in the Secretariat entailed dealing with the 'most varied questions, in particular the economy, commerce, and light industry'. The fact that he did not mention being in charge of cadres proves nothing either way: the subject is not of a kind to be ventilated in the 'bourgeois' press. There is in fact no definite indication that Brezhnev was in charge of cadres either, since neither he nor Podgorny ever conducted any re-shuffle of personnel in the provinces (with Kozlov, the position in this respect was much clearer).

Lastly, the most spectacular rise in Podgorny's influence, in October 1963, coincided with a long illness of Suslov, whereas Brezhnev's rise in 1964 was matched by Suslov's growing activity. It is not impossible that Suslov, who through force of circumstances became the main spokesman of the opposition, placed his confidence in Brezhnev rather than in Podgorny from the start. Khrushchev, in that case, is still more likely to have favoured Podgorny.

In any case, the First Secretary had every reason to be pleased with the situation in June 1963. Instead of one would-be successor who had turned into a rival, he was dealing with two men who were far closer to himself and were, moreover, bound to compete with each other. He had also succeeded in keeping D. F. Ustinov outside the inner circle of the Party. Abroad, Fidel Castro had once more built up his prestige. The 'plenary session on ideology', little as he had wanted it, had turned out much better than could have been expected in April when it had been called. We may now look at its other results.

PLENARY SESSION ON IDEOLOGY

A major shift occurred in relations both with the West and with the East in that month of June 1963. It is very hard to tell whether the decision to sign an agreement with the West on stopping nuclear tests above ground was the cause or the consequence of the break with China. It is known, however, that the one followed the other within a very short time, and with good reason. If the Chinese are to be believed, Moscow was guilty of outright provocation. On June 6 the Chinese Government had, in a memorandum, warned the Soviet rulers 'against any agreement with the United States that would amount to depriving China of the right to equip itself with nuclear weapons'. Moscow is alleged to have replied on June 9: 'The Western position on the suspension of nuclear testing does not at present provide any basis for the conclusion of an agreement.' (*People's Daily*, August 1 and 3 1963.) On the very next day, however, Moscow announced its agreement to the British and American proposal made at the end of April for a tripartite conference on nuclear tests. When, on the same day, Khrushchev was host to Harold Wilson, the leader of the British opposition party, he declared that in his opinion an agreement on the suspension of testing above ground was possible. Khrushchev confirmed this on July 2 and the agreement was concluded practically without any complications at the end of the same month.[1]

This was a *volte-face* as compared to the Soviet position of 1962; but the shift had in fact occurred at the time of the withdrawal from Cuba, since the crisis had amply demonstrated the need for nuclear coexistence. Apart from the probable concern on the part of the military, or at least some of them, the objective grounds for the move had apparently convinced a large majority of the Presidium. It is significant, though, that East–West relations were 'frozen' during the February–March crisis. Any action had had to wait until Khrushchev regained the initiative. Even now, a large section of the Presidium did not seem to feel that the agreement warranted breaking off their holidays and returning to Moscow. The treaty was signed on August 5 in the presence of Khrushchev, Brezhnev, Kirilenko and Podgorny, but no others. Was it accidental that these four comprised the most pro-Khrushchev group of the Presidium?

[1] By December 1962, as noted, Khrushchev had accepted the principle of a certain number of inspections to detect underground nuclear explosions. In his speech of December 12 he had added: 'Means to settle certain pending problems have emerged in the course of exchanges of views on banning nuclear tests.' On April 20 Khrushchev withdrew his agreement concerning on-site inspections (*Pravda*, April 25). But in fact accepting a ban on tests above ground may have been the logical effect of the gesture, since only underground tests required any inspection.

Similarly, the break with China, something unthinkable in February–March, coincided with Khrushchev's resumption of authority. Certainly, the Chinese helped him a good deal with their violent programme-letter of June 14, the celebrated '25 points' replying to the Soviet letter of March 30 (conceivably the document was also meant as a retort to the Soviet 'betrayal' on nuclear testing). This massive attack put an end to the truce that, by and large, both parties had observed for over three months. On June 19, four days after the document was handed in, *Pravda* denounced it as 'libellous'. After a short polemic about a minor matter – the fact that the Soviet press was refusing to publish Chinese views (on June 27 three Chinese diplomats were expelled from Moscow for having tried to disseminate them) – it was announced on July 4, the eve of the bilateral meeting, that the '25 points' were going to be published together with an 'appropriate reply'. This was the no less celebrated 'open letter' of July 14, the start of a polemic whose violence was unexampled since the Soviet–Yugoslav rift fifteen years earlier.

Khrushchev was certainly the inspirer of this new line. In the same way as in 1960, the Chinese excesses put a stop to attempts at appeasement by his entourage and enabled the First Secretary to consolidate his position. The resolution on China adopted at the June plenary session mentioned, for the first and last time in the Khrushchev era, the 'Presidium of the Central Committee headed by comrade Khrushchev'. Instructions on firmness in preparation for the July bilateral meeting were not given to the delegation as such, but to the Presidium of the Party as a whole. Since Khrushchev had just been confirmed as head of the Presidium, the intention was clear. To make doubly sure, the membership of the delegation was changed at the last minute. It had originally consisted of Suslov, Yu. V. Andropov, L. F. Ilyichev, B. N. Ponomarev and S. V. Chervonenko (*Pravda*, June 16 1963); now two more men, obviously close to Khrushchev, were appointed: the President of the trade unions, V. V. Grishin, and the chief editor of *Pravda*, P. A. Satyukov (*Pravda*, July 4).

On the 'ideological' front, the situation had also changed substantially. The attacks against liberal writers had not produced the expected results. The harvest of self-criticism was very scant; abroad, the campaign had merely aroused dissatisfaction within the Communist Parties whose support was more than ever needed in the face of Chinese intrigues. But the main point was that the tough men in cultural matters had lost their most powerful protector – Kozlov. Hence, from May, their campaign abated. On the 12th of that month, *Pravda* had published an interview given by Tvardovsky to the UPI correspondent in Moscow. The editor-in-chief of *Novy Mir* reaffirmed his well-known position and, with appropriate delicacy of phrase, took up the cudgels for many writers who had been under attack in the preceding weeks. Party militants were notified at that time that the interview did not reflect official policy. None the less, *Pravda* sounded a moderating note in an editorial on May 19:

> 'Although the Party directs the development of art and literature in accordance with Leninist principles, it sees no need to control our *intelligentsia* at every step, to explain to it in detail how to write a book, stage a performance, produce a film or compose music. . . . . The creators of art must not be the sort of people who are accustomed to have all their food chewed for them.'

In other words, the emphasis in the cultural field was now on appeasement. The conservatives maintained their pressure, of course, but the worst was over. After the end of May, direct personal attacks against the heretical writers gradually abated, and were replaced by more general and indirect attacks.

Thus the plenary session on ideology met in a wholly changed climate. It had originally been planned in an atmosphere of greater rigidity *vis-à-vis* the West and of *rapprochement* with China. Instead, it ratified the almost complete break with China and helped to prepare the Moscow test-ban treaty. As for the writers and artists, there was not much more to be said to them. In so far as ideology was dealt with, a softening rather than a stiffening was detectable. One fact illustrates the paradox: on the second day of the plenary session, on June 19, the Soviets stopped jamming the Russian-language broadcasts of the Voice of America and the BBC.[1] An odd way indeed of proclaiming the 'non-coexistence of ideologies' to the Agitprop élite.

The 'ideologists' received other indications that their plenary session was being downgraded. Hitherto, all plenary sessions of the Central Committee had produced around fifty speakers – fifty-one at each session in 1962. This time, however, a mere half that number was reached. Twenty-seven speakers dealt with the main item on the agenda – Ilyichev's report on ideology – while four others – Suslov, Ponomarev, Andropov and Khrushchev – spoke on the 'substance of the differences' with China. During the last two days of the session there were only five and four speakers respectively, which must have left a large gap in the timetable. Moreover, the editing of the verbatim record of the

---

[1] The reasons why the Russians stopped jamming the Russian broadcasts of the Voice of America and the BBC on June 19 1963 have never been explained, but this seems to have been a diplomatic gesture, coming as it did when the tripartite negotiations on nuclear testing were about to open. In the past, jamming had been suspended briefly during periods of *détente*, e.g. during Macmillan's visit to Moscow in 1959 and after Khrushchev's visit to the United States in the autumn of the same year. This time, however, the suspension was permanent.

session took a singularly long time. It was put on sale only one year later, in the summer of 1964, by which date records of the following two plenary sessions, those of December 1963 and February 1964, had already been out for a long time.

The plenary session of June 1963 was mentioned subsequently in various comments and articles, but very seldom by Khrushchev himself. He was far more preoccupied with his pet idea of a session on chemistry, which he had mentioned again to the officials in charge of ideology on June 21.[1] As soon as the June meeting was over, he started preparing for it.

DESTALINIZATION AGAIN: EXPLANATIONS BY KRUSHCHEV

The somewhat sketchy plenary session brought no major developments, apart from the break with China, but two facts may be noted:
1 Khrushchev became somewhat cooler towards L. F. Ilyichev. This was probably no more than a tactical attitude, with no bearing on their 'objective' alliance against Suslov, which has been mentioned. A rumour had been circulating for a long time in cultural circles that Ilyichev's conduct of the campaign against the liberal intellectuals was a lesser evil compared to what would have happened had Suslov and his protégé D. A. Polikarpov, the chief of the cultural department of the Central Committee, been in charge of it. Other sources suggest that serious consideration was given to having Suslov instead of Ilyichev deliver the main report at the June plenary.[2] If so, Khrushchev could only have welcomed Ilyichev's appointment. Moreover, Khrushchev did nothing to prevent Ilyichev from building up his 'ideological empire' after December 1962 and from taking control over Polikarpov's department. However, the relative failure of the anti-modernist campaign and the protests from abroad hampered the moves of the Secretary in charge of ideology.

The impression created at the plenary session was that Khrushchev gave Ilyichev his head so that he himself might remain in a middle-of-

[1] On June 21 1963 Khrushchev announced at the plenary session on ideology that the Presidium had 'assigned' to him the task of preparing the report for the next plenary session, on chemistry (*Pravda*, June 29 1963).
[2] *Russkaya Mysl*, published in Paris, reported in its 'Letter from Moscow' on December 3 1964 already mentioned, that Suslov had been thought of instead of Ilyichev for the delivery of the main report at the plenary session in June 1963. It should be noted, however, that Ilyichev was designated rapporteur as soon as the plenary session was announced, on April 10.

the-road position. For instance, Ilyichev had endorsed a suggestion by the ultra-conservatives for the fusion of all existing unions of intellectuals (writers, artists, composers, and so forth) into a single strictly regimented organization. Khrushchev, taking the floor after him, deliberately ignored this by pointedly referring to 'the unions' and suggesting a new one for film-makers, thus giving the distinct impression that he was against the merger.[1] Similarly, Ilyichev had attacked 'the editors of *Novy Mir*' (meaning Tvardovsky) and had suggested that 'they' come up to the rostrum and explain their attitude. In fact, though Tvardovsky (and all other writers who happened to belong to the Central Committee) refrained from speaking at the plenary session, Khrushchev mentioned him favourably. A few weeks later, the poet had the supreme honour of being called upon to recite to the First Secretary and a group of foreign writers in Gagra one of his works that had been awaiting publication for a long time. This was *Vassily Tyorkin in the Other World*, which came out a few days later in *Izvestia* with a laudatory introduction by Adzhubey (August 18 1963).

Adzhubey himself was upgraded during this period, perhaps as a counterpoise to the over-enterprising Ilyichev. Taking the floor at the plenary session, he criticized 'the poor quality of ideological work' performed 'by the functionaries of the Central Committee's ideological department.' He could not have been more disrespectful toward Ilyichev.[2]

2 There was also a revival of destalinization. Speaking in April, Khrushchev retained only what suited him from his March 8 speech, namely, the need for 'Party discipline' among the intellectuals. He took up this theme again in June (even going as far as to threaten the contumacious writer Nekrasov with expulsion from the Party), but

[1] Khrushchev's reference to several unions of intellectuals as against the single one suggested by Ilyichev at the plenary session of June 1963 was as follows: 'The Central Committee of the CPSU has taken a step on behalf of the scenario writers and given its approval for their own creative union. We favour self-government for the arts and for the creative unions. . . . But if certain people believe they can use these unions to fight against the Party line, they are very much mistaken' (*Pravda*, June 29 1963).

The creation of a single union had been suggested not only by Ilyichev but also by G. I. Popov, the First Secretary of the Leningrad Urban Committee. After the plenary session, it was mentioned as well in an article by N. M. Gribachov in *Literaturnaya Gazeta* of June 27 and also in the provinces. According to the Uzbekistan press, unification had been fully achieved in that Republic by the end of June, but from July onwards nothing more was heard of this.

[2] It was learned after the plenary session of June 1963 on ideology that Khrushchev had displayed even greater contempt for the ideological department of the Central Committee than Adzhubey. He is alleged to have said about them: 'They neither sow nor reap, but only eat bread' (speech by F. S. Goriachev to the plenary session of March 1965, verbatim record, p. 83).

apparently no action followed. This time, however, he laid stress on a topic that had still been taboo a few weeks earlier, namely Stalin himself. It may not be quite accurate to describe this as a revival of destalinization: after the many set-backs Khrushchev had suffered on the issue since 1961, he could not afford to launch another strong attack. Rather, this was another swing of the pendulum – essentially a defensive operation on Khrushchev's part, with occasional digs at his adversaries.

First, he attacked Stalin under various pretexts: for his self-delusion about the situation in the countryside, an attitude in which Malenkov had abetted him; for 'distrust of the people', for 'refusing contact with the workers and peasants', and so on. Then Khrushchev made a strong plea in his own defence:

1 For his behaviour during the 'cult' period. Without naming Ehrenburg and Yermilov, but clearly indicating how much their controversy had affected him, he listed his own acts of courage in standing up to Stalin. He asserted that as soon as the film *The Kuban Cossacks* (an idyllic picture of rural life around 1950) had come out, 'we told Stalin that the life of the kolkhoz members had been pictured with complete disregard for the truth'. Who were 'we'? He continued: 'At the time, I told Stalin that those turkeys [that the peasants were feasting on] had been bought by Bolshakov, the Minister for the Film Industry, and that it was the actors who were eating them, not the kolkhoz members'. A year later, toward the end of 1952 apparently, he told Stalin 'during a discussion in the Central Committee': 'Comrade Stalin, the Ukrainians are very displeased about the shortage of white bread.'[1]

Speaking just before Khrushchev, Adzhubey had made the same point, but the example he chose was somewhat forced. He alleged that a resolution voted under Khrushchev's aegis by the Moscow Party Committee in March 1937 ('I repeat, 1937,' said Adzhubey) had already taken a very definite stand against the cult of Stalin's personality. Indeed, the passage he quoted criticized the 'pompous speeches and . . . otiose greetings addressed to the Party leaders'. But a perusal of the full text (*Pravda*, March 17 1937) disclosed that the main purpose of the resolution was to approve Bukharin's and Rykov's expulsion from the Party. It needed a large dose of good will to describe it as even an indirect criticism of Stalin.

It was becoming obvious, in any case, that Khrushchev had been hard hit by the insidious allusions of the Ehrenburg case. The question 'What were you doing during the period of the cult?' had been ad-

[1] To Khrushchev, who claims he told Stalin about dissatisfaction in the Ukraine owing to the lack of white bread, Stalin regally replied, still according to Khrushchev: 'The Ukrainians must be given white bread.'

dressed to him often enough that spring to compel him to reply in public. But he had practically no one save Adzhubey to turn to for his defence.

2 Regarding his destalinization efforts, Khrushchev now gave additional details and took some pains to explain, with at least a semblance of candour, why he had taken the initiative. He said:

> 'I remember that when we discussed this matter [the denunciation of the cult] at the time of the Twentieth Congress, there was a serious clash within the leadership. . . . Certain persons, who felt highly guilty for the crimes they had committed at the same time as Stalin, were afraid of this truth, of being unmasked. After a lengthy dispute they agreed that the matter should be raised at the Congress' (*Pravda* June 19 1963).

This clearly meant the 1957 'anti-party group'. Interestingly enough, Khrushchev was reverting to the highly controversial point of their criminal responsibilities. But why did he not now name these persons? Was it because he did not feel strong enough to give new impetus to the old anti-Molotov campaign, or, on the contrary, because he did not have only the 'anti-party group' in mind? The question needs an answer, because, enlarging on the theme, he proceeded to refute the arguments of yet another opposition:

> 'Certain people who then belonged to the Presidium of the Central Committee were saying: "How will the Congress and the Party interpret this?". . . . Of course, if one cannot help thinking like a *petit bourgeois* (*po-obyvatelski*), one may wonder why the question had to be raised: Stalin is no longer alive, and neither are many people who were victims of the repressions. The country is developing, a leadership has come into existence. Why stir, dig up, reform everything? But this petit-bourgeois attitude is inadmissible in politics. The question had to be brought up and discussed, not for the sake of those who are no longer among us, but for the sake of those who are alive and those who will live. On this issue we fought *not for our personal interests* but for the sake of the Party, for the purity of the Leninist Party. . . .' (*Pravda*, June 29 1963). [Author's italics].

It is quite likely that Molotov and his associates had used the argument in question in 1956, but nothing indicates that they were the only ones. Anyway, if Khrushchev kept harping on the objection, clearly it had not been finally answered. The 'petit bourgeois' attitude of 1956 was obviously still alive in 1963, perhaps even more so than ever, since it had prompted the speech of March 8. As for the probable sources of the objections, one of them at least (apart from Mikoyan) 'belonged to the Presidium of the Central Committee', namely Suslov. It should also be noted that, for the first time, Khrushchev was defending himself against the accusation of having launched the destalinization campaign 'for his personal interests'. He could not have acknowledged more candidly that he had actually been rebuked for this. Of course, far more than this bare denial would have been needed in order to refute the charge.

It was probably because the speech was controversial for all the reasons listed here that it almost met the same fate as Khrushchev's final statement at the preceding plenary session, in November 1962, by remaining unknown to the world. *Pravda* waited for eight days, from 21 to 29 June, before publishing it. Naturally its text may have been censored as well.

The June plenary session put an end to the acute stage of the 1963 crisis, and ushered in a semblance of normal political life. We therefore pause here in our analysis. The next period, a more agitated one, brought about the leader's downfall one year later. No doubt Khrushchev's worries did not cease meanwhile. The main one was the catastrophic harvest of 1963 after which the USSR had to purchase huge quantities of wheat abroad, tell the population of its agricultural difficulties and institute a measure of rationing. Again, Khrushchev could not get off the defensive on that issue. He had to keep 'demonstrating' over and over again the financial soundness of his virgin lands operation,[1] and stress the fact that, under Stalin, people had sometimes died of starvation. To remedy the situation, he planned a new crash programme for the production of mineral fertilizers. The plenary session on chemical problems that he had wanted so long was held in December 1963. But like all his previous campaigns, this one bore the mark of improvisation and 'subjectivism'. Khrushchev had to tone down some of his demands[2]; moreover, he was not allowed time to act on them.

[1] In his report of December 9 1963 to the Central Committee, Khrushchev produced specially prepared figures on the virgin lands programme. Comparison with the figures he had himself given three years earlier disclosed an embarrassing fact: over the entire period the virgin lands may have brought some profit to the State, but since 1960 they were running up a deficit. In his 'theses' of January 1961 Khrushchev had estimated the profit made by the State between 1954 (the start of the land-clearing) and 1960 at 3.2 billion new roubles. The corresponding figure was down to 3 billion for the 1954–1962 period. Besides, the virgin lands had absorbed 2.3 billion roubles in State investments for the years 1961 and 1962, that is, over half what their development had cost (4.4 billion from 1954 to 1960). The deficit would of course have been much larger had the speaker included the figures for 1963 (see *Agricultural Speeches* vol 4 p 240 and vol 8 p 280).

[2] Launching his crash programme on fertilizers just after the plenary session June 1963, Khrushchev suggested a target of 100 million tons for 1970 (as against 20 million in 1963). This was done in a 'note to the Presidium' dated July 12 (*Agricultural*

If the new phase in Khrushchev's reign introduced by the Cuban fiasco and the February–March crisis had to be described in a single word, it would be 'helplessness'. True, things had begun to go wrong in 1960; but until 1962, Khrushchev's moves still bore the mark of his enterprising character. After the Caribbean crisis, the opposition – which had at last found a leader in Kozlov – showed some aggressiveness, but the latter's departure from the scene in April 1963 gave Khrushchev a long respite. Khrushchev's good fortune was that at the very top the opposition was divided, timid, and also shaky because the issue of who should be second to him had been reopened for a considerable time to come. Only Suslov was in a position to crystallize the dissatisfaction within the Party. Circumstances did not help him, and in addition he was ill for over three months at the end of 1963. On occasion he was also made to feel that politically his position was vulnerable.[1]

Khrushchev, on the other hand, was still not strong enough to react drastically. Even in 1960 and 1961 he had not been able to reshuffle the Party Presidium to suit his purposes. He was much less likely to succeed in 1963. Barring an overall change in the situation, he could no longer expect to overcome the inertia of his apparatus, or even its conscious attempts at sabotage. A kind of mournful stability seemed to settle over the country, caused by the helplessness of both the ruler and his opponents. For how long? To all appearances, until nature herself resolved the problem of the succession. But, at this stage, another law of the system may have come into play, namely that authority must either grow or dwindle rapidly.

Speeches vol 8 p 34); two weeks later, he mentioned '80 to 100 million tons' (speech of July 30, vol 8 p 44). Then he again spoke of the 100 million tons in speeches made on September 16 and 26 (pp 129 and 177). But in his report to the December plenary session he brought the figure down to '70–80 million' (p 273).

Khrushchev apparently had a very hazy view of what this would cost the State: on July 12 he had mentioned 5·8 milliard roubles (p 35) but on the 30th of the same month he was speaking of 10 milliard (p 45).

On September 5 he asked 'for an immediate survey of the means of putting a complete stop to or of reducing to a minimum the export [of fertilizers] in 1964' (p 105). By September 26 his memory had returned: 'We must remember the demand from the fraternal socialist countries' (p 177).

[1] The article in *Pravda* of December 1 1963, to commemorate the birthday of the economist Nikolay Voznesensky (see p 202) should be construed as a thrust at Suslov.

Nothing is known as to the nature of Suslov's illness. He was absent throughout August 1963, and again disappeared in mid-September (the last mention of him being on September 16) until January 1 1964. Thus the article was published during his absence.

Part Four
THE FALL 1964

The passing of time gives events their logic. A few years after Khrushchev's overthrow, there is no difficulty in recalling a series of facts and indications pointing to his downfall as if to an inescapable ending. Needless to say, while events were unfolding, they appeared more complex, not only to outside observers, but to the protagonists as well.

Let it be stated at the outset that the palace revolution of October 1964 was not and could not have been foreseen by most of those who must be termed Kremlinologists – with the exception of a few inveterate gamblers who guess right every other time. Their 'science' has its limitations, and in all fairness they should not be asked to do more than it allows them, for they would otherwise be crystal-gazing – which they tend to be identified with as it is. Kremlinology interprets past and present events and makes it possible – or so we hope to have shown – to perceive the moments at which power falters. But our science lacks sufficient means to enable it to identify the various groups operating in each conflict, and it is still less in a position to fathom the intentions of those groups. In this particular case, secrecy was the essential condition of success and was so well achieved that Khrushchev himself was caught off guard. It would have been amazing indeed for the outside world to have been aware of the situation before he was. On the other hand, we can and must try to reconstruct – tentatively, of course, pending the opening of the archives – the main episodes leading up to the denouncement. They appear to fall into two stages. The first began at the end of the winter of 1963 and lasted through the spring of 1964. It brought fresh difficulties to Khrushchev; the progressive and manifest dwindling of his authority, and new major differences within the top leadership. This may have been the time when the idea of a coup first occurred to some people, especially Suslov, who master-minded the action. Then came the stage of execution, which started at the end of September 1964 – the last straw that broke the camel's back. An attempt will be made to find out what that last straw could have been.

1 The Premise:
The Crumbling of Authority

The Central Committee of the Party sat in plenary session in Moscow from the 10th to the 15th of February 1964. This was the last such session of Khrushchev's reign, since it was at the following one, in October, that he fell. The sole item on the agenda was the perennial one of agricultural problems. However, it was the Chinese issue, also debated at the session, that excited attention abroad. Here matters had reached a complete standstill. At the end of October 1963, Khrushchev had made a gesture by unilaterally putting a stop to the polemic that had been raging with Peking throughout the summer. On November 29 he had proposed in a letter to the Chinese a series of 'concrete steps' to improve relations between the two countries, in particular an expansion of commerce, the return of the Soviet technicians to their posts and a settlement of frontier problems. He also affirmed that the conference which the Soviets and their allies were now urging need not lead to a rift. The Chinese refrained from answering the letter (they did so only on February 29 1964) and continued to run in their press a series of lengthy articles in reply to the Soviet 'open letter' of July 14 1963. The seventh and last article appeared on February 4 1964 in *Jenmin Jih Pao* under the outspoken title,'The CPSU leaders are the worst schismatics of our time'.

By January it had become clear in Moscow that official patience was at breaking point and that the plenary session next month was going to strike at the Chinese with the 'decisive retort' that the Soviets had been promising for almost a year. Private information and other signs pointed in that direction. For instance, an anti-Chinese book edited by L. F. Ilyichev, *Conversations on Political Topics*, came out in the middle of January. The order to print had been given at the end of October 1963, just before the truce went into effect, and publication meant the truce was over. On January 30, for the first time in three months, *Pravda* openly attacked a Chinese newspaper.

Events followed their logical course throughout the plenary session. The discussion of the Chinese issue had been scheduled for February 14. By the 12th, the leadership of the Soviet Communist Party had sent a letter to the fraternal Parties (but not to the Chinese) informing them of its intention to publish shortly the anti-Chinese documents and resolutions that the Central Committee was about to adopt.[1] On the morning of February 14 the Moscow papers greeted the anniversary of the Sino-Soviet friendship treaty with rather tart articles, indicating in particular that Peking bore the responsibility for the drop in commercial exchanges. In the afternoon, *Vechernyaya Moskva* announced that the plenary session, after listening to a major speech by Khrushchev in the morning, had continued its proceedings with a complete change in its composition. Instead of the agricultural experts of the beginning of the week, all the political and ideological cadres in the country, ranging from the Central Committee propagandists to the political commissars of the armed forces, and including the press chiefs and the 'old bolsheviks', were now in session. In the afternoon Tass began to publish a summary of Khrushchev's speech, which contained in particular the following sentence: 'We have struggled and will continue to struggle against the latter-day dogmatists, revisionists and Trotskyists who mouth resounding revolutionary phrases, but injure the unity of the Communist movement by their fractious activities.'

Then, still on February 14, a complete switch occurred. The above sentence in Khrushchev's speech about the Chinese issue, although it was fairly mild, disappeared from what was supposed to be the full text of the speech – six newspaper pages – put out by *Izvestia* late that evening. The evening paper's communiqué announcing the change in plenary session participants was ignored by *Izvestia* as well as by *Pravda* on February 15.[2] In other words, whatever concerned the Chinese in any way was suddenly cut out, even to the mention of the problem having been discussed. This situation lasted for six weeks, during which the Soviet press kept silent on the issue far more strictly than during the preceding three months. Ilyichev's work was again relegated to the storage shelves in the bookshops.

The anti-Chinese report delivered by Suslov to the plenary session and the resolution on it were released only on April 3. The explanation, or some attempt at an explanation, of the delay came only later, in the 'April Declaration' by the Rumanian Central Committee, published on April 28. According to this, the Rumanian leaders – who since the summer of 1963 had adopted an attitude of non-alignment in the

---

[1] The Rumanian leaders stated in the resolution adopted by their Central Committee in April 1964 that they received the anti-Chinese letter circulated by the Soviet Central Committee on February 13. The Chinese, however, who in a series of subsequent documents repeatedly demanded to be apprised of its contents, refer to it as having been dated February 12.

[2] The communiqué about the change of participants in the plenary session of February 1964 was published not only by *Vechernyaya Moskva* but also by a few provincial newspapers (for instance, the February 15 issue of *Pravda Vostoka*, in Tashkent) which were presumably notified too late to leave it out.

conflict – had, on February 14, addressed to the leaders of the Soviet Communist Party a 'pressing fraternal' plea not to resume the polemic against the Chinese, as the Soviets had announced they were going to in their message the day before. Curiously enough, the request was acceded to forthwith. That very day, the Bucharest declaration states, the Rumanians were informed that the CPSU had decided 'to postpone publication of the plenary session material and to refrain from publishing polemical matter provided the Chinese comrades also stopped the public polemic'.

Was the Rumanian plea the only reason for Moscow's *volte-face*? This is hard to believe. True, Bucharest's move was accompanied by a final attempt at mediation with Peking, which at first seemed as if it might succeed, since Mao Tse-tung agreed to receive a Rumanian delegation, and in the meantime declared that 'he would be able for the present not to publish polemical material'. On February 14, however, nothing supported such an expectation. Moreover, it is not usual for the Soviet rulers to change a decision simply under pressure by a minor ally, and even less for them to do such a thing at a few hours' notice.

Evidently there were other reasons for the switch, and they were domestic ones. Rumours circulated in Moscow at the time – and suddenly burst out afresh after Khrushchev's downfall – that the audience had balked when the First Secretary had demanded that the plenary session release Suslov's report and resume the polemic with China. Khrushchev had, it was alleged, even had to threaten to resign before calm was restored (it was too early for his resignation to be accepted). These rumours cannot be verified, but certain anomalies in official behaviour do confirm the uneasy situation. For instance, nowhere was it stated that the plenary session resolution on the Chinese issue had been adopted 'unanimously'. Even the *Pravda* editorial of April 3 1964 that published and commented upon it was silent on that point. Besides, the text was adopted on February 15 instead of 14, that is, the day after Suslov had delivered his report, and after the leadership of the Soviet Communist Party had informed the Rumanians that they had decided to postpone the polemic. Possibly, the Central Committee had adopted the resolution only on condition that the polemic was to be suspended. In any event, the outcome was paradoxical: the Party had decided to 'unmask ideologically the anti-Leninist position of the Chinese Communist Party leadership' and deliver 'a decisive retort to its fractious actions', but for six weeks it did just the opposite. Lastly, despite its firm tone, the resolution, in one respect at least, seemed milder than the Suslov report. Suslov, after listing the doctrinal points assumed to be common to all the 'Marxist-

Leninist' parties, had concluded: 'All this has been distorted and virtually thrown overboard by the Chinese leadership.' The resolution, on
the other hand, repeated the points in question textually and added
only: 'All this has been distorted by the Chinese leaders.' Furthermore,
nowhere was it stated, as tradition demanded, that the report had been
'approved'. The plenary session, the resolution declared, had 'heard and
discussed' Suslov's report.

A BAD MOMENT FOR SUSLOV

Suslov's role in the affair raises some issues. Moscow rumour had it
that the report was not his own, that whole passages in it had been
written by a member of Khrushchev's executive office, and that the
Party ideologist had agreed to assume responsibility for it only on
condition that it would remain unpublished. An East European personality who was very well informed on Soviet affairs corroborated this
information in the presence of this writer and added, as an explanation:
'The rule in force in our systems often demands that the minority
carry out the decisions of the majority.' It is difficult to form an opinion
on this matter on the basis of the substance of the debate, namely, the
resumption of the polemic with China. In past years Suslov's position
had not appeared much softer toward Peking than Khrushchev's – as
witness his treatment of Wilcox, the very pro-Chinese leader of the
New Zealand Communist Party, a few months earlier during a private
talk.[1] Other points in his report give a far clearer indication of a non-
Suslovian influence: for example, the compliments paid to Khrushchev – the most emphatic ever to have come from Suslov:

> 'The Chinese leaders, and not only they, must get it into their heads
> that our Central Committee, led by the faithful Leninist Nikita Ser-
> geyevich Khrushchev, is more united and monolithic than ever.
>   'Comrade N. S. Khrushchev, with his inexhaustible energy, his
> ardour and his loyalty to true bolshevik principles, is the recognized
> leader of our Party and people. He expresses the most intimate
> thoughts and feelings of the people. It is impossible to dissociate
> the Leninist line followed by our Party from the Central Committee,
> and from Nikita Sergeyevich Khrushchev. This line has raised to un-

[1] According to Wilcox, Suslov said to him during talks in Moscow in September
1963: 'You are in the wrong. We had hoped that you would remain within the ranks
of the fraternal Parties of the Marxist–Leninist movement. But if you do not change
your attitude, you will be expelled and will remain outside it' (*Peking-Information*,
March 30 1964).

precedented heights the prestige of our country in the international arena and has enhanced its authority in the eyes of the workers of the entire world' (*Pravda*, April 3 1964).

A show of unity around Khrushchev was needed, of course, to impress the Chinese and Khrushchev must have been aware that its by-product would be a personal gain for him. Suslov was also forced to render Khrushchev an even greater service.

Suslov sharply attacked the 1957 'anti-party group' and for the first time disclosed that they had been expelled from the Party. Certain members of that group, he said, bore responsibility for mass repressions against innocent people, in particular Molotov, who had sent to their death several wives of 'enemies of the people' whom Suslov named (Kosyor, Chubar, Eykhe). The mention of expulsion from the Party was a much less direct one:

'Aren't the Chinese leaders eager to revive equally inhuman methods? Isn't it for that reason that they show sympathy to these people who have been thrown out of the ranks of our Party?' (*Pravda*, April 3, 1964).

Apart from Molotov, 'the people' were not identified, but it was clear none the less that, at the beginning of 1964, indirectly as it were, Khrushchev had succeeded where all his efforts had failed in 1961. Suslov's allusion to the Chinese 'sympathy' for the 'anti-party group' is a likely explanation. The conflict with Peking having grown to such proportions, Molotov's collusion with China had probably become the key motive for his expulsion. Three years earlier Molotov had been an accomplice in the Stalinist crimes but was not guilty of treasonable dealings with an outside enemy – a far more serious matter. Still, it had taken a good deal of persistence on Khrushchev's part to reach his objective, although he could not now reap the benefits he had expected in 1961. The victory resulted from attrition on both sides, and it came too late. Furthermore, it was only announced in passing, so to speak, and was never mentioned again.

It is a safe bet, however, that Suslov was not best pleased at having to make the statement, since he had always sided with Khrushchev's adversaries on the issue. The tribute to the First Secretary, the building up of his personal power, the aggressive defensive policy that Khrushchev was initiating on the Chinese issue – all this was too much for a man who had always favoured caution. Was his uneasiness compounded by the audience's reactions? Possibly so, since a decision adopted by the Presidium majority, on February 12 or earlier, to resume the polemic with Peking was rescinded at the session of the Central Committee, most probably under pressure by its members. Although this was an extremely rare occurrence, in this particular case it is not over-surprising, since pro-Chinese sympathies were more widespread among the rank and file than in the top leadership. This must have given Suslov, who had ultimate control over the apparatus, something to think about. Even if he had found himself in a minority within the Presidium, he now had more reason than ever to stiffen his opposition.

After Khrushchev's downfall, the rumour circulated in Moscow – and was apparently disseminated in diplomatic circles by Suslov's entourage – that at the time of the February plenary session, Suslov had gone to see Kozlov in hospital, when the latter allegedly told him that the only way to alleviate the country's problems was to get rid of Khrushchev, since 'no good will come of him any more'. True or false, the anecdote supports what cannot be more than an assumption, namely, that the notion of the October coup started taking shape in Suslov's mind at that moment.

THE 'STEEL-EATERS' AGAIN

The period of the plenary session also brought about interesting incidents on domestic issues. The session itself was rather colourless. It had been called upon to discuss purely technical aspects of agricultural problems and, in particular, the carrying out of the fertilizer programme adopted at the session of December 1963. As usual, the participants were thousands of experts who were not members of the Central Committee or even of the Party itself. The main rapporteur, I. P. Volovchenko, the Minister of Agriculture, was not a Central Committee member, and, out of forty speakers in the debate on agriculture, only five belonged to the Central Committee. However, various problems other than that of China were discussed in committee.

First, there was a resurgence of the debate on economic priorities between 'steel-eaters' and advocates of more consumer goods. At the last plenary session, in December 1963, Khrushchev had asserted that any sacrifices made for the sake of chemistry and fertilizer production were justified and even that 'some temporary slowdown in the rate of growth of certain branches of industry' was necessary. The military budget for 1964 had been cut by 600 million roubles, and the only officer prepared to support the measure was Marshal Grechko, who did so in an article in *Krasnaya Zvezda* on December 22 1963. Khrushchev in his speech of February 14 had chided more sharply than ever before the adversaries of his chemical programme, affirming for instance that 'only dyed-in-the-wool dogmatists can regard it as a departure from the general line'.

This was obviously what Khrushchev was being charged with, but he committed an even greater sacrilege by abandoning the old Stalinist distinction between 'group A' (capital goods) and 'group B' (consumer goods). 'At the present time, there can be no opposition between groups A and B.' As for the 'steel-eaters', he told them in so many words: 'The officials responsible for steel production, for instance, must understand what is new and draw the necessary practical conclusions. However, sufficient understanding of this is lacking among some top officials' (*Pravda*, February 15 1964). A few days later, on February 24 and 25, Arzumanian, a member of the Academy, came to the First Secretary's rescue in two major articles in *Pravda*. Although he did not dare attack the stronghold of heavy industry outright – he acknowledged in his conclusion that 'the law of priority for capital goods still remains in effect' – he was at pains to prove the opposite, citing the example of the United States to show that it was not dangerous to allow 'group B' to gain priority. He mentioned Molotov's name to scare potential opponents.

Such efforts were largely ineffectual, since a few days later, on March 3 1964, a *Pravda* editorial, visibly inspired by the 'steel-eaters', set matters straight. We are willing to develop chemistry, the authors said in substance, but this is just why the metallurgical industry must not be slighted:

'Metal production is growing rapidly, but the demand for metal is growing just as fast. . . . Industry consumes more ferrous and nonferrous metals with every passing year. A great deal is needed in particular for the production of the machines needed to develop agriculture. It is evident that our metallurgical industry must continue to grow and improve.'

The article ended with this remarkable conclusion: 'The Party has set as its most pressing task widespread emphasis on chemistry for the entire economy. Steel, cast iron, rolled metal are in ever greater demand in all sectors' (*Pravda*, March 3 1964).

In short, the quarrel between Khrushchev and the planners was still smouldering. At the end of September, just before his downfall, it broke out in a particularly serious, even crucial form.

SHABLON – PRO AND CON

Another major debate on management methods in agriculture took place at the same time, and Khrushchev was even more directly implicated on that score. It is common knowledge that, immediately after his downfall, he was chided for his continuous interference with producers, his cut-and-dried instructions to all and sundry regardless of local conditions, or – to sum it up in one word – *shablon*, the official term for stereotyped and unintelligent routine. Although he always denied this, Khrushchev was infinitely more prone to indulge in *shablon* than in its opposite – the granting of autonomy to the farms – for the simple reason that he had assumed personal responsibility for agriculture ten years earlier, had drawn the entire Party into the task and regarded any set-back as due to human failure rather than to objective causes. The worsening of the situation only sharpened his authoritarian tendencies. Pushed to its logical conclusion, his principle would have been: 'Agriculture is too important a matter to be left to agriculturists.'

In the beginning of the spring of 1964, however, a series of vacillations was to be observed in that sector. True, the disastrous harvest of 1963 had played into the hands of those who advocated a change in methods. Just before the February plenary session, an article by K. Karpov in *Kommunist* (No 2, cleared for printing on January 31 1964) injected a new note. It recommended greater autonomy for kolkhozes and sovkhozes, financial incentives for farmers, the use of economic levers to regulate production, bank loans, and so on. Apparently these long neglected 'real problems' were at last going to be dealt with by the plenary session. But not at all: every imaginable theme except that was mentioned by the speakers, starting with Khrushchev in his marathon speech of February 14. The resolution adopted at the end of the proceedings brought no increase in farm autonomy, but only additional Party control.

The problem was taken up two weeks later at an 'enlarged meeting' of the Presidium (once again, a horde of Party agricultural cadres had been invited), which looked very much like a supplementary session to cover topics neglected by the plenary session. The meeting was held on February 28 and reported the following day, but Khrushchev's speech, at first vaguely summarized, was published by *Pravda* only on March 7. This time he had dealt at length with material incentives for kolkhoz members, and autonomous farm management. On the latter point, Khrushchev had denounced 'certain local bureaucracies which saddle kolkhozes with plans for sowing every single crop, thereby paralysing the activities of farm directors and curbing the initiative of the kolkhoz members'. To eliminate these practices, he announced a special *ukase* that indeed was promulgated on March 20. The problem was not a new one, obviously, since the *ukase* merely reaffirmed the validity of a decree passed in 1955 to control *shablon*; it threatened officials guilty of excessive interference in kolkhoz activities with 'sanctions'.

All this was still very vague, but the foes of *shablon* regained some hope. One of the most notorious victims of Khrushchev's agricultural fads, the Siberian agronomist T. S. Maltsev, expressed his relief at a session of the Lenin Agricultural Academy. He said:

'It seems to me that after the decisions of the February plenary session [it would have been more accurate to call it the additional meeting of the 28th], stereotyped directives are going to be liquidated in agriculture. I experienced their effects personally when we were being forced to sow too early. . . . When we no longer have stereotyped instructions, there will be more initiative in agriculture and greater responsibility for the harvest . . . When the crop is good, the man responsible is always to hand, but no one wants to be answerable for a bad crop'[1] (*Selskaya Zhizn*, March 14 1964).

Khrushchev had thus apparently had to make some concessions under pressure. This was especially difficult for him, because Maltsev's example had shown that the anti-*shablon* drive had an irritating way of backfiring against his own slogans. Hence, a month later, Khrushchev again managed to change course. Using his old method for promoting controversial projects, on April 13 he sent the Party Presidium a new 'memorandum', which *Pravda* published eleven days later, on the 24th. As usual it contained a good many contradictions. It did censure 'administrative interference' with kolkhozes, but Khrushchev apparently had only the 'bad' kind of interference in mind. The rest of his message was a plea for official planning of a kind which had not been heard since the last bout of activity on this front in March 1962. It was widely believed that the kolkhozes were hampered by controls of all kinds, and here was Khrushchev worrying about the opposite:

'In fact, the kolkhozes and sovkhozes are not being managed, that is, they are not being given concrete instructions on organizing produc-

[1] T. S. Maltsev, a Siberian agronomist who had been prominent under Stalin, had trouble with Khrushchev as early as 1947, when his experiments served as the basis for the drive to encourage the cultivation of spring wheat. Khrushchev, who advocated winter wheat for the Ukraine, was directly affected since Kaganovich came to replace him in Kiev for a few months. The ex-First Secretary defended himself at length on this subject in a speech delivered on November 2 1961 (*Agricultural Speeches* vol 6 p 57 ff.).

During his tenure of power, Khrushchev put pressure on Maltsev on several occasions to support him over growing maize instead of wheat and preferring 'occupied fallows' to 'vacant fallows'. Maltsev somehow withstood the pressure, which brought him the following praise from the regional First Secretary, G. F. Sizov, in *Kommunist* in April 1965 (No 5): 'During the past few years, this kolkhoz expert has suffered many blows. It had been suggested to him that he should undertake the cultivation of maize, although the kolkhoz named *Lenin's Precepts*, where T. S. Maltsev works, is a base for the study of wheat growing. . . . Actually maize cultivation failed and Maltsev was unjustly criticized for this more than once.'

tion, on concrete tasks to be fulfilled within a given time, and the execution of these instructions and tasks is not being checked . . . This is because . . . the kolkhozes are co-operatives . . . that are not subject to Government control . . . and nobody interferes with their production.'

This might have been true in law, but not in fact, since Khrushchev's activity itself for the past ten years was evidence to the contrary. But this was not enough to stop the First Secretary. He went on:

'We are in the presence of full autonomy in each kolkhoz and, to call things by their names, a sort of anarchy prevails. The kolkhoz is left to its own devices, it manages its production as it sees fit. . . . This is the main cause of many shortcomings. . . . Agricultural production must be managed' (*Pravda*, April 24 1964).

No practical measure was announced for the time being, except for the setting up of a commission whose task was to consider the means of carrying out another pet project of Khrushchev's: the processing of animal products on an industrial basis in large specialized sovkhozes. The chairman of the commission was Podgorny, and its membership was announced on April 24, the day when the memorandum was released. It included no fewer than five Presidium members: L. I. Brezhnev, G. I. Voronov, A. N. Kosygin, A. I. Mikoyan and D. S. Polyansky. The meaning of this odd membership will later be discussed at greater length. Suffice it to note here that the commission, which was scheduled to report to the Central Committee within one month, was never mentioned again.

Another sign that the climate was no longer favourable to increased farm autonomy, but rather to a strengthening of State and Party control, was that the traditional slogan about 'kolkhoz democracy' vanished from the list of May Day slogans published by *Pravda* on April 14 1964.

AN ALARM: THE ORENBURG AFFAIR

Was this to be the end of the strange pendulum movement? Not quite. At the end of April, *shablon* was dealt a far less overt but more dangerous blow, with the so-called Orenburg affair. This was officially aimed at a few provincial officials, but through them at their protector in Moscow, G. I. Voronov, a notorious exponent of *shablon*, and behind him, probably at Khrushchev himself.

On April 29 1964 a terse communiqué in *Pravda* announced that V. A. Shurygin, the First Secretary of the Orenburg region, had been dismissed for 'having failed to perform his management functions' in the Oblast Committee. The change had been presided over by L. N. Yefremov, an alternate member of the Party Presidium who, as mentioned previously, had succeeded Voronov in November 1962 as First Deputy Chairman of the RSFSR Bureau in charge of Agriculture. A few days later, on May 3 1964, *Pravda* again reported on the case in a three-column article. Shurygin, it stated, and several other Oblast Committee officials were accused of having 'regulated agricultural production in a high-handed fashion,' 'hampering the initiative' of the farmers with 'stereotyped directives' (*shablon*) and 'administrative pressures.' They had, in particular, protected a careerist named Khairulin, an agronomist of Tatar background, who had, with the backing of the Oblast Committee, become the dictator of agriculture for the entire region. He had been expelled from the Oblast Committee Bureau at the same time as Shurygin, relieved of his duties as head of the Orenburg Livestock Institute, and subjected to 'severe blame' for 'negligence in his work . . . , lack of humility, self-advertisement and careerism'.

The attack on G. I. Voronov, a member of the Party Presidium, Chairman of the Council of Ministers of the RSFSR, was obvious. Not only had he been First Secretary of the Orenburg Oblast Committee from 1957 to 1961, when all the dismissed officials had been his associates, but the pseudo-scientist Khairulin was without any possible doubt his creature and his personal client. Their relationship dated back to 1939 at least, when Voronov had arrived in the Siberian town of Chita as an Oblast Committee Secretary and Khairulin was at the head of one of the region's agricultural departments. Still under the auspices of Voronov, who was then First Secretary of the Oblast Committee, Khairulin had been promoted chief of agricultural management of the regional soviet in 1951. In 1957 he had followed Voronov to Orenburg, where he had become the head of the Livestock Institute, and in fact was in charge of the entire region's agricultural policy.[1] Besides, Voronov had on several occasions praised his adviser and protégé. He had done so at the January 1961 plenary session, when he had recommended to Khrushchev a new type of cattle-shed devised by Khairulin, but which the Moscow scientists opposed. At the Twenty-second Congress he had mentioned Khairulin twice as one of the 'outstanding scientists who are making an invaluable contribution to the kolkhozes and sovkhozes' (*Twenty-second Congress*, vol 1, p 372).

[1] See Khairulin's biography in the 1962 *Encyclopedic Yearbook* (*Yezhegodnik*).

Although Voronov had never been named directly, it was made clear that the agricultural shortcomings in the region, and particularly Khairulin's misdeeds, could not be ascribed solely to the man in charge since 1961 – Shurygin – but had started far earlier, in Voronov's time. Regarding Khairulin, the May 3 1964 article in *Pravda* stated:

'As soon as he [Khairulin] appeared in the region *in 1957* he was hailed as a great specialist on agricultural and livestock problems; he received one appointment after another in various organizations, and administrative orders made it mandatory to comply with his stereotyped recommendations. Those who dared oppose Khairulin were subjected to pressure or even relieved of their functions.' [Author's italics.]

The local press provided fresh details implicating the pre-1961 Oblast Committee leadership, that is, Voronov. A certain S. A. Ambrok reported an incident *in 1958* over an article in which he had advocated spring weeding:

'Comrade Khairulin lashed out at me with a fierce article, declaring that weeding had to be done only in the autumn. [There followed a demonstration that the method was not effective] . . . Nevertheless, the Party Oblast Committee ordered the reprinting of his article in all the Oblast newspapers. Even though the spring was a rainy one, sowing was started without any preparation on fields overgrown with weeds' (*Yuzhny Ural*, May 7 1964).

Khairulin was not the only one. The agricultural recipes on which Voronov had built his political fame were openly questioned, for instance the so-called 'Orenburg technical agricultural system'. Voronov had advocated this first in 1958 (cf. p 132), and then when he was promoted by the January 1961 plenary session. He had said:

'The Party regional organization, drawing inspiration from the instructions of the Twentieth Congress on the liquidation of *shablon* in agriculture [*sic*], caused the introduction into kolkhozes and sovkhozes of a new system of cultivation devised by our scientists, specialists and innovators. The basis of that system is early deep ploughing, smoothed out in the following autumn. . . . We believe in our soil treatment system' (Plenary Session, January 1961, p 274).

And now *Pravda* was going into battle against the 'so-called Orenburg soil treatment and sowing system' which consisted of 'demanding unconditional early sowing' and 'mandatory deep ploughing smoothed out in the following autumn everywhere, regardless of local soil and climate conditions' (*Pravda*, May 3 1964).

In other words, beyond the 'so-called system', *shablon* itself was under attack together with one of its best-known spokesmen. Voronov must have understood, since he discreetly withdrew from the political scene for a few weeks. He was not present at a conference held on May 18 1964 to deal with the industrial problems of the Russian Federation, whereas all the other leaders of the Bureau for the RSFSR, in particular Kirilenko and L. N. Yefremov, took part in it. Voronov was seen in Moscow only once during the whole of May.

Cases of a Presidium member being attacked so overtly are rare enough to indicate a serious underlying political struggle. Furthermore, it is fairly clear that Khrushchev himself was a target. As noted, Voronov did not see eye to eye with Khrushchev on several political issues, but his 'agricultural competence' and his authoritarian methods in this domain probably accounted for his 1961 promotion. Now, such methods were the main cause of complaint against him; and just at the time when Khrushchev's memorandum of April 13 aimed at increasing control over the kolkhozes, advocates of that line were being pilloried. If Khrushchev personally had wanted the Orenburg purge, its victims would no doubt have been reinstated after his downfall, as were so many others. But nothing of the sort occurred, and although Voronov is still active, he no longer deals with agriculture. His protégés, Shurygin and Khairulin, are in minor posts (the former had a seat at the Twenty-third Congress as a Secretary of the Volgograd Oblast Committee but lost his membership of the Central Committee).

Khrushchev himself was somewhat involved in the case of the pseudo-scientist Khairulin. In January 1961 he had made a favourable remark about Khairulin's new cattle-shed design, later described as 'much ado about nothing'. More recently, the same Khairulin had placed Khrushchev in an awkward position. Taking the floor at the plenary session of February 1964, he had made a public show of handing Khrushchev an article and demanding its publication. The First Secretary had rashly agreed, but its publication in *Selskaya Zhizn* on February 21 provoked such a storm among agronomists that Khrushchev must have bitterly regretted his gesture. The following explanation in his speech of February 28 1964 indicates embarrassment, not to say self-criticism.

'Khairulin spoke at the [February] plenary session. Some say that he is an experienced man who knows his business. Others criticize him for his superficial attitude. I shall not presume to judge him, for I do not know him well. In front of all the participants at the plenary session, he handed me his article and asked the editors of *Selskaya Zhizn* to publish it. The editorial staff declared that the article contained potentially harmful stereotyped recommendations [*shablon*];

but since comrade Khairulin insisted, it was decided to publish his article for information's sake. And what happened? Today, many farming experts, agronomists, scientists, sovkhoz and kolkhoz managers sharply criticize the principles outlined in comrade Khairulin's article. They accuse him of imposing upon a huge region of the country identical sowing schedules, and justly point out that sowing dates can only be decided locally, on each farm. They take a stand against *shablon*. It is not difficult to understand what they mean' (*Pravda*, March 7 1964).

As noted, the meeting of February 28 at which these explanations were given inaugurated the new drive against *shablon*, whereas the plenary session two weeks earlier had been silent on the issue. Hence it is safe to assume that the Khairulin case served as a pretext to shake off the control over agriculture imposed by Khrushchev and his favourites. The fact that it took two months for the pseudo-scientist and his Orenburg protectors to be purged confirms that resistance was strong.

In the meantime, Khrushchev had tried to get things back under control by means of his highly authoritarian plans of April 13. The outcome meant that his power had been seriously undermined.

LYSENKO ON THE DOWNGRADE

The Lysenko case, another by-product of *shablon*, illustrates Khrushchev's loss of influence in the spring of 1964. The role Lysenko played in Soviet biology for decades, thanks first to Stalin's and then to Khrushchev's protection, is well known. His swift removal just after the October coup (the most clear-cut case, together with Adzhubey's) confirms that he indeed owed his monopoly to the First Secretary. Lysenko's difficulties in 1964, however, started well before the October plenary session. Several months before Khrushchev fell, he had had to dissociate himself from his protégé, cautiously but firmly.

At the plenary session of February 1964, Lysenko had made a bitter speech. He claimed that his work and discoveries were encountering a wall of incomprehension on the part of the agricultural cadres, at all levels, ranging 'from the federal agencies to local farm managements.' He had noted this in particular with respect to a 'quite important' matter: the process he had devised to increase the fat content of milk. Even Minister Volovchenko in his report to the plenary session had 'not said one word about it'. This was a way of drawing Khrushchev's attention to the latest 'injustice'. Khrushchev, on the other hand, was intimating to the scientist, for the first time in several years, that there were limits to his powers of protection. In his reply of February 14, he paid tribute to Lysenko's research on milk, but added this:

> 'We are not saying that this is the only method for obtaining a high fat content for milk. It is possible that other ways will be found. It is not possible for the Central Committee to say that only this or that method must be used. I, in my capacity as First Secretary of the Central Committee and Chairman of the Council of Ministers, cannot and will not say so. Why? Because on this matter there must be competition among minds, ideas, scientists. . . . When the Party condemned the habits of the cult of personality, it condemned the state of affairs in which one man allegedly understood everything and decided everything on his own' (*Pravda*, February 15 1964).

This refusal was not only a snub to Lysenko, but a change in attitude on Khrushchev's part. Until then he had not hesitated systematically to back the scientist against his foes. It is true that Khrushchev reverted to his earlier attitude in his speech of February 28, by stating his preference for another controversial process of Lysenko's on the use of fertilizers. The struggle was not over and, until the very eve of the October plenary session, Lysenko's backers fought back fiercely.

The anti-Lysenko camp did not yet have the press at its disposal, but it retorted in a secret memorandum circulated during the summer which allegedly contained some perfidious political remarks.[1] Lysenko's

[1] The very pro-Lysenko M. A. Olshansky, then President of the Lenin Agricultural Academy (he lost the post in February 1965), disclosed the existence of the anti-Lysenko text in an article in *Selskaya Zhizn* on August 29 1964.

'Of late, a lengthy memoir written by Zh. A. Medvedev has been circulated. It is full of scurrilous inventions about our biological science. . . . Substituting idle gossip for facts . . . using a condescending, ironical tone, Medvedev destroys the theoretical bases of Michurinian biology. . . . Interpreting arbitrarily, with disregard for historical truth, certain events that occurred during the period of the cult of personality, Medvedev makes monstrous charges according to which scientists of Michurin's school are guilty of repressions inflicted on certain scientific researchers at that time.

'It is clear that this is no longer a farce but a dirty political game. . . . Isn't it time to tell Zh. A. Medvedev and others of his ilk that they must either back up their perfidious accusations with facts or else answer for their slanders before the courts. Of course they cannot back up their accusations with facts, for there are no such facts.'

The same Zh. A. Medvedev had distinguished himself in 1963 by publishing a book close to 'bourgeois concepts' in biology, which brought him under attack, for instance by N. G. Yegorychev, First Secretary of the Moscow Urban Committee (*Moskovskaya Pravda*, June 20 1963). He also published in *Neva* (No 3 1963) another anti-Lysenko article for which Olshansky berated him (*Selskaya Zhizn*, August 18 1963). Probably because Medvedev had overdone it, his name did not appear on the list of biologists 'rehabilitated' after Khrushchev's downfall.

Other indications provided by Olshansky confirm that Medvedev was not alone in his behind-the-scenes fight in the summer of 1964. The well-known physicist and

foes managed to gain some public success. N. P. Dubinin, a biologist whom Khrushchev had identified in 1959 as being 'at the head' of attacks against Lysenko (*Pravda*, July 2 1959) and who was fully rehabilitated after Lysenko's downfall, was allowed to submit his candidacy for membership of the Academy of Science in June 1964 (*Izvestia*, June 8 1964). He was not elected, but among those promoted at the time were some who later, in 1965, distinguished themselves as rabid foes of Lysenko. Among them was B. E. Bykhovsky, the author of the *Pravda* article that rehabilitated Mendel on June 24 1965. Another scientist who dared oppose Khrushchev overtly, P. A. Vlasiuk, a former President of the Academy of Agricultural Science for the Ukraine, who, at Khrushchev's instance, had been dismissed in 1961, again surfaced in May 1964. *Pravda Ukrainy* of May 13 announced his election to the Vice-Presidency of the Society of Knowledge (*Znanie*) of the Republic, and at the same time ran a story about a report he had delivered.

Lysenko's foes went on publishing their work as fast as they could manage. On March 10 1964 *Selskaya Zhizn* expressed astonishment that a book by M. E. Lobashev that 'fully shared the metaphysical views of Mendel and Morgan on problems of genetics' could have been published in Leningrad, not only with the patronage of the University's editorial board, but also with the 'favourable recommendation' of the Ministry of Public Education which was responsible. . . . In short, it was not without reason that the President of the Academy of Science, M. V. Keldysh, reporting on the shaking off of Lysenko's influence, noted in February 1965: 'The situation in biology has *consistently improved in the past few years*' (*Pravda*, February 4 1965. Author's italics). Khrushchev's downfall was the end of a long process, as well as a turning point.

In this uncertainty over the confrontation with the Chinese and the quarrels over agriculture, a downgraded and diminished Khrushchev was being propelled towards the crucial test. His authority, meanwhile, was under increasing dispute and controversy. Wherever one turned, one saw his work more or less insidiously undermined, his projects buried. Here are a few more examples:

1 The 'work passport': someone had hit upon the idea of replacing Soviet citizens' identification papers with a fuller passport containing a

---

member of the Academy, A. D. Sakharov, had 'in a public speech delivered at a meeting of the USSR Academy of Science made an insulting attack, quite remote from science, against the Michurinian scientists, in the style of the libellous letters circulated by Zh. A. Medvedev' (*Selskaya Zhizn*, August 29 1964).

record of any rewards or penalties meted out to the bearer during his working life. This proposal was put forward initially as a so-called 'workers' initiative' in *Izvestia* of February 26 1964 (Moscow edition), then by *Pravda* next day, and was favourably commented upon for three days by all the newspapers. Khrushchev, in his speech of February 28, enthusiastically approved the 'suggestion', with which he was obviously not unfamiliar. That was enough, apparently, to cut the discussion short. After that speech, the matter was never mentioned again.

2 The Lenin Literary prize: Tvardovsky and the *Novy Mir* editorial staff had proposed Solzhenitsyn for the prize on the strength of his study of the forced labour camps, *A Day in the Life of Ivan Denisovich*. After the 1963 storm Khrushchev had had to dissociate himself somewhat from this author whom he had himself probably promoted in 1962, but his prestige was at stake nevertheless. For a while Solzhenitsyn seemed about to receive the prize. The poet Samuil Marshak wrote a warm recommendation in *Pravda* of January 30 1964. But a few weeks later the conservatives had gained the upper hand. Under the guise of 'letters from readers' the same *Pravda* on April 11, the day before the prize committee's vote, ran a full-dress review criticizing *Ivan Denisovich*. The prize went to an obscure Ukrainian writer.

3 The school reform: one of the first grand designs of the reign, in 1958, was to start large-scale 'training in production', in other words, introduce manual work into the secondary and higher schools. This was to be offset by an extension of schooling, and in particular by extending secondary schooling from ten to eleven years. From the start, the reform had caused grumbling within the intelligentsia. But it was only in 1964 that the plan began to be attacked overtly. On May 21 a decree cut the duration of schooling in higher learning institutions and in the specialized secondary schools by six to eighteen months through a corresponding reduction of 'training in production'. The motive given was that the teaching was 'not necessary' since the students had already received it in the middle schools (*Vestnik Vysshey Shkoly* [Higher Schooling Bulletin], No 6 1964). In fact, the turn of the middle schools came on August 10 when a new decree, for the same reasons, shortened the period from eleven to ten years. This naturally did not mean the official rejection of training in production, which was merely supposed to be imparted 'more effectively and within a shorter time' (*Uchitelskaya Gazeta* [Teachers' Newspaper], August 13, 1964). But it did mean cutting manual work instruction by seven hundred hours over the last three years of school (*Uchitelskaya Gazeta*, August 20 1964). Hence, even before Khrushchev was overthrown, not much remained of his achievements in this area.

4 A last humiliation: since 1958 it had become customary to publish a

collection of Khrushchev's foreign policy speeches – one volume, then two, each year as his eloquence grew. The speeches delivered in 1964 are lacking – understandably so – but also those of 1963, since the whole of 1964 went by without the State publishing houses having deemed it fit to fill the gap or to explain the break with tradition. A collection of his speeches on 'communist education' was, however, brought out, as well as volume 8 of his *Agricultural Speeches*.

A GLORIOUS INTERLUDE – THE SEVENTIETH BIRTHDAY

Under these conditions, the ceremonies that marked Khrushchev's seventieth birthday, on April 17, 1964, were only an interlude whose significance should not be overestimated. This was the last great show of unity around the person of the First Secretary and, at the time, it certainly did create an illusion. Looking back, it appears rather ludicrous, and its only interest is to emphasize the very limited importance that attaches to rituals of that kind.

The quarrel with China, which had just flared up again with the publication of the Suslov report on April 3, meant that the brilliance of the ceremony was enhanced. The international aspect of the event was duly emphasized: Gomulka, Ulbricht, Kádár, Zhivkov, Tsedenbal and Novotný were summoned (only the Rumanian leader Gheorghiu-Dej, whose quarrel with Khrushchev was especially serious at the time, had picked that date to call his Central Committee into plenary session; at the last minute he sent his Prime Minister, Maurer). All the guests brought along their country's highest decoration as a present. The Soviets were not to be outdone, and Khrushchev was awarded a new 'Hero of the Soviet Union' medal. A large banquet was given in the Kremlin, at which over twenty speakers drank to his health. An 'exhibition for N. S. Khrushchev's seventieth birthday' was held in Kalinovka, his native village (but not in Moscow). The account of the ceremonies took up seven out of the eight pages of *Pravda* of April 18, and the magazine *Ogonyok* carried seven colour photographs of the event. But no film or major book was brought out for the occasion.[1] There was no comparison with Stalin's seventieth birthday celebration in 1949, and care was taken not to prolong the festivities unduly. Whereas telegrams congratulating Stalin had appeared in *Pravda*'s columns for months on

---

[1] A thirty-minute television documentary did appear, entitled *The Leninist Path*. It stressed the liberal character of Khrushchev's policy, by showing the demolition of the Taganskaya prison in Moscow.

end, after Khrushchev's birthday life returned to normal within a few days.

The 'cult' did, however, make some progress: Khrushchev's military role, not only in World War II but in the Civil War, was particularly stressed. The collective message signed by all the members of the Presidium declared:

> '*During the Civil War*, while performing political work within the Red Army, *you fought with weapons in hand* against the interventionists and the counter-revolutionaries of the White Guard. . . .
>
> 'During the grim years of the Great Patriotic War, you and other personalities of our Party *led directly on the battlefield* the self-sacrificing struggle of the Red Army against the Nazi aggressor. As a member of the military Soviets on a number of active fronts, *you took the most direct part in planning and carrying out vital military operations*, the historic battles of Volgograd, Kursk, Oryol and others. . . .' (*Pravda*, April 17 1964. Author's italics.)

Khrushchev's participation in the Civil War 'with weapons in hand' was a new and mysterious fact to the historians. *Izvestia* of April 17 (Moscow edition) helped by publishing 'a rare photograph' on which Khrushchev was shown surrounded by the political commissars of the Ninth Kuban Army in 1920. Additional details on the period were provided, evidently in order to fill a gap in the distinguished man's biography.

Malinovsky, who joined in as the military spokesman, was more guarded. In his version, Khrushchev had 'taken an active part' in the Civil War, particularly by 'inspiring the Red soldiers through words and personal example.' As to his role in World War II, it was mentioned without any of the above details. For security, Malinovsky gave a long list of other 'eminent personalities of the Party and State' who, like Khrushchev, had served at the front. It included Voroshilov, Zhdanov, Brezhnev and Suslov.[1]

In his tribute, A. V. Sofronov, the editor-in-chief of *Ogonyok*, daringly contrasted the Molotov–Kaganovich–Malenkov group which 'bore, together with Stalin, the responsibility for all the illegal acts perpetrated by the bloodthirsty Beria and his henchmen', and Khrushchev, who on the contrary 'during the period of the cult of Stalin did everything he could, in Moscow and in the Ukraine, to preserve the lives and honour of several thousand persons' (*Ogonyok*, April 12 1964). The cult reached its peak with Galina Serebryakova, Karl Marx's biographer, who had

---

[1] Malinovsky's remarks on the occasion of Khrushchev's seventieth birthday appeared in *Krasnaya Zvezda* of April 17 1964. The passage quoted here is not included in the summarized version of the article published by *Pravda* the same day.

drawn attention to herself in December 1962 by attacking Ehrenburg.[1] Apart from these two authors, the writers' participation in the festivities was minimal. In fact, this was the only organized group that refrained from visiting Khrushchev's house to pay him tribute on the morning of April 17. Moreover, no writer or artist spoke at the official banquet.

The rest of the praise did not go beyond the bounds of ordinary ritual. The collective message from the members of the Presidium and the Secretariat was bombastic enough but, except for the mention of the hero's military achievements, it merely reproduced the most often heard phrases of the past years (close contact with the people, inexhaustible energy, 'profound insight into vital processes' and so on). Several leaders added their personal touch; for instance, A. P. Kirilenko, P. E. Shelest, K. T. Mazurov, A. Ya. Pelshe, and also L. I. Brezhnev and A. I. Mikoyan. Brezhnev, the future First Secretary of the Party who, in his capacity as Head of State, awarded Khrushchev his new 'Hero' medal, was definitely more reserved than he had been in his speech at the Twenty-second Congress. He spoke much more briefly and merely praised 'the heroic life of the communist fighter' who, during the Civil War as well as during the period of the building of socialism and the hard war years, had 'always been in the front line, where the fight for the cause of the Party and of the people was raging most fiercely'. Mikoyan, who had the honour of reading the leaders' collective message, injected this touch of humour – sick humour as it now turns out:

'We are celebrating today the jubilee of a middle-aged man who is, as you see for yourselves, at the peak of his strength and capabilities. . . . We feel, dear friend, that you are only half-way through your life, (*Pravda*, April 18 1964). He went so far as to add: 'Each one of us'

---

[1] The following extract from Galina Serebryakova's remarks on the occasion of Khrushchev's seventieth birthday is worth quoting:

'On reading everything that comrade Khrushchev has said and written concerning his manifold activities, I recognized him as one of the truly superior men of our time. . . . How inexhaustible is the energy of Nikita Sergeyevich Khrushchev! Where has he not been in these past ten years! With chemists he is a chemist, with agronomists he is an agronomist, with power industry experts he is a power industry expert. The earth and the universe occupy his attention at all times. . . . The whole world knows and honours him. It is difficult to imagine a simpler, more approachable, more cheerful man, or one more precise in his language. Nikita Sergeyevich's polemical talent – which shows not only in his speeches but in his remarks and repartees, the swiftness and ingenuity of his answers – is justly appreciated everywhere. Who can forget his devastating verbal assaults in the forum of the United Nations? Khrushchev is one of the most original and outstanding orators of our times. He combines an enormous force of conviction with profound theoretical analysis; clear imagery, precise examples, resounding humour – all are his. To us Soviet people, one and all, he is infinitely dear. When we see him off on a long trip we impatiently count the days till he returns.

'Contact with Nikita Sergeyevich elevates the mind, impels one towards action, towards good . . .', etc. (*Literaturnaya Rossiya*, April 17 1964).

members of the Presidium of the Central Committee, alternates of the Presidium and Secretaries of the Central Committee, harbours equally warm fraternal feelings toward comrade Nikita Sergeyevich Khrushchev. . . .'

The First Secretary's mistake was probably in taking these congratulations at face value. His reply to Brezhnev in front of the television cameras was obviously extemporaneous and betrayed the somewhat smug contentment of the sovereign who believes in the sincerity of his eulogizers. He declared himself, without qualifications, 'pleased with his life and destiny', and glad to have climbed 'step by step' the rungs of the hierarchy before rising to his post 'at the highest possible level.' Of course, it was out of the question for him to retire: the age he had reached was 'not so terrible' and anyway 'he had little need of doctors' services'. Then, thinking perhaps of his political enemies, he added unexpectedly: 'For some statesmen, political death may come before physical death. This is why, if a statesman wishes to live long, he must work with the collective for the good of the people, for the good of the Party' (*Pravda*, April 18 1964 and *Le Monde*, April 19–20 1964).

Finally, since the 'grand designs' of Khrushchev's reign always came back to the surface at moments of sincerity, he again recalled destalinization, and, embroidering on the theme, declared that it caused him many worries. The consequences of the cult had been overcome, he said, 'despite an enormous force of inertia'. He had achieved this 'without surgery and with therapeutic means only'. Was he expressing satisfaction or a touch of regret? Knowing the resistance he had encountered in almost all sectors, it was becoming increasingly obvious that 'surgery' was needed if the task he had set himself was to be fulfilled.

That was Khrushchev's last big manifestation. He might have stood firm at that point, learned from his failures, organized coexistence with his associates on a stabler footing, allowed the substance of power to fall into their hands little by little, retaining for himself only its trappings – for which he also cared, as the April 17 ceremonies showed. Very probably the 'Khrushchev problem' could have been settled that way, and the First Secretary could have gone into honourable retirement. Perhaps, if he had learned a little more restraint, he might even have been allowed to continue in his capacity of roving ambassador, to which the outside world had become so well accustomed. Had he been willing, a dignified solution might have been found with Khrushchev as Head of the Government or, better still, as Head of State.

But Khrushchev wanted everything at once. He wanted to enjoy the frills of power and travel abroad; remain the undisputed master at home, pull all the strings both in the Party and in the State; promote his grand designs, shape and reshape according to his whims one of the most conservative administrative structures in the world. In fact, he travelled more than ever, and this is the main reason for what happened to him. In May he stayed in the Crimea with Ben Bella, then went on a lengthy tour of the United Arab Republic from May 6 to 25; in June he received Tito at Leningrad, then went on a three weeks' pleasant if pointless cruise to Scandinavia; in July he was in Poland, and this was followed by an extended agricultural tour in August topped by nine days in Czechoslovakia, from August 27 to September 5. And to stretch it out, Khrushchev travelled by ship and train rather than by plane. Altogether, not counting week-ends, he was away for about 135 days in the first eight months of 1964, more than half the period.

BREZHNEV BECOMES HEIR PRESUMPTIVE

Only on one point was Khrushchev forced to accept the consequences of his restless mode of life: the arrangement worked out in June 1963 whereby the 'succession' in the Party Secretariat was to be assumed by the Brezhnev–Podgorny team turned out to be short of perfection, since it required the First Secretary to function as arbiter and he was unable to do so on a regular basis. The general staff of the apparatus under the Central Committee demanded a master, and this role naturally fell to Brezhnev, who had greater seniority within the top hierarchy. True, he was not as compliant as Podgorny in his support of Khrushchev, but the First Secretary obviously did not suspect any threat from him.[1] On July 15 1964, on a proposal by Khrushchev, ratified by the Supreme Soviet, A. I. Mikoyan replaced Brezhnev as Chief of State. Unlike Khrushchev himself, Mikoyan was wise enough to accept this disguised demotion and possibly thought that the time had come to withdraw to some extent from real responsibilities.[2]

---

[1] When, on October 31 1963, Khrushchev was host to Guy Mollet, he understood a question of the latter's about the new generation as referring to his own successors, and without embarrassment discussed the men who, as it turned out, supplanted him a year later. Describing them all as 'professional revolutionaries', he listed first Brezhnev, whom he warmly praised, then Kosygin, whom he commended for his competence in economic problems, and lastly Podgorny. During the same conversation, as we know, he was much more off-hand concerning Kozlov.

[2] Mikoyan was not replaced as First Deputy Prime Minister, and the paradoxical situation continued whereby men of different rank held similar posts: Kosygin, who was a member of the Party Presidium, and D. F. Ustinov, who was not. The most likely candidate to succeed Mikoyan was D. S. Polyansky, who was already a member of the Presidium, but merely Deputy Prime Minister. But it took Polyansky more than a year to have his situation regularized.

Was Brezhnev, now invited to 'concentrate on his activities as Secretary of the Central Committee', already contemplating the 'October coup'? One cannot be sure, of course, but it does not seem likely. He had now become the First Secretary's natural heir at the head of the Party, but it was bound to be some time before he could consolidate his new position and manifest a desire for power. Moreover, at the time, it was still quite conceivable that the succession would take place naturally. At the same time men like Suslov, who meant to rush matters whenever they could, must have been pleased with the way in which the stage was now set, with one candidate remaining for each of the two major offices – Brezhnev for the Party and Kosygin for the Government. The temporary abatement of rivalries within the collective leadership would make the crucial confrontation much more straighforward.

This writer left Moscow in September 1964 with a few fleeting impressions and glimpses of the picture. They were not enough to permit definite conclusions, but gave food for thought: Suslov nervously drumming on his desk during an extemporaneous speech by the First Secretary; Suslov and Kosygin, alone among Khrushchev's hearers, failing to applaud a crude joke of his; Malinovsky greeting the First Secretary on his return from a trip without bothering to take his hands out of his pockets; Brezhnev greeted with an ovation lasting for several minutes when he appeared at a rally held in the chief's absence; a whispered remark in a conversation: 'Khrushchev is off somewhere again; in the meantime everybody does what he likes. There is no leadership any more.' Such whispers, indeed, were frequent enough to suggest that they were being encouraged from above. But this kind of thing, after all, had happened before. And by and large, the façade was so smooth. How could anyone believe that the inside of the house had fallen into such disrepair?

2 The Last Straw

The story up to this point shows that Khrushchev's authority was being consistently whittled down, but not that his fall was imminent. It was one thing quietly to sabotage the carrying out of his decisions, and quite another to start compassing his overthrow. Even if a man like Suslov had determined on his course long before, some specific event had to occur in order to bring him into the open and prompt him to take the initiative with all its risks. Some people might call the specific event 'the last straw', others simply a favourable opportunity. But what was this event?

Following the shock in the West caused by his eviction from office, observers feverishly scrutinized the recent past in the hope of finding the reasons for such an unexpected ending. Many of them, applying their own familiar parliamentary procedures to the Soviet system, interpreted the event to mean that Khrushchev had fallen 'over' some specific issue, on account of his agricultural and economic failures, and so on. Although the various hypotheses formulated in this way constitute the background rather than the causes, they should be briefly reviewed.

At first a widely held view was that the leader had to be overthrown in order to save the counter-offensive against the Chinese from running into disaster. On July 30 1964 Moscow had decided to call a meeting of the twenty-six major Communist Parties for December 15, 1964, in order to prepare the way for another communist world council. This brought not only vehement protests from the Chinese, but also some quasi-official expressions of concern from a number of normally pro-Soviet Parties. Obviously, a major failure was looming and for a while the collective leadership seemed to have chosen to get rid of Khrushchev as a way out of their embarrassment. The trouble with this explanation was that the new leaders soon showed they had not the slightest intention of cancelling the conference. They postponed it because of some last-minute difficulties, but it was held in March 1965. Altogether, the Chinese issue cannot be called the cause of the fall. Subsequent events showed that Suslov and his colleagues were telling the truth when they assured the French Communist Party delegation which arrived in Moscow after the coup that nothing would be changed in that domain, except for the few 'exaggerations' in Khrushchev's language.[1] At the

[1] Georges Marchais, who headed the French communist delegation to Moscow after

most, the fall provided the opportunity for a reassessment of relations with Peking and for a new suspension in the polemic.

Since the problems of the communist world were especially acute in the autumn of 1964, the memoir prepared by Togliatti, just before his death in the Crimea at the end of August, for discussion with Khrushchev was also scrutinized. This major document, known as Togliatti's 'Testament', painted a gloomy picture of the situation within the communist world and contained several critical remarks about the Soviet political system. Naturally enough, the Soviets tried to prevent its publication (Brezhnev worked unsuccessfully at this during his stay in Rome for Togliatti's funeral); but it is hard to understand why, once the harm had been done, *Pravda* chose to aggravate it by publishing the text in full on September 10. Explanations differ, but one of them has it that the instigator was Suslov, who – it was suggested – as a good disciple of Machiavelli, wished to draw the attention of Party officials to the sorry state of family affairs. However that may be, this episode too is only part of the background, not the cause we are seeking to discover.

THE *RAPPROCHEMENT* WITH BONN

The disagreement over German policy was more serious. Khrushchev had been host to Ulbricht in Moscow from May 29 to June 13, treated him with the usual honours and signed a new friendship treaty with him on June 12. Conceivably, the gesture was meant to distract attention from the diplomatic move under way in the opposite direction. About the same time, Adzhubey notified the editors of three West German

---

the coup, gave the following report to the Central Committee of the French Communist Party on his talks with the new Soviet rulers regarding their relations with China:

'In this field [problems of unity of the communist movement], comrade Khrushchev's shortcomings took the form of certain extravagances that did not, however, impair application of the correct line. Our comrades told us that "all the documents made public and the letters sent on various occasions to the fraternal Parties retain their full force, without alteration. All of them were approved at every stage by the Presidium.". . . The proposals for a new international conference, which include the meeting of the preparatory committee of the twenty-six Parties set for December 15, remain in force.

'Rejecting insinuations that the Communist Party of the Soviet Union was seeking an ideological compromise with the leaders of the Chinese Communist Party, the Soviet rulers said they were examining signs of new opportunities for discussion aimed at overcoming differences. When we were in Moscow, the presence of a Chinese delegation at the November 7 celebrations already appeared possible' (*L'Humanité*, November 9 1964).

newspapers that he was ready to take up a long-standing invitation to visit their country. The visit of Khrushchev's son-in-law and two other journalists, N. E. Polyanov and V. V. Lednev, which lasted from July 18 to August 2, provoked wide comment at home and abroad. At the beginning of August the travellers wrote three long articles for *Izvestia* that were definitely more moderate than usual about the German Federal Republic and its policy; in the West certain rash statements by Adzhubey (in particular that Ulbricht was suffering from cancer and did not have long to live) created a stir. After the palace revolution in October they were even more widely discussed, and on this point Soviet criticism falls into two categories:

1 In the first place, Khrushchev was blamed for having entrusted his son-in-law with a diplomatic mission, in violation of normal procedure. This was intimated to the French Communist Party delegation at the end of October. ('By-passing elected officials, he entrusted increasingly important missions to members of his personal entourage,' as Georges Marchais reported in *L'Humanité* on November 9 1964.) Gromyko, who no doubt saw things from the point of view of his own job, said bluntly to one of his visitors at the time: 'Why was Khrushchev over-thrown? Because he sent Adzhubey to Bonn, of course.' It is clear that Adzhubey's combined political and pleasure tours, coupled with his personality and the privileges he enjoyed, had been grating on the nerves of high officials for a long time. They must have had a good many other grievances against him as well. In March 1963, in the midst of the political turmoil that followed the Cuban crisis, Adzhubey was entrusted with the important task of paying a visit to the Pope. But, assuming what is not proven – that Khrushchev was blamed for his son-in-law's trip before he was overthrown – this would tend to show mainly that everything was grist to the opposition's mill. It was only one factor among several.

2 Khrushchev was taken to task more sharply over the substance of the issue. No one will ever know exactly what he had in mind as regards West Germany in the summer of 1964, but it is clear that, using the prospect of a marked expansion of commercial relations, he planned to visit Bonn a few months later (Adzhubey spoke of this to Chancellor Erhard) in the hope of achieving a *rapprochement* with the much-vilified exponents of 'militarist revanchism'. No matter how carefully he moved in that direction, he was bound to come up against a hallowed tenet of Soviet foreign policy, a stronghold even more impregnable than that of heavy industry in the economic field. (Khrushchev himself had ascribed the very same 'crime' to his own enemies when he charged Malenkov and Beriya with wanting to sell out the 'German Democratic Republic' after Stalin's death.) To the vigilant watchdogs of the country's

political and military security this was tantamount to treason. Besides, Khrushchev was offending one of the Soviet Union's chief allies – the most dependent, but also the most demanding because most exposed, namely, Ulbricht. This was illustrated at the beginning of October, when Willi Stoph, the East German Prime Minister, ended a stay in the USSR without visiting Khrushchev at Gagra. The statements made during his visit by various members of the collective leadership plainly indicate the extent of the disquiet.

Resistance to Khrushchev's new German policy assumed various forms. Evidently in order to improve the atmosphere for the *rapprochement* with Bonn, a decree dated August 29 1964 had rehabilitated the national group of 'Volga Germans', deported by Stalin in 1941 as pro-Hitler sympathizers. The decree did not reinstate their 'Autonomous Republic', which had been liquidated at the same time, but it requested local authorities to improve their living conditions in their new settlements. The decree was not rescinded after Khrushchev's fall, but neither was it given publicity until January 1965, when it could no longer have any effect on the diplomatic scene (*Le Monde*, January 7 1965). On the other hand, what was publicized and was bound to have adverse diplomatic effects was the incident of September 6 1964 in which the West German diplomat Schwirkmann was injected with a toxic gas by an unidentified assailant while attending a service at the Zagorsk monastery near Moscow. The details were naturally not released, but Moscow's apologies to the West Germans, just before Khrushchev's downfall, were unusually profuse: 'Those who indulge in such actions are trying to undermine the good relations between our two countries'. (It is true that this was not published in Moscow, but only in the German press.)

Suspicion for the incident naturally fell on the KGB – Semichastny's secret police in charge of watching foreigners. Again, on September 28, the police were involved in the 'Khabarovsk incident', when fifteen agents in civilian clothes burst at midnight into the hotel room where three American military attachés and one of their British colleagues were asleep. Their baggage was searched and their notes on their journey confiscated in their presence. On October 6 Moscow rejected the protests of the respective Governments. Whatever the hidden motives may have been, the incidents clearly impaired international relations, and this without the blessing of the political authorities, least of all Khrushchev. Obviously, as during earlier political crises, e.g. that of 1963, the KGB was making itself felt. The spectacular tribute rendered that summer to Richard Sorge, the greatest war-time Soviet spy, provided the police with an additional opportunity – one it had probably itself created – to enhance its prestige.

There was also the episode of the 'dread weapon'. On September 15 Khrushchev declared to a delegation of Japanese parliamentarians, according to their subsequent report: 'Yesterday I was shown a terrible destructive device. I have never seen anything like it. It is a means of destroying and annihilating mankind. It is the most powerful, the strongest device in existence. It has unlimited power.' Two days later, however, speaking at a reception at the Indian Embassy, he ate his words: 'I did not speak of a weapon having unlimited power.' Later, on September 19, Tass published another official version which referred only to 'new types of weapons'. These two corrections, especially the second, point to a minor rumpus among the leaders. This was strange, since even if Khrushchev had made an unauthorized boast, he had not said anything which could harm the national interest. It was not the first or the last time that a Soviet leader bragged about his country's armaments – even those it did not have as yet. What the incident showed was that any pretext was being used to get the First Secretary into trouble.

CLASH WITH THE PLANNERS

The last and most serious warning of the crisis was connected with the planners' meeting held on an unknown date in September. On October 2 1964 *Pravda* and the other newspapers announced that the Party Presidium had 'a few days before' held an enlarged meeting attended by all the Party and State officials in charge of the economy. They had heard a report from A. A. Goregliad, First Vice-President of Gosplan (oddly enough, the President, P. F. Lomako, did not attend). Nothing more was divulged, except that the agencies concerned had 'started drawing up the national economic development plan'. On the other hand, an extensive summary was given of Khrushchev's speech, even if it was not reprinted in full. A few weeks later it was officially reported that it had caused something of a storm. 'Quite recently,' Georges Marchais reported, 'comrade Khrushchev unexpectedly delivered a speech on economic problems, without any previous consultation' (*L'Humanité*, November 9 1964). Although no such drastic judgment was warranted at the time of the speech, it was obvious even then that trouble was afoot:

1 The old debate over priorities was still unresolved. Khrushchev was still sniping at heavy industry, but did not dare attack it outright. On the one hand he declared:

'Although, during the first five-year plans and in the post-war years, we emphasized the development of heavy industry as the basis for the expansion of the country's economy and for the strengthening of its defence capability, at present, when we have a powerful industry, when the country's defence has reached the required level, the Party has as its task a more rapid development of the branches of industry that produce consumer goods' (*Pravda*, October 2 1964).

But at the same time a number of ambiguous statements restricted the scope of the commitment. For instance: 'We must, in drawing up the plan, provide for increased development of consumer goods production. . . . Naturally, we must at the same time take care to maintain the country's defence at the required level.' And again: 'To continue increasing the country's defence potential in order to consolidate peace in the whole world – that is our constant concern' (*Pravda*, October 2 1964).

In short, either the text of the speech had been reviewed and amended and all these qualifications reflected the collective leadership's reservations, or else this was the way Khrushchev himself had worded it, which meant that he was still obliged to beat about the bush.

2 A new disagreement emerged regarding the duration of the next development plan. The seven-year plan adopted in 1959 was to end in 1965 and it was time to decide what to do next. At the beginning of 1963 the resumption of five-year plans had been announced.[1] Either Khrushchev had not succeeded in making his views prevail at the time, or else he had changed his mind since, as he was now asking for a longer-term plan:

'N. S. Khrushchev indicated that, in view of the present scale of the country's economy, it is quite feasible to plan economic development *over a longer period*. . . . The measures taken in the past few years to improve planning and to start scheduling both long-range plans and current plans *over a longer period – seven years* and two years respectively – are fully justified. After the fulfilment of the current Seven-Year Plan, there remains *a fifteen-year period* during which, as provided in the Party programme, the material and technical basis of communism has to be created. It is reasonable to draw up the new long-range development plan *for a longer period'* (*Pravda*, October 2 1964. Author's italics).

Longer than what? This was not specified, and the previous decision to plan for five years was 'overlooked'. It seemed, from the above

[1] A decree on planning dated January 11 1963 stated: 'It has been decided that the national economic development plans shall be drawn up for five years' (*Spravochnik Partiynovo Rabotnika*, 5th edition, 1964, p 77).

quotation, that Khrushchev was considering a fifteen-year plan, but that was not quite clear either. Perhaps seven, perhaps fifteen, anyway 'longer' than something he did not specify. Once again, either Khrushchev was not spelling out what he meant, or else, and this is the most likely alternative, since the speech was 'unexpected', he had given a figure that *Pravda* took care not to divulge. Moreover, on closer inspection, it was obvious that a disagreement had arisen. This is how the communiqué ended:

'The Presidium of the Central Committee of the CPSU and the Council of Ministers of the USSR have instructed the USSR Gosplan to make the necessary calculations and report . . . its proposals regarding the most optimal [*sic*] period for the new long-range plan and the main lines of the economic development of the USSR' (*Pravda*, October 2 1964).

Nowhere was it stated that this 'most optimal period' was to be longer than initially planned – the point Khrushchev had gone to such lengths to maintain. After his speech, it would also have been logical to add that the 'main lines of development' would be laid down in accordance with the directives just described by the First Secretary. But this was not done either. The Presidium merely advocated continuing the survey without committing itself on its substance. In any event the five-year plan (1966–1970) was reinstated as soon as Khrushchev fell.

The only valid explanation is that Khrushchev rejected Gosplan's drafts because of disagreement, not only over the duration of the next plan, but probably over a series of other problems as well – basic orientation, priorities and so on. One of the counts on which he was rebuked immediately after his downfall, namely, his 'reluctance to take into account all that science and practical experiment have already achieved' (*Pravda*, October 17 1964), apparently related to this particular incident. The question whether to publish his speech must also have caused a clash. Khrushchev won only a partial victory on that point, since it was not published immediately or in full. Parts of it were deleted and it had probably been edited besides.

Was this episode the 'last straw'? Our review of the situation leading to his overthrow might conclude, at this point, that with such opposition, such problems and mistakes on Khrushchev's part, he could not fail to be removed from power. In a parliamentary system, all this would indeed have been more than enough to provoke a governmental crisis, and no other explanation would have been necessary; but in the Soviet system and in this particular case, it is not so. Nevertheless, all the episodes mentioned above are essential to an understanding of the facts. Their meaning can be summarized in two main points:

1 They show that Khrushchev was perilously isolated. After having aroused the hostility of the 'steel-eaters' and the military by promoting the large-scale production of consumer goods and of the agronomists and biologists by his fondness for *shablon*, he had outraged the diplomats with his idiosyncratic German policy and the planners with his outburst over the long-range plan. Even for a man in a stronger position, all this would have meant courting danger.

2 These episodes also show that the opposition had stiffened. The First Secretary's controversial moves (for example, regarding Germany and the economy) were being overtly countered. His opponents were even using innocuous incidents, such as the statement about the 'ultimate weapon', to get him into trouble. Clearly, the plot against him was taking shape.

THE REAL DANGER LOOMS:
THE NOVEMBER PLENUM

Something more was needed, however, for the plot to crystallize. In the Soviet system in its present form, and even more so as it existed before October 14 1964, the sudden overthrow of the leader is no routine procedure, to say the least. It had never succeeded in the past. It required conspiratorial, highly dangerous methods. The precedent of 1957 indicated that the price of failure was, at the lowest, 'political death'. Despite all precautions, there could never be a guarantee of success. Khrushchev was in a much weakened position, but he still held many of the strings and was sure to pull them if plans went wrong. To use the 1957 phraseology, the shattering condemnation of a new 'anti-party group' consisting, let us say, of 'Suslov, Kosygin, Brezhnev, and Mikoyan who joined them', was a serious possibility throughout the crisis.

It is hard to imagine a man of Suslov's cautiousness venturing on an enterprise of that kind without some pressing motive and, specifically, a sense of present danger to justify the risks involved. But, in the situation so far described, no danger loomed either for Suslov or for any other members of the collective leadership. Whether the issues concerned Germany, agriculture or planning, Khrushchev's moves needed to be stopped perhaps, as they had often been in the past, but they did not call for open warfare. Even assuming that Suslov regarded the current isolation of the First Secretary as a favourable opportunity to carry out a long-cherished plan, how could he have persuaded his colleagues in the collective leadership to go along? The case for action was definitely too weak to offset the risks.

Our difficulty arises from the fact that we know only the events that preceded the downfall, and not – for obvious reasons – what would have happened if it had not occurred. In other words, the missing link – which is at least as important as all the rest put together – is the sum of the victim's intentions at the moment of his downfall. However, a few facts make it possible to form some idea of this, and they bring out the hitherto unexplained foreboding of danger.

When he was overthrown, Khrushchev was preparing a new plenary session for November 1964, which was supposed to deal with agriculture. He had announced it himself at the start of his agricultural tour at Saratov on August 4, adding that one of the topics to be discussed was the old problem of 'vacant' versus 'occupied' fallow lands (*Pravda*, August 5 1964). This sounds innocuous enough, but it is possible that he said more than *Pravda* reported: for we know that the revelations made that day aroused objections in high quarters (anyway, it was not proper to disclose the date of a plenary session before the special communiqué on the subject, although Khrushchev had already done this when he announced his plenary session on chemistry the year before). This opposition, in turn, toughened Khrushchev's attitude. A few days afterwards, in Northern Ossetia, he declared:

> 'Certain comrades have said to me: perhaps all this material should not be published, and the problems to be discussed in the report to the Central Committee plenary session should not be disclosed beforehand' (*Pravda*, August 10 1964).

He replied to this argument that secrecy about the convening of plenary sessions and the content of the speeches to be delivered was no longer necessary, while publicity was in line with Leninist tradition and so on. He slighted the collective leadership even more by saying:

> 'If we do not speak about it now, we shall waste a lot of time. For people will say: it is good that an important decision has been taken, but it would have been better to talk about it earlier, so that we might have begun to take action this year. . . . This is why I am telling you of it beforehand. . . . Perhaps you will have time to do something before the plenary session (*Pravda*, August 10 1964).

In other words, he was inviting his listeners to carry out his decisions before they had been ratified by the Central Committee or, in all probability, by the Presidium itself. Incidentally, in the same speech he alluded to a memorandum he had addressed to the Presidium on the same problems, and appeared to be displeased at learning that his audience had not known of it. He said: 'The Central Committee distributed it to the Party organizations and the Soviets, and to the agricultural production agencies.' This implied that the memorandum, like other writings of the same nature, had been addressed to the Presidium only for protocol's sake, and that in this particular case its distribution had gone awry. 'But now,' he went on, 'I shall explain to you my ideas on certain questions' (*Pravda*, August 10 1964).

And what were these ideas? Khrushchev gave additional details only on one point:

'Clearly, within each republic, directorates will have to be set up for the production of cereal, sugar beet, cotton, cattle, pigs, poultry and so forth. Scientific institutions, as well as seed and insemination centres, should be concentrated within these directorates. This will make it possible to produce each commodity on a scientific basis, on the basis of modern technological achievements' (*Pravda*, August 10, 1964).

The plan was mentioned several times subsequently, for example in an editorial in the weekly *Ekonomicheskaya Gazeta* dated October 3, where it was presented as one of the points on the agenda of the forthcoming plenary session. It fitted in with an older idea of Khrushchev's – the setting up of giant units for the processing of animal products. On one point at least, the stage of execution was reached: on September 5 *Pravda* announced the creation of a 'federated republican administration' (i.e. having its centre in Moscow and branches in each republic) for the industrial production of poultry.

Outwardly, this was a technical issue, but by its context and spirit it also took on major political importance.

In the first place, it was an example of *shablon*, for which Khrushchev had fought so stubbornly in the spring of 1964. It meant that at least where livestock was concerned, the kolkhozes were going to lose what little autonomy they had retained. Agriculture was increasingly becoming a matter for the State to deal with, at ministerial level and even higher.

Secondly, it heralded another administrative shake-up of even greater scope than that mentioned in August by *Pravda*. The picture resembled that of 1962. At that time, at the March plenary session Khrushchev had first launched a campaign for planning and agricultural centralization, then had muddled along with an initial, half-baked project (territorial agricultural administrations and the call for regional First Secretaries to take personal charge of agriculture), before he finally hit upon his miracle formula during the summer. This was the crowning of his ideas, the radical division of the Party apparatus, which was ratified in November. Two years later the First Secretary was in a similar mood: in the spring, spurred on by the failure of the 1963 harvest, he again advocated a crash programme for centralized planning, but encountered greater difficulties. Again, he stopped midway by setting up Podgorny's 'Livestock Commission'. The summer gave him the opportunity to round off his plans. As in 1962, he chose to divulge them first to kolkhoz audiences, by means of widely circulated memoranda and premature revelations. Clearly, all this was leading to a large-scale reorganization as in 1962. And the 'November plenary session' of 1964 was supposed to top it all.

The only difference was that this time the reshuffle was going to be at a higher level. There was logic in this: since direct assumption of responsibility for agriculture by the Party regional apparatus did not bring the expected results, and since Khrushchev had chosen to solve the problems through increased central planning, the only thing left for him to do was to bring the major central hierarchy into play. A top Party figure with authority and experience, endowed with full powers, must and would succeed where an Oblast Committee Secretary had failed. At least this was so according to Khrushchev's 'Leninist' logic in accordance with which 'the cadres decide everything.'

There is hardly any doubt that, in addition to the various ministers whom he meant to appoint to deal with technical problems, Khrushchev firmly intended to assign Presidium members to handle these matters. The Podgorny Commission set up in April gives an inkling of his designs: as mentioned, besides Podgorny it included five full members of the Presidium (half of its membership), some of whom had only a very distant connection with the breeding of pigs and chickens. Conceivably D. S. Polyansky, the Deputy Chairman of the Council in charge of Agriculture, and G. I. Voronov, the former Orenburg agricultural 'expert' who had become Head of Government of the RSFSR, might have been suited to the task, but how about Kosygin, Mikoyan and Brezhnev? These men must have found it rather humiliating, not only to be nominally supervised by one of their peers, an unheard-of situation, but to deal with matters so remote from major political issues.[1] If this

---

[1] According to *Pravda* of April 24 1964 the other members of the Livestock Commission set up by Khrushchev and headed by Podgorny were: L. N. Yefremov, First Deputy Chairman of the RSFSR Bureau in charge of Agriculture; V. I. Polyakov, Agricultural Secretary of the Central Committee; P. F. Lomako, President of Gosplan; V. E. Dymshits, Chairman of the USSR sovnarkhoz; I. L. Novikov, Chairman of the State Committee for Building, Deputy Chairman of the USSR Council of Ministers; I. P. Volovchenko, Minister of Agriculture; A. A. Yezhevsky, Chairman of the Agricultural Material Distribution Centre; N. P. Gusev, Vice-

went on, even the austere Suslov might one day find himself in charge of sheep-breeding.

The Podgorny Commission was short-lived, but in all likelihood the radical solutions which Khrushchev was contemplating for November would lead in the same direction. All the rumours after he was overthrown agree as to this, although details were forthcoming only on one point. It was widely reported that Khrushchev wanted to promote his son-in-law Adzhubey to the post of Party Secretary in charge of agriculture or of something else. As to his other plans, the following confidence from a reliable Moscow source is indicative enough:

'You will see, the November plenary session is going to be very interesting. There will be many changes at the top. Almost all the leaders *except Khrushchev* will be affected.'

Assuming the prediction was justified, it is easier for us to understand why it was just the opposite that occurred. Using agriculture as a pretext, and for the sake of strengthening central control over that sector, Khrushchev was preparing to divest the members of the collective leadership of true responsibilities. Using a different device, but a far more radical one than in 1962, he was about to endanger the equilibrium maintained with such difficulty for four years. This, in the present writer's opinion, was the last straw, the danger that drove Suslov and the collective leadership to take action. Either Khrushchev or they had to disappear, and if it was to be Khrushchev, it had to be before the November plenary session. In this way, he himself set the date for his overthrow.

President of Gosplan in charge of Agriculture; L. R. Korniets, Chairman of the State Committee for the Transportation of Agricultural Products.

Also included were the First Secretaries and Heads of Government of the federated republics.

The heads of the main economic organizations were also members, but not D. F. Ustinov who, with his 'Supreme Sovnarkhoz', was supposed to co-ordinate the activities of those bodies.

3 The Coup

On September 30 Khrushchev left on holiday. The circumstances were somewhat unusual since, for the first time, it was clearly hinted in Moscow that the First Secretary had been dispatched to the seaside by his colleagues of the collective leadership. ('He's gone for a rest at the Presidium's suggestion,' an American businessman was told at the beginning of October.) L. M. Zamyatin, the head of the press department at the Ministry of Foreign Affairs, gave the information to the newspapers on the evening of Khrushchev's departure.[1] His colleagues may have used the pretext of the 'dread weapon' whose existence had been 'disclosed' to the members of the Japanese parliamentary delegation, or the speech to the planners. The publicity was probably designed to make sure he really would go away.

How did Khrushchev react to what was indisputably a blow to his authority? Not so well as appeared at the outset. He did go to the Crimea, but by October 2 he was off again visiting farms in the region and showering them with 'good advice' (*Pravda*, October 3 1964). Furthermore, it was on October 2, as noted, that the press gave a summary of his speech to the planners. This may well have been done on direct orders from him, carried out unwillingly to be sure, but carried out all the same. The matter had obviously been in abeyance for several days, and in the light of subsequent events it would have been better for the collective leadership to have let it alone.

This may also have been the time when Khrushchev divulged more than he ever had before about his contemplated reorganization. Various Moscow observers, particularly Reuter's correspondent on October 22, mentioned a new memorandum issued by the First Secretary at the beginning of the month from his holiday residence. The document, dealing with the November plenary session, is said to have been very badly received in Moscow. If the information is correct, we may assume that it set out in 'definitive' form Khrushchev's plans as outlined in the

---

[1] The date of Khrushchev's departure on holiday just before the coup is not open to question. That morning he had had a meeting with Sukarno. The day before, September 29, he had presided over the rally held at the Bolshoy Theatre to celebrate the anniversary of the First International. This was the last appearance of the rulers as a group before the crisis. They were seated in the following order: Khrushchev, Mikoyan, Brezhnev, Podgorny, Suslov, Kosygin, Polyansky.

August memorandum. Perhaps he responded in kind to the opposition's aggressiveness and gave the names of the men he intended to remove from responsibility under the guise of putting them in charge of agriculture or something else. This may have sealed his fate.

Whatever the case may be, his enforced departure on holiday on September 30 does not indicate that all the component parts of the plot had fallen into place. Rather, it represented the success of preliminary moves by the most determined elements of the opposition – men who, like Suslov, had made up their mind some time ago. But it was still too early for a showdown. Prudence demanded that Khrushchev should suspect no more than fleeting difficulties, and for this reason it is very unlikely that all members of the Presidium had already been informed or consulted.

On October 3 Tass reported that Khrushchev was in Sochi, on the eastern coast of the Black Sea (the day before, he was still in the Crimea), where he had received another delegation of Japanese MPs who had come to pay him a private visit. The communiqué added:

'At the end of the meeting with the Japanese Members of Parliament, the Chairman of the Presidium of the Supreme Soviet, A. I. Mikoyan, who has just arrived here on holiday, joined N. S. Khrushchev and took part in the interview' (*Pravda*, October 4 1964).

Mikoyan's arrival 'at the end of the meeting' catches the eye, if only because he had already met the same delegation in Moscow the day before (*Pravda*, October 3 1964). Moreover, he was again with Khrushchev at Sochi on October 12, at the height of the crisis, which suggests that he was an important agent in the plot. Was he already playing the part on October 3? It was later explained to the French delegation, headed by Georges Marchais, that, in view of the latest 'aggravation' of the First Secretary's shortcomings, 'several comrades went to see comrade Khrushchev to tell him that working conditions in the Presidium had to be discussed' (*L'Humanité*, November 9 1964). The only one among the 'several' to whom this is likely to apply is Mikoyan. It is not likely that he had been moved solely by the lofty considerations outlined to Georges Marchais. Possibly, Mikoyan's mission did consist in persuading Khrushchev to come and state his case when the time came but, in the meantime, a no less important task was to lull Khrushchev and keep him unaware of the coalition's plans. Only then would the plot have a chance of success.

However, Mikoyan's role at the earlier stage is still unclear. Since no activity on his part was reported between October 3 and 12, it is uncertain whether he was with Khrushchev all that time. On October 4, for instance, Khrushchev saw another delegation, of Pakistani members of parliament, and Mikoyan was not present (*Pravda*, October 5 1964).

SUSLOV ON THE WARPATH

Relations with East Germany, which were particularly animated at the beginning of October, throw some light on the matter. From October 1 to 3, Willi Stoph, the Head of the East German Government, was in Moscow to open an exhibition. On October 5 Brezhnev flew to East Berlin as the head of a six-member delegation (which included K. T. Mazurov and A. Ya. Pelshe) to take part in the festivities marking the fifteenth anniversary of the founding of the new State.[1] As mentioned, the attempts at a *rapprochement* with Bonn and Khrushchev's impending visit to the German Federal Republic were a cause of tension within the collective leadership and also between Khrushchev and Ulbricht. The speeches by the various leaders on the occasions of those visits help one to understand their views on the subject, and to a lesser extent on the 'Khrushchev case'.

Kosygin was fairly friendly to the First Secretary. When he went to meet Stoph at the airport on October 1, he greeted him 'in the name of the Central Committee of the CPSU, the Soviet Government and its chief, N. S. Khrushchev' (*Pravda*, October 2 1964). In another speech, at the opening of the exhibition on October 3, he again mentioned the 'Central Committee of the CPSU, the Soviet Government and its chief, Nikita Sergeyevich Khrushchev'. He again mentioned Khrushchev in connection with Germany: 'As comrade Khrushchev said, the Soviet Union and the other socialist countries, in their capacity as faithful friends and allies in the common struggle for the victory of communism, have always been and will remain by the side of the German Democratic Republic' (*Izvestia*, October 4 1964). Was this a way of reassuring his guest about Khrushchev's intentions, or of reminding the First Secretary about his commitments? In any case, Kosygin was skilful and cautious.

Suslov, in the speech he made two days later at a rally held in Moscow

---

[1] Exchanges with East Germany in September and October 1964 also included a visit to East Berlin at the end of September by a delegation headed by Yu. V. Andropov, Secretary of the Central Committee in charge of relations with fraternal Parties in power. He returned to Moscow on October 1. Then, on October 5, another East German delegation headed by Matern, a member of the Politburo, arrived in Moscow. Neither Matern nor Willi Stoph visited Khrushchev at Sochi. At the end of September, exceptional publicity was given to the ratification by the Presidium of the Supreme Soviet of the USSR–GDR treaty concluded in June 1963.

in honour of the GDR, took a far more definite stand in East Germany's favour. The full text is not known, but in the lengthy summary given by *Pravda* Khrushchev's name is not mentioned once. The speaker was much more eloquent on the German issue than Kosygin had been. He said:

'The treaty between the USSR and GDR puts a stop to the foolish illusions of West German revanchist circles about the possibility of a deal with the Soviet Union at the expense of the GDR. "If the USSR wants good relations with West Germany," it is being said in those circles, "let it give in on the interests of the GDR." It is an understatement to say that such plans are a provocation. They are evidence of their authors' bourgeois narrow-mindedness. . . . In the first place, the GDR is a sovereign State, and no one, except its own people, is entitled to bargain with its interests; in the second place, the fraternal amity and socialist solidarity which link the USSR and the GDR are not to be bought and sold, even for all the gold in the world'[1] (*Pravda*, October 6 1964).

This emphatic reminder was obviously aimed both at Khrushchev's possible attempts or temptations on the subject of a *rapprochement* with Bonn, and at the 'illusions' entertained by the other side. Suslov, incidentally, touched upon the normalization of relations with the other Germany, but only by saying that 'both parties are equally interested in this' – in other words, the USSR did not need to make any concessions to obtain it. 'In any case,' he went on, 'such relations can successfully develop not on the basis of any underhand deals (*sdyelki*) but on the basis of good will directed toward co-operation in the interests of all European States' (*Pravda*, October 6 1964).

Relations with Germany, as already mentioned, were only one of the controversial issues, but served as a touchstone in this instance, showing that Suslov was far more aggressive than usual, and clearly on the warpath.

Brezhnev spoke in East Berlin on October 6 in a more moderate tone, although in substance he was close to Suslov. He mentioned Khrushchev only once, without any amplification or praise, in connection with the planned international conference of Communist Parties.[2] Concern-

---

[1] *Izvestia* in its issue of October 7 (foreign edition) merely mentioned, but did not quote from, Suslov's speech on Germany made on October 6 1964.

[2] The statements about the Chinese issue contained in speeches by the Soviet rulers at the beginning of October 1964 provide no basis whatsoever for linking it with the anti-Khrushchev plot. Kosygin and Brezhnev attacked the Chinese only indirectly, without naming them; the former spoke more sharply than the latter. Suslov, who was the most hostile to Khrushchev, was also the most outspoken against Peking: he denounced the 'schismatic anti-Leninist policy . . . the provocations of the Chinese leaders'.

ing Germany, he merely noted in a neutral tone: 'We also wish, as you know, to normalize our relations with the German Federal Republic.' But he had said before:

'Only short-sighted politicians who have completely lost any sense of realities, such as certain gentlemen on the banks of the Rhine, can lull themselves with the hope of decisions and deals (*sdyelki*) of some kind to be concluded behind the back and at the expense of the GDR and its security. No, my good friends, this will not happen. Do not expect that from us!' (*Pravda*, October 7 1964).

It is difficult, of course, to reach any conclusion on the basis of these fragmentary statements – the only ones available to us. The exact role each man played in the crisis, for example, will remain a secret of history for a long time to come. But the overall impression is that, at that stage, Brezhnev had definitely taken a stance distinguishing him from Khrushchev and was drawing fairly close to Suslov – now unquestionably the spearhead of the opposition. As for Kosygin, he seemed to be his usual self, that is to say, by no means a certain supporter of the First Secretary. The exact moment when each one was apprised of the intended coup and invited to give his assent is also impossible to pinpoint. Brezhnev, who was detained in East Berlin until the 11th, could not have played any active role in the preparations. Moreover, for safety's sake, the moment of truth had to come as late as possible where the less reliable elements were concerned.

There was no rush to inform Podgorny. He had arrived in Kishinyov on October 9 to take part in a local anniversary celebration, and on the 10th started his speech as follows:

'Comrades, on the day I left to come here, I had a telephone conversation with Nikita Sergeyevich Khrushchev who is, at the moment, away from Moscow. He was very sorry to be unable to take advantage of your friendly invitation and participate in your great festivities. Nikita Sergeyevich asked me to present to all the workers, farmers and intelligentsia of flourishing Soviet Moldavia his cordial congratulations and wishes for further success in your work and personal happiness' (*Pravda*, October 11 1964).

At the same rally, an honorary Presidium was elected, consisting of the 'Presidium of the Central Committee of the CPSU headed by comrade Khrushchev'. But that was not all: on the next day, October 11, when in Moscow the plan for the coup had been virtually completed, Podgorny declared before leaving Kishinyov:

'I have also been asked by Nikita Sergeyevich Khrushchev to transmit to the Moldavian people and to the Communist Party of Moldavia his warm congratulations and best wishes for further success. *It gives me great pleasure to carry out this mission. . . .*' (*Pravda*, October 12 1964. Author's italics.)

It is hard to imagine that a man who knew what was afoot would have spoken publicly in that vein. If only for the sake of his ultimate reputation, he would presumably have been more discreet in performing his task.[1] It may be objected, of course, that, by presiding over the ceremonies in Kishinyov, Podgorny was helping the plotters, since this saved Khrushchev from making a personal appearance and thereby prevented any possible outbursts on his part. This is plausible, and Podgorny's remark about the invitation sent to Khrushchev suggests that his participation had been seriously considered. But this still did not make it necessary to inform Podgorny about the plot. Podgorny left Kishinyov only in the evening of October 11 after a series of rather pointless engagements, such as the planting of a new 'friendship boulevard', another rally and a reception. Hence, he reached Moscow only late at night. On Monday morning, the Presidium opened its debate on the 'Khrushchev case', and this is probably when he was initiated. Let us, however, first review the preceding days.

Thursday, October 8
Judging from the press, everything was normal. Khrushchev was mentioned in a routine fashion in editorials and articles: *Pravda* went on with its recently launched column 'Preparations for the plenary session of the Central Committee' (in November). No member of the Party Presidium made an appearance in Moscow on the 7th or 8th. Only Brezhnev's activities in East Berlin were reported.

It was on the 8th, however, that the French Senate first received the list of Soviet members of parliament who were to compose the delegation which, some time before, had been invited to France. The head was P. A. Satiukov, the editor-in-chief of *Pravda* and a member of the Central Committee; his number two was D. A. Polikarpov, an alternate member of the Central Committee and associate head of its ideological department. Their arrival in Paris was scheduled for October 11. We shall revert to this later.

In the meantime, the main press officials, including A. I. Adzhubey,

[1] Like Podgorny, L. N. Yefremov, an alternate member of the Presidium, blundered at a ceremony in the Tuva Republic on October 11 1964 by declaring: 'It gives me great pleasure to carry out the mission entrusted to me, and to present to you the warmest greetings and congratulations from the First Secretary of the Central Committee of the CPSU and Head of the Government, Nikita Sergeyevich Khrushchev' (*Pravda*, October 12 1964).

the editor-in-chief of *Izvestia*, M. A. Kharlamov, the director of radio-television, and Satyukov were reported by *Pravda* of October 8 to have signed in Moscow a co-operation agreement with the Union of Bulgarian Journalists, probably on the day before.

Friday, October 9

The situation was still normal, except that, for the third day in succession, no member of the Presidium was mentioned except for Brezhnev, who was still in Berlin. *Pravda* reprinted several messages and telegrams from Khrushchev, who also headed the list of signatories of the obituary for the economist Eugene Varga, who had died on the 7th.[1]

Also on the 9th, Marshal Malinovsky, who had headed a military delegation to Czechoslovakia, returned to Moscow (*Pravda*, October 10 1964). The day before, another prominent figure, D. F. Ustinov, no supporter of Khrushchev, had returned from a visit to Finland (*Pravda*, October 9 1964).

Saturday, October 10

This, most probably, was the day when the plot took shape. Not that anything particularly abnormal happened. The press presented its usual aspect; Khrushchev was mentioned several times. One leader at last made an appearance in Moscow, namely Kosygin, who was host to the French minister Gaston Palewski. The future Head of Govern-

---

[1] On October 9 1964, *Pravda* carried an interesting article on its 'control page' concerning the Party–State Control Committee by the First Secretary of the Moscow Urban Committee, N. G. Yegorychev, who became influential after the crisis. It contained the first veiled criticism of this Committee, a powerful agency headed by A. N. Shelepin. Yegorychev clearly hinted that its officials should be brought back under Party control. He wrote:

'The Party–State Control organs enjoy wide powers: they inflict sanctions or money fines and remove officials from their posts. They provide a link between the Party sector and the Soviet and State sector. This gives them great strength. *And the Party organizations are in duty bound to use this strength correctly. . . .*'

The meaning of this kind of 'help' in Party phraseology is well known. Yegorychev went on to explain that this in no way implied protecting guilty officials from prosecution by the Control Committee, but he added:

'We have also reminded the staff of the Party–State Control Committee several times, especially in the first few months, that administrative action is an extreme measure and should not be abused. We did so in particular because, during this period, certain officials had regular recourse to administrative action. It is the easiest method, it is true' (*Pravda*, October 9 1964).

This warning against Shelepin's omnipotence just before a crisis that brought him to the very top is difficult to explain. In any case, it shows the unease in the Party caused by the existence of Control Committee officials. This may account for the liquidation of the Control Committee a year later (cf. p. 505).

ment specifically mentioned the meeting that his guest was scheduled to have with Khrushchev, and its exact time was announced that day: Tuesday, October 13, in Sochi at 11 am. It was understood in French circles in Moscow that a luncheon would follow the talks.

However, two incidental facts occurred, which were to some extent related to the coup:

1 A communiqué released in the evening by the Tass agency announced the arrival in Moscow 'within the next few days' of Osvaldo Dorticós, the President of the Cuban Republic (*Pravda*, October 11 1964). In all likelihood, the exact date of the visit was fixed that very day, as was customary. Dorticós arrived on Wednesday, October 14, when the crisis was ending, and was therefore the first official guest of the new Soviet rulers. It was somewhat odd, though, that the visit had been arranged for the 14th. According to the communiqué, Dorticós was coming to Moscow 'on his way back to Havana after the second conference of Heads of States and Governments of the non-aligned nations in Cairo'. But the Cairo conference ended on the evening of October 10, and there was no reason why Dorticós could not be in Moscow by the next day, Sunday. Why make him waste an extra three days in Cairo?

The forthcoming visit may have acted as a catalyst: it could not be put off too long since it was tied to Dorticós's stay in Cairo. On the other hand, the plotters had evidently decided to keep Khrushchev from taking part in any further official visits that he might use for speeches and contacts. Hence the operation had to be over by the time Dorticós arrived. These four days must have been judged sufficient, and they were.[1]

It is also possible, if less likely, that the space flight about to be launched (the orbiting of three men in the *Voskhod* spaceship) contributed to speed up events. The flight started on Monday the 12th and was expected to be a 'long' one, according to the first Tass communiqué. Anyway, there would be no problem in postponing the welcoming ceremonies for the cosmonauts, the only ones of any political significance.

The second fact confirms the hypothesis suggested by the Dorticós visit.

2 On Saturday, the French Senate was notified of a change in the

---

[1] Naturally, the diplomatic stage in Moscow is never completely empty, and there were bound to be a few flaws in the plan. Gaston Palewski's presence was one. Another was the unexpected arrival of Tsedenbal, the chief of the Mongolian Party and Government, who decided to stop once again in Moscow after returning from East Berlin, where he had gone for the GDR anniversary celebrations, and before going on to Hungary. He arrived in Moscow on October 12 and was met only by V. N. Titov, Central Committee Secretary (*Pravda*, October 13 1964). He left on the 14th without meeting any officials or being seen off at the airport (*Pravda*, October 15 1964).

composition of the parliamentary delegation due to arrive in Paris next day. D. A. Polikarpov, the number two man, had been replaced by a shock worker, N. N. Rusakov.

The fact is of some significance. As an alternate member of the Central Committee, Polikarpov was entitled to attend all its 'plenary sessions'. Like Satyukov, he therefore ought to be present at the session held to ratify Khrushchev's downfall. The only difference was that *Pravda's* editor-in-chief was well known to support Khrushchev, whereas Polikarpov, a veteran of Agitprop, was equally well known to be a Suslov man. Polikarpov's presence in Moscow was not only legal, but also useful to the conspiracy, while Satyukov's, although no less legal, was undesirable. That is the clearest sign available to this day in establishing premeditation in the 'October coup' and in pinpointing the dates when the operation assumed concrete shape: viz. between October 8, the date of the first communiqué on the Satyukov delegation, and the 10th, when the list was amended.

This calls for some additional remarks about the role of the press in the entire operation. After the coup, many observers noted that several of the chief information officials had been away from Moscow during the crucial week. For example, Satyukov, *Pravda's* editor-in-chief, was in Paris, and Kharlamov, the radio-television director, had gone to Scandinavia at an unknown date (he returned to Moscow on October 17). Adzhubey's whereabouts are less certain. It was rumoured that he did not attend the plenary meeting of the 14th that overthrew his father-in-law, but this is not confirmed. In any case, these three men had played a larger role in Khrushchev's entourage than their posts called for (they were virtually a permanent part of Khrushchev's staff when he was abroad) and it is no accident that they were the first to be removed after his downfall. Adzhubey was purged within the hour, Kharlamov almost as soon, Satyukov a little later.[1] Realizing that Khrushchev might try to make a last-minute appeal to public

[1] The purging of Satyukov after Khrushchev's downfall probably gave rise to controversy. The report in *Pravda* of October 19 of his return from France on the previous day was much briefer than the news of his departure, and his name was not even mentioned. At the same time, the rumour circulated that A. G. Yegorov, the assistant head of the ideological department, had taken over as *Pravda's* editor-in-chief. On the 19th, however, speaking to foreign journalists, Satyukov denied the news of his replacement, and events, for a while, bore this out. On November 6, for example, Satyukov signed in *Pravda* the obituary of Academician Nemchinov, and his place on the list of signatories was fully appropriate to his functions: he preceded N. N. Inozemtsev, the deputy editor-in-chief of *Pravda*, and A. M. Rumyantsev, the man who later succeeded him in running the paper. His replacement was officially announced only on November 13 (*Le Monde*, November 15 1964).

This can be explained only on the ground that Satyukov was a client of L. F. Ilyichev no less than of Khrushchev, and Ilyichev managed to stay on for several months after the First Secretary was overthrown.

opinion by issuing orders to his faithful henchmen in the press, the plotters probably chose to have them safely out of his reach during the crucial days. But unless one assumes that Polikarpov's appointment to the Satyukov delegation was simply a mistake, this would suggest that the plotters had not originally planned things the way they turned out. Presumably they had not known at the time that the Central Committee would have to be called as early as the following week. After the 10th, on the other hand, this was already clear, and Satyukov was therefore kept on as the head of the delegation to make sure he would be away from Moscow.

Sunday, October 11

Brezhnev came back from Berlin with the rest of his delegation. He was met at Vnukovo airport by Suslov, V. N. Titov, M. A. Lesechko, P. F. Lomako (the two latter were Deputy Chairmen of the Council of Ministers) and N. A. Muravyova, the Chairman of the Auditing Committee (*Pravda*, October 12 1964).

Contrary to an almost unbroken tradition, the 'welcoming group' was different from the one that had seen Brezhnev off on the 5th. The latter had consisted of G. I. Voronov, Kosygin, Podgorny, V. N. Titov and Muravyova. In the second group, the Presidium was represented by only one member instead of three, namely Suslov, who was making his first public appearance since his much talked-about speech on Germany of October 5. The master schemer evidently wanted personally to inform the man who had a key role to play in the operation before he could reap its benefits. Was this the first inkling Brezhnev had of the coup? It is impossible to tell. If its date had been fixed the day before, Brezhnev could, at any rate, not have known that he would have to go into action so soon. Many other details must have been decided in his absence, since he had been away for almost a week. On the substance of the issues, however, he had been close to Suslov for some time. The principle of an anti-Khrushchev operation might have been decided by both of them before Brezhnev left for East Berlin, in which case the meeting with Suslov at Vnukovo was a briefing rather than a revelation.

Monday, October 12

This was the first day of the operation – the moment of frankness for all the members of the collective leadership except Khrushchev, who was still at Sochi. On the basis of the information available so far, it would be useless to try to reconstruct the discussions. It is known only that the Presidium first met on the 12th.[1] This must have been when Podgorny

[1] All information received from Moscow after the crisis confirms that the Presidium

and probably a few other members of the Presidium heard about the scheme for the first time.

Some public events of the day are of interest: in the first place, the flight of the three cosmonauts, Komarov, Feoktistov and Yegorov, who took off from the Baikonur launching pad at 10.30 am Moscow time. The political part of the flight, if it may be so described, proceeded normally that day, and Khrushchev was associated with it at three stages. First, the ritual message sent by the crew after the launching, addressed to 'the Central Committee, the Soviet Government and N. S. Khrushchev personally', and reproduced in the press on October 13; then the telephone call Khrushchev made to the space centre a few minutes before the launching on Monday morning. One departure from the traditional procedure was noted: Brezhnev did the same thing from his Moscow office at about the same time (*Pravda* and *Sovietskaya Rossiya*, October 13 1964). Hitherto Khrushchev had enjoyed a monopoly of sponsoring space flights; now his would-be successor was pointedly showing he was around too. Finally, Khrushchev talked by telephone with the cosmonauts from his Sochi residence in front of the television cameras about 2 pm. Mikoyan was at his side and *Pravda* used this fact to emphasize the 'collective leadership' aspect of the story, which it entitled: 'Conversation of N. S. Khrushchev and A. I. Mikoyan with the crew.' Then, during the conversation, Mikoyan made a move that all the viewers noticed and Khrushchev described thus: 'I'm handing the receiver to Anastasy Ivanovich Mikoyan. *He's literally tearing it out of my hands.* I can't deny him this' (*Pravda*, October 13 1964).

Some observers have construed Mikoyan's unusual behaviour as meaning that he tried to prevent the First Secretary from speaking for fear of some dangerous political improvisation. It is more likely, however, that Mikoyan, like Brezhnev a few hours earlier, simply wanted to assert himself and show that Khrushchev was not exclusively in charge of any particular sector. On the other hand, it may be safely assumed that not only was Mikoyan in the plot, but that his role was a crucial one. Otherwise he would have been in Moscow that day, since Suslov and Brezhnev were busy organizing a 'united front' against the First Secretary within the Presidium. Alternatively, his absence from Moscow could only have meant that the coup was directed against him too, which was later disproved. The fact was that at that stage, the most delicate one in the operation, the plotters needed a reliable man to be near Khrushchev, preferably one trusted by the latter. Mikoyan's

---

met on October 12. Marchais's report, already quoted, even stated that the Presidium sat for two days '*under his chairmanship* [Khrushchev's]'. This cannot possibly be correct, since Khrushchev arrived in Moscow only early in the afternoon of Tuesday, October 13, and by the following morning the Central Committee had taken over.

role was to watch Khrushchev's reactions, supervise his outside contacts and talk him into coming to Moscow at the right moment.

Mikoyan, it goes without saying, was the best man for the job, and obviously his performance was a good one. The telephone episode indicates that his deference toward the First Secretary was a thing of the past, and that he was following the new line decided upon by the collective leadership a few weeks earlier. He probably apprised Khrushchev of the Presidium's grievances, but carefully refrained from letting him guess the intended outcome. Khrushchev naïvely told the cosmonauts about the grandiose welcome that 'we shall organize for you' and ended the conversation by saying 'we are expecting you on earth' (he never did see the three heroes again).

It must also have been Mikoyan who persuaded Khrushchev to come to Moscow to account for his past conduct. In the afternoon of Monday the 10th, the French minister Palewski was informed that his audience with the Head of Government, arranged for the next day, had been advanced from 11 am to 9 am. A few days later, he understood why his host had appeared in such a hurry.[1]

Another event of that day sheds additional light on the situation: on Monday, October 12, a conference on 'the development of production and the use of advanced methods in industrial procurement' was to meet at Izhevsk, an industrial city in the Udmurt Autonomous Republic, about a thousand miles east of Moscow. On October 12 *Pravda* stated that 'the heads of State Committees for branches of industry, the Secretaries of a number of Party Oblast Committees, the heads of sovnarkhozes, scientists, technologists', etc, had already congregated at Izhevsk. K. N. Rudnev, a Deputy Chairman of the Council, was there as well. Evidently, this was to be a fairly high-level conference. *Izvestia* confirmed this in its Monday afternoon Moscow edition (international edition of October 13 1964):

'The conference was opened by the Deputy Chairman of the Council of Ministers of the USSR, K. N. Rudnev. It heard reports by the leaders of State Committees for the branches of industry: A. V. Topchiev, A. I. Kostousov, E. S. Novosyolov and others.'

---

[1] Did Khrushchev let himself be 'recalled' to Moscow willingly? It is doubtful, considering his temperament. On October 31 1963 – in the not so distant past – when telling Guy Mollet about the 1957 crisis, he had dwelt on that very point. When told during his visit to Finland that a Presidium meeting had been called in Moscow, and that his presence was required, he had at first refused to comply and declared: 'What's this? I am the First Secretary of the Central Committee and it is I who convene the Presidium!' It was only after receiving next day a second invitation couched in more pressing language that he decided to return. It is reasonable to assume that he reacted the same way in 1964.

At least two of these speakers, Rudnev and Kostousov, were members of the Central Committee; the two others were chairmen of their respective State Committees. However, when *Pravda* came out on the morning of October 13, it gave a different list of speakers. Rudnev was mentioned, but not Kostousov or any State Committee chairmen. For instance, in place of A. V. Topchiev, the Chairman of the State Committee for Heavy Mechanical Engineering, Power and Transportation, only M. N. Shchukin, the deputy chairman of that committee, was listed. It was also specified that the debates were going to be conducted 'in sections' – in other words, the conference was to be broken up into committees. This was a very rare procedure, or at any rate, very seldom reported for meetings of that type. Moreover, it was soon discovered that Rudnev had not lingered in Izhevsk: the next morning he was back in Moscow, welcoming the Chinese and Vietnamese delegations on their return from Berlin (*Pravda*, October 14 1964).

The explanation is a simple one: the *Izvestia* correspondent had sent in his story on Monday morning for the afternoon edition. As sometimes happens in journalistic work, he had given, so to speak, an advance report and described scheduled speakers as having already spoken. *Pravda*, which goes to press at the end of the day, was more accurate in indicating that the conference had been cut short, probably in the course of the afternoon, and that Rudnev and all the ministers had rushed back to Moscow. Either they had to prepare for the Central Committee session or – and the two are not mutually exclusive – there was some arm-twisting to be done. Since most of these ministers were notorious 'steel-eaters', whose sentiments toward Khrushchev after the previous month's incident over the Plan were not of the friendliest, their presence was especially desirable. Rudnev himself, though he later suffered some setbacks, apparently was in on the plot. He was one of the first emissaries of the new leadership abroad: he was sent to Belgium just after the crucial week, a sign of notable confidence.

It is hard to determine the scale on which officials were mobilized at that stage. It was rumoured that several days before the events, an old enemy of Khrushchev, I. A. Benediktov, a former Minister of Agriculture and currently Ambassador to India, had arrived in Moscow. But at the same time, another prominent Central Committee member, the head of the Komsomol, S. P. Pavlov, was attending the Olympic Games in Tokyo, apparently unaware of an infinitely more important contest going on at home. Satyukov and a few others who were abroad were being deliberately kept in the dark. The same may have been done with Marshals A. I. Yeremenko and I. Kh. Bagramian, who, on the evening of the 13th, were still in Riga for the anniversary festivities of the 'liberation' of the Baltic States (*Pravda*, October 14 1964). Another man entitled to attend the plenary session – Academician M. A. Lavrentiev, an alternate member of the Central Committee – came from Novosibirsk only on October 15, when everything was over. He was a personal friend of the First Secretary. Clearly the mobilization was highly selective.

Tuesday, October 13
This was the second day of the crisis, and Khrushchev was now present. Its main developments are fairly well known.

At 9 am Khrushchev received Gaston Palewski, his last foreign visitor, at his Sochi residence. The meeting lasted for half an hour, less than any previous official meeting. Khrushchev let it go on just long enough to escape the charge of discourtesy, then excused himself explaining that he had to leave on a 'trip', but did not specify that he was going to meet the cosmonauts.

Allowing for translation, the two men did not have time to say much to each other, but it was clear from what Khrushchev did say that he was not expecting his tenure of office to be cut short. He mentioned his trip to West Germany as unlikely to yield any results, but as being necessary all the same. Learning that General de Gaulle was in good health, he remarked: 'Yes, only death can wrest a statesman from his work.' He doubtless realized that his position held some risks (cf. the remark in his birthday speech about 'political death') but he fully intended to carry on. It is also reported that Khrushchev left his visitor several times, probably to telephone (or try to telephone?); but this was normal, since *Voskhod* was expected to land any minute and, in fact, did so at 10.57 Moscow time.

Directly after the meeting with Palewski, Khrushchev boarded the plane for Moscow. A persistent rumour later circulated that he travelled under police escort and was met in Moscow by Semichastny, the head of the KGB in person, as well as by Shelepin. This cannot be verified and, in any case, how is one to distinguish between 'surveillance' and 'protection'? However, it is quite likely that, in this particular case, the 'surveillance' aspect might have overshadowed the other. At that stage, the Presidium was vitally interested in dealing with Khrushchev alone and in preventing him from contacting his rank-and-file supporters as he had done so successfully in 1957.

Khrushchev arrived in Moscow early in the afternoon (at 2.30 pm, according to the *New York Times* correspondent on October 21) and went to face the Presidium. On this point too, all versions concur in their broad outline. Suslov led the attack, seconded by Polyansky, who inveighed mainly against Khrushchev's errors with regard to agriculture.

The charges are of scant interest, for it is clear that there was no shortage of grievances once it had been agreed to hold the trial.

It is not hard to guess what Khrushchev's reaction must have been, and it only aggravated his case. A scanning of the press shows that it was on the evening of Tuesday the 13th, and not earlier, that Khrushchev became the 'political corpse' that he is today. Until then he had been downgraded, but not eliminated. *Pravda* of the 13th – which reflected the views of the collective leadership as of Monday evening, that is after the first day of the proceedings – not only gave full coverage to the First Secretary's activities, but quoted him profusely. The collective character of the leadership was emphasized, it is true, as was shown by the report on the conversation 'of Khrushchev and Mikoyan' with the cosmonauts, and also by the fact that no photograph illustrated the story. This contrasted with June 17 1963, when the entire press had shown Khrushchev talking to Tereshkova after her flight, and with earlier occasions when he had always been shown with the cosmonauts. But the First Secretary was still mentioned in all the major reports of the space exploit, and one of his statements appeared as a caption to the heroes' biography: 'Co-ordination and collective action in space flights are of extreme importance for the conquest of space.' There was another ritual mention of him in an article by A. Ya. Pelshe, the First Secretary of the Latvian Communist Party, on the Baltic States' anniversary. In short, a few anomalies were perceptible, but nothing too alarming.

By the time *Izvestia* came out in Moscow in the evening of Tuesday the 13th, however (foreign edition, October 14 1964), the picture had changed radically. First, an unusual fact had occurred: Khrushchev had not spoken to the cosmonauts after their landing as had been the custom hitherto (he could not have, for the simple reason that he was flying to Moscow at the time under heavy escort). Secondly, Khrushchev was not mentioned in connection with anything whatsoever. For example, an article by the writer Dmiterko on the twenty-fifth anniversary of the liberation of the Ukraine from Hitler's armies contained no mention of the First Secretary – something unheard-of for any piece of writing on that subject. Another abnormal sign: Khrushchev's meeting that same morning with Palewski was not even mentioned. Obviously, this could not be due to forgetfulness on the part of every single member of *Izvestia's* staff. Rather, the impression was that a singularly thorough blue pencil had gone through the newspaper that evening and had erased every mention of the man who, for ten years, had presided over the country's destinies, and who was henceforth an unperson.

This, if only from the ceremonial standpoint, was a little excessive, so *Pravda* softened the blow that night. When the Party daily came out in the morning of Wednesday the 14th, it belatedly reported the Palewski meeting (a few lines at the bottom of page one) and mentioned Khrushchev another three times: as the recipient, together with Mikoyan, of congratulatory messages from the Polish and East German leaders on the occasion of the space flight (two other messages – from Novotný of Czechoslovakia and Waldeck-Rochet for the French Communist Party – had apparently been addressed to the Party's Central Committee or the Council of Ministers, assuming, as we safely may for that day, that telegrams were being reprinted faithfully); lastly, Khrushchev figured as the signatory of a message to the King of Afghanistan on his country's national holiday. This return to protocol does not mean that the leader had made a comeback. An article by Marshal Konev on the anniversary of the liberation of the Ukraine confirmed, on the contrary, that Khrushchev, the former Party chief in Kiev, had been erased from that chapter of the republic's history. In his article, which ran to more than three columns, the Marshal named at least half a dozen people and left out the one whom it had been mandatory to honour only a few days earlier.[1] The same held true for all the other articles, and of course for subsequent issues of the paper. Khrushchev's political death-agony had set in.

The brutal fall within a few hours' time is highly instructive. To be exact, it confirms a major assumption and at the same time raises a question. It confirms that the showdown took place before the start of the Central Committee meeting on the 14th. The Presidium, instead of waiting for its constituents to ratify its decision, was already carrying it out. The fall also proved, in a tangible if modest fashion, that the Kremlinological method had proved its worth, since it disclosed by Tuesday evening, if not the full extent of the crisis, then at least a very serious situation. This was confirmed by the analysts beyond doubt on Wednesday morning, almost two days before the official announcement, which came only on the evening of Thursday the 15th. Khrushchev's absence from the scene after the landing of the cosmonauts, and the

---

[1] For technical or other reasons, the censor did not go over everything with equal thoroughness. For instance, in *Komsomolskaya Pravda* of October 14, still in connection with the liberation of the Ukraine, an article by the chief of the Army's political administration, A. A. Yepishev, gave a clear idea of what the celebration would have been like under normal circumstances. The author first asserted that Khrushchev 'was at that time our direct leader, as a member of the Military Council at the front'. Then he wrote about an old woman who gave Nikita Sergeyevich Khrushchev 'a motherly kiss' to congratulate him on the liberation. Finally, he described the rally presided over by Khrushchev in liberated Kiev and quoted a passage from his speech. The article, which appeared on the morning when the 'October plenary session' opened, was apparently the last manifestation of the Khrushchev cult.

articles by Dmiterko and Konev on the anniversary of the liberation of the Ukraine, both rank as major indications.

The question raised is whether the instigators of the coup had not originally planned a less drastic solution than the one actually carried out, and whether Khrushchev did not court oblivion by rejecting the terms they were willing to grant him. This does not disprove the existence of premeditation and plotting, which have been established beyond doubt. The episodes of Polikarpov's planned journey and the Izhevsk conference indicate that a plenary session was afoot from the beginning. This, in turn, heralded a decision involving Khrushchev's functions as the Party leader. But conceivably, his enemies might have made him leave the Secretariat, cancelling his prospective November reforms and other controversial decisions;[1] they might have been content with inflicting a reproof, in exchange for which he would have remained Head of the Government at least for a while. This might have been preferable for dealings with the outside world, where continuity is a major consideration. Signs pointing to any such intention on the plotters' part are indeed slim, but since in all likelihood they had sealed their alliance by Monday, and since Khrushchev was being held at their disposal, why did they let him have almost normal press coverage until he reached Moscow? Why not find some excuse to cancel his interview with Palewski? – the latter was due to remain in the Soviet Union for several days longer, so why could he not have met Kosygin after the change-over? If the plotters were afraid of trouble with old-time Khrushchev supporters of Podgorny's type, it would surely have been easier to tell them: 'We'll put Khrushchev in his place', rather than 'That dangerous chatterbox must go'.

Here again, the question cannot be answered. But even if the plotters had had any such idea, it would hardly have altered the course of events. It would have been out of keeping with Khrushchev's character to accept such a diminished position, and the plotters doubtless knew this. When he turned down their offer – if it was made – they had to take more drastic measures.

Wednesday, October 14
This was the day of the 'October plenary session', the final ratification

---

[1] The column 'Preparation for the plenary session' (meaning Khrushchev's November session) appeared in *Pravda* of October 12 (Monday) for the last time. All the other newspapers had stopped it even earlier: for instance *Sovietskaya Rossiya* on the 11th and *Selskaya Zhizn* on the 10th. It is true that those papers do not come out on Monday and that, after that date, the space flight had monopolized the news. The fact remains, however, that after the 12th, when the Presidium opened the 'Khrushchev case', the November plenary session ceased to be mentioned, nor was it ever formally convened.

of the coup. It was held in the morning, very early perhaps if, as alleged, Khrushchev went directly from the Presidium chamber to the hall where the Central Committee was waiting (this was the version given by the *New York Times* of October 12 1964). In any case, the collective leadership obviously did not want to give the victim any respite between the two meetings.

There are two versions of what happened at the plenary session.

The official version was given to the French Communist Party delegation and reported by Georges Marchais as follows:

'After the discussion [at the Presidium], comrade Khrushchev acknowledged the validity of the main points of criticism. He mentioned his state of health, his age, and declared that he could no longer perform his duties. He handed in his resignation.

'In these circumstances, the Central Committee, the only body competent to take a decision, was called into session. Comrade Khrushchev took part in the proceedings from start to finish. He addressed to the full members of the Central Committee, the alternates and the members of the Central Credentials Committee[1] a letter in which he asked to be relieved of his functions as Party Secretary, member of the Party Presidium and Chairman of the Council of Ministers, owing to his advanced age and deteriorating health. He promised the Central Committee to devote the rest of his life and strength to work, to the Party, to the welfare of the Soviet people and the building of communism.

'After a discussion of all the problems involved, the Central Committee unanimously decided to comply with N. Khrushchev's request, and elected comrade Brezhnev to the post of First Secretary of the Central Committee of the Communist Party of the Soviet Union' (*L'Humanité*, November 9 1964).

The other version was given by an alternate member of the Central Committee who was present at the meeting: he told it a few weeks later to a Polish personality, who repeated it to this writer.

'Having received my summons very late, I arrived at the plenary session after it had started and slipped into a back row. Suslov had the floor and was saying: "The man has lost all humility, he has lost his conscience!" I first thought he was talking about Ilyichev, for I had been told about that time that he was going to be removed shortly. Then I noticed that Khrushchev was not in his usual chairman's place but was in a side seat at a distance from the Presidium.

[1] I.e. Central Auditing Committee.

He was flushed and was clenching his fists. That is how I understood what was going on.'

According to the same source, Suslov was the only speaker, but a few members of the audience (ten or so) interrupted him to express their indignation over Khrushchev's behaviour and to call for a stiffer penalty. But for fear of starting an avalanche of demands for sterner punishment, and to prevent the discussion taking a pro-Chinese turn, it was decided, according to the informant, to stop the proceedings then and there.

The two versions do not conflict on the last point. The French Communist Party version of a 'discussion of all the problems involved' does not imply a multitude of speakers. Presumably, since the main point was to emphasize the 'democratic nature' of the operation, if there had been more speakers, the fact would have been reported. Even the alleged fear of pro-Chinese arguments seems plausible, considering the way the rank and file had apparently reacted at the previous plenary session. On the other hand, it would have been very difficult for Khrushchev to have sent each member of the Presidium a letter of resignation before the meeting. The story just quoted shows at all events that, even if he had sent such a letter, it had not been duly distributed. It is highly probable, however, that Khrushchev was forced to give in before the plenary session started, realizing that he had no chance of regaining the upper hand.

Anyway, it was all over by early afternoon, when a large group of Central Committee members, including Mikoyan, Voronov, Podgorny, Malinovsky and Semichastny left for Vnukovo Airport to meet President Dorticós. A portrait of Khrushchev was still hanging on the airport building[1] and Dorticós, who of course did not know what had just happened, declared himself happy at the prospect of an exchange of views 'with our friend Nikita Sergeyevich Khrushchev'. Presumably for protocol's sake, *Pravda* of October 15 quoted him on this. It was the only mention of Khrushchev in that particular issue, since all other references, even congratulatory messages from abroad, were reworded as being addressed to 'The Central Committee of the CPSU and the Council of Ministers'.[2] Kosygin still had to be appointed Head of

---

[1] *Krasnaya Zvezda* of October 15 1964. In *Pravda's* version, the airport was decorated only with 'Cuban and Soviet flags'.
[2] On October 15 1964 the message to Khrushchev from Gheorghiu-Dej, the head of the Rumanian Communist Party, was reworded. According to the version broadcast by Radio Bucharest on the 13th, Gheorgiu-Dej concluded his message as follows: 'We congratulate you and, in your name, the Central Committee of the CPSU, the Government of the USSR', etc. In *Pravda* of October 15 this appeared as: 'We congratulate the Central Committee of the CPSU', etc.

Government, and this was done during the day of Thursday the 15th, at a meeting of the Presidium of the Supreme Soviet presided over by Mikoyan. It was only on that day, incidentally, that a large portrait of Khrushchev, which had been put up a few days earlier on a building near Red Square for the cosmonauts' welcome, was taken down. The world press began to stir. The communiqué announcing Khrushchev's resignation 'in view of his advanced age and deteriorating health' appeared in all the newspapers on the morning of the 16th, having been broadcast during the night. The Khrushchev era was officially over.

A FEW QUESTIONS

It remains to answer, or to try to answer, a few questions that were asked all over the world under the shock that followed the event:
1 Why did events take a different turn in 1964 from those of 1957? Why did Khrushchev fail to preserve his power on this occasion, when seven years earlier he had so successfully thwarted an equally strong, if not stronger, coalition against him?

One answer, of course, is that an erosion of power had taken place in the interval, that discontent was much more widespread at the end of the reign than at the beginning and was naturally focused on the man who had embodied power for so long. This explanation is valid, but there are others connected with the technique of the coup itself. For instance, the 1957 plotters had disregarded legality, or more accurately had overlooked the strings their victim could still pull by resorting to virtually forgotten legal procedures. Being accustomed to settle every problem within the Presidium, while they of course intended that the Central Committee should ratify their decision, they had regarded this as a minor matter, to be dealt with after the great ones had settled the quarrel. Khrushchev, however, had insisted on immediately taking the case to the Central Committee. The discussion on this point of procedure had dragged on for six days within the Presidium itself, which enabled Khrushchev to contact his outside supporters, arouse his friends and sway the Party parliament in his favour. He had in this fashion illustrated a basic principle in the operation of the Soviet system, namely, that the golden rule of the average official is to wait and see. Its corollary is that victory goes to the man who takes the initiative of convening the Central Committee.

The 1964 conspirators had learned this lesson. They themselves took the initiative of calling the Central Committee and thereby gained extra time for backstairs manoeuvring. They also took care that the session should open as quickly as possible after the start of the crisis. Khrushchev presumably tried to resort to his 1957 gambit: 'I don't have to account to you; let's call a plenary session', but this time they were able to retort: 'The Central Committee is assembled and waiting for you!' Taken unawares and virtually imprisoned by his colleagues, the First Secretary could not hope, within a few hours, to reverse the situation in his favour.

The relative duration of the crises brings out their basic difference. The 1964 crisis lasted from Monday October 12 to Wednesday the 14th, at noon – less than three days, out of which the victim had only twenty-four hours to put up any resistance. In 1957 there had been over two weeks' discussion in Khrushchev's presence, not to mention the preliminary stage. In one case he was placed before a *fait accompli*, in the other the situation had deteriorated gradually. The outcome in each case could clearly have been foreseen.

2 What role did the military and the police play? Judging from appearances, the army played a minor one: far smaller than in 1957, at any rate. At that time, troop movements were noticed around Moscow, the army mobilized its vehicles to transport the members of the Central Committee, and Marshal Zhukov emerged as the strong man of the hour. Nothing of this sort happened in 1964. As noted, two marshals who belonged to the Central Committee, Bagramian and Yeremenko, were in Riga at the critical time, on the evening of October 13. The former had some influence as commander of the rearward area and Deputy Defence Minister, but the latter, while much more of a Khrushchev supporter, wielded scarcely any power in his capacity as Inspector-General. Moreover, seven marshals were in Moscow on Monday the 12th for a Polish reception. They were Malinovsky, A. A. Grechko, S. S. Biryuzov (the Chief of the General Staff, who was killed in a plane crash at Belgrade a few days later), I. S. Konev, K. S. Moskalenko, V. I. Chuykov and V. D. Sokolovsky – in other words, almost the whole of the high command.

The role of Malinovsky, who as late as April 1964 had hailed Khrushchev as 'Supreme Commander in Chief' of the armed forces (*Krasnaya Zvezda*, April 17 1964), has never been clearly established. It has been reported from various quarters that he was invited to take part in the Presidium debates during the crisis. It seems likely that the plotters would have tried to gain his advance consent or at least his neutrality. Brezhnev, whose connection with the armed forces is known (he has given several proofs of it since his accession to power), must have seemed to the marshals far preferable to Khrushchev, who had been trying for so long to whittle down their appropriations. In any case, there was no sign of any opposition to the plot on their part.

Even if any of the military chiefs had sought to come to Khrushchev's rescue, it is hard to see what he could have done. A military man may well disagree with a Presidium decision, but unless he resorts to *putsch* methods – which so far have never been used in the Soviet Union – it is difficult for him to do anything about it when it has been ratified by a Central Committee plenary session and is therefore virtually public knowledge. Zhukov's role in 1957 can be explained only by the fact that the Molotov–Malenkov group had allowed the situation to deteriorate. In 1964, on the contrary, no one, including Khrushchev himself, had time to take action.

The police played a more important role. It was an instrument that the plotters could not afford to overlook, since it could have wrecked their plans had it taken the wrong side (a leak to Khrushchev at the right moment would have been enough). It was needed both to 'protect' Khrushchev at the crucial stage and to keep an eye on various figures during the preparatory phase. An indication of its part in the coup is the list of promotions at the plenary session of November 1964: V. E. Semichastny was co-opted full member of the Central Committee, while A. N. Shelepin, his predecessor at the head of the KGB, who had kept an eye on that sector, climbed straight up to full membership of the Presidium. One must assume at least that neither of them had hampered the operation, and it is more likely that their promotions were rewards for help.

Equally significant was the promotion of P. E. Shelest, Podgorny's successor as the head of the Ukrainian Communist Party, who, in November, also became a full member of the collective leadership. This may have been done for legality's sake, to make his rank match his actual functions, but even so he had had to wait for it a whole year. A few months earlier, Khrushchev had publicly humiliated him during their visit to Hungary.[1] Shelest had also played his part in the plot by neutralizing Khrushchev supporters, who were particularly numerous in the Ukrainian Party machine.

3 Did some Khrushchev supporters come to their patron's rescue? They may have, but the likelihood should not be overrated. Once the operation had started, it proceeded smoothly and there was no room for any active intervention on behalf of the First Secretary. However, this calls for a few qualifications.

In the first place, it is not at all certain that the resolution of the

[1] When Shelest accompanied Khrushchev to Hungary and it was learned during their visit to a factory that a Ukrainian plant was behindhand in its deliveries, Khrushchev publicly upbraided Shelest and then said, pointing to him: 'Look how glum he is – just as if a hedgehog had been rammed down his throat!' (*Le Monde*, April 10 1964). The Soviet press did not publish this sally.

plenary session that stripped Khrushchev of power was adopted unanimously. Georges Marchais in his report quoted above did mention unanimity, and this point figured in subsequent statements concerning the 'October plenary session'.[1] However, the official communiqué published in *Pravda* of October 16 does not mention it. The fact is striking, especially since, side by side with this communiqué, another one, announcing that the Presidium of the Supreme Soviet had ratified Kosygin's appointment as Head of Government in Khrushchev's place, specifically states that this was voted unanimously. It should also be borne in mind that, under the procedure in force, the resolution was adopted by a show of hands and not by secret ballot.

In the second place, moderating elements apparently made themselves felt on several occasions during the crisis. For example, the 'advanced age and deteriorating health' that Khrushchev allegedly mentioned as grounds for resignation were a sorry fiction that did not serve the interests of the collective leadership abroad. All the same, it did indicate a desire to save appearances. The same applies to the decision to keep Khrushchev in the Central Committee and to postpone action for a month in a case as clear-cut as Adzhubey's (he was expelled from the Central Committee only in November). It is also hard to understand why the first public (though still indirect) criticism of the ex-First Secretary came only on Saturday, October 17, in a *Pravda* editorial which was at the same time the first political manifesto of the new rulers. They had waited for over two days, although one might have expected them to inform the public and the outside world at the time they announced the change in leadership.[2]

If one examines this article, the wording of the positive section, which consists of a statement of allegiance to 'the general line of the Twentieth, Twenty-first and Twenty-second Congresses', appears too general to have given rise to any immediate controversy. The only new element is the criticism of Khrushchev, so that conceivably difficulties had arisen among the new leaders precisely on that point. This is somewhat paradoxical, since a whole week had just been spent disposing of his

---

[1] On the question whether the October plenary session had voted 'unanimously' to strip Khrushchev of power, Brezhnev tried to dissipate any uncertainty by declaring in his report of November 6 1964 that the session had been held 'in an atmosphere (*obstanovka*) of complete unanimity among all participants' (*Pravda*, November 7 1964).

[2] The Soviet rulers' concern to reassure Soviet and foreign opinion after the coup and affirm the continuity in leadership is characteristic of the 'epigones' in matters of this kind. The communiqué announcing Stalin's death in 1953 also embodied his successors' political manifesto. After the 1957 crisis it was unofficially disclosed that Molotov and the other plotters had already drafted their declaration justifying Khrushchev's removal. They had been at pains to do this before calling the Central Committee into session.

case, but of course there were many possible ways of doing this,[1] and some of his colleagues may have believed it was better not to say anything about him at all.

Other tokens of restraint came later. The *Pravda* editorial, superficial though it was, did publicize the case and end the fiction of the 'deteriorating health'. New revelations might have been expected to follow. As a matter of fact, several foreign correspondents in Moscow did announce the forthcoming publication of a 'Khrushchev report'. It was also noted that the Party journal *Kommunist* was late in appearing. But, when the first post-Khrushchev issue came out on October 29, it did not contain the slightest new fact. Debate on the case went on, of course, but only within the Party organizations, and a report was issued to key personnel.[2] To this day, except for a few references in the verbatim record of the plenary session of March 1965,[3] no direct charge has been formally levelled at Khrushchev. The coup only added a new euphemism to the already rich vocabulary of political jargon: the custom of referring to his overthrow simply as the 'October plenum'.

Such circumspection may be due to a variety of reasons, but mainly

[1] The text finally adopted by the drafters of the statement is well known. It especially pilloried Khrushchev's style:

'The Leninist Party is the enemy of subjectivism and complacency in the building of communism. Harebrained scheming, hasty conclusions, rash decisions and actions based on wishful thinking, boasting and empty words, bureaucratism, the refusal to take into account all the achievements of science and practical experience – all these defects are alien to the Party. The building of communism is a living, creative task, it cannot tolerate bureaucratic methods, one-sided decisions, the refusal to take into account the practical experience of the masses.'

The only other noteworthy points were the reaffirmation of the collective principle and the call to 'reinforce the Party's leadership in all areas of the economy and culture' (*Pravda*, October 17 1964).

[2] For example, Georges Marchais wrote: 'The discussion then continued within the Party organizations' (*L'Humanité*, November 9 1964).

[3] The statements by F. S. Goryachev, who claimed that Khrushchev despised the ideologists, and by V. P. Mzhavanadze, who declared that Khrushchev refused to listen to any objections against the division of the Party (cf. p. 356 footnote 2 and p. 256 footnote 2), have been mentioned. The last criticism came from D. A. Kunayev, the First Secretary in Kazakhstan. Denouncing 'wilful' methods in agriculture, Kunayev added: 'Today it's a delicate subject, but everybody knows it was comrade Khrushchev's doing. . . . I must say we had all the bad luck: he used to come to see us often. It's embarrassing (*neudobno*) to disclose all this now to the Central Committee plenary session.' Embarrassing or not, Brezhnev broke in at that point to report that Khrushchev had prevented him from extending the fallow area in Kazakhstan during his term as First Secretary in the Republic (1954–1956) (verbatim record, March 1965 plenary session, p 104).

This overt criticism did not appear in the daily press, but only in the verbatim record, which was published some time later and had markedly less impact. The tone of the speeches also varied: for instance, Goryachev and Kunayev spoke about 'comrade Khrushchev' – the second when speaking of the 'delicacy' of the subject – while Mzhavanadze, by far the most outspoken, said merely 'Khrushchev'. Brezhnev managed to avoid naming his predecessor altogether.

to the wish of the former First Secretary's many clients, disciples or associates (and who, from Brezhnev downwards, had not been one at some point?) to avoid placing themselves in an awkward posture. The average rank-and-file supporter of Khrushchev – an *apparatchik* promoted through patronage by the former Party chief – is unlikely to have had serious qualms about denying old ties, unless he was a sentimentalist, which is most improbable. However, he did have to be assured that no thorough purge was in the offing. What one may call a statutory discretion on the subject of Khrushchev and his works provided the best guarantee in this respect. (The same still holds true. The launching of a large-scale attack against Khrushchev, if it ever occurs, will be a sign of pressure on some politically active figure who is vulnerable on that score, just as the former leader's anti-Stalinist salvoes were directed against the Stalinists in his entourage.)

An even better guarantee seems to have been given initially to pro-Khrushchev elements, namely Podgorny's rise. The analysis of Podgorny's behaviour just before the crisis has suggested that he was not a member of the plot. His declaration stamped him as one of the best and oldest supporters of Khrushchev within the Presidium. To some extent, he even remained one after the crisis: he was one of those who observed most restraint on the subject of the 'October plenum'. Nevertheless, just after that session, he made a spectacular climb: on October 19 1964 he presided over the welcoming rally for the cosmonauts; at the November 7 reception he proposed the first toast on behalf of the Party, after Kosygin but before Brezhnev, and he also delivered the main report at the plenary session of November 1964 – the most important act of the new leadership. Next to a First Secretary who visibly did not yet have the stature, he was definitely more than the new heir presumptive.

The paradox is only on the surface: either the collective leadership had devised this as a reward for a signal *volte face* on Podgorny's part, or else, and this is far more likely, he was merely reaping the benefit of the privileged position in which he had found himself at the time of the showdown. Standing between an opposition that had acted without him but now needed the votes of his protégés, and Khrushchev, whom he was willing to forsake but whose supporters he was inheriting, he had been in an excellent position to dictate terms. Even when the parliamentary game involves only a few dozen players, there is always room for a 'centre party'. Podgorny was the beneficiary of this fact, and also the moderating influence. The guarantee afforded by Podgorny's rise could not last for ever. The power struggle was bound to go on, since conditions were still favourable to it. But this pertains to the internal affairs of the collective leadership.

Part Five
THE COLLECTIVE
LEADERSHIP ON ITS OWN
1964–1966

The best proof that Khrushchev's fall was due to a rebellion over internal 'organizational' issues rather than political differences was the fact that, for a long time, the new leaders appeared to be completely uncertain about their own political line, though they were prodigal with vows of allegiance to the 'lines' of previous congresses. Everyone was agreed in condemning 'subjectivism', 'empty phrases', 'harebrained schemes' and 'rash decisions', and of course to bury for good any projects which Khrushchev had had in store for his November plenum. In short, the new rulers knew roughly what they objected to but, in the three days that the crisis had lasted, they had hardly had time to discuss what they did want. When Khrushchev defeated his adversaries in 1957 he had done so for the sake of a certain policy: he proclaimed that policy as soon as he won, and the accusations he cast at Molotov were essentially political in nature. Brezhnev, Kosygin and Suslov were in a different situation in 1964. It looked as if they had defended their seals of office rather than a policy.

This accounts for the marked waverings of the first days. Even the decisions later described as being the outcome of the 'October plenum' were not taken immediately. For instance, the quarrel with the Chinese seemed fated to go on: on October 17, *Pravda* published a French communist text that was violently hostile to Peking, and, the day after, it encouraged the pro-Soviet elements of the Japanese Communist Party in their rebellion against their 'sectarian' leadership. Apparently 'signs' were required from Peking before the Russians thought of using Khrushchev's downfall for a *rapprochement*. One of the ex-leader's least realistic projects, namely, turning West Berlin into a 'demilitarized free city', remained in its original form in the joint communiqué signed with Cuban President Dorticós (*Pravda*, October 19 1964). Only at the beginning of December, in the joint communiqué signed with Novotný, was a more cautious formula devised (that of a 'self-governing political entity') before the issue was finally buried. On October 17 and 20 *Pravda* violently attacked French policy in Latin America and Vietnam, but on the 27th it published a highly laudatory comment on General de Gaulle. In short, the new team's foreign policy gave an impression of hindsight rather than of a considered rejection of Khrushchev's line.

At that stage, power problems were more important. The first concern of the leadership was to gain acceptance by those who had not been consulted during the operation – that is, the masses. After his 1957 victory Khrushchev had inaugurated a crash programme of housing construction. His successors' bounty took the form of abolishing the 'unfounded limitations' that he had imposed in 1961–1962 on the size of individual peasants' plots of land. Flour was distributed in the cities (it had not been available in the last months of Khrushchev's reign), and lastly, an extra New Year holiday was given (*Pravda*, December 29 1964). The biologists obtained Lysenko's downgrading, the writers and artists the promises that outbursts of the 1963 kind would not recur.[1] In other words the new 'reign' began, as might have been expected, in an atmosphere of *détente*.

This was bound to be temporary: not so much because choices had to be made which favoured this or that group (the new leadership tried for a long time, and is still trying with fair success, to postpone a number of awkward decisions), but because the various rival interest groups were too unequal. It would have been both impossible and illogical to go on pleasing everyone for long. Collective leadership, whose essential characteristic is the absence of the power of personal arbitration at the top, resolved itself in practice into rule by lobbies – groups of organized interests operating behind the scenes. This is the only clue which may enable us to unravel the tangled skein of post-Khrushchev political life. Anticipating our conclusions somewhat, we may say that, out of the several competing lobbies, two main ones emerged – that of the Party *apparatchiki* and that of the high State administration. The two groups clashed fairly sharply in May and June 1965, and the repercussions were felt in the top hierarchy. The outcome was a compromise (plenary session of September 1965 and economic reform) that gave the latter group substantial advantages; but the *apparatchiki* tried to restrict its scope by reasserting their control over all areas in every possible way. It was only at that point that the official line changed markedly on a few major issues, including a reassessment of Stalinism. The ups and downs of the various candidates for power should be viewed in the same light.

[1] As regards the promise that no new attacks would be made against writers and artists after Khrushchev's downfall, see the *Pravda* editorial of January 24 1965. Even before then, liberal writers had felt free to speak out. Those who had been castigated in 1963 – Yevtushenko, Voznesensky, etc. – were fairly outspoken in the autumn of 1964 and the beginning of 1965, while two notorious representatives of the conservative school, the sculptor Vuchetich and the painter Laktyonov, were personally attacked in the press (*Komsomolskaya Pravda*, December 2 1964, and *Pravda*, January 24 1965). However, the new spirit was not exempt from opposition and proved to be short-lived. This will be discussed later.

1 The Lobbies

Lobbies had always existed, even under Stalin, and we have seen how they became active whenever Khrushchev's authority dwindled. His downfall left them a clear field. Instead of one person to approach, there were eleven, each of whom needed outside support in the inevitable power struggle. Besides, it is always easier to form and dissolve a majority coalition than to induce an autocrat to change his mind. Thus any group which felt injured by some decision was inclined to regard it as provisional. It was only a step from there to unruliness, of which there were many signs in 1965 and 1966.

We shall deal first with those lobbies which, for the present, played only a minor role. One of these was the army. Since its contribution to Khrushchev's overthow had been small, it was in no position to thrust its chief into the Party Presidium, as happened with Zhukov after the 1957 crisis. However, the 1964 coup encouraged every group to widen its area of autonomy, as shown by Marshal Malinovsky's toast at the November 7 reception. Malinovsky's excursion into diplomacy was so forceful that Kosygin felt obliged to amend his Minister's utterance for the sake of the diplomats present. Subsequently, however, the military do not appear to have gained much. Their budget was cut by 500 million roubles for the 1965 fiscal year, but was increased by 600 million a year later because of the Vietnam war. The statements on the subject are roughly similar to those heard under Khrushchev. The military played a great part in the campaign for an 'objective' assessment of Stalin's role, which eventually helped other lobbies in promoting outright restalinization. But more of this later.

There is also little to be said about the police lobby, which kept in the background as far as the key issue was concerned. Its publicity efforts in 1964, as already mentioned, were aimed at rehabilitating Sorge; this treatment was extended to heroes of more recent times also. For instance, on March 13 1965, *Izvestia* extolled 'the dangerous life of a Soviet intelligence agent . . . on the American continent in the post-war years'. On May 7, in *Pravda*, V. E. Semichastny, the Chairman of the KGB, paid the first official tribute to 'the agent known under the name of Rudolf Abel', and added, almost apologetically: 'The time has not yet come when we can give the names of all the brave men' following in his footsteps. Apart from this unusual glorification of spying, there were few signs of any upsurge of politically independent KGB activity. In any case, even assuming that police pressure on the population increased in the two first post-Khrushchev years, the Party *apparatchiki* were not affected by it. And the KGB cannot become an element of power as it was under Stalin unless it extends its control to Party officials. For the time being, therefore, it remains a minor lobby.

The 'steel-eaters" lobby, as noted on several occasions, is a permanent institution in Soviet political life, and remained so without any interruption after Khrushchev's downfall. It includes all those who cling to the old Stalinist thesis of priority development for heavy industry – a dogma that will have to be revised some day if the rulers want to catch up with the new technological revolution and to promote consumption. The 'steel-eaters' are the official defenders of metallurgy versus chemistry, of capital goods production versus light industry and agriculture. This lobby did not, any more than those just mentioned, emerge as a candidate for power. Rather, as in Khrushchev's time, it was a silent but stubborn force that did not budge under assault but bided its time in order to sabotage unwelcome policies.

At first, the new rulers pretended that Khrushchev's overthrow had solved this particular problem. In his report to the plenary session of March 1965, Brezhnev termed the blatant shortage of funds allocated to agriculture one of Khrushchev's many errors (verbatim record of the plenary session, p 8). This ignored the struggle Khrushchev had waged for years against the 'steel-eaters', as A. M. Shkolnikov, one of the speakers at the plenary session, pointed out clearly though indirectly.[1] Even assuming, as Shkolnikov did, that the fault lay only with

---

[1] This is what Shkolnikov, the First Secretary of the Volgograd Oblast Committee and a long-standing advocate of an increase in industrial equipment for agriculture, replied to Brezhnev, who was blaming the plight of agriculture on Khrushchev at the March 1965 plenary session:

'One legitimate question arises in this connection: how has it come about that our industry has proved incapable of supplying machinery to agriculture? Who has curtailed the production even of basic agricultural machines? It seems to us that this question must not be left unanswered. The leaders who are responsible to Gosplan and to the federal sovnarkhoz for the construction of agricultural machines must give an explanation to the plenary session. . . .' (verbatim record, March 1965, plenary session, p 69).

One leader whom Shkolnikov singled out as responsible was P. S. Kuchumov who, until December 1962, had been chairman of the agency in charge of agricultural machinery distribution (*soyuzselkhoztekhnika*) and then became head of the Department of Agricultural Mechanical Engineering of the USSR sovnarkhoz. The speaker demanded no less than a 'severe sanction' by 'the Secretariat of the Central Committee or the Party–State Control Committee' against Kuchumov and other officials in similarly responsible posts. This meant going much further than Brezhnev who, by describing this shortcoming as one of the consequences of 'wilfulness' and 'stereotyped directives', had implied that Khrushchev alone had been guilty.

Kuchumov's successor at the head of *soyuzselkhoztekhnika*, A. A. Yezhevsky, defended himself with some skill by disclosing that in 1958–1959, when the seven-

officials in Gosplan and the federal sovnarkhoz, and not in any higher bureaucracy, the fact was that all these men were still at their posts and the problem was still real. Brezhnev himself had to concede a few months later that the sacrifices imposed on other sectors for the sake of agriculture (71 billion roubles to be invested in that sector over the next five years, 41 billion of which were to be supplied by the State) were being frustrated by the bureaucracy.[1] But although these 41 billion (a sum equal to the total amount spent on agriculture during the nineteen post-war years) were later whittled down through backstairs manoeuvring, the decision to allot them was after all a defeat for the 'steel-eaters'. Their spokesmen at the Presidium must have been in the minority and, at the plenary session, the most prominent RSFSR figures, G. I. Voronov and A. P. Kirilenko, both notoriously indifferent to the financial needs of agriculture, were silent.

However, even if the 'steel-eaters'' lobby can no longer dictate policy because the Soviet economy must obey its own inescapable laws, it is still strong enough to prevent other groups from reaching their goals, both in practice and in theory. For instance, the most active advocates of light industry development, such as Kosygin, can hardly go further than speak of 'bringing close together the rates of development' of 'group A' and 'group B', without daring to question the former's privileged position. Every now and then the dogma of the priority of heavy industry is reaffirmed, sometimes aggressively. For instance, in *Pravda* of March 1 1966 it was described as an 'unshakeable principle': 'we have held to it, and we shall continue to do so'. Even Kosygin, addressing the Supreme Soviet in August 1966 about the five-year plan, the

---

year plan was being drafted, a cutback in the production of agricultural machinery had been sought: 'The premise had been that, after the machinery had been sold to the kolkhozes, they would use it so much more rationally that production could be cut drastically.' This, naturally, was a thrust at Khrushchev. Yezhevsky, with even greater skill, implicated I. I. Kuzmin, Kosygin's rival who had been removed in 1960: 'Comrade Kuzmin, who was then President of Gosplan, completely disagreed with those who wanted to step up the production of agricultural machinery. Of course, he is not the only culprit' (verbatim record, March 1965 plenary session, pp 148–150).

This was specious reasoning. It is true that, after the record harvest of 1958, Khrushchev believed the agricultural problem had been solved and began to pare down the appropriations for that sector. But in subsequent years he reached very different conclusions, as his repeated pleas indicated.

[1] 'It must be stressed that, at certain levels of our State apparatus, at Gosplan, in the ministries and various administrations, there is to this day a tendency to alter this or that point, juggle with figures at the expense of agriculture, and slight the interests of the kolkhozes and sovkhozes. And this happens despite the perfectly clearcut decisions of the March plenary session, which stipulate that agriculture has to be given maximum help' (*Pravda*, September 30 1965).

In other words, the administration had had no qualms about transferring to other sectors, as need arose, the appropriations voted for agriculture. As we have seen, the same thing had happened under Khrushchev.

drafting of which was much delayed by this very quarrel, pleaded once again for 'bringing the rates closer together', but added immediately: 'It goes without saying that this in no way means that less attention will be given to heavy industry. The policy of giving priority to the development of that industry - the material basis of our whole economy – will be continued' (*Pravda*, August 4 1966).

In short, there was little change from the ambiguous tone that had prevailed under Khrushchev. The 'heavy industry stronghold' was still holding its own and had plenty of defenders ready to pounce on would-be assailants and accuse them of heresy. Since this fact provided a convenient outlet for the settlement of political scores (Khrushchev, as we know, had used it against Malenkov in 1954) it will be useful in future to keep a look-out for any public attacks on the advocates of heavy industry or their opponents.

THE *APPARATCHIKI*

The lobbies so far discussed were only secondary forces in the competition for political power. We now come to the two major groups on whom that power is at present based: the Party *apparatchiki* and the administrators of the economy.

From the outset, the average *apparatchik* – by which we mean the secretary of a rayon, oblast or republic committee, the head of a department of the Central Committee, etc. – was a major beneficiary of the 'October plenum'. Even under Khrushchev he had in a sense been the mainstay of power, but Khrushchev regarded the *apparat* as a mere conveyor belt for his orders and whims. Its members could be not only criticized but removed at will. Although the force of inertia, encouraged from above by the collective leadership, had gradually enabled it to resist attacks, the *apparat* would not forget in a hurry the humiliation of the famous 'enlarged plenary sessions', the sharp rebukes of the First Secretary, the downgrading of the Party to a mere appendage of the agricultural agencies, etc. It was eager to regain its former prestige, political stability, and security of employment as fast as possible. Since the Party machine sets the tone at the Central Committee – in which its representatives occupy over half the seats – and since at the time in question at least three strong men, Brezhnev, Suslov, and Podgorny, derived their own power from it, its members were in the best possible position to press their demands.

At any rate, these received early attention. The first major decision of the men now in power was to rescind the 1962 reform by reuniting the agricultural and industrial branches of the *apparat*. Although, as noted, the division of the Party had apparently been approved without much opposition by the Presidium in 1962, it was easy to demonstrate that practice had not justified the reform. N. V. Podgorny himself, who in 1962 had been one of the first 'fully to support and approve' the division of the Party (verbatim record of the November 1962 plenary session, p 118), came forward to put an end to it in his report to the plenary session of November 1964. As the traditional Oblast Committees were reinstated, the Party committees of the agricultural territorial administrations, also created in 1962, were abolished. The *raykom* (district or *okrug* Committee) was reinstated as well. Wherever Khrushchev had created over-large territorial units, they were replaced by several Rayon Committees on the former pattern. The Urban Committees (*gorkoms*) were revived wherever they had been abolished, for instance in the Ukraine. Thus, after a brief intermission, the *apparat* regained the form it had possessed for over forty years. The *apparatchik* recovered his status as a local leader enjoying jurisdiction in all fields, and also saw the familiar chain of command restored.

The second demand of the *apparatchik* was security of tenure. The first editorial of *Partiynaya Zhizn* after the October crisis (No 20 1964) declared: 'There is no doubt that bad officials must be replaced. The turnover of personnel is a legitimate phenomenon. However, it still happens that frequent reassignments are presented as an achievement, as a mark of vigilance, whereas they actually betoken inefficiency.' One could sense that this statement was the prelude to a demand for review of the Party statutes of 1961 which, it will be remembered, laid down rules for the 'systematic renewal of cadres'. Such a demand was stated for the first time officially (if not quite publicly) by the First Secretary of the Rostov Oblast Committee, M. S. Solomentsev, at the plenary session of March 1965: 'We communists demand that these provisions be amended.' But this was not known until the verbatim record of the session was published.[1] By September 1965, when elections were being held for the lower echelon committees in preparation

---

[1] Solomentsev also showed plainly how the apparatus had managed to get around the 1961 regulations: instead of promoting new secretaries, the old ones were merely moved from one region to another. He said:

'It is known that, in accordance with the decision of the Twenty-second Party Congress and the statutes then adopted, cell secretaries may be elected only for two terms, which means they may work in a given Party organization only for two years. This, of couse, has led to great fluidity and rotation of Party organization secretaries. It is difficult for us today to recruit a cell secretary, because every two years he has to move from one place to another, from one district to another. I think this is a somewhat artificial and false democracy.' Voices: 'Hear, hear!' (March 1965 plenary session, p 120).

for the Congress, *Partiynaya Zhizn* had in fact given its blessing to those who disregarded these now obsolete provisions. Without once alluding to the principle of 'systematic renewal', it made the decision contingent upon 'concrete conditions in a given organization' and emphasized the 'need to maintain experienced cadres in Party work and to respect the principle of continuity in leadership' (No 17 1965 p 7). Throughout the year, those 'experienced cadres' were the object of flattering comment, with the growing implication that the Stalinist cadres were the most 'experienced' of all. Under the circumstances, it was no surprise when the Twenty-third Congress in April 1966 cancelled the rules laid down five years earlier for the change of elected officials. It was decided, however, probably to avoid giving the impression that the 'new class' was clinging to power, to let the principle of 'systematic renewal' stand in the Party statutes. Since all the provisions designed to give it reality had been eliminated, it was henceforth nothing but a pious wish.

The yearning for stability among the middle cadres was a reaction against Khrushchev's arbitrariness, but it was also meant as a warning to the new leadership. Any high official who tried to use the change to pack the *apparat* with his own people, or to eliminate his rivals' protégés, was going to meet with resistance from the rank and file. That was probably why the new rulers were at first cautious in reassigning personnel (besides, Brezhnev had not yet had time to consolidate his position within the Secretariat). The re-establishment of the Oblast Committees, which might have opened the way for a major reshuffle, resulted almost everywhere in the return of the 'legal' holders (the pre-1962 First Secretaries) to their former posts. In an effort to keep discontent to a minimum, most chiefs of the parallel Oblast Committees set up two years earlier were appointed Second or Third Secretaries. It is likely that the same thing happened lower down at the Rayon Committee level. Return to old structures meant the return of the old faces.

Apart from this normal defensive attitude, there were other signs that the rank and file distrusted the top hierarchy. This does not mean, though, that this attitude was at the root of the many pleas for 'democratization' of the Party after Khrushchev's downfall. Depending on the level at which it is applied, democratization may hurt 'lesser' secretaries as well as 'greater' ones, and there have been many instances where the top hierarchy has used that very slogan against the middle cadres. Nevertheless, some of the proclamations are significant. The first post-Khrushchev editorial in *Partiynaya Zhizn* had, as mentioned, expressed the basic demand of the middle ranks of the *apparat* for security. However, the same editorial demanded that 'the activities of each leader should be on behalf of the Party and the people', and that 'control and if need be correction' of that leader should be provided for; it also asked that a stop be put to a situation where 'every word of the man at the top is regarded as a discovery, and his actions and attitudes are assumed to be infallible'. The result could only be further to curtail the authority of Brezhnev and of the collective leadership, which was meagre to start with. Moreover, by pointing out that each 'collective' 'must be able, whenever necessary, to put the person who has taken liberties back in his place', and by pointedly criticizing an Azerbaijan Rayon Committee which, for three years, had tolerated a leader guilty of nepotism and other sins, the journal seemed to be hinting that the Presidium for its part had been tardy in putting Khrushchev 'back in his place' (*Partiynaya Zhizn*, No 20 1964). A little later, A. Ya. Pelshe, then a member of the Central Committee and the First Secretary of the Party for Latvia, extolled at length in *Pravda* (November 6 1964) the role of the Central Committee and its plenary sessions without once mentioning the existence of the Presidium. Quoting Lenin, in whose day 'no important political or organizational problem was solved without instructions from the Central Committee', Pelshe praised the measures taken 'against an excessive concentration of power in the hands of certain officials' and against their attempts to evade control by the 'collective'. Pelshe, incidentally, also praised the provisions of the statutes concerning the 'systematic renewal of cadres'.[1] All this was undoubtedly a discreet but firm plea to let the Central Committee benefit from its newly regained freedom since, during the October crisis, it had once again been a mere rubber stamp.

Similar appeals were made subsequently as well. Some warnings to the upper hierarchy against exerting pressure on the lower ranks of the *apparat* at election time were particularly emphatic, for instance the following in *Kommunist* of December 1964, (No 18 1964), when the reunified Oblast Committees were being set up:

'There is no shortage of declarations proclaiming that Party members are the masters of their own organization. But no sooner are elections or progress reports due than officious mentors spring up and multiply processes completely alien to democracy; they may try to foist a bad candidate on the Party masses, and resort to crude pressure in order to push him through. Naturally, any higher Party committee can recommend the election of a particular comrade to a Party body, and not only recommend it, but defend the candidate.

[1] Pelshe had the advantage, when pleading for greater power for the Central Committee, of being a veteran Party member (since 1915). He had been an active participant in the 1917 events in Petrograd and at the same time was relatively new as a leader since he had become head of the Party in Latvia only in 1959. This made him the ideal spokesman of the 'Party parliament' *vis-à-vis* the collective leadership.

But no one has the right to transform advice and recommendation into an instrument of pressure upon communists.'

A year later, this warning was repeated with regard to elections by the lower organizations preceding the Party Congress:

'Certain comrades . . . are trying to apply to the election procedure within Party bodies the principle that decisions by higher Party bodies are binding upon lower Party bodies. The recommendation of a Rayon Committee or an Urban Committee on behalf of a particular candidate is not mandatory: it is an opinion that communists should naturally take into consideration, but with which they may disagree. It is wrong to interpret such disagreement as "undermining" the authority of the higher body' (*Partiynaya Zhizn*, No 1 1966).

These proclamations were directed mainly against pressure put on Party cells by the Urban and Rayon Committees, but it is safe to assume that they applied also to any possible pressure by a higher body on a lower one. Bearing in mind that the appointment of an Oblast Committee First Secretary requires a 'recommendation' from the Central Committee (specifically from the Secretariat or the Presidium), we may note that, in at least one case, constituents balked at the official candidate, although they eventually accepted him. This was B. F. Petukhov, who, in December 1964, was elected First Secretary of the reunified Kirov Oblast Committee. 'A number of delegates' at the Party regional conference had said that he 'did not heed collective opinion, did not tolerate objections, permitted himself to shout and make insulting remarks, protected toadies' (*Partiynaya Zhizn*, No 2 1965). According to the same publication, the names of two former secretaries of the industrial and agricultural Oblast Committees in the region, V. I. Trushin and G. Fokin, were struck off the list by the constituents themselves. Presumably, an attempt had been made, upon 'recommendation' from headquarters, to reserve for them posts in the *apparat* of the reunified Oblast Committee.

All this indicates that the Party apparatus should not be regarded as a homogeneous entity. Tensions exist between the various levels of the Party bureaucracy, and any real prospect of 'democratization' might produce quite a few surprises. But group cohesion is restored as soon as a confrontation with the other candidate for power is imminent.

THE MANAGERS

The word 'managers' seems the best equivalent to the Russian *khozyay-stvenniki*. The alternative term 'technocrats', which current trends have made popular abroad, is not quite accurate, because technology is not the sole concern of the men in charge of the Soviet economy. All these officials, ranging from the Chairman of Gosplan to factory managers, are part of an original management system where respect for certain procedures, for example the cult of the plan, are at least as important as technology itself. The term 'administrators' might seem adequate, and indeed the Soviet economy is basically an administered one; but it does not specify the economic sphere, the only one of concern to our argument. For these reasons we shall stick to the term 'managers'.

This group is even less homogeneous than the Party *apparat*. It would be wrong to imagine that most of its members are in favour of reforms, profit, profit-earning capacity (*rentabelnost*) and market operation – in short, everything that is commonly called 'Libermanism'.

This impression was created by the flood of articles propounding 'reforms' and 'progress' that found their way into the press just after the collective leadership had taken over. In fact, however, the trend was not a new one: the 1962 'Liberman debate' had been resumed under Khrushchev when Academician Trapeznikov published an article in *Pravda* of August 17 1964. It is hard to tell whether this was another sign that Khrushchev's authority was dwindling, or merely that he was not interested in the subject. In 1964, however, unlike 1962, a first step towards reform was actually taken. During the summer an experimental programme was started in two plants, a clothing and a shoemaking factory – Bolshevichka in Moscow and Mayak in Gorki. It aimed at organizing production exclusively on the basis of commercial orders without – in principle – any interference from planning agencies. On October 12 1964, two days before Khrushchev's downfall, a *Pravda* editorial affirmed that: 'This experiment deserves wider application, not only within the ready-made clothing industry, but also in other branches of light industry.' Therefore, the decision taken at the beginning of 1965 to convert four hundred consortiums and enterprises in light industry to that system (*Pravda*, January 13 1965) did not come as a surprise.

What was new, on the other hand, was the support that the reformers were finding within the top hierarchy, especially from Kosygin, now free from the constraint imposed by Khrushchev. All Kosygin's declarations of this period indicate that he sided with the reformers. In his first speech, on October 19, the day the cosmonauts were welcomed, he pinpointed the true problem of Soviet economy by saying:

'We cannot hope to exceed the high productivity reached by the most developed capitalist countries unless we increase the workers' initiative and freedom of action' (*Pravda*, October 20 1964). A few weeks later, before the Supreme Soviet, he expressed support for the practice of 'direct links' between enterprises, not only in light industry, but everywhere: 'Exactly the same direct links between suppliers and customers are necessary in the branches that produce capital goods – machinery, equipment, metal' (*Pravda*, December 10 1964). It was obviously with Kosygin's blessing that articles by the most eager advocates of 'Libermanism' multiplied in the press, as well as countless grievances of the men shackled by the 'petty controls' imposed upon them.[1]

All this agitation should not be overestimated. No doubt, then as now, everyone saw the need to 'do something' about the bureaucratic red tape that was strangling the country's economy, with its resultant waste, impairment of productivity and slowing up of technological progress. But it was one thing to call for 'quality' in production, for 'better education of cadres' or for the use of electronic equipment to lighten administrative work, and quite another to go to the root of the evil by advocating a radical change in planning itself, and the replacement of the administrative chain of command by flexible management based on the operation of the market and the laws of profit.

When it came to this basic issue, it became obvious that the representatives of the latter tendency, the only genuine 'reformers', were few indeed. Apart from Liberman himself (although, since his success abroad, his main assignment apparently consisted in explaining to the American press that his suggestions did not amount to a return to capitalism), there were economists such as I. Birman and V. Belkin, but these, on the whole, were theoreticians and professors free from direct managerial duties. They were a mere handful of top men who, thanks to the scope of their responsibilities and their access to broader information, had grown more 'enlightened'. But in between was the formidable power of the managers, the huge Gosplan machine, ministries and industrial branch committees and their multiple ramifications in the provinces. The men staffing all these agencies had been trained in

[1] The following is a statement by an Odessa factory director complaining about administrative controls, published by *Pravda* on December 7 1964:

> 'The plan concerning productivity, salaries, cost, profit and administrative expenses is handed to the factory every year without any previous consultation with its officials. . . . The utilization of the wage fund is prescribed from above down to the last kopek. . . . The manager does not have the right to alter the quarterly distribution of supplies and funds or to transfer them from one sector to another. . . . He does not have the right to issue to a worker a glove or an apron in excess of the quota prescribed by the regulations.'

thirty-five years of Stalinist planning to recognize only one law – that of '*val*' (production expressed in physical units, regardless of quality and cost); only one method – that of direct command; and only one type of hierarchy – absolute obedience by the lower echelons.

It is not even certain that the main victims of this administrative totalitarianism – the heads of enterprises themselves – belonged to the 'enlightened' class of managers. There are many exceptions, of course, but it does seem that, owing to fear of responsibility, lack of training and a general climate that did not promote initiative, they often wanted no more than a readjustment of the same old methods. Many of them wanted to have twenty scattered and contradictory supervisors replaced by a single reliable one (a ministry, for example, or the local Party Committee), but not to have no supervisor at all. Kosygin himself in December 1964 deplored the fact that the few rights granted earlier to the enterprises were 'still far from being fully exercised' (*Pravda*, December 12 1964).

All this explains the resistance encountered by the reformers, and the very limited scope of their 'victory' – the compromise of September 1965, which will be discussed subsequently. But the managers, whether reformers or not, had another basic problem to solve – that of their relations with the first group, the Party *apparatchiki*.

THE PARTY, *PODMYENA* AND PRODUCERS' INITIATIVE

A confrontation between the two groups was inevitable. There no longer existed a single authority which, as under Stalin and more recently under Khrushchev, controlled both Party and State. At the very top were now two men of equal political stature, Brezhnev and Kosygin. Under these conditions, the respective position of each group had to be defined, or at least an attempt had to be made in that direction. The problem went beyond their different attitudes toward reforms and even beyond purely 'Kremlinological' rivalries for political power. It was due to the fact that the Party reaffirmed at the outset its intention of managing the entire life of the country, including its economic life.

The totalitarian attitude of the *apparat* was amply demonstrated throughout the discussions over reform in 1965. A number of Party officials did, indeed, advocate 'initiative for the masses', and also for managers; in fact, the subject was never so much discussed as during this period. But since no spontaneous move independent of the Party's 'organizational work' was conceivable in the eyes of the *apparat*, what it gave with one hand was invariably taken back with the other. Here are a few examples.

Immediately after Khrushchev's overthrow, the press denounced with renewed vigour the phenomenon known as *podmyena* (substitution), meaning that the respective functions of *apparatchiki* and managers overlapped and that, as a result, the latter's responsibilities were usurped by the former. On November 18 1964 *Pravda* in its editorial blamed the division of the Party in 1962 for having 'led in practice to the confusion of the respective functions, rights and duties of the Party organs, the soviets and the economy, and . . . prompted the Party committees to substitute themselves for the economic agencies'. One might have thought that this would have been followed by the suggestion that one group should henceforth take charge of the economy and the other of political work. Not at all. The editorial went on to state that: 'The reorganization (in 1962) meant that in a number of sectors that are very important for the building of the economy, the influence of the Party organs over production activities has weakened.' This started a strange alternation of slogans that went on for months, from anti-*podmyena* proclamations to the cry for 'constant reinforcement of the Party's role':

'Naturally, one must not displace the economic leaders or downgrade their role and their prestige within the "collective". But wherever necessary, the Party organization must intervene in the affairs of the farm, fully using the right of control given it by the CPSU statutes. . . . Practice shows that the best results are obtained where constant care is taken to enhance the role of the Party organizations in brigades and farms' (*Pravda* editorial, December 6 1964).

As a matter of fact, it was in agriculture that, after denouncing Khrushchev for having attempted to impose 'petty control' over production, Brezhnev's *apparat* first showed signs of making the same mistake. For example, by the end of 1964 it had been decided to cut down planning in agriculture: the regional authorities were merely to let the kolkhozes know what amounts and types of products they had to deliver. This is how *Pravda* interpreted the decision on January 5 1964:

'Rural workers themselves . . . can and must set out in their production plan the areas and structure for the most profitable seed-beds, as well as stockbreeding objectives. They must decide what crops to sow and what amount, how much livestock to keep on the farms, how to make the most rational use of the land.'

But the editorial that had started out so well was in fact a cry of alarm. The result of this daring liberation was that 'in some kolkhozes, the sowing of crops that are very important for that particular region has been arbitrarily reduced'. In Krasnodar 'the farms, using their right to plan, have curtailed beet-growing areas without giving a thought to higher yield'. The Novosibirsk farms 'have unjustifiably cut down on buckwheat growing in their plans for 1965'. One could not imagine a better illustration of the principle: You are free provided you do the right thing. And that, indeed, was how the article ended:

> 'This [planning of production by the kolkhozes] must be done intelligently, keeping in mind the interests of the State and actual conditions on the farm. . . . *The ones to direct* (vozglavlat) *this work are the organs of the Party*, the soviets and the agricultural agencies. Their duty is *to help the rural workers* to approach their activities and to draw up plans *from the viewpoint of the State*' (*Pravda*, January 5 1965). [Author's italics.]

The same line prevailed at the plenary session of March 1965. On the one hand, the provisions adopted at the end of 1964 on the relaxation of planning were confirmed. In addition, the volume of compulsory farm deliveries was cut back, with the promise that there would be no increase for the next five years. An explanatory provision published by *Pravda* on April 12 1965 merely invited the kolkhozes and sovkhozes to:

> 'examine the possibility of their selling to the State in 1965, *on a voluntary basis*, additional amounts of wheat and rye.'

It was learned on the same occasion that these estimated surpluses over the official plan would be the subject of 'an additional plan' drafted in high quarters, but that no instructions on the subject would be given to the farms. Even assuming that the State would refrain from interfering, was the Party going to stand by and not do anything about this 'voluntary' programme? Clearly not. The day after the provision was made public, *Pravda* made the following comment:

> 'The fact that the plan fixes the amounts to be delivered over a number of years . . . does not diminish but rather enhances the responsibility of the Party organs and soviets for increasing agricultural production' (*Pravda*, April 13, 1965).

A little later, another newspaper specified how this responsibility was to be discharged:

> 'The farms themselves determine how much grain they can sell in excess of the plan. But *this in no way means that the Rayon Committees*

have to remain on the sidelines. Each collective has to be helped to estimate its needs correctly, while the advantages of a sale of wheat in excess of the plan must be explained as often as necessary' (*Sovyetskaya Rossiya*, August 15, 1965).

This subtle distinction between 'help' and 'substitution' might be legitimate if the Party honestly confined itself to an 'advisory' role. Actually, the same slogans enable it to control all other spheres of activities; its 'recommendations' have always been orders, and its 'help' administrative interference. Therefore the problem is akin to squaring the circle. It was nothing new, but this particular debate illustrated the paradoxes in a particularly striking way. For example, *Pravda's* editorial on June 29 1965:

'The Party has great confidence in agricultural specialists. It regards them as a reliable base in the struggle for progress in agriculture and stockbreeding. But having confidence does not mean letting things drift. . . . Of course, it is out of the question to interfere constantly with the specialist's day-to-day work or to take his place. This practice was condemned once and for all, and it is not to be resumed. What is needed is concrete help, a daily and thorough supervision of the execution of adopted decisions. . . .'

Let those who can differentiate between 'daily and thorough supervision of the execution of adopted decisions' and 'constant interference with day-to-day work'. These explanations show that the Party apparatus, after having 'suffered' at Khrushchev's hand by being confined to administrative tasks, was happy to regain its traditional political and ideological prerogatives. This did not mean, however, that it intended to relinquish its hold over the economy. A Rayon Committee secretary in the Altay made this plain in an article in *Pravda* of June 9, 1965:

'Day after day, the Party Rayon Committee sees to it that all the communists in the kolkhozes and sovkhozes enter continuously and thoroughly into all details of work and study the economy of the farm. We give special attention to this because there are here, in the Altay, officials who believe that it is for the Rayon's agricultural agencies (the State machine, in other words) to deal with the economy, while the Party Rayon Committee and the Party rank and file must deal only with political and propaganda work. But how can political work be carried out, towards what goal are the rural communists to be led, if the Rayon Committee and the Party organizations are not thoroughly familiar with each farm's economic conditions and its prospects of development? . . . The Rayon Committee and the Party cells are responsible for everything. . . . We appeal to all Party cells, to all communists . . . not to shirk economic problems, but to study them continuously and carefully.'

The above examples apply to agriculture, which is traditionally the most 'politicized' branch of the Soviet economy, but the situation was more or less the same in industry. True, the debate in this case was not over 'petty controls' such as those described in the farms (after all, it is harder for the Party to interfere with the management of a steel mill than that of a kolkhoz). In industry the issues were of greater significance, affecting, for instance, the manager's place in the political system. The main point was that, when the Party tried to impose its totalitarian rule over industry, it clashed with the State's industrial bureaucracy, an incomparably stronger one than its agricultural bureaucracy.

THE FUTURE OF THE SOVNARKHOZES

The first difficulty arose at the end of 1964 regarding the sovnarkhozes. These 'regional economic councils' were threatened as soon as Khrushchev's heritage was open for review. The 1957 reform that had set them up was also the one that had made the largest number of victims within the State machine, since all the Moscow industrial ministries had been liquidated to make way for the new councils. In addition, their significance had dwindled as a result of the progressive recentralization which had taken place over the seven years since their establishment. All that was now left of the 1957 'decentralization' was an additional link in the chain of command.

The liquidation of the sovnarkhozes therefore seemed imminent. On December 1 1964 *Pravda* reprinted, 'as a basis for discussion', an article by the director and chief engineer of a Leningrad factory, who raised the problem overtly. Observing that the sovnarkhozes served practically no purpose ('their superficial and formal role actually consists in nothing more than preparing reports and inventories that no one analyses or studies'), the writers proposed that the sovnarkhozes' co-ordination tasks should be restricted to 'local' industries. Everything else, they suggested, should come under the authority of the Moscow industrial State committees. These, by regaining direct managerial powers, would become what the former ministries used to be: 'It is in the State committees that planning and actual management of the entire branch should be concentrated.' The authors did not specifically call for the liquidation of the sovnarkhozes, but the implication was clear enough.

Pravda invited all those interested to 'give their opinion' about the article, thus announcing a major debate which in fact did not occur. On the contrary, at the Supreme Soviet session meeting a few weeks later, it became clear that the wind had completely shifted. N. G. Yegorychev, the First Secretary of the Moscow Urban Committee, attacked the authors of the December 1 article for having set at naught the progress achieved by Soviet factories (*Izvestia*, December 11 1964).[1] G. I. Popov, the First Secretary of the Leningrad Urban Committee (the region whence the debate in *Pravda* had originated), was even more eloquent:

> 'Of late, an increasing number of voices have advocated the liquidation of the sovnarkhozes and a return to the former system of management by ministries. In our opinion, such proposals are unfounded. We believe that the *system of sovnarkhozes is progressive and has fully vindicated itself.* The experience of the Leningrad sovnarkhoz has brought to light the clear advantages of this new form of management. *We advocate sovnarkhozes, but with substantially wider rights and prerogatives*' (*Izvestia*, December 11 1964). [Author's italics.]

As it happens, these two advocates of the sovnarkhozes were the most prominent representatives of their local Party apparatus. Their attitude is not surprising, since the presence of the sovnarkhoz, a State agency at their own level, made it easiest for them to keep the regional industry in their grip. G. I. Popov made this quite clear:

> 'The CPSU programme emphasizes that, under present conditions, the leading role of the Party and its local organs is growing immensely in all sectors of the building of communism. This was particularly stressed at the recent plenary sessions of the Central Committee. But in practice it is not possible to exert effective Party leadership over the economy unless the principle of territorial and branch management is maintained' (*Leningradskaya Pravda*, December 11 1964).

Against the representatives of the local Party apparatus were naturally the managers of the Central State apparatus, the leaders of Gosplan and State committees, who were eager to regain their ministerial seats. Not by accident did both Popov and Yegorychev roundly criticize the representatives of that group, the latter even going so far as to accuse them of being 'unprincipled'.

---

[1] In this and subsequent parts of the book the dates given will be those of the foreign edition of *Izvestia*.

The only surprise was that the two main newspapers took opposite sides. *Pravda* (edited at the time by A. M. Rumyantsev), which usually upholds the interests of the *apparatchiki*, had taken the initiative of questioning the existence of the sovnarkhozes in its article of December 1. *Izvestia* (editor-in-chief, V. I. Stepakov), which was in theory the organ of the central State apparatus, did not support the attack on the sovnarkhozes but, on the contrary, became the only mouthpiece of their supporters. (*Pravda*, for instance, did not reprint the Popov and Yegorychev statements.) In fact, the problem was more complex than appears at first sight. The liquidation of the sovnarkhozes was entirely to the liking of the Moscow managers, but it also meant the dismissal of thousands of local managers employed by sovnarkhozes for the past seven years. Hence the State apparatus could not take a unanimous stand on the issue. The same held true for the *apparatchiki*. The existence of a sovnarkhoz for a single city or region, as in Moscow or Leningrad, fully accounted for the attitude of men like Popov and Yegorychev. But in many other localities the sovnarkhozes, which had been enlarged after 1962 and 1963, covered several oblasts. Hence, the First Secretary of an Oblast Committee would not find a management agency at his own level to which he could issue 'recommendations'. Moreover, the situation was very often reversed and some supra-regional sovnarkhozes tended to regard all regional authorities, even Oblast Committees, as being under their control.[1]

At any rate, the debate dragged on longer than expected. In the beginning of March 1965, a concession was made to the 'privileged managers', i.e. the men in charge of the defence industry, by converting their State committees into ministries (*Pravda*, March 4 1965). But no further steps were taken at that time. Kosygin, speaking on March 19 at a planners' meeting, hinted that the time had not yet come to settle the sovnarkhoz problem. He said:

[1] This was illustrated in *Pravda* of May 29 1965 by an article by V. Baranov, the head of the building department of the Ivanovo Oblast Committee. Four oblasts were grouped within a single economic region, and the Oblast Committees involved were receiving directions and even orders from the building administration of the economic region. Why the Oblast Committees? Because at present, Baranov explained, 'the only organs within the oblast that co-ordinate to some extent the activities of the contractors and the services they run are the Oblast Committees and their branch services, whether they want to or not'.

Subsequently the phenomenon became more widespread, especially after the sovnarkhozes were liquidated and the ministries re-established. The Oblast Committees could not escape the *podmyena* since they 'are responsible for everything' within their region. This turned the Oblast Committees into 'super-managers' – hence, the most authoritative local agencies for the Moscow ministries to deal with. The journal *Kommunist* in July 1966 (no 11 p 126) provided several examples of 'requests' and other injunctions addressed by the ministries to the Oblast Committees.

'Many leaders also express the opinion that proper order will not prevail in planning so long as the industry is subject to the authority of the local organs, so long as the sovnarkhozes exist. Give us a Ministry, these people say, and order will prevail.'

Did Kosygin share this opinion or not? He seemed to be disagreeing with 'these people', but he may have been under pressure when making the statement, since he went on:

'Economic planning is closely tied to the forms and methods of economic management, and there is no doubt that the existing system needs improvement. It would be wrong, however, to ascribe all shortcomings in planning and economic activities to flaws in the management system of industry and building. If we adopt that viewpoint, we shall make many more mistakes' (*Planovoye Khozyaystvo*, no 4 1965).

The plenary session of March 1965 did not change anything in that part of the system. Even the problem of the 'Supreme Sovnarkhoz' was not raised when its chairman, D. F. Ustinov, was promoted to other functions within the Party Secretariat. He was immediately succeeded by V. N. Novikov, one of his associates in the armament industry, who had returned to the scene directly after Khrushchev's overthrow. The sovnarkhoz was somewhat downgraded, however, in so far as Novikov did not inherit Ustinov's functions of First Deputy Prime Minister, and became merely a Deputy Prime Minister. It was only in June that the decision to liquidate the sovnarkhozes was apparently adopted. In its issue No 9, dated June 15, *Kommunist* announced: 'The time has come to cut down the number of echelons in the management apparatus.' The decision was announced only in September 1965, at the same time as the economic reform.

Both problems were, indeed, connected and this did not make the discussion any easier. On February 17 1965 *Pravda* had closed the public debate by announcing that a 'series of special committees' had just been set up within Gosplan and elsewhere in order to draft 'concrete suggestions' for reforms. Agreement still had to be reached at the top.

STEPANOV VERSUS THE 'PRACTICAL MEN'

The managers, as noted, were far from agreeing on the best way of running the economy. But naturally enough, they believed that the problem, if not the exclusive concern of their own group (the Party could not be left out completely), was essentially for them to settle. This was definitely Kosygin's view. In his speech of March 19th to the planners, the new Head of Government sharply upbraided his audience (in particular for an unsatisfactory draft five-year plan for 1966–1970 which they had handed in), but at the same time clearly indicated that Gosplan, and generally speaking the Government as a whole, should thereafter be able to manage the economy without any outside interference. His only reference to Lenin was on that very point:

'Lenin cared about Gosplan's authority, about a certain autonomy, a certain independence that it was meant to enjoy. "Gosplan", he wrote, "is visibly turning into a committee of experts. . . . A certain independence, a certain autonomy are necessary if this scientific institution is to have the necessary authority, and its independence and authority hinge on one single thing: the conscientiousness of its officials, and their honest effort to put our plan for economic and social construction into practice." ' (*Planovoye Khozyaystvo*, no 4, April 1965).

Kosygin also gave a very broad interpretation of planning:

'Properly speaking, planning is not only an economic activity, as people often believe. It is the solving of social problems, problems linked with the raising of the people's standard of living. We regard the plan as a complex of economic and social tasks to be performed during the period covered by it, as a complex of all problems related to man's life' (*ibid.*).

Then he went on to define the criterion which should govern the planners' activity: to serve the interests of the economy, and them alone:

'We have to free ourselves completely . . . from everything that used to tie down the planning officials and obliged them to draft plans otherwise than in accordance with the interests of the economy. . . . In the course of analysing many important problems, we often find ourselves prisoners of laws we ourselves have made, which should have been replaced long ago by new principles corresponding to the modern conditions that govern the development of production' (*ibid.*).

Economy, production, living standards: nowhere had ideology, communism, or even the Party been mentioned. This could not be allowed to go unchallenged. It was noticed that Kosygin's speech was ignored by the major papers. It was published after a month's delay in the Gosplan monthly journal quoted here, which was put on sale about April 19 1965, and the weekly *Ekonomicheskaya Gazeta* of

April 21 1965. But even that was too much for the Party, which could not overlook the slight.

Its answer came on May 17, when *Pravda* published an article by V. P. Stepanov, the editor-in-chief of *Kommunist*. The title, 'The higher ideals of the Party and its daily cares', gave a fair summary of the content. The 'daily cares' were economy and management, while the 'higher ideals' were something much broader – the building of communism, social changes, the disappearance of classes, etc. Hence, *what* to produce was at least as important as *how* to produce:

> 'Lenin's pressing pleas to feel concern over each *pud*[1] of grain, each *pud* of coal, are well known. . . . But the entire meaning of Lenin's appeal consisted in defining *the means whereby* those *puds* would be obtained, in order that they might be produced in a non-capitalist manner, through the conscious, voluntary, heroic and dedicated labour of ordinary workers. Behind this *pud* of coal or wheat, Lenin sensed that new relationships between men were emerging. . . . '
> (*Pravda*, May 17 1965. Author's italics.)

Unless the higher goals were kept in mind (in other words if, as Kosygin wished, only the interests of the economy and the laws of production were considered), there was a risk of falling into a number of sins which, evidently, were those of the average 'manager':

> 'Our Party advocates the concrete and operative character of labour, but at the same time it strongly opposes aimless bustling (*byezgolovoye delyachestvo*) and blind fussing over details, which even today still have their enthusiasts. . . . Lenin . . . used to laugh at the narrow-minded (*uzkolobye*) "practical men" who could not see the wood for the trees, and who would get bogged down in details and lose sight of the overall picture' (*Pravda*, May 17 1965).

Stepanov, naturally, could not accept Kosygin's very broad definition of planning. To start with, the goal was not merely to raise living standards. On this point, Stepanov's criticism was ostensibly aimed at Khrushchev, but in fact at all those who might be tempted to follow in his footsteps:

> 'To equate communism with the mere fulfilment of the "stomach's needs", with a narrow, blind, "practical approach" when we are facing the wide horizons of the future and higher ideals, would be profoundly wrong' (*ibid.*).

---

[1] The *pud*, a Russian unit of weight, is the equivalent of about 36 lbs.

Furthermore, if there was one science embracing 'all problems of man's life' it was not planning but ideology, which alone was capable of foreseeing the future:

'The Soviet people are building a communist society. But it has not been built yet, and this is why, to a large extent, it belongs to the realm of theory rather than reality. For this reason, the working out in theory of all the principles of communism, of the roads that lead to it and the means by which it is to be built, is one of the main tasks of the Party and of our social sciences' (*ibid.*).

It goes without saying that the Party was supposed to guide the entire process with a firm hand, and this was a far cry from the degree of independence for Gosplan advocated by Kosygin. As a last warning, Stepanov again quoted Lenin, theoretically to show the dangers of 'subjectivism' à la Khrushchev, but, in fact, to round out his picture of the 'practical men':

'The machine eludes control: one believes that a man is there, steering the wheel, but the machine does not go where it is driven. . . . It does not operate quite as the man at the wheel imagines, and sometimes quite differently' (*ibid.*).

The laws of Kremlinology are subtle, and it was obvious that none of Stepanov's statements, if taken literally, contradicted Kosygin's directly. On that level, that is usually the case. But the difference in stress told the whole story, and was sufficiently marked to reveal a basic disagreement.

For instance, regarding economic reform Stepanov was expounding the line that the Party propaganda officials were to follow in the coming months. In substance it was this: 'We all agree to seek more flexible, rational methods of management. We advocate a partial return to the mechanisms of profit, prices and credit; in so far as this reform implies a change in attitude on the part of the managers, we shall press for it. But the Party, which by definition represents everything that is most progressive, does not have to change its methods of work or to curtail its prerogatives. On the contrary, it will exert greater vigilance than before to make sure that the "higher ideals" are not betrayed: for instance, the moral incentives that the Party has always upheld – competitive campaigns, educational work, and so on – must not be overlooked under the pretext of reinstating profit incentives.' Put more simply, the Party was willing to agree to a reform provided its own realm was left untouched.

Where political matters were concerned, Stepanov reaffirmed with particular sharpness that the Party, or rather its apparatus, intended to remain in control of the economy. This, furthermore, was not to be merely at the Rayon and Oblast Committee level, as in agriculture, but at the top also. Stepanov was reminding Kosygin, who had proclaimed the Government's right to plan and manage the economy without any outside interference, that such intrusions were going to occur, particularly where ideology was concerned, precisely because the task of ideology was to prevent any relapse into the 'narrow practical approach'. This was the clearest indication so far that the ever-recurring problem of relations between Party and State, and between Brezhnev and Kosygin, was again claiming attention.

THE CONFRONTATION OF MAY 1965

A few signs indicated that a showdown occurred in Moscow in May 1965.

On the afternoon of May 17 (the date of Stepanov's article) and probably for the next few days, the Presidium met in Moscow. Kosygin, who had been in Leningrad since the evening of the 15th together with Shastri, the head of the Indian Government, left his guest at the end of the morning of the 17th instead of accompanying him to Kiev. Shastri duly arrived in Kiev that afternoon, but P. E. Shelest, another member of the Presidium, who was the First Secretary of the Ukrainian Party, was not there. It was not Shelest's capacity as Party official that prevented him greeting a 'bourgeois' visitor, since his counterpart in Leningrad, V. S. Tolstikov, had taken part in the welcoming ceremonies, and in Tashkent a little later Shastri was greeted by Rashidov, the local First Secretary. From Kiev on, Shastri was escorted only by V. E. Dymshits, Prime Minister.

The two members of the Presidium who apparently were most occupied by the session were Brezhnev and Kosygin. Although both were in Moscow, neither made any public appearance on May 18, although many official functions were held on that day. Brezhnev, for instance, did not attend a luncheon given by a delegation of the Algerian FLN 'in honour of the CPSU representatives who had participated in the talks and meetings with the Algerian Party delegation' (*Pravda*, May 19 1965), although he had attended one of these meetings only the day before, on the morning of May 17 (*Pravda*, May 18).

Both Brezhnev and Kosygin reappeared next day, but for three days running *Izvestia* made no mention of Brezhnev, although he had made two public appearances. These were on the 17th, when he had been host to the Algerian delegation, and on the 19th, when he had attended a reception at the Moscow Soviet. Not until after May 21 did the name of the Party First Secretary reappear in *Izvestia*, and then only with Shastri's at the foot of their joint communiqué. On the other hand, Kosygin's considerable activity was faithfully reported, both by *Izvestia* and *Pravda*. For instance, on May 19 he had the honour of presenting the city of Moscow with the emblem of 'heroine-city'. Although this was no time for a detailed comment on economic reform, he said in his speech:

> 'The rate of our forward movement depends on how far we can utilize all the opportunities provided by the technological and scientific revolution now taking place' (*Pravda*, May 20 1965).

He listed among the achievements of the Moscow Communists their 'having always been in the forefront of the struggle for the purity of the Party line' and 'having actively opposed all attempts to make them deviate from the Leninist path' [1] (*ibid.*).

It is impossible to determine the exact meaning of each of these signs. The only possible inference is that, perhaps for the first time since the 'October plenum', serious differences had arisen and that a show-down had probably occurred within the Presidium, mainly between Brezhnev and Kosygin. Whoever came out the loser, it was not Kosygin and his supporters. This became noticeable when a strong editorial appeared in *Izvestia* on the evening of the 20th (international edition, May 21), three days after Stepanov's article. It was a barely disguised challenge to the editor-in-chief of *Kommunist*:

> 'The October plenary session [Khrushchev's downfall] and the following plenary sessions of the Central Committee sharply condemned subjectivism, wilful decisions and *ignorance of economic laws* in the management of the economy. . . . The Party confirmed once again that it is the *economic* methods of management of socialist production that preserve the *basic meaning* and *best ensure* the development of the workers' initiative' (*Izvestia*, May 21 1965. Author's italics).

---

[1] *Pravda* reprinted Kosygin's entire speech at the Moscow city award ceremony, but in its same issue (May 20) there was an anomaly concerning him. According to *Izvestia* (international edition of May 20 1965), the chairman at the meeting of the Moscow Soviet, N. G. Yegorychev, had 'in the name of the deputies and of all the workers in the capital, expressed his cordial gratitude to the Central Committee of the CPSU, the Presidium of the Supreme Soviet and the Council of Ministers of the USSR for the title of "heroine-city" awarded to the capital, and for the cordial greetings to the Moscow workers *expressed by A. N. Kosygin*.'
Pravda reprinted this sentence verbatim except that it omitted the words in italics. [Author's italics.]

In other words, as between priority for economic laws as advocated by Kosygin in his March 19 speech, and Stepanov's thesis of priority for ideology, *Izvestia* had definitely chosen the first. Consequently, profit incentives were to be given first place.

'The March [1965] plenary session of the Central Committee devoted its chief *attention to the reinforcement of profit incentives* in the development of production and the consolidation of the financial basis of agriculture. Such an attitude is wholly *correct also for industry* and other branches of the economy' (*ibid.*).

Needless to say, the portrait of the manager in the editorial was the opposite of Stepanov's caricature:

'The combination of business sense and fidelity to great ideas is characteristic of the Soviet leader, whatever his post. . . . The Soviet economic leader . . . has to watch over the range of production and respond as accurately as possible to fluctuations of demand when drafting the plans for his enterprise. For this, one has to be a good businessman and estimate with scientific accuracy the changes in the overall picture. *With all this, the Soviet director is not a narrow-minded "practical man"* ' (*ibid.* Author's italics).

The 'narrow-minded practical man' (*deliaga s uzenkim gorizontom*) was, of course, an allusion to the 'narrow-minded businessman' whom Stepanov so despised.

It was then up to *Pravda* to reply, and it was obvious that it had no intention of surrendering. An article by László Orban, the Hungarian Agitprop chief, written in just the right vein, was conveniently discovered: its gist was: 'Economic reform, yes, but . . .'

'Further progress depends not only on solving economic problems, but also on the results of ideological and educational work. . . . The strengthening of the workers' power and a thriving economy are inconceivable without the political changes that have occurred in people's minds and consciousness' (*Pravda*, May 21 1965).

The same went for profit incentives:

'We do not forget that, if the principle of profit incentives is envisaged unilaterally, instead of being combined with educational work and moral exhortation, . . . this will give rise to a selfishness that is alien to socialism, and a deviation towards the dominance of private interests at the expense of collective interests' (*ibid.*).

There were countless 'buts':

'Ever-increasing attention is given to the problems of raising profit-earning capacity and productivity. However, this in turn demands an equally high level of organization, discipline and labour.

'The Party organizations fully understand that economic problems are at the centre of the class struggle. Unfortunately not everybody is sufficiently aware that the formation of socialist consciousness and ideological education represent an equally important aspect of Party work, without which it is impossible fully to perform economic tasks' (*ibid.*).

This explains one of the major worries of the *apparatchiki*: so long as the economy had operated under the Stalinist principle of 'command supplemented by enthusiasm', they had naturally found their place in the system by organizing competitive campaigns: first the 'Stakha-novite' movements, then 'communist labour', 'shock brigades', etc. – in short, by surrounding labour with the whole mystique of 'enthusiasm for work' that filled the newspapers. But if the economy was to start operating under its own laws, independently as it were, who was going to need the Party and its *apparatchiki*? Even if they kept their political and ideological functions on the territorial level, they did not like the idea of being shut out of the factories. Hence their efforts at this stage to justify their existence to the managers and prove their 'superiority'. For example, this is how G. I. Popov, First Secretary of the Leningrad Urban Committee, put it:

'The Party leader is a political official, and he approaches the solution of production tasks in a different fashion, uses methods different from those of the economic leader. *He reinforces and complements*, but in no way replaces him' (*Pravda*, May 30 1965. Author's italics).

And here was an almost nostalgic recollection of old-time methods now apparently threatened by the technologists' intrusion:

'The promotion of specialists to head Party organizations does not mean that attention to Party political and organizational work should be allowed to slacken, and that the *tried and true traditions, forms, and methods of leadership* should be abandoned . . . . The Party leader with an engineer's diploma is not worth his salt unless he is at the same time an engineer of human souls . . . if he does not bring a political approach to the solution of problems. . . .' (*Pravda*, May 30 1965. Author's italics).

In the meantime the battle was going on about the respective roles of financial and moral incentives. On June 2 *Izvestia* published an article by a reporter deriding the purely routine competitive campaigns organized in the Donbas (everybody knew they were being organized by the Party) and quoting the following remark by Lenin about competition: 'This is far easier in the political than in the economic sphere, but the one that is important for socialism is precisely the latter.' Still according to *Izvestia*, Lenin stressed enthusiasm as a motive, but 'not enthusiasm directly: the enthusiasm born of the great revolution must inspire calculations of personal interest, personal incentive and economic advancement.'[1] *Pravda* retorted as follows in an editorial on June 21:

> 'The workers and specialists who are producing high-quality industrial goods must be financially encouraged; they need incentives. But *this does not at all mean that moral incentives may be overlooked and that the importance of socialist competition is to be disregarded.* . . . Mass competition among workers is a tried and true method for the building of communism.'[2]

Clearly the dispute had gone rather far. Whereas in Khrushchev's time only more or less veiled remarks against the man in power, and him alone, were permissible, now a regular battle was raging, each side

---

[1] This curiously worded quotation from Lenin about profit incentives is actually only part of a sentence from an article written by him and published by *Pravda* on October 18 1921, i.e. in the early days of the NEP. Lenin wrote that it was a mistake to try to reorganize production 'in a country of small peasant farms' by authoritarian methods. He went on as follows:

'Life has shown us our mistake. We now see the need for a series of intermediate stages – State capitalism and socialism – so that, through many years' work, the transition to communism may be prepared. Try in the first place to build solid bridges which, in a country of small peasant farms, will lead to socialism through State capitalism. Do not rely on enthusiasm pure and simple but, using the enthusiasm born of the great Revolution, build on personal interest, personal incentive, economic calculation. Otherwise you will not achieve communism' (Lenin, *Sobranie Sochineniy* (Collected Works), vol 33 pp 35–36).

In other words, Lenin contemplated resorting to the profit incentives only in the initial stage, the transition from a peasant economy to State capitalism, and possibly in the next stage, leading to socialism. Apparently he did not foresee that profit incentives would still be needed in order to make the transition from socialism to communism. Understandably, the 1965 exegetists omitted what they regarded as superfluous details.

[2] In its editorial of June 21 1965 on socialist competition, *Pravda* called upon all newspapers to give 'systematic daily publicity to all forms of workers' competition' and chided 'certain' papers for 'merely printing communiqués on the results of competition without emphasizing the experience of the participants'. This was an obvious dig at *Izvestia* which, only the day before (Moscow edition of June 19), had given no more than twelve lines to the announcement that the Moscow region had fulfilled its seven-year plan 'before the target date'. *Pravda*, on the other hand, had hailed the achievement with a headline spread over three columns and a lengthy article by V. I. Konotop, the regional secretary (*Pravda*, June 20 1965).

expounding its views publicly, or almost publicly, in its own press organ, and sticking to its positions. How were matters settled at the top? With great difficulty, evidently, since the plenary session which was to ratify the economic reform – the outcome of the discussion – was not held until September, although it had been unofficially fixed for June. According to the Moscow correspondent of the Italian communist paper *Unità*, it had been postponed 'from week to week' (*Unità*, September 5 1965). It has also been virtually proved that the 'Stepanov camp' was eventually defeated, if not completely, at least on major points. Assuming, as seems clear, that all the warnings quoted here were aimed at preventing a change in management methods favoured by the Party, and also at preventing the reconstitution of an unduly strong State apparatus at top level, then the decisions of the September plenary session were a defeat for the Stepanov thesis. The outcome of the plenary session was that the managers in the central apparatus regained all their pre-1957 prerogatives; some changes were made in management methods, and, although of limited scope, they followed the lines advocated in *Izvestia*. Therefore, starting in June, *Pravda* and the other Party publications gradually had to change their tone and begin emphasizing the profit incentives, economic levers, etc. At least until the September plenary session, the 'buts' became a little scarcer.

The distribution of forces within the Presidium is, of course, far more difficult to determine. Although, on the whole, the conflict was between the Party apparatus and the State machine, it would be a gross oversimplification to believe that the representatives of each 'lobby' necessarily and uniformly espoused their group's interests. In theory, the spokesmen of the Party *apparat* were in a slight majority. There were six of them: Brezhnev, Podgorny and Suslov, the Central Committee Secretaries; Shelest, the First Secretary of the Ukrainian Communist Party; Kirilenko, the First Deputy Chairman of the Central Committee Bureau for the RSFSR; and Shvernik, the Chairman of the Party Control Committee. The State machine was represented by five men: Kosygin, Mazurov, Polyansky and Voronov, who were members of the Government, and Mikoyan, the Chief of State. Shelepin, the twelfth man, had a foot in each hierarchy, but his functions drew him closer to the Party. In some respects, though, this distribution was too recent to be decisive. For instance, K. T. Mazurov, the latest addition to the collective leadership, had until March 1965 been strictly a representative of the Party *apparat*.[1] Although he was Kosygin's sole First Deputy at

[1] It was obviously in order to soften or prevent conflicts between the Party and the Government that, in March 1965, transfers of officials from one hierarchy to the other had been carried out. For instance, in Byelorussia, Mazurov left his post as chief of the Party to become the second man in the Government, while D. F. Ustinov,

the head of the Government and, in that capacity, was chosen to explain the details of the industrial reform to the Supreme Soviet at the beginning of October 1965, he may still at that stage have been sympathetic to the grievances of the *apparatchiki*. It is perhaps no accident that, in the summer of 1965, Byelorussia, Mazurov's former stronghold, offered the best examples of Party committees' control over ministries. (See, for example, an article by P. Masherov in *Kommunist*, No 11, 1965.)

DISAGREEMENT BETWEEN SUSLOV AND PODGORNY

Unity did not prevail among the Party Secretaries either; perhaps because their respective interests were not endangered to the same degree and the discussion had crystallized various personal grudges among them, or else because the issue was so complex and offered such a wide range of options. Clearly, Brezhnev's silence about industrial reforms throughout the crucial period[1] and his visible reticence after the decisions had been taken place him in the 'conservative' camp. It is no less clear that his two associates in the Secretariat, Suslov and Podgorny, overtly adopted conflicting positions on the same subject. The former sided with Brezhnev, or maybe even took a stronger stand against reform, while the latter agreed with Kosygin in favouring it.

Suslov's systematic discretion on controversial issues has already been pointed out. It had required a serious crisis to induce the *éminence grise* of the collective leadership actually to engage in battle, as he had in his outburst of October 1964 on the German problem. So it was probably the crisis within the Presidium in May 1965 that prompted him to make a major political speech in Sofia during a visit to Bulgaria. It was his first of this kind since the Twenty-second Congress in 1961, and it took up one and a half pages in *Pravda* (the reply by Zhivkov, the First Secretary of the Bulgarian Party, was condensed into half a page). But the speech was published only three days later, on June 5 – the day

---

who had held the latter post until then, was reassigned to the Party Secretariat. Such measures may serve the purpose for a while, but naturally do not provide a lasting solution. Individuals are quickly shaped by their new functions.

[1] Not until July 10 1965 did Brezhnev announce in a speech that the Party intended to convene a plenary session to deal with 'the work of our industry, in order to provide for its even more successful development and to step up technological progress in the entire economy' (*Pravda*, July 11 1965). Until the September plenary session, the First Secretary did not commit himself any further on the issue of reform.

after Suslov's return to Moscow. Had he personally insisted on its publication?

Suslov was always careful not to make judgments on controversial issues, and in this instance he had performed a *tour de force*. He spoke about all the past and present moves of the collective leadership, about all its 'main preoccupations' for the future, without uttering a single word about the industrial management reform. The only allusion at all connected with the subject was concerned with the experimental reform then under discussion in Bulgaria. He cautiously said:

'We have been deeply interested in the new system of planning and economic management that you have worked out, which, *we have been told*, makes it possible to raise substantially the efficiency of production, to develop creative initiative and the welfare of the workers' (*Pravda*, June 5 1965. Author's italics).

The phrase 'we have been told' injected doubt into a comment that was in any case a little too terse to reflect enthusiasm.[1] With this, Suslov dropped the subject. He did, however, acknowledge in the same speech that one of the current problems was to 'couple correctly the State and Party administrations and to achieve a more clear-cut distribution of the respective functions of Party and State organs'. He added a few general phrases recalling Stepanov's article of May 17:

'Even though material conditions play a large part in the life of society, the problem of the building of communism is not fully resolved by the abundance of material goods. It is also necessary that communist social relationships should establish themselves in all aspects of life. . . . (*Pravda*, June 5 1965).

It is interesting to compare this with Podgorny's statements a few days before, in a speech at Baku. In his opinion, the 'new tasks' confronting the country were 'primarily the problems of profit-earning capacity in industrial and agricultural production'. He said:

'At present, the Central Committee and the Council of Ministers of the USSR are endeavouring to improve the organization and management of industry, by giving equal attention to all aspects of

---

[1] In contrast with Suslov's lukewarm comment in his Sofia speech upon management reform, he expatiated thus on an innovation in Bulgaria which he liked:

'We have been told about an interesting experiment in Party organization by urban districts. This, in our opinion, is an aspect of mass work that is important owing to its significance [sic] and interesting in its form. It broadens the Party's links with strata of the population that are not reached by the activity of Party organizations in enterprises and administrations' (*Pravda*, June 5 1965).

the problem in consultation with economic leaders, specialists and leading producers' (*Pravda*, May 22 1965).

This was obvious enough, and it would have been helpful if Suslov had also mentioned it. But Podgorny went further. Shunning reservations like Suslov's about the Bulgarian experiment, Podgorny warmly praised the far more drastic reforms being carried out in Czechoslovakia (he had just returned from a stay there):

'Our friends are at present carrying out the plan of the Czechoslovak Communist Party for improving the organization and management of the economy. A great creative impetus reigns in that country. The same tireless pursuit of new ways of accelerating the development of society is going on in Poland, in the German Democratic Republic, in Bulgaria, in Hungary, and in other lands of socialism' (*ibid.*).

It also should be noted that, in Podgorny's opinion, the main advantage of the 'October plenum' (i.e. Khrushchev's overthrow) was to have created conditions for 'an objective, scientifically based attitude towards the analysis of the country's economy'. Suslov, on the other hand, had denounced the violation of 'economic laws' only in agriculture. Since the supremacy of economic laws in all fields had been the leitmotiv of Kosygin's speech of March 19, it was clear that Podgorny had sided with the head of the Government on most of the major issues of the day.[1]

Evidently the top Party apparatus had its turncoats. Shelepin's position in the debate is not known, but he too may have taken advantage of the opportunity to display a more 'progressive' attitude than the senior Secretaries. In any case, the problems involved were complex enough to prevent the formation of two rigid groups. It would be an exaggeration to speak of a 'victory' by the reformers, since nothing indicates that Kosygin gained all he wanted in September. However, the decisions definitely represented a setback for the conservative faction, including men like Stepanov (backed by Brezhnev and Suslov), who feared a deviation towards the 'business approach'. Those who had wanted to prevent the liquidation of the sovnarkhozes suffered an even worse set-back.

Another point that may be regarded as proved is that the decisions of the deeply divided Presidium were carried by a narrow margin. The press itself indicated this by mentioning for the first time in many years that differences had occurred 'at the top'. For example, in its issue

[1] Suslov and Podgorny also disagreed in May 1965, on the problem of defence appropriations. This will be further discussed when the ups and downs in Podgorny's political career are analysed (cf. p. 499).

No 12 (June) 1965, the journal *Partiynaya Zhizn*, in an article by N. Lomakin, featured the following quotation from Lenin:

> 'Without discipline we shall perish. The Politburo is a collective organ. There are disagreements among us. Everyone is entitled to defend his opinion. But if the decision has been taken, carry it out. That is elementary.'

It sometimes happened, the article went on, 'that a decision was adopted with which Lenin disagreed. In those cases he submitted to the will of the majority and acted in accordance with the decision taken.' And, in case this was not clear enough, Lomakin further elaborated upon the attitude to be expected from the 'leaders of collegial institutions':

> 'They are called upon to create the conditions for normal, smooth work by all members of the collegium, for serious basic discussion and for the solution of all problems. If the leader is conceited, if he cannot or will not listen to others, if he tolerates no objection, does not take into account the opinion of the members of the "collective", this cannot fail to have an adverse effect on the activity of the entire collegium and vice versa' (*Partiynaya Zhizn*, No 12 June 1965).

It was very tempting to compare the 'leader' here depicted with Brezhnev and draw the conclusion that the First Party Secretary, after having been defeated by a majority in the Presidium, was trying to evade the discipline of the 'collective'. The Party's theoretical journal, *Kommunist*, edited by V. P. Stepanov, also dwelt on the problem of discipline. Like *Partiynaya Zhizn*, it emphasized the necessity, 'once the decision has been taken, to ac together, unanimously and with full responsibility, in carrying out the adopted decision'. But it injected a new note by pointing out that, against the authority of the group of leaders, there stood the higher authority of its constituents. Taking the example of the kolkhoz, where supreme authority is exercised in principle by the 'general assembly' of the members whose 'steering committee' (*pravlenie*) is only an agent, *Kommunist* declared (No 9, 1965, cleared for printing on June 15, 1965):

> 'It is clearly inadmissible that even the most enlarged sessions of the steering committee, or conferences of the active members, should take the place of their parent assemblies. It is inadmissible that the authoritative opinion of the collective master should be overlooked or its decision not be executed.'

Was this an allusion to the fact that the Party Presidium did not have the right to take, even in an 'enlarged session', any decisions contrary to the will of the 'general assembly' of the Party, namely its Congress? Was this a hint that even the plenary session of the Central Committee was not qualified to take such a serious decision, and that it would be for the Congress (whose convening was then expected) to settle the matter? This is a moot point.[1] Agreement was reached finally, but the incident had shown for the first time the flaws and limitations of collective leadership.

Another result of this major confrontation in May and June 1965 was to draw the leaders' attention to the press. Several newspapers had wrangled almost overtly for many weeks and it was time to bring them to heel. The success of the advocates of reform probably accounted for the promotion of their spokesman. V. I. Stepakov, the editor-in-chief of *Izvestia* – the paper that had most firmly supported Kosygin – was named head of the Central Committee Agitprop department in May 1965. *Izvestia* had no chief editor until the beginning of October, when L. N. Tolkunov was appointed to the post. He had been a high official in the Central Committee apparatus, and was First Deputy to Andropov at the head of the department for relations with Communist Parties in power. The editor-in-chief of *Pravda*, A. M. Rumyantsev, had also been replaced in the meantime, but this apparently had more to do with cultural policy, as will be shown subsequently.

The militant V. P. Stepanov apparently paid in instalments for his bold behaviour in May. In December he stepped down as head of *Kommunist*, although he remained on the editorial staff (cf. No 18 1965). His post went to A. G. Yegorychev, another official in charge of ideology. At the Twenty-third Congress Stepanov was removed from his alternate membership of the Central Committee (he had not even been elected a delegate to the Congress). The same happened to E. I. Bugayev, the editor-in-chief of *Partiynaya Zhizn*, who in April 1966 was replaced by M. I. Khaldeyev (cf. No 7 of the journal). Altogether, nearly all the major political organs found themselves under new management within a year. But this was only one aspect of a shake-up such as precedes most Party congresses.

---

[1] Issue No 9 of *Kommunist*, for June 1965, disclosed additional disagreements within the top leadership. For example, considering that one of the major new powers granted to heads of enterprises was the right to dismiss workers without authorization from above, the many references to full employment in the Party organ are significant. M. Sakov, the author of a pro-reform article, places full employment at the head of the list of 'fundamental problems solved by socialism'. An anonymous editorial in the same issue raises this question:

'Are the economic leaders and the Party organizations in those enterprises aware of the impasse that would be created if efforts were not devoted to the maintenance of a constant level of manpower in enterprises?'

2 From the September Plenary Session 1965 to the Twenty-third Congress March 1966

The Central Committee met in plenary session on September 27 1965 and heard a report by Kosygin on economic reform, which appeared in the press next day.[1] After hearing K. T. Mazurov's report, a session of the Supreme Soviet on October 1 and 2 ratified the corresponding decrees. On management methods, the 'modernists'' victory was a limited one: various indicators (*pokazateli*) for mandatory planning purposes had been eliminated (such as those on manpower utilization); State investments were to bear interest, and the share of profit left available to plant managers was to be increased. But on the other hand, mandatory planning was maintained for the 'main production schedule', expansion of capacity and technological policy – three broad areas which, in a market economy, are part of the policy which any plant manager is free to determine for himself. The solution of the problem of prices – the prerequisite of any return to financial 'levers' – was postponed until '1967–68' and there was no mention of the 'direct ties' between enterprises which, in December 1964, Kosygin had advocated for all branches of industry. Instead, the old system of administrative distribution of supplies and products (the so-called *snabsbyt*) was strengthened on the national level through the creation of a large specialized ministry to be headed by V. E. Dymshits, a Deputy Prime Minister. Obviously, the compromise between reformers on the one hand and managers traditionally in favour of centralization on the other had favoured the latter's views to a large extent.

The main point was that the partisans of centralization were being

[1] *Pravda* published Kosygin's report to the Central Committee plenary session on September 28 1965. The prompt publication of the main report contrasts with the procedure at the previous session, in March 1965, when Brezhnev's report was published three days after delivery, when the session had ended (*Pravda*, March 27 1965). Conceivably, the Presidium majority was trying, by means of this innovation, to forestall any obstruction of its decisions by the rank-and-file *apparatchiki*. Also for the first time since Khrushchev's downfall, the plenary session was enlarged – if only to a limited extent – by an admixture of 'First Secretaries of Oblast Committees, Prime Ministers of the Federated Republics, Second Secretaries of the Central Committee of the Federated Republics, Ministers and Chairmen of State committees, members of the *apparat* of the Central Committee and Council of Ministers of the USSR, and editors-in-chief of the central newspapers' (*Pravda*, September 28 1965). It is true that there were no 'vanguard workers', but the Central Committee members had ample grounds to suspect a return to Khrushchevian tactics.

given back unchanged the ministries abandoned in 1957. This was announced quietly at the end of the Kosygin report, together with repeated assurances that the officials in charge would have to work in an 'entirely new' spirit. But for these officials the re-establishment of the ministries was the main aspect of the reform. If the new spirit really had been the goal, this would have been a good opportunity to rejuvenate the cadres by promoting genuinely progressive economists. Nothing of the kind was done. The man picked to head the system as Gosplan President was none other than N. K. Baybakov, who had been removed from that post by Khrushchev in 1957. Five of the re-established ministries were to be headed by the same men as before the reform, which in some cases took quite a bit of doing. For instance S. F. Antonov was brought from Kabul, where he was serving as Ambassador, and given back the post of Minister for the Meat and Dairy Industry which he had occupied until 1957; P. F. Lomako, who was President of Gosplan and Deputy Prime Minister since 1962, was demoted to the rank of Minister for Non-ferrous Metallurgy – merely a return to his pre-1957 status. Altogether, including officials reinstated earlier, for instance V. V. Matskevich, the Minister of Agriculture, or those who had never changed posts, this brought to seventeen, i.e. one out of four, the number of ministers who again found themselves in the posts they had held eight years earlier.[1] The maintenance of old-time Stalinist planners naturally meant the use of the old methods, so it is no wonder that complaints about management methods steadily increased.[2]

The high Party officials apparently had almost stopped worrying about the 'business approach' in enterprises. Their greatest fear now was the political threat represented by the formidable State apparatus that had sprung up. Kosygin had already had to include in his report to the Central Committee reassurances of all kinds about the role of the Party – 'a force for leading and orienting the development of the socialist economy on the way to communism'. He also specified that:

[1] Most of the 'new' ministers appointed after the economic reform of September 1965 were chairmen of the corresponding State committees that had begun to spring up in 1960. Only four officials had had to step aside in favour of regional sovnarkhoz chairmen. Among those demoted was K. N. Rudnev, who had until then been Deputy Chairman of the Council of Ministers and Chairman of the State Committee for the Co-ordination of Scientific Research. He was nevertheless re-elected to the Central Committee at the Twenty-third Congress.

[2] The results of a *Pravda* inquiry published in July 1966 showed that the industrial ministries' main preoccupation was to gather as much data as they could from the enterprises on the subject of their *daily* output and to bombard with orders and instructions those that did not fulfil their promises. *Pravda* added: 'The words "production sold", "profit", "profit-earning capacity" are heard within the walls [of the ministry] far less than those of "gross production" or "units produced". For the time being, the old criteria and notions are the most prevalent around here' (*Pravda*, July 27 1966).

'It follows from the very essence of the measures proposed that the Party's leadership of the economy will grow still further. The Central Committees of the Communist Parties in the Federated Republics, the Party Territorial and Oblast Committees, are assuming considerably greater responsibility for the scientific leadership of industry, freed from parochial influences and from any spirit of administrative compartmentalization (*Pravda*, September 28 1965).

Kosygin warned against confusing the roles of the Party and the State (*podmyena*), but at the same time extolled the function of the Party committees within the plants, especially in using 'moral incentives'.

This no doubt was to the liking of the *apparatchiki*, and furthermore Brezhnev personally spelled things out. In his speech at the plenary session, published 'with a few cuts' in *Pravda* of September 30 1965, he dealt at length with the problem of the ministries and warned that they 'and the ministers personally' would have to bear 'full responsibility before the Party and the State' for the activities of their respective branches of industry. The Party meant to exercise control indirectly, by manipulating cadres. The First Secretary was much more specific than Kosygin and announced that he was going to scrutinize the structure and the staff, both old and new, of each ministry. He advocated placing one of the deputy ministers in charge of 'daily management of cadres' work', which suggested that this official would be the Party's watchdog in his particular sphere. There were to be other Party agents as well, for instance the Party Committees (*Partkom*) to be run by 're-commended', 'highly qualified and experienced Party officials'. 'The Party Committees in the ministries,' Brezhnev added, 'will make periodic progress reports to the Central Committee of the CPSU on the Party organizations and on the measures taken to improve the work of the ministries' (*Pravda*, September 30 1965). The same idea was expressed in *Pravda* of October 4 1965 by N. G. Yegorychev, who, in his capacity as First Secretary of the Moscow Urban Committee, was to be in charge of supervising the activities of these Party Committees. He said:

'The Moscow Urban Committee of the CPSU . . . will try in every way to bring about the setting up of combat Party organizations headed by experienced Party officials within the new ministries and administrations. We shall direct the Party Committees to enhance the role and personal responsibility of every communist, and to co-ordinate the activity of the entire apparatus. Naturally, the work of the Party organizations within the ministries and administrations will be a centre of attention for the Urban Committee and the entire urban Party organization.'

Yegorychev also intended to reinforce Party control at the rank-and-file level, for, he explained, 'extending the rights of the enterprises is primarily extending the rights of the collectives'. Since the 'collective' in fact is the Party, the only authoritative spokesman of the 'masses', the plant director in making his decisions would have 'to rely on the Party and the social organizations.'

No conclusive information is available on the practical results of these suggestions, especially at the level of the ministries and their Party Committees. It appears only that, among the rank and file, Brezhnev's and Yegorychev's instructions were applied fairly strictly. According to an article in *Partiynaya Zhizn* in January 1966, some local *apparatchiki* had even tried to bar management representatives from Party Committees at the plant and higher levels. The Party journal regarded this attitude as excessive, but stated nevertheless that the plant director, or even the chairman of the Soviet or its executive committee, were in no way automatically entitled to membership of the Party Committee; they might have to make do with being represented by one of their deputies.

> 'The presence within a Party organ of representatives of the management and social organizations [i.e. trade unions or Komsomol] undoubtedly has its advantages. Anyone trying to bar economic leaders from election to Party organs – and on occasion this has been suggested – would obviously be wrong. But is it necessarily the top leaders who have to be elected always and everywhere? Is it a secret that as a result of this practice certain comrades have become, as it were, irremovable and permanent members of the bureaux and Party Committees?' (*Partiynaya Zhizn*, No 1 1966).

The Party made other attempts to regain the upper hand over the State apparatus after its September 'defeat':

1 Transfers of personnel from the Party to the Government apparatus. The method had been used in March 1965, but in the reverse direction also. For instance, K. T. Mazurov had been appointed First Deputy to Kosygin while D. F. Ustinov was moved from the Government to the Secretariat. From September onwards the transfers were resumed, but became unilateral. Between October 1965 and January 1966, about ten high-ranking *apparatchiki* were transferred to the Government machine. They included M. T. Yefremov, the First Secretary of the Gorki Oblast Committee, who in November was appointed Deputy Chairman of the USSR Council of Ministers, and A. M. Shkolnikov, the First Secretary of the Volgograd Oblast Committee, who became First Deputy Chairman of the RSFSR Council of Ministers.[1] The only

---

[1] The following officials were also transferred from the Party to the Government

case of a transfer in the opposite direction was that of M. V. Zimyanin, who interrupted a long diplomatic career to take over *Pravda*, the Party's main daily newspaper. This rather anomalous move was apparently due to his connection with K. T. Mazurov, the newcomer to the collective leadership.[1]

2 Withdrawal from Government jurisdiction of all State Committees of an 'ideological' character: radio-television, cinema, publishing and cultural relations with foreign countries. The collective leadership announced in a decree dated October 9 1965 (published in the *Vedomosti Verkhovnovo Sovieta SSR*, No 41/1284) that those four committees

---

apparatus towards the end of 1965: F. F. Kuzyukov, First Secretary of the Chelyabinsk Oblast Committee, who was appointed Deputy Minister for the USSR Coal Industry, and A. G. Dmitrin, First Secretary of the Komi Oblast Committee, who became Deputy Minister for Forestry (*Pravda*, October 30 1965); I. T. Marchenko, First Secretary of the Tomsk Oblast Committee, was appointed Minister of the RSFSR Local Industry, and N. A. Kuznetzov, the Second Secretary of the Moscow Urban Committee, was appointed Minister of Culture of the RSFSR (*Sovyetskaya Rossiya*, November 27 1965); L. Ya. Florentyev, First Secretary of the Kostroma Oblast Committee, was appointed Minister of Agriculture of the RSFSR, and V. K. Mesyats, Secretary of the Moscow Oblast Committee, was appointed his deputy (*Sovyetskaya Rossiya*, December 18 1965); G. I. Vorobyev, First Secretary of the Krasnodar Territorial Committee, was appointed Deputy Minister of Agriculture of the USSR (*Izvestia*, January 16 1966), etc.

[1] Like Mazurov, Zimyanin had spent all his earlier career in Byelorussia. He had become First Secretary of the Byelorussia Komsomol in 1940. His deputy at the time was Mazurov, who became Komsomol Secretary in 1942 and stepped into Zimyanin's post in 1946. They both took part in partisan operations during the war. This for instance is what P. Masherov wrote in *Sovyetskaya Byelorussia* on May 8 1965: 'For a long time, the Komsomol Central Committee Secretaries K. T. Mazurov and M. V. Zimyanin lived behind the enemy lines.' In 1950 Mazurov became First Secretary of the Minsk Oblast Committee, probably with the backing of Zimyanin who, since February 1949, had been Second Secretary of the Republic in charge of cadres policy.

A strange thing happened to Zimyanin in 1953. The *Encyclopedic Yearbook* for 1962 notes in his biography: 'In 1953, First Secretary of the Central Committee in Byelorussia', which had never been reported at the time. In the entry for N. S. Patolichev, the same *Yearbook* states: 'First Secretary of the Central Committee in Byelorussia from 1950 to 1956'. Apparently, Zimyanin was the man picked by Beriya in June 1953 to head the Party in Byelorussia instead of the Russian, Patolichev. Beriya, before his downfall, endeavoured to promote native cadres within the republics. But Beriya fell before the change had been announced, and Patolichev took over the job immediately, while Zimyanin dropped from sight. Zimyanin, indeed, was the only local leader who did not attend the rally held in Minsk in July 1953 to approve Beriya's dismissal (*Pravda*, July 11 1953). It was only in September that he reappeared as head of a department in the USSR Ministry of Foreign Affairs (*Pravda*, September 20 1953).

Zimyanin was not the only Byelorussian who was promoted to a post in Moscow in the wake of Mazurov's rise. In December 1965 V. F. Shauro, until then Secretary of the Central Committee of Byelorussia, was reported to be head of the cultural department of the Central Committee of the CPSU (*Pravda*, December 12 1965), which entitled him to a seat as Central Committee alternate at the Twenty-third Congress.

'would no longer be part of the USSR Council of Ministers' and that their chairmen consequently would no longer bear the title of minister. This suggested a certain inconsistency, since only a few days earlier the Supreme Soviet had amended the Constitution in order to register the new composition of the Government resulting from the September reform, and had expressly confirmed that these four State committees belonged to the Council of Ministers (*Pravda*, October 3 1965). In all likelihood this new way of curtailing even the nominal authority of the Government over these sectors had come as an afterthought. Similarly, at about the same time, the 'Ideological Committee attached to the Central Committee of the CPSU' reappeared. This had been a creation of L. F. Ilyichev in 1962, and had not been mentioned once since Khrushchev's downfall.[1] The Committee's purpose was to place under the same Party authority not only the chairmen of these State committees, but also the ministers for 'ideology' who had remained within the Government (Ye. A. Furtseva, the Minister of Culture, and the various ministers for public education). The revival of the Committee was therefore opportune.

All these measures had the desired effect of strengthening the Party's grip over the State. After the long and difficult confrontation of the summer of 1965, and the laborious compromise of September, it seemed that each of the two major groups had received some satisfaction. The State apparatus had, as Kosygin wished, gained a 'certain autonomy', at least in managerial matters, but definitely remained under Party authority. The Party, on the other hand, had had to abandon some of its attempts to interfere in the managers' current work. It made up for this by reaffirming, with renewed vigour, its monopoly over all other areas of activity. Moreover, the settlement of the problem of economic reform, temporary though it may have been, ended the series of reorganizations that followed Khrushchev's overthrow. The *apparatchiki* were now free to press their other major demands. First they were determined to bring the intelligentsia to heel, and then to wipe out the effects of the destalinization drives.

AN ENLIGHTENED IDEOLOGIST: RUMYANTSEV

The writers, as we saw, were treated fairly well in the period following Khrushchev's downfall. Their liberal wing was in effect one of the

---

[1] It was learned incidentally in October 1965 that Ilyichev's ideological committee had reappeared. This was recorded in the obituary of D. A. Polikarpov, the chief of the Central Committee cultural department, when he was described as 'member of the Ideological Committee attached to the Central Committee of the CPSU' (*Pravda*, November 3 1965).

'lobbies' then in operation and the temporary power gap had helped them, like other groups, to advance their interests somewhat. It is beyond the scope of this book to retrace the cultural events of the period. The most drastic contradictions emerged from the outset, since the conservative lobby also took advantage of circumstances to assert itself. More interesting is the attitude of the Party authorities to these quarrels. It ranged from a 'hands-off' policy to discreet but marked sympathy for the progressive wing. But from August onwards there was a definite shift toward ultra-conservative positions.

It is impossible to determine the positions of the top rulers on this question. Neither is there any solid evidence for the opinion commonly held in the West, that L. F. Ilyichev's successor at the head of the Ideological Department of the Central Committee Secretariat, P. N. Demichev (promoted to alternate membership of the Presidium in November 1964), was a man of 'enlightened' views.[1] The only ascertainable fact is that, during the first months of the new rule, no one prevented the most progressive elements in the apparatus from expressing their views in a manner that gave them a very official character. Among these 'progressives' was the first editor-in-chief of *Pravda* after Khrushchev's fall, A. M. Rumyantsev.[2]

His was the first major declaration of policy in the literary and artistic sphere, embodied in a long article in *Pravda* of February 21 1965.

[1] It was never even officially confirmed that Demichev had taken charge of the Ideological Committee (whose very existence, as noted, remained problematic until November 1965). The fact can be established, however, on the basis of information gathered in Moscow, including various indirect confirmations. For instance, on April 20 1965 *Pravda* reported that Demichev had, at a conference of propaganda officials, delivered a report on the 'Party's ideological tasks'. It is known that until that date and since November 1962, Demichev had been in charge of the Central Committee Bureau for Chemical and Light Industries.

Despite the strange reassignment, Demichev was not quite a newcomer to the ideological scene. As First Secretary of the Moscow Urban Committee from 1960 to 1962, he had on several occasions participated in the stormy debates of the city's intelligentsia. A substantial part of his speech at the Twenty-second Congress in October 1961 was devoted to that subject. In it, he criticized the writers and artists who, 'owing to lack of maturity, especially on the part of the younger members of their group, suffer from diseases such as false innovationism, formalism', etc. He also took to task 'certain prominent literary figures and art critics who, for fear of being considered old-fashioned, flatter and try to imitate those who affect anything new'. The tone, obviously, was not indicative of any 'revolutionary' sympathies.

[2] A. M. Rumyantsev was born in 1905 and started his career in Kharkov, first in agriculture, then in teaching and academic activities. In 1952 he was promoted to Moscow and given a post in the Central Committee apparatus. In 1956 he took over the editorship of *Kommunist*. As an ideologist of the 'pre-Ilyichev' school, he lost some of his influence when Ilyichev took over the Agitprop service in 1958, and was sent to Prague to edit the joint journal of the Communist Parties: *Problems of Peace and Socialism*. Despite his set-backs he was elected member of the Central Committee at all the post-1952 Congresses. He is unquestionably an important figure in the 'hard core' of that body.

Before that the Party had published some pieces on the subject, but they were rather contradictory. For instance, on January 9 an editorial had stressed primarily the Party spirit (*partiynost*) in literature and, except for a few reservations about 'hasty and unqualified judgments', it had in substance justified the 1963 drive against 'erroneous phenomena'. But on January 17 another editorial completely disregarded *partiynost* and, on the contrary, stressed what is usually viewed as its antithesis – search for artistic quality and the condemnation of 'grey, dull' works. Rumyantsev's article attempted for the first time to give a balanced analysis, and it was more 'enlightened' by far than anything the Khrushchev era had produced on these matters.

Partiynost was not mentioned at all, but, instead, Rumyantsev spoke of *narodnost* or 'populism', which, in Soviet terms, connoted patriotism and civic spirit. In addition, the author deprecated the 'vulgar notion according to which *narodnost* involves lowering artistic standards to the level of primitive needs and tastes'. The only tendencies condemned in the article were 'formalism in its pure state' and 'manifestations of bourgeois ideology'. Otherwise, the officially proclaimed policy was of the 'hundred flowers' type:

> 'Artistic creation . . . is always the discovery of something new, something hitherto unknown. . . . It cannot be stimulated to order, it does not tolerate any official's bureaucratic attitude, or meticulous control and regimentation. . . . It is possible only in an *atmosphere of search, experimentation, free expression and the clash of opinions.* . . . The fruitful development of science, literature and art demands *the existence of different schools and tendencies,* of differing and competing styles and genres that are at the same time united by the identity of the dialectic materialist concept of the world, by the unity of the principles of socialist realism.' (*Pravda*, February 21 1965.) [Author's italics.]

Rumyantsev even went so far as to advocate tolerance toward dubious experiments. It was inadvisable, he said, 'to put obstacles in the way of experiments that are not yet sufficiently advanced to permit forming a judgment as to their true value' (*Pravda*, February 21 1965).

The author could not, of course, advocate a complete 'hands-off' attitude for the Party. One must not 'await passively the judgment of time', and therefore a criterion valid under all circumstances was needed. But this criterion was an unexpected one, namely 'the free multilateral development of the personality of each member of society' (*Pravda, ibid.*).

The last statement was truly revolutionary. Of course the authorities had prescribed different criteria in this matter at different times, but they had all been strictly political in character. Rumyantsev's article called for a rejoinder. A few days later, the Writers' Congress of the RSFSR met in Moscow and the message of the Central Committee read from the rostrum by A. P. Kirilenko contained a 'criterion for the value of socialist works of art' which ran:

'... faithfulness to the Leninist principles of *partiynost* and *narodnost*, the indissoluble tie with life, irreconcilable opposition to the enemy bourgeois ideology, the artistic and accurate expression of reality in all its richness and diversity on the basis of the communist conception of the world' (*Pravda*, March 4 1965).

The rapporteur at the Congress, the very conservative L. S. Sobolev, summarized this in the even more lapidary phrase: '*Partiynost* is the sole criterion of our literary activities' (*Pravda*, March 4 1965).

Rumyantsev had obviously gone too far on the subject of the 'criterion', but he did not seem threatened with removal from his post. The fact that he was editing *Pravda* accounts for the 'progressive' position of that newspaper on cultural problems in spring 1965, even though the dogmatist group had lost none of its power in other quarters. This is why, for a while, a veiled quarrel went on between *Pravda* and *Izvestia* on the literary issue, similar to the one waged a few weeks later on economic reform. In this instance, however, the roles were reversed, the Government daily siding with the Party conservatives.

As if by accident, on March 3 1965, *Izvestia* published an editorial berating with the usual vehemence young writers who 'in search of sensationalism' or 'under the pretext of searching for modernism' produce 'an ideological hotchpotch of items from the Vanity Fair of an alien bourgeois culture'. On the same day, *Pravda* dealt with the subject in a much more temperate editorial without mentioning *partiynost* or, for once, even 'socialist realism'. *Pravda* repeatedly attacked the magazine *Oktyabr*, the bastion of the conservative group (but without naming its editor-in-chief, V. A. Kochetov): in particular on February 28 and even more sharply on March 28, when the critic S. Gaysarian wrote a three-column criticism of the magazine and its methods of criticism.[1]

---

[1] *Pravda's* attack on *Oktyabr*, on March 28 1965, included the following:

'One cannot escape the impression that the magazine is clinging to bygone times and would like to maintain its position unchanged. ...

'Very often, *Oktyabr's* judgments are not convincing because of their tendentious and subjective character. ...

'Articles of this kind [*Oktyabr's* attack on Konstantin Simonov], being based on arbitrary judgments of taste and on group prejudices, can only disorient both writers and readers. ...

'[The magazine] publishes many articles that are tedious in content and weak as literature. They are, so to speak, impersonal and indistinguishable ... many of the magazine's positions are characterized by an exaggerated tone. ...'

But when it came to the leader of the opposite camp, namely Tvardov-sky, the editor-in-chief of *Novy Mir*, the task of dealing with him was left to *Izvestia*, which for this purpose commissioned the sculptor Vuchetich, whose article came out on April 15.[1]

A painting exhibition organized at the Manège in Moscow was reviewed in an entirely different light by the two newspapers. On March 7 *Pravda* sharply criticized 'the solemn pompousness of the canvases' and the 'atmosphere of complacency' generated by 'sweepingly favour-able' criticism, and chided the organizers for having 'left outside the boundaries of the exhibition certain works that may be questionable but are evidence of the daring, passionate search without which art cannot live'. *Izvestia*, on the contrary, which had already upbraided the maga-zine *Iskusstvo* (Art) for having harshly criticized the exhibition (*Iskusstvo* had been just a shade sharper than *Pravda*), again ran a completely favourable commentary on April 14, save for a mild reservation on the lack of 'laconism' or economy. Again, *Pravda* and its director Rum-yantsev were disavowed: on March 16, the entire collective leadership, headed by Brezhnev (but without Kosygin) visited the exhibition. The Tass communiqué, which evidently embodied the approved line, stated:

> 'The exhibition . . . is enjoyable owing to its life-affirming optimism, its faithfulness to life. . . . [The artists] make the visitor feel the joys and difficulties of the past years. Many works show great talent and search for novelty' (*Pravda*, March 17 1965).

This praise was coupled with an anodyne reservation, probably in order to avoid falling into the excess of 'subjectivism' that Khrushchev had so blatantly displayed on that very same spot on December 1 1962:

> 'Often while viewing the paintings and sculptures, one hears visitors discuss the qualities and flaws of the works exhibited. . . .' (*ibid.*)

This suggests that the 'progressive' attitude of the main national daily, at the time, was due to Rumyantsev personally, rather than to a con-certed policy of the Party leadership. Conversely, *Izvestia's* militant dogmatism should not be ascribed to a hypothetical special position of the State apparatus – to which the paper belonged, but which wielded no power in cultural matters – but rather to the attitude of its staff and in particular the chief editor, then V. I. Stepakov. As noted,

---

[1] Vuchetich's attack was superficially civil but highly venomous. Taking Tvardovsky to task for his editorial commemorating the fortieth anniversary of *Novy Mir* in its January issue, Vuchetich accused him of being 'tendentious', 'losing his sense of proportion' when he criticized Stalinist literature, and giving too much space to Solzhenitsyn. In conclusion, he asked Tvardovsky to say outright 'what he stands for'.

Stepakov was promoted in May 1965 to the post of head of the Central Committee's Agitprop department.[1] His promotion was due, probably, to his orthodoxy in cultural matters no less than to the flexible views he apparently held on economic problems. In any case, the change could only help those who wanted to put a stop 'once and for all' to the anti-conformist acts of the intelligentsia.

THE SINYAVSKY CASE

In mid-September 1965 the literary critic Andrey Sinyavsky and the translator Yuly Daniel were arrested in Moscow. It is not certain that the timing was premeditated. The State Security Service (KGB) must have unexpectedly had indications enabling it to identify the two authors as 'Abraham Terts' and 'Nikolay Arzhak', the pen-names under which works regarded as 'anti-Soviet' had been published abroad for years past (since 1956 where the former was concerned). On the other hand, at the end of July 1965, the 'Soviet Writer' publishing house in Leningrad had brought out a volume of poetry by Pasternak with a long preface by Sinyavsky (Tass announced this in a special communiqué dated July 30). Evidently, this would not have been done had the slightest suspicion about the critic existed at the time.

It is hardly surprising that the authorities decided to arrest the 'culprits' immediately after their guilt was discovered. Although publishing abroad is not an offence under existing laws, the moral and political crime, according to Soviet standards, was serious enough to warrant police action. If any dilemma existed, it related to the action to be taken after the arrest. Would it take the form of compulsory measures of an 'administrative' nature enforced quietly (banishment from Moscow, forced residence, etc.), or on the contrary a full-dress trial entailing 'exemplary' punishment? The authorities opted in the end for the latter course, which did great harm to the country's prestige abroad. The trial was just public enough to attract the attention of

---

[1] The official title of Stepakov's agency was 'Agitation and Propaganda Department of the Central Committee of the CPSU', or at lest that is what it was called immediately after the name of 'ideological department' introduced by Ilyichev was abandoned. But in May 1966 it became simply 'Propaganda Department' (cf. *Pravda*, May 17 1966), which seemed to reflect a shift in orientation. The term 'agitation' applies to 'mass' work among the population as a whole, whereas 'propaganda' refers to the same activity on a higher level, directed at the cadres. Propaganda (a kind of agitators' agitation) deals in broader and more sophisticated types of information.

world opinion (the Moscow press reported it regularly), and just secret enough (no non-Soviet observer was admitted, not even foreign communist journalists) to remain a travesty of justice. At the last moment, the authorities tried to divert attention from the case by allowing another opposition writer, Valery Tarsis, to leave for the West, but this did not yield the expected results. The Sinyavsky–Daniel trial provoked hostile reactions among most of the West European 'fraternal Parties', and to this day the case may be regarded as a serious blunder on the part of a leadership that prided itself on being 'scientific'.

It is quite possible that the growing tide of reaction abroad contributed to the rulers' stubbornness. Their pathological sensitivity to what they regard as 'foreign interference' has often turned into deliberate policy what may have started as a casual misjudgment. But it is not difficult to perceive the domestic motives that prompted the advocates of a tough line to act as they did. Sinyavsky the critic – the official figure, as distinct from 'Terts' and his secret writings – was well known on the Soviet literary scene and a regular contributor to *Novy Mir*, the chief monthly magazine of the liberal intelligentsia,[1] whose editor, A. T. Tvardovsky, had paid a public tribute to him only a few months earlier.[2] This was, of course, a providential opportunity for the conservatives, who were now able to say: 'You see where the critical realism you advocate is leading: to treason pure and simple and anti-Soviet agitation, immediately exploited by our enemies abroad. All the things that Sinyavsky did in broad daylight – his defence of modernism and the young apolitical poets, the denigration of the period of the cult – were a cloak for anti-communist activity. Finally, it was not difficult to insinuate that any writers who, like Sinyavsky in *Novy Mir*, were bringing out anti-conformist works legally, were potential traitors capable of producing – if they were not already doing so – an entirely different kind of writing 'for their desk drawers'. In the upsurge of

---

[1] See, for instance, Sinyavsky's articles in *Novy Mir* No 3 of 1965, Nos 1, 6, and 12 of 1964, No 3 of 1962, Nos 1 and 8 of 1961, etc. Several of these articles, in particular those of 1961, were written in co-operation with A. Menshutin.

Yuly Daniel, the translator of Ukrainian, Uzbek and other national poetry, was much less known. His latest contribution was a translation of works by the Ukrainian poet Drach, which appeared in *Novy Mir*, No 4 of 1965.

[2] In his editorial of January 1965 on the fortieth anniversary of *Novy Mir*, Tvardovsky wrote about 'young' literary criticism: 'I shall even venture to say that, thanks to the breadth of its ideological and aesthetic range and by enhancing the literary gifts of its exponents, "young" criticism is successfully competing today with "young" poetry and "young" prose, which are receiving far more praise. Since this is *Novy Mir* I shall naturally name first the critics who write for this magazine, for instance, Yu. Burtin, I. Vinogradov, A. Lebedev, I. Solovyova and A. Sinyavsky' (*Novy Mir*, No 1 1965 p 17).

chauvinism bred by the trial, the entire left wing of the intelligentsia was to come under fire.

The case, therefore, was bound to help the conservatives, but apparently the wind was about to shift in their favour anyway. This was shown by another article by A. M. Rumyantsev in *Pravda* of September 9 1965, only a few days before the arrest of Sinyavsky and Daniel. In this, which turned out to be his last piece in *Pravda*, Rumyantsev did not actually disavow his article of February 21, but the tone was entirely different. The title itself – 'Party spirit (*partiynost*) in the work of the Soviet intelligentsia' – emphasized a theme that Rumyantsev had completely disregarded in his initial formulation. True, he still made large allowances for the liberal intelligentsia. For example, he took *Izvestia* to task for its 'incorrect' criticism of the writer Aksyonov, and, something new and particularly interesting, he issued a warning against 'anti-intellectualism', suggesting that this trait was quite widespread among certain Party cadres (the Sinyavsky trial was of course going to encourage it).[1] On the other hand, Rumyantsev warned the intellectuals – and in particular the 'indisputably honest' people who cast 'doubts on the need for Party leadership in art and literature' – that the Party 'can and must have its say' in the matter. 'Party leadership that is flexible and faithful to principles has been, is and will continue to be the prerequisite for the development of Soviet art.' The article's calls to vigilance against 'bourgeois ideology', for the 'class struggle', etc., were much stronger than in February. 'The free multilateral development of everyone's personality' was mentioned, to be sure, as it had been in February, but this time not as the criterion applicable to works of art at present, but only as something the future communist society was to strive for, which made it a very long-range goal. Moreover, Rumyantsev had added the qualification: 'in the interest of all . . . '.

Shortly thereafter Rumyantsev was replaced at the head of *Pravda* by M. V. Zimyanin (Tass announced the change on September 22), and became head of the Institute for World Economy and International

---

[1] Rumyantsev also wrote in his article in *Pravda* of September 9 1965:

'It must be pointed out that, under conditions here, any attempt to oppose intellectualism to *partiynost* and populism (*narodnost*) would be tantamount to adopting a demagogic and illiterate position against culture and against the scientific conception of the world. . . . Only obscurantists and class enemies are afraid of reason, hate intellectualism and seek to develop lower instincts and feelings. . . .

'To reject intellectualism or show scepticism towards it would mean preaching regression and primitivism, advocating lack of education and qualification, the degradation of man. . . . It would mean taking one's stand against, not for, *partiynost* and *narodnost*'.

Relations, a post left open by the death a few months earlier of the Academician Arzumanian. Although this was an enviable position[1] and Rumyantsev kept his seat in the Central Committee at the Twenty-third Congress, his 'excessively liberal' attitude in cultural matters was probably the cause of his removal from *Pravda* just ten months after he had taken over. He may even have been blamed for undue gentleness in telling the intellectuals how things now stood. On September 9, the day when his article was published, *Literaturnaya Gazeta* was far more brutal and assailed three periodicals at once: the weekly *Literaturnaya Rossiya* for having published poetry by Severyanin without making it plain that the poet's attitude was 'hostile to the Soviet Union and decadent'; the Kazakh monthly *Prostor*, for having reprinted poems by Mandelshtam with a similarly inadequate preface by Ilya Ehrenburg; lastly the review *Yunost* for having done the same with Pasternak. It so happened that these were three 'damned' poets whose slow but progressive unofficial rehabilitation over the past few years had been regarded as achieved. Hence the criticism in *Literaturnaya Gazeta* represented a definite setback.

The rest of the story is better known: in cultural matters the Twenty-third Congress was a triumph for the ultra-conservatives such as they had not enjoyed since their orgy in March–April 1963. Coming as the climax of a campaign on the themes of 'heroic labour' and 'imperialism's diversionary tactics in ideology', with a militant plenary session of the Komsomol Central Committee in December 1965 and the Sinyavsky-Daniel trial in February 1966, the attack forced the 'progressives' on to the defensive on all fronts. True, there were no such excesses of language as in 1963, because this was not really a settlement of scores between the two camps of the intelligentsia (only Sholokhov, the Nobel Prize winner, lashed out at Sinyavsky, Daniel and their 'protectors'). It was rather in the nature of a series of reprimands to the writers, emanating exclusively from the Party *apparat*.

As a result, the Party parliament was left without its 'enlightened' member writers. They were Tvardovsky, who was not even elected as a delegate to the Congress and lost his alternate membership in the Central Committee, and A. A. Surkov, a late-comer to 'liberalism' and far less daring than *Novy Mir's* editor-in-chief. Both had been among the oldest Central Committee members.[2] On the other hand,

---

[1] Rumyantsev did not long remain in this post. In July 1966 he took over the Economic Section of the USSR Academy of Science. In May 1967 he was elected Vice-President of the Academy of Science.

[2] Surkov was elected member of the Party Central Auditing Committee in 1952 and alternate Central Committee member in 1956. Tvardovsky also became a member of the Auditing Committee in 1952, but lost his post as director of *Novy Mir* in

the Congress did not re-elect V. A. Kochetov, editor-in-chief of *Oktyabr* and a sworn enemy of Tvardovsky, although he was invited to partici-pate in the discussion as a delegate. Moreover Kochetov was replaced on the Party Auditing Committee by G. M. Markov, a highly orthodox literary *apparatchik*. The only writers who were full members of the Central Committee, M. A. Sholokhov and A. E. Korneychuk, and the alternate member N. M. Gribachev, retained not only their seats but the full confidence of their ultra-conservative friends.

Following these events, one might have expected to see Tvardovsky removed from his post and drastic changes in the staff of *Novy Mir* and *Yunost* (run by Boris Polevoy) and other literary magazines that had been under sharp attack. Despite persistent rumours which circu-lated in Moscow in the spring of 1966, this was not the only time that nothing in fact happened after a campaign of this sort. Either Tvardov-sky was too tough to be broken, or else moderate Party elements had stepped in to prevent the ultras from gaining the upper hand, and the *status quo* prevailed.[1] In summer 1966 *Novy Mir*, and even *Yunost*, which had felt it necessary to publish a humble recantation in April (No 4 1966), reverted almost without change to the line of 'critical realism' which had made their fortune. The ultra-conservatives re-lapsed into the sulky but resigned hostility which had been their attitude for several years. The campaign died down – until the next storm, or even the genuine settlement of scores that might come some day.

DESTALINIZATION STOPPED

Khrushchev's personal motives in conducting his anti-Stalinist drive have been analysed in sufficient detail to make it plain that, with his downfall in October 1964, the whole campaign was called into question. His successors had every reason to wish destalinization to go no further than it had done immediately after the dictator's death in 1953. This entailed respect for collective leadership, the elimination of concen-tration camp 'excesses', Party control over the police, etc. On the

---

1954 and was not elected to any top Party organ at the Twentieth Congress in 1956. At the Twenty-second Congress in 1961 he was elected alternate member of the Central Committee.

[1] According to reliable information, the Party leaders had contemplated replacing Tvardovsky by K. M. Simonov at the head of *Novy Mir*; but the prominent novelist refused so that the operation had to be postponed. Meanwhile the editorial staff had threatened to strike in support of its director.

other hand, the new leaders had no desire to endorse Khrushchev's additions to this, namely: public criticism, the accusation of individual 'Stalinists', spectacular rehabilitations with their many implications, etc.

Of course these problems still exist and will have to be solved some day. But this will require an overt competition for power, a dynamic leader resembling the Khrushchev of 1956, a man bent on fighting the same dangerous battle. Nothing of the sort existed after the 1964 palace revolution, which was a reaction precisely against the 'cult of personality' and the seizure of power. Anyway, even if one of the present leaders had been seeking a device to consolidate his own power, he could not have chosen that one; destalinization had been so discredited that he would have been more likely to choose its opposite, so as to emphasize his dissimilarity with the deposed leader. As a matter of fact, Brezhnev appeared at this time to base his political fortune chiefly on restalinization.

For this, all he had to do was to go along with the 'apparatus'. The basic demand of the average *apparatchik*, apart from seeing the last of agricultural nostrums, hasty reorganizations, reprimands and other humiliations, was a halt to the attacks against 'the period of the cult'. The overwhelming majority of these men were the legitimate heirs of Stalinism: it suffices to scan the biographies to see that, in most cases, their political careers started in 1938, the year when the second wave of purges installed the 'definitive' type of cadre personnel. Even if he had had no hand in the purges, the *apparatchik* of the sixties was still their beneficiary. Furthermore, harping on the errors and crimes of the Stalinist era had resulted in discrediting the Party as a whole, in casting doubts on the wisdom of its decisions and the consistency of its acts. Even for officials who joined the hierarchy later, this was a weighty argument.

Since it is not easy to stop a movement without starting one in the opposite direction, what must be termed a limited restalinization did occur. Roughly, its objectives were the following:

1 To introduce some nuances into Stalin's image and bring out its favourable aspects.

2 To speak as little as possible about purges and victimizations. This did not, as a rule, mean disavowing the rehabilitations of the previous reign. The most illustrious of the executed heroes would still be mentioned, but their tragic deaths would be played down.

3 To denounce the 'anti-cult' literature of the Khrushchev years, from Solzhenitsyn to Yevtushenko. This was to be a major aspect of the drive already mentioned against the liberal intelligentsia.

4 Finally, to extol the favourable aspects of the Stalinist era, the 'heroic memories' of the first five-year plans and of the war, thereby

showing that there had been no break with the past either in 1953 or in 1956. This is where the change was the most striking.

Even this picture needs some modification, as considerable forces resisted and still resist even a verbal restalinization along the lines just described. These forces included the intellectuals, most of the foreign pro-Soviet Communist Parties, and probably also a few career-minded *apparatchiki* of the latest vintage who wanted to keep the weapon in reserve for later use against their elders. Some ambitious men in top circles (Shelepin?) who are still awaiting their hour may share these feelings. This would explain why the movement was apparently neutralized soon after it had gained momentum, and also why its start was slow and beset by contradictions.

At first, everything seemed likely to go on unchanged. At regular intervals the press published articles extolling the chief victims of Stalinism, specifying that they had been the 'victims of arbitrariness and illegality in the period of the cult of personality' (*Izvestia*, November 18 1964 for Kosyor, *Pravda*, November 10 1964 for Odintsov, etc.). On November 17 a long article in *Pravda* dedicated to another victim, A. M. Nazaretyan, inveighed against Stalin and the atmosphere of persecution during the 'cult', and recalled the courageous attitude of men like Ordzhonikidze and Kirov. It is true that, on December 1 1964, *Pravda*, recalling the thirtieth anniversary of Kirov's assassination, did not say a word about the mystery surrounding the event, which Khrushchev had described at length at the Twenty-second Congress. But even though no attempt was being made to throw light on additional cases as Khrushchev had promised at the Congress, there was no hesitation in discussing known cases or the dictator's ideological 'errors'. In an article on leftism, *Kommunist* (No 18 1964) criticized Stalin for mistakes dating back to Lenin's time.

The picture started to change at the beginning of 1965. At first, on the surface at any rate, this seemed due to the military alone. The approach of the twentieth anniversary of victory, in May, produced a spate of historical recollections. It was normal to extol the part played by the Supreme Command of the Soviet armed forces, and Stalin who had led them to victory. His name appeared in several articles; a documentary film about the war showed him on four different occasions; the *Pravda* issue of July 1941, containing his celebrated appeal to fight to the bitter end, was given prominent place in the renovated Red Army Museum in Moscow. This was natural enough, though it contrasted sharply with Khrushchev's assertions that Stalin had never done anything worth while even during the war.

However, the role of the military stopped there. They only aimed at re-establishing historical truth concerning Stalin and other figures, particularly G. K. Zhukov, the marshal demoted in 1957. The writer, S. S. Smirnov, even suggested in a televised interview that Zhukov should head the military parade on Red Square (*Le Monde*, February 15 1965). This was profitable to Stalin's victims too, for *Krasnaya Zvezda*, the Army organ, did not hesitate at the same time to mention the excesses of the 'cult'. On February 16 1965 it described at length the sufferings of one of the first military chiefs, N. I. Podvoysky, who fell from favour in 1933, having clashed with Stalin even before the Revolution (*Pravda*, which published an article about him on the same day, omitted this 'detail'). A highly unusual event was the denunciation of Malenkov and Kaganovich[1] for their failure to respond to Podvoysky's pleas. Furthermore, the military asked for an objective attitude towards certain victims from the early stages of the Soviet régime. For instance, also in February 1965, a colonel, writing in the weekly *Nedelya* (No 8 1965) rehabilitated the memory of the military chief B. Dubenko, who was shot for treason in 1920, having, as the author explained, been the victim of slander. Later, the military asked the historians to be more serious in describing the role of Trotsky, and even of Kerensky who 'must have had some qualities if he was able to gain temporary success and so skilfully mislead the people' (*Krasnaya Zvezda*, November 3 1965).

In short, the military wanted a return to objectivity, and were trying to prevent the politicians from rewriting history to suit the current

---

[1] As might be expected, the 'anti-party' issue disappeared from the news directly after Khrushchev's downfall. Some criticism of the group persisted, however, for instance in *Pravda* of July 19 1965, which accused Malenkov of having refused to believe that a German attack was imminent. It is true that the author was also a military man, and that only Malenkov was taken to task (nowhere was Molotov mentioned, for example). Furthermore, only political errors were brought up. Criminal accusations against the 'anti-party group' were apparently the first to be dropped. An article in *Pravda* of February 20 1965, about A. A. Kuznetsov, a victim of the 'Leningrad affair' in 1950, ascribed that crime to 'Beriya, Abakumov and their accomplices', whereas under Khrushchev, Malenkov's name was invariably added to theirs.

This was confirmed when, in June 1965, a revised and corrected edition of a handbook on the Party and its history came out. The first edition had been published in 1963 (*KPSS–Spravochnik*). All references to the participation of Molotov, Kaganovich and Malenkov in the Stalinist purges, as well as their reluctance to denounce the cult, had been cut out. Moreover, the account of the June 1957 plenary session, which was substantially shortened, only mentioned a 'group' – hence not necessarily an 'anti-party' one – that included Malenkov, Kaganovich, Molotov 'and others'. The previous edition had listed Bulganin, Pervukhin, Saburov and Shepilov after the first series of names. In other words, the 'guilt by association' imposed by Khrushchev in 1959 and later was no longer valid. These alterations confirm our previous conclusion, namely that on these two main points (criminal responsibility of the 'anti-party group' and the inclusion in their group of individuals who had not been denounced in 1957), the collective leadership did not share Khrushchev's views.

political situation. M. V. Zakharov, the new chief of the General Staff, explained this in no uncertain terms.[1] Although these men gave Stalin his due, they pointed out his weakness in military matters. On the anniversary of victory, the same Zakharov criticized the country's state of unpreparedness when the Germans attacked, and in particular the gaps in the disposition of troops along the border (*Izvestia*, May 7 1965). On the same date, Malinovsky did not even mention Stalin in his article on the anniversary of victory (*Pravda*, May 8 1965). Perhaps in the meantime he had realized what effects the movement had produced in Party circles.

FROM OBJECTIVITY TO RESTALINIZATION

A large section of the *apparatchiki* had been waiting for an opportunity to have Stalin's indictment by Khrushchev reviewed. Between 'objective' thinking and the rehabilitation of Stalin and his era, between the cessation of attacks against the cult and the attack on those who castigated the cult, there was only one step, and it was definitely taken.

An indication came with the victory celebrations in May 1965. Objectivity demanded the recognition of Stalin's merits in the conduct of the war; but it demanded that the unpreparedness of the country in 1941 and Stalin's refusal to believe in the imminence of the German invasion be acknowledged as well. That is how the military saw things, but the civilians' attitude was different. In his main report of May 8, Brezhnev called for acclaim of Stalin, 'the Secretary-General of the Central Committee . . . at the head of the State Committee for Defence', which was normal; but he also endeavoured to depict Stalin's entire policy as beyond reproach from beginning to end, which was less normal. Instead of listing the problems posed by the outbreak of the war, he merely stated: 'Our Party and the Soviet people had taken steps to increase the economic and defence potential of the country' (*Pravda*, May 9 1965). He ascribed the initial set-backs only to the suddenness of the German assault, whereas even Malinovsky, in his article written the day before, had mentioned 'a whole series of reasons'. Not only did Brezhnev dismiss any notion of panic in 1941, but he sought to

---

[1] On February 4 1965 Zakharov criticized in *Krasnaya Zvezda* 'certain historians who, in analysing a given operation of World War II, do not pay attention to its true military and strategic importance, but rather consider the posts currently occupied by the people who were in charge of carrying it out. The more exalted their present post, the more the historians think the operation has to be emphasized and inflated. . . . These historians are slipping into the role of court scholars – and where a courtier's attitude prevails, it is the death of scholarship.'

present the Party and people as having steeled themselves for the war effort from the outset. He did not even mention the evacuation of the ministries from Moscow, and only emphasized that 'the political General Staff of the country and the Central Committee of the Party had remained at its combat post in Moscow'.

The object was clearly to rehabilitate Stalin as well as to restore confidence in the wisdom of the top Party leaders, and more specifically in the men of the Stalinist apparatus who had held key posts at the time. One of the veterans, V. M. Ryabikov, First Deputy Minister for Armament at the beginning of the war and currently First Vice-President of Gosplan, lent Brezhnev a hand by writing an article for *Pravda* on April 30 1965, where he stated that none of the steps taken in and after 1939 deserved criticism. Mistakes might have been made earlier through the geographical over-concentration of industrial capabilities, but the evacuation had gone according to plan. On May 7 *Pravda* devoted a whole page to the Party officials' deeds during that period. Several old-timers in the apparatus emerged from the shadows for the occasion. One of them, for instance, was P. K. Ponomarenko, First Secretary of the Party in Byelorussia from 1938 to 1947, who in that capacity headed the central general staff of the partisan movement. He had vanished from the scene after being recalled from the Soviet Embassy at The Hague in 1961. The 'salvaging' of these men was normal enough in the euphoria of the anniversary, especially as a reaction to Khrushchev's and his friends' tendency to monopolize the glory of the past. But behind these manifestations, the real demand was taking shape: no more attacks against the old-timers, whether the pretext be destalinization or anything else.

The first sign of this unofficial rehabilitation of an era came in February 1965, at the time the military launched their own drive. In *Pravda* of February 21 N. Abalkin had criticized a film released in October 1964, *The Chairman*, which described the tribulations of an enterprising kolkhoz chairman in the post-war years. The film was a model of conformism à la Khrushchev (for instance, at Stalin's death, the camera abruptly moved from a scene of wretchedness to opulent wheatfields). Abalkin was on solid ground in claiming that the picture of recent years had been embellished. He also accused the authors of having exaggerated the sorry plight of the countryside during the Stalin years. The film, he explained, depicted the early years of collectivization rather than the post-war period. Any shortages after the war were due to the destruction wrought by the occupation forces. Lastly, the fact that only an outstanding political and social régime could have bred such an outstanding character as Trubnikov, the chief hero, had not been sufficiently emphasized. Despite its cautious and courteous tone, the article was a definite departure from everything said during the preceding ten years about the Stalinist régime and its effects on agriculture.

This was only a beginning, for after the victory celebrations such signs multiplied. In Georgia, where Stalin's museum in his birthplace at Gori reopened, the local First Secretary, V. P. Mzhavanadze, quoted Stalin, who had said in a 'strikingly picturesque fashion': 'Our Party is a fortress whose gates open only for tried and true people' (*Zarya Vostoka*, June 29 1965). Since the quotation came in support of a plea for the rehabilitation of the 'old and experienced officials',[1] it was clearly meant as a call for the promotion of veteran Stalinists. In Leningrad the Party Urban Committee addressed its first warning to the writers against 'giving undue prominence to the cult [*kultovy*] atmosphere', and thus losing sight of the Party's enormous activity in organizational work and in the building of communism (in other words, the credit side of the 1930s) (*Pravda*, June 7 1965). Other indications followed; for instance:

1 The publication in June of the second edition of the *Handbook of Party History* (*KPSS-Spravochnik*, cleared for printing on June 10), replacing the 1963 edition. As expected, the history of the war had been revised and corrected in the light of the May celebrations and, while Stalin's disbelief in an impending invasion was still mentioned (p 268), the following sentence in the first edition (p 271) had been cut out:

'The history of the Great Patriotic War shows that Stalin committed serious mistakes and miscalculations in the period preceding the war and during the war itself, and that their correction cost much effort and some victims.'

There were also corrections of a more political nature. Although still mentioning 'mass repressions', the 'cult of Stalin's personality' and Stalin's 'erroneous' thesis that the class struggle was bound to intensify as socialism progressed', the editors of the second edition had left out a long list of the principal victims at the end of that paragraph (p 244 in the first edition). Similarly, while it was still acknowledged that Kirov's assassination in 1934 had set off 'mass repressions and gross violations of socialist legality', it was no longer stated that 'Stalin used Kirov's assassination for reprisals against many persons he no longer wanted' (1st edition, p 231). The significant change, apparently,

---

[1] 'During the past few years, many young communists who are capable organizers have risen to leadership in the Party organizations. This is good. But sometimes, out of excessive enthusiasm for the renewal of the secretariat staff, we have unjustifiably and unreasonably removed from leadership old and experienced officials, despite the fact that experience is not acquired in one month or even in one year.'

was the slight departure from the rehabilitation process followed under Khrushchev. It was acknowledged that repressions had occurred, but the contention now was that some of the rehabilitated victims should not have been whitewashed, for they had indeed been enemies of the people. This was confirmed by the deletion of a sentence according to which in 1934 a 'united and monolithic' Party had gathered for its Seventeenth Congress and that, after the confessions of Zinoviev, Kamenev and others, 'there were no opposition groups within the Party' (1st edition, p 230). On the other hand, the authors added a new sentence to indicate that the reason why Stalin had been confirmed in his position at the head of the Party in 1924, despite Lenin's warning, was 'his energetic struggle against Trotskyism which, at the time, represented the main danger for the Party' (2nd edition, p 207).

Lastly, new dividing lines for historical periods robbed the year 1953 (Stalin's death) of any significance. The chapters for the 1945–1953 and 1953–1958 periods which in the first edition covered the post-war era were changed to 1945–1958 and 1959–1965, and the critical tone was more pronounced in the second of these chapters than the first. According to this version, then, Stalin's death had not entailed any decisive break, and moreover, in some respects, the recent past was more dubious than the earlier past.

2 On August 29 1965 the First Secretary of the Komsomol, S. P. Pavlov, endorsed the new line in *Pravda*. Characteristically enough, the first 'but' (*odnako*) about destalinization came from this prominent spokesman of the 'young *apparatchiki*' (he was born in 1929). This is what he wrote:

'Unquestionably, the denunciation of the cult of personality has had enormous importance for the education of the young generation. *Nevertheless* one can hardly justify *a certain unilateral* approach by some theoreticians and writers who view entire stages in the history of socialist society exclusively through the prism of the adverse consequences of the cult of personality. Such a unilateral approach does not help to promote patriotism, or to impart to young people a correct understanding of the history of our country. The thirties, for instance, have often been depicted in sombre colours only. Actually, the life of Soviet society during those years was determined *primarily* by industrialization and the cultural revolution, the socialist transformation of agriculture and the masses' enthusiasm for work, the stakhanovist movement and the flights of Chkalov, genuine innovation (*novatorstvo*) and the victory of socialist realism in art and literature.' [Author's italics.]

The article aimed at more than 'salvaging something from the experience of the pre-war years' in Komsomol work (Pavlov even added that the experience was 'rich and interesting'). It meant that the entire history of the thirties was to be reviewed in a favourable light, and the older generation should present itself as an example to youth instead of cowering under the insulting labels affixed to it by destalinization. As for the repressions, it was better to close the chapter for fear of sliding back into the regrettable 'unilateral approach' of recent years. 3 An article in *Pravda* of October 8 1965 by S. P. Trapeznikov, the new head of the Central Committee department for 'Science and Educational Institutions', was one more step in the same direction. Like S. P. Pavlov, he added his 'but' to destalinization (using a formula dating back to Khrushchev's time, he declared that 'neither the cult nor its consequences derived in any way from the nature of the socialist régime') and called for a struggle against the 'unilateral approach'. His version of the thirties was even brighter than Pavlov's:

'The period of the struggle for the industrialization of the country-side, for the socialist transformation of the village, and for the cultural revolution, was *one of the most brilliant* in the history of the Party and of the Soviet State. It was a period of rich experience in theoretical and practical Party activities, *a hard-fought struggle for ideological purity within its ranks*, and the education of communists in the spirit of unconditional faithfulness to Marxism–Leninism. The collapse of the two most dangerous anti-Leninist ideologies, Trotskyism and right-wing opportunism, was of major significance.' [Author's italics.]

In other words, the achievements of that period, 'one of the most brilliant', were now not merely industrialization, collectivization and the 'cultural revolution', but also the 'ideological' purges, assuming that one is willing to close one's eyes to their penal outcome. Trapeznikov, incidentally, did not write one word about those 'excesses', but, on the contrary, corroborated what we have already noted concerning the CPSU handbook:

'An aftertaste of subjectivism has also coloured judgments about certain figures and their role in the period of major transformations [still the 1930s]. On occasion certain people have been extolled although they not only played no significant role in these events, but in some cases even took up hostile positions in the unfolding struggle' (*Pravda*, October 8 1965).

In short, certain 'enemies of the people' had been rehabilitated when they should not have been. Perhaps they had not deserved to be shot – or at least this may be surmised from the author's failure to be more specific on the subject – but neither did they deserve the posthumous honours rendered them. This new note fits in with the deletion of the list of victims from the handbook, and is not accidental.

In any case, after the summer of 1965, notices in the Soviet press commemorating the anniversaries of 'cult' victims appeared at much longer intervals. One of the last was in *Pravda* of September 3 in memory of V. G. Knorin, a Comintern official executed in 1938, but this time the circumstances and even the date of his death were left out. His activities were reported only up to June 1937. True, the provincial press and literary magazines occasionally still carried a notice of that type. But not until after the Twenty-third Congress did the central newspapers again run the usual notices on the victims of the cult and mention their tragic deaths.[1]

4 The peak was reached in the first three months of 1966. A major step was taken on January 30, when *Pravda* reprinted the declaration of three prominent historians, E. Zhukov, V. Trukhanovsky and V. Shunkov:

> 'The denunciation by the Party and the people of the cult of personality – a phenomenon thoroughly alien to Marxism – has had very useful effects. It has had favourable repercussions on the life of Soviet society, in particular the development of social sciences. Unfortunately, however, subjectivist influences foreign to Marxism, which have also been expressed in certain historical works, have found an outlet in this domain. *The erroneous non-Marxist term of "period of the cult of personality" has been disseminated.* The use of that term, exaggerating as it does the role of one person, has resulted, whether this was intended or not, in minimizing the heroic efforts of the Party and people in the struggle for socialism, and in impoverishing history.' [Author's italics.]

Hence, it was permissible, at a pinch, to speak of the 'cult of personality' – preferably as seldom as possible, since the other previously mentioned warnings remained in effect – but no longer of the 'period of the cult', because the expression was regarded as insulting to the Stalinist generation of cadres. This indeed, was the end of an era. And the order must have come from a very high quarter, since the phrase disappeared from the press overnight. As far as is known, it has not reappeared to this day.

[1] For the recrudescence of statements about victims of the cult of personality, see for example *Izvestia* of May 14 and 25 1966. But this return to candour was not universal. For instance, on August 15 1966, Marshal Bagramian gave in *Pravda* a lengthy account of Yakir, the military leader executed during the purges, without a single word about his disgrace and execution.

Lurking behind these quarrels on semantics, a growing threat was overshadowing the entire destalinization policy. As it happened, a date of importance in the history of that policy was approaching – happily or unhappily according to one's opinion – namely the tenth anniversary of the Twentieth Congress, which had met in February 1956. Needless to say, under Khrushchev it would not have gone unnoticed. The collective leadership would have to celebrate it in some way if it was to remain faithful to the line of the 'Twentieth, Twenty-first and Twenty-second Congresses', as it had proclaimed it would. Less important and momentous anniversaries are celebrated daily. Nevertheless, in this case it was decided to abstain. The anniversary of the Congress, February 14, went by without any mention in the press. Next day, the Polish and Czechoslovak allies decided to celebrate it on their own, and their editorials mentioned the event as one 'of enormous importance' (*Trybuna Ludu* and *Rudé Právo*, February 15 1966). The gesture carried a hint of warning, and Moscow finally followed suit in a *Pravda* editorial on February 26. But a passing mention in an editorial on a different topic obviously lacked conviction.[1] As if by accident, the same issue of the paper contained an article praising A. A. Zhdanov, the literary dictator of the Stalinist period, about whom silence had been maintained throughout the preceding years. The day before, a rally had been held to celebrate his seventieth birthday, and had been attended by P. N. Pospelov. One cannot help noticing that 'family celebrations' of this type were easier to hold under Brezhnev than those associated with destalinization.

THE SPOKESMAN OF THE NEW MOVEMENT: BREZHNEV

Among the forces at work behind this insidious but persistent restalinization, Brezhnev is in first place. His role in the victory commemoration ceremonies in May 1965 has been noted in passing, as well as his attitude toward Stalin, which was definitely more favourable than that of the military. Brezhnev also was the first to restore Zhdanov

---

[1] *Pravda* wrote thus about the tenth anniversary of the Twentieth Congress: 'Ten years ago – in February 1956 – the Twentieth Party Congress was held, which played a major role in the life of our Party and of the country.' And a little further: 'The decisions of the Party aimed at restoring Leninist standards in the life of the Party and State, observing and developing the principles of collective leadership and democracy within the Party, were of major importance. Overcoming the consequences of the cult of personality, the Party performed valuable ideological, political and organizational work among the masses and took important measures to promote the development of socialist democracy' (*Pravda*, February 26 1966).

to his former place of eminence: in a speech delivered in Leningrad in July 1965 he described him as 'an outstanding statesman and political leader' (*Pravda*, July 11 1965). One of the forerunners of restalinization, S. P. Trapeznikov, whose article glorifying the 1930s has been quoted, was obviously one of Brezhnev's clients. From 1949 on, Trapeznikov was director of the Higher Party School in Moldavia, and therefore must have had contacts with Brezhnev, who was the First Secretary in that republic from 1950 to 1952. In recent years, Trapeznikov had been Vice-Rector of the Higher Party School in Moscow, and he could not have been promoted to the post of head of the Central Committee department for 'Science and Educational Institutions' (which entitled him to full membership of the Central Committee at the Twenty-third Congress) without the protection of the new Party chief. Nor could he have hailed the Stalinist era as 'one of the most brilliant' periods in Soviet life without Brezhnev's assent.

Brezhnev even gave the impression at times of being ready to go further than his entourage in reviving Stalinist symbols. In a speech at Kiev on October 23 1965 he mentioned Stalingrad twice – not only in connection with the battle, but when listing the cities currently bearing the title of 'heroine-cities' (*Pravda*, October 24 1965). All the speakers who followed him, in particular P. E. Shelest, N. G. Yegorychev and A. I. Shitov, the First Secretary of the City's Urban Committee, consistently used its new name of Volgograd. Shelest, for example, disregarded the name of Stalingrad even with reference to the great battle, using the Khrushchevian device of referring to the 'battle of the Volga'. Brezhnev may even have contemplated restoring the former name, but been prevented from doing so.

Neither was it accidental that the peak of restalinization was reached in the spring of 1966 when Brezhnev, after more or less definitively removing his chief rivals Podgorny and Shelepin (this will be discussed at greater length), was about to receive the prestigious title of 'Secretary-General' and appeared to be at his strongest. His alliance with Suslov, whose action in 1964 has been analysed, must have played a part in his attitude, as also did his desire to build up a clientèle for himself among the *apparatchiki* embittered by destalinization. This may not have required any 'agonizing reappraisal' of Brezhnev's earlier beliefs, since in 1961 he had already held an ambiguous position on the issue.

However, the Secretary-General was about to discover that it was almost as difficult to restalinize in 1966 as it had been to destalinize in earlier years. Justly alarmed by the above signs, all the forces hostile to a return to the past – even a symbolic one – went into action before the Congress opened. Twenty-seven Soviet writers, artists, and scientists signed a petition to the Central Committee against any rehabilitation of Stalin, having first made sure that their move would be known abroad (UPI, March 15 1966).[1] The East European allies, who had at first found it so difficult to adopt the destalinization line in 1956, had no intention of being forced to change course once again. They made their position known discreetly but quite definitely, as indicated by the Polish and Czechoslovak moves in February on the anniversary of the Twentieth Congress. Did all these forces find any response within the Soviet apparatus? Quite probably, as already mentioned. At the beginning of March, one of the most virulent spokesmen of the restalinizers, the Secretary of the Georgian Communist Party, D. G. Sturua, overtly complained at the Congress of his Party that 'discord (*raznoboy*) had arisen regarding the assessment of the past work of our ideological institutions'.[2]

[1] In its issue of September 16 1966 the usually well-informed Russian émigré periodical *Posev* published what it claimed to be the text of the petition to the Central Committee by writers, artists and scientists on the eve of the Twenty-third Congress. Here are some excerpts:

'Respected Leonid Ilyich [Brezhnev],
'Tendencies have recently appeared in certain public speeches and articles in our press, directed towards a partial or indirect rehabilitation of Stalin. We do not know whether these tendencies have a solid basis, but they are growing more frequent as the Twenty-third Congress approaches. Even if this means only a partial review of the decisions of the Twentieth and Twenty-second Congress, it is causing deep apprehension among us. . . .
'Until now we have not been apprised of a single fact or argument which suggests that the condemnation of the cult of personality was mistaken in any way whatsoever. On the contrary, it is hard to doubt that many of the startling, indeed appalling facts about Stalin's crimes have not yet been made public. . . .
'We believe that any attempt to whitewash Stalin involves a threat of serious strife within Soviet society. . . . No explanations or articles will induce the people to believe in Stalin. They will, on the contrary, only foster anger and disorder. Any attempts of that kind are dangerous, in view of the complex economic and political situation in our country. . . .'

Among the twenty-seven signatories were the Academicians L. A. Artsimovich, P. L. Kapitsa, I. M. Maysky, A. D. Sakharov, I. E. Tamm and S. D. Skazkin; the writers V. P. Katayev, V. P. Nekrasov, K. G. Paustovsky, B. A. Slutsky, V. F. Tendriakov and K. I. Chukovsky; the artists O. N. Yefremov, P. D. Korin, Yu. I. Pimenov, M. M. Plisetskaya, M. I. Romm, M. M. Khutsiev, etc.
[2] The speech by D. G. Sturua, one of the high points of the restalinization drive, was delivered on March 3 1966 but published – in abbreviated form – only on March 10 in the provincial daily *Zarya Vostoka*. The orator first castigated, just as *Pravda* had on January 30, the expression 'period of the cult':

'In ideological work, attention has been concentrated on illuminating the areas in the life of our society that were in the shadow during the period when I. V. Stalin was at the head of the Party and of the Soviet State. Moreover, this period came to be labelled "period of the cult of personality", which in practice tended to minimize and denigrate the heroic struggle waged for many years by the Soviet people under the leadership of the Leninist Party.'

Then Sturua took to task those who, taking advantage of the struggle against the 'cult', had attempted to rehabilitate Trotskyism and other deviationist tendencies.

THE CONGRESS OF SILENCES

These influences were no doubt responsible for the neutralization of the restalinizers' campaign at the Twenty-third Congress. When the Congress met at the Kremlin on March 29 1966, the earlier policy was being questioned so overtly that some airing of differences, or at least an attempt at one, seemed imminent. It could have been reasonably assumed that Stalin and perhaps Khrushchev as well were going to be assigned their rightful place in history. Even if their names were still difficult to utter, one might have thought that the substitute euphemisms of 'cult of personality' and 'subjectivism' were going to be analysed in greater detail. Nothing of the sort occurred. Brezhnev's report and the other speeches gave the impression that the future Secretary-General of the Party and his allies were strong enough to stop destalinization, but not strong enough to replace it with anything else. The result was a political vacuum without precedent for many years.

What was the thinking on the last few congresses of the Khrushchev era? It did not take long to find out, since Brezhnev declared in the opening sentence of his report: 'During all these years, the CPSU, inspired by the line defined by the Twentieth and Twenty-second Congresses, unswervingly led the Soviet people towards the building of communism' (*Pravda*, March 30 1966). But that was all. With this fairly safe formula, the collective leadership closed the matter. Stalin and the 'cult' were not mentioned at all. The 'brilliant years' of Stalinism were not either, although, out of a strangely interpreted concern for continuity, the earlier period received better treatment than the recent past. The reproaches addressed to Khrushchev were not new either: the division of the Party and *shablon* in agriculture were mentioned and a brief summary was given of the attempts at correcting his mistakes in the course of the last eighteen months. But the language used on this subject was restrained, far more so, for example, than at the plenary session of March 1965.

Not until the second day of the Congress, when N. G. Yegorychev, the First Secretary of the Moscow Urban Committee, delivered his speech, were some of the gaps filled in. All the Congress had to say on the delicate topic was contained in this statement:

In his opinion, criticism of the cult had also bred 'nihilism', 'cosmopolitanism', 'apoliticism', 'distortions of history', etc. He took this opportunity to call Sinyavsky and Daniel 'agents in the pay of the bourgeoisie', 'drug addicts of literature' and 'ideological black-marketeers'.

It should be noted that D. G. Sturua, the Secretary of the Central Committee of the Georgian Communist Party since 1961, belonged to the generation of *apparatchiki* under thirty-five years old in 1966. This shows how misleading it would be to use only the criterion of generations to differentiate between 'Stalinists' and 'liberals'.

'It has become fashionable of late to seek in the country's political life elements of alleged "Stalinism" and to use it as a scarecrow to frighten public opinion, especially the intelligentsia. We say to such people: 'It won't get you anywhere, gentlemen! . . .' The cult of personality, the violation of Leninist standards and principles in the life of the Party, of socialist legality, everything in short that impeded our forward movement, has been decisively rejected by our Party, and there will never be any return to that past! The course of the Twentieth Congress and of the October plenary session of the Central Committee of the CPSU [Khrushchev's overthrow] securely guarantees this.

'At the same time, the Party rejects with the same determination all attempts to suppress the heroic history of our people. . . . We see now that some things could have been done better, since fifty years have taught us a great deal. But what has been done fills the heart of the Soviet people with pride, and fosters the admiration of our friends all over the world' (*Pravda*, March 31 1966).

This, in theory, was sufficient to reassure doubters abroad or among the intelligentsia. For the first time in several months, the 'cult of personality' and its consequences, including 'violations of legality', were explicitly censured and the 'line of the Twentieth Congress' explicitly reaffirmed. On the other hand, the new line had not been overlooked, since 'the heroic history' and concern for continuity had also been considered. In all likelihood, this clarification by the young chief of the Moscow *apparat* (Yegorychev was born in 1920) had been made with the assent of the top Party leadership, or at least a section of it. To have said nothing whatever on all these issues would have been exceedingly embarrassing to friends abroad. At the same time, one wonders what had prevented a similar statement from being included in the main report to the Congress, delivered by Brezhnev the day before. The procedure adopted not only detracted somewhat from the official character of these assurances, but also suggested that the Party Presidium had failed to reach agreement on them. The phrase 'period of the cult' had already been vetoed, and it now seemed that the mere mention of 'cult of personality' went too far.

In any case, taking into account the work of the Congress as a whole, Yegorychev's declaration fits in as lip-service to destalinization. Since it was followed by practically no additional statement,[1] it appears to be an exception that confirms the rule – namely that the Twentieth

---

[1] At the Twenty-third Congress Podgorny also briefly alluded to the 'cult' in the following terms: 'The Party did a great deal to reinforce the socialist legal order, and eliminate the baneful influences linked with the cult of personality' (*Pravda*, April 1 1966).

Congress, destalinization, in short everything that had been the leit-motiv of the previous congresses, had become taboo. The average speaker at the Twenty-third Congress dealt with his region's economic achievements and problems, as required by the tradition of all con-gresses, and then chided the 'fault-finding writers', which was in line with the new tradition. There was hardly any chance of breaking out of these bounds, especially since the great ones, who might have given a new impetus to the proceedings, kept silent. Breaking with tradition, neither Suslov nor Shelepin nor even the lesser lights, such as Polyansky, Voronov or Mazurov, took the floor. In this heavy silence, explicable only by disagreement within the collective leadership, the rank-and-file speakers could not have been expected to display any great originality.

The vacuum did not affect only the issues of Stalin and Khrushchev. Since 1961 the Party had been living under a programme outlining policy for the establishment of the 'bases' of the communist society from then until 1980. The programme clearly bore Khrushchev's mark and had in fact become obsolete in a number of areas. But no one could say this outright, still less proclaim that it was in need of revision or replacement. Brezhnev mentioned the programme briefly in the introduction to his report ('The entire activity of the Party has been oriented toward the carrying out of the CPSU programme'), but as neither he nor the other speakers reverted to that issue, the con-clusion must be that, as in the case of the Twentieth Congress, this brief reminder too was the exception that confirms the rule.

In some cases, such silences made for awkward situations. For instance, in 1961 Khruschev, as noted, had obtained the banning of the concept of 'dictatorship of the proletariat' and the change from 'the Party of the working class' to 'the Party of the whole people' and from 'the Soviet State' to 'the State of the whole people'. All these innova-tions had been registered in the 1961 programme, and apparently they were strictly observed even after 'the October plenum'. For instance, a long anonymous article in *Pravda* of November 1 1964 professed faith-fulness to all points of the programme, including the concepts of 'Party of the whole people' and 'State of the whole people'. This insistence was especially noticeable because the collective leadership, just then striving for a *rapprochement* with the Chinese, might quite as easily have played down these highly revisionist – and pointless – formulae which had provoked Chinese and Albanian propaganda attacks. Far from it, on December 6 1964, *Pravda* again praised the slogan of 'the State of the whole people', this time in a rebuttal of criticism from abroad. It even reaffirmed that the formula was valid not only for the USSR but, at some stage, for 'every country'.[1]

[1] On December 6 1964 *Pravda* wrote concerning the slogan of 'the State of the whole

It is not known why it was decided to revise these formulae. The fact that, for a few months after taking power the collective leadership decided to maintain Khrushchev's line on this issue, and even reaffirmed it spectacularly, indicates that the subject had certainly not come up for discussion at the 'October plenum', or at the November one. At the same time, one should bear in mind Brezhnev's manifest coolness towards these new ideas at the Twenty-second Congress. The narrow conservatism that he displayed in many areas as soon as he had consolidated his position, and his attachment to the symbols of Stalinism, must have prompted him gradually to jettison that part of Khrushchev's heritage, after he had rejected many others. The revision on this issue was conducted in the greatest secrecy. Only the slogans published twice yearly by Agitprop on the occasion of the two major celebrations of the régime, May Day and November 7, showed that it was going on.

Up to then 'the State of the whole people' had been proclaimed in two slogans which were repeated unchanged on May Day, 1965:

'May the union of the working class and of the kolkhoz peasantry, unshakeable basis of the socialist State *of the whole people*, prosper and grow in strength! . . .

'Long live our socialist State *of the whole people*! May Soviet socialist democracy develop and strengthen, and may the activity of the workers increase in the management of State affairs!' (*Pravda*, April 22 1965, slogans Nos 58 and 101.) [Author's italics.]

For November 7 1965 the correctors stopped mid-way: the second slogan was left unchanged, but the first mentioned only 'the Soviet Socialist State' (*Pravda*, October 23 1965). By the time May Day 1966 arrived, any mention of 'the State of the whole people' had been cut out of both (*Pravda*, April 17 1966). These first post-Congress slogans were also the first to omit any reference to the Party programme. This confirms that despite Brezhnev's polite mention of the programme in his report, the document was doomed to gradual oblivion.[1]

---

people': 'The tasks and processes that require the transformation of the dictatorship of the proletariat into a State of the whole people inevitably arise in every country at a given stage of the building of the new society.'

[1] Other chapters of the 1961 Party programme had been revised as well. One of the leitmotivs, for example, had been that the perfect communist society would be achieved 'essentially' in the eighties and that 'the present Soviet generation was going to live under a communist régime'. All kinds of production targets were announced, including a grandiose expansion of agriculture. As was to be expected, these spectacular promises soon ceased to be mentioned. The slogan: 'Forward to the victory of communism!' disappeared from the October 1965 series, as did other references here and there to the 'builders of communism', who were replaced by 'the Soviet people'. But the slogan which traditionally closed the list – viz. 'Long live

Such a 'revision through silence' has its drawbacks, since it is difficult for the propagandists to carry on their daily task without knowing whether the Soviet State is a 'dictatorship of the proletariat' or a 'State of the whole people'. Where the Party was concerned, apparently the thing to do was to abide by the explanation provided in January 1965 by N. A. Lomakin in *Partiynaya Zhizn* (No 2 1965). According to him, the Party was 'at the same time' the Party of the whole people and the Party of the working class. This was the only officially permitted revision of the 1961 programme. It meant that there had been no transformation of the Party, but that it had merely acquired another feature in addition to its former ones. This explanation might not satisfy everybody, but since none other was given, it had to do.

Thus, in all sectors where a semblance of political initiative was apparent, ranging from restalinization to the curbing of the writers and including the abandonment of some of Khrushchev's doctrinal innovations, the movement was soon neutralized by opposite forces. Any practical move dwindled to the level of a mere impulse. This had already happened under Khrushchev, but to a lesser degree. At that time the opposition tended to interfere with the execution of decisions rather than with their formulation. Under the collective leadership, paralysis set in as soon as a problem had to be put into words. The Albanian leader, Hysni Kapo, was not far from the truth when in Peking, on May 9 1966, he commented on the proceedings of the Twenty-third Congress:

'Whereas at the Twentieth, Twenty-first and Twenty-second Congresses, the Khrushchevian revisionists were on the offensive, at the Twenty-third they have retreated and have been forced into a defensive position all along the line. Under cover of a smoke-screen, they have sidestepped all the most burning issues, such as the problem of Stalin, their relations with the Chinese Communist Party and the Albanian Labour Party, Khrushchev's downfall, their agricultural failure, bourgeois degeneration in the cultural and artistic fields, the German problem, etc. During this Congress they did not even dare allude to their cherished slogan: "The Party of the whole people and the State of the whole people." Many of the present Soviet leaders did not even take the floor' (*Peking-Information*, No 20 1966, p 33).

---

communism, which brings about the reign of peace, labour, liberty, equality, fraternity and the happiness of all peoples on earth' – did not disappear till April 1966.

Finally, in the summer of 1965 when the second edition of the *CPSU Guide* came out, it was noted that all the promises in the Party programme which took the form of figures regarding production in 1980 had been eliminated.

It was, of course, presumptuous to regard this as the product of Sino-Albanian efforts. Superficially such an interpretation corresponded with the course of the 'congress of silences', but, in fact, the causes were essentially domestic ones. Previous congresses had been aggressive in character because Khrushchev was (or was thought to be) in a position of strength and was waging war against his enemies at home. The Twenty-third Congress, on the other hand, was, in the last analysis, not so much aggressive as merely superfluous. A congress had had to be convened, since the statutes required one every four years (and it was already six months late), but no one was in a position to take advantage of it. The only thing to do was to declare a drawn game which reflected the actual balance of forces.

3 The Power Structure

Whatever Khrushchev's successors might say at the time, his downfall did change a great deal in the overall political picture and in the power structure itself. From one day to the next, the rule of the game had been drastically altered. It was no longer a question of accepting or rejecting Khrushchev's moves, but of increasing the chances of success for one's own moves in a situation that, all of a sudden, had become highly fluid. The entire system of alliances was upset and any coalitions were now possible. Even though a hierarchy subsisted because Brezhnev and Kosygin were in a privileged position and because the distinction between senior and junior Presidium members had not been erased, the odds as between individuals had been markedly equalized.

The anonymous style, the sober tone and the stricter secrecy that immediately pervaded political life were more than a psychological reaction against Khrushchev's over-assertive methods. The large majority of the collective leadership was anxious to maintain the pattern of equal opportunity as long as it could, and the only way was to cover the whole group in a veil of anonymity. For instance, both individual and group photographs of the leaders became very rare in the press. This was done not only to hide Brezhnev from view, but also to avoid displaying the hierarchic order of precedence that is so revealing to *apparatchiki* as well as to foreign Kremlinologists. As is almost traditional after a crisis, a new decree was promulgated concerning the nomenclature of communities and geographical sites, including streets and parks (*Vedomosti Verkhovnovo Sovieta RSFSR*, No 5 1965). A similar decree had followed the 1957 crisis, but Khrushchev had disregarded it.

Experience of Stalin's and Khrushchev's régimes had bred distrust for the Party Secretariat. Its huge power and the classic mingling of executive and legislative functions under the Soviet system had always turned the post of Secretary (whether First or not) into a stepping-stone for the conquest of power, and this was bound to remain unchanged. It is not surprising, therefore, that the Presidium made a point of reaffirming its power immediately. As soon as Khrushchev was overthrown, the Presidium rather than the Secretariat became the supreme embodiment of collective leadership. For example, in October 1964, when the agricultural and industrial branches of the apparatus were reunited, it was learned that the Presidium, besides taking the decision, had also determined the procedure for its application. It was also the Presidium and not the Secretariat that assumed the task of 'examining and settling all organizational problems relating to the creation of single Party organizations and their governing bodies, within the *kray* (territory) and *oblast*, as well as the rebuilding of single Soviets' (*Pravda*, November 17 1964). This official intrusion into 'organizational' matters, i.e. those pertaining to cadres, was actually an encroachment upon the Secretariat's powers, since, under the Party statutes, the Secretariat is in charge of 'supervising current work, mainly in the recruitment of cadres, and organizing control over its execution' (*Twenty-second Congress*, vol 3 p 347). It was learned later that, despite the existence of special agencies for given sectors, such as the Central Committee Bureau for the RSFSR, it was in fact the Party Presidium that, along with the Secretariat, was handling 'all the most important problems pertaining to the activity of Party organizations at the *kray* and *oblast* level' of the Russian Federation (Brezhnev's report to the Twenty-third Congress, *Pravda*, March 30 1966). Finally, even when Brezhnev was in the forefront, it was carefully pointed out that he did not take decisions on his own authority. At the plenary session of March 1965, the formula used in most speeches was: 'the measures drafted by the Presidium of the Central Committee of the CPSU and set forth in comrade Brezhnev's report'.

This situation was naturally bound to change, and is still doing so. The predominance of the Presidium over the Secretariat turned out, however, to be its most enduring feature. It was rightly regarded as the best guarantee of the preservation of collective leadership, and it has apparently survived every attempt at encroachment by the Secretariat. The fact that the representatives of the latter body were never in a majority within the Presidium also helped. On the other hand, the respective positions of the leaders within each body were bound to be affected in the long run both by circumstances and by individual ambitions or tendencies.

The liquidation of Khrushchev's empire went smoothly and without affecting the top leadership in any way, so that it requires no special comment. Protégés who had been too involved with the whims of the ex-First Secretary, such as V. I. Polyakov (head of the Agricultural Department of the Central Committee), or with his manoeuvres against the strong men at the time, such as L. F. Ilyichev, naturally disappeared from the scene. The most interesting fact was that no member of the Presidium was ousted for having been an over-zealous Khrushchev supporter. This was not because none was vulnerable to such an accusation, but rather because there were enough of them to defend themselves. In any case, the rule prevailing under Khrushchev, namely that it is easier to enter the Presidium than to leave it, was still valid under the new dispensation.

Everyone remained in his place, even though in some cases the function did not fit the rank. For instance, it is still a mystery why, in March 1965, K. T. Mazurov was picked for the vacant post of First Deputy to Kosygin at the head of the Government, which involved his joining the Presidium, whereas D. S. Polyansky, his senior both in the Presidium and in the Government, continued until October to vegetate in the lowly position of simple Deputy Prime Minister. G. I. Voronov kept both his seat and his function, although he witnessed the undoing of the agricultural policy which he had established, and the promotion of many high officials whom he had excoriated.[1] L. N. Yefremov was kept on for over a year as an alternate member although, having been transferred to Stavropol, he had no reason whatsoever to remain in the Presidium. Altogether, only two veterans of that body, Shvernik and Mikoyan, were removed, and then only at the Twenty-third Congress. Furthermore, in Mikoyan's case this may have been only an indirect and remote consequence of Khrushchev's downfall. Despite his role in the October crisis, Mikoyan was slightly compromised owing to his former position as Khrushchev's privileged confidant. In any case, he was better suited for manoeuvring behind the scenes in

[1] In December 1965 G. I. Voronov had to accept L. Ya. Florentiev, the former First Secretary of the Kostroma Oblast Committee, as Minister of Agriculture of the RSFSR. Voronov had berated him for years for his refusal to engage in the campaign against grass-growing. At the Twenty-second Congress for instance, Voronov had derided the harvest results in the Kostroma region: 'two loaves of bread and one sheep per hectare', adding, 'One might say that it was not even enough for comrade Florentiev's dinner' (*Pravda*, October 21 1961). In August 1961 the Central Committee Bureau for the RSFSR, then run by Voronov, had adopted a special decision criticizing the 'gross errors and oversights' committed by Florentiev in the management of agriculture (*Sovietskaya Rossiya*, January 31 1962).

The rehabilitation of agricultural personnel was not a smooth process, because the officials had been purged at various stages of Khrushchev's reign and the turnover had been high. Each one had come to the fore thanks to a particular campaign before being swept away by the next, and consequently they were at loggerheads with one another. This produced some odd situations: V. V. Matskevich was appointed Minister of Agriculture of the USSR on February 17 1965, less than two days after he had been sharply upbraided by *Izvestia* (February 16). A. V. Bazov took over the Ministry of Agriculture of the RSFSR, but in December became Ambassador to Rumania. K. G. Pyzin, a Minister of Agriculture dismissed by Khrushchev in March 1963, was appointed First Deputy Chairman for Agriculture of the RSFSR Government after Khrushchev's fall. At the plenary session of March 1965, he continued to oppose grass crops rotation on tillable land, which brought him into conflict with P. P. Lobanov, another victim of Khrushchev's who had been rehabilitated. Pyzin even took it upon himself to defend the Orenburg Livestock Institute, i.e. the pseudo-scientist Khairulin who had been demoted in April 1964 (verbatim record of the March 1965 plenary session, p 47). He was probably trying to curry favour with Voronov, but apparently did not succeed.

the shadow of a personal power than for the anonymous management of faceless *apparatchiki*. Various signs indicated that Mikoyan had lost the basis of his influence.[1] Fortunately, he had enough insight to realize this in time and, in December 1965, willingly gave up his post as Chief of State. This enabled him to subside with honour into gilded retirement.

It required subtler, slower, more elaborate scheming to distribute the roles among the handful of men who really counted: Brezhnev, Kosygin, Podgorny and Suslov, plus Shelepin, who belonged to the group thanks to his position and his special 'expectations'. To simplify somewhat, one might say that Brezhnev set about reinforcing his position *vis-à-vis* his rivals or competitors, i.e. most of the men in the group. Kosygin, Podgorny and Shelepin turned out to be the first who stood in his way.

KOSYGIN

The picture here was straightforward. Kosygin was the typical technocrat or 'manager', who had practically never held any Party post.[2] As Head of the Government, he was not at all in the same position as Malenkov *vis-à-vis* Khrushchev in 1953. Any conflict that might arise between him and Brezhnev was less likely to be due to personal rivalry than to differences regarding the respective jurisdiction of Party and Government. Kosygin had neither the capability nor, probably, the ambition to compete with Brezhnev for political leadership. He only wanted the managers to have a free hand in running the economy without interference from the ideologists. This, as we saw, was the meaning of his

[1] It is conceivable that the spate of recollections about Ordzhonikidze which appeared in the press in the last months of 1964 was aimed at embarrassing Mikoyan (cf. *Izvestia*, November 6 1964; *Pravda*, November 17 1964). These articles, like earlier ones about him, purported to show that only Ordzhonikidze and a few others (Kirov and Kuybyshev) had had the courage to step in and see justice done whenever they came to know about unjust 'repressions'. The suggestion was that, after Ordzhonikidze's suicide in 1937, there had been no other 'human being' among the leaders to whom one might turn for help. Mikoyan, who had been a member of the Politburo since 1935, could not have viewed these reminiscences with favour.

It was also noticed that, in the very carefully arranged photograph of the collective leadership congratulating the cosmonauts, which appeared in *Pravda* of March 19 1965, Mikoyan was far below the place befitting his functions. He was in third position to the right of Brezhnev, after Kosygin and Podgorny, and was merely allowed to place one hand on the table at which the VIPs were seated. Even Voronov, sitting next to Suslov on Brezhnev's left, was in a superior place.

[2] Kosygin's only service in the Party apparatus was apparently for a few months in 1938, when he took over an unspecified function at the Leningrad Oblast Committee before becoming the city's mayor (Chairman of the Urban Executive Committee).

speech of March 19 1965, and the cause of the showdown between *apparatchiki* and managers that spring.

The September compromise on the economic reform was original in that both sides won. The managers rebuilt a powerful centralized State machine. Kosygin was not only confirmed as its master, but succeeded in getting some of his theses on the 'business approach' to management adopted over the resistance of the doctrinaires. He unquestionably emerged with added strength.

But Brezhnev, too, consolidated his position, having taken the opportunity to reaffirm the privileged role of the Party in all other areas. Even in economic matters, the Party remained in charge of general supervision and kept the right to oversee day-to-day management. Since the principle of Party primacy was thereby confirmed and since Kosygin had been confirmed as second man, Brezhnev was *ipso facto* confirmed as number one.

This was reflected in matters of protocol. For example, the Soviet delegation at the first post-Khrushchev conference of Warsaw Pact leaders, held in January 1965 in Warsaw, had no chief, which fact made for some difficulty in drafting the communiqués.[1] But at the second such conference in Bucharest in July 1966, it was stated unequivocally that Brezhnev was the head of a delegation that included Kosygin (*Pravda*, July 3 and 5 1966). In fact, Brezhnev had made it a point well before this to assume precedence in foreign policy. On February 24 1965 *Izvestia* showed him in second position (after Mikoyan, the Chief of State, but before Kosygin) at the talks with the Finnish President Kekkonen, although the occasion did not call for negotiations on the Party level. It was at the beginning of April 1965 that for the first time a Soviet delegation went abroad with Brezhnev 'at its head' and Kosygin as a member of the team (*sostav*). This was the visit to Poland reported by *Pravda* on April 5 1965. In June 1966 Brezhnev even preceded Podgorny, the Chief of State, during the talks with General de Gaulle.

This situation seems destined to last, although it entails some anomalies in protocol and some practical inconveniences. Up to now, Brezhnev's presence at diplomatic talks has appeared supererogatory, in view of the revelation of Kosygin's diplomatic talents at the Indo-Pakistani meeting at Tashkent in January 1966. But nothing so far indicates that the Head of Government is disposed to challenge the Secretary-General or to

---

[1] At the Warsaw Pact conference in January 1965 it was announced that the Soviet delegation 'consisted of' Brezhnev, Kosygin, Yu. V. Andropov, R. Ya. Malinovsky and A. A. Gromyko. In order to place everybody on the same footing, the cables from the agencies in the 'fraternal countries' were reworded so as to make it appear that the other delegations had no 'chief' either.

try to shake off the Party's grip over the country's activities. Even if this should occur, he could not possibly succeed unless he were to secure powerful accomplices within the Party apparatus itself.

PODGORNY

In this case the problem was one of persons rather than institutions, since Brezhnev and Podgorny had to come to terms over their mutual relations within the same powerful body – the Secretariat. Rivalry between them was inevitable. As early as 1963, they had competed for the position of heir presumptive. The 'October plenum' gave Brezhnev the title of First Secretary, but Podgorny, as we saw, emerged from the crisis in the strong position of a 'centrist' and moderating influence, backed by a host of protégés not only in the Ukraine, his former stronghold, but among disquieted Khrushchev supporters everywhere. As his role at the plenary session of November 1964 indicated, he had naturally inherited the second place in the Party – indeed much more, since the authority of the new Party chief could hardly compare to Khrushchev's even in the last months of his reign. If Brezhnev wanted to be the unchallenged First Secretary, he would have to find himself a less noteworthy or less ambitious second-in-command. It took him about nine months to do so, by means of various attacks and manoeuvres, some of which became evident.

A first incident occurred in May 1965, over Podgorny's speech delivered at Baku on the 21st (p 457). Besides urging management reform, Podgorny vigorously defended consumer goods production, as he had done consistently throughout Khrushchev's reign. He said in part:

> 'There was a time when the Soviet people consciously accepted material restrictions for the sake of the priority development of heavy industry and the strengthening of our defence capacity. That was fully justified. . . . But now collective wealth is multiplying year by year, while conditions are emerging that make it easier to satisfy the workers' ever-growing domestic and cultural needs' (*Pravda*, May 22 1965).

This recalled Khrushchev's words, in particular in his last speech to the planners at the end of September 1964. Kosygin had expressed similar ideas at the end of 1964, but had to change his tune fairly rapidly because, three months after the beginning of American escalation of the Vietnam war, the USSR had had to increase its military commitments to Hanoi and other allies. It was therefore venturesome, to say the least, to hint that sacrifices for the army's sake were no longer necessary. Suslov took it upon himself to rebut Podgorny in his speech at Sofia on June 2:

> 'We would like the life of the Soviet people to improve at a faster rate. But we have to take into account objective reality that forces us to make considerable expenses for the defence of our country, and not of our country alone. . . .
>
> 'At a time when the imperialist powers are pursuing the arms race and unleashing military aggression first in one and then in another region of the world, our Party and our Government have to maintain the country's defence at the highest level and improve it constantly. . . . All this naturally demands considerable material sacrifices from the Soviet people and the appropriation of a major part of the national revenue for defence' (*Pravda*, June 5 1965).

Thus the 'material restrictions' for the sake of defence, far from being a thing of the past, were more than ever a clear and present need. The admonition was so sharp as to entail some unpleasantness for Podgorny. It had already been noticed that his Baku speech was published one day late by the military organ *Krasnaya Zvezda* (May 23). On June 2, the day of Suslov's speech, first Kosygin and then Podgorny had received a delegation of the Ankara municipal council. Only the former of these meetings was immediately reported by Tass, Radio Moscow and *Pravda*; the second, with Podgorny, was reported only twenty-four hours later (*Pravda*, June 4). Finally, on June 5, the day Suslov's speech was published, Podgorny was scheduled to receive another Turkish delegation. At the last minute, the visitors were told that the meeting was cancelled because Podgorny was 'confined to his house by doctor's orders' (UPI, June 23 1965). This 'illness' lasted until the end of July, i.e. almost two months.[1] Needless to say, it had all the marks of a political disease.

At that time a subtler but equally dangerous manoeuvre against Podgorny came to fruition. This was the attack against what must be termed the 'Kharkov group'.

The affairs of the important Kharkov region started to come under criticism in the Ukrainian and Moscow press around March–April 1965. At first it involved only details, personal matters that did not seem to involve the Oblast Committee leaders. But then, such campaigns generally start that way. In June or July the local First Secretary, G. I.

[1] After his 'illness', in June 1965 Podgorny reappeared for the first time at Sebastopol on July 24, on the occasion of the award of the Order of Lenin to the city (*Pravda*, July 25).

Vashchenko, was called to Moscow to 'account' to the Party Secretariat – i.e. Brezhnev or Suslov, since Podgorny was 'ill' at the time. The result was a special Central Committee decree on 'serious shortcomings in the Kharkov regional Party organization's work of recruitment and education of young communists'. A summary was published by *Partiynaya Zhizn* (No 15 1965) at the beginning of August. In substance, the Oblast Committee was accused of having been over-liberal in its recruitment policy, of having admitted 'undesirable elements' into the Party, of having overlooked cases of misbehaviour etc. The decree set a precedent, since it formed the basis for the more selective recruitment policy adopted at the Twenty-third Congress. It is needless to point out that Khrushchev's policy of large-scale recruitment had caused such 'shortcomings' in all parts of the country.

Why was Kharkov chosen for the demonstration? Before G. I. Vashchenko, the regional First Secretary had been N. A. Sobol, who was promoted Second Secretary of the Party for the entire Ukraine in 1963; before him, from 1953 to 1961, there had been V. N. Titov, who later became head of the 'Party Organs' department of the Central Committee and then Secretary of the Central Committee in charge of 'organizational work'. Earlier still (1950–1953) there had been Podgorny himself, the present second man in the Party. In other words, for several years, the entire system of cadres, in the Ukraine as well as in Moscow, had been in the hands of 'Kharkov men'. There was no better way of attacking the policy than by excoriating the 'bad example' set at Kharkov. Or to put it the other way about: if Podgorny was the target, the best method was to strike at the cadres – the main aspect of his activity – in Kharkov, the region where his followers were concentrated. In this case, the personal links were just right: G. I. Vashchenko had served as Second Secretary under Titov in Kharkov; Titov had served as Second Secretary under Podgorny. Hence it was scarcely necessary to point out that the mistakes of the Oblast Committee dated back 'several years' (as *Pravda* did in a violent article on August 28 1965) in order that the patrons concerned should feel threatened by the move against their clients.

This, indeed, was the result of the operation: while Vashchenko was let off after the usual self-criticism, the patrons did not recant, but instead forfeited the instrument of their power. The first victim was V. N. Titov, who at the beginning of April was transferred to Kazakhstan as Second Secretary of the Republic's Central Committee, and in September was relieved of his functions as federal Secretary. His removal was announced abruptly a week after a plenary session which, to all appearances, had taken no decision on his case. The decision had probably not been easy to push through, and this may have prompted

Brezhnev to intensify his drive against the 'Kharkov group'.[1] The last victim was N. A. Sobol, who in March 1966 was stripped of his key post of Second Secretary of the Ukrainian Communist Party and transferred to the Government apparatus (he became First Deputy Chairman in the Republic's Government).

Podgorny's turn had come in the meantime. His election as Chief of State in Mikoyan's place on December 9 1965 was accompanied by all the ritual honours. Brezhnev made a campaign speech on his behalf before the Supreme Soviet, but none of these courtesies could disguise the facts. The spectacular formal promotion masked eviction from the Secretariat – the true centre of power (the Twenty-third Congress confirmed this three months later). Brezhnev was particularly well placed to know this, since he had suffered the same fate in 1960 at the hands of his rival Kozlov.[2]

True, Podgorny and the Kharkov men received fairly gentle treatment. Vashchenko, Sobol, Titov and Rumyantsev kept their seats in the Central Committee at the Twenty-third Congress; Podgorny himself, ostensibly the first man in the State and a member of the Politburo, retained some influence and, like Brezhnev in 1960, could still look forward to regaining his lost functions at some future time. All the same, he had suffered a blow, thanks to his tactical mistakes and lack of toughness in the power struggle. It is quite possible that, despite his long career as an *apparatchik*, he is best suited for the post of Head of State and will be content to remain there. His relatively

---

[1] Something untoward must have happened to Titov at the March 1965 plenary session, for he was (with Shvernik) the only leader who did not attend the concert given on the last evening of the session, on March 26 1965. He reappeared on April 2 at a reception, and on the 3rd greeted a delegation of Polish lawyers; on the evening of the 4th, he saw Brezhnev and Kosygin off for Warsaw. He must have moved fast to take over his new functions as Second Secretary of the Kazakhstan Central Committee, since the plenary session that 'elected' him met there the next day, April 5 (*Pravda*, April 6).

His meeting with the Polish lawyers was reported on the evening of April 5 by the Moscow edition of *Izvestia*, and Titov was listed under his title of 'Central Committee Secretary'. On the 6th, *Pravda* reported on the lawyers' activities but omitted from the communiqué any mention of their meeting with Titov. These signs suggest that the transfer was pushed through against resistance from some quarters.

[2] The list of Kharkov men demoted in 1965 also includes A. M. Rumyantsev, *Pravda*'s editor-in-chief, whose relatively liberal attitude on cultural problems has been noted, and who was removed from his post in September. For almost ten years, Rumyantsev had held Party functions (most probably as Agitprop chief) in the Kharkov Oblast Committee, and Podgorny was his patron until 1952. In that year, he was promoted to Moscow for ideological work, probably to a position higher than his chief's, since at the Nineteenth Congress he held a seat as full Central Committee member whereas Podgorny was only a member of the Auditing Committee. Therefore Rumyantsev is not, properly speaking, a 'client' of Podgorny's. It is possible, none the less, that he was appointed head of *Pravda* with Podgorny's help in November 1964, since the latter was then at the peak of his power.

advanced age (sixty-three in 1966) will diminish his chances as time goes by.

SHELEPIN

Brezhnev had devised an almost elegant way of getting rid of an over-mighty second-in-command, but he now had to find a replacement. A. N. Shelepin was most spoken of in 1965 as Podgorny's successor, but it soon became clear that Brezhnev, understandably, did not care for this solution.

Shelepin's promotion in 1961, when he represented the younger men in the power struggle, has been discussed (p 197 ff.) and in this connection his assets have been described. With his spectacular promotion, after Khrushchev's overthrow, to full member of a collective leadership whose shape was still somewhat ill-defined, he took on even greater stature. In a team where such figures as Brezhnev, Suslov, Kosygin and Podgorny belonged mostly to the old guard, Shelepin inevitably stood out as the man of the future. Moreover, although unquestionably a junior member of the Presidium, he happened to hold more posts than anyone else. He was Party Secretary, a Deputy Prime Minister and the head of a mysterious Control Committee of wide ramifications with the power – in theory at any rate – to remove both State and Party officials. Shelepin, at the age of forty-six, was in a most favourable position in all respects.

However, prominence was itself a drawback. The rest of the collective leadership could not overlook the fact that such vast powers represented a threat to it, nor could it completely discount the rumours that periodically circulated in Moscow and abroad about Shelepin's promising future. Mere jealousy may have been at work too, but at any rate it seemed clear that some people were striving to thwart Shelepin's expectations and remind him that he was only a junior member of the group.

In fact, Shelepin became the butt of petty harassment as soon as he was promoted to the Presidium, in November 1964. In the communiqué announcing his election (*Pravda*, November 17) he was listed after Shelest, who had been promoted to the same function that same day, although this was contrary to alphabetical order. When, a few days later, Shelepin left for Egypt at the head of a parliamentary delegation, he was seen off only by V. N. Titov, Central Committee Secretary, two Deputy Chairmen of the Council, I. T. Novikov and K. N. Rudnev, and the Presidents of the two Houses of the Soviet

(*Pravda*, December 19 1964). Not one of his colleagues in the Presidium was present. Podgorny, on the other hand, who left for Turkey at the head of a similar delegation, was seen off by Kirilenko and Suslov (*Pravda*, January 5 1965). Then even Shelepin's farewell escort was judged too large, so that upon his return from Cairo he was welcomed at the airport only by the Presidents of the two Houses and two Chairmen of State Committees, but none of his colleagues in the Secretariat or the Council of Ministers (*Pravda*, December 30 1964). Another anomaly occurred at the plenary session of March 1965. Shelepin was the only member of the ruling group, besides Mikoyan (then in Bucharest) and Shvernik, who was not included in the committee in charge of drafting the final resolution, which was presided over by Brezhnev (verbatim record, p 87).

None of this prevented Shelepin from playing a major role during this period. For the first time, he was entrusted with missions of some importance abroad and apparently carried them out with his usual vigour. Following his visit to Cairo, Nasser invited Ulbricht to the UAR on an official visit – a major success for Soviet diplomacy. A year later, Shelepin talked Hanoi into sending a delegation to the Twenty-third Congress. These were not his only activities. Everything indicates that he also retained his power of supervision over the police. In April 1965 he presided over a conference of the 'administrative organs' – and police judiciary – on problems of 'legality' (*Pravda*, April 10 1965).

As regards the dismantling of the 'Party–State' supervisory agencies, it is by no means certain that this was aimed primarily against their chief, Shelepin, for this was not his only responsibility or perhaps even his most important one.[1] But, as noted in the case of Podgorny and the 'Kharkov group', the argument may well be reversed: the best way to attack Shelepin was indirectly, by attacking the activities and status of those bodies. In the first place, it so happened that after the various reorganizations carried out in the wake of the 'October plenum', the Party–State Control Committee was the only remaining institution which traced its origin directly to Khrushchev. Moreover, it was a

---

[1] Interestingly enough, Shelepin was very seldom explicitly referred to as 'Chairman of the Party–State Control Committee of the Central Committee of the CPSU and of the Council of Ministers of the USSR'. Only his other titles were usually listed, namely 'member of the Presidium of the Central Committee', 'Secretary of the Central Committee', or 'Deputy Prime Minister', and sometimes all three at once. His presence at the head of the control organs was mentioned in reference works, such as the *Encyclopedic Yearbook* (*Yezhegodnik*) for 1965, but not in the press, and nowhere else after Khrushchev's downfall. Shelepin himself, in the three years of the existence of the Committee, did not deliver a single public speech on its activities or write a single article on the pages devoted to its work which appeared twice a month in *Pravda* and *Izvestia* from March 1963 onwards.

product of the hated 1962 reform. That reform had been the first thing to go, and the Party–State Control Committee was all that was left of it. Hence it was logical that it should come under fire, especially since the cadres, while basking in their newly regained security, still felt threatened by a committee enjoying such wide powers. (Apparently Shelepin had not used them to the full, but that might always change.) Lastly, the hybrid nature of these agencies raised problems of jurisdiction, hence of power. Straddling the Party and the State machines, they threatened to elude the authority of either, something especially objectionable at the time of the 'strengthening of the Party's role in all areas'.

It was in the summer of 1965 that anxiety first arose about this problem and that Party bodies were invited to give more 'help' to the supervisory officials and in particular the 'assistance groups', which were widely scattered voluntary organizations set up under the aegis of the Shelepin committees.[1] As mentioned earlier, N. G. Yegorychev, the First Secretary of the Moscow Urban Committee, had advocated this just before Khrushchev's downfall. His appeal brought no results at the time (cf. p 405, footnote 1), but on July 6 1965, *Pravda* raised the question again:

> 'The success of their work [that of the 'assistance groups'] depends on the degree of leadership exercised over them by the Party organizations and the Party–State Control Committees. Whenever the Party's continuing leadership, influence and support are not felt, the work of the groups and supervisory posts is weakened. . . .
> Many lower-level Party organizations have given up the task of directing the Party–State supervisory groups and assistance posts and do not give them concrete help.'

At this time the idea was still that of leadership exercised jointly by the Party apparatus and the Shelepin committees. But a few weeks later, the emphasis had shifted and was on the predominant role of the Party. On August 20 *Pravda* recalled that Party–State control was 'an integral part of Party organizational work', and that it was the duty of Party committees to appoint their representatives to the 'assistance groups'. A new demand was advanced, namely that the chairman of each 'assistance group' should in future be one of the deputy secretaries of the corresponding Party organization. Announcing with satisfaction on September 4 1965 that this had been achieved in 'most' of the country's enterprises and institutions, *Pravda* added:

---

[1] In 1965 no less than five million voluntary workers were co-operating with Shelepin's Committee (*Pravda*, September 4 1965).

'It is perfectly understandable that an assistance group under the deputy secretary of the Party organization will be more successful both in carrying out its immediate tasks and in playing the part of an organizing centre for purposes of social control.'

The Party took advantage of the re-election of these 'assistance groups' (they had been set up for two years in the winter of 1962–1963, hence this was their first re-election and *Pravda* was insisting that this should always coincide with regular Party assemblies) to 'delegate' its trusted men to stand as candidates and to place the groups under the leadership of a cell secretary. In this way it was steadily reasserting its hold over the supervisory machine. This can hardly have been to the liking of the officials of Shelepin's committees. Certainly all these appeals for the reinforcement of Party leadership appeared in *Pravda* editorials rather than on the pages of the newspaper devoted to the committees' work.

This, however, was only a groping half-measure. The final settlement of the problem, ratified by the Central Committee on December 6 1965, indicated a complete reversal of attitude. The Party–State Control Committee, instead of being taken over by the Party, was simply to be liquidated. In its place the old Stalinist system was, once again, to be resumed. It consisted, on the one hand, of Party supervision exercised by 'Party Committees' at the lowest level and by the 'Party Control Committee' at the highest: and, on the other hand, of State supervision supervised by a member of the Government. The only difference was that the latter machinery, which used to be called 'Soviet Control', now went under the slightly more ambitious title of 'People's Control'. This meant the complete dismantling of Shelepin's Committee.

It is not known whether this gave rise to dissension at top level, or whether any difficulty was found in justifying the abandonment of an authentically Leninist institution reinstated by Khrushchev.[1] At all events, Brezhnev's explanations seemed very laboured. Rather than announce outright that the two branches of control, 'Party' and 'State', were being separated, he reduced the matter to a mere problem of terminology:

'At present the supervisory organs are called organs of Party–

---

[1] The institution known as 'Workers' and Peasants' Inspection' (Rabkrin or RKI) was reorganized in 1923, that is, in Lenin's lifetime, in order to make it a 'Party–State' body covering both bureaucracies. It remained thus until 1934, when Stalin split it into two organizations. In November 1962 Khrushchev accused Stalin of having 'grossly violated' the teaching of the founder of the Soviet state in this respect (verbatim records of November 1962 plenary session, pp 83–94).

State control. This title is not quite correct. It does not sufficiently reflect the fact that supervision in our country is exercised by the people. This is why it will be more correct to transform these bodies and call them "People's control organs" ' (*Pravda*, December 7 1965).

Brezhnev did announce the true purpose of the change, but at the end of his remarks and in passing:

'It should also be borne in mind that the organs do not supervise the work of the Party organs. That is done by the system of internal Party supervision provided for by the Party statutes. This is why it is indispensable that the Party committees should also intensify their work.' (*ibid.*).

In other words, the Party was going to supervise its own organization, while whatever remained of the Shelepin organization was going to supervise only the work of the State administration on behalf of both the Government and the Party. The resolution of the plenary session specified this by indicating that the People's organs were going to be 'one of the effective means whereby the Party and the Government would supervise the execution of official directives by the organizations of the Soviets, of the economy and others'. The Party was not among these 'others'.

Under the circumstances, the worst blow for Shelepin would have been to leave him at the head of his transformed Committee. Apparently this was not contemplated, and his former deputy, P. V. Kovanov, was chosen to run what was now only one 'State committee' among many others. At Kosygin's suggestion, Shelepin was simply relieved of his functions as Deputy Prime Minister, since 'the Central Committee of the CPSU considered it necessary that comrade A. N. Shelepin should concentrate upon his work within the Central Committee of the CPSU' (*Pravda*, December 10 1965). The fact remained that Shelepin had lost part of his power – a minor part it is true – namely his hold on both the Government and the Party apparatus, something that he alone had enjoyed so far.

Shelepin would have been more than compensated for his loss if he had been destined to inherit Podgorny's post as second man in the Secretariat, as many people thought he would. But a series of minor signs cast doubt on this from the outset. If the change in his functions had been meant as a promotion, this would have been publicized in one way or another. For instance, his work as head of the Control Committee would have been praised, or he would have been given an opportunity of immediately appearing in the role of apparatus chief second only to Brezhnev. In 1960 no time had been wasted in making it known in this way that Kozlov was the man who counted. However, nothing of the kind was done. Brezhnev did not say a word about Shelepin when announcing the dissolution of the latter's Committee on December 6. He did not enlarge on its merits but, after stating that it had performed 'a major task' and had 'helped' the Party and the Government, added: 'naturally this does not mean that there are no shortcomings in its work' (*Pravda*, December 7 1965). It is safe to assume that he would have spoken differently if the Committee's chief was due to receive a spectacular promotion.

Shelepin's position remained obscure. It is definitely known only that he did not become second in the Secretariat. The hierarchy announced by Brezhnev at the end of the Twenty-third Congress even disclosed a major anomaly, since he was listed third in the Secretariat (after Brezhnev and Suslov, but before Kirilenko) and only in seventh place in the Politburo (*after* Kirilenko). Lastly, it was confirmed just after the Congress that Shelepin's new functions were going to take him far from the real bases of power. He was going to deal with light industry, commerce and the food and service industries, and his presence at two conferences on these subjects was duly reported in *Pravda* on June 17 and 23 1966). True, Podgorny was said to have been handling the same matters two years earlier (cf. p 351), but that was in Khrushchev's time, and everything points to the fact that, after the latter's downfall, Podgorny had in addition taken over major Party responsibilities. Furthermore, there was no sign, after the one of April 1965 already noted, that Shelepin had even retained supervision over the police and judiciary.

In short, Shelepin evidently suffered a set-back during the winter of 1965–1966. This, of course, did not prejudge the future, but merely showed that the old guard was anxious to keep him at a safe distance. But if any member of that group, in particular Brezhnev or Suslov, were to disappear, it is highly probable that Shelepin would come to the fore again.

IS SUSLOV THE SECRETARY IN CHARGE OF ORGANIZATIONAL PROBLEMS?

After Mikoyan and Shvernik were gone, Suslov suddenly became the man with greatest seniority in both supreme bodies – the Presidium as well as the Secretariat. He was the only one who had weathered all the crises of the past ten years, from the 'anti-party' affair to Khrushchev's overthrow. Everything suggests that he was the cardinal figure in the collective leadership, although his exact role is not known. Here again, one can only guess, since the 'chief ideologist', faithful to the tactics that had helped him in his career so far, again retreated into the background shortly after his decisive action in October 1964. Only once after that did he step down into the arena – with his speech in Bulgaria on June 2 1965. Except for the rebuke he then administered to Podgorny, it was only by silence that he indicated his lack of enthusiasm for the plans for economic reform that were then under discussion. The only activities which he carried out on his own were, as in the past, meetings with foreign communist leaders, at which the loyal B. N. Ponomarev was invariably at his side.

According to all the signs, Suslov was again playing the same role as between 1955 and 1957, when he first acted as a member of the collective leadership. This is also suggested by his willingness to reminisce about that period. Then, as in 1964, he seemed content to watch the ups and downs of the debates; he seldom engaged in any quarrel, and then only when he was sure of coming out best; he stood out for observance of proper procedures within the eleven-member democracy, and protected the power of the Party and its *apparatchiki*. In addition, on the later occasion he was most probably allied to Brezhnev. By publicly chiding Podgorny in his Sofia speech just when the First Secretary was trying to get rid of him, Suslov rendered Brezhnev a signal service. His role in October 1964, which knitted tight bonds of complicity between the two men, should not be overlooked either. Logically, this should even have made the First Secretary dependent in some degree on the man who had placed him on the throne. Did Brezhnev acknowledge this? Apparently he did at this period, for the two men's speeches were similar in tone and content. On the major issues (economic reform, restalinization, etc.) they evidently saw eye to eye. Besides, until Brezhnev was able to pack the collective leadership with his own men, the next best thing for him was to support a man like Suslov who obviously did not covet supreme power.

The question remains whether Suslov figured as the real second-in-command at and after the Twenty-third Congress. In terms of protocol this was undeniable. Throughout the Congress, he sat immediately on Brezhnev's right; in the Secretariat he was in second place, in the Politburo fourth, after Brezhnev, Kosygin and Podgorny. Since the latter two were entitled to these positions by virtue of being Head of Government and Head of State, Suslov may be regarded as having been virtually in second or third place within the collective leadership, his influence being undoubtedly greater than Podgorny's and possibly even than Kosygin's.

On the other hand, if 'second-in-command' means 'secretary in charge of organizational problems' – a kind of Deputy Secretary-General specifically in charge of cadres, as Kozlov had been before 1963 – Suslov did not indisputably deserve that title, at any rate during the Twenty-third Congress; though a slight indication based on a *Pravda* obituary suggests that he may have occupied such a post just after Podgorny's removal.[1] However, at no time did he take any public action in an affair to do with cadres. It may be added that only in a single case did a member of the Presidium personally preside over an appointment in the provinces – something that had been current under Khrushchev – and this was Brezhnev's replacement of M. T. Yefremov by K. F. Katushev as First Secretary of the Gorki Oblast Committee (*Pravda*, December 28 1965). Conceivably, by overseeing the change in person at a time when Podgorny's departure was raising many questions, the First Secretary meant to show that, provisionally or not as the case might be, he himself was assuming the right to supervise cadres.

The Twenty-third Congress did not clarify this problem; far from it. The silence of the top leaders, and in particular the three main Secretaries – Suslov, Shelepin and Kirilenko – was probably due to political

---

[1] A slight indication that Suslov may at one time have been in charge of cadres is provided by the obituary of I. A. Buyanov, the chairman of a leading kolkhoz in the Moscow region, published by *Pravda* on December 14 1965. The following signatures of Presidium members headed the list: Brezhnev, First Secretary of the Central Committee; Podgorny, Chief of State; Kosygin, Chief of Government; Suslov; G. I. Voronov, Chief of the RSFSR Government; A. P. Kirilenko, First Deputy Chairman of the Central Committee Bureau for the RSFSR; D. S. Polyansky, First Deputy Prime Minister, until then Deputy Chairman in charge of Agriculture; P. N. Demichev, alternate member of the Presidium, Secretary of the Central Committee.

The only two figures whose known functions did not entitle them to sign the obituary of a kolkhoz chairman were P. N. Demichev (in charge of ideology, but a few years earlier First Secretary of the Moscow Oblast Committee) and, especially, Suslov, whose name was included for the first time in a document of this type. In fact, his place on the list seems to be the one normally reserved in such instances for the 'Second Secretary' of the Central Committee in charge of cadres.

A very similar obituary was published by *Pravda* on August 11 1965 for Tursunkulov, the chairman of an Uzbek kolkhoz. The signatures on that occasion were the following: Brezhnev; Mikoyan (then Head of State); Kosygin; Podgorny (then Central Committee Secretary); Polyansky; Sh. Rashidov, First Party Secretary in Uzbekistan.

It was obvious that in Buyanov's obituary, Podgorny's name had been replaced by Suslov's. The fact that Suslov was listed in the capacity of supervisor of cadres was supported by the fact that in both cases, farther down the list, only the names of two Central Committee heads of departments appeared: viz. the head of the agricultural department, which was normal (F. D. Kulakov) and the head of the 'Party Organs' department. In December, this was I. V. Kapitonov and in August it had been P. F. Pigalev, previously assistant head, who became the acting head after V. N. Titov's removal. In other words, the death of a kolkhoz chairman was of equal concern to the men in charge of cadres policy and to those in charge of agriculture. Apparently, at the top level, in Tursunkulov's case Podgorny was regarded as covering the former sector, while in Buyanov's case it was Suslov.

differences that the collective leadership did not wish to advertise. It may also have been due to the fact that major responsibilities had not been definitely assigned within the Secretariat. The subjects of the respective speeches would have been an indication of these, and those concerned were either unable or unwilling to give it. Even more significant was the absence of a special report on the Party statutes. Usage demanded that, whenever statutes were amended – which happens at almost every congress – a leader other than the supreme Party chief should deliver a report on the subject. By so doing, that leader designates himself as the 'Secretary in charge of organizational problems', and in general as the 'second-in-command' or strong man of the Party. Khrushchev came forward in this role in 1952 and Kozlov in 1961.[1] The Twenty-third Congress side-stepped that issue as well, as Brezhnev outlined the changes in the statutes but did not deliver a special report. It is not known whether the reason for this was the Secretary-General's determination to avoid the emergence of any 'Secretary in charge of organizational problems', or an unresolved rivalry between Suslov and Shelepin for that post, or a combination of both.

BREZHNEV CONSOLIDATED

All these circumstances draw attention to Brezhnev, whose rise during this initial period of collective leadership was nothing less than remarkable. He had in turn put Kosygin in his place, removed Podgorny, downgraded Shelepin and apparently, in addition, prevented the emergence of a 'Secretary in charge of organizational problems' who might have assumed the status of an heir apparent. The First Secretary, who was now 'Secretary-General', came out of the Twenty-third Congress with a much stronger image than that of caretaker leader which he bore after the 'October plenum'. This was not because of anything specially decisive about his activities. He was seldom identified with a specific political idea, far more seldom than Khrushchev had been. Even when he was, his policy seemed dominated by conservatism and prudence, by the endeavour to appear 'reliable', and for this purpose to revert to the tried and true methods of the past. He also showed a hitherto unsuspected gift for manoeuvring and a strong determination

---

[1] The only precedent for the absence of a special report on amendments to the Party statutes had been set by the Twentieth Congress, which also had met during a period of collective leadership and power struggle. That Congress amended the statutes without hearing a special report, since Khrushchev had dealt with the question in his main report.

to maintain himself in power, exercise his authority and enlarge and strengthen its bases. Conscious perhaps that he found himself at the head of the Party somewhat by accident in October 1964, Brezhnev was striving stubbornly and not unsuccessfully to transform his power into something permanent.

Such self-assertion is, of course, difficult in the atmosphere of sharp reaction against any personal power that has pervaded the apparatus since the 'October plenum'. The constant tributes to collective leadership have created a bad climate for his ambitions. It is no accident, therefore, that Brezhnev's contribution to the chorus was a half-hearted one. He very seldom praised collective leadership in his speeches, and did so only when he could not help it, for instance in collective reports by the Presidium. Such tributes have been far more numerous in *Pravda's* anonymous editorials and in articles in *Kommunist* or *Partiynaya Zhizn* – in other words in the proclamations issued by the apparatus. Even so, a 'but' began creeping into comments upon collective leadership, while the 'personal responsibility of the leader for the tasks entrusted to him' was presented with growing frequency as the counterpart of the same principle (for example in *Pravda* of May 16 1965).

It was only around May 1965 that Brezhnev, who up to then had been somewhat overshadowed by Podgorny and Kosygin, actually came into his own as number one. At the victory celebrations he definitely played the major role. On that occasion, like Khrushchev in his day, he monopolized the pleasant task of announcing the awards and other favours (titles of 'heroine-cities' to Moscow and Brest-Litovsk, proclamation of a legal holiday on Women's Day (March 8), etc. – all these matters being in fact under the jurisdiction of the Presidium of the Supreme Soviet, of which he was not yet a member). Moreover, it was on May 8 1965 that the first sign of a 'cult' was noticed, when *Pravda* published a major article about a little-known exploit of the last war, namely the capture by the Eighteenth Airborne Army, in February 1943, of the small locality of Malaya Zemlya near Novorossisk on the North Caucasus front. A group of veterans wrote on this subject:

> 'The entire staff of the political section of the Eighteenth Army was constantly with the parachutists, helping them day in and day out. The chief of the political section of the Eighteenth Army, Colonel of the Guard L. I. Brezhnev, was often to be seen amidst the valiant parachutists who were fighting to the death in their hard battle against the enemy. He was the soul of the Army, our comrade in arms and friend in combat' (*Pravda*, May 8 1965).

The highly flattering account of this hitherto unknown episode in

Brezhnev's biography[1] was the first of its kind, and apparently remained the only one. It is noteworthy, however, that the article was picked to appear in *Pravda* on V-E Day rather than for publication as one of the many stories that the paper had been running for weeks. This, of course, had not happened without the First Secretary's knowledge. He even made a point of mentioning the capture of Malaya Zemlya in his victory report of the same day (*Pravda*, May 9 1965).

In foreign relations, Brezhnev progressively created for himself the image of sole authoritative spokesman. As we saw, from the spring of 1965 onwards he became the head of delegations while Kosygin was merely a member. Not long afterwards, he grew strong enough to dispense with any mentors and carried out several missions on his own, particularly in Eastern Europe. At home, he used the system of personnel transfers to broaden the base of his power. The status quo had prevailed in that sector for the first few months of the new era, but things started moving in the summer of 1965, ostensibly in preparation for the forthcoming Congress, but really because of the disturbance of the equilibrium at top level. This ended the standstill in Secretariat work caused by the Brezhnev–Podgorny tug of war. The set-back suffered by Podgorny and his 'Kharkov group' notably helped one section of their opponents, namely the 'Brezhnev group' in Dnepropetrovsk (also in the Ukraine). It was in fact in the Dnepropetrovsk region that Brezhnev had his closest and oldest ties and hence the greatest concentration of his clients. He was born and went to school there and, after holding agricultural posts in Kursk and the Urals, returned to his home town to attend the local Institute of Metallurgy, from which he graduated in 1935. He started his climb in the hierarchy there as well, and in 1939 reached the rank of Secretary of the Dnepropetrovsk Oblast Committee. After the war, he again returned there, this time to serve as First Secretary, from 1947 to 1950. Another member of the present collective leadership, A. P. Kirilenko, succeeded him as head of the Oblast Committee from 1950 to 1955. All this, of course, was more than enough to improve the standing of the 'men of Dnepropetrovsk'. Here are a few examples:

1 M. V. Shcherbitsky: former Dneprodzerzhinsk engineer, appointed in 1948 (under Brezhnev) Second Secretary of that town's Urban Committee. On October 16 1965 promoted Head of the Ukrainian

---

[1] During the capture of Malaya Zemlya, Brezhnev must have been closely associated with M. A. Suslov, then chief of the political leadership of the North Caucasus front. But whereas Suslov spent the entire war in that region (and was also chief of the General Staff of the Stavropol partisans), Brezhnev was sent to the Ukraine in 1943 and, with the rank of major-general, took over political leadership of the Fourth Ukrainian front operating in the Crimea.

Government and, in the following December, to alternate membership of the Party Presidium. The noteworthy fact here was that he had already held these functions until June 1963. Then, just as Podgorny was promoted to Moscow, Shcherbitsky was assigned to another, far less important post, namely First Secretary of the Dnepropetrovsk Oblast Committee. His return to favour at the time when Podgorny suffered a set-back is the significant point.

2 N. A. Tikhonov: engineer in various Dnepropetrovsk factories before the war, director of a factory in the region from 1947 to 1950, i.e. under Brezhnev; chairman of the Dnepropetrovsk sovnarkhoz, then Vice-Chairman of the USSR Gosplan during Khrushchev's reign. On October 2 1965 promoted Deputy Prime Minister of the USSR, which entitled him to rise from alternate to full membership in the Central Committee at the Twenty-third Congress.

3 G. S. Pavlov: student at the Dneprodzerzhinsk Institute of Metallurgy (he graduated in 1936, a year after Brezhnev); Secretary of the Dneprodzerzhinsk Urban Committee during and after the war. His post at the time of Khrushchev's overthrow is not known; at the end of 1965 he was promoted Executive officer (*upravlyayushchy dyelami*) of the Central Committee, which is the equivalent of a head of department mainly for administrative matters but requiring a person of trust.

4 N. A. Shcholokov: Ukrainian, graduated from the Dnepropetrovsk Institute of Metallurgy in the thirties, appointed Secretary of the Rayon Committee in the same region in 1938, mayor of Dnepropetrovsk in 1939. Promoted Second Secretary of the Moldavian Central Committee in December 1965, and on September 17 1966, USSR Minister for the Protection of Public Order – the former MVD, which was now re-established. In this case there was a double connection with Brezhnev, since Shcholokov became First Deputy Prime Minister of Soviet Moldavia in 1951, when Brezhnev was First Secretary in that Republic.

Brezhnev had in fact made connections outside Dnepropetrovsk, both in Moldavia (S. P. Trapeznikov has already been mentioned) and in Kazakhstan. The return to favour of D. A. Kunayev, who was reappointed First Secretary for that Republic in December 1964, was probably due to Brezhnev's patronage.[1] But the 'Dnepropetrovsk

[1] Before being appointed First Secretary in Kazakhstan in December 1964, Kunayev had been President of the Kazakhstan Academy of Science. In 1955 he was appointed Chief of the Kazakhstan Government when Brezhnev was First Secretary in that Republic (1954–1956). In addition, the highly conflicting personnel movements in Kazakhstan reflect the old Kozlov–Brezhnev rivalry.

D. A. Kunayev was for the first time appointed First Secretary of the Party for that Republic in January 1960 in the presence of Brezhnev, who was then still a Central Committee Secretary and seemed destined to succeed Kirichenko as cadres

group' was undoubtedly the most important. Even within the Ukraine, that particular area seemed to gain prestige, as indicated by the election of its First Secretary A. F. Vashenko (also a former associate of Brezhnev, promoted in 1948 to 'leadership work' in the Party in that area), to full membership of the Presidium of the Ukrainian Party in March 1966. He was the only First Secretary of an Oblast Committee to be so promoted. His counterparts in Kharkov and the Donets were only alternate members.[1]

Little by little, Brezhnev managed to inherit various accessory functions that Khrushchev had assumed or that went with his post. For instance, he inherited the Chairmanship of the Constitutional Committee in December 1964 (the drafting of the new Constitution went no faster than under his predecessor), and he gained a seat, though not until October 1965, on the Presidium of the Supreme Soviet (the symbolic State function that in theory entitles him to travel in the West). He obviously encountered greater difficulty in getting himself confirmed in the post of Chairman of the Central Committee Bureau for the RSFSR, which Khrushchev had taken himself when that Bureau was founded in 1956. Brezhnev is mentioned as holding this

---

supervisor (*Pravda*, January 21 1960). On the same day, two other Secretaries were appointed: N. N. Rodionov (Second Secretary) and T. I. Sokolov, who a few months later took over the Territorial (Kray) Committee of the virgin lands.

Kozlov obviously had different ideas about who the top officials in the Republic were to be. After a vigorous campaign, he arrived in person in December 1962 to purge D. A. Kunayev (whom he replaced with the unknown I. Yusupov), and N. N. Rodionov (*Kazakhstanskaya Pravda*, December 27 1962). A few months later, he returned and even more suddenly purged T. I. Sokolov, whom he replaced by F. S. Kolomyets (*Pravda*, February 22 1963).

Brezhnev who, in November 1964, had managed to expel 'Kozlov's ghost' from the collective leadership, at once set about undoing the latter's work in Kazakhstan and rehabilitating his victims. Kunayev again became First Secretary for Kazakhstan at the beginning of December 1964 while, in October 1965, N. N. Rodionov reappeared as First Secretary of the Cheliabinsk Oblast Committee and T. I. Sokolov in the corresponding post in Orel. Yusupov disappeared without a trace, and F. S. Kolomyets was demoted to First Vice-Minister for the USSR Food Industry.

[1] G. E. Tsukanov, the head of Brezhnev's executive office, was undoubtedly also connected with the Dnepropetrovsk group. He was identified for the first time at the Twenty-third Congress as 'assistant' to the First Secretary of the Central Committee of the CPSU (verbatim record, vol 2 p 589) and elected member of the Central Auditing Committee, in the same way as his predecessor, G. T. Shuysky, had been under Khrushchev. His career is not known, but he represented the Dnepropetrovsk organization at the Twenty-third Congress. He was also elected deputy to the Supreme Soviet for Dnepropetrovsk (*Pravda*, June 15 1966).

Another 'Assistant to the First Secretary' who appeared on the list of delegates to the Twenty-third Congress was A. M. Aleksandrov-Agentov. This apparently was a diplomatic adviser who, in Khrushchev's time, had served as an expert on the Soviet delegation to the United Nations. In January 1966 he accompanied Brezhnev to Mongolia (*Pravda*, January 16 1966).

post by the *Encyclopedic Yearbook* for 1965, put on sale in September, but the daily press never reported this. The abolition of the Bureau in April 1966 prevented Brezhnev from trying to use it to build up a personal stronghold, as Khrushchev had done ten years earlier.

THE 'SECRETARY-GENERAL'

The decision approved by the Twenty-third Congress to change the title of 'First Secretary' to that of 'Secretary-General' was a symbolic recognition of Brezhnev's eighteen months of work. The change seemed to be a significant one indeed. Officially it was the counterpart to the revival of the Party Presidium's earlier name of Politburo. Both moves were presented as a restoration of 'Leninist traditions'. This was true in the letter, if not in the spirit: for, although both institutions had been created in Lenin's lifetime, it was hard to forget that the only man who had held the post of Secretary-General in the entire history of the Party had been Stalin. In any case, the changes suggested a return to the traditions and vocabulary of the 'good old times'. In the speeches made at the Congress, their institutional implications were barely touched on:

1 As far as the Presidium was concerned, Brezhnev merely said that the name of Politburo 'reflects more fully the character of the activities of the supreme political organ of our Party, which is in charge of Party work in the intervals between the plenary sessions of the Central Committee of the CPSU' (*Pravda*, March 30 1966). The change applied to one point only: the Politburo was to direct 'the work of the Party' as a whole, whereas according to the existing statutes, it was to direct 'the work of the Central Committee'. Article 38 of the statutes was amended accordingly (*Partiynaya Zhizn*, No 9 May 1966). But apart from slightly enhancing the Politburo's prestige, no practical changes were apparent.

2 Explanations about the revival of the title of Secretary-General were still more evasive. Unlike the previous measure, this one was not proposed by Brezhnev (perhaps on grounds of modesty) but by the first speaker, the First Secretary of the Moscow Urban Committee, N. G. Yegorychev, who used a purely terminological approach.[1] Expressions of approval were couched in similar terms, although a few more zealous

---

[1] Yegorychev, after having approved the transformation of the Presidium into a Politburo, went on: 'Clearly it is proper to reinstate as well the function of Secretary-General of the Central Committee, which was introduced after the Eleventh Congress on the initiative of Vladimir Ilyich' [Lenin] (*Pravda*, March 31 1966).

speakers added a semblance of political explanation. K. F. Katushev, whom Brezhnev had recently appointed First Secretary of the Gorki Oblast Committee, specified that the Secretary-General would 'direct the Central Committee' (*Pravda*, April 1 1966); T. Uzubalyev, chief of the Party in Kirgizia, explained that he was 'the political leader of our Party' (*Pravda*, April 4); K. I. Galanshin commented with greater caution that the title would 'correspond better and more fully to his actual role within the activity of the Central Committee and our entire Party' (*Pravda*, April 5). The prize for 'Brezhnevism' undoubtedly went to Yu. D. Filinova, a Rayon Committee Secretary in the Saratov region, who declared that she approved 'the creation of a *Politburo headed by a Secretary-General*' (*Pravda*, April 3 1966). This ascription of a 'head' to the collective leadership, so reminiscent of past efforts by Khrushchev supporters, was unheard-of since the 'October plenum'. It might have been a mere slip of the tongue on the part of a rank-and-file speaker who was too junior to grasp the fine points; but it is striking that *Pravda* printed her statement.

In any event, the least one can say is that the new title did not curtail Brezhnev's powers. On the other hand, the Stalinist precedent must have seemed ominous to some people, and in fact a large minority of speakers abstained from approving the proposal.[1] The representatives of the major regions – the Ukraine, Leningrad, Kazakhstan and Uzbekistan – took the floor to support the suggestion of their Moscow colleague, but some of the Republic leaders ignored it, e.g. P. M. Masherov for Byelorussia and V. P. Mzhavanadze for Georgia. Podgorny, who, it is true, only dealt with State problems, also abstained on this point. Among those who thus held back, four speakers indicated that their attitude was deliberate by explicitly approving only the changes in statutes 'contained in the progress report' of Brezhnev (i.e. in particular the transformation of the Presidium into the Politburo) and by ignoring 'the proposals made by other delegates', that is to say Yegorychev's. They were A. A. Yepishev, the head of the political administration of the armed forces; I. G. Kebin, First Party Secretary in Estonia; V. E. Chernyshev, First Party Secretary in the Maritime Province (Vladivostok); and finally A. Ya. Pelshe, then chief of the Latvian Party. Pelshe's case is particularly significant because, as mentioned earlier, he was an ardent advocate of collective leadership (his speech at the

---

[1] During the part of the proceedings when the question of the Secretary-General's title was discussed (up to, but not including Kosygin's report), and leaving out of account people whose functions did not cover *apparat* questions (for instance ministers, writers, and shock workers), about ten persons who might have been expected to give their definite approval abstained on the issue, as against twenty-three who expressly approved Yegorychev's proposal.

Congress still further emphasized this) and just after the Congress he was co-opted as full member of the Politburo. The promotion, apparently, was decided very late in the proceedings[1] and must have reflected the leader's desire – and possibly that of the Central Committee as well – to strengthen the more 'democratic' camp against any encroachments by the Secretary-General. Since Pelshe had inherited Shvernik's functions as head of the Party Supervisory Committee, which served in particular as the highest court of appeal for all cases of expulsion from the Party, Pelshe was well placed for the task.

Yegorychev himself had somewhat played down beforehand the political import of his proposal by specifying that the principle of collective leadership applied not only to the Presidium but to all Party organs including the Central Committee Secretariat (*Pravda*, March 31 1966). Before him, N. A. Muravyova had been even more explicit in her report on behalf of the Party Auditing Committee: 'The Secretariat of the Central Committee is a truly executive and collegial organ' (*Pravda*, March 30 1966). Clearly the title of 'Secretary-General' lost a great deal of its weight if its holder had to negotiate with ordinary Secretaries in the same way as with his colleagues in the Politburo. Pushing the argument to its logical conclusion, one might even claim that the title of 'First Secretary' was more exalted, since it officially set Brezhnev above his colleagues. The term 'General', despite the prestigious memories it held, only gave him the right to deal with all matters, without conferring any special arbitral power.

Resistance from the collective leadership was also responsible for the return to alphabetical order in the listing of the leaders, a few hours after Brezhnev had divulged to the Party membership – and to the world at large – another classification based on influence. This hierarchic order (see the verbatim records of the Twenty-third Congress, vol 2 p 292, for a full description of the structure of all the more important Party organs) was announced by the Secretary-General on the morning of April 8. His speech was broadcast live, and Tass made no

---

[1] The assumption that it was decided at a late stage of the Twenty-third Congress to co-opt Pelshe as a full member of the Politburo is based on the fact that his successor in Latvia, A. E. Voss, was not elected to any top party function at the Congress, not even to alternate membership of the Central Committee or membership of the Auditing Committee (he became the only First Secretary of a Republic to be in such a position). This was a sign that it had not been decided to replace him by the time the elections to the Central Committee were held. It is interesting to contrast Pelshe's case with that of G. F. Sizov who, until then, had been first Secretary of the Kurgan Oblast Committee and who, at the end of the Congress, was elected Chairman of the Party Auditing Committee. His successor in Kurgan, F. K. Knyazev, had meanwhile been elected alternate member of the Central Committee although he was only Chairman of the local Oblast Executive Committee, which shows that Sizov's transfer had been planned beforehand.

change in the listing in its initial dispatches. But two hours later, Tass was giving a 'complete' version of the speech, which did not include the first part – the one that dealt with the elections. In the afternoon, a new list appeared, a strictly alphabetical one (except that Brezhnov headed the Secretariat), which was reproduced by the press the next day and subsequently.

This episode was perhaps also an attempted 'return to old traditions'.[1] In any case, it was a marked departure from the procedure strictly enforced since the victory of the collective leadership, and even from the ritual generally observed under Khrushchev. Evidently, it was meant to enhance the Secretary-General's stature (Brezhnev's name headed the Politburo list owing to his political rank rather than because alphabetical order would have required this anyway), and in general to emphasize the gap between seniors and juniors. It goes without saying that true collegial spirit demanded a return to alphabetical listing.

All these signs show that the rise of the Secretary-General was meeting with resistance. Apparently, the Twenty-third Congress and preparations for it had enabled Brezhnev to consolidate his positions to a marked degree; but he had reached a plateau and, from there on, he was to encounter far greater difficulty. This was indicated first by the fact that, as we saw, the political platform on which Brezhnev had built his career – partial rehabilitation of Stalinism, return to doctrinal rigidity, crackdown on the writers, etc. – lost a great deal of its authority following the Twenty-third Congress. In the summer of 1966 the issue of rehabilitation was cautiously brought up again, while 'left-wing' journals (*Novy Mir*, *Yunost*, etc.) renewed their criticism with even greater daring than in the past. In short, the impression grew that the Congress had made hardly any mark on the history of the country. This was also indicated by the new polemic on power problems, conducted almost openly in the press in July 1966, and centring precisely on Brezhnev's role. The episode is revealing as to the dilemma confronting not only the personalities but the institutions of the Soviet state.

---

[1] Top Soviet leaders had been listed in their hierarchic order throughout the Leninist period; alphabetical order appeared for the first time after the Fourteenth Congress in 1926, at the time of the struggle among Lenin's successors. The hierarchic order was resumed in 1934, when Stalin began to establish his absolute domination over the entire apparatus. It was abandoned in 1939 (Eighteenth Congress) when that process had been completed. Some years later, alphabetical order was again abandoned for all practical purposes. It reappeared, except for Stalin himself, at the Nineteenth Congress (1952). After the dictator's death, his successors reverted to the hierarchical order so as to place Malenkov at the head of the list, but this lasted only a short time. In June 1954, without any explanations, the press adopted the alphabetical order which, by and large, was maintained throughout Khrushchev's reign.

'THE SECRETARY IS NOT A CHIEF'

An article by the official historian A. Kolesnikov, published by *Pravda* on July 6 1966, was indisputably a major effort by the Brezhnev supporters to broaden their chief's prerogatives. Its main purport was to extol 'efficiency' (*dyelovitost*), the hallmark of a good Secretary. This key-word appeared in the title of the article and was linked several times with the word 'collegial' in such a fashion as to suggest a degree of opposition between the two. In fact, the author was advocating a large measure of autonomy for the Secretariat:

> 'When plans have been drafted, policy defined and problems eluci-
> dated, there remains, as Lenin taught us, the task of translating
> them into facts. . . . Here, the efficiency and the organizational
> abilities of the cadres must be given *full latitude*' (*Pravda*, July 6 1966.
> Author's italics).

Further on, interestingly enough, one of the conditions of success was claimed to be a 'creative [*tvorcheskoye*] attitude towards the discharge of one's obligations'. This term, used whenever the founders of Marxism have to be updated, is in essence an invitation to interpret the instructions of the legislature. Lenin, it was declared on this occasion, used to 'encourage in every way . . . initiative, daring and self-reliance [*samostoyatelnost*] on the part of officials in solving problems'.

All these terms assume a very definite meaning when applied, as is visibly the intention here, to the execution by the Secretariat of decisions taken by the Politburo. In substance, Brezhnev wanted for himself and for his section of the bureaucracy what Kosygin had asked for on behalf of Gosplan in 1965. That is, he was willing to have the Politburo take the decisions, but did not want it to interfere in the 'self-reliant' and 'creative' execution of those decisions by the Secretariat.

The writer of the article did not stop there. He also gave an equally broad interpretation of another statutory prerogative of the Secretariat, namely 'supervision of execution' by the lower bureaucracies:

> 'In Lenin's mind, this did not just mean supervision in the narrow
> sense of the term. . . . It involved concrete help in organizing execu-
> tive measures, the study of local experience and cadres, and the
> giving of instructions to those cadres' (*ibid.*).

Again Lenin's example was being cited, and this helps to show how his successor viewed his own role:

> 'For Lenin, the method of control was an inherent part of the work
> in major and minor matters. When he gave an order, he never failed

to demand a report on its execution, he specified the form in which it was to be furnished and indicated what interested him most (copies of the instructions given, names of the persons responsible for execution, listing of problems regarded as the most important, supervision of execution, etc.)' (*ibid.*).

All in all, the article presented the picture of a chief enjoying very extensive, not to say officious, powers, which it ascribed to a Secretary in general and to Brezhnev in particular. Unless one assumes that Brezhnev's colleagues in the collective leadership were trying to prod him into being more enterprising – a very unlikely supposition – it was his portrait that Kolesnikov was painting.

The reply was not long in coming. On July 20 1966 another article appeared in *Pravda*, signed by F. Petrenko. Its title was 'Collegiality and Responsibility', and it dealt almost overtly with the same problem of relations between the collective leadership and the Secretary-General, but in an entirely different tone.

'The nature of the relations between the members of a Party Committee or its Bureau on the one hand, and the First Secretary of the Committee on the other, is of special significance if the collective nature of the leadership is to be respected. This latter presupposes respect and support for the leaders who, based on the masses, inflexibly carry out the Party line. But *the collegial spirit asserts itself when respect for authority does not go beyond reasonable limits* and when the Committee Secretaries possess the tact, caution and spirit of self-criticism which are necessary if the collective exchange of opinions is not to be impeded' (*Pravda*, July 20 1966. Author's italics).

A little later comes this key sentence:

'The secretary of the Party committee is not the chief (*nachalnik*), he is not invested with the right to give orders (*komandovat*). He is only the senior (*starshy*) in the organ of collective leadership elected by the communists. A greater responsibility rests upon him. But, in solving problems, he has the same rights as the other members of the committee' (*ibid.*).

Petrenko was thus replying to Kolesnikov, without naming him of course, as regards 'supervision of execution'. He did not deny that the task was necessary, but suggested that it could not be performed by one man or even one institution:

'The responsibility for seeing that Party decisions are carried out does not fall only upon the First Secretary, but also upon the other secretaries, the heads of departments, the members of the Party committee and the ordinary Party members, each of them in the areas entrusted to them directly. To participate personally and actively in the practical work of organizing the execution of the decisions of the Party and the Government and of one's own com- mittee – that is the direct duty of every member of a Party committee and of every communist' (*ibid.*).

The allusion to the 'other secretaries', 'heads of departments', etc., seems pointed at Brezhnev, just as did the passages referring to Lenin in Kolesnikov's article. It may well be, therefore, that this second article expressed the reaction of the Politburo as a whole – not only those of its members who did not belong to the Secretariat, but also including Shelepin, Suslov, and perhaps Kirilenko – against Brezhnev's tendency to take an inflated view of his authority as 'Secretary-General'. The fact that its author was a member of a department under the Central Committee tends to support this hypothesis.[1]

The episode does not merely indicate the barriers which block the paths of anyone ambitious for personal power. It also illustrates an institutional weakness of collective leadership: when personal ambitions lead to a stalemate, the respective responsibilities of the various organs of the body politic become very hard to define. The quarrel between 'Party Committee' and 'First Secretary', or rather 'Politburo' and 'Secretary General', was, of course, nothing new. But this was the first time that it was manifested so openly, which means that it must have grown fairly acute. The same phenomenon occurs in other penumbral areas that are not generally exposed to public view. For example, also in July 1966 *Izvestia* inveighed against a writer who had cast doubt on the fact that the Presidium of the Supreme Soviet has jurisdiction over the parliamentary committees, and took the opportunity to repeat three times that the Government itself is answerable to the Presidium (*Izvestia*, July 30 1966). In other words, Podgorny ranks higher than Kosygin.

This indeed is the law, but the interesting point is that it is being mentioned for the first time. The last episode proves that, two years after Khrushchev's downfall, collective leadership is still solidly entrenched in the Kremlin. But it also proves that collective leadership cannot solve every problem.

[1] *Pravda* of May 27 1965 mentioned an F. F. Petrenko – very probably the same as the writer of the article quoted here – as a 'responsible official in a Central Com- mittee department'. It was in that capacity that he accompanied Suslov to Bulgaria. Petrenko had attracted attention earlier with other articles, in particular in January 1963 when he had replied to criticism about the division of the Party (*Partiynaya Zhizn*, No 2 1963).

EPILOGUE
&
POSTSCRIPT

Epilogue

There will never be an end to the Kremlin's power problems or their poor relation, Kremlinology. One might therefore stop the description at this point and postpone any further analysis until a fresh set of events warrants its resumption; or one could use the results so far achieved to try to picture future developments. What, for instance, if the Brezhnev–Suslov team should split; or if either man should disappear; or if Shelepin should rise to power? Or, in more general terms, what if a new personal power gradually asserts itself and, through a succession of crises, brings about a repetition of the Khrushchev pattern, or indeed the Stalin pattern? Or else the present collegial formula may endure, punctuated by spells of repression, manoeuvring and crises. In other words, a subdued struggle comparable to what has existed for the past seven years may last for decades or even centuries.

But there is no reasonable ground to expect this. True, the power struggle in 1966 seemed to be unfolding as it did in 1960 (or in 1953); but one major fact had occurred in the interval, something that had been unthinkable for over a quarter of a century: namely the overthrow of the supreme leader. Moreover, the struggle is not being waged entirely within a rarified circle. Although none of the various national forces – economic, social or diplomatic – joined in the fray or openly played anything like what is elsewhere regarded as their normal role, they did carry some weight on several occasions. All these forces are pressing for change, and the passage of time can only increase the pressure.

Internally, Soviet society has become a modern society served by a host of researchers, scientists, engineers and technicians. What is needed to bring it into line with the new industrial revolution and up to the level of affluence to which it aspires is the climate of free research and initiative that no official planning can ever replace. This does not apply merely to the physical sciences, where the process has been almost completed, but to the social sciences as well. Despite the 1965 reform, the economy is still waiting to be destalinized. Literature and philosophy, historical and sociological research are still hampered by a variety of taboos that belong to the past. The present system derives from the social demands of the nineteenth-century Russian intelligentsia. It is now under increasing pressure from its own intelligentsia to satisfy the demands of 1789 for human rights and fundamental freedoms.

So far it has succeeded in evading these demands, and it will go on doing so for a long time to come. But this is increasingly difficult because economic and social progress hinges on their fulfilment.

In foreign relations, it is a cliché by now to say that the Cuban crisis robbed the USSR for many years to come of its diplomatic and military dynamism. Barring the collapse of the United States or a European catastrophe, the Soviet Union must now be content for a long time with limited defensive action. It must defend its positions and prestige against outside pressure, but without risking a general conflict provoked, for instance, by war in Vietnam. At the same time, it must delay the action of corrosive elements within its own system of alliances, which it cannot prevent altogether, as indicated by events in China, Rumania, etc. The real dilemma is that, whatever they say, the Soviet rulers have to co-operate with the West economically and even politically, while continuing to protect themselves against ideological infiltration. Barring a victory over the opposite camp, which is inconceivable, the only prospect the population can look forward to is therefore one of endless cold war, a siege never to be lifted.

The Party, meanwhile, can no longer provide satisfactory answers to current problems. Blind faith in its wisdom was shattered by the denunciation of Stalin and the condemnation of Khrushchev. But even in the face of events that constantly belie the Party's claims, the need for continuity forces it to go on asserting its infallibility – past, present and future. For lack of anything better to offer, it clings to Khrushchev's slogans of competition in living standards, revolution through example, and so forth, while the actual facts increasingly cast doubt on such prospects. Ideology, in the past, provided the impulse for major economic and social changes. It has now turned into an encumbrance that the Party cannot discard without at the same time destroying the basis of its authority. Typically, after having half-rejected the thesis of the 'Party of the whole people', but without reverting to that of the 'dictatorship of the proletariat', the Party has suddenly seized upon 'science', which it presents as the basis for its entire action. The Party, it is explained, must control every aspect of national life because it holds the key to social science and 'knows the laws' of all social development. A paradoxical discovery if ever there was one, since the Party's interference with these very branches of science is so glaringly and increasingly frustrating their development. Behind these laboured explanations, the question looms ever more clearly: 'The Party must come first, but for what purpose?'

The Party has at least provided a political system, institutions and a workable cadre system. These are the areas where its usefulness has been the most durable, but even there changes are under way.

First of all, the existence of a totalitarian structure of the Soviet type is justifiable only under revolutionary conditions, or for a few years after the revolution. The cadres, which enjoy full powers over their subordinates and the population, are then still fresh enough or sufficiently inspired by the prevailing enthusiasm to conform to the iron discipline that emanates from headquarters. But, within a few years, power produces its corrosive action. Convictions are blunted by material privilege and by the interplay of alliances, friendships and patronage; anyone who cared to has carved out his own more or less independent political stronghold. The man at the top is forced to deal, even at the regional level, with people who may consider themselves his peers. In a system that rests upon authority, the authority of headquarters is itself challenged.

Hence, the only way the totalitarian system can preserve its inner dynamism is through periodic rejuvenation by means of artificial revolutions: the purges. Stalin set off the great purges with Kirov's assassination in 1934 because, after eliminating his opponents, he had also to get rid of his colleagues. Fifteen years later, in 1953, he was preparing a similar operation against his entourage: although not his peers, they had been part of the system for too long. There is apparently something fateful about this fifteen to twenty-year interval between revolutions. Even Mao Tse-tung's China, which had seemed safe from such upheavals, has been beset by them seventeen years after its revolution. The methods and instruments used may vary, but the goal is always the same – to preserve the chief's authority – and the target is also the same: the Party and its dignitaries.

The USSR has not had its full quota by far: the political generation of 1938 is more secure than ever as its thirtieth year in power approaches. Discipline, which was unduly weak under Khrushchev, can only slacken further when the ruling team cannot boast of any privileged seniority and lacks any special aura. So strong was the need for physical and psychological security within the apparatus after Khrushchev's overthrow that its demand for them was tantamount to a challenge. It has become difficult enough to remove any officials at the local level, not to speak of the top hierarchy where it has long been virtually impossible. The Party's grip over the population is as firm as ever, but the machinery of power now tends to split into separate entities (major State administrations, 'steel-eaters', army, police, regional groups). None of them can as yet either gain the upper hand or be subdued. Only through a purge conducted by an outside force – the police for instance – can resistance from these groups be overcome and totalitarian discipline again be imposed upon the entire power structure in order to bring back its inner logic and dynamism. But intervention by the police is just what the Party wants to avoid at all costs. Needless to say, Red Guards are out of the question also.

At the top, this situation has produced the collective leadership which has been operating ever since the 'October plenum', and in fact much longer. For several years before Khrushchev's downfall it had become clear that his personal power had dwindled until it was a mere relic of the past, an island of helpless rhetoric that no longer matched the social structure of the apparatus. At least, the overthrow of the leader brought the top of the apparatus into harmony with its lower levels, though at the price of hampering the exercise of power. It is indeed easy to show that Brezhnev, or any other member of the collective leadership, enjoys far fewer prerogatives than the chief executive in a Western democracy.

For instance, he has no decision-making power. In Great Britain, for example, the Prime Minister is responsible to the House of Commons, but not to his ministerial advisers, whose opinions he is free to disregard. Brezhnev, on the other hand, may have a decision imposed on him by a Politburo majority.

Secondly, he cannot alter the composition of the Government team. As chief of the Secretariat, he may have a say in the appointment of an official of intermediate rank, but he cannot bring any member into the Politburo or have him removed without the assent of his colleagues. In fact, the co-optation rule dictates the composition of his entourage.

Furthermore, his own team may dismiss him at a moment's notice. Elsewhere, the man in charge is designated, by a public and universally accepted procedure, for a period often determined beforehand. In the Soviet Union a few dozen persons, meeting whenever they choose, can make and unmake any man's power without his knowledge or that of the public. Is it conceivable that in the United States a member of the National Security Council, the Secretary of Defence, for instance, should decide to depose President Johnson by forming a coalition against him within the Council? That is more or less what Suslov did to Khrushchev in October 1964.

The drawbacks of the situation have been described earlier. Despite the pressure of circumstances and Kosygin's determined efforts to push through the economic reform of September 1965, it took several months to overcome blocking tactics, and the final result was an anaemic compromise. Furthermore, that compromise was concluded between powerful competing interest groups rather than between conflicting opinions. The Party resigned itself to the new measures provided none of its own functions was affected, which markedly reduced the scope of the reform. On the other hand, the campaign conducted by the conservative wing for the whitewashing of the 'cult' period was not successful either. The phenomena of Stalinism and Khrushchevism have not yet been defined. Official language is more and more dominated by euphemisms, while the major problems of the régime are cloaked in silence.

It is true that the main problems left over from the Khrushchev period (economic reform, Twenty-third Congress, etc.), have been settled after a fashion, and that the ruling group can now 'wait and see'. Collective leadership may be quite capable of coping with current managerial tasks. But if a decision on a more serious issue is necessary or if a more acute conflict arises between some of its members, all the real flaws of collegial power will be exposed. Consequently the system seems most unlikely to last very long in its present form. In theory, two types of development are possible.

Firstly, a return to undisputed one-man rule. In a while, the climate will probably have grown more favourable to this. Once the anti-Khrushchev reaction has blown itself out, all the drawbacks of the absence of a single authority will have become evident. One member of the team may also have drawn ahead of his colleagues and be ready to take over. Khrushchev's experience should serve as a reminder, however: no one can secure absolute power without paying the price, namely without conducting a drastic purge, a new revolution which, as in the 'thirties, must sweep away the bulk of the existing apparatus. Barring this, the new power can be no more than a more pronounced version of Khrushchevism, which the apparatus would not stand for. Who might attempt such a coup, and how? The question cannot be answered at present, which does not mean that it should be dismissed altogether. Indeed, the paradoxical fact is that a coup would be the safest way for the régime to preserve its totalitarian structure for a lasting period and regain its lost dynamism. The only point to keep in mind is that the new master might well be an outsider to the Party apparatus. A police or army officer, for instance, might try to take charge if grave confusion set in.

However, return to one-man rule may be out of the question for a long time because the respective leaders' ambitions will continue to neutralize one another as they do now, and block any individual's attempt to take over. In that case, the collective will have to be broadened and eventually accept true democratization.

It is easy to understand why this curious enclave of democracy embodied in the Politburo and the few dozen privileged lobbies it rests upon cannot preserve its shape: it must either develop or be submerged. In the summer of 1966 the Soviet press started discussing the respective roles of the Secretariat and the Politburo, of the Presidium of the Supreme Soviet and the Government. This was the first indication of the path that might be followed. It means that the exercise of collective leadership may lead progressively to a general review of Soviet institutions, or rather of their operation. If it does, anything might happen.

The entire Soviet political system rests on a number of fictions. In theory, a very liberal Constitution has given 'all power to the Soviets', has established an electoral law that is no more and no less democratic than in many Western nations (two-ballot majority voting for a single candidate, as in France) and has even given its constituent republics the right to secede. In practice, however, the Soviets wield no power *vis-à-vis* the Party, elections provide no choice of candidates, the Supreme Soviet sits for less than one week a year to ratify – when it is asked to – ready-made decisions of a body that is not even recognized by the Constitution, namely the Party Politburo. Neither is the Party itself immune from inner contradictions: in theory, its Congress, endowed with supreme power, freely elects the Central Committee which, in turn, freely chooses the Politburo and the Secretariat. In fact, these 'elections' disguise a system of appointments by higher authority and of co-optation by the main bureaucratic institutions. At all levels, power is exercised through 'recommendations' that are really orders, through 'assistance' that is really interference, and through 'initiatives' dictated from above. Officially, the secretariats only execute the decisions of the assemblies and their committees, but in fact they make those decisions. Moreover, dictatorial interpretation of the principle of 'democratic centralism' has turned all public debates into well-orchestrated ceremonies precluding any surprises.

The discrepancy between reality and fiction dwindles to manageable proportions when a single individual holds all the strings of power, non-official as well as official; for example, when the same man heads both the Party and the Government. Or else, if that is not the case, the personal authority of the supreme leader must be far above average. He needs it because his power and the channels through which it operates are determined at best by custom and not by statutory law. Whenever the leader lacks such authority, there will be a temptation to ignore his recommendations, since legally speaking they are not orders, and to resist the attempts of the Secretariat, then of the Politburo and finally of the Party itself to interfere with any matter whatsoever. In short, legal institutions will begin to be taken seriously. The fact that each chain of command is headed by a different individual, all of whom are of equal political stature and probably competing for power, is in itself enough to foster unruliness. Moreover, it tends to strengthen pressure from the rank and file for freer discussion as laid down by the Party statutes.

The collective leadership itself will not be able to forestall this evolution for very long. Meanwhile, the prolonged existence of a situation where no man can expel another from the top hierarchy despite disagreements and rivalries amounts, in fact, to the legalization of factionalism, whose existence is bound to become known outside the magic circle. It is quite conceivable, however, that some day a Politburo minority will refuse to bow before the majority and will bring its dispute before a plenary session or even a congress. These assemblies will then really discuss the issues at stake instead of being confronted with ready-made decisions. The process seems already to have started in the Central Committee. Since its proceedings are again being held behind closed doors, the public is no wiser than before, but it does appear that the discussions themselves are freer. The provision adopted at the Twenty-third Congress to resume 'Union All-Party conferences' (extraordinary congresses convened outside the legal intervals) may also hold some promise of increased parliamentary influence.

In short, the day will come when legality, under the Constitution and the Party statutes, will cease to be fiction and become reality. The process will not be a smooth one, naturally. It is difficult to imagine how the Party could obtain democracy for itself without extending it to wider strata of the population; and it is even harder to imagine how the power of the *apparat* could survive a free confrontation with the living forces that make up the nation.

Whichever the solution – totalitarianism under one-man rule, or an extended parliamentary system – major transformations will have to take place. The Party will be the first to feel their strong political and social impact. Today this may seem highly problematic, but each of the two main communist countries independent of Moscow has taken one of these two paths: China the first, Yugoslavia the second. The only room left between the two is for rearguard action by a narrow conservatism.

Postscript

The Soviet scene did not stop changing after this book was finished, and shattering events have taken place in the interval. The international crisis – the Six Days' War between Israel and the Arab nations in June 1967 – was comparable to the 1962 Cuban crisis in its gravity and possible consequences. The crisis is not yet over, and although it has not produced all of its consequences, the signs are that it will leave its mark on the collective leadership just as the Cuban fiasco ushered in the last stage of Khrushchev's reign. The continuing but slow and gradual confrontation in Vietnam has not involved a 'moment of truth' for Khrushchev's successors; but the Middle East crisis did, and the Kremlin strategists made a poor showing.

This is not to discount the major differences between the two crises. The USSR was less committed *vis-à-vis* the Arabs in 1967 than *vis-à-vis* Cuba five years earlier. There was no threat of global confrontation involving a direct challenge for Moscow. The issue was a local one and the Kremlin was not directly a party to it. Nevertheless, Moscow's losses were as large if not larger, because it found itself in the losers' camp. Huge Soviet supplies were squandered within a few days and the prestige of Soviet diplomacy was at stake on several occasions – when it reversed its attitude at the United Nations Security Council and when it was defeated in the General Assembly. In 1962 the settlement was a local one, namely simple return to the *status quo ante*. This time, on the contrary, the crisis brought about a complete upheaval in the Middle East. The territory of Moscow's official protégés was occupied by the enemy, and neither the Arabs nor the Kremlin can hope to redress the situation in the foreseeable future.

Moscow had tried to find consolation in the thought that the Arab military débâcle would be offset by the consolidation of friendly 'progressive' régimes and the expansion of Soviet influence in the region, coupled with the wiping out of Western influence. But these conclusions soon had to be revised. The 'progressive' régimes turned out to be shakier than ever; Moscow had to make it plain that it did not approve of Egypt's power structure, and to disavow the extremist diplomacy of Syria and Algeria, with whose régimes it had become closely involved before the crisis. Far from being jeopardized, Western influence is looked upon as indispensable in the search for a political settlement.

No matter where one turns, one does not see any durable gain for the USSR, whereas its losses are plain.

A more serious matter is at stake: the top men in the collective leadership are no longer masters of the crises in which they intervene. Moreover, when they do so, it is not out of deliberate calculation, but rather through a kind of collective involvement whose mechanism is apparently beyond their control.

Khrushchev at least knew what he was trying to do. When he decided to advance a pawn in Berlin, Cuba or even the Middle East (in 1957, for instance, when he started denouncing alleged Turkish troop concentrations on the Syrian frontier) he was deliberately building up a crisis. He shouted louder than anybody else, but kept his finger on the pawn. If anything went wrong or if he thought the game had lasted long enough, he withdrew it. He was not always successful, but he was always the master of his own moves.

In contrast to this, a close scrutiny of the events that preceded June 5 1967 has failed to disclose how, through whom, or at what moment, Soviet diplomacy became so deeply involved in the disastrous crisis. Virtually no answer could be found, probably because no answer existed.

The background was this: for over ten years the general line, by and large, was support of Nasser and the other 'progressive' Arab régimes. From 1966 onwards this prompted the Kremlin leaders to cater to the most dangerous new régime of all, namely al-Atassi's left-wing Baathist group in Syria. It was a risky game, because in encouraging Damascus in its anti-Western 'non-capitalist' path, the Russians were blinding themselves to the most sombre and explosive aspect of the Syrian régime, namely its demagogical fanaticism. This is what prompted the Syrian leaders to swear they were going to attack Israel, and to say so outright.

The date of April 21 1967 should be kept in mind. This is when Moscow addressed its first protest note to Israel for the reprisal air raid on Damascus a fortnight earlier. Why the delayed charge of aggression in respect of something which, until then, the Soviet press had cautiously described as mere border 'clashes'? The only explanation was the stay in Moscow, from April 17 to 22, of the Iraqi Minister for Foreign Affairs, and perhaps also the talks that N. G. Yegorychev (First Secretary of the Moscow Urban Committee, who was removed a few weeks later) held in Cairo on April 20 with Ali Sabri, the Secretary-General of the Arab Socialist Alliance. The Arab leaders probably chided the Soviet leaders for failing to react to an incident that had aroused indignation in the Middle East. The Kremlin then responded with the protest note, probably without realizing that by giving in to pressure, it was letting itself be drawn into something it could not control. It was still more irresponsible to inform the delegates of the Egyptian parliament who arrived in Moscow at the end of April that Israel was concentrating troops on the Syrian frontier with 'the premeditated intent of attacking Syria'. Nasser, who disclosed this in his June 9 speech after the defeat, did not specify who the well-intentioned 'Soviet friend' had been. Perhaps it was Kosygin himself who, on April 29, had had a *tête-à-tête* with Anvar Sadat, the leader of the delegation.

This had been enough to touch off the crisis. In the meantime, the Israeli troop concentrations that were allegedly at the root of the trouble were apparently not taken over-seriously in Moscow. Not until May 16 did *Pravda* mention them, although Nasser was already getting his war machine into gear. Moscow's declaration on the crisis on May 23 only alluded very discreetly to the troop concentrations. Evidence of Tel-Aviv's 'aggressive' intentions was being sought in General Rabin's declarations or in the Knesset debates. Again, one can hardly help recalling that when Khrushchev unleashed his propaganda attacks against Turkish troop concentrations in October 1957, he behaved more responsibly. He was directing the campaign, of course, but he knew he could stop it any day. He could always ascribe his own excessive language to Marshal Zhukov's adventurism and thus bring the whole thing to an end. In 1967, on the contrary, the Arabs had the initiative, and they drew their Moscow protectors in deeper and deeper after them.

After the disaster, the Soviet leaders hastened to state – that is, they intimated orally to rank-and-file Party members, since it was awkward to admit it publicly – that Nasser had not consulted Moscow about the blockade of the Gulf of Aqaba. In fact, from June 5 onwards, the Soviet press maintained that it would have been possible to conduct negotiations on this point before starting the hostilities. No doubt this is true, but one would look in vain through all Soviet comments and declarations before the hostilities for so much as a hint of disavowal of Nasser's move or for any encouragement of such negotiations. It is true that Moscow never condoned the Aqaba blockade. Both declarations of the Soviet Government, on May 23 and June 5, were silent on that point, and so was Fedorenko in his speeches at the United Nations. But undisguised sympathy was expressed everywhere else, and this was tantamount to unofficial support. The subject was not taboo for the Soviet press, as always happens when friendly powers adopt an attitude disapproved of by the Soviets. (For instance, calls for the destruction of Israel always met with total silence.) The Soviet newspapers described in detail the closing of the Gulf and the motives that prompted the move, stressed the full support it was receiving from the other Arab nations, and overtly pictured it as a success. For example, on May 29 *Pravda* ran a story on Israeli and even United States ships turning back from the Strait of Tiran.

At first, Soviet support for the Arabs was barely disguised. *Pravda* of May 26 stated that the Gulf waters 'cannot, under any United Nations decision, be regarded as Israeli territorial waters'. In vain one awaited the nuance, the acknowledgment that riparian States may have some rights – a position that the Soviet Union has always taken up in cases involving maritime law. As for negotiations, it is no understatement to say that the Kremlin was in no hurry. Fedorenko opposed convening the first meeting of the Security Council on the issue and refused any consultations. Even when the crisis grew hotter, the 'blockade' (*Pravda* used quotation marks, as if to deny it was a fact) was alleged not to be a serious matter – a poor way of promoting negotiations. On June 1 in *Pravda*, Mayevsky derided the problem of whether 'two or four ships will or will not go through the Tiran Strait each day'. *Pravda*'s last comment before hostilities started on June 5 was to ridicule Anglo-American efforts to form a group of maritime powers. One might have expected some counter-proposal, if only a suggestion for talks. Nothing came. One may well wonder, echoing Mayevsky, who the 'irresponsible' people really were.

It is true that, on some days, the Soviet delegation to the United Nations seemed ready to listen to compromise suggestions. But its receptiveness was fleeting and, in the week before the conflict in particular, the delegation refused to consider any such possibility. It is also true that, on May 26, Kosygin sent to Nasser as well as to Levi Eshkol messages whose tone is alleged to have been 'very conciliatory', requesting them not to open hostilities. His sincerity is unquestionable. The Soviets did not want war, although they took the easy way out and were irresponsible where their true motives and behaviour were concerned.

The easy way out was not to resist the pleasure of helping Nasser win a diplomatic victory and later claiming credit for it. They had probably not ruled out negotiations but contemplated their being conducted much later at a slow pace, on the basis of Nasser's gains and his new positions of strength. Roughly speaking, this was a miniature Cuban operation. It had not been deliberately fomented as in 1962, but, so to speak, caught on the wing of history. Like the Cuban operation five years earlier, it was meant to help the so-called progressive camp to alter the balance of power. Specifically, it was supposed to help Nasser restore the pre-1956 situation. The picture was different from 1962 in that the prospective gain for the USSR was slight. The installation of missiles in Cuba was assuredly more worth while than the

Aqaba blockade, and Nasser was an infinitely less reliable ally than Castro. Yet, in spite of these drawbacks, Soviet prestige was as much at stake in the Middle Eastern crisis as it had been in Cuba.

This brings up the question of irresponsibility. Anyone meddling with a Middle East powder-keg – particularly Arab-Israeli relations, the most explosive aspect of all – must take the elementary precaution of considering the possibility, if not the likelihood, of war ensuing as a result of the slightest change. One more possibility should have been considered: that of a third Arab defeat. Now, everything points to the fact that this calculation was not made in Moscow, or that if it was, the collective leadership ignored it. The evidence is that the only action taken was to exhort the adversaries not to open fire – something that almost all heads of State in the world did at the time. The only way out would have been to force Nasser to negotiate (or at least make it plain to him that he must), and make serious proposals to the Israelis instead of insulting them. The Soviets were the only ones that could have played that role, and this had to be done as quickly as possible. Obviously, the Kremlin rulers did not show proper concern, as Khrushchev might have done. It was noted with astonishment that on May 31 Brezhnev, Kosygin and Grechko, the New Defence Minister, left on a four-day inspection of the Soviet fleet in Murmansk and Arkhangelsk. They returned to Moscow on June 4, just in time to face the war that they should have foreseen and could have prevented.

This helps to explain why the individual responsibilities of each leader cannot be clearly assessed and why there was no question of any 'punishment' such as Khrushchev was made to suffer in 1962. The reason is that this time the crisis in Moscow had not been provoked by one man's gamble. Instead, the entire collective but headless leadership had drifted along on the routine pattern set by past decisions and was engulfed in events beyond its control. In 1962 Khrushchev miscalculated; in 1967 it would be more accurate to say that no one calculated at all. A review of the crisis does not disclose any particular fatal or irreversible decision by Soviet diplomacy, but rather a series of 'non-decisions' (to restrain al-Atassi or Nasser, to impose an arrangement over Aqaba, etc.) that led to the disastrous impasse step by step. This might have been expected. It fitted in with the style of the collective leadership, since inaction is the most probable result of opposite impulses. No particular member of the group can be blamed for having failed to make any specific necessary decision, since the group as a whole is in charge.

It is no accident, therefore, that the first cracks did not occur at the very top, in the Politburo, but at a lower level. Just after the Central Committee plenary session in June 1967, after the fight was over, N. G. Yegorychev, the First Secretary of the Moscow Urban Committee, was abruptly removed, apparently because he had criticized Soviet policy on the Middle East. Some information also indicates that he had advocated a tough line and had wanted firmer support for the Arabs after the start of the conflict. This is possible and even probable, since he had visited Egypt in April and since the rank-and-file communists were concerned primarily with the Soviet losses in prestige and military equipment. Moreover, it is an important principle that, whenever a collective leadership manages to preserve its cohesion and keep its disagreements secret, the political debate tends to shift toward a lower hierarchy. Thus the Politburo clashes with the Central Committee just as Khrushchev once used to clash with the Politburo. Yegorychev's swift removal also shows how far criticism is allowed to go: a parliamentary régime is still in the distant future.

Up to now, this collective solidarity of the Politburo *vis-à-vis* its constituents and all other outside forces has overshadowed any disagreements among its members. This is the prerequisite for its survival, and perhaps even for the survival of the régime. It will therefore take a great deal more strain to break the solidarity. This does not mean that disagreements are fading. Some of them even come to the surface occasionally, for instance the old conflict between Brezhnev and Kosygin over economic reforms. The long-standing rivalries described in this book have not disappeared either. In the past few months, Shelepin's power has been steadily dwindling. He must have represented a major threat for Brezhnev to have pursued him and his Komsomol group with such assiduity for two years. Even before Shelepin was reassigned to trade-union leadership, the last of his former associates had been removed. They were D. P. Goryunov, the director of the Tass agency, and especially V. E. Semichastny, his successor as the head of the State Security agency. Brezhnev now reigns almost undisputed over the Secretariat with the support of Kirilenko (whose behaviour and statements show that he is closely allied to the Secretary-General) and of Suslov (for how much longer, one may wonder). Even now, in matters of protocol and prestige Brezhnev's stature is incomparably greater than at the end of 1964. He is clearly above all the other members of the collective leadership.

It is true that after the removal of several Secretariat representatives, this body has only a small fraction of its members left in the Politburo, which fully intends to remain in control. Furthermore, various signs that it would take too long to enumerate here suggest that Brezhnev's authority is not equally strong in all the regions of the country and that the 'Dnepropetrovsk men' cannot do everything they want. Altogether, Brezhnev is still in the position in which Khrushchev found himself in

1956, that is, when he already had the Secretariat under his thumb while the Politburo was the same as after Stalin's death – packed with his rivals, adversaries or simply old-timers who did not support him. Brezhnev therefore still has a long way to go if he wants to build up for himself even the nominal authority of his predecessor. It is doubtful that he will succeed, since by 1955 Khrushchev was a political figure, already identified with an impulse that reflected his underlying imagination and dynamism. One would in vain seek these qualities under the narrowly conservative approach and the flowery but empty eloquence of his successor. And any man who wishes to wield something more than the purely 'organizational' influence of the *apparatchik* and to become a political leader must have both imagination and dynamism.

Our conclusions therefore remain unchanged. Of the alternatives of the Soviet system moving towards parliamentarism and its reverting to a one-man dictatorship, the first is more probable with one qualification. A movement toward a parliamentary régime, or rather toward true liberalization, cannot fail to occur – but only some day in the distant future. Such an evolution must occur, because it corresponds to the overall evolution of Soviet society. In the meantime, however, the possibility of 'accidents' such as military or police dictatorships must certainly more than ever be contemplated. Even now, despite insistent reaffirmations of the Party's leading role, the army and the police are gradually gaining ground. The army is gaining since, thanks to international tension and ideological impoverishment, militant patriotism is about the only surviving reliable value. The police is gaining because it has to step in with growing frequency to keep a recalcitrant population under control; it is no accident that its chief has just joined the Politburo (as an alternate, it is true) for the first time since Beriya's day. Even under present conditions, things are probably doomed to get worse before they get better. The defensive conservatism of the régime has still not produced its full effects, and we shall see more and more writers' trials, signs of dissatisfaction and 'special laws'. New societies cannot make their way without paying the price.

Only one thing is certain: the power of the Party *apparatchiki*, or rather of the Stalinist generation that has been in charge for almost a quarter of a century now, is drawing to an end, and the change-over to their successors will probably be chaotic. One statistical fact speaks for itself: the average age of the voting members of the Central Committee has risen from 49 in 1952 to 51 in 1956, 52 in 1961 and 56 in 1966, when the last elections were held. Just before the next congress, it will be around 60, an age that 35 per cent of the Central Committee members have already reached or passed. Far from worrying about this, the collective leadership is apparently contriving to keep younger men away and to fill any post of responsibility from among the steadily shrinking circle of old-timers. 'Young' Semichastny (43 in 1967) has been replaced at the head of the KGB by Yu. V. Andropov, his elder by ten years and a senior dignitary of the Central Committee apparatus. N. G. Yegorychev, who at 47 was also one of the most prominent representatives of the new generation of cadres, has also been removed; although there were enough young Rayon Committee secretaries in Moscow who could have succeeded him at the head of the Urban Committee, the leaders picked V. V. Grishin, who was older by six years but, more important, was one of the veterans in the hierarchy and a member of the sacrosanct 'hard core' of 1952. N. N. Organov, another member of that same group, was rescued from the diplomatic functions where he had been relegated by Khrushchev and, at 66, was appointed head of a still unspecified department of the Central Committee. Even S. G. Lapin, the new director of Tass, although only three years older than his predecessor, was also a figure from the past, since he had been in charge of political broadcasting during World War II.

In other words, the new ruling group is clearly and increasingly restricting its trust to the few old-timers whom Khrushchev had removed (Organov) and to the few dozen people who have been very close to the collective leadership for the past ten or fifteen years (Grishin, Andropov). This is due either to the rulers' natural inclinations or to the fact that the patronage extended by members of the ruling group to their respective clients cancels out. The young have no place in this scheme. With the noteworthy exception of K. F. Katushev, who happens to be a client of Brezhnev and has been appointed First Secretary of the Gorki Oblast Committee at 38, in the past few years not a single young official has been promoted to any post of importance.

It happens elsewhere too, of course, that venerable old men preside over their nations' destinies; but the political machines, the administrations – not to mention the business world – are in the hands of other generations. In the USSR, Brezhnev and Kosygin are not particularly old considering the posts they occupy; but the point is that all the country's cadres belong to the same age-group as they. All the main cogs of the administration, the army, the economy and all the other components of the system are in the hands of that generation alone. This highly restrictive state of affairs has its part in enforcing the paralysing conservatism that is shackling the country. This does not foreshadow a glorious ending for those individuals who are now benefiting from the system.

Vienna, September 1967

MAIN EVENTS SINCE
STALIN'S DEATH

Main Events since Stalin's Death

1953
March 5 Stalin's death. Malenkov appointed Head of Government; Khrushchev relieved of his functions as First Secretary for the Moscow region in order to 'concentrate upon his work within the Secretariat'.
March 14 Malenkov relieved of his functions within the Secretariat.
March 27 First amnesty measure.
April 4 Rehabilitation of the Kremlin doctors whose arrest had been announced in January on a charge of plotting to assassinate Stalin.
July 7 Fall of Beriya.
July 27 Armistice in Korea.
September 3–7 Central Committee plenary session on the agricultural situation. Khrushchev appointed First Secretary.

1954
February 23–March 2 A Central Committee plenary session, on a proposal by Khrushchev, announces a campaign for the cultivation of the virgin lands in Kazakhstan and Siberia. 101,270,000 acres to be developed between 1954 and 1960.
July 20 Armistice in Indochina.

1955
February 8 Malenkov performs 'self-criticism' and is replaced as Head of Government by Bulganin, but remains a member of the Presidium.
July 4–12 A plenary session ratifies the Soviet–Yugoslav *rapprochement*. Suslov and Kirilenko elected members of the Presidium.
July 17–24 Big Four Conference at Geneva.

1956
February 14–25 Twentieth Congress. Khrushchev's secret report on 'the cult of personality and its consequences'.
October 23–November 4 Hungarian rising.

1957
February 13–14 Upon Khrushchev's proposal a plenary session ratifies an industrial reform: abolition of a number of industrial ministries, creation of about one hundred regional Economic Councils (sovnarkhozes).

June 22–29 Condemnation by a Central Committee plenary session of the 'anti-party group'. Malenkov, Kaganovich and Molotov expelled from the Presidium and the Central Committee, Shepilov from the Secretariat and the Central Committee, Saburov from the Presidium. Pervukhin demoted to alternate membership of the Presidium.

October 4 First sputnik.

October 15 Moscow promises China a model of the atom bomb and secret data on its production.

End of October After hearing Suslov's report, the Central Committee expels from its membership Marshal Zhukov, Defence Minister.

November 14–16 Conference of Party chiefs of twelve communist countries in Moscow, attended by Mao Tse-tung.

1958

February 25–26 Upon Khrushchev's proposal, a plenary session ratifies the 'reorganization of Machine Tractor Stations' (MTS) in the countryside. The Stations are dissolved and their machinery sold to the kolkhozes.

March 27 Khrushchev succeeds Bulganin as Head of Government.

September 5 Bulganin expelled from the Presidium.

November 12 The Central Committee ratifies a school reform: a period of several years' factory training is mandatory for all applicants for higher schooling.

November 27 Khrushchev announces his intention to cure the Berlin 'tumour' within six months.

December 15–19 Plenary session on agriculture. Bulganin accused.

1959

January 27–February 5 Twenty-first Congress. Adoption of the 1959–1965 Seven-Year Plan. Pervukhin and Saburov accused.

May 16 Khrushchev awarded the Lenin Peace Prize.

June 20 Moscow rescinds the 1957 Sino-Soviet agreement on atomic co-operation.

September 9 Tass statement deploring the Sino-Indian border conflict.

September 15–27 Khrushchev's visit to the United States. Talks with Eisenhower at Camp David.

September 30–October 4 Khrushchev's trip to China. Talks with Mao Tse-tung.

December 22–25 Plenary session on agriculture.

1960

January 14 Demobilization of 1,200,000 men – one third of the armed forces.

May 1 U-2 incident.

May 16 Collapse of the Paris summit meeting.

June Bucharest conference of Communist Parties in power, attended by Khrushchev.

July 13–16 Central Committee plenary session on industrial problems.

July 17 Soviet experts recalled from China.

November Moscow conference of chiefs of the eighty-one Communist Parties.

1961

January 10–18 Plenary session on agriculture.

June 2–5 Khrushchev–Kennedy meeting in Vienna. Start of the second Berlin crisis: the German peace treaty must be signed 'this year'.

October 17–31 Twenty-second Congress. First public criticism of Albania. Voroshilov accused.

1962

March 5–9 Plenary session on agriculture. Setting up of territorial administrations for agriculture.

June 1 Price increase for animal products.

October 22–28 Cuban crisis.

November 19–23 Central Committee plenary session. Division of the Party apparatus and of the Soviets into industrial and agricultural branches; creation of a Party–State Supervisory Committee.

December 1 Khrushchev's visit to the Manège exhibition. Start of the drive against 'modernist' art.

1963

March 8 Khrushchev's speech to the writers.

April Kozlov's illness.

June 18–21 Central Committee plenary session on ideological problems.

July 14 Open letter initiating the public polemic with Peking.

August 5 Signing of Moscow treaty on the banning of nuclear tests.

End of October Khrushchev announces a truce in anti-Chinese polemics.

December 9–13 Central Committee plenary session on the chemical industry and fertilizer production.

1964

February 10–15 Plenary session on agriculture. Suslov's report on the Chinese issue: resumption of the quarrel with Peking (in April).

April 17 Khrushchev's seventieth birthday.

July 15 Brezhnev replaced by Mikoyan as Head of State.

October 14 Khrushchev's fall.

November 16 Central Committee plenary session. Reuniting of the industrial and agricultural branches of the Party apparatus and of the Soviets.

1965

March 24–26 Plenary session on agriculture.

September 27–29 A Central Committee plenary session, upon Kosygin's proposal, ratifies industrial reform. Liquidation of the sovnarkhozes and reinstatement of the industrial ministries.

December 9 Podgorny succeeds Mikoyan as Head of State. Liquidation of the Party–State Supervisory Committee.

1966

March 29–April 8 Twenty-third Congress. Brezhnev assumes the title of Secretary-General.

BIOGRAPHIES

Biographies

ARISTOV, Averki Borisovich: born in 1903, member of the Party since 1921, of the C.C. since 1952, of the Presidium in 1952–1953 and from 1957 to 1961; in 1943–1944, Secretary of the Kemerovo Oblast Committee; 1944–1950: First Secretary of the Krasnoyarsk Territorial Committee; 1950–1952, First Secretary of the Cheliabinsk Oblast Committee; 1952–1953: Secretary of the C.C.; 1953–1954: Chairman of the Khabarovsk Territorial Executive Committee; 1954–1955: First Secretary of the Khabarovsk Territorial Committee; 1955–1960: Secretary of the C.C.; since 1961, Ambassador in Warsaw.

BELIAYEV, Nikolay Ilyich: born in 1903, member of the Party from 1921, of the C.C. from 1952 to 1961, of the Presidium from 1957 to 1960; 1940: Secretary of the Novosibirsk Oblast Committee; 1943–1955: First Secretary of the Altai Territorial Committee; 1955–1958: Secretary of the C.C.; in February 1956: Deputy Chairman of the C.C. Bureau for the RSFSR; 1957–1960: First Secretary of the Kazakhstan C.C.; in 1960, First Secretary of the Stavropol Territorial Committee. Purged in June 1960. Died in October 1966.

BREZHNEV, Leonid Ilyich: born in 1906, member of the Party since 1931, of the C.C. since 1952; alternate member of the Presidium in 1952–1953 and in 1956–1957, full member since 1957; 1939: Secretary of the Dnepropetrovsk Oblast Committee; 1946–1947: First Secretary of the Zaporozhye Oblast Committee; 1947–1950: First Secretary of the Dnepropetrovsk Oblast Committee; 1950–1952: First Secretary in Moldavia; 1952–1953: Secretary of the C.C.; 1953–1954: First Assistant Chief of the Armed Forces Political Administration; 1954–1956: First Secretary of the Kazakhstan C.C.; 1956–1960: Secretary of the C.C.; 1960–1964: Chairman of the Presidium of the USSR Supreme Soviet; 1963–1964: Secretary of the C.C.; 1964–1966: First Secretary of the C.C.; since 1966, Secretary-General of the C.C.

DEMICHEV, Pyotr Nilovich: born in 1918, member of the Party since 1939, of the C.C. since 1961, alternate member of the Presidium since 1964; 1950–1956: Moscow Oblast Committee, then C.C. apparatus; 1956–1958: Secretary of the Moscow Oblast Committee;

1958–1959: executive officer of the USSR Council of Ministers; 1959–1960: First Secretary of the Moscow Oblast Committee; 1960–1962: First Secretary of the Moscow Urban Committee. In 1962, Chairman of the C.C. Bureau for chemical and light industry. Since 1961, Secretary of the C.C. After 1965, Chairman (probably) of the C.C. ideological committee.

FURTSEVA, Yekaterina Alekseyevna: born in 1910, member of the Party since 1930, alternate member of the C.C. from 1952 to 1956, full member since 1956; alternate member of the Presidium in 1956–1957, full member from 1957 to 1961; 1942–1950: Secretary of a Moscow Rayon Committee; 1950–1954: Second Secretary of the Moscow Urban Committee; 1954–1957: First Secretary of the Moscow Urban Committee; 1956–1960: Secretary of the C.C.; since 1960 Minister of Culture.

IGNATOV, Nikolay Grigoryevich: born in 1901, member of the Party from 1924, alternate member of the C.C. from 1939 to 1941, full member from 1952; alternate member of the Presidium in 1952–1953, full member from 1957 to 1961; 1938–1940: First Secretary of the Kuybyshev Oblast Committee; 1940–1948: Secretary, then First Secretary of the Oryol Oblast Committee; 1949–1952: First Secretary of the Krasnodar Territorial Committee; 1952–1953: Minister for the Transportation of Agricultural Products and C.C. Secretary; 1953: Secretary of the Leningrad Oblast Committee; 1953–1955: First Secretary of the Voronezh Oblast Committee; 1955–1957: First Secretary of the Gorki Oblast Committee; 1957–1960: Secretary of the C.C. In 1959 Chairman of the Presidium of the RSFSR Supreme Soviet for a few months; 1960–1962: Deputy Chairman of the USSR Council of Ministers; after 1962, Chairman of the Presidium of the RSFSR Supreme Soviet. Died in November 1966.

ILYICHEV, Leonid Fyodorovich: born in 1906, member of the Party since 1923, alternate member of the C.C. from 1952 to 1956, of the Auditing Committee from 1956 to 1961, member of the C.C. from 1961 to 1966; 1940–1944: Secretary on *Pravda*'s editorial staff; 1944–1948: editor-in-chief of *Izvestia*; 1948–1949: Assistant Chief of the Agitprop department of the C.C.; 1949–1950: deputy editor-in-chief of *Pravda*; 1950–1952: editor-in-chief; 1953–1958: head of the press department of the Ministry of Foreign Affairs; 1958–1965: chief of the C.C. Agitprop department; 1961–1965: Secretary of the C.C. Since 1965, Deputy Minister of Foreign Affairs.

KAPITONOV, Ivan Vassilievich: born in 1915, member of the Party since 1939, of the C.C. since 1952; 1951–1952: Secretary of the

Moscow Oblast Committee; 1952–1954: First Secretary of the Moscow Urban Committee; 1954–1959: First Secretary of the Moscow Oblast Committee; 1959–1964: First Secretary of the Ivanovo Oblast Committee; 1964–1965: chief of the Party Organs department for the RSFSR; since 1965 Secretary of the C.C. and C.C. head of department for Party organizational work.

KHRUSHCHEV, Nikita Sergeyevich: born in 1894, member of the Party since 1918, of the C.C. from 1934 to 1966; alternate member of the Presidium in 1938–1939, full member from 1939 to 1964; 1931–1932: Secretary of a Rayon Committee in Moscow; 1932–1934: Second, then First Secretary of the Moscow Urban Committee; 1935–1938: First Secretary of the Moscow Oblast Committee; 1938–1947: First Secretary of the Ukraine C.C.; 1947: chief of the Ukrainian Government; 1947–1949: again First Secretary of the Ukraine C.C.; 1949–1953: Secretary of the C.C. and First Secretary of the Moscow Oblast Committee; 1953–1964: First Secretary of the C.C.; from 1958 to 1964 Chairman of the USSR Council of Ministers (Prime Minister).

KIRICHENKO, Aleksey Ilarionovich: born in 1908, member of the Party since 1930, of the C.C. from 1952 to 1961; alternate member of the Presidium from 1953 to 1955, full member from 1955 to 1960; 1938–1941: in the apparatus of the Ukraine C.C.; 1941–1945: Secretary of the Ukraine C.C.; 1945–1949: First Secretary of the Odessa Oblast Committee; 1949–1953: Second Secretary of the Ukraine C.C.; 1953–1957: First Secretary of the Ukraine C.C.; 1957–1960: Secretary of the C.C.; in 1960 First Secretary of the Rostov Oblast Committee; removed in June 1960.

KIRILENKO, Andrey Pavlovich: born in 1906, member of the Party since 1931, of the C.C. since 1956; alternate member of the Presidium from 1957 to 1961, full member since 1962; 1938–1941: Rayon Committee Secretary, Second Secretary of the Zaporozhye Oblast Committee; 1943–1947: Second Secretary of the Zaporozhye Oblast Committee; 1947–1950: First Secretary of the Nikolayevsk Oblast Committee; 1950–1955: First Secretary of the Dnepropetrovsk Oblast Committee; 1955–1962: First Secretary of the Sverdlovsk Oblast Committee; 1962–1966: First Vice-President of the C.C. Bureau for the RSFSR; since 1966 Secretary of the C.C.

KOSYGIN, Aleksey Nikolayevich: born in 1904, member of the Party since 1927, of the C.C. since 1939; alternate member of the Presidium from 1946 to 1948, full member from 1948 to 1952, alternate in 1952–1953 and again from 1957 to 1960, full member of the Presidium since 1960; 1938: mayor of Leningrad; 1939–1940:

Minister of the USSR Textile Industry. Deputy Chairman of the Council of Ministers of the USSR from 1940 to March 1953 (also, from 1943 to 1946, Chairman of the Council of Ministers of the RSFSR); ditto from December 1953 to December 1956 and from July 1957 to May 1960; 1960–1964: First Deputy Chairman of the USSR Council of Ministers; since 1964 Chairman of the USSR Council of Ministers (Prime Minister).

KOZLOV, Frol Romanovich: born in 1908, died in 1965. Member of the Party from 1926, of the C.C. from 1952; alternate member of the Presidium in 1957, full member from 1957 to 1964; 1940–1944: Secretary of the Izhevsk Urban Committee; 1944–1947: in the C.C. apparatus; 1947–1949: Second Secretary of the Kuybyshev Oblast Committee; 1949–1952: Secretary of the Leningrad Urban Committee; 1952–1953: Secretary of the Leningrad Oblast Committee; 1953–1957: First Secretary of the Leningrad Oblast Committee; 1957–1958: Chairman of the RSFSR Council of Ministers; 1958–1960: First Deputy Chairman of the USSR Council of Ministers; 1960–1964: Secretary of the C.C. Onset of illness in April 1963; died November 1965.

KUUSINEN, Otto Vilgelmovich: born in 1881, died May 1964; member of the Party since 1904, of the C.C. since 1941; member of the Presidium in 1952–1953 and from 1957 till his death. Member of the Finnish revolutionary government in 1918, chief of the Finnish 'Government' set up in the USSR in 1939; 1940–1958: Chairman of the Presidium of the Finno–Karelian Supreme Soviet. From 1957 until his death, Secretary of the C.C.

MAZUROV, Kirili Trofimovich: born in 1914, member of the Party since 1940, of the C.C. since 1956; alternate member of the Presidium from 1957 to 1965, full member since 1965; 1939–1941: Komsomol work in Byelorussia; 1942–1946: Byelorussia Komsomol Secretary; 1946–1949: First Secretary of the Byelorussia Komsomol; 1949–1950: Secretary of the Minsk Urban Committee; 1950–1953: First Secretary of the Minsk Oblast Committee; 1953–1956: Chairman of the Council of the Byelorussia Council of Ministers; 1956–1965: First Secretary of the Byelorussia C.C.; since 1965 First Deputy Chairman of the USSR Council of Ministers.

MIKOYAN, Anastasy Ivanovich: born in 1895, member of the Party since 1915, of the C.C. since 1923; alternate member of the Presidium from 1926 to 1935, full member from 1935 to 1966; 1926–1930: Minister of Domestic and Foreign Commerce of the USSR; 1930–1934: Minister of Supplies; 1934–1938: Minister of Food Industry; Deputy Chairman of the USSR Council of Ministers from 1937 to 1955 and in 1957–1958; First Deputy Chairman from

1955 to 1957 and from 1958 to 1964; 1964–1965: Chairman of the Presidium of the USSR Supreme Soviet.

MUKHITDINOV, Nuritdin Akramovich: born in 1917, member of the Party since 1942, of the C.C. from 1952 to 1966; alternate member of the Presidium in 1956–1957, full member from 1957 to 1961; 1947–1950: Secretary, First Secretary of the Namangan Oblast Committee; 1950: Secretary of the Uzbekistan C.C.; 1950–1951: First Secretary of the Tashkent Oblast Committee; 1951–1955: Chairman of the Council of Ministers of Uzbekistan; 1955–1957: First Secretary of the Uzbekistan C.C.; 1957–1961: Secretary of the C.C.; 1961–1966: Deputy Chairman of Soviet Co-operatives. Since 1966 First Deputy Chairman of the Committee on Foreign Cultural Relations.

PELSHE, Arvid Yanovich: born in 1899, member of the Party since 1915, of the C.C. since 1961, of the Presidium since 1966; 1940: in the Party apparatus in Latvia; 1941–1959: Secretary of the Latvian C.C.; 1959–1966: First Secretary of the Latvian C.C. Since 1966, Chairman of the Party Control Committee (KPK).

PODGORNY, Nikolay Viktorovich: born in 1903, member of the Party since 1930, of the Auditing Committee from 1952 to 1956, of the C.C. since 1956; alternate member of the Presidium from 1958 to 1960, full member since 1960; 1939–1940: Deputy Minister of the Ukraine Food Industry; 1940–1942: Deputy Minister of the USSR Food Industry; 1942–1944: Director of the Moscow Institute of Food Industry; 1944–1946: Deputy Minister of the Ukraine Food Industry; 1946–1950: representative of the Ukraine Council of Ministers at the USSR Government; 1950–1953: First Secretary of the Kharkov Oblast Committee; 1953–1957: Second Secretary of the Ukraine C.C.; 1957–1963: First Secretary of the Ukraine C.C.; 1963–1965: Secretary of the C.C.; since 1965, Chairman of the Presidium of the USSR Supreme Soviet.

POLYANSKY, Dmitri Stepanovich: born in 1917, member of the Party since 1939, of the C.C. since 1956; alternate member of the Presidium from 1958 to 1960, full member since 1960; 1945–1949: cadres supervision work at the C.C.; 1949–1952: Second Secretary of the Crimea Oblast Committee; 1952–1953: Chairman of the Crimea Oblast Executive Committee; 1953–1955: First Secretary of the Crimea Oblast Committee; 1955–1957: First Secretary of the Orenburg Oblast Committee; 1957–1958: First Secretary of the Krasnodar Territorial Committee; 1958–1962: Chairman of the RSFSR Council of Ministers; 1962–1965: Deputy Chairman of the USSR Council of Ministers; since 1965, First Deputy Chairman of the USSR Council of Ministers.

SHELEPIN, Aleksandr Nikolayevich: born in 1918, member of the Party since 1940, of the C.C. since 1952, of the Presidium since 1964; 1940–1943: Moscow Komsomol; 1943–1952: Secretary of the Komsomol C.C., First Secretary from 1952 to 1958; 1958: chief of the Party Organs department of the Party C.C.; 1958–1961: Chairman of the State Security Committee. Since October 1961, Secretary of the C.C.; from 1962 to 1965 Chairman of the Party-State Control Committee and Deputy Chairman of the Council of Ministers.

SHELEST, Piotr Yefimovich: born in 1908, member of the Party since 1928, of the C.C. since 1961; alternate member of the Presidium in 1963–1964, full member since 1964; 1954–1957: Second Secretary of the Kiev Urban Committee, then of its Oblast Committee; 1957–1962: First Secretary of the Kiev Oblast Committee; 1962–1963: Secretary of the Ukraine C.C.; since 1963, First Secretary of the Ukraine C.C.

SHVERNIK, Nikolay Mikhailovich: born in 1888, member of the Party since 1905, of the C.C. since 1925; alternate member of the Presidium from 1939 to 1952 and from 1953 to 1957, full member in 1952–1953 and from 1957 to 1966. In 1926, Secretary of the C.C.; 1927–1928: Secretary of the Ural Oblast Committee; 1930–1944: First Secretary of the trade unions; 1944–1946: Chairman of the Presidium of the RSFSR Supreme Soviet; 1946–1953: Chairman of the Presidium of the USSR Supreme Soviet; 1953–1956: Chairman of the trade unions; from 1956 to 1966 Chairman of the Party Control Committee (KPK).

SUSLOV, Mikhail Andreyevich: born in 1902, member of the Party since 1921, of the Auditing Committee from 1939 to 1941, of the C.C. since 1941, of the Presidium since 1955; 1939–1939: Secretary of the Rostov Oblast Committee; 1939–1944: First Secretary of the Stavropol Territorial Committee; 1944–1946: President of the C.C. Bureau for Lithuania; 1949–1950: *Pravda*'s editor-in-chief; since 1947, Secretary of the C.C.

TITOV, Vitaly Nikolayevich: born in 1907, member of the Party since 1938, of the C.C. since 1956; 1944–1950: Rayon Committee Secretary in Kharkov, Second Secretary of the Kharkov Urban Committee; 1950–1953: Second Secretary of the Kharkov Oblast Committee; 1953–1961: First Secretary of the Kharkov Oblast Committee; 1961–1965: Chief of the C.C. Party Organs service; from 1962 to 1965, Secretary of the C.C.; since 1965 Second Secretary of the Kazakhstan C.C.

USTINOV, Dmitri Fyodorovich: born in 1908, member of the Party since 1927, of the C.C. since 1952; alternate member of the

Presidium since 1965; 1941–1953 Minister of Armament; 1953–1957: Minister of Defence Industry; 1957–1963: Deputy Chairman of the USSR Council of Ministers; 1963–1965: First Deputy Chairman of the Council of Ministers and Chairman of the Supreme Sovnarkhoz. Since 1965 Secretary of the C.C.

VORONOV, Gennady Ivanovich: born in 1910, member of the Party since 1931, of the C.C. since 1952; alternate member of the Presidium in 1961, full member since 1961; 1939–1948: Second Secretary of the Chita Oblast Committee; 1948–1955: First Secretary of the Chita Oblast Committee; 1955–1957, Deputy Minister of Agriculture of the USSR; 1957–1961: First Secretary of the Orenburg Oblast Committee; 1961–1962: First Vice-President of the C.C. Bureau for the RSFSR; since 1962, Chairman of the RSFSR Council of Ministers.

VOROSHILOV, Kliment Yefremovich: born in 1881, member of the Party since 1903, of the C.C. from 1921 to 1961 and since 1966; of the Presidium from 1926 to 1960; 1925–1934: Minister of Military and Naval Affairs; 1934–1940: Defence Minister; 1940–1953: Deputy Chairman of the Council of Ministers; 1953–1960: Chairman of the Presidium of the Supreme Soviet of the USSR.

INDEX

Index

Abakumov, 245, 478 *n*
Abalin, S. M., 202 *n*
Abalkin, N. A., 246, 480
Abel, Elie, 266 *n*
Abel, Rudolf, 429
Abramov, G. G., 153, 161
Adzhubey, A. I., 19, 20, 62, 64,
 114 *n*, 191 *n*, 201, 296, 300, 310,
 326 *n*, 356, 357, 358, 377, 388–389,
 398, 404, 407, 421
Afanaseyev, S. A., 137
Agriculture, 23, 27, 36, 87, 96, 97 *n*,
 109–110, 114, 132–134, 139, 166–
 175, 177, 214–217, 219, 220, 224,
 250–251, 252–256, 258, 282, 291,
 292, 296, 370–377, 387, 395–398,
 428, 430–432, 440–443
Akhundov, V. Yu., 82, 165
Aksyonov, A. N., 247, 473
al-Atassi, 533, 536
Albania, 19, 34 *n*, 46, 77, 98, 101 *n*,
 102, 103 *n*, 147, 149, 154, 157,
 164–165, 205, 213, 232, 262 *n*, 320,
 321 *n*, 322, 323, 339, 490, 492, 493
Aleksandrov-Agentov, A. M., 515 *n*
Alferov, P. N., 22 *n*
Algeria, 450, 532
Ali Sabri, 533
Allkhverdev, T., 82
Alpatov, 247 *n*
Alsop, Stewart, 218
Ambrok, S. A., 375
Ampleyev, N. A., 258, 259
Andreyev, A. A., 52, 320
Andrianov, V. M., 26
Andronov, 299
Andropov, Yu. V., 102, 289, 296, 353,
 354, 401 *n*, 460, 498 *n*, 539
anti-party Group, 16, 21, 24, 25,
 26–27, 29, 30–31, 32, 51, 90, 92–93,
 94, 125, 138–140, 145–147, 150,
 151 *et seq.*, 158, 159–164, 185,
 187, 193, 196, 197, 198, 203, 204,

206, 211–214, 220, 222, 223, 244,
 278, 350, 358, 368
Antonov, General, 237
Antonov, S. F., 462
Arab-Israeli Conflict (1967), 532–537
Arabs, see Algeria, Egypt, Iraq,
 Syria and United Arab Republic
Aragonez, 240
Aristov, A. B., 24, 25, 30, 35, 85, 86,
 89, 90 *n*, 100 *n*, 112, 113, 115 *n*,
 131–132, 133, 138 *n*, 156, 157,
 165 *n*, 193, 194
Artsimovich, L. A., 487 *n*
Arzhak, Nikolaj, see Danyiel Yuly
Arzumanian, 370, 474
Avkhimovich, N. E., 22 *n*
Aydit, 350

Bagirov, 139, 144 *n*
Bagramyan, Marshal I. Kh., 411,
 419, 484 *n*
Baranov, V., 445 *n*
Barudzin, S., 318 *n*
Batov, General P. L., 36
Baybakov, N. K., 22 *n*, 23, 118,
 192 *n*, 331, 462
Bazov, A. V., 496 *n*
Beliayev, N. I., 24, 25, 30, 34 *n*, 36,
 37, 85, 87, 109, 190
Belishova, Lira, 98, 102, 103 *n*
Belkin, Y., 438
Belyutin, Professor, 299, 306
Ben Bella, Ahmed, 385
Benediktov, I. A., 22 *n*, 23, 138 *n*,
 190, 411
Berclav, Edward, 35 *n*
Beriya, L. B., 31, 139, 142, 245, 314 *n*,
 315, 325, 382, 389, 478 *n*, 538
Berlin problem, 19, 43, 50, 58, 70,
 72, 75, 170–171, 177, 229, 232–233,
 234, 238, 241, 273, 303, 401, 402,
 403, 533
Beshchev, B. P., 152

Birman, I., 438
Biryukov, Marshal S. S., 236, 311 *n*, 419
Bochkarev, G. N., 289, 292 *n*
Bodyul, I. I., 153, 161
Bolshakov, G. N., 242, 357
Boytsov, I. P., 22 *n*
Brezhnev, D. D., 22 *n*
Brezhnev, L. I., attitude to Stalinism, 152, 156, 157, 161–162, 476, 485–486, 488
  relations with Khrushchev, 24–25, 80, 90–91, 176, 178–179, 180–181, 284, 382, 383, 385–386, 402–403, 423, 430–431
  relations with Kosygin, 439, 450–451, 497–499
  relations with Kozlov, 86–88, 156, 157, 293, 334–335, 342, 349–351
  relations with Podgorny, 349–351, 397, 499–503
  relations with Suzlov, 408–409, 509–510, 513 *n*
  other references, 41, 49, 75, 83, 85, 89, 95, 100, 103 *n*, 112, 113, 155 *n*, 173, 292 *n*, 336, 341, 343, 352, 373. 399 *n*, 401, 404, 416, 419, 421 *n*, 422 *n*, 427, 432, 434, 435, 440, 455, 456, 458, 461 *n*, 463, 464, 470, 491, 494, 495, 506, 507, 508, 511–516, 517, 519, 520–522, 536, 537–538, 539
Bubnovsky, N. D., 97 *n*
Bucharest Conference (1960), 101–104, 106, 108, 110, 201
Bugayev, E. I., 259, 460
Bukharin, N. I., 245, 314, 357
Bulganin, N. A., 22 *n*, 23, 27, 28, 30, 92, 100 *n*, 109 *n*, 142, 146, 152 *n*, 189, 249, 478 *n*
Bulgaria, 101 *n*, 138, 218, 234, 238, 245, 246, 405, 456–458
Burtin, Yu., 472 *n*
Buyanov, I. A., 510 *n*
Buzinov, Colonel V., 325
Byedny, Demyan, 340
Bykhovsky, B. E., 379

Camp David Talks (1959), 44, 46, 48, 49, 54, 58, 62, 64, 65, 67, 68, 77, 78, 84, 95 *n*, 100, 198 *n*, 201, 232

Castro, Fidel, 230, 235, 264, 265, 272, 273, 343, 347, 348 *n*, 349, 351, 536
Castro, Raul, 239, 240
Chakovsky, A. B., 300, 318 *n*
Cheplakov, P. F., 136, 139
Chernyshev, V. E., 517
Chervonenko, S. V., 46, 190 *n*, 322, 353
China, 19, 34 *n*, 44, 45–49, 51, 57 *n*, 61, 66, 69, 73, 78, 79–80, 100, 101–105, 107, 110–111, 112, 113, 122, 141, 146, 147, 165 *n*, 205, 213, 235, 236 *n*, 238, 263 *n*, 274, 303, 319–324, 332, 336, 339, 343, 349, 352, 353–355, 364–369, 379, 381, 387, 417, 427, 490, 492, 526, 527, 531
Choilbalsan, 276
Chou En-lai, 165 *n*
Chubar, 368
Chukanov, O. A., 136
Chukhray, G., 148, 333
Chukovsky, Korney, 301, 303, 487 *n*
Churayev, V. M., 134, 135, 190 *n*, 191 *n*
Chuykov, Marshal V. I., 71, 177, 419
Cienfuegos, 234
Clay, General Lucius, 236
Congress (Party)
  Seventeenth (1934), 73, 125, 482
  Eighteenth (1939), 86 *n*, 182, 191, 519 *n*
  Nineteenth (1952), 86 *n*, 92, 125, 131, 189, 191, 519 *n*
  Twentieth (1956), 22, 24, 27, 29, 30, 31, 51, 97 *n*, 125, 141, 143, 148, 149, 150, 159, 180, 189, 191, 201, 204, 421, 475 *n*, 485, 488, 489, 490, 492
  Twenty-first (1959), 21, 22–23, 25, 26, 27, 29, 31, 32, 33, 34, 35, 37, 87, 93, 94, 125, 138, 152 *n*, 160, 199, 421, 485, 492
  Twenty-second (1961), 17, 21, 28, 30, 31, 51, 90, 94, 97, 117, 119, 125–225, 244, 245, 246, 249, 277, 279, 295, 298, 309, 314, 336, 341, 383, 421, 433 *n*, 456, 475 *n*, 477, 485, 488, 491, 492
  Twenty-third (1966), 139 *n*, 192 *n*, 434, 465 *n*, 486, 487 *n*, 488–493, 495, 496, 502, 504, 508, 509, 510,

511, 514, 515 *n*, 516, 519, 529, 531
Conquest, Robert, 26, 34
Cousins, Norman, 49
Cuba Crisis, 15, 43, 229–244, 246, 249, 255, 260, 261–276, 278, 280, 281–282, 283, 284, 285, 293, 298, 303, 319, 323, 332, 336, 352, 360, 532, 533, 535, 536
Czechoslovakia, 54, 59, 101 *n*, 177 *n*, 274–275, 320, 335, 339, 385, 414, 458, 485, 487; see also Novotny, Antonin

Danyel (Marcovich), Yuly, 471–475, 488 *n*
Demichev, P. N., 149, 153, 158, 189 *n*, 196–197, 204, 247, 287, 289, 291, 467, 510 *n*
Denisov, G. A., 138, 139 *n*, 192 *n*
Deriugin, B. I., 22 *n*
Dillon, 50
Djuanda, 111
Dmiterko, 413, 415
Dmitrin, A. G., 465 *n*
Dobrynin, A. F., 241
Doliniuk, 130
Dorochenko, P. E., 167 *n*
Dorticós Torrado, Oswaldo, 406, 417, 427
Dovgopol, V. I., 58
Drach, 472 *n*
Drygin, A. S., 137
Dubenko, B., 478
Dubinin, N. P., 329
Dulles, Allen, 45, 67, 122
Dymshits, Aleksandr, 282 *n*
Dymshits, V. E., 175, 286, 290, 330 *n*, 331, 397 *n*, 450, 461
Dzhavkhishvili, G. D., 158, 292 *n*

Egypt, 406, 503, 532 *et seq.*; see also Nasser, Gamal al—
Ehrenburg, Ilya, 283 *n*, 300, 301–302, 303, 304, 308, 310, 314–315, 316, 357, 383, 474
Eikhe, 368
Eisenhower, Dwight M., 19, 42, 43, 44, 48, 51, 54, 57–59, 61, 62, 63–67, 77, 95 *n*, 122
Engels, Friedrich, 165

Erhard, Ludwig, 389
Eshkol, Levi, 535

Falk, 299
Favorsky, 303
Fedorenko, 534, 535
Fedoseyev, P. N., 49, 202 *n*, 257 *n*
Feoktistov (cosmonaut), 409
Féron, Bernard, 351
Filinova, Yu. D., 517
Florentyev, L. Ya., 465 *n*, 496 *n*
Fokin, G., 436
Fomenko, Lydia, 308
Fomin, A. S., 266, 267, 268, 270
Frantsev, Yu. P., 259
Frost, Robert, 240, 308, 314
Furtseva, Ye. A., attitude to Stalin, 143–144, 150, 152, 160, 161
relations with Khrushchev, 24, 180, 194,
other references, 25, 83, 85, 89, 92 *n*, 95, 100, 112, 113, 156, 193, 220, 294, 318, 466

Gafurov, B. G., 22 *n*
Gagarin (cosmonaut), 177, 341
Gaile, G. I., 120
Galanshin, K. I., 517
Ganenko, I. P., 136
Garst, Mr., 110
Gatovsky, L. M., 202 *n*
Gaulle, Charles de, 43, 412, 427, 498
Gay Sarian, S., 469
Georgiev, A. V., 152
Gerasimov, Aleksandr, 300
Gerasimov, K. M., 85, 118–119, 120, 121 *n*
Germany (East), 43, 50, 70, 71, 101 *n*, 170, 194, 213, 232, 234, 236, 303, 310, 389–390, 401–402, 414, 456, 458
(West), 170, 232, 241, 301, 337, 350, 389–391, 394, 401–403, 412, 427, 456; see also Berlin
Gheorghe, D. E. J., 274, 381, 417 *n*
Gladyrevsky, A. V., 291 *n*
Glezerman, G. E., 260
Golikov, Marshal F. I., 75, 161, 236, 237
Golovko, Admiral, 237
Gomulka, Wladyslaw, 32, 159 *n*, 275, 284, 381

Goreglyad, A. A., 117, 391
Goriachev, F. S., 152, 356 n, 422 n
Gorkin, A. F., 149, 153
Gorny, General A. G., 325 n
Goryunov, D. P., 114 n, 537
Grafov, L. E., 115 n
Grechko, Marshal A. A., 54, 71, 72–73, 74, 76, 79, 190 n, 369, 419
Gribachev, N. M., 19, 247, 301, 356 n, 475, 536
Grishin, V. V., 108 n, 152, 161, 353, 559
Grishmanov, I. A., 137, 290
Gromyko A. A., 67, 77, 233, 237, 242, 321, 389, 498 n
Gronchi, 327 n
Guevara, Ernesto ('Che'), 233, 239, 240
Guishiani, D. M., 327
Gusev, N. P., 397 n

Herter, Christian A., 42, 43, 49, 50, 53, 60, 61, 62, 63
Hitler, Adolf, 240 n, 413
Hoxha, Enver, 46, 98, 164
Hungary, 19, 32, 101 n, 339, 341, 406 n, 420, 452, 458

Ignatiev, S. D., 138
Ignatov, N. F., 35
Ignatov, N. G., attitude to Stalin, 150, 152, 156–157
  relations with Khrushchev, 24–26, 180, 185
  other references, 35, 85, 86, 87, 88, 89, 100, 145, 160, 162, 175, 193, 194, 220, 290
Ilyichev, L. F., attitude to Stalin, 150, 153, 161–162, 208–210, 245, 307, 314–315
  ideological views, 51, 89, 289, 292, 293, 295, 300, 303 n, 305, 307, 308, 314–315, 337, 465–466
  relations with Khrushchev, 19, 186, 354–356
  relations with Suzlov, 112, 200–204, 495
  other references, 102 131 n, 175, 195, 196, 217, 318, 353, 364, 365, 407 n, 416
India, 46, 263–264, 339, 391, 450
Indonesia, 46, 111, 339, 350

Inozemtsev, N. N., 407 n
Iraq, 533
Isakov, Professor, 66
Isayev, P. N., 115 n

Jacobs, Richard, 324
John XXIII, Pope, 141, 327 n
Johnson, Lyndon B., 528
Johnson, Priscilla, 299 n, 313 n
Julien, Claude, 230

Kabanov, I. G., 22 n
Kádár, Janos, 275, 284, 341, 381
Kaganovich, L. M., 16, 21, 28, 30, 31, 32, 97, 98, 109 n, 139, 140, 142, 143, 144, 146, 147, 149, 150, 151, 152 n, 154, 155 n, 157, 159, 160, 206, 223, 314, 315, 372 n, 382, 478
Kalchenko, N. T., 36, 96 n, 136
Kaln Berzin, Ya. N., 34 n, 193
Kamenev, L. B., 245, 482
Kapitonov, I. V., 35, 36, 196, 510 n
Kapitsa, P. L., 487 n
Kapo, Hysini, 102, 492
Karpov, K., 371
Katayev, V. P., 487 n
Katsman, Y., 305
Katushev, K. F., 510, 517, 539
Kaverin, 303
Kazakov, Yury, 301
Kazanets, I. P., 160 n
Kebin, I. G., 153, 165, 517
Kekkonen, Urho Kaleva, 274, 498
Keldysh, M. V., 379
Kennedy, John F., 44, 110 n, 170, 218, 230, 232, 233, 239, 241–242, 255, 261, 262, 264–267, 269–273
Kennedy, Robert, 271
Kerensky, A. F., 478
Khairulin, 374, 375–377, 496 n
Khaldeyev, M. I., 460
Kharlamov, M. A., 114 n, 305 n, 405, 407
Khrushchev, N. S. (principal topical references only)
  attitude to art, literature and science, 19–20, 246–249, 298–311, 312, 316–319, 353–355, 377–381, 383
  attitude to China, 45–49, 101–106, 263–264, 319–324, 353, 364–367, 387–388

attitude to economic affairs, 114–
121, 128–130, 133, 166–170,
171–175, 214–217, 328–332,
369–377, 391–398
attitude to foreign policy, 19,
43–44, 50, 53–68, 69, 74, 112,
229, 230–233, 239–243, 244, 245–
246, 260–275, 339, 387–391
attitude to Stalin (Stalinism),
19–20, 21–22, 28, 82, 141–145,
149, 150–151, 157–159, 166, 186,
206, 245, 246–249, 298–311,
311–317, 356–359, 423
criticisms of, 63–68, 99 n, 129–130,
180–181, 256, 268–271, 273–279,
304–306, 317, 346–347, 375,
376, 377, 402–403, 416–417, 418
et seq., 482–484
personality cult of, 19–20, 72, 80,
94, 95, 99, 112, 178–181, 311,
367–368, 381–384, 404, 414 n
visits abroad: Albania 19, 77;
Austria, 177 n – see also Vienna
Conference; Bulgaria, 218, 238,
245, 246; China, 19; Czechoslovakia, 177 n, 385; East
Germany, 303, 310; France, see
Paris Conference; Hungary, 19;
Indonesia, Poland, 19, 303, 310;
Roumania, 19–see also Bucharest
Conference: United Arab
Republic, 385; USA, 19–see
also Camp David Talks
his love of travel, 177 n, 384–385
Khrushcheva, Nina Petrovna, 20, 274
Khutsiev, M. N., 487 n
Kirichenko, A. I., 24, 25, 27, 30, 31,
33–37, 83, 85, 86, 87–88, 94, 95,
96, 100, 109, 190, 197, 291
Kirilenko, A. P., 54, 106, 121, 135,
152, 161, 190 n, 193, 222–223, 239,
272 n, 286, 291, 293, 333 n, 335,
336, 348, 352, 376, 383, 431, 455,
469, 504, 508, 510, 513, 537
Kirilin, V. A., 292
Kirov, S. N., 82, 150, 151, 156, 477,
481, 497 n, 527
Kiselev, N. V., 34
Kiselev, T. Ya., 58, 69, 95 n
Knorin, V. G., 484
Knox, William, 263, 271 n
Knyazev, F. K., 518 n

Kobelev, B. M., 22 n
Kochetov, V. A., 65–66, 67, 69, 78,
104, 247, 282, 319, 469, 475
Kohler, Foy, 242
Kolesnikov, A., 520–522
Kolomyets, F. S., 515 n
Kolushchinsky, E. P., 138, 139
Komarov, V. N., 71
Komarov (cosmonaut), 409
Konenkov, 303
Konev, Marshal I. S., 70, 71, 72, 73,
74, 75, 78, 234, 236, 414, 415, 419
Konotop, V. I., 454 n
Konovalov, N. S., 137
Korin, P. D., 487 n
Korneychuk, A. E., 475
Korniets, L. R., 398 n
Korochenko, D. S., 54, 92 n, 106,
114, 193
Korytkov, N. G., 137
Koshevoy, P. K., 71
Kosolapov, V. A., 300
Kostandov, L. A., 331 n
Kostousov, A. I., 410, 411
Kosygin, A. N., attitude to Stalin,
153, 154, 156, 157, 161, 162
attitude to economic affairs, 117,
118, 119, 121, 139, 173–174, 216,
219, 253, 260, 283–286, 287,
288, 373, 385 n, 431–432, 437–
438, 439, 445–450, 458, 460–462,
528
relations with Brezhnev, 386, 408,
450–451, 456, 497–499, 511–513,
520, 537
relations with Khrushchev, 92–94,
99–100, 110–111, 112–113, 147,
176, 179, 181, 207, 224, 225,
274, 342, 385 n, 386, 394, 397,
399 n, 401–403, 405, 415
other references, 41, 85, 91, 106,
165 n, 275, 326, 334, 336, 345,
348 n, 423, 429, 455, 464, 500,
503, 507, 509, 517 n, 522, 534,
535, 536, 539
Kosyor, 368, 477
Kovalenko, A. V., 190 n
Kovanov, P. V., 507
Kovrigina, M. D., 22 n
Kozlov, F. R., attitude to Stalin, 21,
25–26, 152, 155, 156, 157, 161
196

Kozlov, F, R.—*cont.*
  relations with Brezhnev, 85–88,
    113, 207, 224, 274, 293, 335, 342,
    349–351, 502, 575 *n*
  relations with Khrushchev, 24,
    34 *n*, 79–80, 83, 88–89, 100,
    105–106, 110, 113, 131, 176, 177,
    179, 181, 183, 195, 207, 224–225,
    248, 272, 281, 293, 297, 312,
    333–335, 337, 338, 360
  other references, 41, 81, 85, 98,
    103, 112, 118, 134 *n*, 135, 137,
    165 *n*, 173, 191, 192, 193, 211,
    216, 239, 249, 251, 254, 267, 283,
    284, 285, 286, 291, 353, 369, 511
Kozlov, I. I., 291 *n*
Kroll, 241
Kruglev, 245
Kucherenko, V. A., 137, 190, 191 *n*
Kuchumov, P. S., 430 *n*
Kulakov, F. D., 510 *n*
Kunayev, D. A., 36, 111 *n*, 153, 161,
  165, 256 *n*, 336 *n*, 422 *n*, 514
Kurachev, S. V., 284
Kuusinen, O. V., 24, 25, 48, 85,
  100 *n*, 146, 147, 153, 155, 156, 157,
  160, 162, 165 *n*, 166, 179, 195,
  210 *n*, 224, 286, 291, 296, 335, 350
Kuybyshev, N. V., 497 *n*
Kuzmin, I. I., 23, 93, 117, 118, 138,
  139, 288, 431 *n*
Kuznetsov, A. A., 26 *n*, 478 *n*
Kuznetsov, A. N., 220 *n*
Kuznetsov, N. A., 465 *n*
Kuzyukov, F. F., 465 *n*

Laktyonov, A., 300, 318, 318 *n*, 428 *n*
Langelle, Russell, 198 *n*, 326
Lapin, S. G., 539
Larionov, Alexis, 128–129
Lavochkin, 108
Lavrentiev, M. A., 412
Lazarkina, D. A., 158
Lebedev, A., 422 *n*
Lebedev, V. S., 108 *n*, 248, 296
Lehi, Hadji, 103 *n*
Lenin, V. I., 20, 47, 48, 51, 52, 102,
  146, 149, 165, 187, 217, 258–260,
  305, 347, 435, 448, 449, 454, 459,
  477, 482, 516, 520, 522
Leningrad Affair (1949), 26, 28,
  153 *n*, 197, 201, 314, 315, 478 *n*

Leninism (Marxist–Leninism), 148,
  149, 154, 155, 157, 165 *n*, 175, 176,
  179, 180, 186, 209, 258–60, 277, 279,
  280, 305, 308, 334, 354, 366, 395,
  397, 483, 484, 489, 516, 519 *n*, 520
Leonov, P. A., 187
Leontyev, Leon., 208, 211 *n*, 267–268
Leseychko, M. A., 284, 287, 290,
  330 *n*, 344, 408
Liberman, Professor Y. G., 253–254,
  285, 286, 437, 438
Lippmann, Walter, 63–64, 66, 81,
  95 *n*, 278
Liu-Shao-tsi, 103 *n*
Liu-Siao, 79, 235, 274
Lobanov, P. P., 496 *n*
Lobashev, M. E., 379
Lodge, Henry Cabot, 67
Lomakin, N. A., 459, 492
Lomako, P. F., 120, 224, 286, 290,
  329, 391, 397 *n*, 408, 462
Lomonosov, V. G., 256, 291
Lubennikov, L. I., 169
Lunacharsky, A. V., 308
Lu-Ting-Yi, 48
Lysenko, T. D., 133, 377–379, 428

Machiavelli, Niccolo, 388
Macmillan, Harold, 43, 234, 354 *n*
Malenkov, G. M., 16, 21, 25, 26, 28,
  30, 31, 92, 93, 94, 109 *n*, 118, 131,
  136, 139, 140, 142, 143, 144, 146,
  149, 150, 151, 152 *n*, 159, 160, 161,
  163, 166, 175, 286, 295 *n*, 314, 316,
  357, 382, 389, 420, 432, 478, 497,
  519 *n*
Malinovsky, Marshal A. R., 43, 53,
  60, 69, 70, 72, 74–75, 77–79, 152,
  161, 217, 218, 237, 311 *n*, 323, 382,
  386, 405, 417, 419, 429, 479, 498
Maltsev, T. S., 372
Mandelshtam, 474
Mao-Tse-tung, 46, 48, 49, 57 *n*, 60,
  66, 101, 105, 322, 323, 366, 527
Marchais, Georges, 178 *n*, 388 *n*, 389,
  400, 416, 421, 422 *n*
Marchenko, I. I., 465
Markov, G. M., 318, 475
Markov, I. V., 71
Marshak, Samuil, 380
Marx, Karl, 165, 382; see also
  Leninism

Masherov, P. M., 456, 465 *n*, 517
Matern, 401 *n*
Matkovsky, N. V., 102, 108
Matskevich, V. V., 109, 110 *n*, 138, 139, 175, 462, 496 *n*
Matveyev, V., 268–269, 270
Maurer, 381
Mayakovsky, V. V., 305 *n*
Mayevsky, 535
Maysky, I. N., 487 *n*
Mazurov, K. T., 64 *n*, 89, 95 *n*, 150, 152, 161, 170, 174, 180, 197, 254, 312, 383, 401, 455, 456, 461, 464, 465
Medvedyev, Z. A., 378 *n*
Melnikov, L. G., 34, 36, 37, 96, 136
Mendel, Gregor Johann, 379
Menshutin, A., 472 *n*
Mesyats, V. K., 465 *n*
Michurin, I. V., 378 *n*
Mikhailov, N. A., 85, 91 *n*, 190, 197
Mikhailov, S. V., 333
Mikoyan, A. I., attitude to Stalin, 28–29, 146, 147, 153, 154, 155, 156, 157, 161, 162
   relations with Khrushchev, 23, 24, 26–29, 31, 32, 33, 34, 45, 51, 80–84, 100, 107, 108, 113, 179, 194, 207, 225, 383, 385, 394, 399 *n*, 400–401, 409–410, 413, 414, 418
   relations with Kosygin, 81, 92, 147, 181, 239, 284–285, 293, 342
   other references, 46, 60, 87, 106, 109, 111, 112, 146, 165 *n*, 166, 173, 185, 192, 217, 224, 231, 232, 239, 272, 275, 283, 284, 294, 330, 334, 335, 336, 341, 343 *n*, 345, 358, 373, 397, 417, 455, 497 *n*, 504
Mobotu, Hugh, 134
Mollet, Guy, 33 *n*, 184, 342, 385 *n*, 410 *n*
Molotov, V. M., 16, 25, 30, 31, 32, 51, 52, 93, 94, 97, 109 *n*, 116, 125, 137, 138, 139, 140, 142, 143, 145–147, 149, 150, 151, 152, 153, 154, 155, 156, 159, 160, 161, 162, 163, 176, 185, 187, 199, 206, 212, 223, 316, 358, 368, 370, 478 *n*, 382, 420, 421 *n*, 427
Morgan, Conway Lloyd, 379

Moskalenko, Marshal K. S., 236–237, 419
Moskvin, V. A., 22 *n*
Mukhitdinov, N. A., 24, 86, 92 *n*, 100 *n*, 144 *n*, 156, 157, 161, 165, 180, 192 *n*, 193, 194
Muratov, Z. I., 22 *n*
Muravyova, N. A., 408, 518
Mussolini, Benito, 240 *n*
Mustafayev, I. D., 22 *n*
Mylarshchikov, V. P., 133, 134 *n*
Mzhavanadze, V. P., 54, 64, 153, 161, 190 *n*, 254, 256 *n*, 272 *n*, 292 *n*, 312, 422 *n*, 481, 517

Nagibin, Yury, 300
Nagy, Imre, 32
Nasser, Gamal-Abl-al, 504, 533, 534, 535, 536
Naydek, L. I., 37
Nazaretyan, A. M., 477
Nekrasov, V. P., 301, 310, 356, 478 *n*
Nemchinov, 407 *n*
Nikolayev, K. K., 222 *n*
Nikolayev (cosmonaut), 252, 350
Nikonov, 299
Nosenko, A., 67, 95 *n*
Novikov, I. T., 290, 330 *n*, 397 *n*, 503
Novikov, V. N., 85, 118, 169, 170, 175, 217, 287, 288, 294, 446
Novosyolov, E. S., 118, 410
Novotný, Antonin, 54, 274, 275, 283, 285, 320, 381, 414, 427

Obichkin, G. D., 259 *n*
Odintsov, 477
Oganessian (bandit), 327 *n*
Okudzhava, Bulat, 300
Olshansky, 175, 378 *n*
Onika, D. G., 115 *n*
Orban, László, 452
Ordzhonikidze, G. K., 28, 82, 150, 154, 477, 497 *n*
Organov, N. N., 290, 539
Orlov, Vladimir, 177 *n*

Pakistan, 41, 401, 498
Palewski, Gaston, 405, 406 *n*, 410, 412, 413–414, 415
Pan-Tsin-li, 321
Pappas, 80

Paris Summit Conference (1960), 41, 43, 44, 49, 57, 60–62, 64, 67, 73, 76, 77, 101, 201
Pasternak, Boris L., 471, 474
Patolichev, N. S., 138 *n*, 465 *n*
Paustovsky, K. G., 303, 478 *n*
Pavlov, G. S., 514
Pavlov, G. P., 411, 482–483
Pegov, N. M., 190
Pelshe, A. Ya., 34 *n*, 383, 401, 435, 517–518
Penkovsky, O. V., 324, 325–327
Pervukhin, M. G., 17, 21, 22 *n*, 23, 27, 28, 32, 92, 93, 116, 138, 150, 152 *n*, 193, 196, 199, 478 *n*
Petrenko, F. F., 521, 522 *n*
Petrochenko, V. V., 325
Petukhov, B. F., 436
Petukhov, K. D., 147, 331
Pietro, Italo, 346 *n*
Pigalev, P. F., 292 *n*, 510 *n*
Pilipets, S. M., 115 *n*
Pimenov, Y. I., 487 *n*
Pittermann, Dr. Bruno, 240, 241
Plissetskaya, M. N., 487 *n*
Podgorny, N. I., attitude to Stalin, 149, 152, 156, 157, 158, 160, 162, 489 *n*
  attitude to economic affairs, 174, 216, 260, 397, 403–404, 432–433, 456–60, 499–503, 508
  relations with Brezhnev, 349–351, 385, 498, 499–503, 508, 512, 517
  relations with Khrushchev, 64, 94–99, 100, 130, 179, 223, 342, 349–351, 385, 403–404, 415, 423
  other references, 41, 60, 85, 91, 102, 106, 165 *n*, 190, 197, 221, 255, 312, 334, 341, 352, 399 *n*, 408, 417, 455, 486, 497, 504, 507, 509, 510, 513, 514, 522
Podvoysky, N. I., 478
Pokrass (brothers), 313
Poland, 19, 101 *n*, 159 *n*, 211, 303, 310, 339, 414, 419, 485, 487, 498
Polekhin, M. A., 292 *n*
Polevoy, Boris, 301, 310, 319, 475
Polianov, N. E., 232, 389
Polikarpov, D. A., 292, 355, 404, 407, 415, 465 *n*, 495
Polyakov, V. I., 289, 296, 333 *n*, 343, 347 *n*, 397 *n*, 495

Polyansky, D. S., attitude to Stalin, 150, 152, 156, 157
  relations with Khrushchev, 97–99, 130, 179, 297, 412
  other references, 41, 60, 85, 91, 100 *n*, 132 *n*, 162, 170, 174, 190 *n*, 191, 192, 193, 217, 223, 267, 290, 291, 294, 330 *n*, 335, 341, 346, 348 *n*, 373, 385 *n*, 397, 399 *n*, 455, 490, 496
Ponomarenko, P. K., 138 *n*, 480
Ponomarev, B. N., 102, 153, 161, 195, 196, 203–204, 208, 280, 296, 314, 347, 353
Popkov, P. S., 26 *n*
Popov, G. I., 356 *n*, 444, 445, 453
Popovich (cosmonaut), 252
Poskrebyshev, A. N., 191 *n*, 300, 309, 316
Pospelov, P. N., 85, 89–90, 92 *n*, 102, 114, 146, 153, 161, 163, 193, 202 *n*, 211, 259 *n*, 485
Powers, Francis Gary, 41, 42, 53–54, 77, 110 *n*
Pozovny, Major-General A., 325
Pyryev, A. I., 333
Pyzin, K. G., 496 *n*

Rabin, General, 534
Ragimov, S. G., 22 *n*
Rashidov, Sh., 153, 161, 194, 235, 272 *n*, 312, 450, 510 *n*
Razumov, E. Z., 115 *n*
RB–47 affair, 110, 295 *n*
Reimann, Max, 337, 350
Rodionov, M. I., 26 *n*
Rodionov, N. N., 152, 155, 161, 515 *n*
Roifman, 327 *n*
Rokosovsky, Marshal K., 237
Rokotov, Ian, 130
Romanov, A. V., 318
Romanovsky, S. K., 221 *n*
Romm, M. I., 487 *n*
Roumania, 19, 101–102, 274, 287 *n*, 365–366, 381, 417 *n*, 526
Rudakov, A. P., 289, 296
Rudenko, R. A., 190 *n*
Rudnev, K. N., 137, 326, 330 *n*, 326, 410, 411, 462 *n*, 503
Rumyantsev, A. M., 190 *n*, 407 *n*, 445, 460, 462 *n*, 466–471, 473, 474, 502

Rusakov, N. N., 407
Rusk, Dean, 266
Russell, Bertrand, 263
Ryabikov, V. M., 120, 137, 480
Rykov, A. I., 357

Saburov, M. Z., 17, 21, 22 n, 23, 27, 28, 32, 33 n, 92, 93, 138, 150, 152 n, 196, 199, 478 n
Sadat, Anvar, 534
Sakharov, A. D., 379 n
Sakov, M., 460 n
Satyukov, P. A., 19, 64, 102, 114 n, 146, 150, 152, 161, 185, 201, 202, 209, 210, 353, 404, 405, 407, 411
Scali, John, 266, 270
Scheyven, Raymond, 241
Schlesinger, Arthur M., 262 n, 265, 266, 270 n
Schwirkmann, 390
Semichastny, V. E., 200 n, 390, 412, 417, 420, 429, 537, 539
Senin, I. S., 95 n, 120
Serdyuk, Z. T., 136, 137, 150, 152, 161, 163, 190 n, 194, 199
Serebrovskaya, E., 318
Serebryakova, Galina I., 300, 303 n, 308, 309, 383 n
Serov, General I. A., 190, 198, 245, 304, 324, 325
Serov, V. A., 299, 318
Severyanin, 474
Shakerman, 327 n
Shapiro, Henry, 307 n
Shastri, Lal Bahadur, 450
Shauro, V. F., 465 n
Shcherbitsky, V. V., 194, 254, 312, 513-514
Shchipachov, S. P., 318
Shchukin, N. M., 411
Shelepin, A. N., attitude to Stalin, 152, 154, 163, 477
relations with Khrushchev, 180, 412, 420
other references, 196, 197-200, 287, 290, 330 n, 455, 486, 503-508, 537
Shelest, P. Y., 257, 383, 420, 455, 486, 503
Shelipov, D. T., 17, 30, 140, 150, 152 n, 161, 180, 202 n, 204, 478 n,
Sheynin, 282 n

Shikin, I. V., 26 n
Shitarev, G. I., 347
Shitov, A. I., 486
Shkolnikov, A. M., 153, 170, 430, 464
Sholokhov, M. A., 152, 163, 303 n, 315, 316, 474
Shostakovich, Dmitri, 303
Shunkov, V., 484
Shurygin, V. A., 374-376
Shuysky, G. T., 191 n, 296, 515 n
Shvernik, N. M., attitude to Stalinism, 21, 150, 152, 155, 156, 157, 161, 162, 163, 164, 198
relations with Khrushchev, 24, 25, 83,
other references, 83, 100 n, 180, 192, 267, 334, 348, 496, 504, 518
Simonov, K. M., 303, 469 n, 475 n
Sinyavsky, Andrey, 471-474, 488 n
Sizov, G. F., 372 n, 518 n
Skazkin, G. D., 487 n
Slutsky, B. A., 487 n
Smirnov, L. V., 330, 344, 346 n
Smirnov, N. I., 133, 134 n
Smirnov, S. S., 478
Smirtiukov, M. S., 196
Snastin, V. I., 211
Sobol, N. A., 121, 502
Sobolev, L. S., 246, 469
Sofronov, A. V., 247, 382
Sokolov, A., 316 n, 317
Sokolov, T. I., 336 n
Sokolovsky, Marshal V. D., 70, 71, 72, 73, 74, 75, 78, 217, 237, 419
Solomentsev, M. S., 433
Solovyova, I., 472 n
Solzhenitsyn, Aleksandr, 158 n, 247-248, 277, 282, 306, 307-308, 314, 380, 470 n, 476
Sorensen, Theodore C., 231, 238 n, 241, 262, 263, 264, 266, 270 n
Sorge, Richard, 390, 429
Sorokin, G. M., 202 n
Spiridonov, I. V., 23, 58, 138, 139, 150, 152, 154, 155, 158, 160, 161, 162, 196, 197, 199, 204, 222, 223
Stalin, J. V., 16, 17, 19, 21, 25, 26, 27, 28, 30, 31, 64, 72, 73 n, 82, 83 n, 86, 90, 91 n, 92, 98, 125, 127, 131, 138 n, 141 et seq., 157-158, 166, 178, 181, 183, 186, 190, 194,

196, 197, 198, 201, 202, 208, 209, 210, 229, 245, 246, 249, 276, 279, 280, 283, 298–299, 300, 302, 307, 308, 309, 313–316, 347, 357–359, 377, 381, 382, 389, 429, 430, 476–482, 485, 487 *n*, 488, 492, 494, 516

Stalinism, 22, 25, 29, 127, 131, 133, 142, 143, 144, 189, 194, 197, 200, 201, 214, 246, 247, 248, 277, 301, 304, 305, 308, 309, 317–319, 326, 334, 368, 370, 423, 434, 439, 488–489, 506, 517, 529

Destalinization, 28, 141–175, 206, 213, 244–246, 282, 345, 355–360, 384, 475–479, 487, 489–490

Restalinization, 298 *et seq.*, 310, 312–316, 332, 479–487

Sterenberg, 299

Stevenson, Adlai E., 262 *n*

Stoph, Willi, 390, 401

Struyev, A. I., 58

Stuchebnikova, M. D., 208

Sturua, D. G., 487, 488 *n*

Sukarno, President, 399 *n*

Sun-Sin-lin, Mrs., 46

Surkov, A. A., 303, 308, 474

Suslov, M. A., attitude to Stalinism, 29, 156, 157, 161, 162, 201–203, 209–211, 245, 248, 359

relations with Brezhnev, 351, 386, 403, 408, 486, 508–511, 513 *n*, 522

relations with Khrushchev, 29–31, 88, 100, 105–109, 111–113, 147, 179, 181, 186, 207, 275, 281, 297, 342, 346, 360, 367–369, 394–395, 398, 401–402, 412, 416, 417, 528

views on agriculture and industry, 216, 286, 456–458, 500

views on China, 106–109, 152 *n*, 353, 365–367, 387

other references, 23, 24, 75, 79, 83, 85, 86, 87, 90 *n*, 94, 104, 152, 153, 155, 157, 165 *n*, 173, 176, 181, 186, 188, 194, 195, 199, 200, 224, 225, 239, 248, 251, 291, 293, 335, 336, 337, 341, 348 *n*, 351, 381, 382, 386, 388, 400, 407, 408, 409, 427, 432, 490, 497, 501

Suslov, V. M., 22 *n*

Syria, 532, 533, 534

Tamm, I. E., 487 *n*

Tarasov, A. M., 331

Tarsis, Valery, 472

Tendriakov, V. F., 487 *n*

Tereshkova, V. V. (cosmonaut), 350, 413

Tertz, Abraham, see Sinyavsky, A.

Thant, U., 263, 265, 267

Thompson, Llewellyn, 233

Tikhomirov, S. M., 118, 345

Tikhonov, N. A., 118

Tikhonov, N. S., 303

Tikunov, V. S., 200 *n*, 327 *n*

Timoshenko, Marshal S. K., 71, 72

Tito (Josip Broz) (Titoism), 26 *n*, 29, 47, 246, 275, 279, 280, 285, 339, 385

Titov, V. N., 135, 153, 161, 190 *n*, 194, 289, 291, 292 *n*, 296, 406 *n*, 408, 501, 502, 510 *n*

Togliatti, P., 320, 388

Tolkunov, L. N., 460

Tolstikov, V. S., 153, 161, 223, 333, 450

Topchiev, A. V., 410, 411

Tovmasian, S. A., 138

Trapeznikov, S. P., 286 *n*, 437, 483, 486, 514

Trotsky, L. D. (Trotskyists), 21, 127, 245, 365, 478, 482

Troyanovsky, 201

Trukhanovsky, 484

Trushin, V. I., 436

Tsedenbal, 276, 277, 278, 381, 406 *n*

Tsukanov, G. E., 515 *n*

Tukhachevsky, Marshal N. M., 28, 143, 144, 150, 154, 248

Tumur-Ochir, 276, 277

Turbin, 247 *n*

Turkey, 241, 242, 268–271, 500, 504, 533

Tursunkulov, 177, 510 *n*

Tvardovsky, A. T., 248, 301, 307 *n*, 310, 319, 353, 356, 380, 470, 472, 474 *n*, 475

Twentieth, Twenty-first, Twenty-second and Twenty-third Congress, see Congress

Twining, General Nathan F., 54, 55

U-2 incident, 15, 41 *et seq.*, 53 *et seq.*, 73, 74, 76, 77, 78, 79, 81, 83, 84, 88, 95 *n*,

101, 110, 122, 205, 230, 240, 268, 295
Uboldi, Rafaello, 346 *n*
Uborevich, I. P., 28, 143
Ulbricht, Walter, 43, 213, 232, 275, 284, 381, 388, 389, 504
Uldzhabayev, T., 138, 139
United Arab Republic, 385, 504
USA, 19, 20, 27, 41 *et seq.*, 53 *et seq.*, 73, 77, 78, 79, 80, 84, 94, 110, 122, 171, 198 *n*, 218, 229, 230 *et seq.*, 261–73, 276, 284, 323, 324, 326, 346, 352, 354, 526, 528, 535
Ustinov, D. F., 80, 118, 120, 137, 343–344, 346 *n*, 351, 385 *n*, 398 *n*, 405, 446, 455 *n*, 464
Ustinov, V. I., 58, 69
Usubalyev, T., 517

Vannikov, B. L., 22 *n*
Varentsov, S. S., 324, 325
Varga, Eugene, 405
Vashchenko, G. I., 501, 502
Vashenko, A. F., 515
Vasnetsov, Andrey, 299
Venizelos, S., 107
Vershinin, Air Marshal K. A., 55, 60
Vienna Meeting (1961), 44, 170, 171
Vietnam, 101 *n*, 138, 321 *n*, 411, 427, 499, 532
Vinogradov, I., 472 *n*
Vlasiuk, P. A., 379
Volovchenko, I. P., 369, 377, 397 *n*
Vorobyev, G. I., 130, 294, 465 *n*
Voronov, G. I., attitude to Stalin régime, 152, 153, 157, 161, 162, 194
    relations with Khrushchev, 132–134, 179, 194, 257, 297, 373, 376
    other references, 86, 127, 135, 136, 165 *n*, 175, 193, 222, 223–224, 272 *n*, 289, 290, 291, 293, 333 *n*, 335, 348 *n*, 373–377, 397, 408, 417, 431, 455, 496
Voroshilov, Marshal K. E., 17, 21, 24, 27, 28, 30, 31, 32, 33, 41, 72, 83, 85, 87, 90, 91 *n*, 97, 98, 99, 100 *n*, 106, 107, 108, 111, 143, 144, 149, 152, 154–155, 157, 185, 212, 220, 237, 278, 382
Voss, A. E., 518 *n*

Voznesensky, A. A. (poet), 247, 301, 317, 428 *n*
Voznesensky, N. A., 26 *n*, 30, 201–202, 209, 360 *n*
Vuchetich, E. V., 301 *n*, 428 *n*, 470
Vukmanovich-Tempo, 337

Waldeck-Rochet, Pierre, 337, 414
Warsaw Pact, 46, 50 *n*, 70, 71, 72, 231, 232, 234, 498
White, General, 55
Wilcox, 367
Wilson, Harold, 343 *n*, 352
Wynne, Greville, 324, 325

Yakir, I. E., 28, 143, 154, 314, 484 *n*
Yakovev, I. D., 139
Yakovlev, M. D., 134
Yakubovsky, I. I., 71
Yashim, Aleksandr, 301
Yefremov, L. M., 152, 161, 289, 293, 294–295, 374, 376, 397 *n*, 404 *n*, 496
Yefremov, M. T., 132, 133 *n*, 161, 171, 175, 319 *n*, 464, 510
Yefremov, O. N., 487 *n*
Yegorov, A. G., 407 *n*, 460
Yegorov (cosmonaut), 409
Yegorychev, N. G., 153, 161, 289, 378 *n*, 405 *n*, 444, 445, 451 *n*, 463, 464, 486, 489, 510, 516, 517, 518, 533, 537, 539
Yeniutin, G. V., 190 *n*
Yenukidze, A. S., 29 *n*
Yepishev, A. A., 102, 237, 414 *n*
Yeremenko, Marshal A. I., 177, 311 *n*, 411, 419
Yermilov, V. V., 112 *n*, 283 *n*, 301–302, 304, 308, 314–315, 357
Yesenin-Volpin, 300
Yevtushenko, Y., 247, 248–249, 278, 301, 303, 306, 307, 313, 317, 319, 428 *n*, 476
Yezhevsky, A. A., 397 *n*, 430 *n*, 431 *n*
Yohanson, B. V., 318
Yudin, P. E., 22 *n*
Yugoslavia, 101 *n*, 157, 211, 237, 246, 279–280, 323, 337, 338–340, 341, 353, 531
Yunak, I. K., 136, 190 *n*
Yusopov, I., 515 *n*

Zademidko, A. V., 22 *n*, 115 *n*
Zakharov, Marshal, M. V., 70, 71, 72–74, 479
Zaluzhny, V. I., 200 *n*
Zamchevsky, I. K., 138 *n*
Zamyatin, L. M., 399
Zapylayev, 327 *n*
Zarobyan, Y. N., 136, 152, 161, 190 *n*
Zasyadko, A. F., 80, 93, 118, 190 *n*, 286, 287, 288, 290, 294
Zemlyansky, D. P., 292 *n*
Zeven, P., 259 *n*
Zhadov, General, A. S., 76
Zhdanov, A. A., 26 *n*, 29, 382, 485

Zhegalin, I. K., 139 *n*, 192 *n*
Zhibarev, Professor P. B., 208
Zhigalin, V. F., 331
Zhivkov, T., 275, 381, 456
Zhukov, Y., 484
Zhukov, G. A., 49, 201, 221 *n*, 317
Zhukov, Marshal G. K., 17, 72, 75, 76, 78, 311 *n*, 419, 420, 429, 478, 534
Zimyanin, M. V., 192 *n*, 464–465, 473
Zinoviev, G. E., 245, 482
Zorin, V. A., 218, 267, 268, 274
Zverev, S. A., 330